MEASURING GLOBALISATION

The Role of Multinationals in OECD Economies

1999 Edition

MESURER LA MONDIALISATION

Le poids des multinationales dans les économies de l'OCDE

ORGANISATION FOR ECONOMIC CO-OPERATION AND DEVELOPMENT
ORGANISATION DE COOPÉRATION ET DE DÉVELOPPEMENT ÉCONOMIQUES

ORGANISATION FOR ECONOMIC CO-OPERATION AND DEVELOPMENT

Pursuant to Article 1 of the Convention signed in Paris on 14th December 1960, and which came into force on 30th September 1961, the Organisation for Economic Co-operation and Development (OECD) shall promote policies designed:

- to achieve the highest sustainable economic growth and employment and a rising standard of living in Member countries, while maintaining financial stability, and thus to contribute to the development of the world economy;
- to contribute to sound economic expansion in Member as well as non-member countries in the process of economic development; and
- to contribute to the expansion of world trade on a multilateral, non-discriminatory basis in accordance with international obligations.

The original Member countries of the OECD are Austria, Belgium, Canada, Denmark, France, Germany, Greece, Iceland, Ireland, Italy, Luxembourg, the Netherlands, Norway, Portugal, Spain, Sweden, Switzerland, Turkey, the United Kingdom and the United States. The following countries became Members subsequently through accession at the dates indicated hereafter: Japan (28th April 1964), Finland (28th January 1969), Australia (7th June 1971), New Zealand (29th May 1973), Mexico (18th May 1994), the Czech Republic (21st December 1995), Hungary (7th May 1996), Poland (22nd November 1996) and Korea (12th December 1996). The Commission of the European Communities takes part in the work of the OECD (Article 13 of the OECD Convention).

ORGANISATION DE COOPÉRATION ET DE DÉVELOPPEMENT ÉCONOMIQUES

En vertu de l'article 1er de la Convention signée le 14 décembre 1960, à Paris, et entrée en vigueur le 30 septembre 1961, l'Organisation de Coopération et de Développement Économiques (OCDE) a pour objectif de promouvoir des politiques visant :

- à réaliser la plus forte expansion de l'économie et de l'emploi et une progression du niveau de vie dans les pays Membres, tout en maintenant la stabilité financière, et à contribuer ainsi au développement de l'économie mondiale ;
- à contribuer à une saine expansion économique dans les pays Membres, ainsi que les pays non membres, en voie de développement économique ;
- à contribuer à l'expansion du commerce mondial sur une base multilatérale et non discriminatoire conformément aux obligations internationales.

Les pays Membres originaires de l'OCDE sont : l'Allemagne, l'Autriche, la Belgique, le Canada, le Danemark, l'Espagne, les États-Unis, la France, la Grèce, l'Irlande, l'Islande, l'Italie, le Luxembourg, la Norvège, les Pays-Bas, le Portugal, le Royaume-Uni, la Suède, la Suisse et la Turquie. Les pays suivants sont ultérieurement devenus Membres par adhésion aux dates indiquées ci-après : le Japon (28 avril 1964), la Finlande (28 janvier 1969), l'Australie (7 juin 1971), la Nouvelle-Zélande (29 mai 1973), le Mexique (18 mai 1994), la République tchèque (21 décembre 1995), la Hongrie (7 mai 1996), la Pologne (22 novembre 1996) et la Corée (12 décembre 1996). La Commission des Communautés européennes participe aux travaux de l'OCDE (article 13 de la Convention de l'OCDE).

FOREWORD

This publication is the first to present statistical data on the share of OECD economies controlled by multinationals. It has been prepared by the Economic Analysis and Statistics Division of the OECD Directorate for Science, Technology and Industry, under the auspices of the Working Party on Industrial Statistics of the Industry Committee (Expert Group on Globalisation). It is designed to supply reliable and relatively detailed information to governments, investors, globalisation researchers and the public at large.

The database used for this publication is regularly updated and serves as a reference for analysis of the economic impact of international direct investment on the economies of OECD countries.

The country tables and accompanying technical notes were revised by national experts. The Secretariat wishes to thank representatives of all national administrations who helped in the preparation of this publication.

This book is published on the responsibility of the Secretary-General of the OECD.

AVANT-PROPOS

Cette publication présente pour la première fois des données statistiques sur la part des économies de l'OCDE contrôlée par les firmes multinationales. Elle a été préparée par la Division des analyses économiques et statistiques de la Direction de la science, de la technologie et de l'industrie du Secrétariat de l'OCDE sous les auspices du Groupe de travail sur les statistiques industrielles du Comité de l'industrie (Groupe d'experts sur la mondialisation). Elle a comme objectif de fournir des informations fiables et relativement détaillées aux autorités des pays de l'OCDE, aux investisseurs, aux chercheurs qui s'intéressent à la mondialisation ainsi qu'un grand public.

La base de données qui a été mise au point pour cette publication est régulièrement mise à jour et constitue une base de référence pour l'analyse de l'impact économique de l'investissement direct international sur les économies des pays de l'OCDE.

Les tableaux par pays et les notes techniques qui les accompagnent ont été révisés par des experts nationaux. Le Secrétariat tient à remercier les représentants de toutes les administrations nationales qui ont apporté leur concours à la préparation de cette publication.

Cet ouvrage est publié sous la responsabilité du Secrétaire général de l'OCDE.

TABLE OF CONTENTS/TABLE DES MATIÈRES

Part I -- Partie I

Share of foreign affiliates in manufacturing output, employment, labour productivity, R&D, exports, wages and salaries
Part de la production, de l'emploi, de la productivité, de la R-D, des exportations et des salaires sous contrôle étranger dans l'industrie manufacturière

Part II -- Partie II

Activity of foreign affiliates and share of OECD economies controlled by multinationals
Activité des filiales étrangères et part des économies de l'OCDE
contrôlée par les firmes multinationales

INTRODUCTION

Since the mid-1980s and with the quickening pace of economic globalisation, foreign direct investment has become central to worldwide industrial restructuring and one of the most dynamic elements of international transactions.

Until recently, the only internationally available information on foreign investment was on capital stocks and flows, collected for balance of payments statistics. It is still published by the OECD in its *International Direct Investment Statistics Yearbook.*

The need to assess the role and impact of direct investment not only in financial terms but also in terms of industrial production has underlined the importance of data that reflects the industrial activity of multinational firms.

To meet these new needs for analysing the globalisation process, the OECD's Industry Committee requested its Working Party on Statistics to collect data on the performance of foreign affiliates in the manufacturing sectors of OECD countries as from 1990.

More recently, at the request of the Industry Committee, the OECD's surveys have been extended to cover the activities of multinational firms abroad (outward investment) in the manufacturing sector, on the one hand, and the activities of multinational firms in the services sector, on the other. The latter type of data are collected using a questionnaire prepared jointly by the OECD and Eurostat.

The data in this volume relate mainly to the manufacturing industry and inward investment. The next edition will also include detailed information on services and outward investment.

Most of the countries that cannot as yet reply to the OECD surveys are preparing their own national surveys so as to be able to take part as soon as possible.

The 18 variables requested in the OECD questionnaires are covered in a somewhat uneven manner across countries. Data in this volume relate to the years 1992-1996/97 and are classified according to ISIC Revision 3.

For the first time, the publication gives not only basic data but also the share of various industrial activities (*e.g.* production, employment, R&D) that are "controlled" by foreign multinationals in each country. To obtain these percentages, the same surveys were used to collect data on the activity of all firms (domestic and foreign) in each country and for each of the variables available. This has been essential since the data on the "national total" and on multinational firms are not always based on the same statistical unit. While most of the industrial variables correspond to "establishments", data on multinational firms are collected at a higher level, *i.e.* "firms", each of which may include several establishments. This means that the figures for a sector's production or employment, for instance, will differ depending on whether the sectoral data refer to "establishments" or "firms".

For certain variables, in particular exports or imports, it has not been possible to produce data on the activity of multinational firms and on all of the firms in a country on a comparable basis (firms or establishments). Work is under way in the countries concerned to solve this problem.

Also, unlike data on direct investment flows, which cover any investment representing more than 10% of a firm's capital, data on the activity of affiliates are based on the concept of controlling interest. This is more difficult to assess, which is why the statistical test for data collection is that of a majority interest (over 50% of shares that carry voting rights on a company's board of management). It is assumed that ownership of more than 50% of the shares in a company gives real control over its management, even though such control may sometimes be exercised with less than 50% of the shares. The United States, for instance, includes in its data firms under minority control (between 10% and 50%), where investors may influence the management of firms without necessarily having a controlling interest.

The publication is in two parts. Part I presents a series of diagrams showing trends in the different variables (output, employment, productivity, R&D, etc.) displayed by foreign multinationals and domestic firms in total manufacturing industry and leading sectors. Part II provides basic data but also details of the share of each sector controlled by foreign multinationals for all the industrial variables available and the country of origin of those multinational firms. Technical notes giving details of sources and definitions accompany the data.

INTRODUCTION

Depuis la seconde moitié des années 80 et l'accélération du processus de globalisation de l'économie, l'investissement direct étranger est au coeur de la restructuration industrielle mondiale et un des éléments les plus dynamiques des transactions internationales.

Jusqu'à récemment, les seules informations diffusées au plan international relatives aux investissements étrangers concernaient les flux et les stocks de capitaux recueillis dans le cadre des balances des paiements. Ces données sont toujours publiées par l'OCDE sous le titre *Annuaire des statistiques d'investissement direct international.*

Le besoin d'évaluer le rôle et l'impact des investissements directs non seulement sur le plan financier mais aussi dans le cadre de l'économie réelle, a mis en évidence la nécessité de disposer également de données qui caractérisent l'activité industrielle des firmes multinationales.

Pour répondre à ces nouveaux besoins analytiques du processus de globalisation, le Comité de l'Industrie de l'OCDE, dès 1990, a demandé à son groupe de travail statistique d'organiser sur une base régulière la collecte de données concernant au départ l'activité des filiales étrangères dans les pays de l'OCDE dans le secteur manufacturier.

Plus récemment, à la demande du Comité de l'Industrie, les enquêtes du Secrétariat ont été étendues afin de couvrir d'une part les activités des firmes multinationales à l'étranger (investissements sortants) et d'autre part les activités des firmes multinationales dans le secteur des services. La collecte de cette dernière catégorie de données est organisée à partir d'un questionnaire établi conjointement par l'OCDE et Eurostat.

Les résultats présentés dans ce volume concernent essentiellement l'industrie manufacturière et se réfèrent aux investissements entrants. La prochaine édition comprendra également des données détaillées sur les services et sur l'activité des investissements sortants.

La plupart des pays qui ne sont pas encore en mesure de répondre aux enquêtes du Secrétariat organisent la préparation de telles enquêtes afin de pouvoir y participer dans les meilleurs délais.

Les 18 variables demandées dans les questionnaires de l'OCDE sont couvertes de manière assez inégale de la part des pays. Les données présentées dans ce volume concernent la période 1992-1996/97 et sont classées selon la CITI révision 3.

Pour la première fois, avec les données de base, est également présentée pour tous les pays, la part de chaque industrie qui est « contrôlée » par des multinationales étrangères. Pour pouvoir calculer ces pourcentages, il a fallu collecter dans le cadre des mêmes enquêtes des données concernant l'activité de l'ensemble des firmes (nationales et étrangères) dans chaque pays et pour chacune des variables disponibles. Cette collecte s'est avérée indispensable dans la mesure où les données concernant le « total national » et celles des firmes multinationales ne se réfèrent pas systématiquement à la même unité statistique. Tandis que la plupart des variables industrielles correspondent aux « établissements », les données sur les firmes multinationales sont collectées à un niveau plus élevé, celui des « firmes » dont chacune peut disposer de nombreux établissements. Ainsi la production ou l'emploi par exemple d'un secteur prendront des valeurs différentes selon que le secteur est constitué à partir de données sur les « établissements » ou sur les « firmes ».

Les données concernant l'activité des firmes multinationales et celles de l'ensemble des firmes d'un pays n'ont pas pu être établies sur une base comparable (firmes ou établissements) pour certaines variables notamment celles des exportations et des importations. Des travaux sont en cours dans les pays concernés pour résoudre cette difficulté.

Par ailleurs, contrairement aux données sur les flux d'investissements directs qui concernent tous les investissements supérieurs à 10 % du capital des firmes, les données sur l'activité des filiales reposent sur la notion de contrôle. Il s'agit d'une notion plus difficile à mesurer, c'est la raison pour laquelle le critère statistique choisi pour la collecte des données est celui du contrôle majoritaire (plus de 50 % des actions d'une société donnant droit de vote au conseil d'administration). On suppose que le fait de posséder plus de 50 % des actions d'une société permet d'exercer un réel contrôle sur sa gestion, même si dans certains cas ce contrôle peut être exercé avec la possession de moins de 50 % des actions. Les États-Unis, par exemple, incluent dans leurs données les firmes sous contrôle minoritaire (entre 10 et 50 %), ce qui correspond aux investisseurs qui exercent une certaine influence sur la gestion des firmes en question mais pas nécessairement un véritable contrôle.

La publication comprend deux parties. La partie I présente une série de graphiques concernant l'évolution des différentes caractéristiques (production, emploi, productivité, R-D, etc.) des multinationales étrangères et des firmes nationales du total manufacturier et des principaux secteurs. La partie II présente les données de base mais également des données détaillées concernant la part de chaque secteur contrôlée par des multinationales étrangères pour toutes les variables industrielles disponibles ainsi que les pays d'origine de ces firmes multinationales. Ces données sont accompagnées de notes techniques qui fournissent des précisions quant aux sources et aux définitions utilisées.

Part I - Partie I

Share of foreign affiliates in manufacturing output, employment, labour productivity, R&D, exports, wages and salaries

Part de la production, de l'emploi, de la productivité, de la R-D, des exportations et des salaires sous contrôle étranger dans l'industrie manufacturière

Graph 1. **Share of foreign affiliates in manufacturing production (or turnover)**

1997 or latest year available

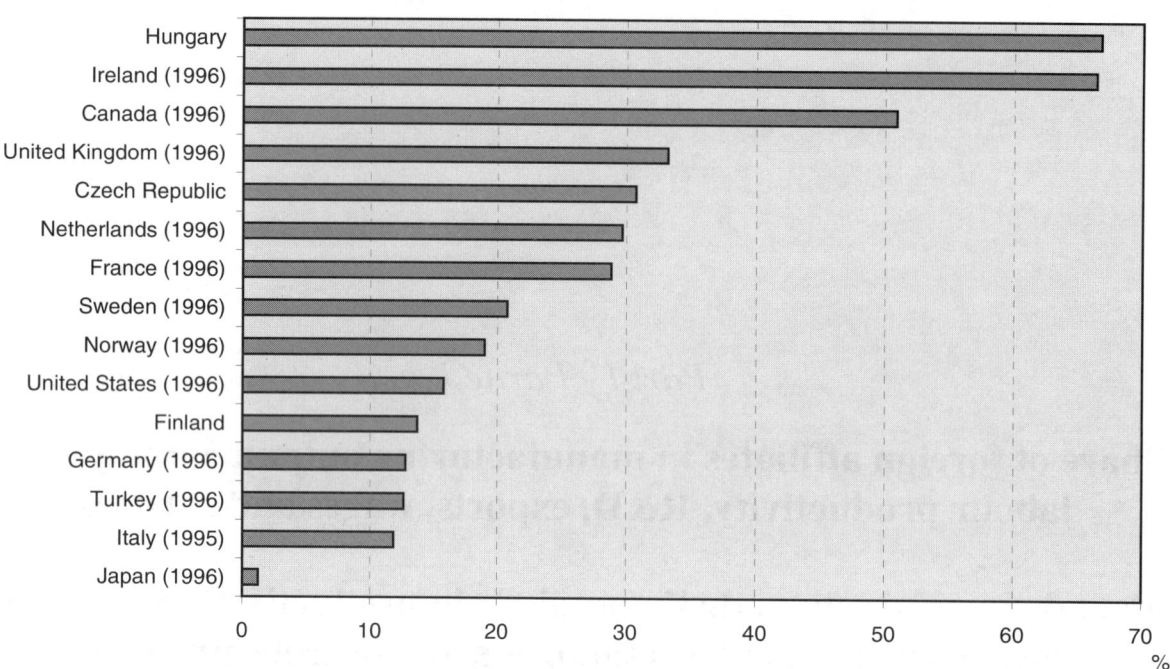

Source: OECD, Activities of Foreign Affiliates database.

Graph 2. **Share of foreign affiliates in manufacturing employment**

1997 or latest year available

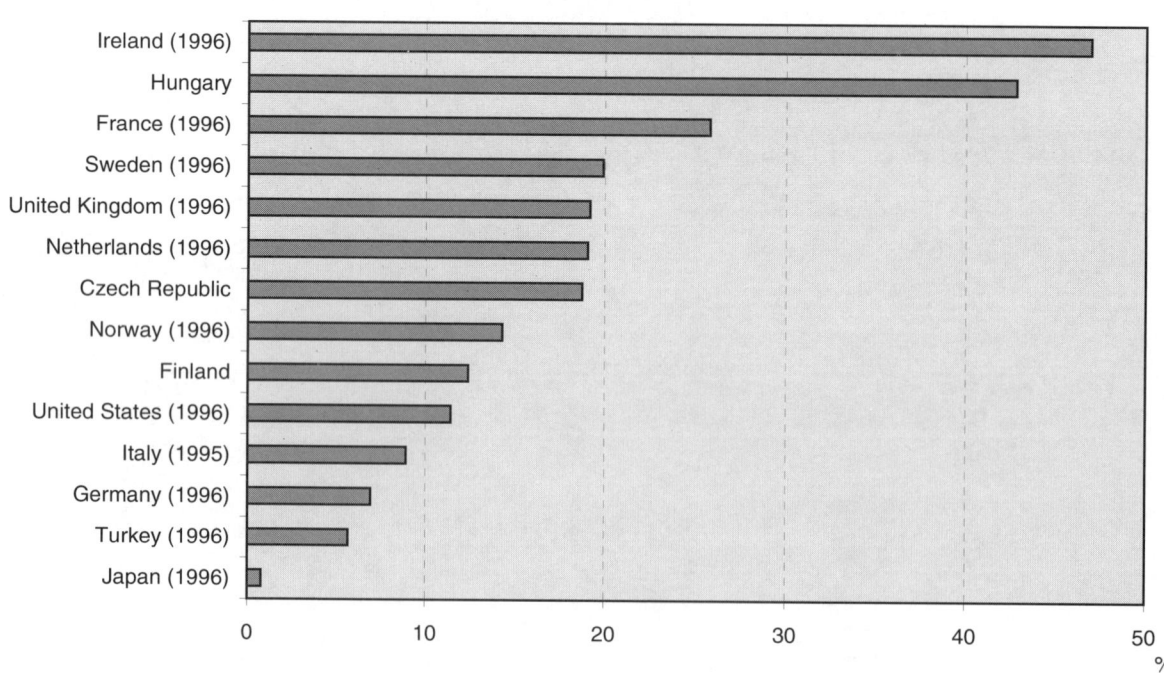

Source: OECD, Activities of Foreign Affiliates database.

Graphique 1. **Part de la production (ou du chiffre d'affaires) sous contrôle étranger dans l'industrie manufacturière**

1997 ou dernière année disponible

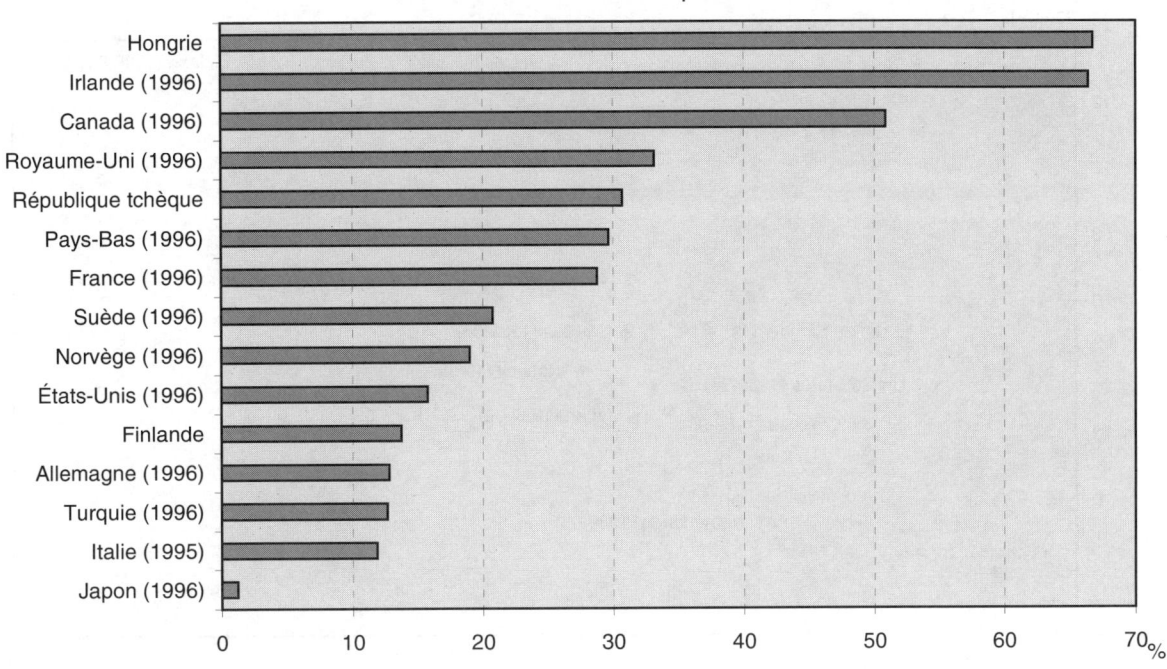

Source : OCDE, base de données sur l'Activité des filiales étrangères.

Graphique 2. **Part de l'emploi sous contrôle étranger dans l'industrie manufacturière**

1997 ou dernière année disponible

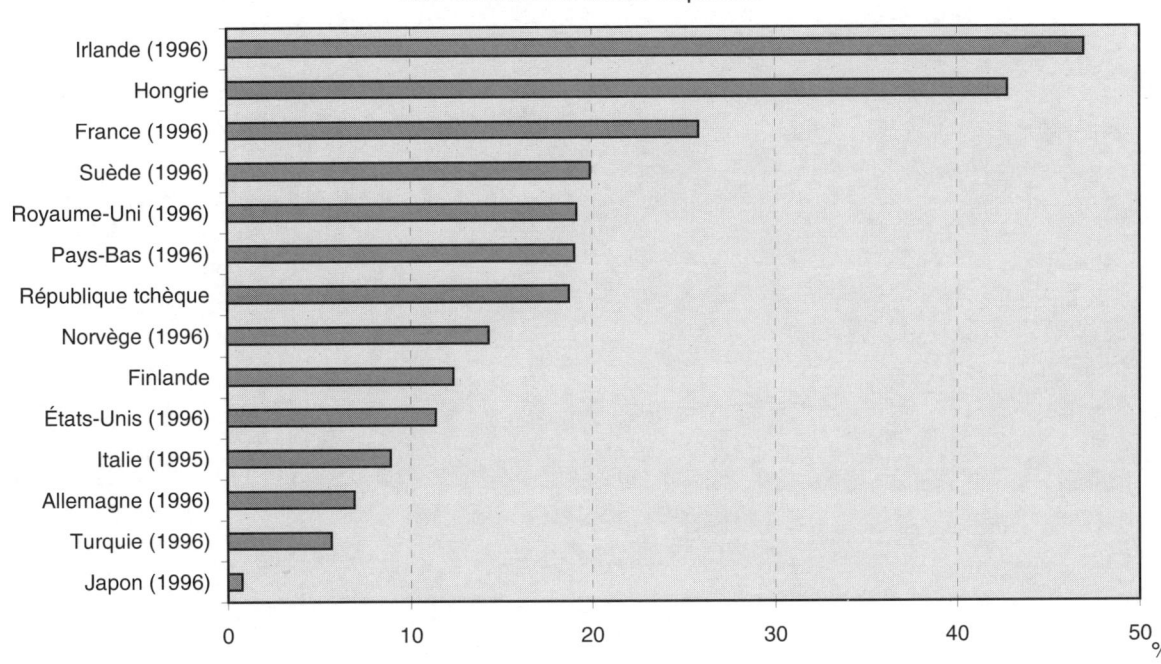

Source : OCDE, base de données sur l'Activité des filiales étrangères.

Graph 3. **Trends in the share of foreign affiliates in manufacturing**

Average annual growth rate, 1989-97 or nearest years

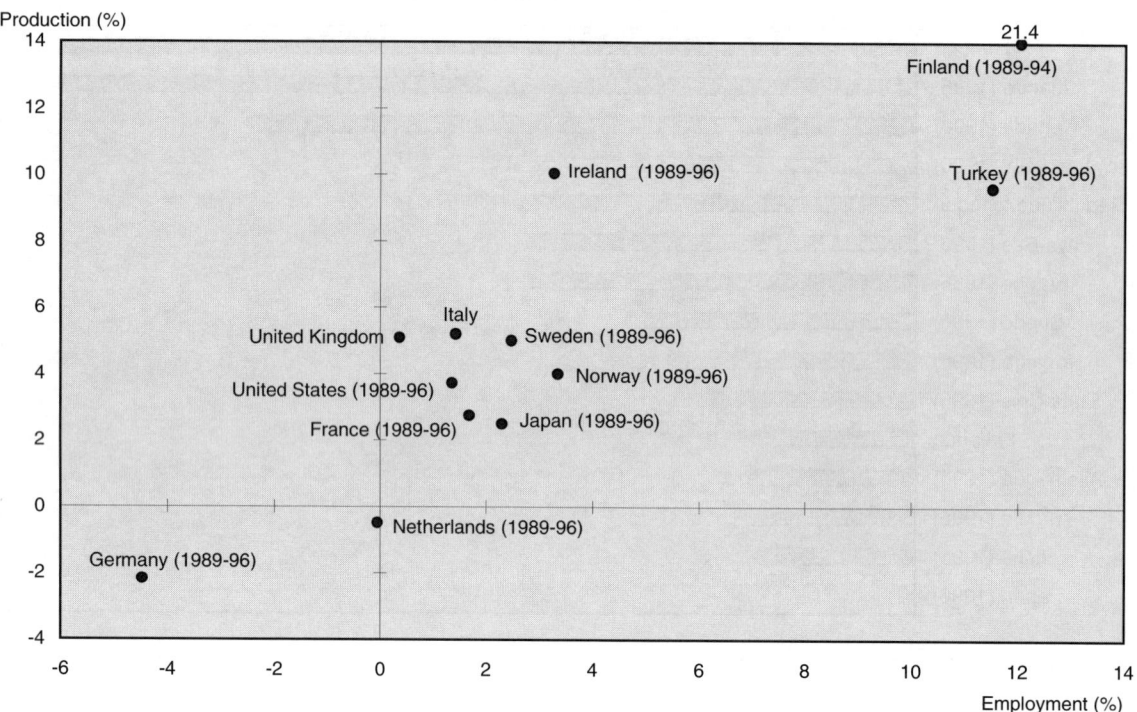

Source: OECD, Activities of Foreign Affiliates database.

Graphique 3. **Évolution du poids des firmes sous contrôle étranger dans l'industrie manufacturière**

Taux de croissance annuel moyen, 1989-97 ou années les plus proches

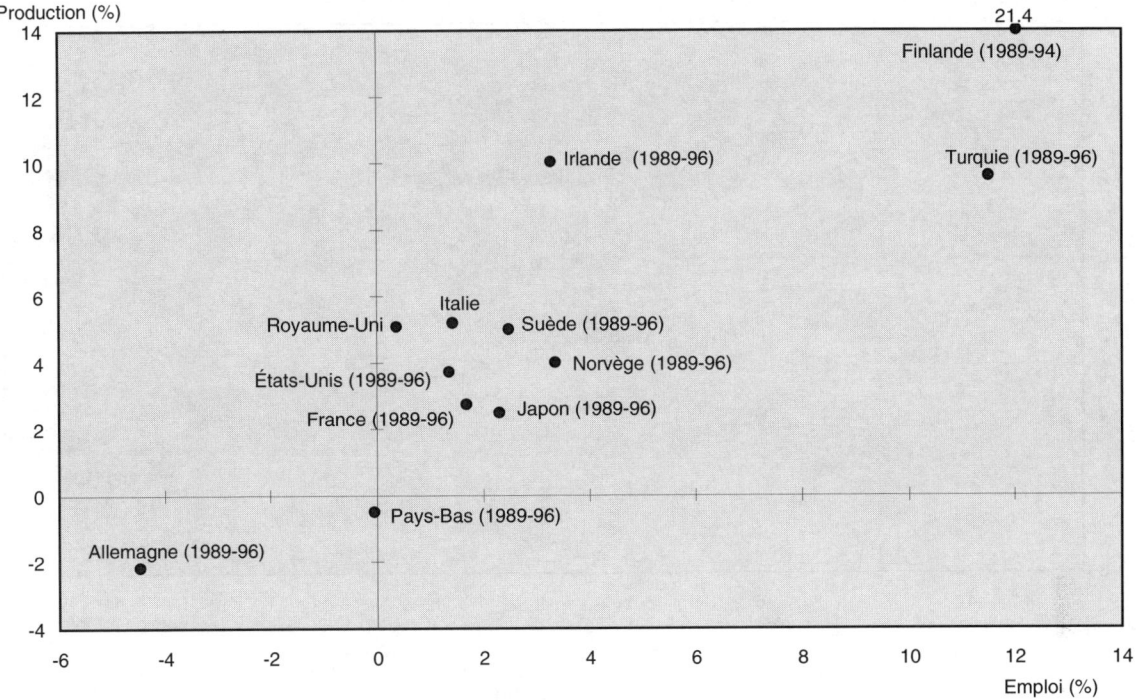

Source : OCDE, base de données sur l'Activité des filiales étrangères.

Graph 4. **Trends in employment in the manufacturing industry**

Average annual growth rate, 1989-96 or nearest years

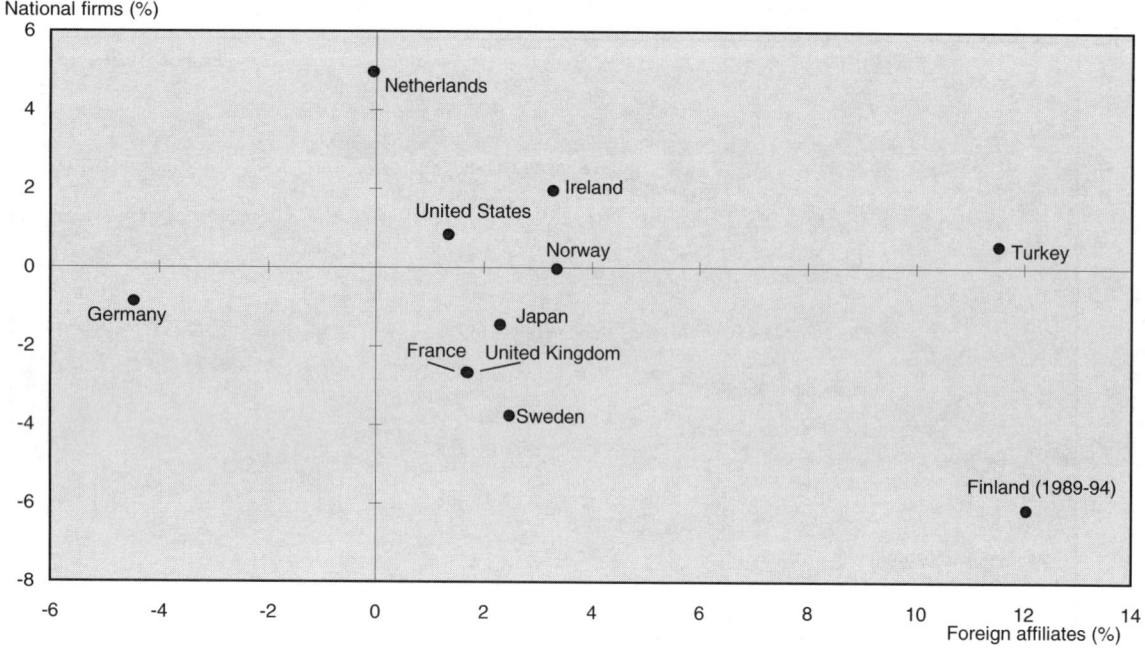

Source: OECD, Activities of Foreign Affiliates database.

Graph 5. **Numbers employed by foreign affiliates in manufacturing**

Change between 1989 and 1997 or nearest years, in thousands

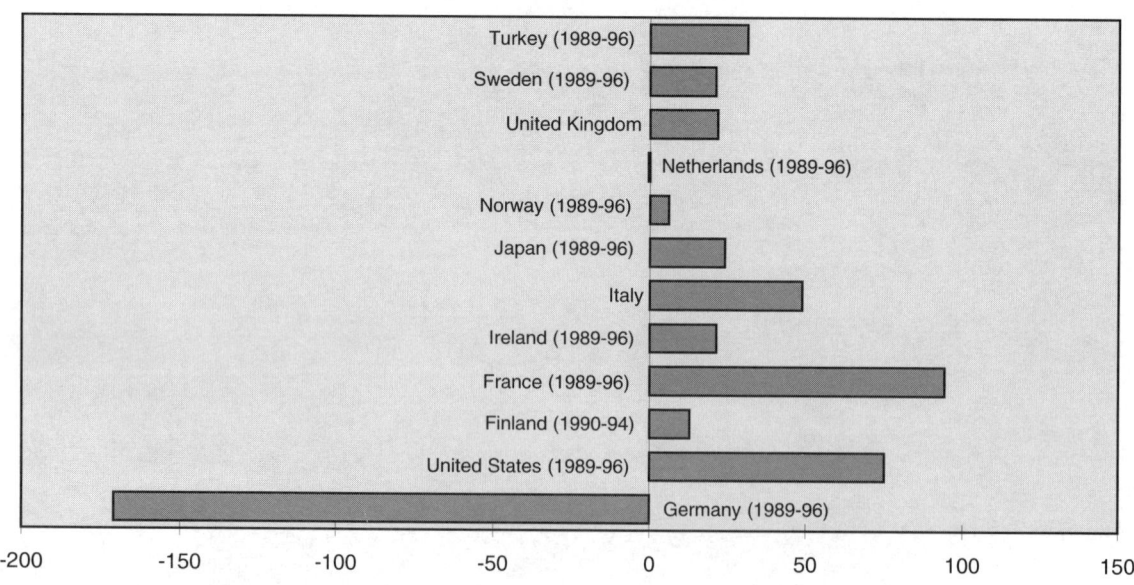

Source: OECD, Activities of Foreign Affiliates database.

Graphique 4. **Évolution de l'emploi dans l'industrie manufacturière**

Taux de croissance annuel moyen, 1989-96 ou années les plus proches

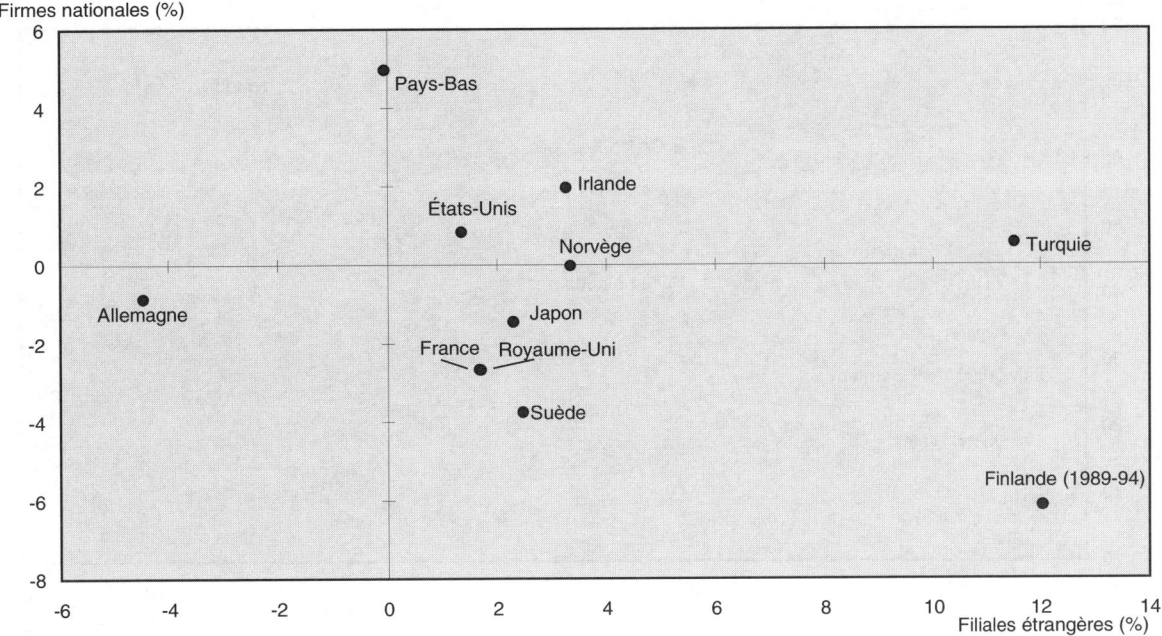

Source : OCDE, base de données sur l'Activité des filiales étrangères.

Graphique 5. **Nombre de salariés des firmes sous contrôle étranger dans l'industrie manufacturière**

Variation entre 1989 et 1996 ou années les plus proches, en milliers

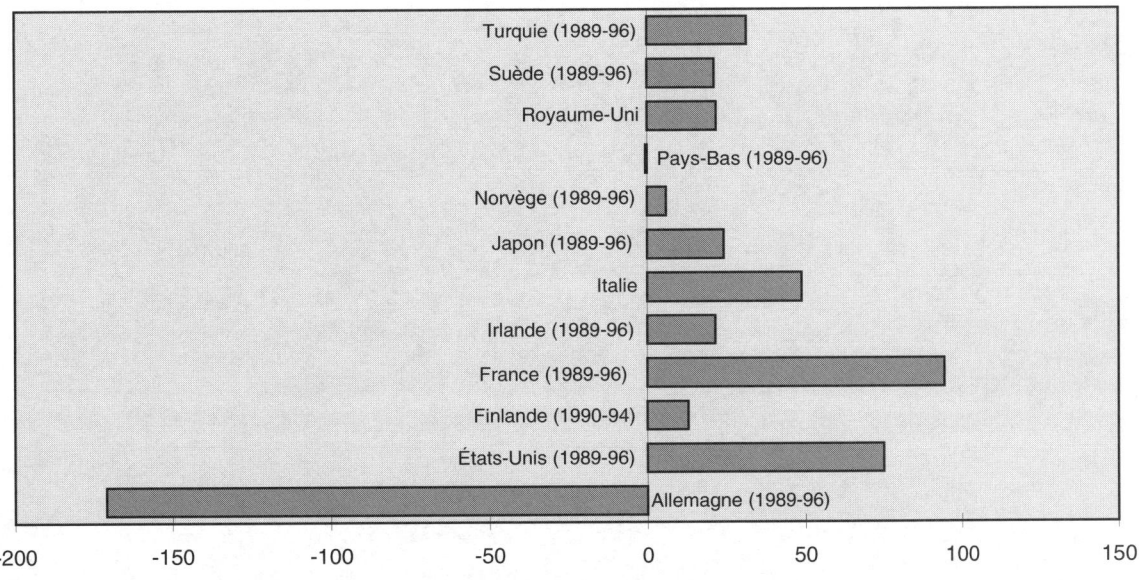

Source : OCDE, base de données sur l'Activité des filiales étrangères.

Graph 6. **Exposure of domestic markets to manufactures**

1996 or latest year available

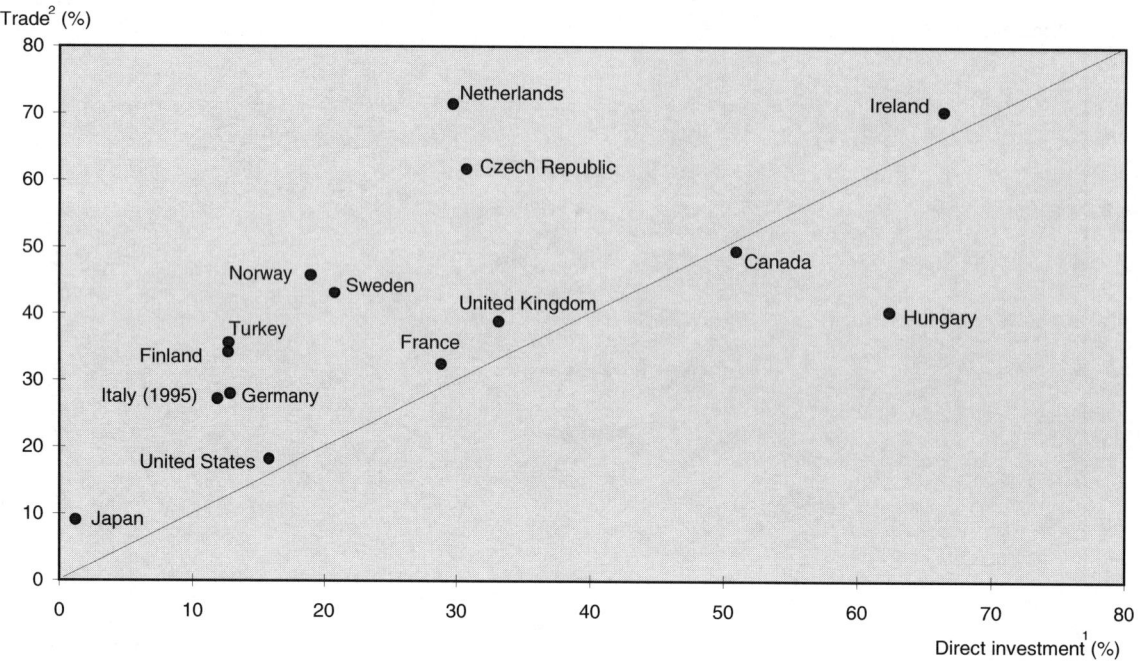

1. Production (or turnover) of foreign affiliates/total production (or turnover).
2. Imports/domestic demand.

Source: OECD, Activities of Foreign Affiliates and STAN databases.

Graphique 6. **Degré d'ouverture des marchés intérieurs pour les produits manufacturés**

1996 ou dernière année disponible

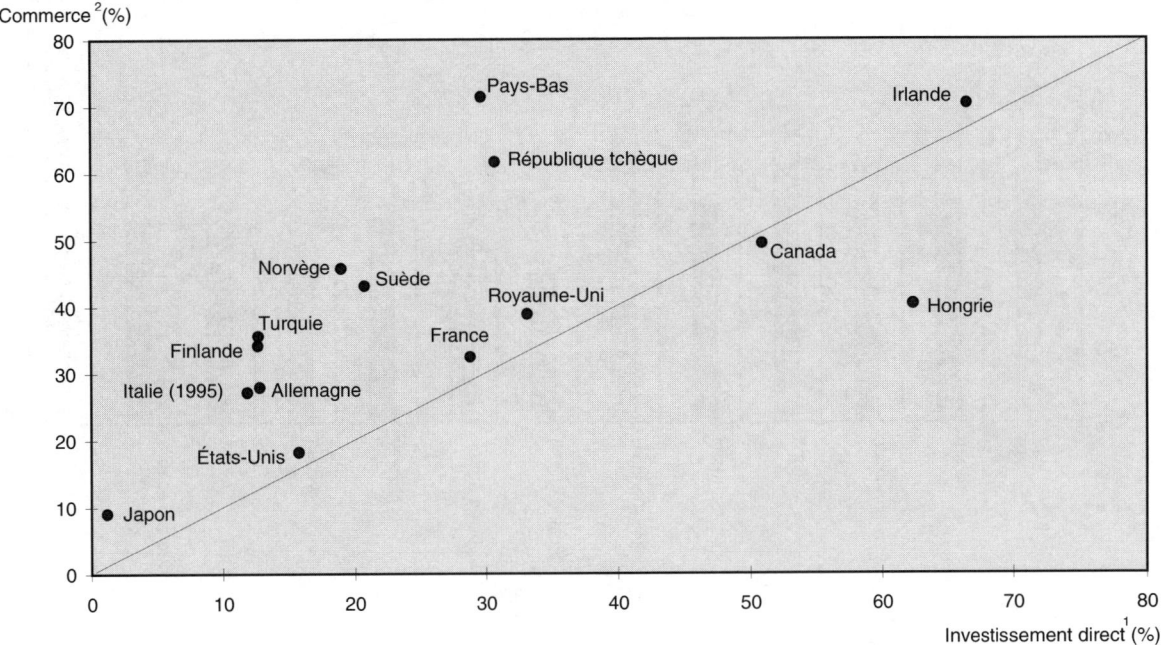

1. Production (ou chiffre d'affaires) des filiales étrangères/production (ou chiffre d'affaires) total.
2. Importations/demande intérieure.

Source : OCDE, bases de données sur l'Activité des filiales étrangères et STAN.

Graph 7. **Gross output per employee in manufacturing**

National firms = 100

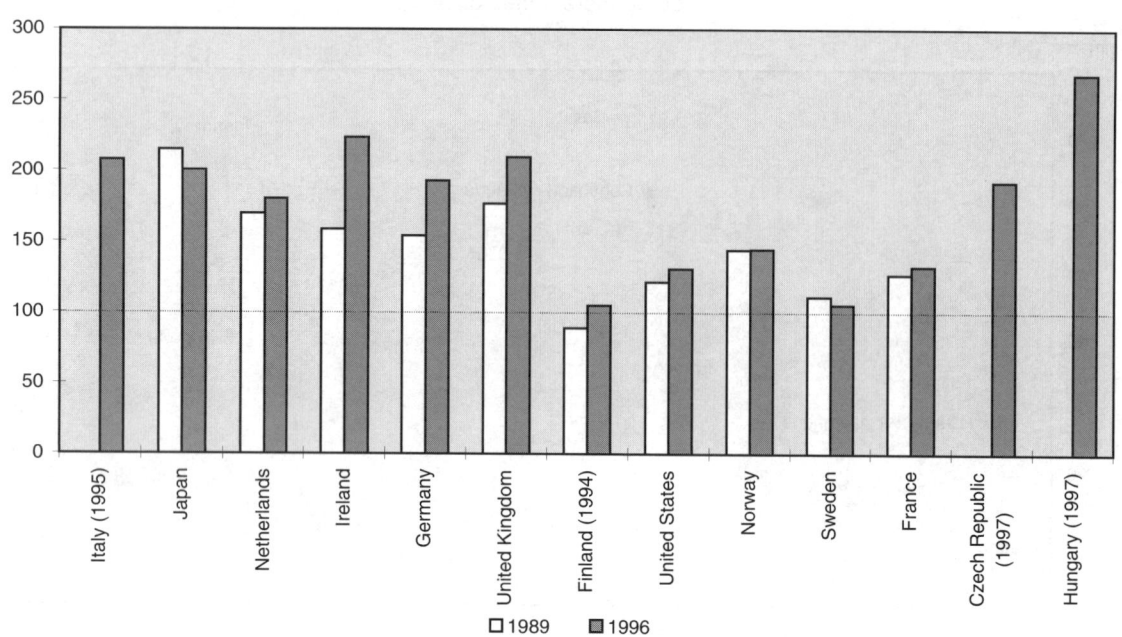

□ 1989   ■ 1996

Source: OECD, Activities of Foreign Affiliates database.

Graph 8. **Compensation per employee of foreign affiliates in manufacturing**

National firms = 100

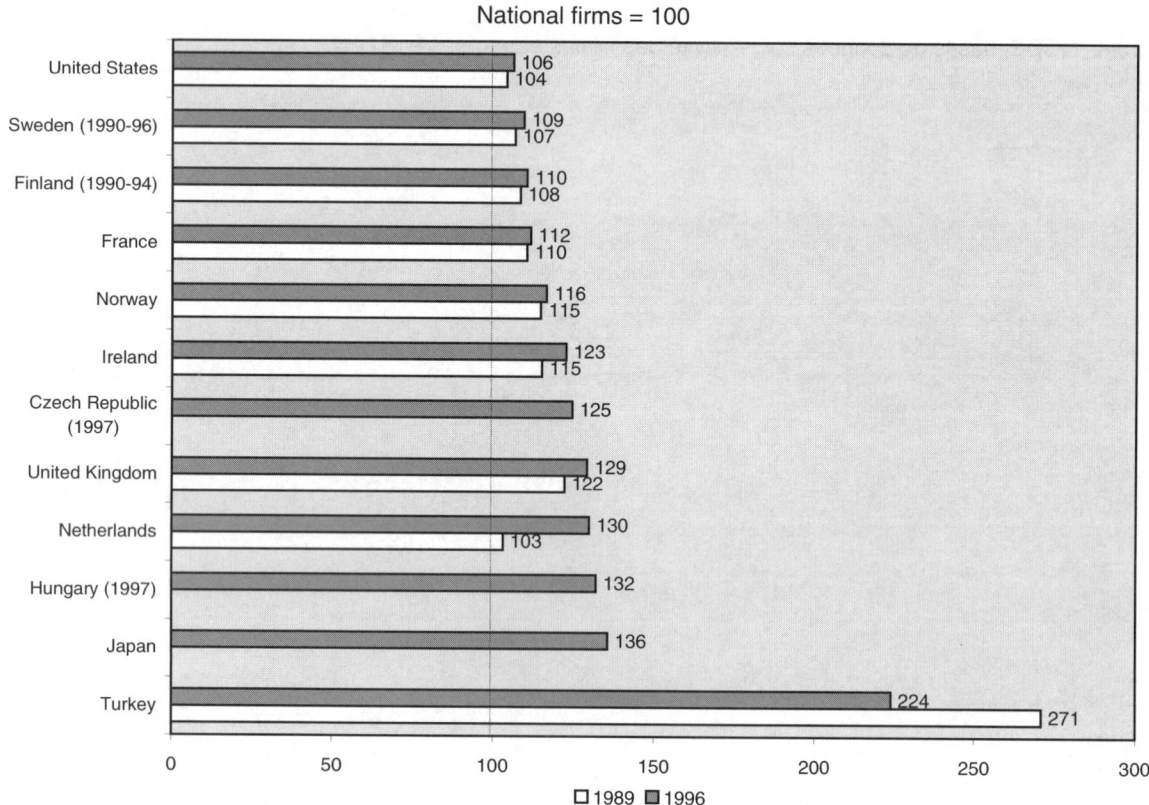

□ 1989   ■ 1996

Source: OECD, Activities of Foreign Affiliates database.

Graphique 7. **Production brute par employé dans l'industrie manufacturière**

Firmes nationales = 100

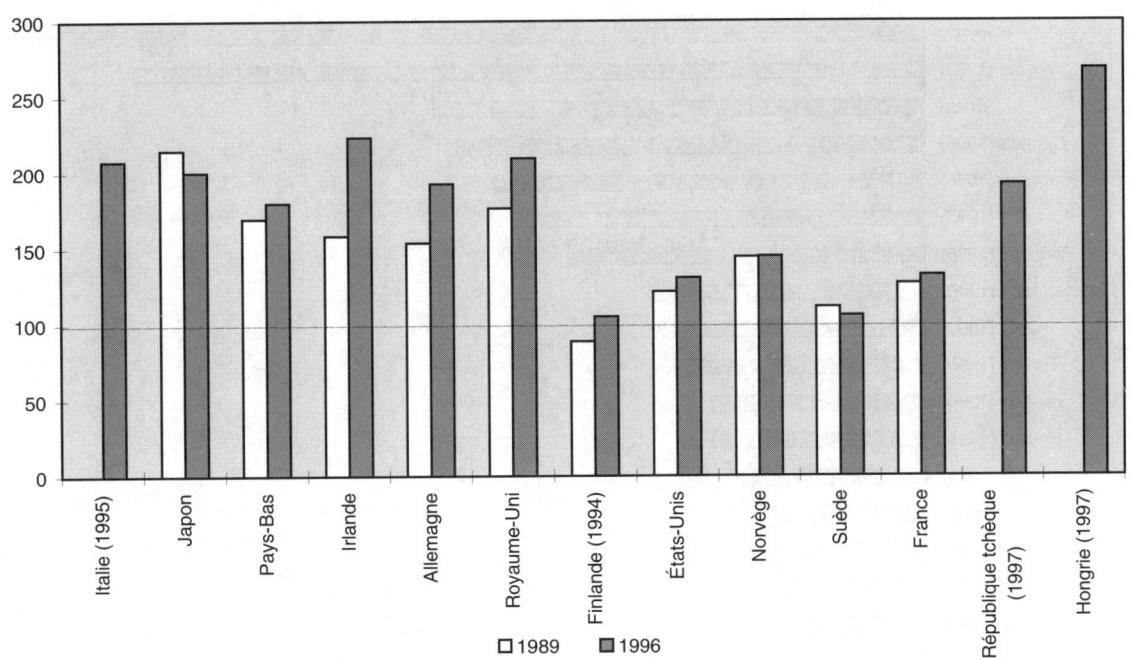

Graphique 8. **Rémunération par employé des firmes sous contrôle étranger dans l'industrie manufacturière**

Firmes nationales = 100

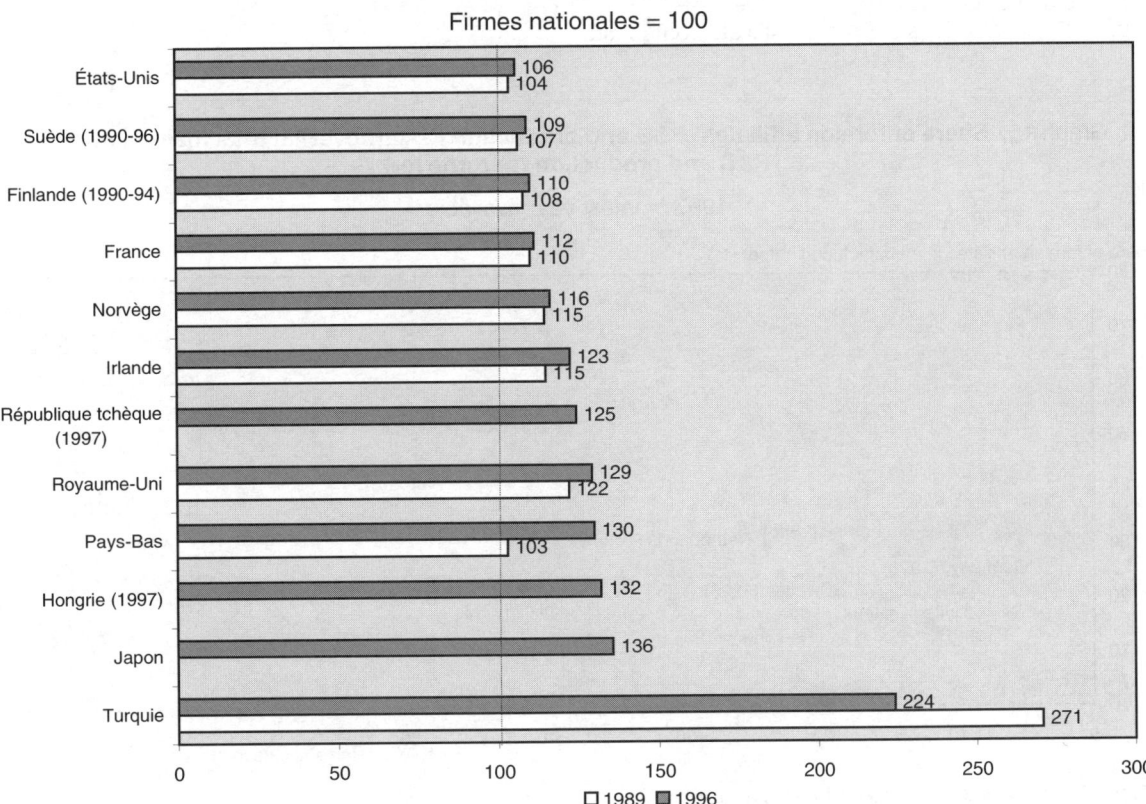

Source : OCDE, base de données sur l'Activité des filiales étrangères.

Graph 9. **Share of foreign affiliates in manufacturing R&D**

1997 or latest year available

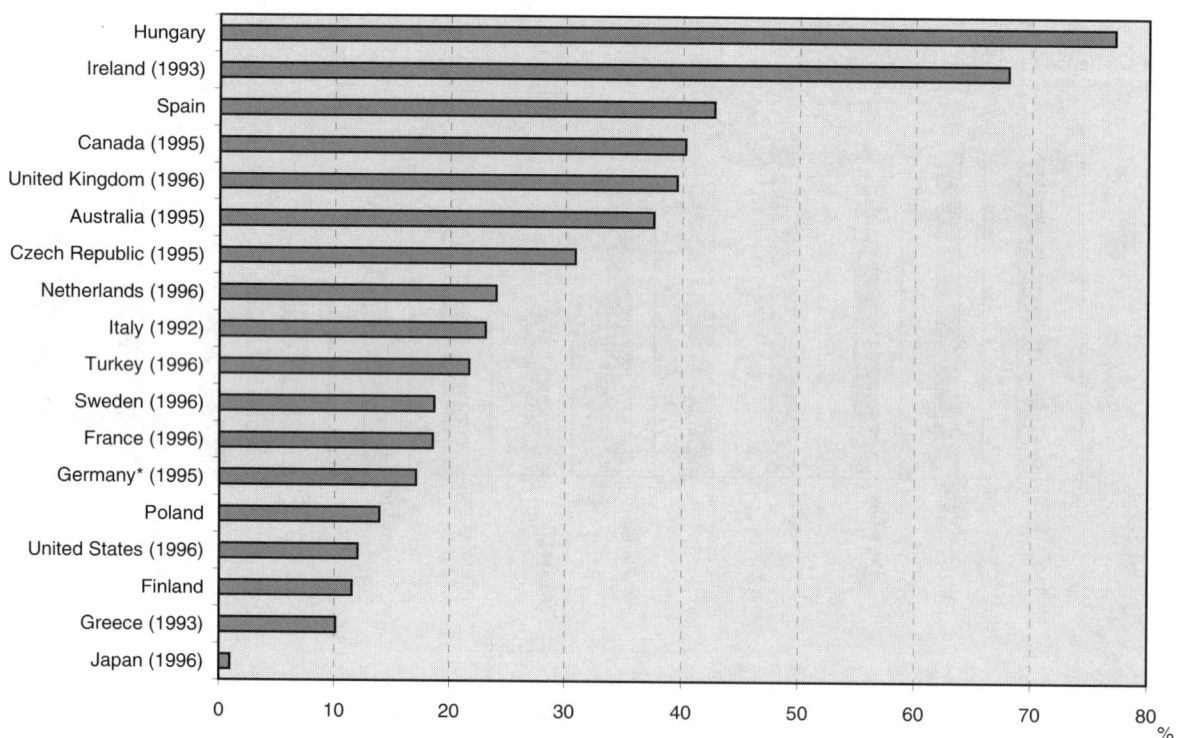

*   Sample of the 500 most R&D-intensive firms.
Source: OECD, Activities of Foreign Affiliates database.

Graph 10. **Share of foreign affiliates' R&D and production (or turnover) in total manufacturing R&D and production (or turnover)**

1997 or latest year available

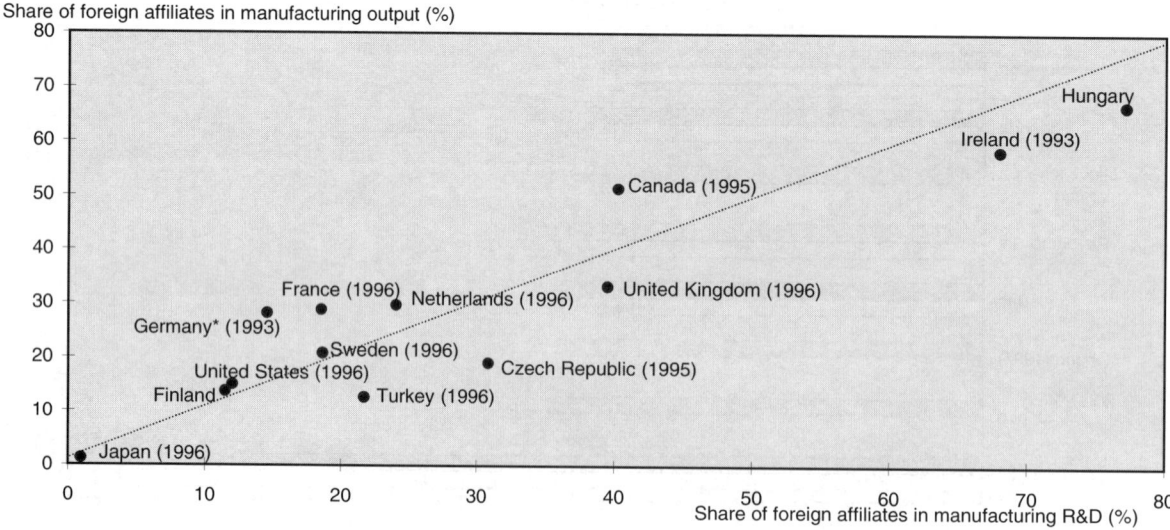

*   Sample of the 500 most R&D-intensive firms.
Source: OECD, Activities of Foreign Affiliates database.

Graphique 9. **Part des firmes sous contrôle étranger dans la R-D manufacturière**

1997 ou année la plus proche

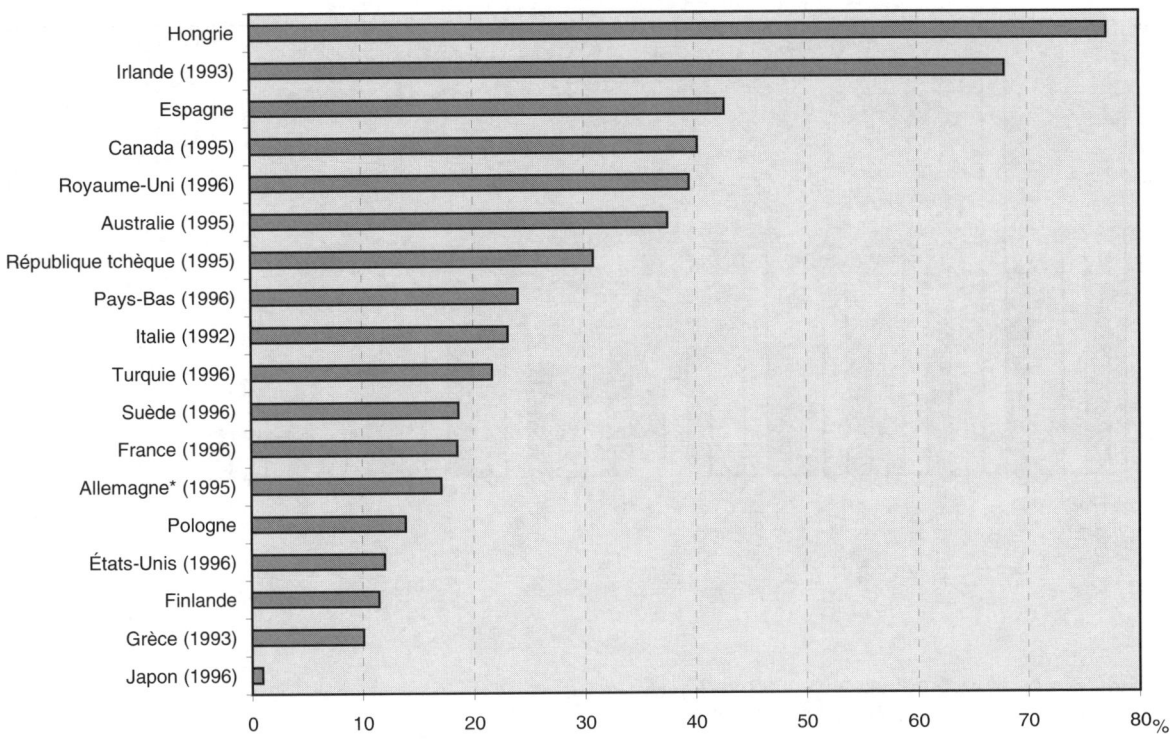

* Échantillon des 500 firmes les plus intensives en R-D.
Source : OCDE, base de données sur l'Activité des filiales étrangères.

Graphique 10. **Part de la R-D et de la production (ou du chiffre d'affaires) des filiales étrangères dans la R-D et la production totales de l'industrie manufacturière**

1997 ou année la plus proche

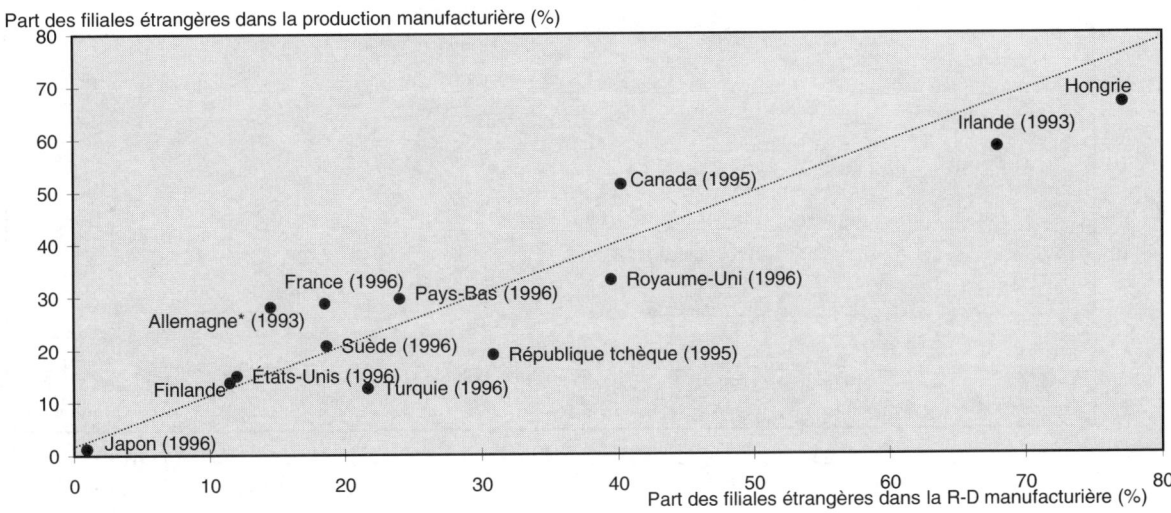

* Échantillon des 500 firmes les plus intensives en R-D.
Source : OCDE, base de données sur l'Activité des filiales étrangères.

Graph 11. **R&D intensities[1] of foreign affiliates and national firms in manufacturing**

1997 or latest year available

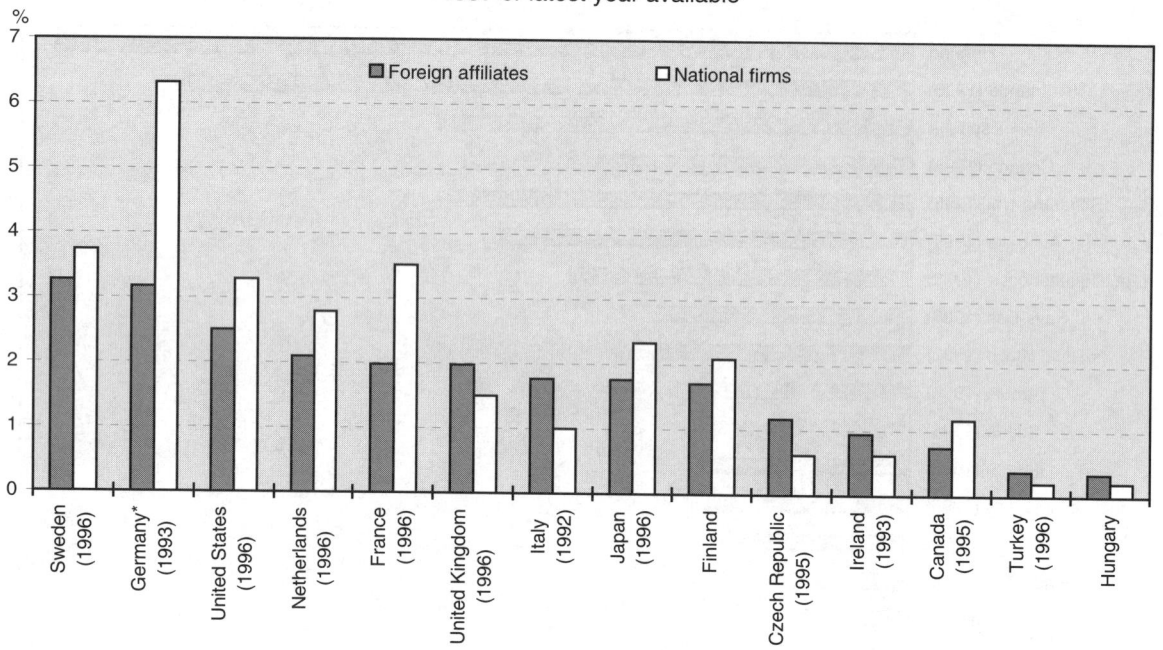

1. R&D expenditure/production (or turnover).
* Sample of the 500 most R&D-intensive firms.

Source: OECD, Activities of Foreign Affiliates database.

Graph 12. **Share of foreign financing of industrial R&D and share of foreign affiliates in total manufacturing R&D**

1997 or latest year available

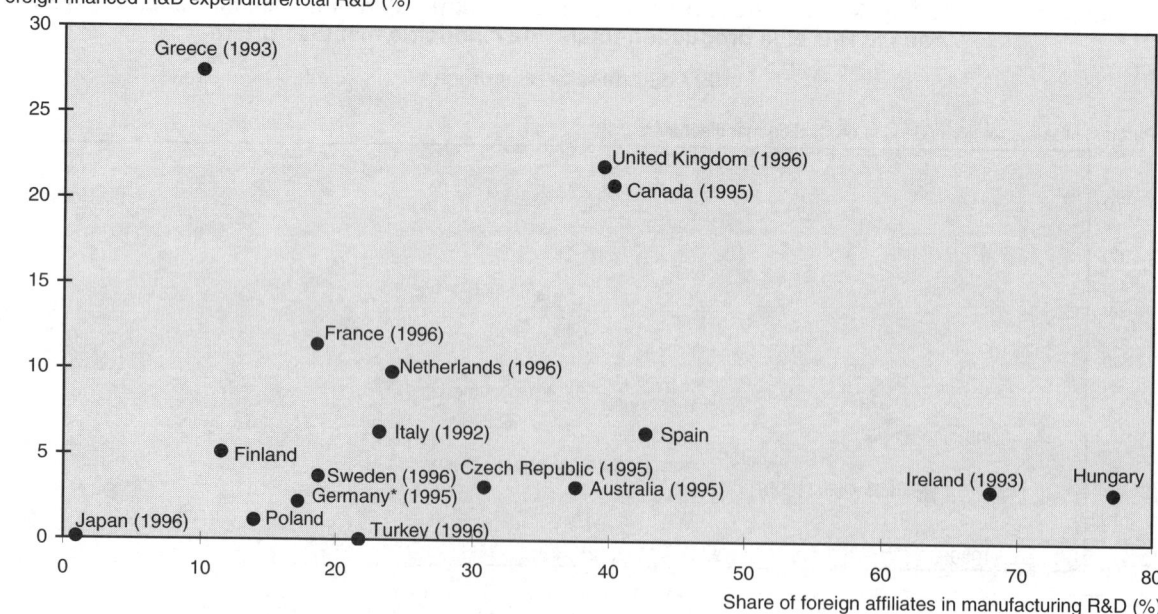

Source: OECD, Activities of Foreign Affiliates and MSTI databases.

26

Graphique 11. **Intensités[1] de R-D des firmes sous contrôle étranger et des firmes sous contrôle national dans l'industrie manufacturière**

1997 ou année la plus proche

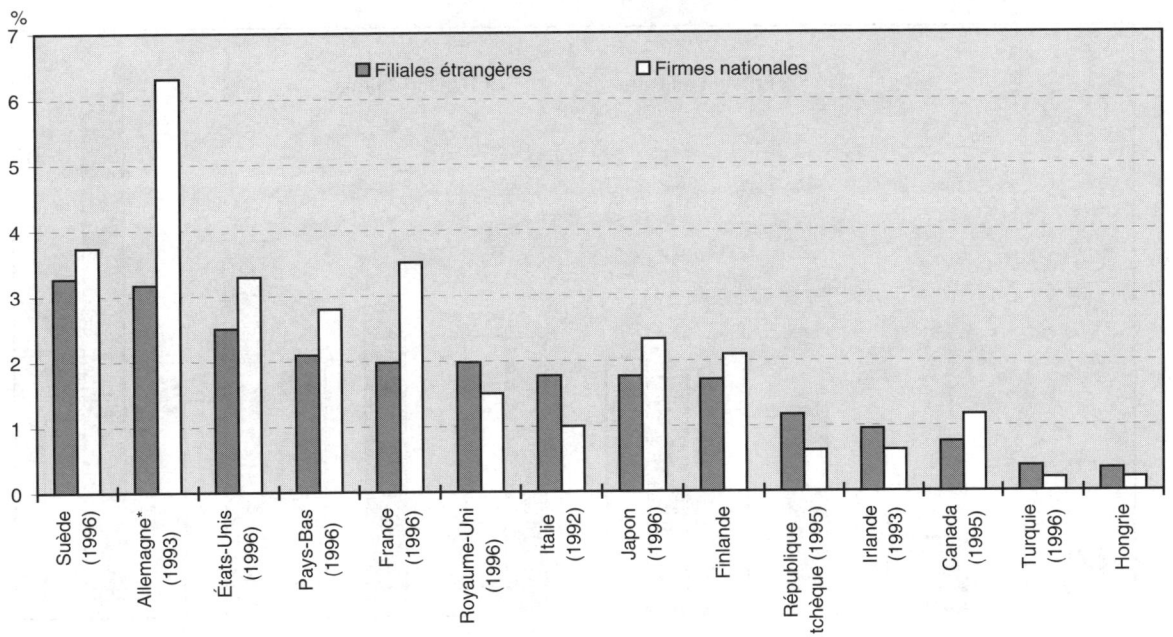

1. Dépenses de R-D/production (ou chiffre d'affaires).
* Échantillon des 500 firmes les plus intensives en R-D.

Source : OCDE, base de données sur l'Activité des filiales étrangères.

Graphique 12. **Part du financement de la R-D industrielle par l'étranger et part des firmes sous contrôle étranger dans la R-D du secteur manufacturier**

1997 ou année la plus proche

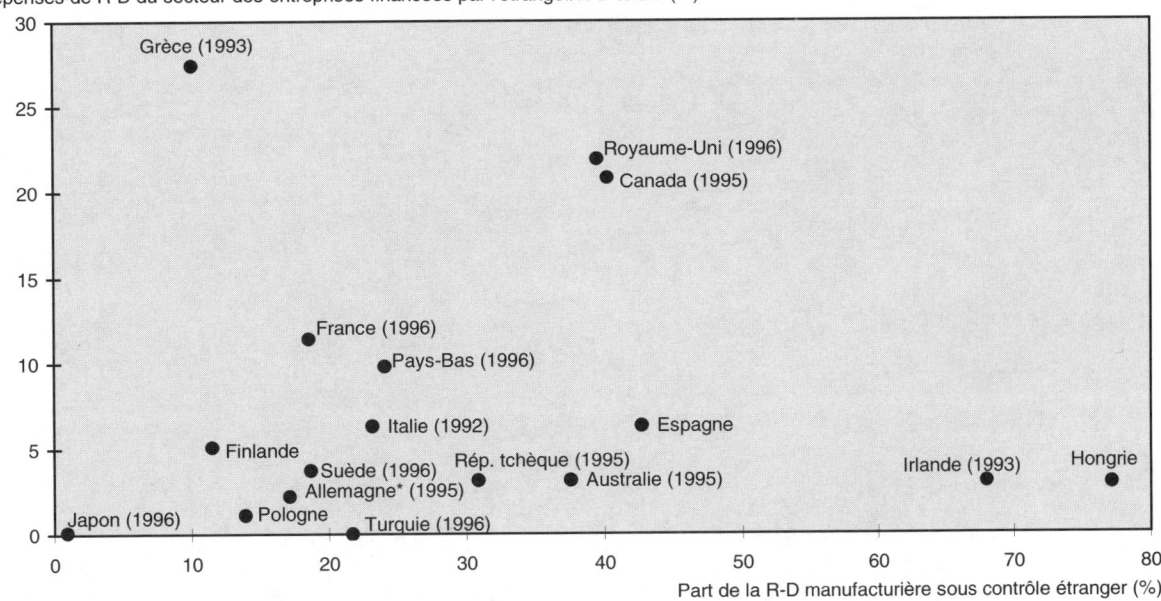

Source : OCDE, bases de données sur l'Activité des filiales étrangères et MSTI.

Graph 13. **Export propensities[1] in manufacturing**

1996 or latest year available

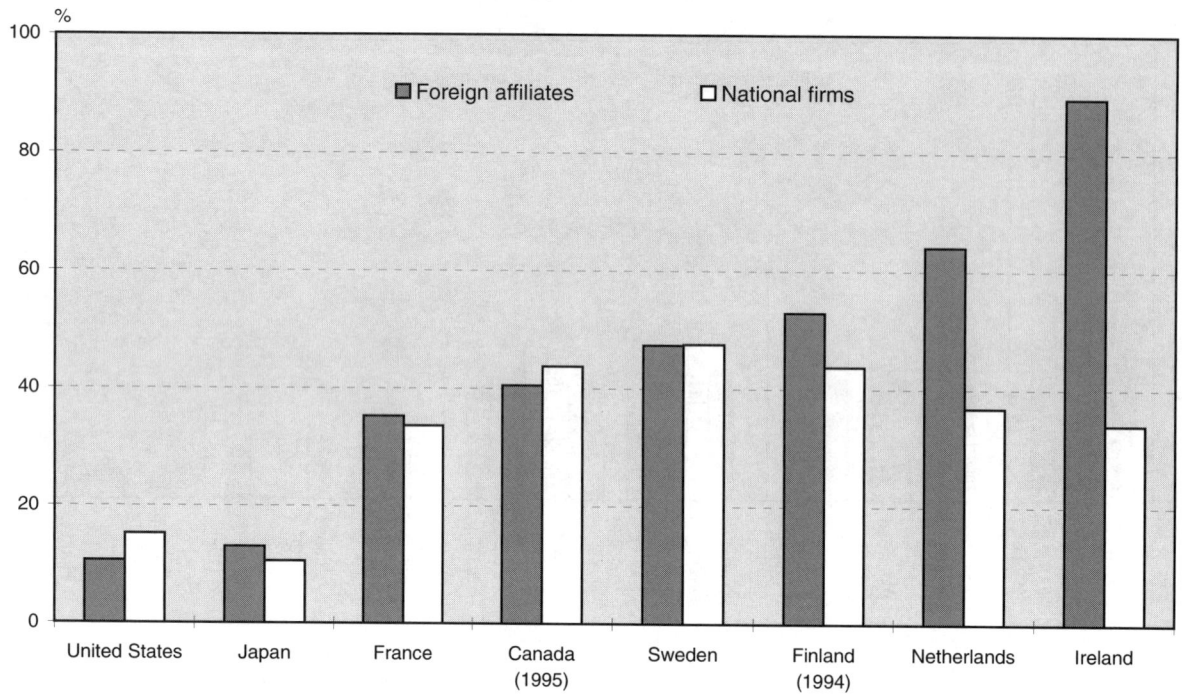

1. Exports/production (or turnover).

Source: OECD, Activities of Foreign Affiliates database.

Graphique 13. **Propension à exporter[1] de l'industrie manufacturière**

1996 ou dernière année disponible

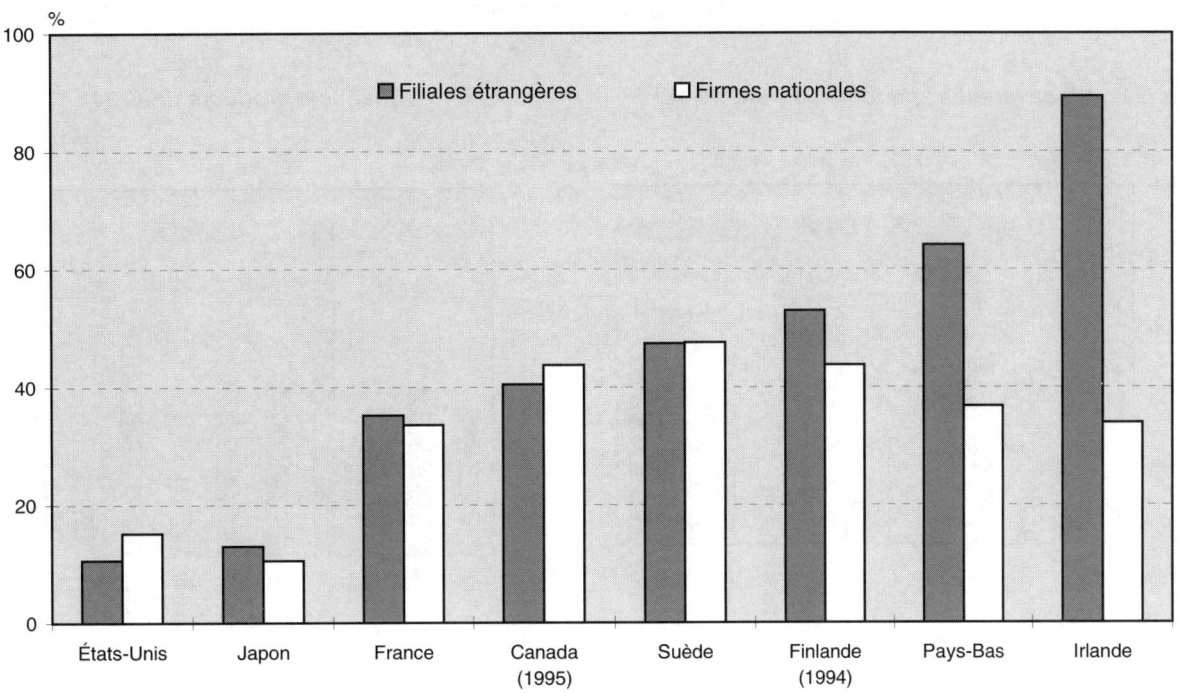

1. Exportations/production (ou chiffre d'affaires).

Source : OCDE, base de données sur l'Activité des filiales étrangères.

Graph 14. **Share of production (or turnover) of foreign affiliates
in selected industrial sectors**

1997 or latest year available

Food, beverages and tobacco (ISIC 15/16)

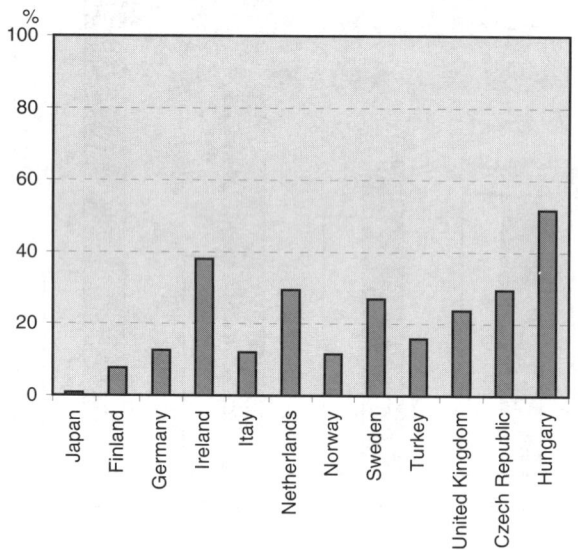

Chemical products (ISIC 24)

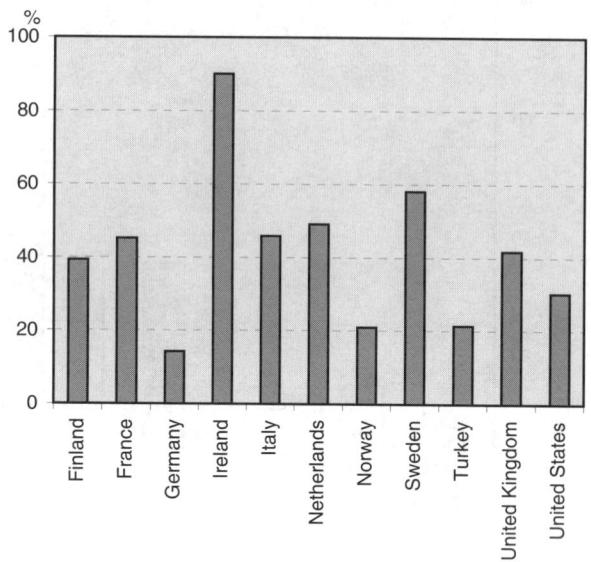

Pharmaceuticals (ISIC 2423)

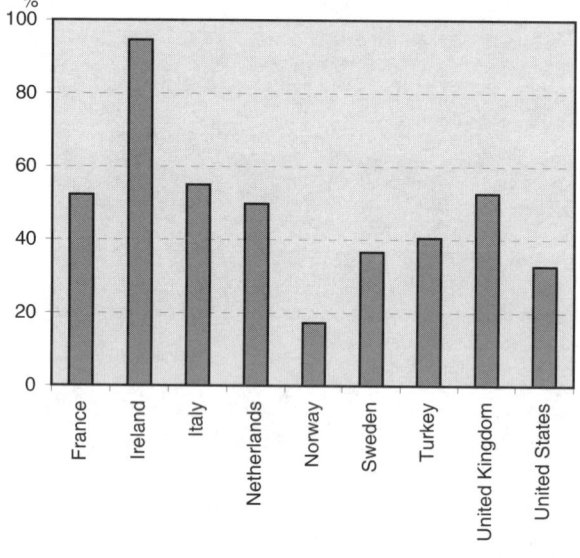

Motor vehicles (ISIC 34)

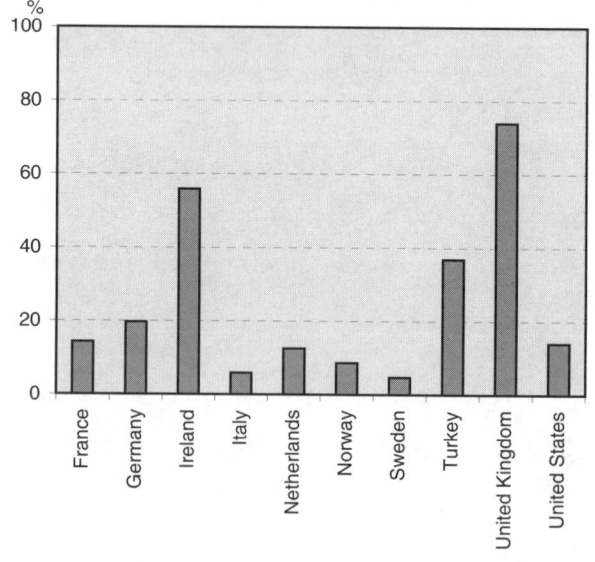

30

Graph 14. **Share of production (or turnover) of foreign affiliates**
in selected industrial sectors *(continued)*

1997 or latest year available

Non-electrical machinery (ISIC 29/30)

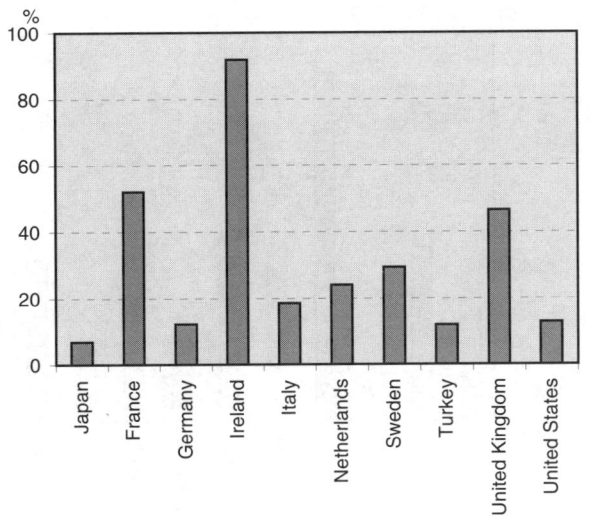

Computers (ISIC 30)

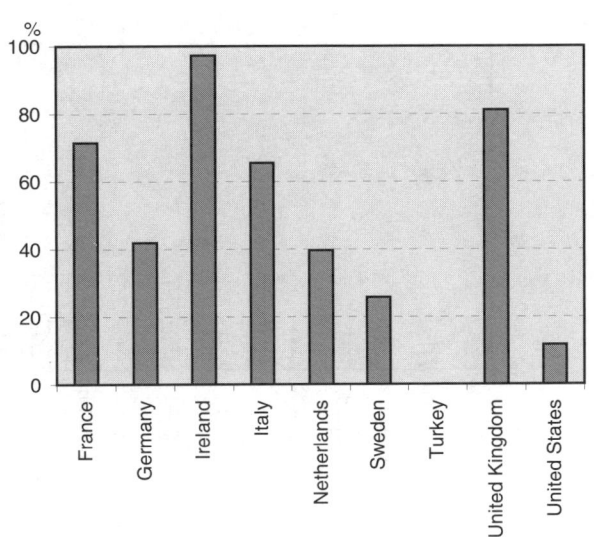

Electronic equipment (ISIC 32)

Instruments (ISIC 33)

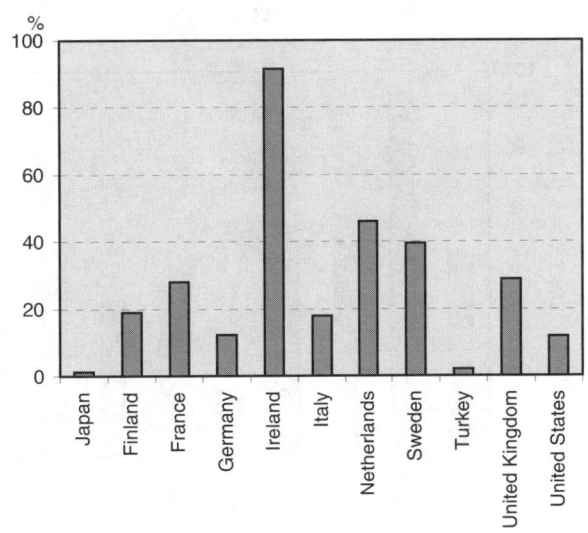

Note: 1992 for the United States, 1995 for Italy, 1996 for France, Germany, Ireland, Netherlands, Norway, Sweden, Turkey and the United Kingdom.

Source: OECD, Activities of Foreign Affiliates database.

Graphique 14. **Part de la production (ou du chiffre d'affaires) des firmes sous contrôle étranger dans quelques secteurs industriels**

1997 ou dernière année disponible

Alimentation, boissons, tabac (CITI 15/16)

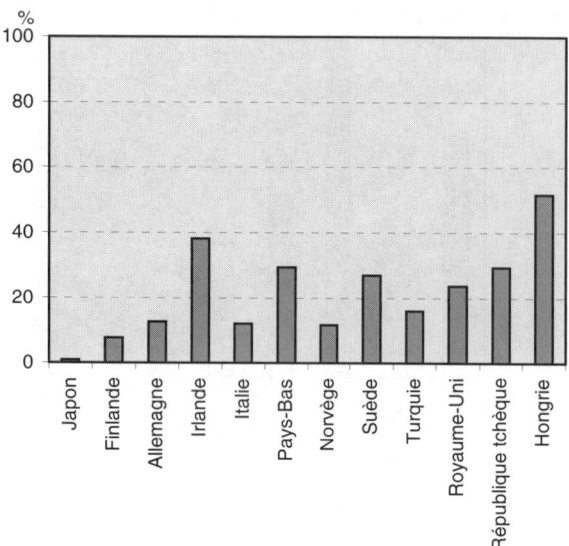

Produits chimiques (CITI 24)

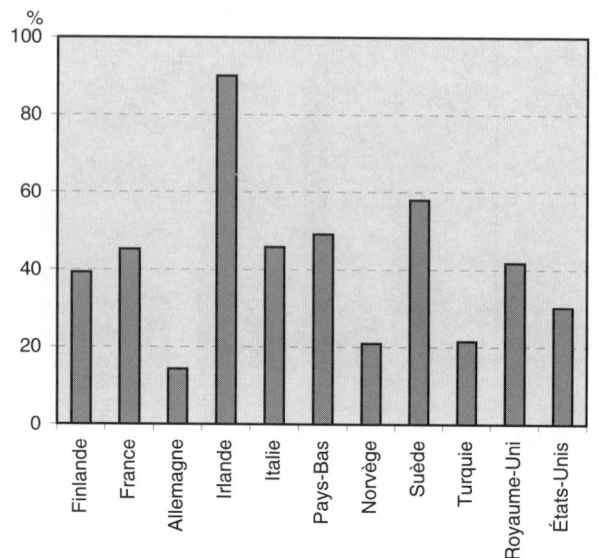

Produits pharmaceutiques (CITI 2423)

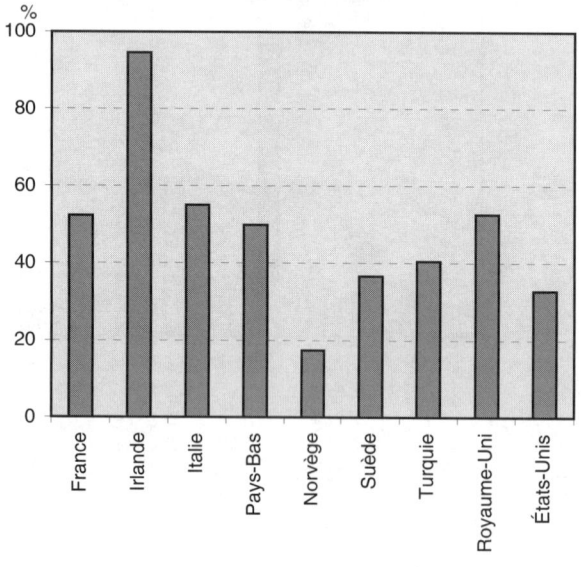

Automobile (CITI 34)

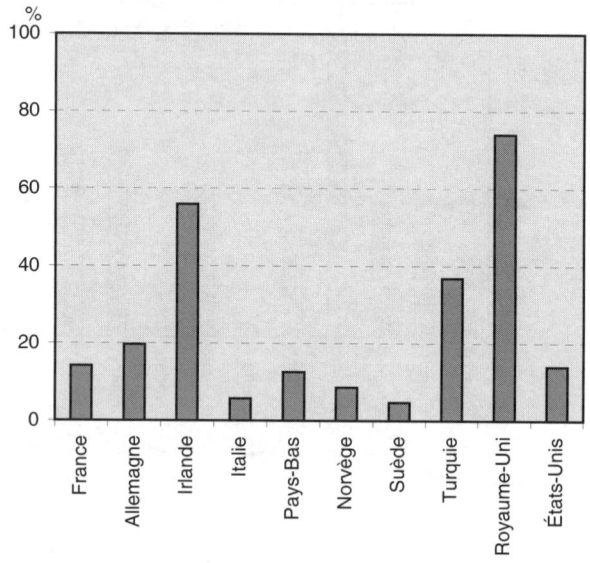

1997 ou dernière année disponible

Machines non électriques (CITI 29/30)

Ordinateurs (CITI 30)

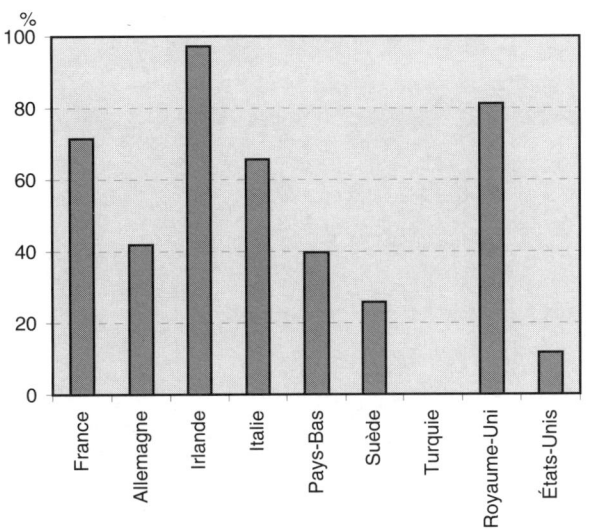

Électronique (CITI 32)

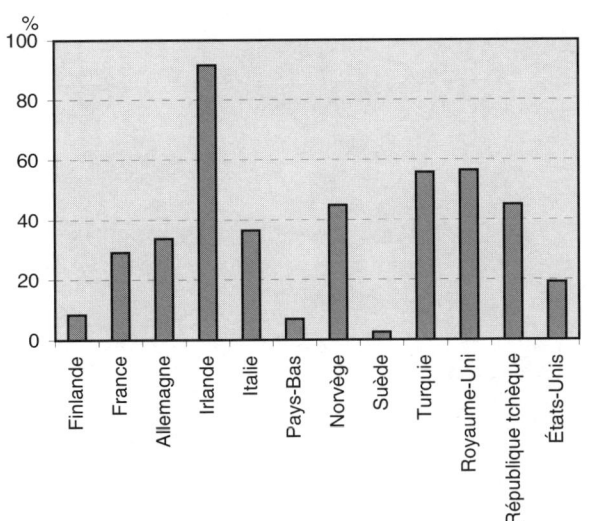

Instruments (CITI 33)

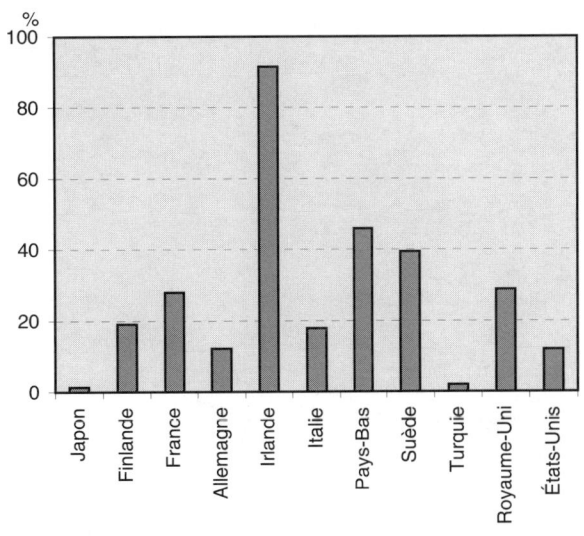

Note : 1992 pour les États-Unis, 1995 pour l'Italie, 1996 pour la France, l'Allemagne, l'Irlande, les Pays-Bas, la Norvège, la Suède, la Turquie et le Royaume-Uni.

Source : OCDE, base de données sur l'Activité des filiales étrangères.

Part II - Partie II

**Activity of foreign affiliates and share of OECD economies
controlled by multinational firms**

**Activité des filiales étrangères et part des économies de l'OCDE
contrôlée par les firmes multinationales**

List of variables and availability of data by country

Liste des variables et disponibilité des données par pays

	Table - Tableau																	
	1	2	3	4	5	6	7	8	9	10	11	12	13	14	15	16	17	18
Canada / Canada	X		X				X	X		X		X						
Czech Republic / République tchèque	X	X	X	X	X	X			X									
Finland / Finlande	X	X	X	X	X	X	X	X	X	X				X			X	X
France / France	X	X	X	X	X	X	X		X	X				X				
Germany / Allemagne	X	X		X			X	X							X	X	X	X
Hungary / Hongrie	X	X		X	X	X	X		X	X	X						X	
Ireland / Irlande	X	X	X		X	X	X			X	X							
Italy / Italie	X	X		X		X												
Japan / Japon	X	X		X	X	X	X	X	X	X	X	X	X	X	X		X	X
Mexico / Mexique	X	X	X	X	X	X			X	X	X			X	X	X	X	X
Netherlands / Pays-Bas	X	X	X	X	X	X	X		X	X	X			X				
Norway / Norvège	X	X	X	X	X	X			X					X				
Sweden / Suède	X	X		X	X	X	X		X	X	X	X		X				X
Turkey / Turquie	X	X	X	X	X	X	X	X	X									
United Kingdom / Royaume-Uni	X	X	X	X	X	X	X		X					X				
United States / États-Unis	X	X		X	X	X	X	X	X	X	X	X	X	X	X	X	X	

Table 1.   Number of enterprises/establishments
Table 2.   Number of employees
Table 3.   Production
Table 4.   Turnover
Table 5.   Value added
Table 6.   Wages and salaries
Table 7.   R&D expenditure
Table 8.   Number of researchers
Table 9.   Gross fixed capital formation
Table 10. Total exports
Table 11. Total imports
Table 12. Intra-firm exports
Table 13. Intra-firms imports
Table 14. Gross operating surplus
Table 15. Technological payments
Table 16. Technological receipts
Table 17. Stock of foreign direct investment
Table 18. Capital under foreign influence

Tableau 1.   Nombre d'entreprises/établissements
Tableau 2.   Nombre de salariés
Tableau 3.   Production
Tableau 4.   Chiffre d'affaires
Tableau 5.   Valeur ajoutée
Tableau 6.   Salaires et traitements
Tableau 7.   Dépenses de R-D
Tableau 8.   Nombre de chercheurs
Tableau 9.   Formation brute de capital fixe
Tableau 10. Exportations totales
Tableau 11. Importations totales
Tableau 12. Exportations intra-firme
Tableau 13. Importations intra-firme
Tableau 14. Excédent brut d'exploitation
Tableau 15. Paiements technologiques
Tableau 16. Recettes technologiques
Tableau 17. Stock d'investissement direct étranger
Tableau 18. Capital sous influence étrangère

CANADA

Sources and Methods

CANADA

Sources et méthodes

Table 1. CANADA

NUMBER OF ENTERPRISES / NOMBRE D'ENTREPRISES

By industry (ISIC Rev. 3)	FOREIGN AFFILIATES (Units)					AS A % OF NATIONAL TOTAL				
	1992	1993	1994	1995	1996	1992	1993	1994	1995	1996
10/14 Mining & quarrying	204	198	207	198	178	..	..	..	..	..
15/37 TOTAL MANUFACTURING	**1570**	**1645**	**1894**	**1946**	**1816**	**24.6**	**26.1**	**25.1**	**25.1**	**26.4**
15/16 Food, beverages, tobacco	124	123	145	147	144	..	..	..	..	..
17/19 Textiles, clothing, leather, footwear	66	69	74	77	78	..	..	..	..	..
20/22 Wood and paper products	175	183	213	213	211	..	..	..	..	..
20 Wood products	56	61	59	61	59	..	..	..	..	..
21/22 Paper, printing and publishing	119	122	154	152	152	..	..	..	..	..
23/25 Chemicals, Total	299	311	335	332	308	..	..	..	..	..
23 Refined petroleum, nuclear fuel	73	73	85	81	75	..	..	..	..	..
24/25 Chemicals, rubber & plastics prod.	226	238	250	251	233	..	..	..	..	..
24 Chemical products	140	147	149	147	143	..	..	..	..	..
2423 Pharmaceuticals	..	..	..	..	..	..	..	..	..	..
25 Rubber and plastics products	86	91	101	104	90	..	..	..	..	..
26 Non-metallic mineral products	101	105	119	125	117	..	..	..	..	..
27/28 Basic & fabricated metals	162	184	232	233	203	..	..	..	..	..
27 Basic metals	46	52	69	70	64	..	..	..	..	..
28 Fabricated metal products	116	132	163	163	139	..	..	..	..	..
29/32 Machinery, Total	236	233	274	295	266	..	..	..	..	..
29/30 Non-electrical machinery	134	131	156	168	150	..	..	..	..	..
29 Non-electrical machinery nec	..	..	..	..	..	..	..	..	..	..
30 Office and computing machinery	..	..	..	..	..	..	..	..	..	..
31/32 Electrical & electronic equipment	102	102	118	127	116	..	..	..	..	..
31 Electrical machinery nec	61	62	70	69	62	..	..	..	..	..
32 Radio, TV & communications eq.	41	40	48	58	54	..	..	..	..	..
33 Scientific instruments	43	47	51	51	44	..	..	..	..	..
34/35 Transportation equipment	138	144	159	166	157	..	..	..	..	..
34 Motor vehicles	109	115	125	133	124	..	..	..	..	..
35 Other transport equipment	29	29	34	33	33	..	..	..	..	..
351 Shipbuilding & repairing	..	..	..	..	..	..	..	..	..	..
353 Aircraft and spacecraft	..	..	..	..	..	..	..	..	..	..
36/37 Other manufacturing	226	246	292	307	288	..	..	..	..	..
40/45 Construction, electricity, gas & water	457	469	520	536	519	..	..	..	..	..
50/55 Trade, repair, hotels & restaurants	1700	1789	2121	2202	2102	..	..	..	..	..
65/74 Finance, insurance, business services	2444	2559	2648	2766	2693	..	..	..	..	..
OTHER ACTIVITIES	109	123	146	156	145	..	..	..	..	..
01/99 GRAND TOTAL	**6484**	**6783**	**7536**	**7804**	**7453**	**18.3**	**19.1**	**19.4**	**19.5**	**20.7**

Total manufacturing by investing country						As a % of total manufacturing by foreign affiliates				
All countries	1570	1645	1894	1946	1816	100.0	100.0	100.0	100.0	100.0
United States	714	746	985	1002	888	45.5	45.3	52.0	51.5	48.9
Canada	..	..	..	..	..	..	..	..	..	..
Mexico	..	..	..	..	..	..	..	..	..	..
Japan	95	105	109	113	123	6.1	6.4	5.8	5.8	6.8
Europe	674	694	692	701	686	42.9	42.2	36.5	36.0	37.8
European Union (15)	591	608	602	603	587	37.6	37.0	31.8	31.0	32.3
Belgium	..	..	..	..	..	..	..	..	..	..
France	91	93	91	86	89	5.8	5.7	4.8	4.4	4.9
Germany	117	126	126	126	123	7.5	7.7	6.7	6.5	6.8
Italy	21	21	22	22	22	1.3	1.3	1.2	1.1	1.2
Netherlands	39	41	41	48	47	2.5	2.5	2.2	2.5	2.6
Spain	..	..	..	..	..	..	..	..	..	..
Sweden	31	33	30	30	27	2.0	2.0	1.6	1.5	1.5
United Kingdom	241	246	244	245	233	15.4	15.0	12.9	12.6	12.8
Switzerland	57	55	60	63	63	3.6	3.3	3.2	3.2	3.5
Australia and New Zealand	27	24	29	32	28	1.7	1.5	1.5	1.6	1.5
Asia (non-OECD)	26	38	36	44	43	1.7	2.3	1.9	2.3	2.4
Latin America	..	..	..	..	..	..	..	..	..	..

Note: Majority foreign-owned firms.
Firmes sous contrôle étranger majoritaire.

Table 3. CANADA

PRODUCTION

By industry (ISIC Rev. 3)		FOREIGN AFFILIATES (Millions of C$)					AS A % OF NATIONAL TOTAL				
		1992	1993	1994	1995	1996	1992	1993	1994	1995	1996
10/14	Mining & quarrying	12921	13806	16174	17083	21242	..	..	..	..	..
15/37	**TOTAL MANUFACTURING**	**177977**	**197478**	**223848**	**253025**	**263527**	**49.9**	**51.4**	**51.4**	**51.3**	**50.9**
15/16	Food, beverages, tobacco	19214	20839	22140	21959	24543	..	..	..	..	..
17/19	Textiles, clothing, leather, footwear	4277	4761	5370	5769	5916	..	..	..	..	..
20/22	Wood and paper products	12786	14328	18001	23169	20337	..	..	..	..	..
20	Wood products	7542	8939	10687	13983	10569	..	..	..	..	..
21/22	Paper, printing and publishing	5244	5389	7314	9186	9768	..	..	..	..	..
23/25	Chemicals, Total	40159	42926	45941	47816	53973	..	..	..	..	..
23	Refined petroleum, nuclear fuel	20908	22152	22689	22799	27422	..	..	..	..	..
24/25	Chemicals, rubber & plastics prod.	19251	20774	23252	25017	26551	..	..	..	..	..
24	Chemical products	14413	15586	17306	18379	19529	..	..	..	..	..
2423	Pharmaceuticals	..	..	..	..	..	..	..	..	..	..
25	Rubber and plastics products	4838	5188	5946	6638	7022	..	..	..	..	..
26	Non-metallic mineral products	6684	7417	7902	8484	9321	..	..	..	..	..
27/28	Basic & fabricated metals	7305	8317	11322	13208	13172	..	..	..	..	..
27	Basic metals	2513	2955	4650	5818	5796	..	..	..	..	..
28	Fabricated metal products	4792	5362	6672	7390	7376	..	..	..	..	..
29/32	Machinery, Total	13093	13465	14540	15049	25989	..	..	..	..	..
29/30	Non-electrical machinery	4448	4946	6122	7290	7133	..	..	..	..	..
29	Non-electrical machinery nec	..	..	..	..	..	..	..	..	..	..
30	Office and computing machinery	..	..	..	..	..	..	..	..	..	..
31/32	Electrical & electronic equipment	8645	8519	8418	7759	18856	..	..	..	..	..
31	Electrical machinery nec	6435	6052	5973	4573	6627	..	..	..	..	..
32	Radio, TV & communications eq.	2210	2467	2445	3186	12229	..	..	..	..	..
33	Scientific instruments	1734	1765	1840	2117	2023	..	..	..	..	..
34/35	Transportation equipment	61945	73279	85093	92286	94372	..	..	..	..	..
34	Motor vehicles	57885	69746	81243	88182	89910	..	..	..	..	..
35	Other transport equipment	4060	3533	3850	4104	4462	..	..	..	..	..
351	Shipbuilding & repairing	..	..	..	..	..	..	..	..	..	..
353	Aircraft and spacecraft	..	..	..	..	..	..	..	..	..	..
36/37	Other manufacturing	10780	10381	11699	23168	13881	..	..	..	..	..
40/45	Construction, electricity, gas & water	8920	9279	8839	11531	12695	..	..	..	..	..
50/55	Trade, repair, hotels & restaurants	67031	75892	87196	97108	108424	..	..	..	..	..
65/74	Finance, insurance, business services	45498	47333	50233	49069	52451	..	..	..	..	..
	OTHER ACTIVITIES	7020	8300	9909	13955	16350					
01/99	**GRAND TOTAL**	**319367**	**352088**	**396199**	**441771**	**474689**	**32.3**	**33.4**	**34.1**	**35.0**	**35.0**

Total manufacturing by investing country						As a % of total manufacturing by foreign affiliates				
All countries	177977	197478	223848	253025	263527	100.0	100.0	100.0	100.0	100.0
United States	123895	139205	160022	185303	190433	69.6	70.5	71.5	73.2	72.3
Canada	..	..	..	..	..	..	..	..	..	..
Mexico	..	..	..	..	..	..	..	..	..	..
Japan	6803	7862	9345	10439	10992	3.8	4.0	4.2	4.1	4.2
Europe	40506	40166	46529	47547	52362	22.8	20.3	20.8	18.8	19.9
European Union (15)	36377	39583	42107	42818	47066	20.4	20.0	18.8	16.9	17.9
Belgium	..	..	..	..	..	..	..	..	..	..
France	5396	5751	7052	7225	7649	3.0	2.9	3.2	2.9	2.9
Germany	6026	7354	8102	8407	9027	3.4	3.7	3.6	3.3	3.4
Italy	1001	1137	1369	1959	2415	0.6	0.6	0.6	0.8	0.9
Netherlands	6244	6477	6888	7476	8408	3.5	3.3	3.1	3.0	3.2
Spain	..	..	..	..	..	..	..	..	..	..
Sweden	2690	2898	1733	2177	2271	1.5	1.5	0.8	0.9	0.9
United Kingdom	13245	14465	15334	13431	13718	7.4	7.3	6.9	5.3	5.2
Switzerland	3701	3656	3834	3906	4225	2.1	1.9	1.7	1.5	1.6
Australia and New Zealand	3665	3053	3582	4072	3855	2.1	1.5	1.6	1.6	1.5
Asia (non-OECD)	1703	1946	2422	2921	2786	1.0	1.0	1.1	1.2	1.1
Latin America	..	..	..	..	..	..	..	..	..	..

Note: Majority foreign-owned firms.
        Firmes sous contrôle étranger majoritaire.

Table 7. CANADA

R&D EXPENDITURE / DÉPENSES DE R-D

By industry (ISIC Rev. 3)	FOREIGN AFFILIATES (Millions of C$)					AS A % OF NATIONAL TOTAL				
	1992	1993	1994	1995	1996	1992	1993	1994	1995	1996
10/14 Mining & quarrying	..	53	..	33	..	..	29.0	..	16.9	..
15/37 **TOTAL MANUFACTURING**	..	1505	..	1900	..	..	40.3	..	40.3	..
15/16 Food, beverages, tobacco	..	44	..	49	..	..	57.1	..	50.0	..
17/19 Textiles, clothing, leather, footwear	..	41	..	44	..	..	83.7	..	81.5	..
20/22 Wood and paper products	..	..	..	3	..	..	..	..	2.2	..
20 Wood products	..	..	..	..	..	..	..	..	..	..
21/22 Paper, printing and publishing	..	..	..	..	..	..	..	..	..	..
23/25 Chemicals, Total	..	..	..	..	..	..	..	..	..	..
23 Refined petroleum, nuclear fuel	..	..	..	..	..	..	..	..	..	..
24/25 Chemicals, rubber & plastics prod.	..	428	..	526	..	..	80.6	..	76.9	..
24 Chemical products	..	418	..	516	..	..	84.4	..	79.6	..
2423 Pharmaceuticals	..	287	..	372	..	..	86.7	..	80.5	..
25 Rubber and plastics products	..	10	..	10	..	..	27.8	..	27.8	..
26 Non-metallic mineral products	..	5	..	4	..	..	41.7	..	40.0	..
27/28 Basic & fabricated metals	..	16	..	..	..	..	6.7	..	..	..
27 Basic metals	..	2	..	..	..	..	1.1	..	..	..
28 Fabricated metal products	..	14	..	11	..	..	21.9	..	14.7	..
29/32 Machinery, Total	..	..	..	636	..	..	..	..	26.5	..
29/30 Non-electrical machinery	..	232	..	246	..	..	55.2	..	49.7	..
29 Non-electrical machinery nec	..	20	..	45	..	..	15.5	..	26.0	..
30 Office and computing machinery	..	212	..	201	..	..	72.9	..	62.4	..
31/32 Electrical & electronic equipment	..	..	..	390	..	..	..	..	20.5	..
31 Electrical machinery nec	..	31	..	43	..	..	53.4	..	54.4	..
32 Radio, TV & communications eq.	..	..	..	347	..	..	..	..	19.0	..
33 Scientific instruments	..	16	..	13	..	..	24.6	..	15.5	..
34/35 Transportation equipment	..	..	..	535	..	..	..	..	59.4	..
34 Motor vehicles	..	99	..	124	..	..	87.6	..	80.0	..
35 Other transport equipment	..	..	..	411	..	..	..	..	55.1	..
351 Shipbuilding & repairing	..	..	..	..	..	..	..	..	..	..
353 Aircraft and spacecraft	..	..	..	410	..	..	..	..	55.3	..
36/37 Other manufacturing	..	..	..	13	..	..	..	..	27.1	..
40/45 Construction, electricity, gas & water	..	..	..	5	..	..	..	..	2.3	..
50/55 Trade, repair, hotels & restaurants	..	..	..	210	..	..	..	..	45.6	..
65/74 Finance, insurance, business services	..	..	..	261	..	..	..	..	15.8	..
OTHER ACTIVITIES	..	..	..	43	..	..	..	..	10.4	..
01/99 **GRAND TOTAL**	..	1895	..	2452	..	..	31.7	..	32.0	..

Total manufacturing by investing country						*As a % of total manufacturing by foreign affiliates*				
All countries	..	1505	..	1900	..	..	100.0	..	100.0	..
United States	..	..	..	1409	..	..	..	..	74.2	..
Canada	..	..	..	..	..	..	..	..	..	..
Mexico	..	..	..	..	..	..	..	..	..	..
Japan	..	..	..	10	..	..	..	..	0.5	..
Europe	..	..	..	454	..	..	..	..	23.9	..
European Union (15)	..	..	..	417	..	..	..	..	21.9	..
Belgium	..	..	..	2	..	..	..	..	0.1	..
France	..	..	..	52	..	..	..	..	2.7	..
Germany	..	..	..	72	..	..	..	..	3.8	..
Italy	..	..	..	6	..	..	..	..	0.3	..
Netherlands	..	..	..	21	..	..	..	..	1.1	..
Spain	..	..	..	0	..	..	..	..	0.0	..
Sweden	..	..	..	..	..	..	..	..	..	..
United Kingdom	..	..	..	219	..	..	..	..	11.5	..
Switzerland	..	..	..	36	..	..	..	..	1.9	..
Australia and New Zealand	..	..	..	..	..	..	..	..	..	..
Asia (non-OECD)	..	..	..	..	..	..	..	..	..	..
Latin America	..	..	..	0	..	..	..	..	0.0	..

Note: Majority foreign-owned firms.
Firmes sous contrôle étranger majoritaire.

Table 8. CANADA

NUMBER OF RESEARCHERS / NOMBRE DE CHERCHEURS

By industry (ISIC Rev. 3)		FOREIGN AFFILIATES (Units)					AS A % OF NATIONAL TOTAL				
		1992	1993	1994	1995	1996	1992	1993	1994	1995	1996
10/14	Mining & quarrying	..	..	..	89	..	..	..	..	14.3	..
15/37	**TOTAL MANUFACTURING**	..	..	..	**7940**	..	..	..	..	**33.3**	..
15/16	Food, beverages, tobacco	..	..	..	260	..	..	..	..	47.3	..
17/19	Textiles, clothing, leather, footwear	..	..	..	135	..	..	..	..	67.5	..
20/22	Wood and paper products	..	..	..	14	..	..	..	..	2.2	..
20	Wood products	..	..	..	..	..	..	..	..	..	..
21/22	Paper, printing and publishing	..	..	..	..	..	..	..	..	..	..
23/25	Chemicals, Total	..	..	..	..	..	..	..	..	..	..
23	Refined petroleum, nuclear fuel	..	..	..	..	..	..	..	..	..	..
24/25	Chemicals, rubber & plastics prod.	..	..	..	1732	..	..	..	..	69.4	..
24	Chemical products	..	..	..	1691	..	..	..	..	73.2	..
2423	Pharmaceuticals	..	..	..	1139	..	..	..	..	81.8	..
25	Rubber and plastics products	..	..	..	41	..	..	..	..	22.2	..
26	Non-metallic mineral products	..	..	..	23	..	..	..	..	26.7	..
27/28	Basic & fabricated metals	..	..	..	..	..	..	..	..	..	..
27	Basic metals	..	..	..	..	..	..	..	..	..	..
28	Fabricated metal products	..	..	..	57	..	..	..	..	11.2	..
29/32	Machinery, Total	..	..	..	4035	..	..	..	..	26.8	..
29/30	Non-electrical machinery	..	..	..	1661	..	..	..	..	50.6	..
29	Non-electrical machinery nec	..	..	..	162	..	..	..	..	20.4	..
30	Office and computing machinery	..	..	..	1499	..	..	..	..	60.2	..
31/32	Electrical & electronic equipment	..	..	..	2374	..	..	..	..	20.2	..
31	Electrical machinery nec	..	..	..	217	..	..	..	..	43.9	..
32	Radio, TV & communications eq.	..	..	..	2157	..	..	..	..	19.1	..
33	Scientific instruments	..	..	..	76	..	..	..	..	11.6	..
34/35	Transportation equipment	..	..	..	1357	..	..	..	..	53.0	..
34	Motor vehicles	..	..	..	295	..	..	..	..	67.4	..
35	Other transport equipment	..	..	..	1062	..	..	..	..	50.1	..
351	Shipbuilding & repairing	..	..	..	..	..	..	..	..	..	..
353	Aircraft and spacecraft	..	..	..	1053	..	..	..	..	50.3	..
36/37	Other manufacturing	..	..	..	106	..	..	..	..	26.1	..
40/45	Construction, electricity, gas & water	..	..	..	53	..	..	..	..	5.9	..
50/55	Trade, repair, hotels & restaurants	..	..	..	1058	..	..	..	..	33.9	..
65/74	Finance, insurance, business services	..	..	..	1935	..	..	..	..	15.8	..
	OTHER ACTIVITIES	..	..	..	141	..	..	..	..	6.3	..
01/99	**GRAND TOTAL**	..	..	..	**11216**	..	..	..	..	**26.1**	..

Total manufacturing by investing country							*As a % of total manufacturing by foreign affiliates*				
All countries		..	..	..	**7940**	..	..	..	..	**100.0**	..
United States		..	..	..	6130	..	..	..	..	77.2	..
Canada		..	..	..	..	..	..	..	..	..	..
Mexico		..	..	..	..	..	..	..	..	..	..
Japan		..	..	..	56	..	..	..	..	0.7	..
Europe		..	..	..	1654	..	..	..	..	20.8	..
European Union (15)		..	..	..	1500	..	..	..	..	18.9	..
Belgium		..	..	..	13	..	..	..	..	0.2	..
France		..	..	..	160	..	..	..	..	2.0	..
Germany		..	..	..	236	..	..	..	..	3.0	..
Italy		..	..	..	38	..	..	..	..	0.5	..
Netherlands		..	..	..	89	..	..	..	..	1.1	..
Spain		..	..	..	0	..	..	..	..	0.0	..
Sweden		..	..	..	..	..	..	..	..	..	..
United Kingdom		..	..	..	742	..	..	..	..	9.3	..
Switzerland		..	..	..	147	..	..	..	..	1.9	..
Australia and New Zealand		..	..	..	..	..	..	..	..	..	..
Asia (non-OECD)		..	..	..	..	..	..	..	..	..	..
Latin America		..	..	..	0	..	..	..	..	0.0	..

Note: Majority foreign-owned firms.
Firmes sous contrôle étranger majoritaire.

Table 10. CANADA

TOTAL EXPORTS / EXPORTATIONS TOTALES

By industry (ISIC Rev. 3)	FOREIGN AFFILIATES (Millions of C$)					AS A % OF NATIONAL TOTAL				
	1992	1993	1994	1995	1996	1992	1993	1994	1995	1996
10/14 Mining & quarrying	7620	7968	9223	11023	..	..	..	..	..	..
15/37 TOTAL MANUFACTURING	**65551**	**78501**	**91957**	**102405**	..	**53.4**	**54.1**	**52.3**	**49.4**	..
15/16 Food, beverages, tobacco	1823	2219	2032	2075	..	..	..	..	..	..
17/19 Textiles, clothing, leather, footwear	1195	1424	1714	1791	..	..	..	..	..	..
20/22 Wood and paper products	7616	8436	9758	12196	..	..	..	..	..	..
20 Wood products	5728	6475	7309	9454	..	..	..	..	..	..
21/22 Paper, printing and publishing	1888	1961	2449	2743	..	..	..	..	..	..
23/25 Chemicals, Total	5776	6521	7367	8289	..	..	..	..	..	..
23 Refined petroleum, nuclear fuel	2498	2717	2595	2689	..	..	..	..	..	..
24/25 Chemicals, rubber & plastics prod.	3279	3804	4773	5601	..	..	..	..	..	..
24 Chemical products	2082	2321	2831	2666	..	..	..	..	..	..
2423 Pharmaceuticals	..	..	..	..	..	..	..	..	..	..
25 Rubber and plastics products	1197	1483	1942	2935	..	..	..	..	..	..
26 Non-metallic mineral products	1111	1230	1498	2604	..	..	..	..	..	..
27/28 Basic & fabricated metals	2310	2948	3728	4673	..	..	..	..	..	..
27 Basic metals	336	575	754	987	..	..	..	..	..	..
28 Fabricated metal products	1974	2373	2974	3686	..	..	..	..	..	..
29/32 Machinery, Total	4308	5025	6434	8035	..	..	..	..	..	..
29/30 Non-electrical machinery	2271	2835	4002	5342	..	..	..	..	..	..
29 Non-electrical machinery nec	..	..	..	..	..	..	..	..	..	..
30 Office and computing machinery	..	..	..	..	..	..	..	..	..	..
31/32 Electrical & electronic equipment	2037	2190	2432	2693	..	..	..	..	..	..
31 Electrical machinery nec	1233	1359	1553	1693	..	..	..	..	..	..
32 Radio, TV & communications eq.	804	831	879	1000	..	..	..	..	..	..
33 Scientific instruments	489	527	630	670	..	..	..	..	..	..
34/35 Transportation equipment	39255	47908	56269	59250	..	..	..	..	..	..
34 Motor vehicles	36270	45112	53583	56386	..	..	..	..	..	..
35 Other transport equipment	2985	2796	2686	2864	..	..	..	..	..	..
351 Shipbuilding & repairing	..	..	..	..	..	..	..	..	..	..
353 Aircraft and spacecraft	..	..	..	..	..	..	..	..	..	..
36/37 Other manufacturing	1667	2264	2528	2822	..	..	..	..	..	..
40/45 Construction, electricity, gas & water	610	689	696	645	..	..	..	..	..	..
50/55 Trade, repair, hotels & restaurants	3009	3906	4576	6133	..	..	..	..	..	..
65/74 Finance, insurance, business services	4908	5018	6758	8123	..	..	..	..	..	..
OTHER ACTIVITIES	995	1407	1754	1985	..	..	..	..	..	..
01/99 GRAND TOTAL	**82691**	**97488**	**114964**	**130313**	..	..	..	..	..	..

Total manufacturing by investing country						As a % of total manufacturing by foreign affiliates				
All countries	**65551**	**78501**	**91957**	**102405**	..	**100.0**	**100.0**	**100.0**	**100.0**	..
United States	53300	63812	75824	84096	..	81.3	81.3	82.5	82.1	..
Canada	..	..	..	..	..	..	..	..	..	..
Mexico	..	..	..	..	..	..	..	..	..	..
Japan	2899	3667	4241	4629	..	4.4	4.7	4.6	4.5	..
Europe	6958	8135	9124	10759	..	10.6	10.4	9.9	10.5	..
European Union (15)	5806	6918	7608	8877	..	8.9	8.8	8.3	8.7	..
Belgium	..	..	..	..	..	..	..	..	..	..
France	1335	1534	1700	1934	..	2.0	2.0	1.8	1.9	..
Germany	1648	1835	2172	2803	..	2.5	2.3	2.4	2.7	..
Italy	343	497	807	1082	..	0.5	0.6	0.9	1.1	..
Netherlands	283	266	315	585	..	0.4	0.3	0.3	0.6	..
Spain	..	..	..	..	..	..	..	..	..	..
Sweden	..	..	..	..	..	..	..	..	..	..
United Kingdom	2129	2739	2558	2580	..	3.2	3.5	2.8	2.5	..
Switzerland	390	422	432	487	..	0.6	0.5	0.5	0.5	..
Australia and New Zealand	1030	1032	1099	1463	..	1.6	1.3	1.2	1.4	..
Asia (non-OECD)	342	491	442	730	..	0.5	0.6	0.5	0.7	..
Latin America	..	..	..	..	..	..	..	..	..	..

Note: Majority foreign-owned firms.
Firmes sous contrôle étranger majoritaire.

Table 12. CANADA

INTRA-FIRM EXPORTS / EXPORTATIONS INTRA-FIRME

By industry (ISIC Rev. 3)	FOREIGN AFFILIATES (Millions of C$)									
	1987	1988	1989	1990	1991	1992	1993	1994	1995	1996
10/14 Mining & quarrying	..	..	..	..	1184	1464	1443	2953	..	..
15/37 TOTAL MANUFACTURING	..	..	..	..	34636	40264	48081	55773	..	..
15/16 Food, beverages, tobacco	..	..	..	..	486	564	571	669	..	..
17/19 Textiles, clothing, leather, footwear	..	..	..	..	428	475	643	802	..	..
20/22 Wood and paper products	..	..	..	..	999	984	1350	1325	..	..
20 Wood products	..	..	..	..	696	650	824	746	..	..
21/22 Paper, printing and publishing	..	..	..	..	303	334	526	579	..	..
23/25 Chemicals, Total	..	..	..	..	2631	2960	3350	3736	..	..
23 Refined petroleum, nuclear fuel	..	..	..	..	1009	1036	1166	1126	..	..
24/25 Chemicals, rubber & plastics prod.	..	..	..	..	1622	1925	2184	2611	..	..
24 Chemical products	..	..	..	..	996	1215	1288	1519	..	..
2423 Pharmaceuticals	..	..	..	..	..	..	..	..	..	..
25 Rubber and plastics products	..	..	..	..	626	709	896	1092	..	..
26 Non-metallic mineral products	..	..	..	..	460	471	612	728	..	..
27/28 Basic & fabricated metals	..	..	..	..	917	910	944	1342	..	..
27 Basic metals	..	..	..	..	102	62	133	182	..	..
28 Fabricated metal products	..	..	..	..	815	848	811	1160	..	..
29/32 Machinery, Total	..	..	..	..	2058	2002	2290	3197	..	..
29/30 Non-electrical machinery	..	..	..	..	1367	1223	1472	2363	..	..
29 Non-electrical machinery nec	..	..	..	..	..	..	..	..	..	..
30 Office and computing machinery	..	..	..	..	..	..	..	..	..	..
31/32 Electrical & electronic equipment	..	..	..	..	691	779	818	835	..	..
31 Electrical machinery nec	..	..	..	..	450	530	580	615	..	..
32 Radio, TV & communications eq.	..	..	..	..	241	249	238	220	..	..
33 Scientific instruments	..	..	..	..	234	315	363	380	..	..
34/35 Transportation equipment	..	..	..	..	26067	31181	37356	42787	..	..
34 Motor vehicles	..	..	..	..	25220	30326	36620	41996	..	..
35 Other transport equipment	..	..	..	..	847	855	736	791	..	..
351 Shipbuilding & repairing	..	..	..	..	..	..	..	..	..	..
353 Aircraft and spacecraft	..	..	..	..	..	..	..	..	..	..
36/37 Other manufacturing	..	..	..	..	357	402	604	807	..	..
40/45 Construction, electricity, gas & water	..	..	..	..	..	..	..	..	..	..
50/55 Trade, repair, hotels & restaurants	..	..	..	..	856	1034	1203	1044	..	..
65/74 Finance, insurance, business services	..	..	..	..	..	..	..	..	..	..
OTHER ACTIVITIES	..	..	..	..	36	63	130	213	..	..
01/99 GRAND TOTAL	..	..	..	..	42021	47209	55107	65209	..	..

Total manufacturing by investing country

	1987	1988	1989	1990	1991	1992	1993	1994	1995	1996
All countries	..	..	..	..	34636	40264	48081	55773	..	..
United States	..	..	..	..	31327	37049	43917	50006	..	..
Canada	..	..	..	..	..	..	..	..	..	..
Mexico	..	..	..	..	..	..	..	..	..	..
Japan	..	..	..	..	959	703	1300	2651	..	..
Europe	..	..	..	..	1959	2123	2470	2771	..	..
European Union (15)	..	..	..	..	1213	1416	1700	1846	..	..
Belgium	..	..	..	..	..	..	..	..	..	..
France	..	..	..	..	669	832	865	731	..	..
Germany	..	..	..	..	295	355	600	730	..	..
Italy	..	..	..	..	..	..	..	..	..	..
Netherlands	..	..	..	..	..	..	..	..	..	..
Spain	..	..	..	..	..	..	..	..	..	..
Sweden	..	..	..	..	..	..	..	..	..	..
United Kingdom	..	..	..	..	431	359	377	419	..	..
Switzerland	..	..	..	..	142	169	190	176	..	..
Australia and New Zealand	..	..	..	..	152	169	170	229	..	..
Asia (non-OECD)	..	..	..	..	217	191	218	108	..	..
Latin America	..	..	..	..	..	..	..	..	..	..

Note: Majority foreign-owned firms.
Firmes sous contrôle étranger majoritaire.

Table 14. CANADA

GROSS OPERATING SURPLUS / EXCÉDENT BRUT D'EXPLOITATION

By industry (ISIC Rev. 3)	FOREIGN AFFILIATES (Millions of C$)					AS A % OF NATIONAL TOTAL				
	1992	1993	1994	1995	1996	1992	1993	1994	1995	1996
10/14 Mining & quarrying	926	1522	2000	1621	3021	..	..	..	..	..
15/37 TOTAL MANUFACTURING	**4675**	**7854**	**13545**	**19198**	**16730**	**46.6**	**52.5**	**50.8**	**50.2**	**53.0**
15/16 Food, beverages, tobacco	1997	2058	2284	2229	2506	..	..	..	..	..
17/19 Textiles, clothing, leather, footwear	365	452	678	748	625	..	..	..	..	..
20/22 Wood and paper products	-209	263	1955	3977	1357	..	..	..	..	..
20 Wood products	-274	285	1518	2654	938	..	..	..	..	..
21/22 Paper, printing and publishing	65	-22	437	1323	419	..	..	..	..	..
23/25 Chemicals, Total	1808	2779	3785	4774	4790	..	..	..	..	..
23 Refined petroleum, nuclear fuel	377	1246	1870	2079	2130	..	..	..	..	..
24/25 Chemicals, rubber & plastics prod.	1431	1533	1915	2695	2660	..	..	..	..	..
24 Chemical products	1173	1282	1554	2226	2109	..	..	..	..	..
2423 Pharmaceuticals	..	..	..	..	..	..	..	..	..	..
25 Rubber and plastics products	258	251	361	469	551	..	..	..	..	..
26 Non-metallic mineral products	177	486	509	820	984	..	..	..	..	..
27/28 Basic & fabricated metals	70	151	569	1130	678	..	..	..	..	..
27 Basic metals	2	53	355	795	299	..	..	..	..	..
28 Fabricated metal products	68	98	214	335	379	..	..	..	..	..
29/32 Machinery, Total	145	168	559	941	1748	..	..	..	..	..
29/30 Non-electrical machinery	105	129	314	449	405	..	..	..	..	..
29 Non-electrical machinery nec	..	..	..	..	..	..	..	..	..	..
30 Office and computing machinery	..	..	..	..	..	..	..	..	..	..
31/32 Electrical & electronic equipment	40	39	245	492	1343	..	..	..	..	..
31 Electrical machinery nec	8	-22	131	251	353	..	..	..	..	..
32 Radio, TV & communications eq.	32	61	114	241	990	..	..	..	..	..
33 Scientific instruments	152	118	115	172	121	..	..	..	..	..
34/35 Transportation equipment	-224	1117	2618	3389	3197	..	..	..	..	..
34 Motor vehicles	-412	954	2438	3094	2825	..	..	..	..	..
35 Other transport equipment	188	163	180	295	372	..	..	..	..	..
351 Shipbuilding & repairing	..	..	..	..	..	..	..	..	..	..
353 Aircraft and spacecraft	..	..	..	..	..	..	..	..	..	..
36/37 Other manufacturing	394	262	473	1018	724	..	..	..	..	..
40/45 Construction, electricity, gas & water	461	492	399	391	567	..	..	..	..	..
50/55 Trade, repair, hotels & restaurants	1193	1020	2645	2842	3634	..	..	..	..	..
65/74 Finance, insurance, business services	3771	4309	5988	7973	9536	..	..	..	..	..
OTHER ACTIVITIES	874	906	891	39	1396	..	..	..	..	..
01/99 GRAND TOTAL	**11900**	**16103**	**25468**	**32064**	**34884**	**22.8**	**24.3**	**27.6**	**28.6**	**30.3**

Total manufacturing by investing country						As a % of total manufacturing by foreign affiliates				
All countries	**4675**	**7854**	**13545**	**19198**	**16730**	**100.0**	**100.0**	**100.0**	**100.0**	**100.0**
United States	3146	5665	9377	13303	11316	67.3	72.1	69.2	69.3	67.6
Canada	..	..	..	..	..	..	..	..	..	..
Mexico	..	..	..	..	..	..	..	..	..	..
Japan	-165	6	363	629	367	-3.5	0.1	2.7	3.3	2.2
Europe	1443	1780	3019	3945	4111	30.9	22.7	22.3	20.5	24.6
European Union (15)	1337	1674	2848	3783	3860	28.6	21.3	21.0	19.7	23.1
Belgium	..	..	..	..	..	..	..	..	..	..
France	70	78	327	381	432	1.5	1.0	2.4	2.0	2.6
Germany	228	396	548	741	754	4.9	5.0	4.0	3.9	4.5
Italy	-29	30	44	91	92	-0.6	0.4	0.3	0.5	0.5
Netherlands	-64	110	625	816	672	-1.4	1.4	4.6	4.3	4.0
Spain	..	..	..	..	..	..	..	..	..	..
Sweden	65	-83	54	224	144	1.4	-1.1	0.4	1.2	0.9
United Kingdom	1042	1079	1154	1360	1463	22.3	13.7	8.5	7.1	8.7
Switzerland	-46	82	148	104	188	-1.0	1.0	1.1	0.5	1.1
Australia and New Zealand	217	207	411	643	228	4.6	2.6	3.0	3.3	1.4
Asia (non-OECD)	-47	-4	130	311	262	-1.0	-0.1	1.0	1.6	1.6
Latin America	..	..	..	..	..	..	..	..	..	..

Note: Majority foreign-owned firms.
Firmes sous contrôle étranger majoritaire.

44

CANADA

Source

For *Number of enterprises*, *Production* and *Gross operating surplus*, the data are prepared by the Industrial Organization and Finance Division of Statistics Canada. These data are collected on an annual basis from the Survey of Financial Statistics which covers firms with foreign control of more than 50% of the voting equity. The results are published in the report entitled *Financial and Taxation Statistics for Enterprises*. Data on the country of control of enterprises are derived from the CALURA survey which is conducted annually. The results of this survey are reported in the publication entitled *Parliamentary Report, Foreign Control in the Canadian Economy*.

For *Total exports* and *Intra-firm exports*, the data are collected by the International Trade Division of Statistics Canada. International trade data is compiled using administrative records provided by Revenue Canada – Customs and Excise and the US Bureau of the Census. The data are derived from administrative sources and therefore are a census of all international trade transactions of merchandise goods trade.

For *R&D expenditure*, the data come from the report *Industrial Research and Development*, Statistics Canada.

Industrial classification

For all variables, the data are classified according to the principal industrial activity of the affiliate.

The industrial classification used for Canadian tables is the national classification converted to ISIC Revision 3.

Variables

- *Production* is defined as the operating revenue, *i.e.* the revenue derived from the sales of goods and services.

- *R&D expenditure* refer to current R&D expenditure only.

- *Total exports* refer to merchandise exports only.

- *Intra-firm exports* are Related Party Exports to the United States.

- *Gross operating surplus* corresponds to operating profit.

Geographical breakdown

The country of origin is that of the immediate controller.

CANADA

Source

Pour le *Nombre d'entreprises*, la *Production* et l'*Excédent brut d'exploitation*, les données émanent de la Division de l'Organisation et des Finances de l'Industrie, Statistique Canada. Elles sont collectées à partir de l'enquête annuelle des Statistiques financières, qui couvre les entreprises dans lesquelles la participation étrangère dépasse 50 % des actions avec droit de vote. Les résultats sont publiés dans le rapport *Financial and Taxation Statistics for Enterprises*. Les données sur le pays de contrôle des entreprises sont issues de l'enquête CALURA qui est effectuée tous les ans. Les résultats de cette enquête sont rapportés dans la publication *Rapport au Parlement, Contrôle étranger de l'économie canadienne*.

Pour les *Exportations totales* et les *Exportations intra-firme*, les données sont collectées par la division du Commerce International, Statistique Canada. Ces données sont issues d'enregistrements administratifs fournis par Revenu Canada – Service des douanes et accise et le US Bureau of the Census. Elles sont dérivées de sources administratives et par conséquent sont un recensement de toutes les transactions internationales de marchandises.

Pour les *Dépenses de R-D*, les données sont issues du rapport de Statistique Canada *Recherche et développement industriel*.

Classification industrielle

Pour toutes les variables, les données sont classées selon l'activité industrielle principale de l'entreprise affiliée.

La classification industrielle utilisée pour les tableaux canadiens est la classification nationale adaptée pour correspondre à la CITI révision 3.

Variables

- La *Production* est définie par le revenu d'exploitation, c'est-à dire le revenu provenant de la vente de biens et services.

- Les *Dépenses de R-D* concernent les dépenses courantes seulement.

- Les *Exportations totales* se réfèrent uniquement aux exportations de marchandises.

- Les *Exportations intra-firme* concernent les exportations aux États-Unis.

- L'*Excédent brut d'exploitation* correspond au bénéfice d'exploitation.

Ventilation géographique

Le pays d'origine est celui où se situe le contrôle immédiat.

CZECH REPUBLIC

Table 1.   Number of enterprises

Table 2.   Number of employees

Table 3.   Production

Table 4.   Turnover

Table 5.   Value added

Table 6.   Wages and salaries

Table 9.   Gross fixed capital formation

Sources and Methods

RÉPUBLIQUE TCHÈQUE

Tableau 1.   Nombre d'entreprises

Tableau 2.   Nombre de salariés

Tableau 3.   Production

Tableau 4.   Chiffre d'affaires

Tableau 5.   Valeur ajoutée

Tableau 6.   Salaires et traitements

Tableau 9.   Formation brute de capital fixe

Sources et méthodes

Table 1. CZECH REPUBLIC / RÉPUBLIQUE TCHÈQUE

NUMBER OF ENTERPRISES / NOMBRE D'ENTREPRISES

By industry (ISIC Rev. 3)	FOREIGN AFFILIATES (Units)					AS A % OF NATIONAL TOTAL				
	1993	1994	1995	1996	1997	1993	1994	1995	1996	1997
10/14 Mining & quarrying	..	..	..	..	10	..	..	..	..	20.4
15/37 TOTAL MANUFACTURING	..	..	**227**	**268**	**373**	..	..	**10.2**	**12.0**	**16.3**
15/16 Food, beverages, tobacco	..	..	23	25	35	..	..	6.3	6.5	9.0
17/19 Textiles, clothing, leather, footwear	..	..	21	..	..	..	..	7.5	..	..
20/22 Wood and paper products	..	..	24	29	41	..	..	12.7	16.8	24.0
20 Wood products	..	..	..	..	..	..	..	..	..	..
21/22 Paper, printing and publishing	..	..	..	..	..	..	..	..	..	..
23/25 Chemicals, Total	..	..	..	..	..	..	..	..	..	..
23 Refined petroleum, nuclear fuel	..	..	..	..	..	..	..	..	..	..
24/25 Chemicals, rubber & plastics prod.	..	..	..	..	30	..	..	..	..	18.9
24 Chemical products	..	..	..	..	..	..	..	..	..	..
2423 Pharmaceuticals	..	..	..	..	..	..	..	..	..	..
25 Rubber and plastics products	..	..	..	..	..	..	..	..	..	..
26 Non-metallic mineral products	..	..	32	..	..	..	..	21.6	..	..
27/28 Basic & fabricated metals	..	..	..	21	..	..	..	..	6.7	..
27 Basic metals	..	..	..	8	..	..	..	..	9.3	..
28 Fabricated metal products	..	..	..	13	..	..	..	..	5.7	..
29/32 Machinery, Total	..	..	53	..	..	..	..	11.9	..	..
29/30 Non-electrical machinery	..	..	19	..	..	..	..	5.8	..	..
29 Non-electrical machinery nec	..	..	19	..	31	..	..	5.8	..	9.3
30 Office and computing machinery	..	..	0	..	..	..	..	0.0	..	..
31/32 Electrical & electronic equipment	..	..	34	..	52	..	..	29.3	..	28.1
31 Electrical machinery nec	..	..	28	..	44	..	..	25.5	..	30.3
32 Radio, TV & communications eq.	..	..	6	7	8	..	..	15.4	17.5	20.0
33 Scientific instruments	..	..	5	10	..	..	..	8.9	18.2	..
34/35 Transportation equipment	..	..	..	..	..	..	..	..	..	..
34 Motor vehicles	..	..	..	..	..	..	..	..	..	..
35 Other transport equipment	..	..	..	..	..	..	..	..	..	..
351 Shipbuilding & repairing	..	..	..	..	..	..	..	..	..	..
353 Aircraft and spacecraft	..	..	..	..	..	..	..	..	..	..
36/37 Other manufacturing	..	..	..	..	..	..	..	..	..	..
40/45 Construction, electricity, gas & water	..	..	21	20	32	..	..	3.1	3.0	5.2
50/55 Trade, repair, hotels & restaurants	..	..	46	46	76	..	..	8.3	10.8	15.0
65/74 Finance, insurance, business services	..	..	47	47	60	..	..	13.5	13.6	15.8
OTHER ACTIVITIES	..	..	8	32	17	..	..	0.8	3.3	1.6
01/99 GRAND TOTAL	..	..	**353**	**421**	**568**	..	..	**7.2**	**8.9**	**11.6**

Total manufacturing by investing country						*As a % of total manufacturing by foreign affiliates*				
All countries	..	..	**227**	**268**	**373**	..	..	**100.0**	**100.0**	**100.0**
United States	..	..	..	..	..	..	..	..	..	..
Canada	..	..	..	..	..	..	..	..	..	..
Mexico	..	..	..	..	..	..	..	..	..	..
Japan	..	..	..	..	..	..	..	..	..	..
Europe	..	..	..	..	..	..	..	..	..	..
European Union (15)	..	..	..	224	311	..	..	..	83.6	83.4
Belgium	..	..	..	..	..	..	..	..	..	..
France	..	..	..	..	..	..	..	..	..	..
Germany	..	..	..	..	..	..	..	..	..	..
Italy	..	..	..	..	..	..	..	..	..	..
Netherlands	..	..	..	..	..	..	..	..	..	..
Spain	..	..	..	..	..	..	..	..	..	..
Sweden	..	..	..	..	..	..	..	..	..	..
United Kingdom	..	..	..	..	..	..	..	..	..	..
Switzerland	..	..	..	..	..	..	..	..	..	..
Australia and New Zealand	..	..	..	..	..	..	..	..	..	..
Asia (non-OECD)	..	..	..	..	..	..	..	..	..	..
Latin America	..	..	..	..	..	..	..	..	..	..

Note: Majority foreign-owned firms.
Firmes sous contrôle étranger majoritaire.

Table 2. CZECH REPUBLIC / RÉPUBLIQUE TCHÈQUE

NUMBER OF EMPLOYEES / NOMBRE DE SALARIÉS

By industry (ISIC Rev. 3)	FOREIGN AFFILIATES (Full-time Eq.)					AS A % OF NATIONAL TOTAL				
	1993	1994	1995	1996	1997	1993	1994	1995	1996	1997
10/14 Mining & quarrying	..	..	..	..	1 914	..	..	..	..	2.5
15/37 TOTAL MANUFACTURING	..	..	**126 430**	**149 847**	**171 000**	..	..	**12.4**	**15.4**	**18.7**
15/16 Food, beverages, tobacco	..	..	15 855	17 015	21 228	..	..	15.1	15.4	20.2
17/19 Textiles, clothing, leather, footwear	..	..	7 212	..	..	..	..	5.4	..	..
20/22 Wood and paper products	..	..	6 695	10 812	12 928	..	..	11.6	19.7	26.6
20 Wood products	..	..	..	..	..	..	..	..	..	..
21/22 Paper, printing and publishing	..	..	..	..	..	..	..	..	..	..
23/25 Chemicals, Total	..	..	..	..	..	..	..	..	..	..
23 Refined petroleum, nuclear fuel	..	..	..	..	..	..	..	..	..	..
24/25 Chemicals, rubber & plastics prod.	..	..	..	..	14 639	..	..	..	..	19.1
24 Chemical products	..	..	..	..	..	..	..	..	..	..
2423 Pharmaceuticals	..	..	..	..	..	..	..	..	..	..
25 Rubber and plastics products	..	..	..	..	..	..	..	..	..	..
26 Non-metallic mineral products	..	..	14 794	..	..	..	..	23.0	..	..
27/28 Basic & fabricated metals	..	..	..	10 982	..	..	..	..	6.5	..
27 Basic metals	..	..	..	4 258	..	..	..	..	4.1	..
28 Fabricated metal products	..	..	..	6 724	..	..	..	..	10.2	..
29/32 Machinery, Total	..	..	28 410	..	..	..	..	13.0	..	..
29/30 Non-electrical machinery	..	..	9 512	..	..	..	..	5.8	..	..
29 Non-electrical machinery nec	..	..	9 512	..	9 585	..	..	5.9	..	7.0
30 Office and computing machinery	..	..	0	..	..	..	..	0.0	..	..
31/32 Electrical & electronic equipment	..	..	18 898	..	26 560	..	..	34.4	..	36.7
31 Electrical machinery nec	..	..	16 174	..	22 038	..	..	31.0	..	38.8
32 Radio, TV & communications eq.	..	..	2 724	2 880	4 522	..	..	15.8	18.3	29.1
33 Scientific instruments	..	..	1 810	3 036	..	..	..	9.4	17.2	..
34/35 Transportation equipment	..	..	..	..	..	..	..	..	..	..
34 Motor vehicles	..	..	..	..	..	..	..	..	..	..
35 Other transport equipment	..	..	..	..	..	..	..	..	..	..
351 Shipbuilding & repairing	..	..	..	..	..	..	..	..	..	..
353 Aircraft and spacecraft	..	..	..	..	..	..	..	..	..	..
36/37 Other manufacturing	..	..	..	..	..	..	..	..	..	..
40/45 Construction, electricity, gas & water	..	..	9 177	10 967	15 396	..	..	3.8	4.7	7.4
50/55 Trade, repair, hotels & restaurants	..	..	18 000	25 286	34 461	..	..	12.1	19.8	27.4
65/74 Finance, insurance, business services	..	..	14 100	15 931	19 013	..	..	10.0	11.5	13.9
OTHER ACTIVITIES	..	..	1 257	11 175	3 160	..	..	0.3	2.8	0.8
01/99 GRAND TOTAL	..	..	**170 596**	**214 621**	**244 944**	..	..	**8.3**	**11.0**	**13.1**

Total manufacturing by investing country						As a % of total manufacturing by foreign affiliates				
All countries	..	..	**126 430**	**149 847**	**171 000**	..	..	**100.0**	**100.0**	**100.0**
United States	..	..	..	..	..	..	..	..	..	..
Canada	..	..	..	..	..	..	..	..	..	..
Mexico	..	..	..	..	..	..	..	..	..	..
Japan	..	..	..	..	..	..	..	..	..	..
Europe	..	..	..	..	..	..	..	..	..	..
European Union (15)	..	..	..	118 044	143 059	..	..	..	78.8	83.7
Belgium	..	..	..	..	..	..	..	..	..	..
France	..	..	..	..	..	..	..	..	..	..
Germany	..	..	..	..	..	..	..	..	..	..
Italy	..	..	..	..	..	..	..	..	..	..
Netherlands	..	..	..	..	..	..	..	..	..	..
Spain	..	..	..	..	..	..	..	..	..	..
Sweden	..	..	..	..	..	..	..	..	..	..
United Kingdom	..	..	..	..	..	..	..	..	..	..
Switzerland	..	..	..	..	..	..	..	..	..	..
Australia and New Zealand	..	..	..	..	..	..	..	..	..	..
Asia (non-OECD)	..	..	..	..	..	..	..	..	..	..
Latin America	..	..	..	..	..	..	..	..	..	..

Note: Majority foreign-owned firms.
Firmes sous contrôle étranger majoritaire.

Table 3. CZECH REPUBLIC / RÉPUBLIQUE TCHÈQUE

PRODUCTION

By industry (ISIC Rev. 3)	FOREIGN AFFILIATES (Millions of CK)					AS A % OF NATIONAL TOTAL				
	1993	1994	1995	1996	1997	1993	1994	1995	1996	1997
10/14 Mining & quarrying	..	..	..	..	2 036	..	..	..	..	3.4
15/37 TOTAL MANUFACTURING	..	..	**180 689**	**236 677**	**342 734**	..	..	**19.0**	**24.3**	**30.7**
15/16 Food, beverages, tobacco	..	..	32 148	38 377	58 174	..	..	20.7	21.2	29.4
17/19 Textiles, clothing, leather, footwear	..	..	2 952	..	..	..	..	4.9	..	..
20/22 Wood and paper products	..	..	9 138	17 751	25 080	..	..	14.6	29.4	40.2
20 Wood products	..	..	..	..	..	..	..	..	..	..
21/22 Paper, printing and publishing	..	..	..	..	..	..	..	..	..	..
23/25 Chemicals, Total	..	..	..	..	..	..	..	..	..	..
23 Refined petroleum, nuclear fuel	..	..	..	..	..	..	..	..	..	..
24/25 Chemicals, rubber & plastics prod.	..	..	..	..	31 043	..	..	..	..	24.5
24 Chemical products	..	..	..	..	..	..	..	..	..	..
2423 Pharmaceuticals	..	..	..	..	..	..	..	..	..	..
25 Rubber and plastics products	..	..	..	..	..	..	..	..	..	..
26 Non-metallic mineral products	..	..	19 395	..	..	..	..	38.9	..	..
27/28 Basic & fabricated metals	..	..	..	16 820	..	..	..	..	9.8	..
27 Basic metals	..	..	..	5 587	..	..	..	..	4.6	..
28 Fabricated metal products	..	..	..	11 233	..	..	..	..	22.2	..
29/32 Machinery, Total	..	..	23 267	..	..	..	..	18.5	..	..
29/30 Non-electrical machinery	..	..	7 797	..	..	..	..	9.0	..	..
29 Non-electrical machinery nec	..	..	7 797	..	10 831	..	..	9.1	..	10.9
30 Office and computing machinery	..	..	0	..	..	..	..	0.0	..	..
31/32 Electrical & electronic equipment	..	..	15 470	..	29 885	..	..	39.6	..	47.6
31 Electrical machinery nec	..	..	14 201	..	25 140	..	..	37.5	..	48.0
32 Radio, TV & communications eq.	..	..	1 269	2 625	4 745	..	..	15.7	30.1	45.1
33 Scientific instruments	..	..	1 171	2 109	..	..	..	14.4	23.7	..
34/35 Transportation equipment	..	..	..	..	..	..	..	..	..	..
34 Motor vehicles	..	..	..	..	..	..	..	..	..	..
35 Other transport equipment	..	..	..	..	..	..	..	..	..	..
351 Shipbuilding & repairing	..	..	..	..	..	..	..	..	..	..
353 Aircraft and spacecraft	..	..	..	..	..	..	..	..	..	..
36/37 Other manufacturing	..	..	..	..	..	..	..	..	..	..
40/45 Construction, electricity, gas & water	..	..	12 899	17 562	27 646	..	..	3.5	4.7	7.5
50/55 Trade, repair, hotels & restaurants	..	..	12 698	16 050	29 506	..	..	17.0	24.9	37.7
65/74 Finance, insurance, business services	..	..	11 723	28 776	37 379	..	..	8.2	20.1	22.4
OTHER ACTIVITIES	..	..	3 216	9 775	9 409	..	..	1.8	4.7	3.7
01/99 GRAND TOTAL	..	..	**222 645**	**310 377**	**448 710**	..	..	**12.6**	**17.1**	**22.0**

Total manufacturing by investing country						As a % of total manufacturing by foreign affiliates				
All countries	..	..	**180 689**	**236 677**	**342 734**	..	..	**100.0**	**100.0**	**100.0**
United States	..	..	..	..	..	..	..	..	..	..
Canada	..	..	..	..	..	..	..	..	..	..
Mexico	..	..	..	..	..	..	..	..	..	..
Japan	..	..	..	..	..	..	..	..	..	..
Europe	..	..	..	..	..	..	..	..	..	..
European Union (15)	..	..	..	201 842	296 158	..	..	..	85.3	86.4
Belgium	..	..	..	..	..	..	..	..	..	..
France	..	..	..	..	..	..	..	..	..	..
Germany	..	..	..	..	..	..	..	..	..	..
Italy	..	..	..	..	..	..	..	..	..	..
Netherlands	..	..	..	..	..	..	..	..	..	..
Spain	..	..	..	..	..	..	..	..	..	..
Sweden	..	..	..	..	..	..	..	..	..	..
United Kingdom	..	..	..	..	..	..	..	..	..	..
Switzerland	..	..	..	..	..	..	..	..	..	..
Australia and New Zealand	..	..	..	..	..	..	..	..	..	..
Asia (non-OECD)	..	..	..	..	..	..	..	..	..	..
Latin America	..	..	..	..	..	..	..	..	..	..

Note: Majority foreign-owned firms.
Firmes sous contrôle étranger majoritaire.

Table 4. CZECH REPUBLIC / RÉPUBLIQUE TCHÈQUE

TURNOVER / CHIFFRE D'AFFAIRES

By industry (ISIC Rev. 3)	FOREIGN AFFILIATES (Millions of CK)					AS A % OF NATIONAL TOTAL				
	1993	1994	1995	1996	1997	1993	1994	1995	1996	1997
10/14 Mining & quarrying	..	..	..	..	1 944	..	..	..	..	3.1
15/37 TOTAL MANUFACTURING	..	..	**185 652**	**251 385**	**361 121**	..	..	**19.2**	**24.8**	**31.0**
15/16 Food, beverages, tobacco	..	..	32 114	39 140	60 552	..	..	19.0	19.2	26.9
17/19 Textiles, clothing, leather, footwear	..	..	2 790	..	..	..	..	4.6	..	..
20/22 Wood and paper products	..	..	9 363	18 393	26 192	..	..	15.1	29.8	41.0
20 Wood products	..	..	..	..	..	..	..	..	..	..
21/22 Paper, printing and publishing	..	..	..	..	..	..	..	..	..	..
23/25 Chemicals, Total	..	..	..	..	..	..	..	..	..	..
23 Refined petroleum, nuclear fuel	..	..	..	..	..	..	..	..	..	..
24/25 Chemicals, rubber & plastics prod.	..	..	..	..	33 897	..	..	..	..	25.9
24 Chemical products	..	..	..	..	..	..	..	..	..	..
2423 Pharmaceuticals	..	..	..	..	..	..	..	..	..	..
25 Rubber and plastics products	..	..	..	..	..	..	..	..	..	..
26 Non-metallic mineral products	..	..	19 638	..	..	..	..	39.8	..	..
27/28 Basic & fabricated metals	..	..	..	17 523	..	..	..	..	10.4	..
27 Basic metals	..	..	..	5 717	..	..	..	..	5.1	..
28 Fabricated metal products	..	..	8 888	11 806	..	..	..	16.3	21.4	..
29/32 Machinery, Total	..	..	22 948	..	..	..	..	17.5	..	..
29/30 Non-electrical machinery	..	..	7 663	..	..	..	..	8.4	..	..
29 Non-electrical machinery nec	..	..	7 663	..	11 000	..	..	8.5	..	9.9
30 Office and computing machinery	..	..	0	..	..	..	..	0.0	..	..
31/32 Electrical & electronic equipment	..	..	15 285	..	32 207	..	..	37.9	..	48.7
31 Electrical machinery nec	..	..	13 645	..	26 775	..	..	35.3	..	49.0
32 Radio, TV & communications eq.	..	..	1 640	3 783	5 432	..	..	19.6	38.2	47.0
33 Scientific instruments	..	..	1 243	2 180	..	..	..	15.1	23.7	..
34/35 Transportation equipment	..	..	..	..	..	..	..	..	..	..
34 Motor vehicles	..	..	..	..	..	..	..	..	..	..
35 Other transport equipment	..	..	..	..	..	..	..	..	..	..
351 Shipbuilding & repairing	..	..	..	..	..	..	..	..	..	..
353 Aircraft and spacecraft	..	..	..	..	..	..	..	..	..	..
36/37 Other manufacturing	..	..	..	..	..	..	..	..	..	..
40/45 Construction, electricity, gas & water	..	..	10 492	18 740	31 587	..	..	2.8	3.2	8.6
50/55 Trade, repair, hotels & restaurants	..	..	46 981	58 912	105 419	..	..	13.1	19.4	27.1
65/74 Finance, insurance, business services	..	..	3 755	11 144	28 947	..	..	8.0	19.8	33.9
OTHER ACTIVITIES	..	..	3 223	9 910	9 410	..	..	1.9	3.9	3.1
01/99 GRAND TOTAL	..	..	**251 519**	**351 629**	**538 428**	..	..	**12.7**	**15.4**	**22.7**

Total manufacturing by investing country						As a % of total manufacturing by foreign affiliates				
All countries	..	..	185 652	251 385	361 121	..	..	100.0	100.0	100.0
United States	..	..	..	..	..	..	..	..	..	..
Canada	..	..	..	..	..	..	..	..	..	..
Mexico	..	..	..	..	..	..	..	..	..	..
Japan	..	..	..	..	..	..	..	..	..	..
Europe	..	..	..	..	..	..	..	..	..	..
European Union (15)	..	..	..	215 767	312 038	..	..	..	85.8	86.4
Belgium	..	..	..	..	..	..	..	..	..	..
France	..	..	..	..	..	..	..	..	..	..
Germany	..	..	..	..	..	..	..	..	..	..
Italy	..	..	..	..	..	..	..	..	..	..
Netherlands	..	..	..	..	..	..	..	..	..	..
Spain	..	..	..	..	..	..	..	..	..	..
Sweden	..	..	..	..	..	..	..	..	..	..
United Kingdom	..	..	..	..	..	..	..	..	..	..
Switzerland	..	..	..	..	..	..	..	..	..	..
Australia and New Zealand	..	..	..	..	..	..	..	..	..	..
Asia (non-OECD)	..	..	..	..	..	..	..	..	..	..
Latin America	..	..	..	..	..	..	..	..	..	..

Note: Majority foreign-owned firms.
Firmes sous contrôle étranger majoritaire.

Table 5. CZECH REPUBLIC / RÉPUBLIQUE TCHÈQUE

VALUE ADDED / VALEUR AJOUTÉE

By industry (ISIC Rev. 3)		FOREIGN AFFILIATES (Millions of CK)					AS A % OF NATIONAL TOTAL				
		1993	1994	1995	1996	1997	1993	1994	1995	1996	1997
10/14	Mining & quarrying	..	..	..	..	963	..	..	..	..	3.3
15/37	**TOTAL MANUFACTURING**	..	..	**37 615**	**54 223**	**90 517**	..	..	**25.4**	**34.4**	**30.8**
15/16	Food, beverages, tobacco	..	..	8 937	9 986	16 226	..	..	36.4	35.9	38.2
17/19	Textiles, clothing, leather, footwear	..	..	764	..	..	..	..	10.3	..	..
20/22	Wood and paper products	..	..	2 575	4 520	5 944	..	..	17.3	33.3	36.3
20	Wood products	..	..	..	..	..	..	..	..	..	..
21/22	Paper, printing and publishing	..	..	..	..	..	..	..	..	..	..
23/25	Chemicals, Total	..	..	..	..	..	..	..	..	..	..
23	Refined petroleum, nuclear fuel	..	..	..	..	..	..	..	..	..	..
24/25	Chemicals, rubber & plastics prod.	..	..	..	..	10 801	..	..	..	..	30.9
24	Chemical products	..	..	..	..	..	..	..	..	..	..
2423	Pharmaceuticals	..	..	..	..	..	..	..	..	..	..
25	Rubber and plastics products	..	..	..	..	..	..	..	..	..	..
26	Non-metallic mineral products	..	..	5 805	..	..	..	..	36.1	..	..
27/28	Basic & fabricated metals	..	..	..	908	..	..	..	..	-6.2	..
27	Basic metals	..	..	..	1 208	..	..	..	..	-4.7	..
28	Fabricated metal products	..	..	..	- 300	..	..	..	..	-2.8	..
29/32	Machinery, Total	..	..	6 033	..	..	..	..	16.8	..	..
29/30	Non-electrical machinery	..	..	2 047	..	..	..	..	7.7	..	..
29	Non-electrical machinery nec	..	..	2 047	..	3 383	..	..	7.7	..	10.1
30	Office and computing machinery	..	..	0	..	..	..	..	0.0	..	..
31/32	Electrical & electronic equipment	..	..	3 986	..	8 957	..	..	43.5	..	45.4
31	Electrical machinery nec	..	..	3 534	..	7 542	..	..	40.6	..	46.0
32	Radio, TV & communications eq.	..	..	452	835	1 415	..	..	15.8	28.4	42.2
33	Scientific instruments	..	..	371	659	..	..	..	11.2	19.3	..
34/35	Transportation equipment	..	..	..	..	..	..	..	..	..	..
34	Motor vehicles	..	..	..	..	..	..	..	..	..	..
35	Other transport equipment	..	..	..	..	..	..	..	..	..	..
351	Shipbuilding & repairing	..	..	..	..	..	..	..	..	..	..
353	Aircraft and spacecraft	..	..	..	..	..	..	..	..	..	..
36/37	Other manufacturing	..	..	..	..	..	..	..	..	..	..
40/45	Construction, electricity, gas & water	..	..	3 906	4 791	7 095	..	..	4.1	5.3	7.5
50/55	Trade, repair, hotels & restaurants	..	..	5 313	6 292	12 285	..	..	17.9	22.4	33.7
65/74	Finance, insurance, business services	..	..	5 036	20 408	24 500	..	..	5.8	22.3	23.1
	OTHER ACTIVITIES	..	..	1 876	4 671	2 649	..	..	2.9	5.8	2.4
01/99	**GRAND TOTAL**	..	..	**54 449**	**91 148**	**138 009**	..	..	**13.1**	**20.7**	**20.6**

Total manufacturing by investing country							*As a % of total manufacturing by foreign affiliates*				
All countries		..	..	37 615	54 223	90 517		..	..	100.0	100.0	100.0
United States		..	..	..	..	..		..	..	..	..	..
Canada		..	..	..	..	..		..	..	..	..	..
Mexico		..	..	..	..	..		..	..	..	..	..
Japan		..	..	..	..	..		..	..	..	..	..
Europe		..	..	..	..	..		..	..	..	..	..
European Union (15)		..	..	..	45 536	77 873		..	..	..	84.0	86.0
Belgium		..	..	..	..	..		..	..	..	..	..
France		..	..	..	..	..		..	..	..	..	..
Germany		..	..	..	..	..		..	..	..	..	..
Italy		..	..	..	..	..		..	..	..	..	..
Netherlands		..	..	..	..	..		..	..	..	..	..
Spain		..	..	..	..	..		..	..	..	..	..
Sweden		..	..	..	..	..		..	..	..	..	..
United Kingdom		..	..	..	..	..		..	..	..	..	..
Switzerland		..	..	..	..	..		..	..	..	..	..
Australia and New Zealand		..	..	..	..	..		..	..	..	..	..
Asia (non-OECD)		..	..	..	..	..		..	..	..	..	..
Latin America		..	..	..	..	..		..	..	..	..	..

Note: Majority foreign-owned firms.
Firmes sous contrôle étranger majoritaire.

Table 6. CZECH REPUBLIC / RÉPUBLIQUE TCHÈQUE

WAGES AND SALARIES / SALAIRES ET TRAITEMENTS

By industry (ISIC Rev. 3)		FOREIGN AFFILIATES *(Millions of CK)*					AS A % OF NATIONAL TOTAL				
		1993	1994	1995	1996	1997	1993	1994	1995	1996	1997
10/14	Mining & quarrying	..	..	..	..	260	..	..	..	..	2.2
15/37	**TOTAL MANUFACTURING**	..	..	**14 239**	**19 777**	**26 143**	..	..	**14.7**	**18.2**	**22.3**
15/16	Food, beverages, tobacco	..	..	1 901	2 481	3 689	..	..	19.0	19.8	26.8
17/19	Textiles, clothing, leather, footwear	..	..	555	..	..	..	..	5.8	..	..
20/22	Wood and paper products	..	..	868	1 514	2 007	..	..	15.3	23.7	31.3
20	Wood products	..	..	..	..	..	..	..	..	..	..
21/22	Paper, printing and publishing	..	..	..	..	..	..	..	..	..	..
23/25	Chemicals, Total	..	..	..	..	..	..	..	..	..	..
23	Refined petroleum, nuclear fuel	..	..	..	..	..	..	..	..	..	..
24/25	Chemicals, rubber & plastics prod.	..	..	..	..	2 326	..	..	..	..	21.5
24	Chemical products	..	..	..	..	..	..	..	..	..	..
2423	Pharmaceuticals	..	..	..	..	..	..	..	..	..	..
25	Rubber and plastics products	..	..	..	..	..	..	..	..	..	..
26	Non-metallic mineral products	..	..	1 815	..	..	..	..	28.5	..	..
27/28	Basic & fabricated metals	..	..	..	1 480	..	..	..	..	7.1	..
27	Basic metals	..	..	..	524	..	..	..	..	3.9	..
28	Fabricated metal products	..	..	..	956	..	..	..	..	12.9	..
29/32	Machinery, Total	..	..	2 820	..	..	..	..	13.6	..	..
29/30	Non-electrical machinery	..	..	1 052	..	..	..	..	6.8	..	..
29	Non-electrical machinery nec	..	..	1 052	..	1 379	..	..	6.9	..	7.8
30	Office and computing machinery	..	..	0	..	..	..	..	0.0	..	..
31/32	Electrical & electronic equipment	..	..	1 768	..	3 697	..	..	33.8	..	39.3
31	Electrical machinery nec	..	..	1 514	..	3 093	..	..	30.4	..	40.8
32	Radio, TV & communications eq.	..	..	254	380	604	..	..	17.4	23.1	32.9
33	Scientific instruments	..	..	178	327	..	..	..	10.3	17.5	..
34/35	Transportation equipment	..	..	..	..	..	..	..	..	..	..
34	Motor vehicles	..	..	..	..	..	..	..	..	..	..
35	Other transport equipment	..	..	..	..	..	..	..	..	..	..
351	Shipbuilding & repairing	..	..	..	..	..	..	..	..	..	..
353	Aircraft and spacecraft	..	..	..	..	..	..	..	..	..	..
36/37	Other manufacturing	..	..	..	..	..	..	..	..	..	..
40/45	Construction, electricity, gas & water	..	..	1 079	1 483	2 486	..	..	4.0	4.9	8.1
50/55	Trade, repair, hotels & restaurants	..	..	1 963	3 038	4 995	..	..	14.6	22.5	31.7
65/74	Finance, insurance, business services	..	..	2 035	2 895	4 039	..	..	10.6	12.4	15.7
	OTHER ACTIVITIES	..	..	255	1 643	715	..	..	0.6	3.6	1.4
01/99	**GRAND TOTAL**	..	..	**19 756**	**29 025**	**38 638**	..	..	**9.6**	**12.5**	**15.2**

Total manufacturing by investing country							As a % of total manufacturing by foreign affiliates				
All countries		..	..	14 239	19 777	26 143	..	..	100.0	100.0	100.0
United States		..	..	..	..	..	..	..	..	..	..
Canada		..	..	..	..	..	..	..	..	..	..
Mexico		..	..	..	..	..	..	..	..	..	..
Japan		..	..	..	..	..	..	..	..	..	..
Europe		..	..	..	..	..	..	..	..	..	..
European Union (15)		..	..	..	16 039	22 153	..	..	..	81.1	84.7
Belgium		..	..	..	..	..	..	..	..	..	..
France		..	..	..	..	..	..	..	..	..	..
Germany		..	..	..	..	..	..	..	..	..	..
Italy		..	..	..	..	..	..	..	..	..	..
Netherlands		..	..	..	..	..	..	..	..	..	..
Spain		..	..	..	..	..	..	..	..	..	..
Sweden		..	..	..	..	..	..	..	..	..	..
United Kingdom		..	..	..	..	..	..	..	..	..	..
Switzerland		..	..	..	..	..	..	..	..	..	..
Australia and New Zealand		..	..	..	..	..	..	..	..	..	..
Asia (non-OECD)		..	..	..	..	..	..	..	..	..	..
Latin America		..	..	..	..	..	..	..	..	..	..

Note: Majority foreign-owned firms.
Firmes sous contrôle étranger majoritaire.

Table 9. CZECH REPUBLIC / RÉPUBLIQUE TCHÈQUE

GROSS FIXED CAPITAL FORMATION / FORMATION BRUTE DE CAPITAL FIXE

By industry (ISIC Rev. 3)	FOREIGN AFFILIATES (Millions of CK)					AS A % OF NATIONAL TOTAL				
	1993	1994	1995	1996	1997	1993	1994	1995	1996	1997
10/14 Mining & quarrying	..	..	..	..	175	..	..	..	..	13.8
15/37 TOTAL MANUFACTURING	..	..	**27 361**	**35 306**	**4 273**	..	..	**36.3**	**44.9**	**19.0**
15/16 Food, beverages, tobacco	..	..	5 917	4 423	1 010	..	..	50.0	35.6	41.0
17/19 Textiles, clothing, leather, footwear	..	..	191	..	..	..	..	5.3	..	..
20/22 Wood and paper products	..	..	1 202	3 278	297	..	..	16.8	43.9	43.1
20 Wood products	..	..	..	..	..	..	..	..	..	..
21/22 Paper, printing and publishing	..	..	..	..	..	..	..	..	..	..
23/25 Chemicals, Total	..	..	..	..	..	..	..	..	..	..
23 Refined petroleum, nuclear fuel	..	..	..	..	..	..	..	..	..	..
24/25 Chemicals, rubber & plastics prod.	..	..	..	..	797	..	..	..	..	21.1
24 Chemical products	..	..	..	..	..	..	..	..	..	..
2423 Pharmaceuticals	..	..	..	..	..	..	..	..	..	..
25 Rubber and plastics products	..	..	..	..	..	..	..	..	..	..
26 Non-metallic mineral products	..	..	4 799	..	..	..	..	51.3	..	..
27/28 Basic & fabricated metals	..	..	..	1 251	..	..	..	..	15.6	..
27 Basic metals	..	..	..	438	..	..	..	..	8.9	..
28 Fabricated metal products	..	..	..	813	..	..	..	..	26.2	..
29/32 Machinery, Total	..	..	2 412	..	..	..	..	30.9	..	..
29/30 Non-electrical machinery	..	..	711	..	..	..	..	14.2	..	..
29 Non-electrical machinery nec	..	..	711	..	123	..	..	14.3	..	3.5
30 Office and computing machinery	..	..	0	..	..	..	..	0.0	..	..
31/32 Electrical & electronic equipment	..	..	1 701	..	383	..	..	60.6	..	24.2
31 Electrical machinery nec	..	..	1 377	..	383	..	..	55.5	..	24.2
32 Radio, TV & communications eq.	..	..	324	578	0	..	..	51.6	78.1	0.0
33 Scientific instruments	..	..	656	488	..	..	..	75.8	46.3	..
34/35 Transportation equipment	..	..	..	..	..	..	..	..	..	..
34 Motor vehicles	..	..	..	..	..	..	..	..	..	..
35 Other transport equipment	..	..	..	..	..	..	..	..	..	..
351 Shipbuilding & repairing	..	..	..	..	..	..	..	..	..	..
353 Aircraft and spacecraft	..	..	..	..	..	..	..	..	..	..
36/37 Other manufacturing	..	..	..	..	..	..	..	..	..	..
40/45 Construction, electricity, gas & water	..	..	673	855	..	..	..	1.0	1.6	..
50/55 Trade, repair, hotels & restaurants	..	..	4 660	5 857	2 518	..	..	40.0	45.9	32.6
65/74 Finance, insurance, business services	..	..	2 052	10 788	2 074	..	..	5.6	28.1	4.8
OTHER ACTIVITIES	..	..	134	363	2 205	..	..	0.2	0.6	21.6
01/99 GRAND TOTAL	..	..	**35 149**	**53 457**	**10 085**	..	..	**13.7**	**20.7**	**11.9**

Total manufacturing by investing country						As a % of total manufacturing by foreign affiliates				
All countries	..	..	**27 361**	**35 306**	**4 273**	..	..	**100.0**	**100.0**	**100.0**
United States	..	..	..	..	..	..	..	..	..	..
Canada	..	..	..	..	..	..	..	..	..	..
Mexico	..	..	..	..	..	..	..	..	..	..
Japan	..	..	..	..	..	..	..	..	..	..
Europe	..	..	..	..	..	..	..	..	..	..
European Union (15)	..	..	..	30 705	2 958	..	..	..	87.0	69.2
Belgium	..	..	..	..	..	..	..	..	..	..
France	..	..	..	..	..	..	..	..	..	..
Germany	..	..	..	..	..	..	..	..	..	..
Italy	..	..	..	..	..	..	..	..	..	..
Netherlands	..	..	..	..	..	..	..	..	..	..
Spain	..	..	..	..	..	..	..	..	..	..
Sweden	..	..	..	..	..	..	..	..	..	..
United Kingdom	..	..	..	..	..	..	..	..	..	..
Switzerland	..	..	..	..	..	..	..	..	..	..
Australia and New Zealand	..	..	..	..	..	..	..	..	..	..
Asia (non-OECD)	..	..	..	..	..	..	..	..	..	..
Latin America	..	..	..	..	..	..	..	..	..	..

Note: Majority foreign-owned firms.
Firmes sous contrôle étranger majoritaire.

CZECH REPUBLIC

Source

The data are prepared by the Czech Statistical Office. They are extracted from the annual structural survey, covering all enterprises with 100 or more employees. No special survey on enterprises with foreign participation is conducted. Foreign-owned enterprises are identified via a question included in the annual survey on investments. Data are available separately for majority foreign-owned firms, minority foreign-owned firms and national firms. The data in this publication refer to majority foreign-owned establishments, which have a foreign capital share of more than 50%.

National totals: data come from the Czech Statistical Office and are compatible with foreign affiliates' data.

Industrial classification

For all variables, the data are classified according to the principal industrial activity of the affiliate.

The data are converted from the national industrial classification (OKEC) based on NACE Revision 1 to ISIC Revision 3.

Variables

- *Number of enterprises*: all enterprises with 100 or more employees where the foreign participation may be identified.

- *Number of employees* is expressed on a full-time equivalent basis.

- *Production* (gross output) is the sum of market and non-market outputs produced by domestic producers over a given period. It is equal to the sum of revenues from sales of own products, goods, works and services provided to the other establishments within the enterprise and includes also changes in stocks of own production and work in progress. Costs incurred on sold goods and VAT are excluded. The valuation is in producer prices, excluding VAT.

- *Value added* is obtained by subtracting the value of inputs (the cost of materials, fuel and other supplies) from the value of gross output.

Geographical breakdown

The country of origin is the country of the immediate controller. For confidentiality reasons, only data for the European Union area are available.

RÉPUBLIQUE TCHÈQUE

Source

Les données émanent de l'office tchèque de la statistique. Elles sont extraites de l'enquête structurelle annuelle, couvrant toutes les entreprises de 100 salariés ou plus. Aucune enquête spécifique relative aux entreprises à participation étrangère n'est réalisée. Les entreprises sous contrôle étranger sont identifiées par une question contenue dans l'enquête annuelle sur les investissements. Des données sont disponibles séparément pour les entreprises à participation étrangère majoritaire, minoritaire, ainsi que pour les entreprises nationales. Les données de cette publication font référence aux établissements sous contrôle étranger où la part du capital en mains étrangères est de plus de 50 %.

Totaux nationaux : les données sont fournies par l'office tchèque de la statistique et sont compatibles avec les données relatives aux filiales étrangères.

Classification industrielle

Pour toutes les variables, les données sont classées selon l'activité industrielle principale de l'entreprise affiliée.

Les données sont converties de la classification industrielle nationale (OKEC) fondée sur la NACE révision 1 vers la CITI révision 3.

Variables

- *Nombre d'entreprises* : toutes les entreprises d'au moins 100 salariés pour lesquelles une participation étrangère a pu être identifiée.

- Le *Nombre de salariés* est exprimé en équivalent plein-temps.

- La *Production* (production brute) est la somme des biens et services marchands et non marchands élaborés par des producteurs intérieurs sur une période donnée. Elle est égale à la somme des revenus tirés des ventes des produits de l'entreprise, des biens, travaux et services fournis à d'autres établissements de l'entreprise et inclut les variations de stocks de sa propre production et des travaux en cours. Les frais encourus sur les produits vendus et la TVA sont exclus. L'évaluation se fait au prix départ-usine, non compris la TVA.

- La *Valeur ajoutée* est obtenue en soustrayant la valeur des consommations intermédiaires (coût des matières premières, combustible et autres fournitures) de la valeur de la production brute.

Ventilation géographique

Le pays d'origine est celui où se situe le contrôle immédiat. Pour des raisons de confidentialité, seules les données de la zone Union européenne sont disponibles.

FINLAND

Sources and Methods

FINLANDE

NUMBER OF ESTABLISHMENTS / NOMBRE D'ÉTABLISSEMENTS

By industry (ISIC Rev. 3)	FOREIGN AFFILIATES (Units)					AS A % OF NATIONAL TOTAL				
	1992	1993	1994	1995	1996	1992	1993	1994	1995	1996
10/14 Mining & quarrying	0	..	21	..	..	0.0	..	13.0	..	..
15/37 TOTAL MANUFACTURING	194	..	287	..	..	3.3	..	5.4	..	..
15/16 Food, beverages, tobacco	8	..	13	..	..	1.0	..	1.9	..	..
17/19 Textiles, clothing, leather, footwear	12	..	7	..	..	2.6	..	1.8	..	..
20/22 Wood and paper products	15	..	16	..	..	1.1	..	1.3	..	..
20 Wood products	..	..	..	..	..	..	..	..	..	..
21/22 Paper, printing and publishing	..	..	..	..	..	..	..	..	..	..
23/25 Chemicals, Total	54	..	65	..	..	11.3	..	15.0	..	..
23 Refined petroleum, nuclear fuel	6	..	5	..	..	25.0	..	50.0	..	..
24/25 Chemicals, rubber & plastics prod.	48	..	60	..	..	10.5	..	14.2	..	..
24 Chemical products	36	..	42	..	..	13.7	..	22.5	..	..
2423 Pharmaceuticals	2	..	2	..	..	9.5	..	10.5	..	..
25 Rubber and plastics products	12	..	18	..	..	6.2	..	7.7	..	..
26 Non-metallic mineral products	8	..	55	..	..	2.0	..	18.0	..	..
27/28 Basic & fabricated metals	24	..	28	..	..	3.0	..	4.4	..	..
27 Basic metals	1	..	9	..	..	1.3	..	10.6	..	..
28 Fabricated metal products	23	..	19	..	..	3.2	..	3.4	..	..
29/32 Machinery, Total	54	..	84	..	..	5.6	..	8.3	..	..
29/30 Non-electrical machinery	33	..	51	..	..	4.7	..	6.9	..	..
29 Non-electrical machinery nec	31	..	48	..	..	4.6	..	6.7	..	..
30 Office and computing machinery	2	..	3	..	..	7.4	..	13.0	..	..
31/32 Electrical & electronic equipment	21	..	33	..	..	8.2	..	12.3	..	..
31 Electrical machinery nec	17	..	26	..	..	9.3	..	14.3	..	..
32 Radio, TV & communications eq.	4	..	7	..	..	5.4	..	8.0	..	..
33 Scientific instruments	4	..	6	..	..	3.9	..	5.0	..	..
34/35 Transportation equipment	8	..	6	..	..	3.7	..	3.5	..	..
34 Motor vehicles	5	..	3	..	..	4.8	..	3.7	..	..
35 Other transport equipment	3	..	3	..	..	2.8	..	3.3	..	..
351 Shipbuilding & repairing	..	..	3	..	..	..	..	4.8	..	..
353 Aircraft and spacecraft	0	..	0	..	..	0.0	..	0.0	..	..
36/37 Other manufacturing	7	..	7	..	..	1.7	..	1.9	..	..
40/45 Construction, electricity, gas & water	..	..	..	..	..	..	..	..	..	..
50/55 Trade, repair, hotels & restaurants	..	..	..	..	..	..	..	..	..	..
65/74 Finance, insurance, business services	..	..	..	..	..	..	..	..	..	..
OTHER ACTIVITIES	..	..	..	..	..	..	..	..	..	..
01/99 GRAND TOTAL	..	..	..	..	..	..	..	..	..	..

Total manufacturing by investing country						As a % of total manufacturing by foreign affiliates				
All countries	194	..	287	..	..	100.0	..	100.0	..	..
United States	..	..	..	..	..	..	..	..	..	..
Canada	..	..	..	..	..	..	..	..	..	..
Mexico	..	..	..	..	..	..	..	..	..	..
Japan	..	..	..	..	..	..	..	..	..	..
Europe	..	..	..	..	..	..	..	..	..	..
European Union (15)	..	..	..	..	..	..	..	..	..	..
Belgium	..	..	..	..	..	..	..	..	..	..
France	..	..	..	..	..	..	..	..	..	..
Germany	..	..	..	..	..	..	..	..	..	..
Italy	..	..	..	..	..	..	..	..	..	..
Netherlands	..	..	..	..	..	..	..	..	..	..
Spain	..	..	..	..	..	..	..	..	..	..
Sweden	..	..	..	..	..	..	..	..	..	..
United Kingdom	..	..	..	..	..	..	..	..	..	..
Switzerland	..	..	..	..	..	..	..	..	..	..
Australia and New Zealand	..	..	..	..	..	..	..	..	..	..
Asia (non-OECD)	..	..	..	..	..	..	..	..	..	..
Latin America	..	..	..	..	..	..	..	..	..	..

Note: Majority foreign-owned establishments. Based on the **Annual Industrial Statistics** of Statistics Finland.
Etablissements sous contrôle étranger majoritaire. Données fondées sur les **Statistiques industrielles annuelles** de l'office finlandais de statistiques.

Table 1b. FINLAND / FINLANDE

NUMBER OF ENTERPRISES / NOMBRE D'ENTREPRISES

By industry (ISIC Rev. 3)	FOREIGN AFFILIATES (Units)					AS A % OF NATIONAL TOTAL				
	1993	1994	1995	1996	1997	1993	1994	1995	1996	1997
10/14 Mining & quarrying	0	0	5	7	10	0.0	0.0	0.4	0.5	0.8
15/37 **TOTAL MANUFACTURING**	**128**	**160**	**257**	**288**	**321**	**0.6**	**0.7**	**1.1**	**1.1**	**1.2**
15/16 Food, beverages, tobacco	6	10	19	13	18	0.4	0.6	1.1	0.7	0.9
17/19 Textiles, clothing, leather, footwear	7	8	8	9	11	0.3	0.3	0.3	0.3	0.4
20/22 Wood and paper products	14	15	25	28	35	0.3	0.3	0.5	0.5	0.6
20 Wood products	..	..	..	..	..	..	..	..	..	..
21/22 Paper, printing and publishing	..	..	..	..	..	..	..	..	..	..
23/25 Chemicals, Total	29	31	46	53	63	3.5	3.7	5.3	5.7	6.5
23 Refined petroleum, nuclear fuel	1	1	2	2	2	14.3	14.3	25.0	25.0	22.2
24/25 Chemicals, rubber & plastics prod.	28	30	44	51	61	3.5	3.6	5.1	5.5	6.3
24 Chemical products	22	22	32	36	44	9.4	8.8	12.5	12.7	14.4
2423 Pharmaceuticals	1	1	2	3	6	5.9	5.3	14.3	13.6	27.3
25 Rubber and plastics products	6	8	12	15	17	1.0	1.4	2.0	2.3	2.6
26 Non-metallic mineral products	12	16	20	28	22	1.6	1.9	2.3	3.1	2.3
27/28 Basic & fabricated metals	15	20	29	37	41	0.4	0.5	0.7	0.9	0.9
27 Basic metals	5	8	8	7	10	4.5	6.8	6.5	5.2	7.0
28 Fabricated metal products	10	12	21	30	31	0.3	0.3	0.5	0.7	0.7
29/32 Machinery, Total	31	39	81	92	94	0.9	1.0	2.0	2.1	2.1
29/30 Non-electrical machinery	22	26	54	61	59	0.7	0.8	1.6	1.7	1.6
29 Non-electrical machinery nec	21	25	50	57	55	0.7	0.8	1.5	1.6	1.6
30 Office and computing machinery	1	1	4	4	4	2.8	2.5	7.4	7.0	6.7
31/32 Electrical & electronic equipment	9	13	27	31	35	1.3	1.8	3.6	3.9	4.2
31 Electrical machinery nec	6	9	19	22	24	1.3	2.0	4.1	4.4	4.8
32 Radio, TV & communications eq.	3	4	8	9	11	1.3	1.6	2.9	2.9	3.4
33 Scientific instruments	5	9	12	12	13	0.7	1.6	1.6	1.5	1.6
34/35 Transportation equipment	3	5	9	9	14	0.4	0.7	1.2	1.1	1.6
34 Motor vehicles	2	3	4	3	6	0.8	1.2	1.5	1.1	2.2
35 Other transport equipment	1	2	5	6	8	0.2	0.4	1.0	1.1	1.4
351 Shipbuilding & repairing	0	1	4	5	7	0.0	0.2	0.9	1.0	1.3
353 Aircraft and spacecraft	0	0	0	0	0	0.0	0.0	0.0	0.0	0.0
36/37 Other manufacturing	6	7	8	7	10	0.3	0.3	0.3	0.3	0.4
40/45 Construction, electricity, gas & water	11	12	38	52	63	0.1	0.1	0.2	0.2	0.2
50/55 Trade, repair, hotels & restaurants	434	550	781	843	957	0.9	1.1	1.4	1.4	1.6
65/74 Finance, insurance, business services	83	130	256	264	342	0.5	0.5	0.8	0.7	0.9
OTHER ACTIVITIES	50	67	139	148	195	0.4	0.2	0.3	0.3	0.3
01/99 **GRAND TOTAL**	**706**	**919**	**1 476**	**1 602**	**1 888**	**0.6**	**0.6**	**0.8**	**0.8**	**0.9**

Total manufacturing by investing country						*As a % of total manufacturing by foreign affiliates*				
All countries	**128**	**160**	**257**	**288**	**321**	**100.0**	**100.0**	**100.0**	**100.0**	**100.0**
United States	..	..	34	51	62	..	..	13.2	17.7	19.3
Canada	..	..	..	4	4	..	..	..	1.4	1.2
Mexico	..	..	0	0	0	..	..	0.0	0.0	0.0
Japan	..	..	6	2	7	..	..	2.3	0.7	2.2
Europe	..	..	..	229	245	..	..	..	79.5	76.3
European Union (15)	..	..	168	183	194	..	..	65.4	63.5	60.4
Belgium	..	..	..	0	1	..	..	..	0.0	0.3
France	..	..	..	8	11	..	..	..	2.8	3.4
Germany	..	..	..	16	23	..	..	..	5.6	7.2
Italy	..	..	..	2	3	..	..	..	0.7	0.9
Netherlands	..	..	..	22	22	..	..	..	7.6	6.9
Spain	..	..	0	0	0	..	..	0.0	0.0	0.0
Sweden	..	..	..	88	83	..	..	..	30.6	25.9
United Kingdom	..	..	..	22	22	..	..	..	7.6	6.9
Switzerland	..	..	..	24	25	..	..	..	8.3	7.8
Australia and New Zealand	..	..	0	0	0	..	..	0.0	0.0	0.0
Asia (non-OECD)	..	..	..	1	2	..	..	..	0.3	0.6
Latin America	..	..	0	0	1	..	..	0.0	0.0	0.3

Note: Majority foreign-owned enterprises. Based on the **Business Register** of Statistics Finland. From 1995 onwards data on indirectly from abroad owned firms are included.
Entreprises sous contrôle étranger majoritaire. Données fondées sur le **registre du commerce** de l'office finlandais de statistiques. Les données à partir de 1995 comprennent les firmes contrôlées indirectement par l'étranger.

NUMBER OF EMPLOYEES / NOMBRE DE SALARIÉS

By industry (ISIC Rev. 3)	FOREIGN AFFILIATES (Units)					AS A % OF NATIONAL TOTAL				
	1992	1993	1994	1995	1996	1992	1993	1994	1995	1996
10/14 Mining & quarrying	0	..	152	..	..	0.0	..	4.5	..	..
15/37 TOTAL MANUFACTURING	**22 495**	**..**	**29 606**	**..**	**..**	**6.2**	**..**	**8.6**	**..**	**..**
15/16 Food, beverages, tobacco	854	..	2 037	..	..	1.8	..	4.9	..	..
17/19 Textiles, clothing, leather, footwear	..	..	344	..	..	..	..	2.0	..	..
20/22 Wood and paper products	1 517	..	1 436	..	..	1.6	..	1.6	..	..
20 Wood products	..	..	..	..	..	..	..	..	..	..
21/22 Paper, printing and publishing	..	..	..	..	..	..	..	..	..	..
23/25 Chemicals, Total	2 929	..	3 750	..	..	8.5	..	11.5	..	..
23 Refined petroleum, nuclear fuel	257	..	208	..	..	6.5	..	6.5	..	..
24/25 Chemicals, rubber & plastics prod.	2 672	..	3 542	..	..	8.7	..	12.0	..	..
24 Chemical products	1 822	..	2 379	..	..	8.3	..	13.4	..	..
2423 Pharmaceuticals	..	..	..	..	..	..	..	..	..	..
25 Rubber and plastics products	850	..	1 163	..	..	9.7	..	9.9	..	..
26 Non-metallic mineral products	..	..	2 206	..	..	..	..	19.1	..	..
27/28 Basic & fabricated metals	..	..	1 852	..	..	..	..	5.5	..	..
27 Basic metals	..	..	385	..	..	..	..	2.4	..	..
28 Fabricated metal products	..	..	1 467	..	..	..	..	8.1	..	..
29/32 Machinery, Total	..	..	11 956	..	..	..	..	15.7	..	..
29/30 Non-electrical machinery	..	..	5 121	..	..	..	..	10.8	..	..
29 Non-electrical machinery nec	..	..	3 880	..	..	..	..	8.8	..	..
30 Office and computing machinery	..	..	1 241	..	..	..	..	37.4	..	..
31/32 Electrical & electronic equipment	..	..	6 835	..	..	..	..	23.7	..	..
31 Electrical machinery nec	..	..	6 139	..	..	..	..	45.6	..	..
32 Radio, TV & communications eq.	..	..	696	..	..	..	..	4.5	..	..
33 Scientific instruments	..	..	928	..	..	..	..	16.2	..	..
34/35 Transportation equipment	..	..	4 692	..	..	..	..	21.4	..	..
34 Motor vehicles	276	..	244	..	..	4.0	..	3.8	..	..
35 Other transport equipment	..	..	4 448	..	..	..	..	28.6	..	..
351 Shipbuilding & repairing	..	..	4 448	..	..	..	..	47.4	..	..
353 Aircraft and spacecraft	0	..	0	..	..	0.0	..	0.0	..	..
36/37 Other manufacturing	..	..	405	..	..	..	..	3.4	..	..
40/45 Construction, electricity, gas & water	..	..	..	..	..	..	..	..	..	..
50/55 Trade, repair, hotels & restaurants	..	..	..	..	..	..	..	..	..	..
65/74 Finance, insurance, business services	..	..	..	..	..	..	..	..	..	..
OTHER ACTIVITIES	..	..	..	..	..	..	..	..	..	..
01/99 GRAND TOTAL	**..**	**..**	**..**	**..**	**..**	**..**	**..**	**..**	**..**	**..**

Total manufacturing by investing country						As a % of total manufacturing by foreign affiliates				
All countries	**22 495**	**..**	**29 606**	**..**	**..**	**100.0**	**..**	**100.0**	**..**	**..**
United States	..	..	..	..	..	..	..	..	..	..
Canada	..	..	..	..	..	..	..	..	..	..
Mexico	..	..	..	..	..	..	..	..	..	..
Japan	..	..	..	..	..	..	..	..	..	..
Europe	..	..	..	..	..	..	..	..	..	..
European Union (15)	..	..	..	..	..	..	..	..	..	..
Belgium	..	..	..	..	..	..	..	..	..	..
France	..	..	..	..	..	..	..	..	..	..
Germany	..	..	..	..	..	..	..	..	..	..
Italy	..	..	..	..	..	..	..	..	..	..
Netherlands	..	..	..	..	..	..	..	..	..	..
Spain	..	..	..	..	..	..	..	..	..	..
Sweden	..	..	..	..	..	..	..	..	..	..
United Kingdom	..	..	..	..	..	..	..	..	..	..
Switzerland	..	..	..	..	..	..	..	..	..	..
Australia and New Zealand	..	..	..	..	..	..	..	..	..	..
Asia (non-OECD)	..	..	..	..	..	..	..	..	..	..
Latin America	..	..	..	..	..	..	..	..	..	..

Note: Majority foreign-owned establishments. Based on the **Annual Industrial Statistics** of Statistics Finland.
Etablissements sous contrôle étranger majoritaire. Données fondées sur les **Statistiques industrielles annuelles** de l'office finlandais de statistiques.

Table 2b. FINLAND / FINLANDE

NUMBER OF EMPLOYEES / NOMBRE DE SALARIÉS

By industry (ISIC Rev. 3)	FOREIGN AFFILIATES (Full-time Eq.)					AS A % OF NATIONAL TOTAL				
	1993	1994	1995	1996	1997	1993	1994	1995	1996	1997
10/14 Mining & quarrying	0	0	..	853	897	0.0	0.0	..	17.6	16.7
15/37 **TOTAL MANUFACTURING**	**17 818**	**20 381**	**37 892**	**44 838**	**50 627**	**4.7**	**5.4**	**9.7**	**11.3**	**12.4**
15/16 Food, beverages, tobacco	2 153	2 195	2 796	2 238	2 895	4.3	4.6	6.1	4.9	6.4
17/19 Textiles, clothing, leather, footwear	329	356	349	420	682	1.6	1.9	1.9	2.4	3.9
20/22 Wood and paper products	1 220	1 367	1 448	1 438	1 701	1.2	1.4	1.5	1.5	1.7
20 Wood products	..	..	..	..	..	..	..	..	..	..
21/22 Paper, printing and publishing	..	..	..	..	..	..	..	..	..	..
23/25 Chemicals, Total	..	..	..	..	..	..	..	..	..	..
23 Refined petroleum, nuclear fuel	..	..	..	..	..	..	..	..	..	..
24/25 Chemicals, rubber & plastics prod.	2 641	3 771	3 441	5 465	7 066	9.1	12.3	11.0	17.5	22.2
24 Chemical products	1 991	3 235	2 288	4 069	5 488	11.7	18.0	12.3	22.1	30.5
2423 Pharmaceuticals	..	..	..	..	..	..	..	..	..	..
25 Rubber and plastics products	650	536	1 153	1 396	1 578	5.4	4.3	9.1	10.8	11.5
26 Non-metallic mineral products	3 822	3 787	3 482	4 487	3 267	26.4	27.9	25.6	36.2	24.3
27/28 Basic & fabricated metals	2 404	2 362	3 610	4 931	5 471	5.5	5.4	8.3	10.6	10.7
27 Basic metals	1 159	1 091	1 194	..	284	7.3	6.7	7.1	..	1.6
28 Fabricated metal products	1 245	1 271	2 416	..	5 187	4.4	4.6	9.0	..	15.5
29/32 Machinery, Total	..	..	..	..	..	..	..	..	..	..
29/30 Non-electrical machinery	..	..	..	..	..	..	..	..	..	..
29 Non-electrical machinery nec	1 759	1 833	6 037	7 414	8 562	4.0	4.2	11.4	13.5	15.3
30 Office and computing machinery	..	..	..	..	..	..	..	..	..	..
31/32 Electrical & electronic equipment	..	..	7 673	10 381	10 967	..	..	21.4	25.5	25.0
31 Electrical machinery nec	217	799	6 055	9 062	8 704	1.7	5.8	41.2	54.4	51.6
32 Radio, TV & communications eq.	..	..	1 618	1 319	2 263	..	..	7.6	5.5	8.4
33 Scientific instruments	616	979	1 386	1 451	1 694	8.0	12.3	16.1	15.5	17.7
34/35 Transportation equipment	..	..	..	..	..	..	..	..	..	..
34 Motor vehicles	..	..	..	..	..	..	..	..	..	..
35 Other transport equipment	..	..	..	..	..	..	..	..	..	..
351 Shipbuilding & repairing	0	..	..	..	..	0.0	..	..	..	..
353 Aircraft and spacecraft	0	0	0	0	0	0.0	0.0	0.0	0.0	0.0
36/37 Other manufacturing	415	403	729	650	1 189	3.1	3.0	5.0	4.4	7.5
40/45 Construction, electricity, gas & water	486	1 324	4 819	6 098	6 365	0.6	1.6	5.3	6.2	5.9
50/55 Trade, repair, hotels & restaurants	14 854	15 312	23 113	24 081	27 340	6.2	6.8	9.9	9.9	10.9
65/74 Finance, insurance, business services	5 062	5 152	8 208	11 241	14 676	3.5	3.3	4.9	6.7	8.3
OTHER ACTIVITIES	1 581	1 518	..	5 694	6 915	1.0	0.9	..	2.6	3.1
01/99 **GRAND TOTAL**	**39 800**	**43 697**	**79 682**	**92 805**	**106 820**	**3.9**	**4.3**	**7.4**	**8.2**	**9.1**

Total manufacturing by investing country						As a % of total manufacturing by foreign affiliates				
All countries	**17 818**	**20 381**	**37 892**	**44 838**	**50 627**	**100.0**	**100.0**	**100.0**	**100.0**	**100.0**
United States	..	..	4 224	7 115	9 113	..	..	11.1	15.9	18.0
Canada	..	..	..	..	..	..	..	..	..	..
Mexico	..	..	0	0	0	..	..	0.0	0.0	0.0
Japan	..	..	..	..	..	..	..	..	..	..
Europe	..	..	..	36 728	38 894	..	..	..	81.9	76.8
European Union (15)	..	..	17 524	20 993	22 989	..	..	46.2	46.8	45.4
Belgium	..	..	..	..	..	..	..	..	..	..
France	..	..	..	631	1 029	..	..	..	1.4	2.0
Germany	..	..	690	2 602	2 716	..	..	1.8	5.8	5.4
Italy	..	..	..	..	..	..	..	..	..	..
Netherlands	..	..	3 714	3 865	4 231	..	..	9.8	8.6	8.4
Spain	..	..	0	0	0	..	..	0.0	0.0	0.0
Sweden	..	..	8 038	8 483	8 849	..	..	21.2	18.9	17.5
United Kingdom	..	..	2 957	3 701	3 199	..	..	7.8	8.3	6.3
Switzerland	..	..	7 924	8 682	8 643	..	..	20.9	19.4	17.1
Australia and New Zealand	..	..	0	0	0	..	..	0.0	0.0	0.0
Asia (non-OECD)	..	..	..	..	..	..	..	..	..	..
Latin America	..	..	0	0	..	..	..	0.0	0.0	..

Note: Majority foreign-owned enterprises. Based on the **Business Register** of Statistics Finland. From 1995 onwards data on indirectly from abroad owned firms are included.
Entreprises sous contrôle étranger majoritaire. Données fondées sur le **registre du commerce** de l'office finlandais de statistiques. Les données à partir de 1995 comprennent les firmes contrôlées indirectement par l'étranger.

Table 3. FINLAND / FINLANDE

PRODUCTION

By industry (ISIC Rev. 3)	FOREIGN AFFILIATES (Millions of Mk)					AS A % OF NATIONAL TOTAL				
	1992	1993	1994	1995	1996	1992	1993	1994	1995	1996
10/14 Mining & quarrying	0	..	192	..	..	0.0	..	6.1	..	..
15/37 **TOTAL MANUFACTURING**	**16 973**	..	**28 295**	..	..	**6.6**	..	**9.0**	..	..
15/16 Food, beverages, tobacco	1 118	..	2 031	..	..	2.3	..	4.2	..	..
17/19 Textiles, clothing, leather, footwear	..	..	273	..	..	..	..	3.8	..	..
20/22 Wood and paper products	1 425	..	1 792	..	..	2.0	..	2.0	..	..
20 Wood products	..	..	..	..	..	..	..	..	..	..
21/22 Paper, printing and publishing	..	..	..	..	..	..	..	..	..	..
23/25 Chemicals, Total	2 798	..	5 160	..	..	8.4	..	12.9	..	..
23 Refined petroleum, nuclear fuel	581	..	601	..	..	5.1	..	4.8	..	..
24/25 Chemicals, rubber & plastics prod.	2 218	..	4 559	..	..	10.1	..	16.5	..	..
24 Chemical products	1 813	..	3 863	..	..	10.0	..	19.1	..	..
2423 Pharmaceuticals	..	..	..	..	..	..	..	..	..	..
25 Rubber and plastics products	405	..	696	..	..	10.4	..	9.4	..	..
26 Non-metallic mineral products	..	..	1 653	..	..	..	..	23.5	..	..
27/28 Basic & fabricated metals	..	..	1 635	..	..	..	..	4.4	..	..
27 Basic metals	..	..	551	..	..	..	..	2.1	..	..
28 Fabricated metal products	..	..	1 084	..	..	..	..	9.7	..	..
29/32 Machinery, Total	..	..	11 210	..	..	..	..	18.1	..	..
29/30 Non-electrical machinery	..	..	5 676	..	..	..	..	16.2	..	..
29 Non-electrical machinery nec	..	..	2 854	..	..	..	..	9.4	..	..
30 Office and computing machinery	..	..	2 822	..	..	..	..	59.0	..	..
31/32 Electrical & electronic equipment	..	..	5 534	..	..	..	..	20.6	..	..
31 Electrical machinery nec	..	..	4 835	..	..	..	..	50.7	..	..
32 Radio, TV & communications eq.	..	..	699	..	..	..	..	4.0	..	..
33 Scientific instruments	..	..	534	..	..	..	..	14.3	..	..
34/35 Transportation equipment	..	..	3 835	..	..	..	..	32.4	..	..
34 Motor vehicles	218	..	178	..	..	5.8	..	5.5	..	..
35 Other transport equipment	..	..	3 657	..	..	..	..	42.7	..	..
351 Shipbuilding & repairing	..	..	3 657	..	..	..	..	58.3	..	..
353 Aircraft and spacecraft	0	..	0	..	..	0.0	..	0.0	..	..
36/37 Other manufacturing	..	..	172	..	..	..	..	3.4	..	..
40/45 Construction, electricity, gas & water	..	..	..	..	..	..	..	..	..	..
50/55 Trade, repair, hotels & restaurants	..	..	..	..	..	..	..	..	..	..
65/74 Finance, insurance, business services	..	..	..	..	..	..	..	..	..	..
OTHER ACTIVITIES	..	..	..	..	..	..	..	..	..	..
01/99 **GRAND TOTAL**	..	..	..	..	..	..	..	..	..	..

Total manufacturing by investing country						As a % of total manufacturing by foreign affiliates				
All countries	**16 973**	..	**28 295**	..	..	**100.0**	..	**100.0**	..	..
United States	..	..	..	..	..	..	..	..	..	..
Canada	..	..	..	..	..	..	..	..	..	..
Mexico	..	..	..	..	..	..	..	..	..	..
Japan	..	..	..	..	..	..	..	..	..	..
Europe	..	..	..	..	..	..	..	..	..	..
European Union (15)	..	..	..	..	..	..	..	..	..	..
Belgium	..	..	..	..	..	..	..	..	..	..
France	..	..	..	..	..	..	..	..	..	..
Germany	..	..	..	..	..	..	..	..	..	..
Italy	..	..	..	..	..	..	..	..	..	..
Netherlands	..	..	..	..	..	..	..	..	..	..
Spain	..	..	..	..	..	..	..	..	..	..
Sweden	..	..	..	..	..	..	..	..	..	..
United Kingdom	..	..	..	..	..	..	..	..	..	..
Switzerland	..	..	..	..	..	..	..	..	..	..
Australia and New Zealand	..	..	..	..	..	..	..	..	..	..
Asia (non-OECD)	..	..	..	..	..	..	..	..	..	..
Latin America	..	..	..	..	..	..	..	..	..	..

Note: Majority foreign-owned establishments. Based on the **Annual Industrial Statistics** of Statistics Finland.

Etablissements sous contrôle étranger majoritaire. Données fondées sur les **Statistiques industrielles annuelles** de l'office finlandais de statistiques.

Table 4. FINLAND / FINLANDE

TURNOVER / CHIFFRE D'AFFAIRES

By industry (ISIC Rev. 3)	FOREIGN AFFILIATES (Millions of Mk)					AS A % OF NATIONAL TOTAL				
	1993	1994	1995	1996	1997	1993	1994	1995	1996	1997
10/14 Mining & quarrying	0	0	..	1 045	1 305	0.0	0.0	..	22.8	25.3
15/37 TOTAL MANUFACTURING	**17 660**	**26 317**	**38 427**	**50 366**	**61 646**	**5.5**	**7.5**	**10.1**	**12.7**	**13.7**
15/16 Food, beverages, tobacco	2 287	2 517	3 109	2 831	3 724	3.9	4.5	6.7	6.0	7.7
17/19 Textiles, clothing, leather, footwear	231	296	303	352	564	3.1	3.7	3.6	4.3	6.4
20/22 Wood and paper products	1 289	1 632	2 378	2 509	3 114	1.7	1.7	2.2	2.3	2.4
20 Wood products	..	..	..	..	..	..	..	..	..	..
21/22 Paper, printing and publishing	..	..	..	..	..	..	..	..	..	..
23/25 Chemicals, Total	..	..	..	..	..	..	..	..	..	..
23 Refined petroleum, nuclear fuel	..	..	..	..	..	..	..	..	..	..
24/25 Chemicals, rubber & plastics prod.	3 192	8 930	5 122	8 075	11 661	13.5	28.7	15.8	24.9	30.0
24 Chemical products	2 808	8 484	4 187	6 894	10 346	17.9	38.0	18.2	30.3	39.3
2423 Pharmaceuticals	..	..	..	..	..	..	..	..	..	..
25 Rubber and plastics products	384	446	935	1 181	1 315	4.8	5.1	9.9	12.1	10.4
26 Non-metallic mineral products	2 610	3 079	2 526	3 829	3 485	32.7	36.1	29.1	44.9	34.2
27/28 Basic & fabricated metals	1 776	1 994	2 968	4 718	5 235	5.7	5.8	7.8	11.7	11.5
27 Basic metals	932	1 066	1 163	..	290	5.6	5.5	5.1	..	1.2
28 Fabricated metal products	844	928	1 805	..	4 945	5.8	6.0	11.6	..	23.8
29/32 Machinery, Total	..	..	..	..	..	..	..	..	..	..
29/30 Non-electrical machinery	..	..	..	..	..	..	..	..	..	..
29 Non-electrical machinery nec	1 632	1 901	5 471	6 831	8 288	5.9	6.2	13.1	14.7	16.8
30 Office and computing machinery	..	..	..	..	..	..	..	..	..	..
31/32 Electrical & electronic equipment	..	..	7 738	10 666	13 061	..	..	21.7	23.9	23.4
31 Electrical machinery nec	168	546	5 946	9 159	9 662	2.0	5.5	50.9	62.1	62.0
32 Radio, TV & communications eq.	..	..	1 792	1 507	3 399	..	..	7.5	5.1	8.4
33 Scientific instruments	458	600	771	1 024	1 387	9.8	12.4	13.6	15.7	19.0
34/35 Transportation equipment	..	..	..	..	..	..	..	..	..	..
34 Motor vehicles	..	244	..	..	..	..	6.7	..	..	..
35 Other transport equipment	..	..	..	..	..	..	..	..	..	..
351 Shipbuilding & repairing	0	..	..	..	..	0.0	..	..	..	..
353 Aircraft and spacecraft	0	0	0	0	0	0.0	0.0	0.0	0.0	0.0
36/37 Other manufacturing	201	215	308	307	616	3.9	3.4	4.3	4.0	7.0
40/45 Construction, electricity, gas & water	204	1 007	4 905	6 062	7 212	0.3	1.5	6.4	7.0	7.7
50/55 Trade, repair, hotels & restaurants	30 804	36 159	48 980	60 987	75 872	9.7	10.7	13.6	15.6	17.7
65/74 Finance, insurance, business services	2 019	2 721	5 249	6 989	6 723	4.9	5.3	8.9	11.3	9.8
OTHER ACTIVITIES	689	1 511	..	7 473	8 764	1.0	1.7	..	6.5	6.7
01/99 GRAND TOTAL	**51 376**	**67 715**	**103 079**	**132 922**	**161 520**	**6.3**	**7.5**	**10.6**	**12.6**	**13.7**

Total manufacturing by investing country						As a % of total manufacturing by foreign affiliates				
All countries	**17 660**	**26 317**	**38 427**	**50 366**	**61 646**	**100.0**	**100.0**	**100.0**	**100.0**	**100.0**
United States	..	..	5 002	8 764	12 248	..	..	13.0	17.4	19.9
Canada	..	..	..	..	..	..	..	..	..	..
Mexico	..	..	0	0	0	..	..	0.0	0.0	0.0
Japan	..	..	..	..	..	..	..	..	..	..
Europe	..	..	..	39 050	43 996	..	..	..	77.5	71.4
European Union (15)	..	..	16 824	21 849	26 743	..	..	43.8	43.4	43.4
Belgium	..	..	..	..	..	..	..	..	..	..
France	..	..	..	558	1 094	..	..	..	1.1	1.8
Germany	..	..	531	2 493	2 980	..	..	1.4	4.9	4.8
Italy	..	..	..	..	..	..	..	..	..	..
Netherlands	..	..	4 869	5 880	7 106	..	..	12.7	11.7	11.5
Spain	..	..	0	0	0	..	..	0.0	0.0	0.0
Sweden	..	..	7 511	7 885	9 255	..	..	19.5	15.7	15.0
United Kingdom	..	..	2 265	3 508	3 367	..	..	5.9	7.0	5.5
Switzerland	..	..	7 937	8 276	8 997	..	..	20.7	16.4	14.6
Australia and New Zealand	..	..	0	0	0	..	..	0.0	0.0	0.0
Asia (non-OECD)	..	..	..	..	..	..	..	..	..	..
Latin America	..	..	0	0	..	..	..	0.0	0.0	..

Note: Majority foreign-owned enterprises. Based on the **Business Register** of Statistics Finland. From 1995 onwards data on indirectly from abroad owned firms are included.
Entreprises sous contrôle étranger majoritaire. Données fondées sur le **registre du commerce** de l'office finlandais de statistiques. Les données à partir de 1995 comprennent les firmes contrôlées indirectement par l'étranger.

Table 5a. FINLAND / FINLANDE

VALUE ADDED / VALEUR AJOUTÉE

By industry (ISIC Rev. 3)		FOREIGN AFFILIATES (Millions of Mk)					AS A % OF NATIONAL TOTAL				
		1992	1993	1994	1995	1996	1992	1993	1994	1995	1996
10/14	Mining & quarrying	0	..	55	..	..	0.0	..	3.2	..	..
15/37	**TOTAL MANUFACTURING**	7 128	..	9 735	..	..	7.8	..	8.9	..	..
15/16	Food, beverages, tobacco	373	..	550	..	..	2.9	..	4.4	..	..
17/19	Textiles, clothing, leather, footwear	..	..	124	..	..	..	..	3.7	..	..
20/22	Wood and paper products	474	..	627	..	..	1.9	..	1.8	..	..
20	Wood products	..	..	..	..	..	..	..	..	..	..
21/22	Paper, printing and publishing	..	..	..	..	..	..	..	..	..	..
23/25	Chemicals, Total	1 237	..	2 059	..	..	10.7	..	14.8	..	..
23	Refined petroleum, nuclear fuel	224	..	205	..	..	10.9	..	7.7	..	..
24/25	Chemicals, rubber & plastics prod.	1 013	..	1 854	..	..	10.7	..	16.4	..	..
24	Chemical products	821	..	1 544	..	..	10.8	..	19.2	..	..
2423	Pharmaceuticals	..	..	..	..	..	..	..	..	..	..
25	Rubber and plastics products	191	..	310	..	..	10.2	..	9.6	..	..
26	Non-metallic mineral products	..	..	688	..	..	..	..	20.9	..	..
27/28	Basic & fabricated metals	..	..	595	..	..	..	..	5.2	..	..
27	Basic metals	..	..	138	..	..	..	..	2.0	..	..
28	Fabricated metal products	..	..	457	..	..	..	..	10.1	..	..
29/32	Machinery, Total	..	..	3 538	..	..	..	..	16.2	..	..
29/30	Non-electrical machinery	..	..	1 352	..	..	..	..	10.8	..	..
29	Non-electrical machinery nec	..	..	1 056	..	..	..	..	8.9	..	..
30	Office and computing machinery	..	..	296	..	..	..	..	47.0	..	..
31/32	Electrical & electronic equipment	..	..	2 186	..	..	..	..	23.3	..	..
31	Electrical machinery nec	..	..	1 835	..	..	..	..	50.9	..	..
32	Radio, TV & communications eq.	..	..	351	..	..	..	..	6.1	..	..
33	Scientific instruments	..	..	240	..	..	..	..	13.6	..	..
34/35	Transportation equipment	..	..	1 226	..	..	..	..	26.4	..	..
34	Motor vehicles	67	..	68	..	..	4.5	..	4.7	..	..
35	Other transport equipment	..	..	1 158	..	..	..	..	36.1	..	..
351	Shipbuilding & repairing	..	..	1 158	..	..	..	..	55.8	..	..
353	Aircraft and spacecraft	0	..	0	..	..	0.0	..	0.0	..	..
36/37	Other manufacturing	..	..	89	..	..	..	..	3.8	..	..
40/45	Construction, electricity, gas & water	..	..	..	..	..	..	..	..	..	..
50/55	Trade, repair, hotels & restaurants	..	..	..	..	..	..	..	..	..	..
65/74	Finance, insurance, business services	..	..	..	..	..	..	..	..	..	..
	OTHER ACTIVITIES	..	..	..	..	..	..	..	..	..	..
01/99	**GRAND TOTAL**	..	..	..	..	..	..	..	..	..	..

Total manufacturing by investing country					As a % of total manufacturing by foreign affiliates				
All countries	7 128	..	9 735	..	..	100.0	..	100.0	..	..
United States	..	..	..	..	..	..	..	..	..	..
Canada	..	..	..	..	..	..	..	..	..	..
Mexico	..	..	..	..	..	..	..	..	..	..
Japan	..	..	..	..	..	..	..	..	..	..
Europe	..	..	..	..	..	..	..	..	..	..
European Union (15)	..	..	..	..	..	..	..	..	..	..
Belgium	..	..	..	..	..	..	..	..	..	..
France	..	..	..	..	..	..	..	..	..	..
Germany	..	..	..	..	..	..	..	..	..	..
Italy	..	..	..	..	..	..	..	..	..	..
Netherlands	..	..	..	..	..	..	..	..	..	..
Spain	..	..	..	..	..	..	..	..	..	..
Sweden	..	..	..	..	..	..	..	..	..	..
United Kingdom	..	..	..	..	..	..	..	..	..	..
Switzerland	..	..	..	..	..	..	..	..	..	..
Australia and New Zealand	..	..	..	..	..	..	..	..	..	..
Asia (non-OECD)	..	..	..	..	..	..	..	..	..	..
Latin America	..	..	..	..	..	..	..	..	..	..

Note: Majority foreign-owned establishments. Based on the **Annual Industrial Statistics** of Statistics Finland.
Etablissements sous contrôle étranger majoritaire. Données fondées sur les **Statistiques industrielles annuelles** de l'office finlandais de statistiques.

Table 5b. FINLAND / FINLANDE

VALUE ADDED / VALEUR AJOUTÉE

By industry (ISIC Rev. 3)	FOREIGN AFFILIATES (Millions of Mk)					AS A % OF NATIONAL TOTAL				
	1993	1994	1995	1996	1997	1993	1994	1995	1996	1997
10/14 Mining & quarrying	..	..	..	315	403	..	..	..	18.6	20.9
15/37 TOTAL MANUFACTURING	..	..	**12 100**	**15 653**	**19 387**	..	..	**9.7**	**12.6**	**13.8**
15/16 Food, beverages, tobacco	..	..	816	722	1 056	..	..	6.8	6.1	8.6
17/19 Textiles, clothing, leather, footwear	..	..	107	135	184	..	..	3.3	4.1	5.5
20/22 Wood and paper products	..	..	541	571	716	..	..	1.3	1.6	1.7
20 Wood products	..	..	..	..	..	..	..	..	..	..
21/22 Paper, printing and publishing	..	..	..	..	..	..	..	..	..	..
23/25 Chemicals, Total	..	..	..	..	..	..	..	..	..	..
23 Refined petroleum, nuclear fuel	..	..	..	..	..	..	..	..	..	..
24/25 Chemicals, rubber & plastics prod.	..	..	1 603	2 455	3 626	..	..	14.1	21.5	28.7
24 Chemical products	..	..	1 270	2 019	3 138	..	..	16.0	26.2	36.9
2423 Pharmaceuticals	..	..	..	..	..	..	..	..	..	..
25 Rubber and plastics products	..	..	333	436	488	..	..	9.6	11.8	11.8
26 Non-metallic mineral products	..	..	996	1 449	1 297	..	..	28.3	42.8	31.7
27/28 Basic & fabricated metals	..	..	1 043	1 441	1 696	..	..	7.2	10.3	10.8
27 Basic metals	..	..	413	..	97	..	..	5.0	..	1.3
28 Fabricated metal products	..	..	630	..	1 599	..	..	10.1	..	19.5
29/32 Machinery, Total	..	..	..	..	..	..	..	..	..	..
29/30 Non-electrical machinery	..	..	..	..	..	..	..	..	..	..
29 Non-electrical machinery nec	..	..	1 769	2 266	2 932	..	..	11.6	13.7	17.2
30 Office and computing machinery	..	..	..	..	..	..	..	..	..	..
31/32 Electrical & electronic equipment	..	..	2 468	3 845	4 680	..	..	20.7	26.7	23.9
31 Electrical machinery nec	..	..	1 950	3 040	3 163	..	..	48.8	61.1	59.5
32 Radio, TV & communications eq.	..	..	518	805	1 517	..	..	6.6	8.5	10.6
33 Scientific instruments	..	..	349	440	617	..	..	13.9	15.3	18.9
34/35 Transportation equipment	..	..	..	..	..	..	..	..	..	..
34 Motor vehicles	..	..	..	..	..	..	..	..	..	..
35 Other transport equipment	..	..	..	..	..	..	..	..	..	..
351 Shipbuilding & repairing	..	..	..	..	..	..	..	..	..	..
353 Aircraft and spacecraft	..	..	0	0	0	..	..	0.0	0.0	0.0
36/37 Other manufacturing	..	..	144	161	269	..	..	5.1	5.5	8.4
40/45 Construction, electricity, gas & water	..	..	1 261	1 614	1 566	..	..	5.0	5.9	5.3
50/55 Trade, repair, hotels & restaurants	..	..	8 106	8 761	9 738	..	..	14.5	15.3	16.1
65/74 Finance, insurance, business services	..	..	2 192	2 995	3 212	..	..	8.3	9.4	9.6
OTHER ACTIVITIES	..	..	..	1 558	1 649	..	..	..	2.8	2.8
01/99 GRAND TOTAL	..	..	**25 240**	**30 896**	**35 955**	..	..	**9.0**	**10.4**	**11.1**

Total manufacturing by investing country						As a % of total manufacturing by foreign affiliates				
All countries	..	..	**12 100**	**15 653**	**19 387**	..	..	**100.0**	**100.0**	**100.0**
United States	..	..	..	2 952	4 467	..	..	..	18.9	23.0
Canada	..	..	..	..	..	..	..	..	..	..
Mexico	..	..	0	0	0	..	..	0.0	0.0	0.0
Japan	..	..	..	..	..	..	..	..	..	..
Europe	..	..	..	12 273	14 201	..	..	..	78.4	73.3
European Union (15)	..	..	5 213	7 170	8 684	..	..	43.1	45.8	44.8
Belgium	..	..	..	..	..	..	..	..	..	..
France	..	..	..	208	426	..	..	..	1.3	2.2
Germany	..	..	..	844	944	..	..	..	5.4	4.9
Italy	..	..	..	..	..	..	..	..	..	..
Netherlands	..	..	..	1 515	1 952	..	..	..	9.7	10.1
Spain	..	..	0	0	0	..	..	0.0	0.0	0.0
Sweden	..	..	..	2 784	3 352	..	..	..	17.8	17.3
United Kingdom	..	..	..	1 253	1 006	..	..	..	8.0	5.2
Switzerland	..	..	..	2 885	3 146	..	..	..	18.4	16.2
Australia and New Zealand	..	..	0	0	0	..	..	0.0	0.0	0.0
Asia (non-OECD)	..	..	..	..	..	..	..	..	..	..
Latin America	..	..	0	0	..	..	..	0.0	0.0	..

Note: Majority foreign-owned enterprises. Based on the **Business Register** of Statistics Finland.
Entreprises sous contrôle étranger majoritaire. Données fondées sur le **registre du commerce** de l'office finlandais de statistiques.

Table 6a. FINLAND / FINLANDE

WAGES AND SALARIES / SALAIRES ET TRAITEMENTS

By industry (ISIC Rev. 3)		FOREIGN AFFILIATES (Millions of Mk)					AS A % OF NATIONAL TOTAL				
		1992	1993	1994	1995	1996	1992	1993	1994	1995	1996
10/14	Mining & quarrying	0	..	20	..	..	0.0	..	4.6	..	..
15/37	**TOTAL MANUFACTURING**	2 955	..	4 189	..	..	6.8	..	9.5	..	..
15/16	Food, beverages, tobacco	128	..	277	..	..	2.4	..	5.5	..	..
17/19	Textiles, clothing, leather, footwear	..	..	50	..	..	..	..	3.2	..	..
20/22	Wood and paper products	207	..	209	..	..	1.7	..	1.7	..	..
20	Wood products	..	..	..	..	..	..	..	..	..	..
21/22	Paper, printing and publishing	..	..	..	..	..	..	..	..	..	..
23/25	Chemicals, Total	383	..	552	..	..	8.7	..	12.3	..	..
23	Refined petroleum, nuclear fuel	38	..	32	..	..	6.1	..	5.9	..	..
24/25	Chemicals, rubber & plastics prod.	345	..	520	..	..	9.2	..	13.2	..	..
24	Chemical products	249	..	376	..	..	8.8	..	14.9	..	..
2423	Pharmaceuticals	..	..	..	..	..	..	..	..	..	..
25	Rubber and plastics products	96	..	143	..	..	10.4	..	10.1	..	..
26	Non-metallic mineral products	..	..	306	..	..	..	..	21.8	..	..
27/28	Basic & fabricated metals	..	..	246	..	..	..	..	5.5	..	..
27	Basic metals	..	..	51	..	..	..	..	2.3	..	..
28	Fabricated metal products	..	..	195	..	..	..	..	8.8	..	..
29/32	Machinery, Total	..	..	1 722	..	..	..	..	16.9	..	..
29/30	Non-electrical machinery	..	..	755	..	..	..	..	11.9	..	..
29	Non-electrical machinery nec	..	..	560	..	..	..	..	9.4	..	..
30	Office and computing machinery	..	..	195	..	..	..	..	48.0	..	..
31/32	Electrical & electronic equipment	..	..	967	..	..	..	..	25.1	..	..
31	Electrical machinery nec	..	..	865	..	..	..	..	49.3	..	..
32	Radio, TV & communications eq.	..	..	102	..	..	..	..	4.9	..	..
33	Scientific instruments	..	..	131	..	..	..	..	16.2	..	..
34/35	Transportation equipment	..	..	655	..	..	..	..	23.9	..	..
34	Motor vehicles	27	..	30	..	..	3.5	..	4.4	..	..
35	Other transport equipment	..	..	625	..	..	..	..	30.4	..	..
351	Shipbuilding & repairing	..	..	625	..	..	..	..	50.5	..	..
353	Aircraft and spacecraft	0	..	0	..	..	0.0	..	0.0	..	..
36/37	Other manufacturing	..	..	42	..	..	..	..	3.5	..	..
40/45	Construction, electricity, gas & water	..	..	..	..	..	..	..	..	..	..
50/55	Trade, repair, hotels & restaurants	..	..	..	..	..	..	..	..	..	..
65/74	Finance, insurance, business services	..	..	..	..	..	..	..	..	..	..
	OTHER ACTIVITIES	..	..	..	..	..	..	..	..	..	..
01/99	**GRAND TOTAL**	..	..	..	..	..	..	..	..	..	..

Total manufacturing by investing country	1992	1993	1994	1995	1996	As a % of total manufacturing by foreign affiliates				
						1992	1993	1994	1995	1996
All countries	2 955	..	4 189	..	..	100.0	..	100.0	..	..
United States	..	..	..	..	..	..	..	..	..	..
Canada	..	..	..	..	..	..	..	..	..	..
Mexico	..	..	..	..	..	..	..	..	..	..
Japan	..	..	..	..	..	..	..	..	..	..
Europe	..	..	..	..	..	..	..	..	..	..
European Union (15)	..	..	..	..	..	..	..	..	..	..
Belgium	..	..	..	..	..	..	..	..	..	..
France	..	..	..	..	..	..	..	..	..	..
Germany	..	..	..	..	..	..	..	..	..	..
Italy	..	..	..	..	..	..	..	..	..	..
Netherlands	..	..	..	..	..	..	..	..	..	..
Spain	..	..	..	..	..	..	..	..	..	..
Sweden	..	..	..	..	..	..	..	..	..	..
United Kingdom	..	..	..	..	..	..	..	..	..	..
Switzerland	..	..	..	..	..	..	..	..	..	..
Australia and New Zealand	..	..	..	..	..	..	..	..	..	..
Asia (non-OECD)	..	..	..	..	..	..	..	..	..	..
Latin America	..	..	..	..	..	..	..	..	..	..

Note: Majority foreign-owned establishments. Based on the **Annual Industrial Statistics** of Statistics Finland.
Etablissements sous contrôle étranger majoritaire. Données fondées sur les **Statistiques industrielles annuelles** de l'office finlandais de statistiques.

Table 6b. FINLAND / FINLANDE

WAGES AND SALARIES / SALAIRES ET TRAITEMENTS

By industry (ISIC Rev. 3)	FOREIGN AFFILIATES (Millions of Mk)					AS A % OF NATIONAL TOTAL				
	1993	1994	1995	1996	1997	1993	1994	1995	1996	1997
10/14 Mining & quarrying	0	0	..	177	191	0.0	0.0	..	22.5	21.5
15/37 TOTAL MANUFACTURING	**2 403**	**2 903**	**7 580**	**9 175**	**10 607**	**5.2**	**5.9**	**10.8**	**12.7**	**14.0**
15/16 Food, beverages, tobacco	302	331	530	456	603	5.0	5.5	7.0	6.1	8.0
17/19 Textiles, clothing, leather, footwear	46	54	72	79	117	2.7	3.1	3.2	3.6	5.3
20/22 Wood and paper products	180	217	312	316	365	1.3	1.6	1.6	1.6	1.8
20 Wood products	..	..	..	..	..	..	..	..	..	..
21/22 Paper, printing and publishing	..	..	..	..	..	..	..	..	..	..
23/25 Chemicals, Total	..	..	..	..	..	..	..	..	..	..
23 Refined petroleum, nuclear fuel	..	..	..	..	..	..	..	..	..	..
24/25 Chemicals, rubber & plastics prod.	370	563	711	1 122	1 490	10.1	..	12.2	19.1	24.1
24 Chemical products	290	488	507	869	1 207	12.5	18.9	13.9	23.7	32.0
2423 Pharmaceuticals	..	..	..	..	..	..	..	..	..	..
25 Rubber and plastics products	80	75	204	253	283	5.8	4.9	9.4	11.5	11.7
26 Non-metallic mineral products	497	504	623	900	659	29.2	30.3	27.3	42.4	27.8
27/28 Basic & fabricated metals	314	330	698	998	1 109	6.0	5.9	8.7	11.9	12.2
27 Basic metals	161	160	240	..	56	7.4	6.7	6.6	..	1.5
28 Fabricated metal products	153	170	458	..	1 053	5.0	5.2	10.6	..	19.7
29/32 Machinery, Total	..	..	..	..	..	..	..	..	..	..
29/30 Non-electrical machinery	..	..	..	..	..	..	..	..	..	..
29 Non-electrical machinery nec	248	273	1 229	1 576	1 875	4.5	4.7	12.0	14.6	16.8
30 Office and computing machinery	..	..	..	..	..	..	..	..	..	..
31/32 Electrical & electronic equipment	..	..	1 579	2 184	2 393	..	..	25.1	29.8	29.7
31 Electrical machinery nec	27	106	1 258	1 921	1 909	1.7	5.9	47.0	60.4	59.5
32 Radio, TV & communications eq.	..	..	321	263	484	..	..	8.9	6.3	10.0
33 Scientific instruments	97	159	284	301	379	9.2	14.1	17.4	17.8	19.6
34/35 Transportation equipment	..	..	..	..	..	..	..	..	..	..
34 Motor vehicles	..	35	..	..	..	..	4.8	..	..	..
35 Other transport equipment	..	..	..	..	..	..	..	..	..	..
351 Shipbuilding & repairing	0	..	..	..	..	0.0	..	..	..	..
353 Aircraft and spacecraft	0	0	0	0	0	0.0	0.0	0.0	0.0	0.0
36/37 Other manufacturing	48	44	94	102	188	3.9	3.2	4.7	5.1	8.7
40/45 Construction, electricity, gas & water	62	140	1 013	1 213	1 226	0.7	1.6	7.1	8.0	7.3
50/55 Trade, repair, hotels & restaurants	2 527	2 811	5 087	5 534	6 209	10.4	11.6	15.1	15.9	16.9
65/74 Finance, insurance, business services	729	844	1 627	2 204	2 276	3.7	4.1	9.0	11.3	10.9
OTHER ACTIVITIES	230	216	..	997	1 173	1.1	1.0	..	3.3	3.8
01/99 GRAND TOTAL	**5 950**	**6 914**	**16 301**	**19 300**	**21 683**	**5.0**	**5.6**	**10.0**	**11.2**	**11.9**

Total manufacturing by investing country						*As a % of total manufacturing by foreign affiliates*				
All countries	**2 403**	**2 903**	**7 580**	**9 175**	**10 607**	**100.0**	**100.0**	**100.0**	**100.0**	**100.0**
United States	..	..	..	1 560	2 020	..	..	..	17.0	19.0
Canada	..	..	..	..	..	..	..	..	..	..
Mexico	..	..	0	0	0	..	..	0.0	0.0	0.0
Japan	..	..	..	..	..	..	..	..	..	..
Europe	..	..	..	7 447	8 048	..	..	..	81.2	75.9
European Union (15)	..	..	..	4 229	4 688	..	..	..	46.1	44.2
Belgium	..	..	..	..	..	..	..	..	..	..
France	..	..	..	116	209	..	..	..	1.3	2.0
Germany	..	..	..	545	589	..	..	..	5.9	5.6
Italy	..	..	..	..	..	..	..	..	..	..
Netherlands	..	..	..	840	934	..	..	..	9.2	8.8
Spain	..	..	0	0	0	..	..	0.0	0.0	0.0
Sweden	..	..	..	1 657	1 804	..	..	..	18.1	17.0
United Kingdom	..	..	..	762	600	..	..	..	8.3	5.7
Switzerland	..	..	..	1 826	1 903	..	..	..	19.9	17.9
Australia and New Zealand	..	..	0	0	0	..	..	0.0	0.0	0.0
Asia (non-OECD)	..	..	..	..	..	..	..	..	..	..
Latin America	..	..	0	0	..	..	..	0.0	0.0	..

Note: Majority foreign-owned enterprises. Based on the **Business Register** of Statistics Finland. From 1995 onwards data on indirectly from abroad owned firms are included.
Entreprises sous contrôle étranger majoritaire. Données fondées sur le **registre du commerce** de l'office finlandais de statistiques. Les données à partir de 1995 comprennent les firmes contrôlées indirectement par l'étranger.

Table 7. FINLAND / FINLANDE

R&D EXPENDITURE / DÉPENSES DE R-D

By industry (ISIC Rev. 3)		FOREIGN AFFILIATES (Millions of Mk)					AS A % OF NATIONAL TOTAL				
		1993	1994	1995	1996	1997	1993	1994	1995	1996	1997
10/14	Mining & quarrying	..	..	..	..	10	..	..	..	..	32.3
15/37	**TOTAL MANUFACTURING**	..	..	815	..	1 054	..	..	12.1	..	11.5
15/16	Food, beverages, tobacco	..	..	12	..	7	..	..	4.6	..	2.4
17/19	Textiles, clothing, leather, footwear	..	..	..	..	..	..	..	..	..	..
20/22	Wood and paper products	..	..	3	..	..	..	..	0.7	..	..
20	Wood products	..	..	..	..	..	..	..	..	..	..
21/22	Paper, printing and publishing	..	..	..	..	..	..	..	..	..	..
23/25	Chemicals, Total	..	..	..	..	..	..	..	..	..	..
23	Refined petroleum, nuclear fuel	..	..	..	..	..	..	..	..	..	..
24/25	Chemicals, rubber & plastics prod.	..	..	..	..	..	..	..	..	..	..
24	Chemical products	..	..	48	..	195	..	..	5.6	..	23.0
2423	Pharmaceuticals	..	..	..	..	..	..	..	..	..	..
25	Rubber and plastics products	..	..	..	..	..	..	..	..	..	..
26	Non-metallic mineral products	..	..	23	..	26	..	..	29.1	..	34.7
27/28	Basic & fabricated metals	..	..	..	..	..	..	..	..	..	..
27	Basic metals	..	..	..	..	..	..	..	..	..	..
28	Fabricated metal products	..	..	4	..	53	..	..	2.4	..	38.4
29/32	Machinery, Total	..	..	..	..	..	..	..	..	..	..
29/30	Non-electrical machinery	..	..	..	..	..	..	..	..	..	..
29	Non-electrical machinery nec	..	..	61	..	86	..	..	7.6	..	7.7
30	Office and computing machinery	..	..	..	..	..	..	..	..	..	..
31/32	Electrical & electronic equipment	..	..	402	..	497	..	..	14.4	..	..
31	Electrical machinery nec	..	..	267	..	293	..	..	69.2	..	..
32	Radio, TV & communications eq.	..	..	135	..	204	..	..	5.6	..	..
33	Scientific instruments	..	..	27	..	104	..	..	6.0	..	16.9
34/35	Transportation equipment	..	..	..	..	..	..	..	..	..	..
34	Motor vehicles	..	..	..	..	..	..	..	..	..	..
35	Other transport equipment	..	..	..	..	..	..	..	..	..	..
351	Shipbuilding & repairing	..	..	..	..	..	..	..	..	..	..
353	Aircraft and spacecraft	..	..	..	..	..	..	..	..	..	..
36/37	Other manufacturing	..	..	..	..	..	..	..	..	..	..
40/45	Construction, electricity, gas & water	..	..	..	..	22	..	..	..	..	8.0
50/55	Trade, repair, hotels & restaurants	..	..	..	..	42	..	..	..	..	27.3
65/74	Finance, insurance, business services	..	..	..	..	379	..	..	..	..	..
	OTHER ACTIVITIES	..	..	..	..	3	..	..	..	..	..
01/99	**GRAND TOTAL**	..	..	..	..	1 510	..	..	..	..	13.3

Total manufacturing by investing country						As a % of total manufacturing by foreign affiliates				
All countries	..	..	815	..	1 054	..	..	100.0	..	100.0
United States	..	..	..	..	380	..	..	..	..	36.1
Canada	..	..	..	..	..	..	..	..	..	..
Mexico	..	..	..	..	..	..	..	..	..	..
Japan	..	..	..	..	..	..	..	..	..	..
Europe	..	..	..	..	..	..	..	..	..	..
European Union (15)	..	..	..	..	338	..	..	..	..	32.1
Belgium	..	..	..	..	..	..	..	..	..	..
France	..	..	..	..	..	..	..	..	..	..
Germany	..	..	..	..	..	..	..	..	..	..
Italy	..	..	..	..	..	..	..	..	..	..
Netherlands	..	..	..	..	..	..	..	..	..	..
Spain	..	..	..	..	..	..	..	..	..	..
Sweden	..	..	..	..	..	..	..	..	..	..
United Kingdom	..	..	..	..	..	..	..	..	..	..
Switzerland	..	..	..	..	..	..	..	..	..	..
Australia and New Zealand	..	..	..	..	..	..	..	..	..	..
Asia (non-OECD)	..	..	..	..	..	..	..	..	..	..
Latin America	..	..	..	..	..	..	..	..	..	..

Note: Majority foreign-owned enterprises. Based on the **R&D survey** of Statistics Finland.
Entreprises sous contrôle étranger majoritaire. Données fondées sur **l'enquête R-D** de l'office finlandais de statistiques.

Table 8. FINLAND / FINLANDE

NUMBER OF RESEARCHERS / NOMBRE DE CHERCHEURS

By industry (ISIC Rev. 3)	FOREIGN AFFILIATES (Full-time Eq.)					AS A % OF NATIONAL TOTAL				
	1993	1994	1995	1996	1997	1993	1994	1995	1996	1997
10/14 Mining & quarrying	..	..	..	..	34	..	..	..	..	44.2
15/37 TOTAL MANUFACTURING	..	..	**2 076**	..	**2 934**	..	..	**11.0**	..	**13.3**
15/16 Food, beverages, tobacco	..	..	31	..	25	..	..	4.2	..	3.3
17/19 Textiles, clothing, leather, footwear	..	..	..	..	..	..	..	..	..	..
20/22 Wood and paper products	..	..	23	..	..	..	..	1.6	..	..
20 Wood products	..	..	..	..	..	..	..	..	..	..
21/22 Paper, printing and publishing	..	..	..	..	..	..	..	..	..	..
23/25 Chemicals, Total	..	..	..	..	..	..	..	..	..	..
23 Refined petroleum, nuclear fuel	..	..	..	..	..	..	..	..	..	..
24/25 Chemicals, rubber & plastics prod.	..	..	..	..	..	..	..	..	..	..
24 Chemical products	..	..	121	..	504	..	..	5.2	..	21.9
2423 Pharmaceuticals	..	..	..	..	..	..	..	..	..	..
25 Rubber and plastics products	..	..	..	..	..	..	..	..	..	..
26 Non-metallic mineral products	..	..	82	..	116	..	..	32.5	..	47.2
27/28 Basic & fabricated metals	..	..	..	..	..	..	..	..	..	..
27 Basic metals	..	..	..	..	..	..	..	..	..	..
28 Fabricated metal products	..	..	26	..	144	..	..	4.0	..	27.7
29/32 Machinery, Total	..	..	..	..	..	..	..	..	..	..
29/30 Non-electrical machinery	..	..	..	..	..	..	..	..	..	..
29 Non-electrical machinery nec	..	..	186	..	248	..	..	8.9	..	8.4
30 Office and computing machinery	..	..	..	..	..	..	..	..	..	..
31/32 Electrical & electronic equipment	..	..	888	..	1 280	..	..	12.0	..	..
31 Electrical machinery nec	..	..	564	..	759	..	..	58.8	..	..
32 Radio, TV & communications eq.	..	..	324	..	521	..	..	5.0	..	..
33 Scientific instruments	..	..	103	..	296	..	..	8.5	..	18.6
34/35 Transportation equipment	..	..	..	..	..	..	..	..	..	..
34 Motor vehicles	..	..	..	..	..	..	..	..	..	..
35 Other transport equipment	..	..	..	..	..	..	..	..	..	..
351 Shipbuilding & repairing	..	..	..	..	..	..	..	..	..	..
353 Aircraft and spacecraft	..	..	..	..	..	..	..	..	..	..
36/37 Other manufacturing	..	..	..	..	..	..	..	..	..	..
40/45 Construction, electricity, gas & water	..	..	..	..	135	..	..	..	..	13.7
50/55 Trade, repair, hotels & restaurants	..	..	..	..	80	..	..	..	..	13.4
65/74 Finance, insurance, business services	..	..	..	..	823	..	..	..	..	..
OTHER ACTIVITIES	..	..	..	..	10	..	..	..	..	..
01/99 GRAND TOTAL	..	..	..	..	**4 016**	..	..	..	..	**13.8**

Total manufacturing by investing country						As a % of total manufacturing by foreign affiliates				
All countries	..	..	**2 076**	..	**2 934**	..	..	**100.0**	..	**100.0**
United States	..	..	..	..	923	..	..	..	..	31.5
Canada	..	..	..	..	..	..	..	..	..	..
Mexico	..	..	..	..	..	..	..	..	..	..
Japan	..	..	..	..	..	..	..	..	..	..
Europe	..	..	..	..	..	..	..	..	..	..
European Union (15)	..	..	..	..	1 067	..	..	..	..	36.4
Belgium	..	..	..	..	..	..	..	..	..	..
France	..	..	..	..	..	..	..	..	..	..
Germany	..	..	..	..	..	..	..	..	..	..
Italy	..	..	..	..	..	..	..	..	..	..
Netherlands	..	..	..	..	..	..	..	..	..	..
Spain	..	..	..	..	..	..	..	..	..	..
Sweden	..	..	..	..	..	..	..	..	..	..
United Kingdom	..	..	..	..	..	..	..	..	..	..
Switzerland	..	..	..	..	..	..	..	..	..	..
Australia and New Zealand	..	..	..	..	..	..	..	..	..	..
Asia (non-OECD)	..	..	..	..	..	..	..	..	..	..
Latin America	..	..	..	..	..	..	..	..	..	..

Note: Majority foreign-owned enterprises. Based on the **R&D survey** of Statistics Finland. Total R&D personnel rather than researchers.
Entreprises sous contrôle étranger majoritaire. Données fondées sur **l'enquête R-D** de l'office finlandais de statistiques. Ensemble du personnel de R-D plutôt que chercheurs.

GROSS FIXED CAPITAL FORMATION / FORMATION BRUTE DE CAPITAL FIXE

By industry (ISIC Rev. 3)	FOREIGN AFFILIATES (Millions of Mk)					AS A % OF NATIONAL TOTAL				
	1992	1993	1994	1995	1996	1992	1993	1994	1995	1996
10/14 Mining & quarrying	0	..	2	..	..	0.0	..	1.3	..	..
15/37 TOTAL MANUFACTURING	**864**	**..**	**1 231**	**..**	**..**	**6.2**	**..**	**9.2**	**..**	**..**
15/16 Food, beverages, tobacco	29	..	37	..	..	1.1	..	2.6	..	..
17/19 Textiles, clothing, leather, footwear	..	..	12	..	..	..	..	6.6	..	..
20/22 Wood and paper products	236	..	73	..	..	4.0	..	1.4	..	..
20 Wood products	..	..	..	..	..	..	..	..	..	..
21/22 Paper, printing and publishing	..	..	..	..	..	..	..	..	..	..
23/25 Chemicals, Total	234	..	290	..	..	12.8	..	16.7	..	..
23 Refined petroleum, nuclear fuel	120	..	17	..	..	16.9	..	13.6	..	..
24/25 Chemicals, rubber & plastics prod.	114	..	273	..	..	10.2	..	16.9	..	..
24 Chemical products	84	..	254	..	..	8.7	..	22.6	..	..
2423 Pharmaceuticals	..	..	..	..	..	..	..	..	..	..
25 Rubber and plastics products	30	..	19	..	..	19.5	..	3.9	..	..
26 Non-metallic mineral products	..	..	55	..	..	..	..	15.9	..	..
27/28 Basic & fabricated metals	..	..	64	..	..	..	..	6.5	..	..
27 Basic metals	..	..	20	..	..	..	..	2.7	..	..
28 Fabricated metal products	..	..	44	..	..	..	..	17.4	..	..
29/32 Machinery, Total	..	..	322	..	..	..	..	12.7	..	..
29/30 Non-electrical machinery	..	..	65	..	..	..	..	7.2	..	..
29 Non-electrical machinery nec	..	..	51	..	..	..	..	6.2	..	..
30 Office and computing machinery	..	..	14	..	..	..	..	18.4	..	..
31/32 Electrical & electronic equipment	..	..	257	..	..	..	..	15.8	..	..
31 Electrical machinery nec	..	..	205	..	..	..	..	46.7	..	..
32 Radio, TV & communications eq.	..	..	52	..	..	..	..	4.4	..	..
33 Scientific instruments	..	..	18	..	..	..	..	12.6	..	..
34/35 Transportation equipment	..	..	354	..	..	..	..	50.6	..	..
34 Motor vehicles	3	..	17	..	..	3.8	..	30.4	..	..
35 Other transport equipment	..	..	337	..	..	..	..	52.3	..	..
351 Shipbuilding & repairing	..	..	337	..	..	..	..	64.9	..	..
353 Aircraft and spacecraft	0	..	0	..	..	0.0	..	0.0	..	..
36/37 Other manufacturing	..	..	5	..	..	..	..	3.2	..	..
40/45 Construction, electricity, gas & water	..	..	..	..	..	..	..	..	..	..
50/55 Trade, repair, hotels & restaurants	..	..	..	..	..	..	..	..	..	..
65/74 Finance, insurance, business services	..	..	..	..	..	..	..	..	..	..
OTHER ACTIVITIES	..	..	..	..	..	..	..	..	..	..
01/99 GRAND TOTAL	**..**	**..**	**..**	**..**	**..**	**..**	**..**	**..**	**..**	**..**

Total manufacturing by investing country						As a % of total manufacturing by foreign affiliates				
All countries	864	..	1 231	..	..	100.0	..	100.0	..	..
United States	..	..	..	..	..	..	..	..	..	..
Canada	..	..	..	..	..	..	..	..	..	..
Mexico	..	..	..	..	..	..	..	..	..	..
Japan	..	..	..	..	..	..	..	..	..	..
Europe	..	..	..	..	..	..	..	..	..	..
European Union (15)	..	..	..	..	..	..	..	..	..	..
Belgium	..	..	..	..	..	..	..	..	..	..
France	..	..	..	..	..	..	..	..	..	..
Germany	..	..	..	..	..	..	..	..	..	..
Italy	..	..	..	..	..	..	..	..	..	..
Netherlands	..	..	..	..	..	..	..	..	..	..
Spain	..	..	..	..	..	..	..	..	..	..
Sweden	..	..	..	..	..	..	..	..	..	..
United Kingdom	..	..	..	..	..	..	..	..	..	..
Switzerland	..	..	..	..	..	..	..	..	..	..
Australia and New Zealand	..	..	..	..	..	..	..	..	..	..
Asia (non-OECD)	..	..	..	..	..	..	..	..	..	..
Latin America	..	..	..	..	..	..	..	..	..	..

Note: Majority foreign-owned establishments. Based on the **Annual Industrial Statistics** of Statistics Finland.
Etablissements sous contrôle étranger majoritaire. Données fondées sur les **Statistiques industrielles annuelles** de l'office finlandais de statistiques.

Table 9b. FINLAND / FINLANDE

GROSS FIXED CAPITAL FORMATION / FORMATION BRUTE DE CAPITAL FIXE

By industry (ISIC Rev. 3)	FOREIGN AFFILIATES (Millions of Mk)					AS A % OF NATIONAL TOTAL				
	1993	1994	1995	1996	1997	1993	1994	1995	1996	1997
10/14 Mining & quarrying	..	..	..	57	86	..	..	..	13.8	18.0
15/37 TOTAL MANUFACTURING	..	..	**1 844**	**1 599**	**2 131**	..	..	**8.2**	**6.5**	**7.8**
15/16 Food, beverages, tobacco	..	..	87	170	123	..	..	3.0	7.4	5.7
17/19 Textiles, clothing, leather, footwear	..	..	14	4	26	..	..	3.8	1.5	6.7
20/22 Wood and paper products	..	..	91	126	105	..	..	1.2	1.1	1.0
20 Wood products	..	..	..	..	..	..	..	..	..	..
21/22 Paper, printing and publishing	..	..	..	..	..	..	..	..	..	..
23/25 Chemicals, Total	..	..	..	..	..	..	..	..	..	..
23 Refined petroleum, nuclear fuel	..	..	..	..	..	..	..	..	..	..
24/25 Chemicals, rubber & plastics prod.	..	..	634	352	731	..	..	32.4	17.8	24.7
24 Chemical products	..	..	595	291	684	..	..	42.1	20.7	29.9
2423 Pharmaceuticals	..	..	..	..	..	..	..	..	..	..
25 Rubber and plastics products	..	..	39	61	47	..	..	7.2	10.6	6.9
26 Non-metallic mineral products	..	..	105	163	151	..	..	18.9	34.9	16.8
27/28 Basic & fabricated metals	..	..	214	152	188	..	..	6.8	5.1	4.6
27 Basic metals	..	..	143	..	9	..	..	6.2	..	0.3
28 Fabricated metal products	..	..	71	..	179	..	..	8.3	..	15.6
29/32 Machinery, Total	..	..	..	..	..	..	..	..	..	..
29/30 Non-electrical machinery	..	..	..	..	..	..	..	..	..	..
29 Non-electrical machinery nec	..	..	161	150	210	..	..	9.1	7.3	12.5
30 Office and computing machinery	..	..	..	..	..	..	..	..	..	..
31/32 Electrical & electronic equipment	..	..	305	342	420	..	..	10.7	22.5	20.0
31 Electrical machinery nec	..	..	202	275	268	..	..	44.2	55.4	44.4
32 Radio, TV & communications eq.	..	..	103	67	152	..	..	4.3	6.5	10.1
33 Scientific instruments	..	..	23	30	39	..	..	13.6	16.2	12.0
34/35 Transportation equipment	..	..	..	..	..	..	..	..	..	..
34 Motor vehicles	..	..	..	..	..	..	..	..	..	..
35 Other transport equipment	..	..	..	..	..	..	..	..	..	..
351 Shipbuilding & repairing	..	..	..	..	..	..	..	..	..	..
353 Aircraft and spacecraft	..	..	0	0	0	..	..	0.0	0.0	0.0
36/37 Other manufacturing	..	..	9	5	22	..	..	3.0	1.7	5.1
40/45 Construction, electricity, gas & water	..	..	82	153	555	..	..	1.1	3.2	4.6
50/55 Trade, repair, hotels & restaurants	..	..	879	1 239	1 676	..	..	13.7	15.9	20.1
65/74 Finance, insurance, business services	..	..	972	1 125	499	..	..	10.9	22.4	9.5
OTHER ACTIVITIES	..	..	..	155	257	..	..	..	1.2	2.1
01/99 GRAND TOTAL	..	..	**4 024**	**4 329**	**5 205**	..	..	**7.2**	**7.8**	**7.9**

Total manufacturing by investing country						*As a % of total manufacturing by foreign affiliates*				
All countries	..	..	**1 844**	**1 599**	**2 131**	..	..	**100.0**	**100.0**	**100.0**
United States	..	..	..	364	503	..	..	..	22.8	23.6
Canada	..	..	..	..	..	..	..	..	..	..
Mexico	..	..	0	0	0	..	..	0.0	0.0	0.0
Japan	..	..	..	..	..	..	..	..	..	..
Europe	..	..	..	1 201	1 532	..	..	..	75.1	71.9
European Union (15)	..	..	..	801	1 184	..	..	..	50.1	55.6
Belgium	..	..	..	..	..	..	..	..	..	..
France	..	..	..	33	189	..	..	..	2.1	8.9
Germany	..	..	..	86	135	..	..	..	5.4	6.3
Italy	..	..	..	..	..	..	..	..	..	..
Netherlands	..	..	..	163	240	..	..	..	10.2	11.3
Spain	..	..	0	0	0	..	..	0.0	0.0	0.0
Sweden	..	..	..	299	371	..	..	..	18.7	17.4
United Kingdom	..	..	..	176	136	..	..	..	11.0	6.4
Switzerland	..	..	..	238	186	..	..	..	14.9	8.7
Australia and New Zealand	..	..	0	0	0	..	..	0.0	0.0	0.0
Asia (non-OECD)	..	..	..	..	..	..	..	..	..	..
Latin America	..	..	0	0	..	..	..	0.0	0.0	..

Note: Majority foreign-owned enterprises. Based on the **Business Register** of Statistics Finland.
Entreprises sous contrôle étranger majoritaire. Données fondées sur le **registre du commerce** de l'office finlandais de statistiques.

Table 10. FINLAND / FINLANDE

TOTAL EXPORTS / EXPORTATIONS TOTALES

By industry (ISIC Rev. 3)	FOREIGN AFFILIATES (Millions of Mk)					AS A % OF NATIONAL TOTAL				
	1992	1993	1994	1995	1996	1992	1993	1994	1995	1996
10/14 Mining & quarrying	0	..	..	..	..	0.0	..	..	..	..
15/37 TOTAL MANUFACTURING	**7 889**	..	**14 969**	..	..	**7.9**	..	**10.7**	..	..
15/16 Food, beverages, tobacco	72	..	407	..	..	1.5	..	7.7	..	..
17/19 Textiles, clothing, leather, footwear	..	..	133	..	..	..	..	5.2	..	..
20/22 Wood and paper products	310	..	800	..	..	0.8	..	1.6	..	..
20 Wood products	..	..	..	..	..	..	..	..	..	..
21/22 Paper, printing and publishing	..	..	..	..	..	..	..	..	..	..
23/25 Chemicals, Total	520	..	1 887	..	..	4.6	..	12.6	..	..
23 Refined petroleum, nuclear fuel	86	..	86	..	..	2.3	..	2.6	..	..
24/25 Chemicals, rubber & plastics prod.	435	..	1 801	..	..	5.7	..	15.5	..	..
24 Chemical products	265	..	1 631	..	..	4.2	..	18.8	..	..
2423 Pharmaceuticals	..	..	..	..	..	..	..	..	..	..
25 Rubber and plastics products	169	..	170	..	..	13.0	..	5.8	..	..
26 Non-metallic mineral products	..	..	762	..	..	..	..	39.2	..	..
27/28 Basic & fabricated metals	..	..	808	..	..	..	..	5.3	..	..
27 Basic metals	..	..	241	..	..	..	..	2.1	..	..
28 Fabricated metal products	..	..	567	..	..	..	..	14.8	..	..
29/32 Machinery, Total	..	..	7 451	..	..	..	..	18.7	..	..
29/30 Non-electrical machinery	..	..	3 954	..	..	..	..	17.7	..	..
29 Non-electrical machinery nec	..	..	1 346	..	..	..	..	7.3	..	..
30 Office and computing machinery	..	..	2 608	..	..	..	..	65.8	..	..
31/32 Electrical & electronic equipment	..	..	3 497	..	..	..	..	20.1	..	..
31 Electrical machinery nec	..	..	3 023	..	..	..	..	61.0	..	..
32 Radio, TV & communications eq.	..	..	474	..	..	..	..	3.8	..	..
33 Scientific instruments	..	..	449	..	..	..	..	17.4	..	..
34/35 Transportation equipment	..	..	2 169	..	..	..	..	42.8	..	..
34 Motor vehicles	112	..	170	..	..	5.0	..	9.4	..	..
35 Other transport equipment	..	..	1 999	..	..	..	..	61.5	..	..
351 Shipbuilding & repairing	..	..	1 999	..	..	..	..	73.3	..	..
353 Aircraft and spacecraft	0	..	0	..	..	0.0	..	0.0	..	..
36/37 Other manufacturing	..	..	104	..	..	..	..	5.6	..	..
40/45 Construction, electricity, gas & water	..	..	..	..	..	..	..	..	..	..
50/55 Trade, repair, hotels & restaurants	..	..	..	..	..	..	..	..	..	..
65/74 Finance, insurance, business services	..	..	..	..	..	..	..	..	..	..
OTHER ACTIVITIES	..	..	..	..	..	..	..	..	..	..
01/99 GRAND TOTAL	..	..	..	..	..	..	..	..	..	..

Total manufacturing by investing country						As a % of total manufacturing by foreign affiliates				
All countries	7 889	..	14 969	..	..	100.0	..	100.0	..	..
United States	..	..	..	..	..	..	..	..	..	..
Canada	..	..	..	..	..	..	..	..	..	..
Mexico	..	..	..	..	..	..	..	..	..	..
Japan	..	..	..	..	..	..	..	..	..	..
Europe	..	..	..	..	..	..	..	..	..	..
European Union (15)	..	..	..	..	..	..	..	..	..	..
Belgium	..	..	..	..	..	..	..	..	..	..
France	..	..	..	..	..	..	..	..	..	..
Germany	..	..	..	..	..	..	..	..	..	..
Italy	..	..	..	..	..	..	..	..	..	..
Netherlands	..	..	..	..	..	..	..	..	..	..
Spain	..	..	..	..	..	..	..	..	..	..
Sweden	..	..	..	..	..	..	..	..	..	..
United Kingdom	..	..	..	..	..	..	..	..	..	..
Switzerland	..	..	..	..	..	..	..	..	..	..
Australia and New Zealand	..	..	..	..	..	..	..	..	..	..
Asia (non-OECD)	..	..	..	..	..	..	..	..	..	..
Latin America	..	..	..	..	..	..	..	..	..	..

Note: Majority foreign-owned establishments. Based on the **Annual Industrial Statistics** of Statistics Finland.
Etablissements sous contrôle étranger majoritaire. Données fondées sur les **Statistiques industrielles annuelles** de l'office finlandais de statistiques.

Table 14. FINLAND / FINLANDE

GROSS OPERATING SURPLUS / EXCÉDENT BRUT D'EXPLOITATION

By industry (ISIC Rev. 3)	FOREIGN AFFILIATES (Millions of Mk)					AS A % OF NATIONAL TOTAL				
	1993	1994	1995	1996	1997	1993	1994	1995	1996	1997
10/14 Mining & quarrying	..	..	..	138	212	..	..	..	15.2	20.3
15/37 TOTAL MANUFACTURING	..	..	**4 520**	**6 478**	**8 780**	..	..	**8.2**	**12.6**	**13.5**
15/16 Food, beverages, tobacco	..	..	287	266	453	..	..	6.4	5.9	9.6
17/19 Textiles, clothing, leather, footwear	..	..	35	56	67	..	..	3.4	5.2	6.0
20/22 Wood and paper products	..	..	230	255	351	..	..	1.1	1.5	1.6
20 Wood products	..	..	..	..	..	..	..	..	..	..
21/22 Paper, printing and publishing	..	..	..	..	..	..	..	..	..	..
23/25 Chemicals, Total	..	..	..	..	..	..	..	..	..	..
23 Refined petroleum, nuclear fuel	..	..	..	..	..	..	..	..	..	..
24/25 Chemicals, rubber & plastics prod.	..	..	890	1 334	2 136	..	..	16.0	24.0	33.0
24 Chemical products	..	..	762	1 151	1 931	..	..	17.9	28.5	40.8
2423 Pharmaceuticals	..	..	..	..	..	..	..	..	..	..
25 Rubber and plastics products	..	..	128	183	205	..	..	9.8	12.1	11.8
26 Non-metallic mineral products	..	..	373	550	639	..	..	30.1	43.7	37.1
27/28 Basic & fabricated metals	..	..	345	444	586	..	..	5.3	7.9	8.8
27 Basic metals	..	..	174	..	40	..	..	3.8	..	1.0
28 Fabricated metal products	..	..	171	..	546	..	..	8.9	..	19.3
29/32 Machinery, Total	..	..	..	..	..	..	..	..	..	..
29/30 Non-electrical machinery	..	..	..	..	..	..	..	..	..	..
29 Non-electrical machinery nec	..	..	540	689	1 057	..	..	10.9	11.9	18.0
30 Office and computing machinery	..	..	..	..	..	..	..	..	..	..
31/32 Electrical & electronic equipment	..	..	889	1 661	2 287	..	..	15.9	23.4	19.9
31 Electrical machinery nec	..	..	692	1 119	1 254	..	..	52.3	62.2	59.6
32 Radio, TV & communications eq.	..	..	197	542	1 033	..	..	4.6	10.2	11.0
33 Scientific instruments	..	..	64	139	238	..	..	7.2	11.7	17.9
34/35 Transportation equipment	..	..	..	..	..	..	..	..	..	..
34 Motor vehicles	..	..	..	..	..	..	..	..	..	..
35 Other transport equipment	..	..	..	..	..	..	..	..	..	..
351 Shipbuilding & repairing	..	..	..	..	..	..	..	..	..	..
353 Aircraft and spacecraft	..	..	0	0	0	..	..	0.0	0.0	0.0
36/37 Other manufacturing	..	..	51	59	81	..	..	6.2	6.3	7.9
40/45 Construction, electricity, gas & water	..	..	248	400	339	..	..	2.3	3.3	2.7
50/55 Trade, repair, hotels & restaurants	..	..	3 019	3 227	3 529	..	..	13.7	14.3	14.9
65/74 Finance, insurance, business services	..	..	565	792	936	..	..	6.8	6.4	7.5
OTHER ACTIVITIES	..	..	..	562	476	..	..	..	2.3	1.7
01/99 GRAND TOTAL	..	..	**8 940**	**11 596**	**14 272**	..	..	**7.6**	**9.3**	**10.0**

Total manufacturing by investing country						*As a % of total manufacturing by foreign affiliates*				
All countries	..	..	**4 520**	**6 478**	**8 780**	..	..	**100.0**	**100.0**	**100.0**
United States	..	..	..	1 392	2 448	..	..	..	21.5	27.9
Canada	..	..	..	..	..	..	..	..	..	..
Mexico	..	..	0	0	0	..	..	0.0	0.0	0.0
Japan	..	..	..	..	..	..	..	..	..	..
Europe	..	..	..	4 826	6 153	..	..	..	74.5	70.1
European Union (15)	..	..	..	2 941	3 996	..	..	..	45.4	45.5
Belgium	..	..	..	..	..	..	..	..	..	..
France	..	..	..	93	218	..	..	..	1.4	2.5
Germany	..	..	..	299	355	..	..	..	4.6	4.0
Italy	..	..	..	..	..	..	..	..	..	..
Netherlands	..	..	..	676	1 018	..	..	..	10.4	11.6
Spain	..	..	0	0	0	..	..	0.0	0.0	0.0
Sweden	..	..	..	1 128	1 548	..	..	..	17.4	17.6
United Kingdom	..	..	..	490	406	..	..	..	7.6	4.6
Switzerland	..	..	..	1 059	1 243	..	..	..	16.3	14.2
Australia and New Zealand	..	..	0	0	0	..	..	0.0	0.0	0.0
Asia (non-OECD)	..	..	..	..	..	..	..	..	..	..
Latin America	..	..	0	0	..	..	..	0.0	0.0	..

Note: Majority foreign-owned enterprises. Based on the **Business Register** of Statistics Finland.
Entreprises sous contrôle étranger majoritaire. Données fondées sur le **registre du commerce** de l'office finlandais de statistiques.

Table 17. FINLAND / FINLANDE

STOCK OF FOREIGN DIRECT INVESTMENT / STOCK D'INVESTISSEMENT DIRECT ÉTRANGER

	FOREIGN AFFILIATES (Millions of Mk)									
By industry (ISIC Rev. 3)	1987	1988	1989	1990	1991	1992	1993	1994	1995	1996
10/14 Mining & quarrying	..	..	..	..	..	..	..	..	..	..
15/37 TOTAL MANUFACTURING	..	..	..	..	..	**8915**	**12122**	**17460**	..	..
15/16 Food, beverages, tobacco	..	..	..	..	..	691	765	770	..	..
17/19 Textiles, clothing, leather, footwear	..	..	..	..	..	242	241	..	..	..
20/22 Wood and paper products	..	..	..	..	..	414	337	447	..	..
20 Wood products	..	..	..	..	..	..	..	95	..	..
21/22 Paper, printing and publishing	..	..	..	..	..	..	..	352	..	..
23/25 Chemicals, Total	..	..	..	..	..	996	1664	..	..	..
23 Refined petroleum, nuclear fuel	..	..	..	..	..	0	0	..	..	..
24/25 Chemicals, rubber & plastics prod.	..	..	..	..	..	996	1664	5315	..	..
24 Chemical products	..	..	..	..	..	..	..	5048	..	..
2423 Pharmaceuticals	..	..	..	..	..	..	..	..	..	..
25 Rubber and plastics products	..	..	..	..	..	..	..	267	..	..
26 Non-metallic mineral products	..	..	..	..	..	..	..	..	..	..
27/28 Basic & fabricated metals	..	..	..	..	..	..	..	1552	..	..
27 Basic metals	..	..	..	..	..	..	..	745	..	..
28 Fabricated metal products	..	..	..	..	..	599	565	807	..	..
29/32 Machinery, Total	..	..	..	..	..	..	..	..	..	..
29/30 Non-electrical machinery	..	..	..	..	..	..	..	..	..	..
29 Non-electrical machinery nec	..	..	..	..	..	..	..	1056	..	..
30 Office and computing machinery	..	..	..	..	..	..	..	..	..	..
31/32 Electrical & electronic equipment	..	..	..	..	..	3906	4848	4911	..	..
31 Electrical machinery nec	..	..	..	..	..	..	..	..	..	..
32 Radio, TV & communications eq.	..	..	..	..	..	..	..	..	..	..
33 Scientific instruments	..	..	..	..	..	..	..	..	..	..
34/35 Transportation equipment	..	..	..	..	..	..	..	..	..	..
34 Motor vehicles	..	..	..	..	..	..	..	..	..	..
35 Other transport equipment	..	..	..	..	..	..	..	..	..	..
351 Shipbuilding & repairing	..	..	..	..	..	..	..	..	..	..
353 Aircraft and spacecraft	..	..	..	..	..	..	..	..	..	..
36/37 Other manufacturing	..	..	..	..	..	..	244	221	..	..
40/45 Construction, electricity, gas & water	..	..	..	..	..	..	..	..	..	..
50/55 Trade, repair, hotels & restaurants	..	..	..	..	..	5911	6769	8192	..	..
65/74 Finance, insurance, business services	..	..	..	..	..	1359	2220	2090	..	..
OTHER ACTIVITIES	..	..	..	..	..	..	905	644	..	..
01/99 GRAND TOTAL	..	..	..	..	..	**16440**	**22128**	**28667**	..	..

Total Manufacturing by investing country										
All countries	..	..	..	..	..	8915	12122	17460	..	..
United States	..	..	..	..	..	..	1023	1600	..	..
Canada	..	..	..	..	..	..	0	0	..	..
Mexico	..	..	..	..	..	..	0	0	..	..
Japan	..	..	..	..	..	..	..	..	..	..
Europe	..	..	..	..	..	..	11154	15809	..	..
European Union (15)	..	..	..	..	..	..	6236	11154	..	..
Belgium	..	..	..	..	..	..	..	..	..	..
France	..	..	..	..	..	..	372	..	..	..
Germany	..	..	..	..	..	..	341	798	..	..
Italy	..	..	..	..	..	..	..	..	..	..
Netherlands	..	..	..	..	..	..	..	..	..	..
Spain	..	..	..	..	..	..	..	0	..	..
Sweden	..	..	..	..	..	..	2645	3386	..	..
United Kingdom	..	..	..	..	..	..	106	75	..	..
Switzerland	..	..	..	..	..	..	..	..	..	..
Australia and New Zealand	..	..	..	..	..	..	0	0	..	..
Asia (non-OECD)	..	..	..	..	..	..	0	7	..	..
Latin America	..	..	..	..	..	..	0	0	..	..

Note: All foreign-owned firms (10% or more of capital share). Based on Bank of Finland's **direct investment statistics**. *Office and computing machinery* (ISIC 30) and *Scientific instruments* (33) are included in *Electrical and electronic equipment* (31/32).

Toutes les firmes sous contrôle étranger (10% au moins du capital détenu par l'étranger). Données fondées sur les **statistiques d'investissement direct** de la Banque de Finlande. Les *Machines de bureau et ordinateurs* (CITI 30) et les *Instruments* (33) sont compris dans le *Matériel électrique et électronique* (31/32).

Table 18. FINLAND / FINLANDE

CAPITAL UNDER FOREIGN INFLUENCE / CAPITAL SOUS INFLUENCE ÉTRANGÈRE

By industry (ISIC Rev. 3)		1987	1988	1989	1990	1991	1992	1993	1994	1995	1996
		FOREIGN AFFILIATES *(Millions of Mk)*									
10/14	Mining & quarrying	..	..	..	..	..	..	..	..	..	..
15/37	**TOTAL MANUFACTURING**	..	..	..	..	..	21252	29194	38880	..	..
15/16	Food, beverages, tobacco	..	..	..	..	..	1264	1460	1457	..	..
17/19	Textiles, clothing, leather, footwear	..	..	..	..	..	518	400	..	..	..
20/22	Wood and paper products	..	..	..	..	..	1052	1035	1274	..	..
20	Wood products	..	..	..	..	..	..	..	260	..	..
21/22	Paper, printing and publishing	..	..	..	..	..	..	..	1014	..	..
23/25	Chemicals, Total	..	..	..	..	..	1981	3296	..	..	..
23	Refined petroleum, nuclear fuel	..	..	..	..	..	0	0	..	..	..
24/25	Chemicals, rubber & plastics prod.	..	..	..	..	..	1981	3296	8258	..	..
24	Chemical products	..	..	..	..	..	..	..	7746	..	..
2423	Pharmaceuticals	..	..	..	..	..	..	..	..	..	..
25	Rubber and plastics products	..	..	..	..	..	..	..	512	..	..
26	Non-metallic mineral products	..	..	..	..	..	..	..	..	..	..
27/28	Basic & fabricated metals	..	..	..	..	..	..	..	2467	..	..
27	Basic metals	..	..	..	..	..	..	..	1008	..	..
28	Fabricated metal products	..	..	..	..	..	1007	1020	1459	..	..
29/32	Machinery, Total	..	..	..	..	..	..	..	..	..	..
29/30	Non-electrical machinery	..	..	..	..	..	..	..	..	..	..
29	Non-electrical machinery nec	..	..	..	..	..	..	..	2863	..	..
30	Office and computing machinery	..	..	..	..	..	..	..	..	..	..
31/32	Electrical & electronic equipment	..	..	..	..	..	9723	11577	13289	..	..
31	Electrical machinery nec	..	..	..	..	..	..	..	..	..	..
32	Radio, TV & communications eq.	..	..	..	..	..	..	..	..	..	..
33	Scientific instruments	..	..	..	..	..	..	..	..	..	..
34/35	Transportation equipment	..	..	..	..	..	..	..	..	..	..
34	Motor vehicles	..	..	..	..	..	..	..	..	..	..
35	Other transport equipment	..	..	..	..	..	..	..	..	..	..
351	Shipbuilding & repairing	..	..	..	..	..	..	..	..	..	..
353	Aircraft and spacecraft	..	..	..	..	..	..	..	..	..	..
36/37	Other manufacturing	..	..	..	..	..	..	439	365	..	..
40/45	Construction, electricity, gas & water	..	..	..	..	..	..	..	..	..	..
50/55	Trade, repair, hotels & restaurants	..	..	..	..	..	15259	14464	18923	..	..
65/74	Finance, insurance, business services	..	..	..	..	..	10402	9918	16566	..	..
	OTHER ACTIVITIES	..	..	..	..	..	..	2805	3179	..	..
01/99	**GRAND TOTAL**	..	..	..	..	..	48147	56669	78656	..	..

Total Manufacturing by investing country

	1987	1988	1989	1990	1991	1992	1993	1994	1995	1996
All countries	..	..	..	..	..	21252	29194	38880	..	..
United States	..	..	..	..	..	..	1765	2660	..	..
Canada	..	..	..	..	..	..	0	0	..	..
Mexico	..	..	..	..	..	..	0	0	..	..
Japan	..	..	..	..	..	..	..	..	..	..
Europe	..	..	..	..	..	..	27102	35967	..	..
European Union (15)	..	..	..	..	..	..	14869	21831	..	..
Belgium	..	..	..	..	..	..	..	..	..	..
France	..	..	..	..	..	..	487	..	..	..
Germany	..	..	..	..	..	..	936	1407	..	..
Italy	..	..	..	..	..	..	..	..	..	..
Netherlands	..	..	..	..	..	..	..	..	..	..
Spain	..	..	..	..	..	..	..	0	..	..
Sweden	..	..	..	..	..	..	6142	7182	..	..
United Kingdom	..	..	..	..	..	..	464	334	..	..
Switzerland	..	..	..	..	..	..	..	..	..	..
Australia and New Zealand	..	..	..	..	..	..	0	0	..	..
Asia (non-OECD)	..	..	..	..	..	..	0	12	..	..
Latin America	..	..	..	..	..	..	0	0	..	..

Note: All foreign-owned firms (10% or more of capital share). Based on Bank of Finland's **direct investment statistics**. *Office and computing machinery* (ISIC 30) and *Scientific instruments* (33) are included in *Electrical and electronic equipment* (31/32).

Toutes les firmes sous contrôle étranger (10% au moins du capital détenu par l'étranger). Données fondées sur les **statistiques d'investissement direct** de la Banque de Finlande. Les *Machines de bureau et ordinateurs* (CITI 30) et les *Instruments* (33) sont compris dans le *Matériel électrique et électronique* (31/32).

FINLAND

Source

The data are prepared by Statistics Finland for all variables except financial variables, prepared by the Bank of Finland.

Statistics Finland provides data on majority foreign-owned firms from two sources:

- The Annual Industrial Statistics relate to the manufacturing sector only and are establishment-level data. The variables covered are: *Number of establishments* (Table 1*a*), *Number of employees* (Table 2*a*), *Production, Value added* (Table 5*a*), *Wages and salaries* (Table 6*a*), *Gross fixed capital formation* (Table 9*a*) and *Total exports*. These data cannot be broken down by investor's country.

- The Business Register, combined with survey results, provides complementary information on non-manufacturing sectors; the basic unit is the enterprise. The variables covered are: *Number of enterprises* (Table 1*b*), *Number of employees* (Table 2*b*), *Turnover, Value added* (Table 5*b*), *Wages and salaries* (Table 6*b*), *Gross fixed capital formation* (Table 9*b*) and *Gross operating surplus*. Information on the investor's country is collected by the Bank of Finland and is available from 1995.

Data from 1995 onwards are not comparable with those for previous years because they include firms which are owned indirectly from abroad. These data are published in *Financial Statements Statistics*.

The Bank of Finland is responsible for the balance of payments statistics and it collects data on the stock of direct investment in Finland and on the balance sheet totals of foreign-owned companies through an annual survey. In this survey, Finland-based foreign-owned companies provide data on capital stock and balance sheet totals in consolidated form. The investor's share is at least 10 %. The survey covers all manufacturing companies, financial institutions and other large direct investment enterprises. Small direct investment enterprises are covered by sampling. However, the values of balance sheet totals in this publication do not include the values of small direct investment enterprises.

For R&D expenditure and *Number of researchers*, data come from the biennial R&D survey (annual from 1997 onwards) conducted by Statistics Finland, which covers all enterprises in the manufacturing sector with more than 10 employees.

Data from different sources should not be mixed.

National totals: provided by Statistics Finland and fully compatible with foreign affiliates' data.

Industrial classification

For all variables, the data are classified according to the principal industrial activity of the affiliate.

The industrial classification used for the Finnish tables is ISIC Revision 3.

In Tables 17 and 18, *Office and computing machinery* (30) and *Scientific instruments* (33) are included in *Electrical and electronic equipment* (31/32).

Variables

- *Number of establishments/enterprises*: the Annual Industrial Statistics provide data at the establishment level; the Business Register provides data at the enterprise level.

- *Number of employees* is expressed on a full-time equivalent basis (applies only to data from the Business Register).

- *Production* is valued in factor values, excluding all indirect taxes and including all subsidies.

- *Value added* (Annual Industrial Statistics) is valued in producer prices, indirect taxes included, subsidies excluded.

- *Wages and salaries* (Annual Industrial Statistics) include employers' contributions to social security schemes and pension funds.

- *R&D expenditure* refers to expenditure by the affiliate itself.

- *Number of researchers* refers to all employees engaged in research and development, and is expressed in full-time equivalent.

- *Gross fixed capital formation* (Annual Industrial Statistics): expenditure on the purchase of fixed assets plus own-account construction of assets, less sales of fixed assets. The valuation is at full cost incurred, including delivered price, cost of installation and fees and taxes.

- *Stock of foreign direct investment* is defined as capital stock = the investor's share in the shareholders' equity of the direct investment enterprise (including reserve and valuation items) + the investor's loans to the direct investment enterprise – the direct investment enterprise's loans to the investor. Intra-group trade credits and intra-group debt securities tradeable in organised financial markets are not, for the present, classified as direct investment capital, contrary to the recommendations given in the new IMF Balance of Payments Manual.

- *Capital under foreign influence* is defined as the consolidated balance sheet totals of directly foreign-owned companies in Finland. Non-renewable assets are included in the balance sheet figures. The values represent the whole of the companies' activities and are not prorated by degree of foreign control. If the foreign-owned company in Finland has subsidiaries and branches abroad, the consolidated balance sheet total includes the assets of these foreign subsidiaries and branches.

Geographical breakdown

The country of origin is that of the "ultimate beneficial owner".

The detail by investor's country is only available from 1995 for data from the Business Register.

FINLANDE

Source

Les données émanent de l'office finlandais de statistiques pour toutes les variables, sauf les variables financières qui sont fournies par la Banque de Finlande.

L'office finlandais de statistiques fournit des données sur les entreprises à participation étrangère majoritaire provenant de deux sources :

- Les Statistiques industrielles annuelles concernent le secteur manufacturier seulement et sont des données qui se situent au niveau de l'établissement. Les variables couvertes sont : *Nombre d'établissements* (tableau 1*a*), *Nombre de salariés* (tableau 2*a*), *Production, Valeur ajoutée* (tableau 5*a*), *Salaires* (tableau 6*a*), *Formation brute de capital fixe* (tableau 9*a*) et *Exportations totales*. Ces données ne peuvent pas être ventilées par pays de l'investisseur.

- Le Registre du commerce, combiné avec des résultats d'enquête, donne des informations complémentaires sur les secteurs non manufacturiers ; l'unité de base est l'entreprise. Les variables couvertes sont : *Nombre d'entreprises* (tableau 1*b*), *Nombre de salariés* (tableau 2*b*), *Chiffre d'affaires*, *Valeur ajoutée* (tableau 5*b*), *Salaires* (tableau 6*b*), *Formation brute de capital fixe* (tableau 9*b*) et *Excédent brut d'exploitation*. Les informations sur le pays d'origine de l'investissement sont collectées par la Banque de Finlande et sont disponibles à partir de 1995.

Les données à partir de 1995 ne sont pas comparables avec celles des années précédentes, car elles comprennent également les firmes détenues indirectement par l'étranger. Elles sont publiées dans *Financial Statements Statistics*.

La Banque de Finlande est responsable des statistiques de balance des paiements et, au moyen d'une enquête annuelle, elle collecte des données sur le stock d'investissement direct en Finlande et sur le total du bilan des sociétés à capitaux étrangers en Finlande. Dans cette enquête, les sociétés à capitaux étrangers basées en Finlande fournissent des données sur leur stock de capital et le total de leur bilan sous une forme consolidée. La participation de l'investisseur est d'au moins 10 %. L'enquête couvre toutes les sociétés manufacturières, institutions financières et autres grandes entreprises recevant des investissements directs, ainsi qu'un échantillon de petites entreprises bénéficiant d'investissements directs. Cependant, la valeur du total du bilan dans cette publication ne comprend pas les chiffres des petites entreprises bénéficiaires d'investissements directs.

Pour les *Dépenses de R-D* et le *Nombre de chercheurs*, les données sont issues de l'enquête biennale sur la R-D (annuelle à compter de 1997) de l'office finlandais de statistiques, qui couvre toutes les entreprises du secteur manufacturier employant plus de 10 salariés.

Les données de sources différentes ne doivent pas être mélangées.

Totaux nationaux : fournis par l'office finlandais de statistiques et entièrement compatibles avec les données relatives aux filiales étrangères.

Classification industrielle

Pour toutes les variables, les données sont classées selon l'activité industrielle principale de l'entreprise affiliée.

La classification industrielle utilisée pour les tableaux de la Finlande est la CITI révision 3.

Dans les tableaux 17 et 18, les *Machines de bureau et à calculer* (30) et les *Instruments* (33) sont inclus dans le secteur *Machines électriques et électroniques* (31/32).

Variables

- *Nombre d'établissements/d'entreprises* : les Statistiques industrielles annuelles fournissent des données à l'échelon de l'établissement ; le Registre du commerce fournit des données au niveau de l'entreprise.

- Le *Nombre de salariés* est exprimé en équivalent plein-temps (uniquement pour les données issues du Registre du commerce).

- La *Production* est évaluée au coût des facteurs, à l'exclusion de tous les impôts indirects, mais y compris toutes les subventions.

- La *Valeur ajoutée* (Statistiques industrielles annuelles) est évaluée aux prix à la production, y compris les impôts indirects, mais à l'exclusion des subventions.

- Les *Salaires* (Statistiques industrielles annuelles) comprennent les cotisations patronales aux caisses de sécurité sociale et de retraite.

- La *Formation brute de capital fixe* (Statistiques industrielles annuelles) correspond aux acquisitions d'actifs fixes, y compris ceux fabriqués par le personnel de l'établissement pour l'usage de ce dernier et déduction faite de la valeur des ventes de ces mêmes biens. L'évaluation est faite au prix de revient total, y compris le prix rendu, les frais d'installation et les droits et redevances.

- Les *Dépenses de R-D* concernent les dépenses effectuées par les filiales pour elles-mêmes.

- Le *Nombre de chercheurs* fait référence à l'ensemble des salariés travaillant dans la recherche-développement, et est exprimé en équivalent plein-temps.

- Le *Stock d'investissement direct étranger* est défini comme le stock de capital, c'est-à-dire la participation de l'investisseur au capital de l'entreprise faisant l'objet de l'investissement direct (y compris les réserves et les provisions pour réévaluation) + les prêts de l'investisseur à l'entreprise destinataire de l'investissement direct – les prêts de la même entreprise à l'investisseur. Les crédits commerciaux intra-groupe et les titres de créance intra-groupe négociables sur des marchés financiers organisés ne sont pas, pour l'instant, classés comme capitaux d'investissement direct, contrairement aux recommandations données dans le nouveau Manuel de la balance des paiements du FMI.

- Le *Capital sous influence étrangère* est défini comme le total du bilan consolidé de sociétés sous contrôle direct de l'étranger en Finlande. Les actifs non renouvelables sont inclus dans les chiffres du bilan. Les chiffres englobent l'ensemble des activités des sociétés et ne sont pas répartis au prorata du degré de contrôle. Si la société sous contrôle étranger en Finlande possède des filiales et succursales à l'étranger, le total du bilan consolidé comprend les actifs de ces filiales et succursales étrangères.

Ventilation géographique

Le pays d'origine est celui du "bénéficiaire ultime de l'investissement".

Le détail par pays de l'investisseur est seulement disponible à partir de 1995 pour les données issues du Registre du commerce.

FRANCE

FRANCE

Table 1. FRANCE

NUMBER OF ENTERPRISES / NOMBRE D'ENTREPRISES

By industry (ISIC Rev. 3)	FOREIGN AFFILIATES (Units)					AS A % OF NATIONAL TOTAL				
	1993	1994	1995	1996	1997	1993	1994	1995	1996	1997
10/14 Mining & quarrying	48	45	54	49	..	13.6	12.8	15.0	15.0	..
15/37 TOTAL MANUFACTURING	**2 618**	**2 446**	**2 730**	**2 787**	..	**11.5**	**10.8**	**12.2**	**12.6**	..
15/16 Food, beverages, tobacco	..	..	..	..	..	..	..	..	..	..
17/19 Textiles, clothing, leather, footwear	204	173	195	203	..	5.1	4.5	5.3	5.7	..
20/22 Wood and paper products	274	263	328	333	..	8.4	7.9	9.8	10.1	..
20 Wood products	44	..	..	..	..	6.4	..	..	..	..
21/22 Paper, printing and publishing	230	..	..	..	..	8.9	..	..	..	..
23/25 Chemicals, Total	654	627	658	652	..	25.6	24.1	25.2	25.0	..
23 Refined petroleum, nuclear fuel	..	..	..	..	..	..	..	..	..	..
24/25 Chemicals, rubber & plastics prod.	654	627	658	652	..	25.6	24.1	25.2	25.0	..
24 Chemical products	441	420	409	389	..	37.1	34.3	34.2	32.9	..
2423 Pharmaceuticals	128	109	106	101	..	41.6	35.9	37.7	37.7	..
25 Rubber and plastics products	213	207	249	263	..	15.6	15.0	17.6	18.5	..
26 Non-metallic mineral products	128	118	134	152	..	12.9	12.0	14.3	16.6	..
27/28 Basic & fabricated metals	301	281	312	329	..	6.2	5.8	6.4	6.7	..
27 Basic metals	74	72	82	84	..	15.5	14.9	16.8	17.5	..
28 Fabricated metal products	227	209	230	245	..	5.2	4.8	5.2	5.5	..
29/32 Machinery, Total	598	579	653	673	..	16.0	16.3	18.4	18.9	..
29/30 Non-electrical machinery	396	391	460	461	..	15.9	17.2	20.6	20.3	..
29 Non-electrical machinery nec	378	375	438	438	..	15.6	17.1	20.4	19.9	..
30 Office and computing machinery	18	16	22	23	..	24.3	19.8	25.0	31.5	..
31/32 Electrical & electronic equipment	202	188	193	212	..	16.2	14.8	14.7	16.5	..
31 Electrical machinery nec	134	130	131	143	..	17.6	17.1	17.3	19.5	..
32 Radio, TV & communications eq.	68	58	62	69	..	14.0	11.4	11.2	12.6	..
33 Scientific instruments	149	131	147	143	..	16.4	14.0	15.9	15.6	..
34/35 Transportation equipment	160	145	162	154	..	19.1	17.3	19.5	19.4	..
34 Motor vehicles	124	112	124	122	..	23.0	20.6	22.9	23.4	..
35 Other transport equipment	36	33	38	32	..	12.1	11.3	13.1	11.7	..
351 Shipbuilding & repairing	10	10	11	5	..	9.3	9.9	11.3	5.7	..
353 Aircraft and spacecraft	9	4	7	7	..	9.8	4.3	7.2	7.7	..
36/37 Other manufacturing	102	84	87	99	..	8.3	6.7	7.2	8.3	..
40/45 Construction, electricity, gas & water	..	..	..	..	..	..	..	..	..	..
50/55 Trade, repair, hotels & restaurants	..	..	..	..	..	..	..	..	..	..
65/74 Finance, insurance, business services	..	..	..	..	..	..	..	..	..	..
OTHER ACTIVITIES	..	..	..	..	..	..	..	..	..	..
01/99 GRAND TOTAL	..	..	..	..	..	..	..	..	..	..

Total manufacturing by investing country						As a % of total manufacturing by foreign affiliates				
All countries	**2 618**	**2 446**	**2 730**	**2 787**	..	**100.0**	**100.0**	**100.0**	**100.0**	..
United States	512	491	561	589	..	19.6	20.1	20.5	21.1	..
Canada	32	..	..	..	..	1.2	..	..	..	..
Mexico	..	..	..	..	..	..	..	..	..	..
Japan	71	73	78	78	..	2.7	3.0	2.9	2.8	..
Europe	1 781	..	..	..	..	68.0	..	..	..	..
European Union (15)	..	1 471	1 676	1 717	..	..	60.1	61.4	61.6	..
Belgium	194	..	..	..	..	7.4	..	..	..	..
France	..	..	..	..	..	..	..	..	..	..
Germany	504	506	576	569	..	19.3	20.7	21.1	20.4	..
Italy	111	..	..	..	..	4.2	..	..	..	..
Netherlands	108	146	168	160	..	4.1	6.0	6.2	5.7	..
Spain	21	..	..	..	..	0.8	..	..	..	..
Sweden	95	..	..	..	..	3.6	..	..	..	..
United Kingdom	317	328	353	388	..	12.1	13.4	12.9	13.9	..
Switzerland	309	275	300	281	..	11.8	11.2	11.0	10.1	..
Australia and New Zealand	..	..	..	..	..	..	..	..	..	..
Asia (non-OECD)	..	17	20	29	..	..	0.7	0.7	1.0	..
Latin America	..	2	2	5	..	..	0.1	0.1	0.2	..

Note: Majority foreign-owned firms. Food (ISIC 15/16), energy industries (ISIC 23 and parts of 10/14) and *Recycling* (37) are excluded. *Total Manufacturing* includes *Mining & quarrying* (ISIC 10/14). Firmes sous contrôle étranger majoritaire. L'industrie agro-alimentaire (CITI 15/16), l'énergie (CITI 23 et une partie de 10/14) et la *Récupération* (37) ne sont pas couvertes. Le *Total manufacturier* comprend les *Activités extractives* (CITI 10/14).

Table 2. FRANCE

NUMBER OF EMPLOYEES / NOMBRE DE SALARIÉS

By industry (ISIC Rev. 3)		FOREIGN AFFILIATES (Full-time Eq.)					AS A % OF NATIONAL TOTAL				
		1993	1994	1995	1996	1997	1993	1994	1995	1996	1997
10/14	Mining & quarrying	..	6 205	6 756	6 513	..	..	24.9	27.2	27.1	..
15/37	**TOTAL MANUFACTURING**	**698 000**	**659 420**	**715 932**	**742 663**	..	**24.3**	**23.1**	**25.1**	**25.8**	..
15/16	Food, beverages, tobacco	..	..	..	..	..	..	..	..	..	..
17/19	Textiles, clothing, leather, footwear	36 000	31 832	35 582	36 496	..	12.0	10.9	12.6	13.5	..
20/22	Wood and paper products	63 000	58 544	66 699	65 582	..	22.2	20.5	23.4	23.1	..
20	Wood products	6 000	..	..	..	..	14.0	..	..	..	..
21/22	Paper, printing and publishing	57 000	..	..	..	..	23.7	..	..	..	..
23/25	Chemicals, Total	..	171 535	179 475	185 165	..	..	36.9	38.5	38.9	..
23	Refined petroleum, nuclear fuel	..	..	..	..	..	..	..	..	..	..
24/25	Chemicals, rubber & plastics prod.	..	171 535	179 475	185 165	..	..	36.9	38.5	38.9	..
24	Chemical products	..	121 332	123 938	124 125	..	..	43.6	44.9	44.3	..
2423	Pharmaceuticals	55 000	45 916	47 500	49 964	..	61.1	51.1	54.0	55.8	..
25	Rubber and plastics products	49 000	50 203	55 537	61 040	..	26.6	26.9	29.1	31.3	..
26	Non-metallic mineral products	..	33 364	37 250	40 283	..	..	25.3	28.4	30.5	..
27/28	Basic & fabricated metals	..	48 391	52 280	59 910	..	..	11.3	12.0	13.3	..
27	Basic metals	..	17 951	19 570	20 276	..	..	13.7	14.7	15.4	..
28	Fabricated metal products	33 000	30 440	32 710	39 634	..	11.1	10.2	10.7	12.5	..
29/32	Machinery, Total	..	193 945	210 847	222 289	..	..	34.5	36.5	37.3	..
29/30	Non-electrical machinery	..	125 505	132 698	137 232	..	..	42.1	44.3	44.8	..
29	Non-electrical machinery nec	..	99 274	107 759	112 578	..	..	38.9	41.8	42.2	..
30	Office and computing machinery	..	26 231	24 939	24 654	..	..	60.7	59.9	62.2	..
31/32	Electrical & electronic equipment	..	68 440	78 149	85 057	..	..	26.0	28.2	29.3	..
31	Electrical machinery nec	..	42 592	45 699	49 863	..	..	27.5	29.3	31.5	..
32	Radio, TV & communications eq.	..	25 848	32 450	35 194	..	..	23.7	26.8	26.6	..
33	Scientific instruments	..	27 774	31 086	30 938	..	..	23.2	27.4	27.8	..
34/35	Transportation equipment	..	70 651	77 617	75 142	..	..	16.8	18.3	18.1	..
34	Motor vehicles	..	61 446	68 195	66 568	..	..	20.8	22.6	22.6	..
35	Other transport equipment	..	9 205	9 422	8 574	..	..	7.3	7.7	7.1	..
351	Shipbuilding & repairing	..	..	1 286	347	..	..	..	8.7	2.3	..
353	Aircraft and spacecraft	..	..	1 624	1 720	..	..	..	2.0	2.1	..
36/37	Other manufacturing	..	17 179	18 340	20 345	..	..	14.7	16.1	17.3	..
40/45	Construction, electricity, gas & water	..	..	..	..	..	..	..	..	..	..
50/55	Trade, repair, hotels & restaurants	..	..	..	..	..	..	..	..	..	..
65/74	Finance, insurance, business services	..	..	..	..	..	..	..	..	..	..
	OTHER ACTIVITIES	..	..	..	..	..	..	..	..	..	..
01/99	**GRAND TOTAL**	..	..	..	..	..	..	..	..	..	..

Total manufacturing by investing country						As a % of total manufacturing by foreign affiliates				
All countries	698 000	659 420	715 932	742 663	..	100.0	100.0	100.0	100.0	..
United States	209 000	208 606	224 113	235 421	..	29.9	31.6	31.3	31.7	..
Canada	10 000	9 160	11 128	11 860	..	1.4	1.4	1.6	1.6	..
Mexico	..	..	..	..	..	..	..	..	..	..
Japan	20 000	21 212	22 496	23 873	..	2.9	3.2	3.1	3.2	..
Europe	406 000	411 036	446 218	460 729	..	58.2	62.3	62.3	62.0	..
European Union (15)	..	350 621	382 409	398 326	..	..	53.2	53.4	53.6	..
Belgium	32 000	32 297	32 681	32 142	..	4.6	4.9	4.6	4.3	..
France	..	..	..	..	..	..	..	..	..	..
Germany	119 000	116 284	128 502	135 172	..	17.0	17.6	17.9	18.2	..
Italy	37 000	39 497	43 582	40 555	..	5.3	6.0	6.1	5.5	..
Netherlands	29 000	39 438	46 470	44 711	..	4.2	6.0	6.5	6.0	..
Spain	..	3 021	3 330	2 289	..	..	0.5	0.5	0.3	..
Sweden	23 000	20 817	22 837	27 497	..	3.3	3.2	3.2	3.7	..
United Kingdom	75 000	76 504	77 989	87 371	..	10.7	11.6	10.9	11.8	..
Switzerland	65 000	57 159	61 102	59 805	..	9.3	8.7	8.5	8.1	..
Australia and New Zealand	..	885	1 018	1 021	..	..	0.1	0.1	0.1	..
Asia (non-OECD)	..	2 127	3 301	4 952	..	..	0.3	0.5	0.7	..
Latin America	..	98	..	273	..	..	0.0	..	0.0	..

Note: Majority foreign-owned firms. Food (ISIC 15/16), energy industries (ISIC 23 and parts of 10/14) and *Recycling* (37) are excluded. *Total Manufacturing* includes *Mining & quarrying* (ISIC 10/14).
Firmes sous contrôle étranger majoritaire. L'industrie agro-alimentaire (CITI 15/16), l'énergie (CITI 23 et une partie de 10/14) et la *Récupération* (37) ne sont pas couvertes. Le *Total manufacturier* comprend les *Activités extractives* (CITI 10/14).

Table 3. FRANCE

PRODUCTION

By industry (ISIC Rev. 3)	FOREIGN AFFILIATES (Millions of FF)					AS A % OF NATIONAL TOTAL				
	1993	1994	1995	1996	1997	1993	1994	1995	1996	1997
10/14 Mining & quarrying	..	6 765	7 417	6 952	..	..	38.4	34.6	35.0	..
15/37 TOTAL MANUFACTURING	..	**682 212**	**789 484**	**803 822**	..	..	**31.5**	**28.6**	**28.8**	..
15/16 Food, beverages, tobacco	..	..	..	..	..	..	..	..	..	..
17/19 Textiles, clothing, leather, footwear	..	20 246	23 766	25 259	..	..	14.5	13.6	14.7	..
20/22 Wood and paper products	..	75 873	96 626	91 073	..	..	36.6	34.0	32.8	..
20 Wood products	..	..	..	..	..	..	..	..	..	..
21/22 Paper, printing and publishing	..	..	..	..	..	..	..	..	..	..
23/25 Chemicals, Total	..	229 327	255 862	254 278	..	..	53.1	43.5	42.5	..
23 Refined petroleum, nuclear fuel	..	..	..	..	..	..	..	..	..	..
24/25 Chemicals, rubber & plastics prod.	..	229 327	255 862	254 278	..	..	53.1	43.5	42.5	..
24 Chemical products	..	192 168	212 961	208 219	..	..	57.6	47.2	45.2	..
2423 Pharmaceuticals	..	68 104	72 919	75 386	..	..	76.4	50.6	52.2	..
25 Rubber and plastics products	..	37 159	42 901	46 060	..	..	38.0	31.3	33.4	..
26 Non-metallic mineral products	..	30 087	34 179	34 306	..	..	36.2	32.1	32.8	..
27/28 Basic & fabricated metals	..	42 733	50 368	57 443	..	..	14.6	13.9	15.8	..
27 Basic metals	..	21 543	26 478	27 843	..	..	14.6	16.0	16.9	..
28 Fabricated metal products	..	21 191	23 890	29 600	..	..	14.6	12.2	15.0	..
29/32 Machinery, Total	..	185 717	214 761	226 844	..	..	48.8	40.6	41.4	..
29/30 Non-electrical machinery	..	127 930	144 853	149 652	..	..	56.9	51.1	52.0	..
29 Non-electrical machinery nec	..	81 411	96 098	99 518	..	..	48.5	45.5	45.7	..
30 Office and computing machinery	..	46 519	48 755	50 135	..	..	81.7	67.6	71.5	..
31/32 Electrical & electronic equipment	..	57 787	69 908	77 191	..	..	37.1	28.5	29.6	..
31 Electrical machinery nec	..	31 958	36 682	39 348	..	..	38.1	28.2	30.1	..
32 Radio, TV & communications eq.	..	25 829	33 227	37 843	..	..	35.9	28.7	29.1	..
33 Scientific instruments	..	19 887	22 553	26 719	..	..	25.1	25.8	28.0	..
34/35 Transportation equipment	..	60 372	70 987	66 389	..	..	12.7	13.4	12.4	..
34 Motor vehicles	..	53 280	64 048	60 234	..	..	14.5	15.2	14.2	..
35 Other transport equipment	..	7 092	6 939	6 155	..	..	6.4	6.3	5.5	..
351 Shipbuilding & repairing	..	..	1 119	271	..	..	..	9.5	2.9	..
353 Aircraft and spacecraft	..	..	1 185	1 259	..	..	..	1.5	1.5	..
36/37 Other manufacturing	..	11 206	12 964	14 560	..	..	20.8	17.5	19.4	..
40/45 Construction, electricity, gas & water	..	..	..	..	..	..	..	..	..	..
50/55 Trade, repair, hotels & restaurants	..	..	..	..	..	..	..	..	..	..
65/74 Finance, insurance, business services	..	..	..	..	..	..	..	..	..	..
OTHER ACTIVITIES	..	..	..	..	..	..	..	..	..	..
01/99 GRAND TOTAL	..	..	..	..	..	..	..	..	..	..

Total manufacturing by investing country						As a % of total manufacturing by foreign affiliates				
All countries	..	**682 212**	**789 484**	**803 822**	..	..	**100.0**	**100.0**	**100.0**	..
United States	..	238 817	264 852	271 513	..	..	35.0	33.5	33.8	..
Canada	..	..	..	..	..	..	..	..	..	..
Mexico	..	..	..	..	..	..	..	..	..	..
Japan	..	20 976	24 580	26 553	..	..	3.1	3.1	3.3	..
Europe	..	..	..	..	..	..	..	..	..	..
European Union (15)	..	346 129	406 321	414 478	..	..	50.7	51.5	51.6	..
Belgium	..	..	..	..	..	..	..	..	..	..
France	..	..	..	..	..	..	..	..	..	..
Germany	..	108 704	125 147	135 926	..	..	15.9	15.9	16.9	..
Italy	..	..	..	..	..	..	..	..	..	..
Netherlands	..	42 657	52 737	49 359	..	..	6.3	6.7	6.1	..
Spain	..	..	..	..	..	..	..	..	..	..
Sweden	..	..	..	..	..	..	..	..	..	..
United Kingdom	..	75 389	79 198	90 056	..	..	11.1	10.0	11.2	..
Switzerland	..	56 735	63 039	60 938	..	..	8.3	8.0	7.6	..
Australia and New Zealand	..	..	..	..	..	..	..	..	..	..
Asia (non-OECD)	..	1 666	2 694	3 827	..	..	0.2	0.3	0.5	..
Latin America	..	..	..	..	..	..	..	..	..	..

Note: Majority foreign-owned firms. Food (ISIC 15/16), energy industries (ISIC 23 and parts of 10/14) and *Recycling* (37) are excluded. *Total Manufacturing* includes *Mining & quarrying* (ISIC 10/14).
Firmes sous contrôle étranger majoritaire. L'industrie agro-alimentaire (CITI 15/16), l'énergie (CITI 23 et une partie de 10/14) et la *Récupération* (37) ne sont pas couvertes. Le *Total manufacturier* comprend les *Activités extractives* (CITI 10/14).

Table 4. FRANCE

TURNOVER / CHIFFRE D'AFFAIRES

By industry (ISIC Rev. 3)		FOREIGN AFFILIATES (Millions of FF)					AS A % OF NATIONAL TOTAL				
		1993	1994	1995	1996	1997	1993	1994	1995	1996	1997
10/14	Mining & quarrying	..	7 260	7 820	7 459	..	..	32.8	34.7	35.6	..
15/37	**TOTAL MANUFACTURING**	810 051	826 880	952 329	965 840	..	30.0	28.7	31.0	31.2	..
15/16	Food, beverages, tobacco	..	..	..	..	..	..	..	..	..	..
17/19	Textiles, clothing, leather, footwear	25 001	22 677	25 629	27 354	..	13.7	12.2	13.5	14.9	..
20/22	Wood and paper products	79 097	82 953	102 440	96 113	..	29.8	29.6	34.0	32.8	..
20	Wood products	5 272	..	..	..	..	17.0	..	..	..	..
21/22	Paper, printing and publishing	73 825	..	..	..	..	31.5	..	..	..	..
23/25	Chemicals, Total	..	277 175	313 327	305 866	..	..	44.5	46.1	44.9	..
23	Refined petroleum, nuclear fuel	..	..	..	..	..	..	..	..	..	..
24/25	Chemicals, rubber & plastics prod.	..	277 175	313 327	305 866	..	..	44.5	46.1	44.9	..
24	Chemical products	..	234 627	264 627	254 135	..	..	48.5	49.9	48.0	..
2423	Pharmaceuticals	93 104	77 350	86 265	92 516	..	62.7	51.7	53.3	55.2	..
25	Rubber and plastics products	39 280	42 548	48 700	51 732	..	30.4	30.6	32.7	34.2	..
26	Non-metallic mineral products	..	35 526	39 697	40 206	..	..	30.4	33.5	34.5	..
27/28	Basic & fabricated metals	..	48 122	55 038	62 257	..	..	13.7	14.2	16.2	..
27	Basic metals	..	24 126	28 152	29 400	..	..	15.5	15.7	16.8	..
28	Fabricated metal products	23 795	23 997	26 886	32 857	..	12.8	12.2	12.9	15.7	..
29/32	Machinery, Total	..	227 644	266 337	283 257	..	..	42.2	44.9	45.6	..
29/30	Non-electrical machinery	..	153 267	177 096	182 915	..	..	51.8	54.9	55.4	..
29	Non-electrical machinery nec	..	97 709	117 023	119 991	..	..	43.9	48.9	48.6	..
30	Office and computing machinery	..	55 558	60 073	62 924	..	..	75.8	72.0	75.7	..
31/32	Electrical & electronic equipment	..	74 377	89 242	100 342	..	..	30.5	33.0	34.5	..
31	Electrical machinery nec	..	37 367	42 180	47 029	..	..	28.7	30.4	33.2	..
32	Radio, TV & communications eq.	..	37 010	47 061	53 313	..	..	32.6	35.9	35.7	..
33	Scientific instruments	..	27 237	30 975	32 636	..	..	28.5	31.0	31.4	..
34/35	Transportation equipment	..	85 916	96 855	94 585	..	..	14.6	16.2	15.6	..
34	Motor vehicles	..	78 430	89 689	87 962	..	..	16.7	18.4	17.8	..
35	Other transport equipment	..	7 486	7 166	6 623	..	..	6.3	6.4	5.8	..
351	Shipbuilding & repairing	..	..	1 187	271	..	..	..	9.9	2.9	..
353	Aircraft and spacecraft	..	..	1 166	1 271	..	..	..	1.4	1.5	..
36/37	Other manufacturing	..	12 369	14 211	16 107	..	..	15.5	17.7	19.5	..
40/45	Construction, electricity, gas & water	..	..	..	..	..	..	..	..	..	..
50/55	Trade, repair, hotels & restaurants	..	..	..	..	..	..	..	..	..	..
65/74	Finance, insurance, business services	..	..	..	..	..	..	..	..	..	..
	OTHER ACTIVITIES	..	..	..	..	..	..	..	..	..	..
01/99	**GRAND TOTAL**	..	..	..	..	..	..	..	..	..	..

Total manufacturing by investing country	1993	1994	1995	1996	1997	As a % of total manufacturing by foreign affiliates				
						1993	1994	1995	1996	1997
All countries	810 051	826 880	952 329	965 840	..	100.0	100.0	100.0	100.0	..
United States	279 651	302 234	336 213	343 469	..	34.5	36.6	35.3	35.6	..
Canada	8 864	7 991	12 446	14 411	..	1.1	1.0	1.3	1.5	..
Mexico	..	..	..	..	..	..	..	..	..	..
Japan	25 693	27 873	32 563	36 646	..	3.2	3.4	3.4	3.8	..
Europe	435 909	479 759	555 954	558 714	..	53.8	58.0	58.4	57.8	..
European Union (15)	..	406 863	474 852	479 954	..	..	49.2	49.9	49.7	..
Belgium	32 633	37 332	40 956	37 188	..	4.0	4.5	4.3	3.9	..
France	..	..	..	..	..	..	..	..	..	..
Germany	125 262	127 037	147 490	155 914	..	15.5	15.4	15.5	16.1	..
Italy	37 115	44 562	53 552	44 928	..	4.6	5.4	5.6	4.7	..
Netherlands	47 564	55 485	68 070	61 357	..	5.9	6.7	7.1	6.4	..
Spain	..	2 652	2 728	2 006	..	..	0.3	0.3	0.2	..
Sweden	24 556	26 638	35 193	39 178	..	3.0	3.2	3.7	4.1	..
United Kingdom	77 541	88 023	92 789	104 024	..	9.6	10.6	9.7	10.8	..
Switzerland	63 977	67 151	74 483	72 355	..	7.9	8.1	7.8	7.5	..
Australia and New Zealand	..	562	836	894	..	..	0.1	0.1	0.1	..
Asia (non-OECD)	..	2 105	2 786	4 187	..	..	0.3	0.3	0.4	..
Latin America	..	43	..	472	..	..	0.0	..	0.0	..

Note: Majority foreign-owned firms. Food (ISIC 15/16), energy industries (ISIC 23 and parts of 10/14) and Recycling (37) are excluded. Total Manufacturing includes Mining & quarrying (ISIC 10/14).
Firmes sous contrôle étranger majoritaire. L'industrie agro-alimentaire (CITI 15/16), l'énergie (CITI 23 et une partie de 10/14) et la Récupération (37) ne sont pas couvertes. Le Total manufacturier comprend les Activités extractives (CITI 10/14).

Table 5. FRANCE

VALUE ADDED / VALEUR AJOUTÉE

By industry (ISIC Rev. 3)	FOREIGN AFFILIATES (Millions of FF)					AS A % OF NATIONAL TOTAL				
	1993	1994	1995	1996	1997	1993	1994	1995	1996	1997
10/14 Mining & quarrying	..	2 591	2 821	2 609	..	..	29.1	30.9	31.1	..
15/37 TOTAL MANUFACTURING	**248 943**	**251 265**	**288 216**	**286 970**	..	**28.7**	**27.2**	**30.0**	**30.4**	..
15/16 Food, beverages, tobacco	..	..	..	..	..	..	..	..	..	..
17/19 Textiles, clothing, leather, footwear	8 509	7 494	8 272	8 444	..	13.6	11.9	13.6	14.7	..
20/22 Wood and paper products	24 892	24 843	30 905	28 736	..	26.9	25.9	30.7	29.3	..
20 Wood products	1 527	..	..	..	..	15.1	..	..	..	..
21/22 Paper, printing and publishing	23 365	..	..	..	..	28.4	..	..	..	..
23/25 Chemicals, Total	..	81 597	93 968	93 559	..	..	42.1	44.8	45.1	..
23 Refined petroleum, nuclear fuel	..	..	..	..	..	..	..	..	..	..
24/25 Chemicals, rubber & plastics prod.	..	81 597	93 968	93 559	..	..	42.1	44.8	45.1	..
24 Chemical products	..	65 744	76 741	74 888	..	..	46.8	49.4	49.2	..
2423 Pharmaceuticals	31 282	26 656	30 346	32 208	..	64.6	55.2	57.1	58.6	..
25 Rubber and plastics products	14 753	15 853	17 227	18 671	..	29.3	29.8	31.7	33.7	..
26 Non-metallic mineral products	..	13 262	15 278	14 578	..	..	28.5	32.1	31.9	..
27/28 Basic & fabricated metals	..	14 592	15 948	18 032	..	..	12.1	12.2	14.5	..
27 Basic metals	..	5 882	6 717	6 693	..	..	13.9	13.8	15.3	..
28 Fabricated metal products	8 772	8 709	9 231	11 340	..	11.7	11.0	11.3	14.0	..
29/32 Machinery, Total	..	70 261	80 624	80 237	..	..	37.7	41.0	40.5	..
29/30 Non-electrical machinery	..	48 114	54 108	53 370	..	..	47.6	51.7	51.2	..
29 Non-electrical machinery nec	..	31 864	35 630	36 622	..	..	41.0	44.6	45.3	..
30 Office and computing machinery	..	16 250	18 478	16 749	..	..	69.6	74.5	71.4	..
31/32 Electrical & electronic equipment	..	22 147	26 516	26 867	..	..	25.9	28.9	28.7	..
31 Electrical machinery nec	..	13 137	14 680	15 619	..	..	27.0	29.5	31.8	..
32 Radio, TV & communications eq.	..	9 010	11 836	11 247	..	..	24.5	28.2	25.2	..
33 Scientific instruments	..	9 541	10 687	10 893	..	..	24.7	28.3	28.7	..
34/35 Transportation equipment	..	22 557	24 912	24 606	..	..	16.0	17.9	17.9	..
34 Motor vehicles	..	20 494	22 478	22 357	..	..	20.8	22.8	23.2	..
35 Other transport equipment	..	2 062	2 434	2 249	..	..	4.8	6.0	5.5	..
351 Shipbuilding & repairing	..	..	336	78	..	..	..	9.4	2.5	..
353 Aircraft and spacecraft	..	..	523	562	..	..	..	1.8	1.8	..
36/37 Other manufacturing	..	4 529	4 801	5 276	..	..	15.5	16.8	18.5	..
40/45 Construction, electricity, gas & water	..	..	..	..	..	..	..	..	..	..
50/55 Trade, repair, hotels & restaurants	..	..	..	..	..	..	..	..	..	..
65/74 Finance, insurance, business services	..	..	..	..	..	..	..	..	..	..
OTHER ACTIVITIES	..	..	..	..	..	..	..	..	..	..
01/99 GRAND TOTAL	..	..	..	..	..	..	..	..	..	..

Total manufacturing by investing country						As a % of total manufacturing by foreign affiliates				
All countries	**248 943**	**251 265**	**288 216**	**286 970**	..	**100.0**	**100.0**	**100.0**	**100.0**	..
United States	83 630	90 185	101 960	101 086	..	33.6	35.9	35.4	35.2	..
Canada	2 723	..	..	..	..	1.1	..	..	..	..
Mexico	..	..	..	..	..	..	..	..	..	..
Japan	6 576	7 134	8 427	9 287	..	2.6	2.8	2.9	3.2	..
Europe	137 164	..	..	..	..	55.1	..	..	..	..
European Union (15)	..	125 806	144 205	145 519	..	..	50.1	50.0	50.7	..
Belgium	10 742	..	..	..	..	4.3	..	..	..	..
France	..	..	..	..	..	..	..	..	..	..
Germany	41 298	41 398	46 966	49 303	..	16.6	16.5	16.3	17.2	..
Italy	10 143	..	..	..	..	4.1	..	..	..	..
Netherlands	11 139	14 674	16 964	15 513	..	4.5	5.8	5.9	5.4	..
Spain	..	..	..	..	..	..	..	..	..	..
Sweden	8 535	..	..	..	..	3.4	..	..	..	..
United Kingdom	25 685	27 971	29 170	31 821	..	10.3	11.1	10.1	11.1	..
Switzerland	21 700	22 121	23 462	22 949	..	8.7	8.8	8.1	8.0	..
Australia and New Zealand	..	..	..	..	..	..	..	..	..	..
Asia (non-OECD)	..	464	857	936	..	..	0.2	0.3	0.3	..
Latin America	..	..	..	..	..	..	..	..	..	..

Note: Majority foreign-owned firms. Food (ISIC 15/16), energy industries (ISIC 23 and parts of 10/14) and *Recycling* (37) are excluded. *Total Manufacturing* includes *Mining & quarrying* (ISIC 10/14).
Firmes sous contrôle étranger majoritaire. L'industrie agro-alimentaire (CITI 15/16), l'énergie (CITI 23 et une partie de 10/14) et la *Récupération* (37) ne sont pas couvertes. Le *Total manufacturier* comprend les *Activités extractives* (CITI 10/14).

Table 6. FRANCE

WAGES AND SALARIES / SALAIRES ET TRAITEMENTS

By industry (ISIC Rev. 3)	FOREIGN AFFILIATES (Millions of FF)					AS A % OF NATIONAL TOTAL				
	1993	1994	1995	1996	1997	1993	1994	1995	1996	1997
10/14 Mining & quarrying	..	1 395	1 531	1 512	..	..	25.0	27.0	27.3	..
15/37 TOTAL MANUFACTURING	**112 136**	**161 180**	**176 095**	**181 996**	..	**26.3**	**25.2**	**27.1**	**27.7**	..
15/16 Food, beverages, tobacco	..	..	..	..	..	..	..	..	..	..
17/19 Textiles, clothing, leather, footwear	4 393	5 667	6 321	6 419	..	13.5	12.3	13.9	15.0	..
20/22 Wood and paper products	10 212	14 815	16 928	17 153	..	23.1	22.2	25.1	25.5	..
20 Wood products	761	..	..	..	..	15.7	..	..	..	..
21/22 Paper, printing and publishing	9 451	..	..	..	..	24.0	..	..	..	..
23/25 Chemicals, Total	..	47 098	50 583	50 992	..	..	40.5	42.3	42.2	..
23 Refined petroleum, nuclear fuel	..	..	..	..	..	..	..	..	..	..
24/25 Chemicals, rubber & plastics prod.	..	47 098	50 583	50 992	..	..	40.5	42.3	42.2	..
24 Chemical products	..	36 910	39 167	38 654	..	..	46.1	47.6	46.7	..
2423 Pharmaceuticals	11 215	14 730	15 802	16 355	..	63.6	55.3	57.5	59.9	..
25 Rubber and plastics products	6 637	10 188	11 417	12 338	..	27.4	28.2	30.5	32.5	..
26 Non-metallic mineral products	..	7 857	8 791	9 155	..	..	27.5	30.4	31.5	..
27/28 Basic & fabricated metals	..	10 094	10 903	12 743	..	..	11.2	11.7	13.6	..
27 Basic metals	..	4 046	4 372	4 751	..	..	13.0	13.7	15.0	..
28 Fabricated metal products	4 384	6 048	6 531	7 993	..	11.1	10.3	10.7	12.8	..
29/32 Machinery, Total	..	48 886	53 066	55 814	..	..	36.2	37.9	38.4	..
29/30 Non-electrical machinery	..	33 863	35 320	36 337	..	..	46.0	47.9	48.6	..
29 Non-electrical machinery nec	..	22 859	25 389	26 558	..	..	40.5	43.8	44.4	..
30 Office and computing machinery	..	11 005	9 931	9 778	..	..	64.0	63.4	65.3	..
31/32 Electrical & electronic equipment	..	15 022	17 746	19 478	..	..	24.4	26.8	27.7	..
31 Electrical machinery nec	..	8 906	9 866	10 964	..	..	26.1	28.2	30.7	..
32 Radio, TV & communications eq.	..	6 117	7 880	8 513	..	..	22.4	25.3	24.6	..
33 Scientific instruments	..	7 428	8 300	8 487	..	..	23.6	27.4	28.3	..
34/35 Transportation equipment	..	14 615	16 031	15 675	..	..	14.7	16.1	15.6	..
34 Motor vehicles	..	12 833	14 096	13 904	..	..	19.9	21.6	21.1	..
35 Other transport equipment	..	1 782	1 935	1 771	..	..	5.1	5.6	5.1	..
351 Shipbuilding & repairing	..	..	244	81	..	..	..	8.4	2.8	..
353 Aircraft and spacecraft	..	315	402	425	..	..	1.2	1.5	1.6	..
36/37 Other manufacturing	..	3 325	3 642	4 045	..	..	16.0	17.6	19.4	..
40/45 Construction, electricity, gas & water	..	..	..	..	..	..	..	..	..	..
50/55 Trade, repair, hotels & restaurants	..	..	..	..	..	..	..	..	..	..
65/74 Finance, insurance, business services	..	..	..	..	..	..	..	..	..	..
OTHER ACTIVITIES	..	..	..	..	..	..	..	..	..	..
01/99 GRAND TOTAL	..	..	..	..	..	..	..	..	..	..

Total manufacturing by investing country						As a % of total manufacturing by foreign affiliates				
All countries	**112 136**	**161 180**	**176 095**	**181 996**	..	**100.0**	**100.0**	**100.0**	**100.0**	..
United States	..	56 789	59 804	62 304	..	..	35.2	34.0	34.2	..
Canada	..	..	..	..	..	..	..	..	..	..
Mexico	..	..	..	..	..	..	..	..	..	..
Japan	..	4 623	4 960	5 295	..	..	2.9	2.8	2.9	..
Europe	..	..	..	..	..	..	..	..	..	..
European Union (15)	..	81 077	89 762	93 586	..	..	50.3	51.0	51.4	..
Belgium	..	..	..	..	..	..	..	..	..	..
France	..	..	..	..	..	..	..	..	..	..
Germany	..	27 328	30 659	32 503	..	..	17.0	17.4	17.9	..
Italy	..	..	..	..	..	..	..	..	..	..
Netherlands	..	9 677	11 576	10 525	..	..	6.0	6.6	5.8	..
Spain	..	..	..	..	..	..	..	..	..	..
Sweden	..	..	..	..	..	..	..	..	..	..
United Kingdom	..	17 630	18 217	20 798	..	..	10.9	10.3	11.4	..
Switzerland	..	14 059	15 218	14 925	..	..	8.7	8.6	8.2	..
Australia and New Zealand	..	..	..	..	..	..	..	..	..	..
Asia (non-OECD)	..	377	647	879	..	..	0.2	0.4	0.5	..
Latin America	..	..	..	..	..	..	..	..	..	..

Note: Majority foreign-owned firms. Food (ISIC 15/16), energy industries (ISIC 23 and parts of 10/14) and *Recycling* (37) are excluded. *Total Manufacturing* includes *Mining & quarrying* (ISIC 10/14).
Firmes sous contrôle étranger majoritaire. L'industrie agro-alimentaire (CITI 15/16), l'énergie (CITI 23 et une partie de 10/14) et la *Récupération* (37) ne sont pas couvertes. Le *Total manufacturier* comprend les *Activités extractives* (CITI 10/14).

Table 7. FRANCE

R&D EXPENDITURE / DÉPENSES DE R-D

By industry (ISIC Rev. 3)		FOREIGN AFFILIATES (Millions of FF)					AS A % OF NATIONAL TOTAL				
		1993	1994	1995	1996	1997	1993	1994	1995	1996	1997
10/14	Mining & quarrying	..	8	3	10	..	..	4.7	1.7	7.2	..
15/37	**TOTAL MANUFACTURING**	..	**13 121**	**16 027**	**15 900**	..	..	**15.7**	**19.4**	**18.6**	..
15/16	Food, beverages, tobacco	..	284	265	320	..	..	22.9	20.9	24.1	..
17/19	Textiles, clothing, leather, footwear	..	152	161	241	..	..	24.6	25.2	37.7	..
20/22	Wood and paper products	..	218	199	199	..	..	69.9	64.4	71.6	..
20	Wood products	..	..	..	..	..	..	..	..	..	..
21/22	Paper, printing and publishing	..	..	..	..	..	..	..	..	..	..
23/25	Chemicals, Total	..	5 875	6 576	6 343	..	..	38.7	42.3	34.4	..
23	Refined petroleum, nuclear fuel	..	83	82	83	..	..	14.1	13.7	13.9	..
24/25	Chemicals, rubber & plastics prod.	..	5 792	6 494	6 260	..	..	39.7	43.5	35.1	..
24	Chemical products	..	5 536	6 171	5 940	..	..	44.0	48.4	39.4	..
2423	Pharmaceuticals	..	3 800	4 289	4 220	..	..	55.7	63.5	47.8	..
25	Rubber and plastics products	..	257	323	320	..	..	12.8	14.8	11.6	..
26	Non-metallic mineral products	..	78	142	191	..	..	10.8	18.0	22.7	..
27/28	Basic & fabricated metals	..	220	224	254	..	..	9.5	9.2	10.8	..
27	Basic metals	..	78	70	74	..	..	6.9	6.1	6.4	..
28	Fabricated metal products	..	142	154	180	..	..	12.1	11.9	15.2	..
29/32	Machinery, Total	..	4 142	5 954	..	..	..	17.7	26.2	..	..
29/30	Non-electrical machinery	..	2 162	2 259	..	..	..	26.1	29.2	..	..
29	Non-electrical machinery nec	..	1 082	1 178	1 256	..	..	20.8	24.4	26.4	..
30	Office and computing machinery	..	1 080	1 081	..	..	..	35.0	37.3	..	..
31/32	Electrical & electronic equipment	..	1 980	3 695	3 352	..	..	13.1	24.6	22.0	..
31	Electrical machinery nec	..	681	827	1 184	..	..	18.0	20.0	30.7	..
32	Radio, TV & communications eq.	..	1 299	2 868	2 168	..	..	11.4	26.4	19.0	..
33	Scientific instruments	..	1 225	1 263	1 253	..	..	10.6	11.5	11.9	..
34/35	Transportation equipment	..	862	1 166	1 206	..	..	3.1	4.2	4.3	..
34	Motor vehicles	..	748	1 014	1 068	..	..	5.7	7.6	8.5	..
35	Other transport equipment	..	114	152	138	..	..	0.8	1.0	0.9	..
351	Shipbuilding & repairing	..	..	..	..	..	..	..	..	..	..
353	Aircraft and spacecraft	..	..	83	88	..	..	..	0.6	0.6	..
36/37	Other manufacturing	..	65	77	61	..	..	19.6	22.3	18.3	..
40/45	Construction, electricity, gas & water	..	24	20	19	..	..	0.9	0.7	0.5	..
50/55	Trade, repair, hotels & restaurants	..	311	337	429	..	..	35.3	41.9	50.6	..
65/74	Finance, insurance, business services	..	1 881	2 225	2 353	..	..	10.6	11.7	13.1	..
	OTHER ACTIVITIES	..	55	42	54	..	..	1.5	1.1	1.4	..
01/99	**GRAND TOTAL**	..	**15 400**	**18 663**	**18 765**	..	..	**14.2**	**17.1**	**16.7**	..

Total manufacturing by investing country						As a % of total manufacturing by foreign affiliates				
All countries	..	13 121	16 027	15 900	..	..	100.0	100.0	100.0	..
United States	..	..	..	..	..	..	..	..	..	..
Canada	..	..	..	..	..	..	..	..	..	..
Mexico	..	..	..	..	..	..	..	..	..	..
Japan	..	..	..	..	..	..	..	..	..	..
Europe	..	..	..	..	..	..	..	..	..	..
European Union (15)	..	..	..	..	..	..	..	..	..	..
Belgium	..	..	..	..	..	..	..	..	..	..
France	..	..	..	..	..	..	..	..	..	..
Germany	..	..	..	..	..	..	..	..	..	..
Italy	..	..	..	..	..	..	..	..	..	..
Netherlands	..	..	..	1 428	..	..	..	..	9.0	..
Spain	..	..	..	..	..	..	..	..	..	..
Sweden	..	..	..	..	..	..	..	..	..	..
United Kingdom	..	..	..	..	..	..	..	..	..	..
Switzerland	..	..	..	..	..	..	..	..	..	..
Australia and New Zealand	..	..	..	..	..	..	..	..	..	..
Asia (non-OECD)	..	..	..	..	..	..	..	..	..	..
Latin America	..	..	..	..	..	..	..	..	..	..

Note: Majority foreign-owned firms.
Firmes sous contrôle étranger majoritaire.

Table 9. FRANCE

GROSS FIXED CAPITAL FORMATION / FORMATION BRUTE DE CAPITAL FIXE

By industry (ISIC Rev. 3)		FOREIGN AFFILIATES (Millions of FF)					AS A % OF NATIONAL TOTAL				
		1993	1994	1995	1996	1997	1993	1994	1995	1996	1997
10/14	Mining & quarrying	..	718	884	683	..	..	40.3	43.1	36.2	..
15/37	**TOTAL MANUFACTURING**	**30 943**	**28 465**	**36 676**	**37 882**	**..**	**30.5**	**28.3**	**32.1**	**30.8**	**..**
15/16	Food, beverages, tobacco	..	..	..	..	..	..	..	..	..	..
17/19	Textiles, clothing, leather, footwear	889	623	846	949	..	18.2	13.4	15.8	18.9	..
20/22	Wood and paper products	2 654	2 923	3 691	3 936	..	31.1	32.2	36.8	34.9	..
20	Wood products	165	..	..	..	..	16.5	..	..	..	..
21/22	Paper, printing and publishing	2 489	..	..	..	..	33.1	..	..	..	..
23/25	Chemicals, Total	..	9 739	10 994	12 077	..	..	44.6	44.0	42.7	..
23	Refined petroleum, nuclear fuel	..	..	..	..	..	..	..	..	..	..
24/25	Chemicals, rubber & plastics prod.	..	9 739	10 994	12 077	..	..	44.6	44.0	42.7	..
24	Chemical products	..	7 828	8 320	9 083	..	..	48.2	46.5	44.3	..
2423	Pharmaceuticals	3 639	2 813	2 650	3 169	..	61.6	57.3	55.0	56.4	..
25	Rubber and plastics products	2 053	1 911	2 673	2 994	..	35.0	33.9	37.7	38.6	..
26	Non-metallic mineral products	..	1 300	2 061	2 232	..	..	26.1	33.6	34.7	..
27/28	Basic & fabricated metals	..	1 587	1 849	2 144	..	..	14.7	14.9	15.4	..
27	Basic metals	..	607	793	845	..	..	13.5	15.2	13.2	..
28	Fabricated metal products	1 050	980	1 056	1 299	..	15.3	15.5	14.7	17.2	..
29/32	Machinery, Total	..	7 494	11 215	10 450	..	..	41.1	52.7	46.0	..
29/30	Non-electrical machinery	..	4 687	5 717	5 845	..	..	60.0	62.3	59.9	..
29	Non-electrical machinery nec	..	2 271	3 476	3 378	..	..	44.9	52.8	48.3	..
30	Office and computing machinery	..	2 416	2 240	2 467	..	..	87.7	86.2	89.4	..
31/32	Electrical & electronic equipment	..	2 807	5 498	4 605	..	..	26.9	45.4	35.5	..
31	Electrical machinery nec	..	1 374	1 524	1 929	..	..	30.6	31.0	35.0	..
32	Radio, TV & communications eq.	..	1 433	3 974	2 676	..	..	24.1	55.3	35.8	..
33	Scientific instruments	..	874	973	1 050	..	..	32.1	38.0	39.7	..
34/35	Transportation equipment	..	2 875	3 785	3 928	..	..	11.9	14.0	14.0	..
34	Motor vehicles	..	2 719	3 576	3 611	..	..	12.8	15.0	14.7	..
35	Other transport equipment	..	155	209	316	..	..	5.4	6.5	8.8	..
351	Shipbuilding & repairing	..	..	23	10	..	..	..	7.9	2.2	..
353	Aircraft and spacecraft	..	..	31	50	..	..	..	1.3	2.0	..
36/37	Other manufacturing	..	332	379	434	..	..	14.9	15.3	16.6	..
40/45	Construction, electricity, gas & water	..	..	..	..	..	..	..	..	..	..
50/55	Trade, repair, hotels & restaurants	..	..	..	..	..	..	..	..	..	..
65/74	Finance, insurance, business services	..	..	..	..	..	..	..	..	..	..
	OTHER ACTIVITIES	..	..	..	..	..	..	..	..	..	..
01/99	**GRAND TOTAL**	**..**	**..**	**..**	**..**	**..**	**..**	**..**	**..**	**..**	**..**

Total manufacturing by investing country						As a % of total manufacturing by foreign affiliates				
All countries	30 943	28 465	36 676	37 882	..	100.0	100.0	100.0	100.0	..
United States	10 997	10 412	11 637	13 436	..	35.5	36.6	31.7	35.5	..
Canada	251	..	..	..	..	0.8	..	..	..	..
Mexico	..	..	..	..	..	..	..	..	..	..
Japan	966	993	1 308	1 298	..	3.1	3.5	3.6	3.4	..
Europe	16 641	..	..	..	..	53.8	..	..	..	..
European Union (15)	..	13 561	18 307	18 772	..	..	47.6	49.9	49.6	..
Belgium	944	..	..	..	..	3.1	..	..	..	..
France	..	..	..	..	..	..	..	..	..	..
Germany	4 817	4 502	5 492	6 469	..	15.6	15.8	15.0	17.1	..
Italy	1 197	..	..	..	..	3.9	..	..	..	..
Netherlands	1 736	1 980	2 564	2 202	..	5.6	7.0	7.0	5.8	..
Spain	..	..	..	..	..	..	..	..	..	..
Sweden	1 008	..	..	..	..	3.3	..	..	..	..
United Kingdom	2 988	2 964	3 332	3 620	..	9.7	10.4	9.1	9.6	..
Switzerland	2 714	2 451	2 789	2 884	..	8.8	8.6	7.6	7.6	..
Australia and New Zealand	..	..	..	..	..	..	..	..	..	..
Asia (non-OECD)	..	91	200	218	..	..	0.3	0.5	0.6	..
Latin America	..	..	..	..	..	..	..	..	..	..

Note: Majority foreign-owned firms. Food (ISIC 15/16), energy industries (ISIC 23 and parts of 10/14) and *Recycling* (37) are excluded. *Total Manufacturing* includes *Mining & quarrying* (ISIC 10/14).
Firmes sous contrôle étranger majoritaire. L'industrie agro-alimentaire (CITI 15/16), l'énergie (CITI 23 et une partie de 10/14) et la *Récupération* (37) ne sont pas couvertes. Le *Total manufacturier*
comprend les *Activités extractives* (CITI 10/14).

Table 10. FRANCE

TOTAL EXPORTS / EXPORTATIONS TOTALES

By industry (ISIC Rev. 3)	FOREIGN AFFILIATES (Millions of FF)					AS A % OF NATIONAL TOTAL				
	1993	1994	1995	1996	1997	1993	1994	1995	1996	1997
10/14 Mining & quarrying	..	1 208	1 402	1 207	..	..	47.5	50.5	46.9	..
15/37 TOTAL MANUFACTURING	**271 171**	**280 017**	**346 789**	**362 801**	**..**	**33.6**	**31.0**	**35.3**	**35.2**	**..**
15/16 Food, beverages, tobacco	..	..	..	..	..	..	..	..	..	..
17/19 Textiles, clothing, leather, footwear	8 633	8 137	9 109	10 056	..	18.5	16.0	16.9	18.7	..
20/22 Wood and paper products	18 674	21 720	29 441	27 070	..	49.4	51.6	60.4	58.9	..
20 Wood products	1 684	..	..	..	..	39.5	..	..	..	..
21/22 Paper, printing and publishing	16 990	..	..	..	..	50.7	..	..	..	..
23/25 Chemicals, Total	..	84 384	100 402	104 401	..	..	43.9	47.4	47.3	..
23 Refined petroleum, nuclear fuel	..	..	..	..	..	..	..	..	..	..
24/25 Chemicals, rubber & plastics prod.	..	84 384	100 402	104 401	..	..	43.9	47.4	47.3	..
24 Chemical products	..	72 488	86 851	88 438	..	..	46.4	50.2	49.4	..
2423 Pharmaceuticals	18 871	15 962	18 390	20 925	..	66.5	55.7	57.3	58.6	..
25 Rubber and plastics products	10 459	11 896	13 551	15 963	..	31.3	33.1	34.9	38.2	..
26 Non-metallic mineral products	..	6 998	8 994	8 969	..	..	29.8	35.6	34.7	..
27/28 Basic & fabricated metals	..	16 777	18 866	20 317	..	..	15.6	16.2	17.8	..
27 Basic metals	..	9 490	11 780	12 215	..	..	14.0	14.6	15.7	..
28 Fabricated metal products	6 423	7 287	7 087	8 102	..	22.1	18.3	19.8	22.1	..
29/32 Machinery, Total	..	96 213	123 666	135 094	..	..	47.6	53.7	53.7	..
29/30 Non-electrical machinery	..	67 843	84 386	88 821	..	..	57.2	63.1	63.8	..
29 Non-electrical machinery nec	..	44 220	54 877	56 633	..	..	49.0	55.7	55.6	..
30 Office and computing machinery	..	23 623	29 509	32 188	..	..	83.2	84.0	85.8	..
31/32 Electrical & electronic equipment	..	28 370	39 280	46 273	..	..	34.0	40.7	41.3	..
31 Electrical machinery nec	..	12 465	15 525	18 111	..	..	30.3	33.2	35.9	..
32 Radio, TV & communications eq.	..	15 905	23 755	28 162	..	..	37.7	47.7	45.6	..
33 Scientific instruments	..	11 764	13 561	14 509	..	..	36.7	40.2	36.7	..
34/35 Transportation equipment	..	29 760	37 834	37 205	..	..	12.8	15.6	14.5	..
34 Motor vehicles	..	27 288	35 051	34 483	..	..	15.4	18.5	17.2	..
35 Other transport equipment	..	2 471	2 783	2 721	..	..	4.4	5.3	4.9	..
351 Shipbuilding & repairing	..	..	554	125	..	..	..	8.0	2.7	..
353 Aircraft and spacecraft	..	..	546	622	..	..	..	1.4	1.4	..
36/37 Other manufacturing	..	3 057	3 513	3 971	..	..	17.3	18.7	20.1	..
40/45 Construction, electricity, gas & water	..	..	..	..	..	..	..	..	..	..
50/55 Trade, repair, hotels & restaurants	..	..	..	..	..	..	..	..	..	..
65/74 Finance, insurance, business services	..	..	..	..	..	..	..	..	..	..
OTHER ACTIVITIES	..	..	..	..	..	..	..	..	..	..
01/99 GRAND TOTAL	..	..	..	..	..	..	..	..	..	..

Total manufacturing by investing country						As a % of total manufacturing by foreign affiliates				
All countries	**271 171**	**280 017**	**346 789**	**362 801**	**..**	**100.0**	**100.0**	**100.0**	**100.0**	**..**
United States	107 301	117 910	141 292	148 172	..	39.6	42.1	40.7	40.8	..
Canada	2 707	1 948	3 861	5 467	..	1.0	0.7	1.1	1.5	..
Mexico	..	..	..	..	..	..	..	..	..	..
Japan	10 987	11 677	13 632	17 685	..	4.1	4.2	3.9	4.9	..
Europe	131 500	145 688	179 925	184 727	..	48.5	52.0	51.9	50.9	..
European Union (15)	..	120 585	151 733	157 746	..	..	43.1	43.8	43.5	..
Belgium	9 333	11 530	13 206	13 017	..	3.4	4.1	3.8	3.6	..
France	..	..	..	..	..	..	..	..	..	..
Germany	38 133	38 492	47 738	54 523	..	14.1	13.7	13.8	15.0	..
Italy	11 355	9 909	14 530	11 009	..	4.2	3.5	4.2	3.0	..
Netherlands	15 049	17 641	20 048	20 693	..	5.5	6.3	5.8	5.7	..
Spain	..	744	789	708	..	..	0.3	0.2	0.2	..
Sweden	7 905	8 374	13 735	14 557	..	2.9	3.0	4.0	4.0	..
United Kingdom	20 433	25 822	29 621	30 695	..	7.5	9.2	8.5	8.5	..
Switzerland	20 477	23 342	26 746	25 606	..	7.6	8.3	7.7	7.1	..
Australia and New Zealand	..	78	185	210	..	..	0.0	0.1	0.1	..
Asia (non-OECD)	..	972	1 431	2 602	..	..	0.3	0.4	0.7	..
Latin America	..	4	..	238	..	..	0.0	..	0.1	..

Note: Majority foreign-owned firms. Food (ISIC 15/16), energy industries (ISIC 23 and parts of 10/14) and *Recycling* (37) are excluded. *Total Manufacturing* includes *Mining & quarrying* (ISIC 10/14).
Firmes sous contrôle étranger majoritaire. L'industrie agro-alimentaire (CITI 15/16), l'énergie (CITI 23 et une partie de 10/14) et la *Récupération* (37) ne sont pas couvertes. Le *Total manufacturier* comprend les *Activités extractives* (CITI 10/14).

Table 14. FRANCE

GROSS OPERATING SURPLUS / EXCÉDENT BRUT D'EXPLOITATION

By industry (ISIC Rev. 3)		FOREIGN AFFILIATES (Millions of FF)					AS A % OF NATIONAL TOTAL				
		1993	1994	1995	1996	1997	1993	1994	1995	1996	1997
10/14	Mining & quarrying	..	1 027	1 098	902	..	..	37.4	38.3	39.6	..
15/37	**TOTAL MANUFACTURING**	**81 924**	**75 575**	**94 624**	**86 533**	**..**	**35.3**	**32.3**	**37.4**	**37.7**	**..**
15/16	Food, beverages, tobacco	..	..	..	..	..	..	..	..	..	..
17/19	Textiles, clothing, leather, footwear	2 560	1 407	1 471	1 506	..	15.9	10.3	12.2	13.0	..
20/22	Wood and paper products	10 027	8 659	12 139	9 765	..	36.3	34.9	42.9	37.6	..
20	Wood products	392	..	..	..	..	14.5	..	..	..	..
21/22	Paper, printing and publishing	9 635	..	..	..	..	38.7	..	..	..	..
23/25	Chemicals, Total	..	29 487	37 226	36 101	..	..	44.6	48.5	49.4	..
23	Refined petroleum, nuclear fuel	..	..	..	..	..	..	..	..	..	..
24/25	Chemicals, rubber & plastics prod.	..	29 487	37 226	36 101	..	..	44.6	48.5	49.4	..
24	Chemical products	..	24 749	32 490	31 015	..	..	47.6	51.5	52.5	..
2423	Pharmaceuticals	12 485	10 136	12 176	13 216	..	64.9	54.5	55.8	56.2	..
25	Rubber and plastics products	4 384	4 738	4 736	5 087	..	34.2	33.5	34.7	36.3	..
26	Non-metallic mineral products	..	4 616	5 520	4 418	..	..	30.4	34.9	32.3	..
27/28	Basic & fabricated metals	..	3 611	4 011	4 106	..	..	15.0	13.6	17.9	..
27	Basic metals	..	1 445	1 882	1 425	..	..	17.1	14.3	16.1	..
28	Fabricated metal products	2 178	2 166	2 129	2 681	..	14.0	13.8	13.1	19.1	..
29/32	Machinery, Total	..	17 590	23 143	19 766	..	..	41.7	50.2	47.7	..
29/30	Non-electrical machinery	..	11 686	15 906	13 969	..	..	51.7	62.5	59.2	..
29	Non-electrical machinery nec	..	7 219	8 176	7 858	..	..	42.4	47.2	48.6	..
30	Office and computing machinery	..	4 467	7 730	6 111	..	..	80.6	95.1	82.2	..
31/32	Electrical & electronic equipment	..	5 904	7 237	5 797	..	..	30.1	35.1	32.5	..
31	Electrical machinery nec	..	3 491	3 948	3 672	..	..	29.3	33.3	35.1	..
32	Radio, TV & communications eq.	..	2 414	3 289	2 125	..	..	31.4	37.5	28.8	..
33	Scientific instruments	..	1 567	1 740	1 700	..	..	32.2	32.7	30.2	..
34/35	Transportation equipment	..	6 655	7 413	7 364	..	..	20.0	24.6	27.4	..
34	Motor vehicles	..	6 520	7 072	7 039	..	..	23.1	26.5	30.0	..
35	Other transport equipment	..	134	341	325	..	..	2.7	9.8	9.5	..
351	Shipbuilding & repairing	..	..	78	- 10	..	..	..	15.2	-34.5	..
353	Aircraft and spacecraft	..	..	79	94	..	..	..	5.4	4.4	..
36/37	Other manufacturing	..	956	864	905	..	..	14.0	13.6	15.1	..
40/45	Construction, electricity, gas & water	..	..	..	..	..	..	..	..	..	..
50/55	Trade, repair, hotels & restaurants	..	..	..	..	..	..	..	..	..	..
65/74	Finance, insurance, business services	..	..	..	..	..	..	..	..	..	..
	OTHER ACTIVITIES	..	..	..	..	..	..	..	..	..	..
01/99	**GRAND TOTAL**	**..**	**..**	**..**	**..**	**..**	**..**	**..**	**..**	**..**	**..**

Total manufacturing by investing country						As a % of total manufacturing by foreign affiliates				
All countries	81 924	75 575	94 624	86 533	..	100.0	100.0	100.0	100.0	..
United States	..	28 443	36 352	32 569	..	..	37.6	38.4	37.6	..
Canada	..	..	..	..	..	..	..	..	..	..
Mexico	..	..	..	..	..	..	..	..	..	..
Japan	..	2 060	2 990	3 392	..	..	2.7	3.2	3.9	..
Europe	..	..	..	..	..	..	..	..	..	..
European Union (15)	..	37 298	45 394	42 330	..	..	49.4	48.0	48.9	..
Belgium	..	..	..	..	..	..	..	..	..	..
France	..	..	..	..	..	..	..	..	..	..
Germany	..	11 639	13 307	13 476	..	..	15.4	14.1	15.6	..
Italy	..	..	..	..	..	..	..	..	..	..
Netherlands	..	4 195	4 325	4 015	..	..	5.6	4.6	4.6	..
Spain	..	..	..	..	..	..	..	..	..	..
Sweden	..	..	..	..	..	..	..	..	..	..
United Kingdom	..	8 703	9 142	8 806	..	..	11.5	9.7	10.2	..
Switzerland	..	6 741	6 706	6 539	..	..	8.9	7.1	7.6	..
Australia and New Zealand	..	..	..	..	..	..	..	..	..	..
Asia (non-OECD)	..	68	171	15	..	..	0.1	0.2	0.0	..
Latin America	..	..	..	..	..	..	..	..	..	..

Note: Majority foreign-owned firms. Food (ISIC 15/16), energy industries (ISIC 23 and parts of 10/14) and *Recycling* (37) are excluded. *Total Manufacturing* includes *Mining & quarrying* (ISIC 10/14).
Firmes sous contrôle étranger majoritaire. L'industrie agro-alimentaire (CITI 15/16), l'énergie (CITI 23 et une partie de 10/14) et la *Récupération* (37) ne sont pas couvertes. Le *Total manufacturier* comprend les *Activités extractives* (CITI 10/14).

FRANCE

Source

The data are prepared by the *Service des Statistiques Industrielles* (SESSI), Ministry of Industry, for all variables except *R&D expenditure*. They are derived from the register containing declarations of foreign participation at the *Direction du Trésor*. This file is complemented with results from the INSEE (French statistical office) survey on financial ties. Only the manufacturing sector and mining and quarrying are covered, except food and energy industries. The data refer to majority foreign-owned firms (foreign participating interests of more than 50%). The results are published annually in *L'implantation étrangère dans l'industrie*.

Data on *R&D expenditure* come from the annual survey on the resources devoted to R&D in the business sector conducted by the Ministry of Higher Education, Research and Technology.

National totals: come from the annual business survey conducted by the SESSI, which covers all firms with 20 or more employees.

Industrial classification

For all variables, the data are classified according to the principal industrial activity of the affiliate.

The industrial classification used for French tables is the national classification converted to ISIC Revision 3.

The following notes concern all variables except *R&D expenditure*. Energy industries – i.e. *Coke and refined petroleum products* (23) and *Crude petroleum, natural gas production* and *Coal mining* (10 to 12) –, *Food, beverages and tobacco* (15/16) and *Recycling* (37) are not covered. *Total manufacturing* includes *Mining and quarrying* (13 to 14).

Variables

Ten variables are available: *Number of enterprises, Number of employees, Production, Turnover, Value added, Wages and salaries, R&D expenditure, Gross fixed capital formation, Total exports* and *Gross operating surplus*. The data for *R&D expenditure* come from a specific study and are not comparable with other variables.

Geographical breakdown

The country of origin is that of the "ultimate beneficial owner".

The detail by country is available when a country controls at least three firms in a given sector.

FRANCE

Source

Les données émanent du Service des Statistiques Industrielles (SESSI) du Ministère de l'Industrie pour toutes les variables, sauf les *Dépenses de R-D*. Elles proviennent du fichier des déclarations de prises de participations étrangères de la Direction du Trésor, auquel s'ajoutent les résultats de l'enquête de l'INSEE sur les liaisons financières. Seules les industries manufacturières et extractives sont couvertes, hors agro-alimentaire et énergie. Les données sont relatives aux entreprises sous contrôle étranger majoritaire (participation strictement supérieure à 50 %). Les résultats sont publiés chaque année dans *L'implantation étrangère dans l'industrie*.

Les données sur les *Dépenses de R-D* proviennent de l'enquête annuelle sur les moyens consacrés à la R-D dans les entreprises menée par le Ministère de l'Éducation Nationale, de la Recherche et de la Technologie.

Totaux nationaux : les données proviennent de l'enquête annuelle d'entreprise du SESSI, qui s'adresse à toutes les entreprises employant au moins 20 salariés.

Classification industrielle

Pour toutes les variables, les données sont classées selon l'activité industrielle principale de l'entreprise affiliée.

La classification industrielle utilisée pour les tableaux français est la classification nationale adaptée pour correspondre à la CITI révision 3.

Les notes suivantes concernent toutes les variables sauf les *Dépenses de R-D*. L'énergie – c'est-à-dire *Cokéfaction et produits pétroliers raffinés* (23) et *Extraction de pétrole, de gaz naturel et de charbon* (10 à 12) –, les *Produits alimentaires, boissons et tabac* (15/16) et la *Récupération* (37) ne sont pas couverts. Le *Total manufacturier* comprend les *Activités extractives* (13 à 14).

Variables

Dix variables sont disponibles : *Nombre d'entreprises*, *Nombre de salariés*, *Production*, *Chiffre d'affaires*, *Valeur ajoutée*, *Salaires*, *Dépenses de R-D*, *Formation brute de capital fixe*, *Exportations totales* et *Excédent brut d'exploitation*. Les données concernant les *Dépenses de R-D* viennent d'une étude spécifique et ne sont pas comparables avec les autres variables.

Ventilation géographique

Le pays d'origine est celui du "bénéficiaire ultime de l'investissement".

Le détail par pays est disponible quand un pays contrôle au moins trois entreprises dans un secteur donné.

GERMANY

ALLEMAGNE

Table 1. GERMANY / ALLEMAGNE

NUMBER OF ENTERPRISES / NOMBRE D'ENTREPRISES

By industry (ISIC Rev. 3)	FOREIGN AFFILIATES (Units)					AS A % OF NATIONAL TOTAL				
	1992	1993	1994	1995	1996	1992	1993	1994	1995	1996
10/14 Mining & quarrying	9	7	8	20	18	1.9	1.5	1.6	4.0	3.6
15/37 TOTAL MANUFACTURING	**1 571**	**1 510**	**1 451**	**1 516**	**1 454**	**3.9**	**3.9**	**3.8**	**4.1**	**4.0**
15/16 Food, beverages, tobacco	108	105	96	94	91	2.4	2.4	2.2	2.2	2.2
17/19 Textiles, clothing, leather, footwear	80	82	74	68	69	2.4	2.7	2.6	2.7	3.0
20/22 Wood and paper products	68	65	57	124	116	..	..	..	2.5	2.4
20 Wood products	..	..	..	17	..	..	..	..	1.2	..
21/22 Paper, printing and publishing	..	..	..	107	..	..	..	..	3.0	..
23/25 Chemicals, Total	318	298	294	291	275	7.8	7.3	7.2	7.6	7.2
23 Refined petroleum, nuclear fuel	10	8	8	7	7	16.7	13.8	12.9	12.5	13.5
24/25 Chemicals, rubber & plastics prod.	308	290	286	284	268	7.7	7.2	7.1	7.5	7.1
24 Chemical products	198	195	184	179	167	14.3	14.0	13.4	14.1	13.2
2423 Pharmaceuticals	..	..	..	..	..	..	..	..	..	..
25 Rubber and plastics products	110	95	102	105	101	4.2	3.6	3.9	4.2	4.0
26 Non-metallic mineral products	70	75	72	64	57	3.3	3.5	3.3	3.0	2.7
27/28 Basic & fabricated metals	198	192	180	180	171	2.8	2.8	2.7	2.8	2.7
27 Basic metals	30	27	24	43	45	3.4	3.2	3.0	4.6	4.9
28 Fabricated metal products	168	165	156	137	126	2.7	2.7	2.6	2.5	2.3
29/32 Machinery, Total	582	555	539	513	493	5.9	5.8	5.8	6.3	6.2
29/30 Non-electrical machinery	345	330	335	358	344	5.4	5.4	5.7	6.1	6.0
29 Non-electrical machinery nec	319	309	315	330	316	5.1	5.2	5.5	5.8	5.7
30 Office and computing machinery	26	21	20	28	28	16.9	13.9	13.0	18.4	17.9
31/32 Electrical & electronic equipment	237	225	204	155	149	6.8	6.7	6.1	6.9	6.8
31 Electrical machinery nec	..	..	..	124	108	..	..	..	6.9	6.2
32 Radio, TV & communications eq.	..	..	..	31	41	..	..	..	6.8	9.2
33 Scientific instruments	56	54	47	92	93	4.5	4.4	4.0	5.3	5.5
34/35 Transportation equipment	42	43	41	44	44	4.0	4.1	3.9	4.1	4.2
34 Motor vehicles	26	30	29	29	27	3.4	3.9	3.8	3.6	3.5
35 Other transport equipment	16	13	12	15	17	5.3	4.5	4.2	5.3	6.4
351 Shipbuilding & repairing	..	..	..	..	..	..	..	..	..	..
353 Aircraft and spacecraft	12	11	10	..	..	21.1	22.0	18.2	..	..
36/37 Other manufacturing	49	41	38	46	45	..	..	..	2.0	2.1
40/45 Construction, electricity, gas & water	162	166	171	176	157	..	..	..	0.7	0.6
50/55 Trade, repair, hotels & restaurants	4 279	3 749	3 729	3 761	3 596	..	..	..	..	..
65/74 Finance, insurance, business services	2 297	2 189	2 260	2 212	2 182	..	..	..	..	..
OTHER ACTIVITIES	304	251	254	357	310	..	..	..	..	..
01/99 GRAND TOTAL	**8 622**	**7 872**	**7 860**	**8 042**	**7 717**	..	..	..	..	..

Total manufacturing by investing country						As a % of total manufacturing by foreign affiliates				
All countries	1 571	1 510	1 451	1 516	1 454	100.0	100.0	100.0	100.0	100.0
United States	340	328	296	311	308	21.6	21.7	20.4	20.5	21.2
Canada	20	21	18	17	..	1.3	1.4	1.2	1.1	..
Mexico	..	..	..	..	..	..	..	..	..	..
Japan	61	60	58	59	56	3.9	4.0	4.0	3.9	3.9
Europe	1 154	1 114	1 073	1 137	..	73.5	73.8	73.9	75.0	..
European Union (15)	741	738	720	771	762	47.2	48.9	49.6	50.9	52.4
Belgium	54	54	59	59	..	3.4	3.6	4.1	3.9	..
France	129	126	122	127	119	8.2	8.3	8.4	8.4	8.2
Germany	..	..	..	..	..	..	..	..	..	..
Italy	41	47	46	50	..	2.6	3.1	3.2	3.3	..
Netherlands	217	213	206	214	215	13.8	14.1	14.2	14.1	14.8
Spain	9	7	9	10	..	0.6	0.5	0.6	0.7	..
Sweden	49	43	35	37	..	3.1	2.8	2.4	2.4	..
United Kingdom	99	94	91	104	104	6.3	6.2	6.3	6.9	7.2
Switzerland	431	397	372	357	311	27.4	26.3	25.6	23.5	21.4
Australia and New Zealand	5	5	4	4	..	0.3	0.3	0.3	0.3	..
Asia (non-OECD)	14	12	13	10	15	0.9	0.8	0.9	0.7	1.0
Latin America	22	24	26	28	24	1.4	1.6	1.8	1.8	1.7

Note: Majority foreign-owned firms. Data by country of origin may not add because of double countings for multinational enterprises.
Firmes sous contrôle étranger majoritaire. Les données par pays investisseur peuvent ne pas s'additionner en raison de doubles comptages pour les entreprises multinationales.

Table 2. GERMANY / ALLEMAGNE

NUMBER OF EMPLOYEES / NOMBRE DE SALARIÉS

By industry (ISIC Rev. 3)	FOREIGN AFFILIATES (Units)					AS A % OF NATIONAL TOTAL				
	1992	1993	1994	1995	1996	1992	1993	1994	1995	1996
10/14 Mining & quarrying	0	0	4 000	4 000	4 000	0.0	0.0	2.0	2.2	2.4
15/37 TOTAL MANUFACTURING	**611 000**	**539 000**	**501 000**	**494 000**	**453 000**	**7.7**	**7.4**	**7.3**	**7.2**	**6.9**
15/16 Food, beverages, tobacco	38 000	39 000	37 000	35 000	30 000	6.2	6.6	6.4	6.3	5.4
17/19 Textiles, clothing, leather, footwear	10 000	8 000	7 000	9 000	10 000	2.4	2.2	2.1	3.1	3.9
20/22 Wood and paper products	18 000	16 000	14 000	18 000	15 000	..	..	..	2.7	2.3
20 Wood products	..	..	..	2 000	..	..	..	..	..	..
21/22 Paper, printing and publishing	..	..	..	16 000	..	..	..	..	..	..
23/25 Chemicals, Total	125 000	113 000	98 000	98 000	81 000	11.3	11.0	10.0	10.4	8.9
23 Refined petroleum, nuclear fuel	7 000	7 000	6 000	6 000	6 000	21.3	21.7	20.1	24.3	26.2
24/25 Chemicals, rubber & plastics prod.	118 000	106 000	91 000	92 000	75 000	11.0	10.6	9.6	10.0	8.5
24 Chemical products	87 000	84 000	69 000	70 000	55 000	13.2	13.8	12.0	12.7	10.3
2423 Pharmaceuticals	..	..	..	..	..	..	..	..	..	..
25 Rubber and plastics products	31 000	22 000	22 000	22 000	20 000	7.5	5.7	5.9	6.0	5.7
26 Non-metallic mineral products	14 000	15 000	15 000	12 000	11 000	4.6	5.1	5.3	4.2	4.2
27/28 Basic & fabricated metals	44 000	41 000	39 000	38 000	37 000	3.9	4.0	4.1	4.2	4.3
27 Basic metals	13 000	12 000	13 000	14 000	14 000	3.4	3.7	4.5	4.7	5.0
28 Fabricated metal products	30 000	28 000	26 000	24 000	23 000	4.1	4.0	4.0	4.0	4.0
29/32 Machinery, Total	219 000	172 000	162 000	152 000	136 000	8.9	7.8	7.9	8.4	7.9
29/30 Non-electrical machinery	118 000	84 000	84 000	86 000	81 000	9.0	7.3	8.1	7.7	7.6
29 Non-electrical machinery nec	78 000	75 000	73 000	73 000	68 000	6.4	7.0	7.5	7.0	6.7
30 Office and computing machinery	41 000	10 000	10 000	13 000	13 000	39.3	13.3	16.3	19.5	23.1
31/32 Electrical & electronic equipment	101 000	87 000	79 000	67 000	55 000	8.7	8.1	7.8	9.5	8.4
31 Electrical machinery nec	..	..	..	28 000	26 000	..	..	..	5.2	5.1
32 Radio, TV & communications eq.	..	..	..	39 000	29 000	..	..	..	23.6	19.3
33 Scientific instruments	15 000	15 000	11 000	19 000	16 000	9.2	10.3	8.0	8.8	7.6
34/35 Transportation equipment	124 000	116 000	109 000	107 000	110 000	12.4	12.8	12.8	11.9	12.5
34 Motor vehicles	119 000	112 000	105 000	102 000	101 000	14.3	14.9	14.7	13.5	13.5
35 Other transport equipment	5 000	4 000	4 000	5 000	9 000	3.0	2.6	2.8	3.6	6.7
351 Shipbuilding & repairing	..	..	..	..	..	..	..	..	..	..
353 Aircraft and spacecraft	5 000	4 000	4 000	..	..	6.8	5.8	6.2	..	..
36/37 Other manufacturing	6 000	5 000	5 000	6 000	6 000	..	..	..	2.4	2.5
40/45 Construction, electricity, gas & water	24 000	19 000	20 000	18 000	17 000	..	..	..	1.0	1.0
50/55 Trade, repair, hotels & restaurants	206 000	198 000	189 000	177 000	173 000	..	..	..	..	..
65/74 Finance, insurance, business services	80 000	71 000	70 000	65 000	65 000	..	..	..	..	..
OTHER ACTIVITIES	21 000	22 000	20 000	39 000	36 000	..	..	..	..	..
01/99 GRAND TOTAL	**943 000**	**849 000**	**799 000**	**796 000**	**748 000**	..	..	..	..	..

Total manufacturing by investing country						As a % of total manufacturing by foreign affiliates				
All countries	611 000	539 000	501 000	494 000	453 000	100.0	100.0	100.0	100.0	100.0
United States	274 000	230 000	213 000	211 000	207 000	44.8	42.7	42.5	42.7	45.7
Canada	10 000	8 000	7 000	7 000	800	1.6	1.5	1.4	1.4	0.2
Mexico	..	..	..	..	0	..	..	..	..	0.0
Japan	18 000	17 000	15 000	16 000	15 000	2.9	3.2	3.0	3.2	3.3
Europe	323 000	304 000	278 000	276 000	245 000	52.9	56.4	55.5	55.9	54.1
European Union (15)	234 000	221 000	202 000	205 000	185 000	38.3	41.0	40.3	41.5	40.8
Belgium	4 000	5 000	7 000	8 000	9 000	0.7	0.9	1.4	1.6	2.0
France	43 000	37 000	36 000	36 000	33 000	7.0	6.9	7.2	7.3	7.3
Germany	..	..	..	..	..	..	..	..	..	..
Italy	12 000	10 000	10 000	12 000	11 000	2.0	1.9	2.0	2.4	2.4
Netherlands	125 000	118 000	103 000	102 000	89 000	20.5	21.9	20.6	20.6	19.6
Spain	2 000	2 000	2 000	2 000	3 000	0.3	0.4	0.4	0.4	0.7
Sweden	14 000	12 000	11 000	11 000	11 000	2.3	2.2	2.2	2.2	2.4
United Kingdom	24 000	27 000	21 000	19 000	19 000	3.9	5.0	4.2	3.8	4.2
Switzerland	101 000	94 000	87 000	76 000	62 000	16.5	17.4	17.4	15.4	13.7
Australia and New Zealand	1 000	0	0	0	..	0.2	0.0	0.0	0.0	..
Asia (non-OECD)	3 000	3 000	3 000	3 000	3 000	0.5	0.6	0.6	0.6	0.7
Latin America	16 000	17 000	9 000	8 000	5 000	2.6	3.2	1.8	1.6	1.1

Note: Majority foreign-owned firms. Data by country of origin may not add because of double countings for multinational enterprises.
Firmes sous contrôle étranger majoritaire. Les données par pays investisseur peuvent ne pas s'additionner en raison de doubles comptages pour les entreprises multinationales.

Table 4. GERMANY / ALLEMAGNE

TURNOVER / CHIFFRE D'AFFAIRES

By industry (ISIC Rev. 3)		FOREIGN AFFILIATES (Millions of DM)					AS A % OF NATIONAL TOTAL				
		1992	1993	1994	1995	1996	1992	1993	1994	1995	1996
10/14	Mining & quarrying	0	0	800	800	1 100	0.0	0.0	1.9	2.0	3.8
15/37	**TOTAL MANUFACTURING**	**298 900**	**251 300**	**259 600**	**272 400**	**269 700**	**14.8**	**13.3**	**13.3**	**13.1**	**12.8**
15/16	Food, beverages, tobacco	31 600	31 800	33 600	33 200	31 600	12.7	12.8	13.6	13.3	12.6
17/19	Textiles, clothing, leather, footwear	2 800	2 100	2 000	2 400	2 400	3.7	3.0	3.0	3.9	4.0
20/22	Wood and paper products	6 600	6 100	6 100	7 500	6 500	..	..	..	4.9	4.2
20	Wood products	..	..	..	700		..	..	..	2.3	..
21/22	Paper, printing and publishing	..	..	..	6 800	..	..	..	..	5.6	..
23/25	Chemicals, Total	101 500	81 900	80 400	85 300	83 000	25.5	21.5	19.6	19.8	19.2
23	Refined petroleum, nuclear fuel	57 800	41 500	41 400	40 900	45 500	53.2	39.9	35.8	35.2	37.5
24/25	Chemicals, rubber & plastics prod.	43 800	40 400	39 000	44 400	37 500	15.1	14.6	13.2	14.1	12.1
24	Chemical products	35 100	35 000	33 300	38 400	31 700	17.2	17.8	15.9	17.0	14.2
2423	Pharmaceuticals	..	..	..	..	..	..	..	..	..	..
25	Rubber and plastics products	8 700	5 400	5 700	6 000	5 700	10.2	6.6	6.7	6.8	6.5
26	Non-metallic mineral products	3 800	4 200	4 400	3 700	3 600	5.8	6.2	6.0	5.0	5.1
27/28	Basic & fabricated metals	12 400	11 500	11 200	12 000	12 000	5.2	5.4	5.1	5.1	5.4
27	Basic metals	5 200	4 600	4 900	6 400	6 400	5.4	5.6	5.7	6.0	6.6
28	Fabricated metal products	7 200	6 900	6 200	5 500	5 600	5.1	5.2	4.6	4.3	4.4
29/32	Machinery, Total	74 200	55 900	58 500	61 800	59 400	14.6	11.6	12.1	13.1	12.5
29/30	Non-electrical machinery	40 800	27 100	29 900	35 700	35 000	15.2	11.3	12.7	12.7	12.2
29	Non-electrical machinery nec	19 000	18 400	19 900	23 000	22 800	8.2	8.7	9.5	9.1	8.9
30	Office and computing machinery	21 700	8 600	10 000	12 700	12 200	58.5	30.8	38.9	41.8	41.9
31/32	Electrical & electronic equipment	33 500	28 800	28 600	26 100	24 400	14.0	12.0	11.6	13.8	13.0
31	Electrical machinery nec	..	..	..	8 200	8 000	..	..	..	5.9	5.7
32	Radio, TV & communications eq.	..	..	..	17 800	16 400	..	..	..	36.2	33.7
33	Scientific instruments	4 000	3 900	3 300	6 000	5 400	15.3	16.2	13.5	14.1	12.3
34/35	Transportation equipment	60 500	52 700	56 800	58 800	64 100	19.8	20.1	20.4	18.7	18.7
34	Motor vehicles	57 200	49 300	54 200	56 400	60 300	21.1	21.4	22.0	20.1	19.7
35	Other transport equipment	3 400	3 400	2 600	2 500	3 800	9.9	10.6	8.1	7.5	10.1
351	Shipbuilding & repairing	..	..	..	..	..	..	..	..	..	..
353	Aircraft and spacecraft	3 300	3 400	2 500	..	..	19.3	22.4	15.9	..	..
36/37	Other manufacturing	1 400	1 300	1 000	1 700	1 600	..	..	..	3.2	3.0
40/45	Construction, electricity, gas & water	3 200	3 100	4 300	4 000	4 200	..	..	..	0.8	0.9
50/55	Trade, repair, hotels & restaurants	202 100	192 900	193 700	197 300	199 700	..	..	..	..	..
65/74	Finance, insurance, business services	36 000	36 000	38 800	35 200	36 200	..	..	..	..	..
	OTHER ACTIVITIES	11 400	9 900	9 500	11 700	11 500	..	..	..	..	..
01/99	**GRAND TOTAL**	**551 600**	**493 300**	**504 300**	**521 400**	**522 400**	..	..	..	..	..

Total manufacturing by investing country	1992	1993	1994	1995	1996	As a % of total manufacturing by foreign affiliates				
All countries	**298 900**	**251 300**	**259 600**	**272 400**	**269 700**	**100.0**	**100.0**	**100.0**	**100.0**	**100.0**
United States	148 100	127 000	131 500	141 700	148 100	49.5	50.5	50.7	52.0	54.9
Canada	5 000	4 000	3 900	3 800	5 100	1.7	1.6	1.5	1.4	1.9
Mexico	..	..	..	..	0	..	..	..	..	0.0
Japan	6 100	5 600	5 500	7 100	7 400	2.0	2.2	2.1	2.6	2.7
Europe	141 900	125 600	130 300	135 300	127 800	47.5	50.0	50.2	49.7	47.4
European Union (15)	114 600	101 400	103 400	108 800	105 400	38.3	40.4	39.8	39.9	39.1
Belgium	1 900	2 000	2 800	3 200	3 400	0.6	0.8	1.1	1.2	1.3
France	13 800	11 400	11 300	12 300	10 400	4.6	4.5	4.4	4.5	3.9
Germany	..	..	..	..	..	..	..	..	..	..
Italy	6 700	5 800	5 500	6 300	6 800	2.2	2.3	2.1	2.3	2.5
Netherlands	64 100	65 200	66 200	68 300	67 400	21.4	25.9	25.5	25.1	25.0
Spain	2 300	1 800	1 400	1 400	1 900	0.8	0.7	0.5	0.5	0.7
Sweden	4 900	5 200	5 200	4 600	4 800	1.6	2.1	2.0	1.7	1.8
United Kingdom	43 500	30 500	29 100	28 600	31 900	14.6	12.1	11.2	10.5	11.8
Switzerland	32 100	28 800	31 500	28 800	24 200	10.7	11.5	12.1	10.6	9.0
Australia and New Zealand	200	100	100	100	..	0.1	0.0	0.0	0.0	..
Asia (non-OECD)	700	700	700	700	800	0.2	0.3	0.3	0.3	0.3
Latin America	8 200	5 800	3 900	4 000	1 600	2.7	2.3	1.5	1.5	0.6

Note: Majority foreign-owned firms. Data by country of origin may not add because of double countings for multinational enterprises.

Firmes sous contrôle étranger majoritaire. Les données par pays investisseur peuvent ne pas s'additionner en raison de doubles comptages pour les entreprises multinationales.

Table 7. GERMANY / ALLEMAGNE

R&D EXPENDITURE / DÉPENSES DE R-D

By industry (ISIC Rev. 3)	FOREIGN AFFILIATES (Millions of DM)					AS A % OF NATIONAL TOTAL				
	1992	1993	1994	1995	1996	1992	1993	1994	1995	1996
10/14 Mining & quarrying	..	..	..	..	..	..	..	..	..	..
15/37 TOTAL MANUFACTURING	..	**6 740**	..	**6 778**	..	..	**16.4**	..	**16.4**	..
15/16 Food, beverages, tobacco	..	..	..	..	..	..	..	..	..	..
17/19 Textiles, clothing, leather, footwear	..	..	..	..	..	..	..	..	..	..
20/22 Wood and paper products	..	..	..	..	..	..	..	..	..	..
20 Wood products	..	..	..	..	..	..	..	..	..	..
21/22 Paper, printing and publishing	..	..	..	..	..	..	..	..	..	..
23/25 Chemicals, Total	..	..	..	..	..	..	..	..	..	..
23 Refined petroleum, nuclear fuel	..	..	..	..	..	..	..	..	..	..
24/25 Chemicals, rubber & plastics prod.	..	..	..	..	..	..	..	..	..	..
24 Chemical products	..	604	..	537	..	..	6.5	..	6.1	..
2423 Pharmaceuticals	..	..	..	..	..	..	..	..	..	..
25 Rubber and plastics products	..	..	..	..	..	..	..	..	..	..
26 Non-metallic mineral products	..	..	..	..	..	..	..	..	..	..
27/28 Basic & fabricated metals	..	..	..	..	..	..	..	..	..	..
27 Basic metals	..	..	..	..	..	..	..	..	..	..
28 Fabricated metal products	..	..	..	..	..	..	..	..	..	..
29/32 Machinery, Total	..	..	..	..	..	..	..	..	..	..
29/30 Non-electrical machinery	..	..	..	..	..	..	..	..	..	..
29 Non-electrical machinery nec	..	409	..	474	..	..	13.2	..	17.6	..
30 Office and computing machinery	..	..	..	..	..	..	..	..	..	..
31/32 Electrical & electronic equipment	..	2 480	..	2 410	..	..	23.3	..	23.1	..
31 Electrical machinery nec	..	..	..	..	..	..	..	..	..	..
32 Radio, TV & communications eq.	..	..	..	..	..	..	..	..	..	..
33 Scientific instruments	..	..	..	..	..	..	..	..	..	..
34/35 Transportation equipment	..	..	..	..	..	..	..	..	..	..
34 Motor vehicles	..	2 056	..	2 071	..	..	20.0	..	19.3	..
35 Other transport equipment	..	..	..	..	..	..	..	..	..	..
351 Shipbuilding & repairing	..	..	..	..	..	..	..	..	..	..
353 Aircraft and spacecraft	..	..	..	..	..	..	..	..	..	..
36/37 Other manufacturing	..	..	..	..	..	..	..	..	..	..
40/45 Construction, electricity, gas & water	..	..	..	..	..	..	..	..	..	..
50/55 Trade, repair, hotels & restaurants	..	..	..	..	..	..	..	..	..	..
65/74 Finance, insurance, business services	..	..	..	..	..	..	..	..	..	..
OTHER ACTIVITIES	..	..	..	..	..	..	..	..	..	..
01/99 GRAND TOTAL	..	**6 788**	..	**6 811**	..	..	**15.9**	..	**16.1**	..

Total manufacturing by investing country						As a % of total manufacturing by foreign affiliates				
All countries	..	6 740	..	6 778	..	..	100.0	..	100.0	..
United States	..	3 078	..	3 473	..	..	45.7	..	51.2	..
Canada	..	..	..	..	..	..	..	..	..	..
Mexico	..	..	..	..	..	..	..	..	..	..
Japan	..	..	..	..	..	..	..	..	..	..
Europe	..	..	..	..	..	..	..	..	..	..
European Union (15)	..	..	..	2 090	..	..	..	..	30.8	..
Belgium	..	..	..	..	..	..	..	..	..	..
France	..	1 179	..	..	..	..	17.5	..	..	..
Germany	..	..	..	..	..	..	..	..	..	..
Italy	..	..	..	..	..	..	..	..	..	..
Netherlands	..	..	..	..	..	..	..	..	..	..
Spain	..	..	..	..	..	..	..	..	..	..
Sweden	..	..	..	..	..	..	..	..	..	..
United Kingdom	..	..	..	..	..	..	..	..	..	..
Switzerland	..	1 143	..	..	..	..	17.0	..	..	..
Australia and New Zealand	..	..	..	..	..	..	..	..	..	..
Asia (non-OECD)	..	..	..	..	..	..	..	..	..	..
Latin America	..	..	..	..	..	..	..	..	..	..

Note: Sample of 500 R&D-intensive companies. Majority foreign-owned firms.
Échantillon de 500 sociétés à forte intensité de R-D. Firmes sous contrôle étranger majoritaire.

Table 8. GERMANY / ALLEMAGNE

NUMBER OF RESEARCHERS / NOMBRE DE CHERCHEURS

By industry (ISIC Rev. 3)	FOREIGN AFFILIATES (Full-time Eq.)					AS A % OF NATIONAL TOTAL				
	1992	1993	1994	1995	1996	1992	1993	1994	1995	1996
10/14 Mining & quarrying	..	..	..	..	..	..	..	..	..	..
15/37 **TOTAL MANUFACTURING**	..	**34 386**	..	**32 314**	..	..	**15.5**	..	**15.9**	..
15/16 Food, beverages, tobacco	..	..	..	..	..	..	..	..	..	..
17/19 Textiles, clothing, leather, footwear	..	..	..	..	..	..	..	..	..	..
20/22 Wood and paper products	..	..	..	..	..	..	..	..	..	..
20 Wood products	..	..	..	..	..	..	..	..	..	..
21/22 Paper, printing and publishing	..	..	..	..	..	..	..	..	..	..
23/25 Chemicals, Total	..	..	..	..	..	..	..	..	..	..
23 Refined petroleum, nuclear fuel	..	..	..	..	..	..	..	..	..	..
24/25 Chemicals, rubber & plastics prod.	..	..	..	..	..	..	..	..	..	..
24 Chemical products	..	3 253	..	3 027	..	..	6.5	..	7.0	..
2423 Pharmaceuticals	..	..	..	..	..	..	..	..	..	..
25 Rubber and plastics products	..	..	..	..	..	..	..	..	..	..
26 Non-metallic mineral products	..	..	..	..	..	..	..	..	..	..
27/28 Basic & fabricated metals	..	..	..	..	..	..	..	..	..	..
27 Basic metals	..	..	..	..	..	..	..	..	..	..
28 Fabricated metal products	..	..	..	..	..	..	..	..	..	..
29/32 Machinery, Total	..	..	..	..	..	..	..	..	..	..
29/30 Non-electrical machinery	..	..	..	..	..	..	..	..	..	..
29 Non-electrical machinery nec	..	2 334	..	2 460	..	..	12.8	..	16.1	..
30 Office and computing machinery	..	..	..	..	..	..	..	..	..	..
31/32 Electrical & electronic equipment	..	13 167	..	11 862	..	..	20.2	..	20.1	..
31 Electrical machinery nec	..	..	..	..	..	..	..	..	..	..
32 Radio, TV & communications eq.	..	..	..	..	..	..	..	..	..	..
33 Scientific instruments	..	..	..	..	..	..	..	..	..	..
34/35 Transportation equipment	..	..	..	..	..	..	..	..	..	..
34 Motor vehicles	..	9 516	..	9 237	..	..	19.6	..	19.1	..
35 Other transport equipment	..	..	..	..	..	..	..	..	..	..
351 Shipbuilding & repairing	..	..	..	..	..	..	..	..	..	..
353 Aircraft and spacecraft	..	..	..	..	..	..	..	..	..	..
36/37 Other manufacturing	..	..	..	..	..	..	..	..	..	..
40/45 Construction, electricity, gas & water	..	..	..	..	..	..	..	..	..	..
50/55 Trade, repair, hotels & restaurants	..	..	..	..	..	..	..	..	..	..
65/74 Finance, insurance, business services	..	..	..	..	..	..	..	..	..	..
OTHER ACTIVITIES	..	..	..	..	..	..	..	..	..	..
01/99 **GRAND TOTAL**	..	**34 612**	..	**32 442**	..	..	**15.1**	..	**15.5**	..

Total manufacturing by investing country	FOREIGN AFFILIATES (Full-time Eq.)					*As a % of total manufacturing by foreign affiliates*				
All countries	..	**34 386**	..	**32 314**	..	..	**100.0**	..	**100.0**	..
United States	..	14 024	..	15 607	..	..	40.8	..	48.3	..
Canada	..	..	..	..	..	..	..	..	..	..
Mexico	..	..	..	..	..	..	..	..	..	..
Japan	..	..	..	..	..	..	..	..	..	..
Europe	..	19 735	..	..	..	..	57.4	..	..	..
European Union (15)	..	13 074	..	10 051	..	..	38.0	..	31.1	..
Belgium	..	..	..	..	..	..	..	..	..	..
France	..	5 671	..	..	..	..	16.5	..	..	..
Germany	..	..	..	..	..	..	..	..	..	..
Italy	..	..	..	..	..	..	..	..	..	..
Netherlands	..	5 088	..	..	..	..	14.8	..	..	..
Spain	..	..	..	..	..	..	..	..	..	..
Sweden	..	..	..	..	..	..	..	..	..	..
United Kingdom	..	..	..	..	..	..	..	..	..	..
Switzerland	..	6 239	..	..	..	..	18.1	..	..	..
Australia and New Zealand	..	..	..	..	..	..	..	..	..	..
Asia (non-OECD)	..	..	..	..	..	..	..	..	..	..
Latin America	..	..	..	..	..	..	..	..	..	..

Note: Sample of 500 R&D-intensive companies. Majority foreign-owned firms. Total R&D personnel rather than researchers.
Échantillon de 500 sociétés à forte intensité de R-D. Firmes sous contrôle étranger majoritaire. Ensemble du personnel de R-D plutôt que chercheurs.

Table 15. GERMANY / ALLEMAGNE

TECHNOLOGICAL PAYMENTS / PAIEMENTS TECHNOLOGIQUES

By industry (ISIC Rev. 3)	FOREIGN AFFILIATES (Millions of DM)					AS A % OF NATIONAL TOTAL				
	1993	1994	1995	1996	1997	1993	1994	1995	1996	1997
10/14 Mining & quarrying	0	0	..	2	2	..	..	..	..	..
15/37 TOTAL MANUFACTURING	**3 111**	**3 082**	**3 226**	**1 897**	**1 400**	..	..	..	**54.2**	**46.7**
15/16 Food, beverages, tobacco	453	394	351	324	249	..	..	..	94.2	94.0
17/19 Textiles, clothing, leather, footwear	26	8	10	4	3	..	..	..	..	..
20/22 Wood and paper products	9	6	..	..	..	..	..	..	..	..
20 Wood products	1	1	..	..	..	..	..	..	..	..
21/22 Paper, printing and publishing	8	5	..	..	..	..	..	..	..	..
23/25 Chemicals, Total	735	631	675	605	..	..	..	..	..	..
23 Refined petroleum, nuclear fuel	4	3	2	2	..	..	..	..	..	..
24/25 Chemicals, rubber & plastics prod.	731	628	677	603	350	..	..	..	..	..
24 Chemical products	585	570	624	570	311	..	..	..	36.8	30.4
2423 Pharmaceuticals	..	..	..	..	..	..	..	..	..	..
25 Rubber and plastics products	147	58	53	33	39	..	..	..	..	..
26 Non-metallic mineral products	..	..	28	27	28	..	..	..	..	..
27/28 Basic & fabricated metals	122	117	83	..	82	..	..	..	..	..
27 Basic metals	20	17	14	..	25	..	..	..	..	..
28 Fabricated metal products	102	100	69	54	57	..	..	..	..	..
29/32 Machinery, Total	1 693	1 845	2 013	780	560	..	..	..	63.1	42.7
29/30 Non-electrical machinery	1 292	1 521	1 617	407	135	..	..	..	..	..
29 Non-electrical machinery nec	..	..	48	46	104	..	..	..	26.3	48.8
30 Office and computing machinery	1 292	1 521	1 569	361	31	..	..	..	..	..
31/32 Electrical & electronic equipment	400	325	396	373	456	..	..	..	..	..
31 Electrical machinery nec	..	..	320	58	84	..	..	..	..	..
32 Radio, TV & communications eq.	400	325	76	315	372	..	..	..	..	..
33 Scientific instruments	..	..	24	26	28	..	..	..	..	..
34/35 Transportation equipment	26	17	..	38	32	..	..	..	61.3	38.1
34 Motor vehicles	25	16	27	37	24	..	..	..	..	..
35 Other transport equipment	1	1	..	1	8	..	..	..	..	..
351 Shipbuilding & repairing	..	..	..	..	..	..	..	..	..	..
353 Aircraft and spacecraft	1	1	..	..	..	..	..	..	..	..
36/37 Other manufacturing	47	64	6	24	17	..	..	..	..	..
40/45 Construction, electricity, gas & water	8	11	13	4	3	..	..	..	..	..
50/55 Trade, repair, hotels & restaurants	349	422	343	258	194	..	..	..	65.2	74.6
65/74 Finance, insurance, business services	44	61	229	1 343	1 578	..	..	..	90.1	92.3
OTHER ACTIVITIES	434	136	..	15	7	..	..	..	..	..
01/99 GRAND TOTAL	**3 945**	**3 711**	**3 828**	**3 520**	**3 191**	**78.3**	**74.1**	**66.6**	**64.9**	**63.8**

Total manufacturing by investing country						As a % of total manufacturing by foreign affiliates				
All countries	3 111	3 082	3 226	1 897	1 400	100.0	100.0	100.0	100.0	100.0
United States	1 988	2 162	..	..	..	63.9	70.1	..	..	..
Canada	1	3	..	..	..	0.0	0.1	..	..	..
Mexico	0	0	..	..	..	0.0	0.0	..	..	..
Japan	68	65	..	..	..	2.2	2.1	..	..	..
Europe	..	..	..	..	..	..	..	..	..	..
European Union (15)	589	449	..	..	..	18.9	14.6	..	..	..
Belgium	49	60	..	..	..	1.6	1.9	..	..	..
France	148	101	..	..	..	4.8	3.3	..	..	..
Germany	..	..	..	..	..	..	..	..	..	..
Italy	20	7	..	..	..	0.6	0.2	..	..	..
Netherlands	283	208	..	..	..	9.1	6.7	..	..	..
Spain	2	0	..	..	..	0.1	0.0	..	..	..
Sweden	4	5	..	..	..	0.1	0.2	..	..	..
United Kingdom	48	28	..	..	..	1.5	0.9	..	..	..
Switzerland	458	397	..	..	..	14.7	12.9	..	..	..
Australia and New Zealand	2	1	..	..	..	0.1	0.0	..	..	..
Asia (non-OECD)	1	2	..	..	..	0.0	0.1	..	..	..
Latin America	0	0	..	..	..	0.0	0.0	..	..	..

Note: **All foreign-owned firms** with foreign participating interests of more than 20%. Up to 1994, ISIC 28 includes 33 and ISIC 36/37 includes 26. See country notes.
Toutes les firmes sous contrôle étranger pour lesquelles la participation étrangère dépasse 20%. Jusqu'en 1994, la CITI 28 comprend 33 et la CITI 36/37 comprend 26. Voir les notes par pays.

Table 16. GERMANY / ALLEMAGNE

TECHNOLOGICAL RECEIPTS / RECETTES TECHNOLOGIQUES

By industry (ISIC Rev. 3)	FOREIGN AFFILIATES (Millions of DM)					AS A % OF NATIONAL TOTAL				
	1993	1994	1995	1996	1997	1993	1994	1995	1996	1997
10/14 Mining & quarrying	0	0	..	0	0	..	..	..	..	..
15/37 **TOTAL MANUFACTURING**	597	563	751	688	799	..	..	..	22.4	22.7
15/16 Food, beverages, tobacco	3	2	2	1	7	..	..	..	3.8	22.6
17/19 Textiles, clothing, leather, footwear	90	100	138	1	0	..	..	..	..	..
20/22 Wood and paper products	0	7	..	..	..	..	..	..	..	..
20 Wood products	0	0	..	..	..	..	..	..	..	..
21/22 Paper, printing and publishing	0	7	..	..	..	..	..	..	..	..
23/25 Chemicals, Total	320	295	216	272	..	..	..	..	..	..
23 Refined petroleum, nuclear fuel	0	0	0	0	..	..	..	..	..	..
24/25 Chemicals, rubber & plastics prod.	320	295	216	272	220	..	..	..	..	..
24 Chemical products	319	292	214	272	215	..	..	..	16.6	13.0
2423 Pharmaceuticals	..	..	..	..	..	..	..	..	..	..
25 Rubber and plastics products	2	3	2	0	5	..	..	..	..	..
26 Non-metallic mineral products	..	..	1	3	3	..	..	..	..	..
27/28 Basic & fabricated metals	10	24	4	..	6	..	..	..	..	..
27 Basic metals	0	0	0	..	0	..	..	..	..	..
28 Fabricated metal products	9	24	4	3	6	..	..	..	..	..
29/32 Machinery, Total	84	91	85	80	66	..	..	..	9.5	6.4
29/30 Non-electrical machinery	51	23	44	37	20	..	..	..	..	..
29 Non-electrical machinery nec	..	..	11	6	18	..	..	..	2.8	9.2
30 Office and computing machinery	51	23	33	31	2	..	..	..	..	..
31/32 Electrical & electronic equipment	33	68	41	43	46	..	..	..	..	..
31 Electrical machinery nec	..	..	38	24	24	..	..	..	..	..
32 Radio, TV & communications eq.	33	68	3	19	22	..	..	..	..	..
33 Scientific instruments	..	..	0	4	9	..	..	..	..	..
34/35 Transportation equipment	70	39	..	319	470	..	..	..	67.3	69.8
34 Motor vehicles	70	39	300	319	463	..	..	..	..	..
35 Other transport equipment	0	0	..	0	7	..	..	..	..	..
351 Shipbuilding & repairing	..	..	..	..	..	..	..	..	..	..
353 Aircraft and spacecraft	0	0	..	..	..	..	..	..	..	..
36/37 Other manufacturing	19	5	0	0	0	..	..	..	..	..
40/45 Construction, electricity, gas & water	0	0	0	0	0	..	..	..	..	..
50/55 Trade, repair, hotels & restaurants	179	213	110	192	31	..	..	..	91.9	72.1
65/74 Finance, insurance, business services	2	3	23	102	57	..	..	..	27.1	16.4
OTHER ACTIVITIES	46	14	..	0	0	..	..	..	..	..
01/99 **GRAND TOTAL**	823	793	884	983	888	31.2	28.4	27.7	26.6	22.4

Total manufacturing by investing country						As a % of total manufacturing by foreign affiliates				
All countries	597	563	751	688	799	100.0	100.0	100.0	100.0	100.0
United States	234	161	..	..	..	39.2	28.6	..	..	..
Canada	3	2	..	..	..	0.5	0.4	..	..	..
Mexico	6	4	..	..	..	1.0	0.7	..	..	..
Japan	62	68	..	..	..	10.4	12.1	..	..	..
Europe	..	..	..	..	..	..	..	..	..	..
European Union (15)	177	190	..	..	..	29.6	33.7	..	..	..
Belgium	2	3	..	..	..	0.3	0.5	..	..	..
France	38	33	..	..	..	6.4	5.9	..	..	..
Germany	..	..	..	..	..	..	..	..	..	..
Italy	22	22	..	..	..	3.7	3.9	..	..	..
Netherlands	10	43	..	..	..	1.7	7.6	..	..	..
Spain	48	15	..	..	..	8.0	2.7	..	..	..
Sweden	5	8	..	..	..	0.8	1.4	..	..	..
United Kingdom	29	43	..	..	..	4.9	7.6	..	..	..
Switzerland	30	38	..	..	..	5.0	6.7	..	..	..
Australia and New Zealand	8	7	..	..	..	1.3	1.2	..	..	..
Asia (non-OECD)	29	44	..	..	..	4.9	7.8	..	..	..
Latin America	34	27	..	..	..	5.7	4.8	..	..	..

Note: **All foreign-owned firms** with foreign participating interests of more than 20%. Up to 1994, ISIC 28 includes 33 and ISIC 36/37 includes 26. See country notes.
Toutes les firmes sous contrôle étranger pour lesquelles la participation étrangère dépasse 20%. Jusqu'en 1994, la CITI 28 comprend 33 et la CITI 36/37 comprend 26. Voir les notes par pays.

Table 17. GERMANY / ALLEMAGNE

STOCK OF FOREIGN DIRECT INVESTMENT / STOCK D'INVESTISSEMENT DIRECT ÉTRANGER

					FOREIGN AFFILIATES (Millions of DM)					
By industry (ISIC Rev. 3)		1987	1988	1989	1990	1991	1992	1993	1994	1995	1996
10/14	Mining & quarrying	..	..	..	- 26	..	- 38	- 45	845	1 249	1 229
15/37	**TOTAL MANUFACTURING**	**39 013**	..	**38 455**	**38 821**	**39 891**	**35 858**	**31 357**	**33 434**	**54 762**	**49 281**
15/16	Food, beverages, tobacco	..	..	..	3 357	..	3 087	3 431	3 947	5 928	4 807
17/19	Textiles, clothing, leather, footwear	..	..	..	414	..	600	393	380	537	597
20/22	Wood and paper products	..	..	..	960	..	762	856	1 261	1 580	1 513
20	Wood products	..	..	..	..	..	..	..	..	75	..
21/22	Paper, printing and publishing	..	..	..	..	..	..	..	..	1 505	..
23/25	Chemicals, Total	..	..	..	13 080	..	13 302	11 637	11 950	18 914	15 794
23	Refined petroleum, nuclear fuel	..	..	..	4 785	..	4 555	3 271	3 634	4 984	3 205
24/25	Chemicals, rubber & plastics prod.	..	..	..	8 295	..	8 747	8 366	8 317	13 930	12 589
24	Chemical products	..	..	..	6 910	..	7 223	7 387	7 108	12 432	11 098
2423	Pharmaceuticals	..	..	..	..	..	..	..	..	..	..
25	Rubber and plastics products	..	..	..	1 385	..	1 524	979	1 208	1 498	1 491
26	Non-metallic mineral products	..	..	..	593	..	737	882	1 073	1 443	1 550
27/28	Basic & fabricated metals	..	..	..	2 422	..	2 337	2 472	1 668	3 676	3 636
27	Basic metals	..	..	..	1 083	..	1 158	1 343	846	2 200	2 009
28	Fabricated metal products	..	..	..	1 339	..	1 179	1 129	822	1 476	1 627
29/32	Machinery, Total	..	..	..	11 660	..	9 685	7 397	6 962	13 006	12 591
29/30	Non-electrical machinery	..	..	..	7 301	..	5 103	3 368	4 083	8 156	7 109
29	Non-electrical machinery nec	..	..	..	3 029	..	2 676	2 654	3 276	5 168	5 056
30	Office and computing machinery	..	..	..	4 272	..	2 427	714	807	2 988	2 053
31/32	Electrical & electronic equipment	..	..	..	4 359	..	4 583	4 029	2 879	4 850	5 482
31	Electrical machinery nec	..	..	..	4 359	..	..	..	..	1 966	2 346
32	Radio, TV & communications eq.	..	..	..	..	..	..	..	..	2 884	3 136
33	Scientific instruments	..	..	..	1 055	..	581	593	504	1 809	1 465
34/35	Transportation equipment	..	..	..	5 133	..	4 610	3 528	4 720	7 439	6 985
34	Motor vehicles	..	..	..	5 108	..	4 250	3 167	4 363	6 815	5 548
35	Other transport equipment	..	..	..	25	..	360	361	357	624	1 437
351	Shipbuilding & repairing	..	..	..	22	..	..	..	..	..	..
353	Aircraft and spacecraft	..	..	..	..	..	356	358	356	..	..
36/37	Other manufacturing	..	..	..	147	..	157	168	132	431	344
40/45	Construction, electricity, gas & water	..	..	..	137	..	130	48	645	1 015	1 004
50/55	Trade, repair, hotels & restaurants	..	..	..	8 993	..	10 868	11 099	12 066	36 932	35 872
65/74	Finance, insurance, business services	..	..	..	46 468	..	55 156	65 358	72 718	150 091	171 064
	OTHER ACTIVITIES	..	..	..	265	..	205	88	104	2 182	2 624
01/99	**GRAND TOTAL**	..	..	..	**94 658**	..	**102 179**	**107 904**	**118 977**	**246 231**	**261 075**

Total Manufacturing by investing country

	1987	1988	1989	1990	1991	1992	1993	1994	1995	1996
All countries	**39 013**	..	**38 455**	**38 821**	**39 891**	**35 858**	**31 357**	**33 434**	**54 762**	**49 281**
United States	..	..	..	18 313	..	14 935	12 612	14 365	22 790	20 861
Canada	..	..	..	..	..	651	370	372	675	..
Mexico	..	..	..	..	..	..	..	..	..	..
Japan	..	..	..	1 007	..	1 159	990	971	1 726	1 795
Europe	..	..	..	..	..	20 170	18 743	18 131	28 669	..
European Union (15)	..	..	..	14 000	..	15 955	15 030	14 316	23 492	21 089
Belgium	..	..	..	..	..	338	409	744	975	..
France	..	..	..	1 642	..	2 492	2 158	2 068	3 620	3 110
Germany	..	..	..	..	..	..	..	..	..	..
Italy	..	..	..	..	..	993	562	816	1 043	..
Netherlands	..	..	..	7 563	..	8 975	8 953	7 791	11 180	9 413
Spain	..	..	..	..	..	70	104	116	181	..
Sweden	..	..	..	..	..	635	688	924	564	..
United Kingdom	..	..	..	2 393	..	3 941	3 057	3 493	1 808	1 801
Switzerland	..	..	..	4 116	..	4 645	4 204	4 355	4 731	3 876
Australia and New Zealand	..	..	..	..	..	37	30	34	21	..
Asia (non-OECD)	..	..	..	5	..	281	420	397	532	522
Latin America	..	..	..	603	..	730	887	504	342	258

Note: Majority foreign-owned firms. Data by country of origin may not add because of double countings for multinational enterprises. New definition from 1995. See country notes.
Firmes sous contrôle étranger majoritaire. Les données par pays investisseur peuvent ne pas s'additionner en raison de doubles comptages pour les entreprises multinationales. Changement de définition à partir de 1995. Voir les notes par pays.

Table 18. GERMANY / ALLEMAGNE

CAPITAL UNDER FOREIGN INFLUENCE / CAPITAL SOUS INFLUENCE ÉTRANGÈRE

By industry (ISIC Rev. 3)		FOREIGN AFFILIATES (Millions of DM)									
		1987	1988	1989	1990	1991	1992	1993	1994	1995	1996
10/14	Mining & quarrying	..	..	..	- 26	..	- 38	- 45	837	1 145	1 015
15/37	**TOTAL MANUFACTURING**	37 572	..	37 303	37 611	38 216	34 349	30 431	32 055	32 992	30 284
15/16	Food, beverages, tobacco	..	..	..	3 203	..	2 941	3 362	3 864	4 017	3 530
17/19	Textiles, clothing, leather, footwear	..	..	..	371	..	551	355	341	349	397
20/22	Wood and paper products	..	..	..	911	..	749	850	1 251	1 004	998
20	Wood products	..	..	..	..	..	..	..	..	50	..
21/22	Paper, printing and publishing	..	..	..	..	..	..	..	..	955	..
23/25	Chemicals, Total	..	..	..	12 823	..	13 066	11 476	11 688	11 752	9 810
23	Refined petroleum, nuclear fuel	..	..	..	4 761	..	4 555	3 271	3 634	3 815	2 186
24/25	Chemicals, rubber & plastics prod.	..	..	..	8 062	..	8 512	8 205	8 055	7 937	7 624
24	Chemical products	..	..	..	6 696	..	7 016	7 247	6 877	7 013	6 668
2423	Pharmaceuticals	..	..	..	..	..	..	..	..	..	..
25	Rubber and plastics products	..	..	..	1 366	..	1 496	958	1 178	924	956
26	Non-metallic mineral products	..	..	..	556	..	609	748	955	1 168	1 115
27/28	Basic & fabricated metals	..	..	..	2 239	..	2 235	2 349	1 545	1 650	1 873
27	Basic metals	..	..	..	1 066	..	1 143	1 328	834	939	939
28	Fabricated metal products	..	..	..	1 173	..	1 092	1 021	711	711	934
29/32	Machinery, Total	..	..	..	11 219	..	8 895	7 066	6 593	6 770	6 943
29/30	Non-electrical machinery	..	..	..	7 032	..	4 408	3 084	3 772	3 722	3 942
29	Non-electrical machinery nec	..	..	..	2 762	..	2 286	2 370	2 965	2 910	2 983
30	Office and computing machinery	..	..	..	4 270	..	2 122	714	807	811	959
31/32	Electrical & electronic equipment	..	..	..	4 187	..	4 487	3 983	2 822	3 048	3 001
31	Electrical machinery nec	..	..	..	4 187	..	..	..	..	1 017	1 384
32	Radio, TV & communications eq.	..	..	..	..	..	..	..	..	2 031	1 617
33	Scientific instruments	..	..	..	1 033	..	558	554	490	1 103	888
34/35	Transportation equipment	..	..	..	5 122	..	4 604	3 518	4 709	4 911	4 557
34	Motor vehicles	..	..	..	5 100	..	4 248	3 162	4 355	4 660	3 593
35	Other transport equipment	..	..	..	22	..	356	356	354	252	964
351	Shipbuilding & repairing	..	..	..	..	..	..	..	..	..	..
353	Aircraft and spacecraft	..	..	..	19	..	353	354	353	..	..
36/37	Other manufacturing	..	..	..	134	..	141	153	115	268	174
40/45	Construction, electricity, gas & water	..	..	..	33	..	124	44	552	415	407
50/55	Trade, repair, hotels & restaurants	..	..	..	8 803	..	10 671	10 808	11 783	12 105	11 961
65/74	Finance, insurance, business services	..	..	..	44 280	..	52 852	61 978	69 731	81 753	97 017
	OTHER ACTIVITIES	..	..	..	249	..	198	77	98	- 264	60
01/99	**GRAND TOTAL**	..	..	..	90 950	..	98 155	103 293	114 552	128 147	140 744

Total Manufacturing by investing country

	1987	1988	1989	1990	1991	1992	1993	1994	1995	1996
All countries	37 572	..	37 303	37 611	38 216	34 349	30 431	32 055	32 992	30 284
United States	..	..	..	18 048	..	13 758	11 361	13 304	14 024	13 359
Canada	..	..	..	..	..	351	297	308	331	..
Mexico	..	..	..	..	..	..	..	..	..	..
Japan	..	..	..	902	..	1 005	834	724	976	1 052
Europe	..	..	..	..	..	18 847	17 254	16 509	17 120	..
European Union (15)	..	..	..	13 533	..	14 823	13 509	12 638	14 072	12 550
Belgium	..	..	..	..	..	273	344	569	739	..
France	..	..	..	1 586	..	2 141	1 868	1 796	2 053	1 966
Germany	..	..	..	..	..	..	..	..	..	..
Italy	..	..	..	..	..	803	375	390	668	..
Netherlands	..	..	..	7 325	..	7 392	7 425	6 385	6 875	5 776
Spain	..	..	..	..	..	66	95	107	108	..
Sweden	..	..	..	..	..	312	360	300	327	..
United Kingdom	..	..	..	2 351	..	2 070	1 183	1 076	1 147	1 012
Switzerland	..	..	..	3 764	..	3 743	3 448	3 493	2 893	2 119
Australia and New Zealand	..	..	..	..	..	21	19	22	20	..
Asia (non-OECD)	..	..	..	5	..	248	389	406	405	428
Latin America	..	..	..	588	..	99	270	275	113	145

Note: Majority foreign-owned firms. Data by country of origin may not add because of double countings for multinational enterprises.
Firmes sous contrôle étranger majoritaire. Les données par pays investisseur peuvent ne pas s'additionner en raison de doubles comptages pour les entreprises multinationales.

GERMANY

Source

For all variables except *R&D expenditure* and *Number of researchers*, the data are prepared by the Deutsche Bundesbank. The data are based on annual stock surveys of direct investment, which cover all enterprises in Germany with a cross-border capital interest amounting to more than 20% and with a balance sheet total of the investment enterprise exceeding DM 1 million. The results are published in Statistical Special Publication No. 10 *Kapitalverflechtung mit dem Ausland* (International capital links). The data on technological receipts and payments come from the balance of payments statistics and are published every two years in *Technologische Dienstleistungen in der Zahlungsbilanz* (Technological services in the balance of payments).

The data refer to firms with a foreign majority participating interest for *Number of enterprises, Number of employees, Turnover, Stock of foreign direct investment* and *Capital under foreign influence*. The data refer to firms with foreign participating interest of at least 20% for *Technological payments* and *receipts*. For all foreign-owned firms, the figures are affected in full and not prorata of the level of ownership.

For *R&D expenditure* and *Number of researchers*, data come from a survey on the R&D activities of foreign affiliates operating in Germany conducted by SV-Wissenschaftsstatistik. This survey analyses the performance of 500 R&D-intensive companies according to their nationality (majority-owned). In 1995, these firms accounted for 83% of the total R&D carried out in Germany and employed 75% of all R&D personnel.

National totals:

- *Number of enterprises, Number of employees* and *Turnover:* the results come from a survey conducted by the Federal Statistical Office, which covers enterprises in the mining and manufacturing industry with 20 or more employees.

- All other variables: same source as foreign affiliates' data.

Industrial classification

For all variables, the data are classified according to the principal industrial activity of the affiliate.

The industrial classification used for German tables is the national industrial classification, converted to Revision 3 up to 1994. From 1995, data have been directly processed using ISIC Revision 3.

The following notes concern the variables *Number of enterprises, Number of employees* and *Turnover*, and refer to data up to 1994:

- *Mining and quarrying* (10/14) excludes *Quarrying* and includes *Coke oven products* (231).

- *Wood and paper products* (20/22) excludes *Publishing* (221) and *Reproduction of recorded media* (223).

- *Refined petroleum and coal products manufacturing* (23) excludes *Processing of nuclear fuel* (233) and *Coke oven products* (231).

- *Chemical products* (24) includes *Processing of nuclear fuel* (233).

- *Pharmaceuticals* (2423) is not available separately.

- *Non-metallic products* (26) includes *Quarrying*.

- *Fabricated metal products* (28) includes *Manufacturing of weapons and ammunitions* (2927).

- *Non-electrical machinery n.e.c.* (29) excludes *Manufacturing of weapons and ammunitions* (2927) and *Manufacturing of domestic appliances n.e.c.* (293).

- *Electrical machinery* (31) includes *Electronic equipment* (32), *Reproduction of recorded media* (223) and *Manufacturing of domestic appliances n.e.c.* (293).

- *Motor vehicles* (34) includes *Transport equipment n.e.c.* (359).

- *Finance, insurance, real estate and business services* (65/74) includes *Publishing* (221) and *Property administration* (75).

The following notes concern the variables *Technological payments* and *receipts*, and refer to data prior to 1995:

- *Fabricated metal products* (28) includes *Scientific instruments* (33).

- *Other manufacturing* (36/37) includes *Non-metallic mineral products* (26).

Variables

- *Number of employees* is based on the figures provided by enterprises on a voluntary basis. It is partly estimated for each economic sector. No distinction is made between full-time and part-time employees.

- *Number of researchers* is in fact the total number of employees working on R&D expressed in full-time equivalent.

- *Technological payments* and *receipts* correspond to expenditures on and receipts from patents, inventions and processes by enterprises in which foreigners hold participating interests of more than 20%.

- Up to 1994, *Stock of foreign direct investment* is defined as the capital stock, and is based on the current balance sheets of the affiliates, taking account of the capital share of the investor. From 1995, it is defined as the primary foreign investment capital and the lending by foreign shareholders and by other affiliated enterprises abroad.

- *Capital under foreign influence* is defined as the primary foreign investment capital excluding lending.

Geographical breakdown

The investor's country is the country of the immediate controller.

The data are processed separately for each individual investing country. Therefore, double countings are not eliminated in all tables for reasons of consistency, *i.e.* in the case of majority interests involving several countries, the variables are assigned in full to each country.

ALLEMAGNE

Source

Pour l'ensemble des variables à l'exception des *Dépenses de R-D* et du *Nombre de chercheurs*, les données émanent de la Deustche Bundesbank. Elles sont basées sur les enquêtes annuelles de stocks d'investissement direct qui couvrent toutes les entreprises d'Allemagne dont les intérêts en capitaux transfrontières s'élèvent à plus de 20 % et dont le total du bilan de l'entreprise bénéficiaire de l'investissement dépasse 1 million de DM. Les résultats paraissent dans la publication statistique spéciale *Kapitalverflechtung mit dem Ausland* (Participations croisées internationales). Les données sur les recettes et paiements technologiques proviennent des statistiques de la balance des paiements et sont publiées tous les deux ans dans *Technologische Dienstleistungen in der Zahlungsbilanz* (Services technologiques dans la balance des paiements).

Les données font référence aux entreprises dans lesquelles l'étranger détient une participation majoritaire et concernent les variables suivantes : *Nombre d'entreprises*, *Nombre de salariés*, *Chiffre d'affaires*, *Stock d'investissement direct étranger* et *Capital sous influence étrangère*. Pour les *Paiements* et *Recettes technologiques*, les données font référence aux entreprises à participation étrangère d'au moins 20 %. Pour toutes les entreprises sous contrôle étranger, les chiffres sont affectés en totalité et non au prorata du niveau de participation au capital.

Pour les *Dépenses de R-D* et le *Nombre de chercheurs*, les données proviennent d'une enquête sur les activités de R-D des filiales étrangères opérant en Allemagne menée par SV-Wissenschaftsstatistik. Elle analyse les résultats de 500 sociétés à forte intensité de R-D en tenant compte de leur nationalité (contrôle majoritaire). En 1995, ces firmes représentaient 83 % de la R-D totale effectuée en Allemagne et 75 % du personnel de R-D.

Totaux nationaux :

- *Nombre d'entreprises*, *Nombre de salariés* et *Chiffre d'affaires* : les résultats proviennent d'une enquête menée par l'office statistique fédéral, qui couvre les entreprises de l'industrie extractive et manufacturière employant au moins 20 salariés.

- Autres variables : même source que les données relatives aux filiales étrangères.

Classification industrielle

Pour toutes les variables, les données sont classées selon l'activité industrielle principale de l'entreprise affiliée.

La classification industrielle utilisée pour les tableaux allemands est la classification industrielle nationale adaptée pour correspondre à la CITI révision 3 jusqu'en 1994. A partir de 1995, les données ont été compilées directement en CITI révision 3.

Les notes suivantes concernent les variables *Nombre d'entreprises*, *Nombre de salariés* et *Chiffre d'affaires* et se réfèrent aux données jusqu'en 1994 :

- *Industries extractives* (10/14) à l'exclusion des *Carrières* et y compris la *Cokéfaction* (231).

- *Production de bois et papier* (20/22) à l'exclusion de l'*Édition* (221) et de la *Reproduction de supports enregistrés* (223).

- *Fabrication de produits pétroliers raffinés et de produits du charbon* (23) à l'exclusion du *Traitement de combustibles nucléaires* (233) et de la *Cokéfaction* (231).

- *Produits chimiques* (24), y compris le *Traitement de combustibles nucléaires* (233).

- *Produits pharmaceutiques* (2423) non disponible séparément.

- *Produits non métalliques* (26) y compris les *Carrières*.

- *Ouvrages en métaux* (28) y compris la *Fabrication d'armes et de munitions* (2927).

- *Machines et matériel n.c.a.* (29) à l'exclusion de la *Fabrication d'armes et de munitions* (2927) et de la *Fabrication d'appareils domestiques n.c.a.* (293).

- *Machines et appareils électriques* (31) y compris l'*Équipement électronique* (32), la *Reproduction de supports enregistrés* (223) et la *Fabrication d'appareils domestiques n.c.a.* (293).

- *Véhicules automobiles* (34) y compris les *Autres équipements de transport* (359).

- *Finance, assurance, immobilier et services aux entreprises* (65/74) y compris l'*Édition* (221) et l'*Administration publique* (75).

Les notes suivantes concernent les variables *Paiements* et *Recettes technologiques*, et se réfèrent aux données avant 1995 :

- *Ouvrages en métaux* (28) y compris les *Instruments scientifiques* (33).

- *Autres industries manufacturières* (36/37) y compris les *Produits minéraux non métalliques* (26).

Variables

- Le *Nombre de salariés* est fondé sur les chiffres fournis par les entreprises sur la base du volontariat. Il est partiellement estimé pour chaque secteur économique. Il n'est fait aucune distinction entre les salariés à temps plein et à temps partiel.

- Le *Nombre de chercheurs* est en fait le nombre total de salariés travaillant dans le domaine de la R-D exprimé en équivalent plein-temps.

- Les *Paiements* et *Recettes technologiques* correspondent aux montants dépensés pour et encaissés sur brevets, inventions et procédés par les entreprises dans lesquelles des étrangers détiennent des participations de plus de 20 %.

113

- Jusqu'en 1994, le *Stock d'investissement direct étranger* est défini comme le stock de capital et s'appuie sur les bilans actuels des filiales, compte tenu de la participation en capital de l'investisseur. A partir de 1995, il est défini comme l'investissement direct primaire en capital plus les prêts accordés par les actionnaires étrangers et par les autres firmes affiliées à l'étranger.

- Le *Capital sous influence étrangère* est défini comme l'investissement direct primaire en capital, à l'exclusion des prêts.

Ventilation géographique

Le pays de l'investisseur est le pays où s'exerce le contrôle immédiat.

Les données sont traitées séparément pour chaque pays investisseur. C'est pourquoi les doubles comptages ne sont pas éliminés dans tous les tableaux pour des raisons de cohérence, c'est-à-dire que dans le cas d'intérêts majoritaires impliquant plusieurs pays, les variables sont attribuées pleinement à chacun.

HUNGARY

Sources and Methods

HONGRIE

Sources et méthodes

Table 1. HUNGARY / HONGRIE

NUMBER OF ENTERPRISES / NOMBRE D'ENTREPRISES

By industry (ISIC Rev. 3)	FOREIGN AFFILIATES (Units)					AS A % OF NATIONAL TOTAL				
	1993	1994	1995	1996	1997	1993	1994	1995	1996	1997
10/14 Mining & quarrying	54	55	69	77	82	25.8	25.7	27.6	26.6	25.9
15/37 TOTAL MANUFACTURING	**3 828**	**3 992**	**4 195**	**4 312**	**4 363**	**14.9**	**14.2**	**13.9**	**12.8**	**12.4**
15/16 Food, beverages, tobacco	493	537	577	544	530	15.7	15.4	15.6	14.0	13.4
17/19 Textiles, clothing, leather, footwear	492	518	559	601	613	15.9	15.5	15.6	15.2	15.0
20/22 Wood and paper products	656	680	751	744	756	13.2	12.0	11.8	10.1	9.4
20 Wood products	..	..	..	..	..	..	..	..	..	..
21/22 Paper, printing and publishing	..	..	..	..	..	..	..	..	..	..
23/25 Chemicals, Total	393	392	393	402	421	20.8	19.7	18.8	18.0	18.1
23 Refined petroleum, nuclear fuel	..	..	..	4	..	..	..	..	..	..
24/25 Chemicals, rubber & plastics prod.	..	..	..	398	..	..	..	..	..	..
24 Chemical products	..	..	..	162	..	..	..	..	..	..
2423 Pharmaceuticals	..	..	..	31	..	..	..	..	..	..
25 Rubber and plastics products	..	..	..	236	..	..	..	..	..	..
26 Non-metallic mineral products	170	174	170	178	191	21.7	19.9	18.4	17.0	17.4
27/28 Basic & fabricated metals	434	452	479	518	533	12.5	12.0	11.9	11.6	11.7
27 Basic metals	..	..	..	52	..	..	..	..	..	..
28 Fabricated metal products	..	..	..	466	..	..	..	..	..	..
29/32 Machinery, Total	..	..	..	841	..	..	..	..	..	..
29/30 Non-electrical machinery	..	..	..	544	..	..	..	..	..	..
29 Non-electrical machinery nec	..	..	..	509	..	..	..	..	..	..
30 Office and computing machinery	..	..	..	35	..	..	..	..	..	..
31/32 Electrical & electronic equipment	..	..	..	297	..	..	..	..	..	..
31 Electrical machinery nec	..	..	..	153	..	..	..	..	..	..
32 Radio, TV & communications eq.	..	..	..	144	..	..	..	..	..	..
33 Scientific instruments	..	..	..	171	..	..	..	..	..	..
34/35 Transportation equipment	..	..	..	108	..	..	..	..	..	..
34 Motor vehicles	..	..	..	73	..	..	..	..	..	..
35 Other transport equipment	..	..	..	35	..	..	..	..	..	..
351 Shipbuilding & repairing	..	..	..	15	..	..	..	..	..	..
353 Aircraft and spacecraft	..	..	..	5	..	..	..	..	..	..
36/37 Other manufacturing	184	189	199	204	193	13.7	12.4	12.0	10.7	9.7
40/45 Construction, electricity, gas & water	1 108	1 199	1 254	1 261	1 221	8.5	8.0	7.7	6.9	6.2
50/55 Trade, repair, hotels & restaurants	10 940	12 517	13 347	13 897	13 933	19.9	19.1	18.5	17.2	16.9
65/74 Finance, insurance, business services	3 027	3 422	3 734	4 041	4 355	9.8	8.8	8.6	7.6	8.2
OTHER ACTIVITIES	2 042	2 372	2 497	2 542	2 573	12.0	10.1	8.4	7.0	6.8
01/99 GRAND TOTAL	**20 999**	**23 557**	**25 096**	**26 130**	**26 527**	**14.8**	**13.8**	**13.1**	**11.8**	**11.6**

Grand total by investing country						As a % of grand total by foreign affiliates				
All countries	20 999	23 557	25 096	26 130	26 527	100.0	100.0	100.0	100.0	100.0
United States	..	..	..	..	..	..	..	..	..	..
Canada	..	..	..	..	..	..	..	..	..	..
Mexico	..	..	..	..	..	..	..	..	..	..
Japan	..	..	..	..	..	..	..	..	..	..
Europe	..	..	..	..	..	..	..	..	..	..
European Union (15)	..	..	..	..	..	..	..	..	..	..
Belgium	..	..	..	..	..	..	..	..	..	..
France	..	..	..	..	..	..	..	..	..	..
Germany	..	..	..	..	..	..	..	..	..	..
Italy	..	..	..	..	..	..	..	..	..	..
Netherlands	..	..	..	..	..	..	..	..	..	..
Spain	..	..	..	..	..	..	..	..	..	..
Sweden	..	..	..	..	..	..	..	..	..	..
United Kingdom	..	..	..	..	..	..	..	..	..	..
Switzerland	..	..	..	..	..	..	..	..	..	..
Australia and New Zealand	..	..	..	..	..	..	..	..	..	..
Asia (non-OECD)	..	..	..	..	..	..	..	..	..	..
Latin America	..	..	..	..	..	..	..	..	..	..

Note: All foreign-owned firms (over 10% of capital share).
Toutes les firmes sous contrôle étranger (plus de 10% du capital détenu par l'étranger).

Table 2. HUNGARY / HONGRIE

NUMBER OF EMPLOYEES / NOMBRE DE SALARIÉS

By industry (ISIC Rev. 3)		FOREIGN AFFILIATES (Units)					AS A % OF NATIONAL TOTAL				
		1993	1994	1995	1996	1997	1993	1994	1995	1996	1997
10/14	Mining & quarrying	2 825	2 635	2 483	5 589	5 168	11.6	13.4	14.0	33.8	38.7
15/37	TOTAL MANUFACTURING	234 425	265 970	288 294	297 448	336 603	30.6	35.3	37.4	35.6	42.8
15/16	Food, beverages, tobacco	55 992	58 870	60 927	52 198	52 367	36.0	38.3	40.8	34.7	38.1
17/19	Textiles, clothing, leather, footwear	35 510	36 578	43 031	43 694	51 784	27.4	29.6	32.6	30.3	36.8
20/22	Wood and paper products	16 779	16 785	18 029	17 950	19 125	25.5	24.1	26.7	27.2	29.2
20	Wood products	..	..	..	..	..	..	..	..	..	..
21/22	Paper, printing and publishing	..	..	..	..	..	..	..	..	..	..
23/25	Chemicals, Total	28 218	49 370	49 986	57 385	56 936	31.1	53.2	55.1	63.5	64.0
23	Refined petroleum, nuclear fuel	..	..	..	..	..	..	..	..	..	..
24/25	Chemicals, rubber & plastics prod.	..	..	..	..	..	..	..	..	..	..
24	Chemical products	..	..	..	..	..	..	..	..	..	..
2423	Pharmaceuticals	..	..	..	..	..	..	..	..	..	..
25	Rubber and plastics products	..	..	..	..	..	..	..	..	..	..
26	Non-metallic mineral products	12 997	12 228	16 609	14 983	15 961	40.0	40.0	46.7	42.8	46.3
27/28	Basic & fabricated metals	15 766	17 285	18 959	20 157	23 409	19.6	21.7	21.2	22.7	27.2
27	Basic metals	..	..	..	..	..	..	..	..	..	..
28	Fabricated metal products	..	..	..	..	..	..	..	..	..	..
29/32	Machinery, Total	..	..	..	..	..	..	..	..	..	..
29/30	Non-electrical machinery	..	..	..	..	..	..	..	..	..	..
29	Non-electrical machinery nec	..	..	..	..	..	..	..	..	..	..
30	Office and computing machinery	..	..	..	..	..	..	..	..	..	..
31/32	Electrical & electronic equipment	..	..	..	..	..	..	..	..	..	..
31	Electrical machinery nec	..	..	..	..	..	..	..	..	..	..
32	Radio, TV & communications eq.	..	..	..	..	..	..	..	..	..	..
33	Scientific instruments	..	..	..	..	..	..	..	..	..	..
34/35	Transportation equipment	..	..	..	..	..	..	..	..	..	..
34	Motor vehicles	..	..	..	..	..	..	..	..	..	..
35	Other transport equipment	..	..	..	..	..	..	..	..	..	..
351	Shipbuilding & repairing	..	..	..	..	..	..	..	..	..	..
353	Aircraft and spacecraft	..	..	..	..	..	..	..	..	..	..
36/37	Other manufacturing	5 738	6 383	6 194	6 116	6 322	20.5	23.7	22.9	21.3	23.3
40/45	Construction, electricity, gas & water	25 840	24 964	56 364	52 360	52 389	10.1	9.7	22.8	22.7	23.5
50/55	Trade, repair, hotels & restaurants	82 270	123 310	88 249	86 647	92 761	21.1	21.6	22.1	20.5	22.8
65/74	Finance, insurance, business services	18 786	21 112	21 513	28 129	29 769	14.2	13.0	14.0	15.1	16.9
	OTHER ACTIVITIES	41 503	45 350	44 910	45 958	48 960	7.6	7.9	8.9	9.3	10.2
01/99	GRAND TOTAL	405 649	483 341	501 813	516 131	565 650	19.2	21.9	24.0	23.6	27.1

Grand total by investing country	1993	1994	1995	1996	1997	As a % of grand total by foreign affiliates				
All countries	405 649	483 341	501 813	516 131	565 650	100.0	100.0	100.0	100.0	100.0
United States	..	..	..	..	..	..	..	..	..	..
Canada	..	..	..	..	..	..	..	..	..	..
Mexico	..	..	..	..	..	..	..	..	..	..
Japan	..	..	..	..	..	..	..	..	..	..
Europe	..	..	..	..	..	..	..	..	..	..
European Union (15)	..	..	..	..	..	..	..	..	..	..
Belgium	..	..	..	..	..	..	..	..	..	..
France	..	..	..	..	..	..	..	..	..	..
Germany	..	..	..	..	..	..	..	..	..	..
Italy	..	..	..	..	..	..	..	..	..	..
Netherlands	..	..	..	..	..	..	..	..	..	..
Spain	..	..	..	..	..	..	..	..	..	..
Sweden	..	..	..	..	..	..	..	..	..	..
United Kingdom	..	..	..	..	..	..	..	..	..	..
Switzerland	..	..	..	..	..	..	..	..	..	..
Australia and New Zealand	..	..	..	..	..	..	..	..	..	..
Asia (non-OECD)	..	..	..	..	..	..	..	..	..	..
Latin America	..	..	..	..	..	..	..	..	..	..

Note: All foreign-owned firms (over 10% of capital share). *Financial intermediation* (ISIC 65 to 67) is excluded.
Toutes les firmes sous contrôle étranger (plus de 10% du capital détenu par l'étranger). Les *Activités financières* (CITI 65 à 67) sont exclues.

Table 4. HUNGARY / HONGRIE

TURNOVER / CHIFFRE D'AFFAIRES

By industry (ISIC Rev. 3)	FOREIGN AFFILIATES (Billions of Ft)					AS A % OF NATIONAL TOTAL				
	1993	1994	1995	1996	1997	1993	1994	1995	1996	1997
10/14 Mining & quarrying	6	11	14	28	41	12.1	24.9	27.2	43.5	54.1
15/37 TOTAL MANUFACTURING	**886**	**1 537**	**2 244**	**3 142**	**4 478**	**40.2**	**54.0**	**56.6**	**62.4**	**66.7**
15/16 Food, beverages, tobacco	289	388	537	641	743	49.2	49.3	52.9	51.4	51.7
17/19 Textiles, clothing, leather, footwear	49	62	89	108	142	36.2	40.9	45.1	45.3	47.9
20/22 Wood and paper products	79	106	159	258	249	43.3	44.2	48.2	65.9	51.9
20 Wood products	..	..	..	..	..	..	..	..	..	..
21/22 Paper, printing and publishing	..	..	..	..	..	..	..	..	..	..
23/25 Chemicals, Total	144	479	633	935	1 213	27.1	73.0	71.3	83.6	85.0
23 Refined petroleum, nuclear fuel	..	..	..	..	..	..	..	..	..	..
24/25 Chemicals, rubber & plastics prod.	..	..	..	..	..	..	..	..	..	..
24 Chemical products	..	..	..	..	..	..	..	..	..	..
2423 Pharmaceuticals	..	..	..	..	..	..	..	..	..	..
25 Rubber and plastics products	..	..	..	..	..	..	..	..	..	..
26 Non-metallic mineral products	39	57	82	102	139	52.5	58.1	58.2	65.0	69.0
27/28 Basic & fabricated metals	65	102	145	162	228	29.1	35.2	32.4	34.7	36.4
27 Basic metals	..	..	..	..	..	..	..	..	..	..
28 Fabricated metal products	..	..	..	..	..	..	..	..	..	..
29/32 Machinery, Total	..	..	..	..	..	..	..	..	..	..
29/30 Non-electrical machinery	..	..	..	..	..	..	..	..	..	..
29 Non-electrical machinery nec	..	..	..	..	..	..	..	..	..	..
30 Office and computing machinery	..	..	..	..	..	..	..	..	..	..
31/32 Electrical & electronic equipment	..	..	..	..	..	..	..	..	..	..
31 Electrical machinery nec	..	..	..	..	..	..	..	..	..	..
32 Radio, TV & communications eq.	..	..	..	..	..	..	..	..	..	..
33 Scientific instruments	..	..	..	..	..	..	..	..	..	..
34/35 Transportation equipment	..	..	..	..	..	..	..	..	..	..
34 Motor vehicles	..	..	..	..	..	..	..	..	..	..
35 Other transport equipment	..	..	..	..	..	..	..	..	..	..
351 Shipbuilding & repairing	..	..	..	..	..	..	..	..	..	..
353 Aircraft and spacecraft	..	..	..	..	..	..	..	..	..	..
36/37 Other manufacturing	11	15	22	26	30	24.8	29.2	34.3	33.0	30.3
40/45 Construction, electricity, gas & water	105	164	487	680	977	12.1	15.4	37.0	40.6	44.8
50/55 Trade, repair, hotels & restaurants	798	1 079	1 447	1 933	2 442	32.1	33.5	35.2	37.2	39.2
65/74 Finance, insurance, business services	128	134	197	266	491	29.8	23.8	26.3	26.8	35.3
OTHER ACTIVITIES	193	267	367	523	689	22.2	23.2	24.4	27.1	28.6
01/99 GRAND TOTAL	**2 116**	**3 192**	**4 756**	**6 573**	**9 117**	**30.6**	**35.9**	**40.7**	**44.1**	**48.0**

Grand total by investing country						As a % of grand total by foreign affiliates				
All countries	2 116	3 192	4 756	6 573	9 117	100.0	100.0	100.0	100.0	100.0
United States	..	..	..	..	..	..	..	..	..	..
Canada	..	..	..	..	..	..	..	..	..	..
Mexico	..	..	..	..	..	..	..	..	..	..
Japan	..	..	..	..	..	..	..	..	..	..
Europe	..	..	..	..	..	..	..	..	..	..
European Union (15)	..	..	..	..	..	..	..	..	..	..
Belgium	..	..	..	..	..	..	..	..	..	..
France	..	..	..	..	..	..	..	..	..	..
Germany	..	..	..	..	..	..	..	..	..	..
Italy	..	..	..	..	..	..	..	..	..	..
Netherlands	..	..	..	..	..	..	..	..	..	..
Spain	..	..	..	..	..	..	..	..	..	..
Sweden	..	..	..	..	..	..	..	..	..	..
United Kingdom	..	..	..	..	..	..	..	..	..	..
Switzerland	..	..	..	..	..	..	..	..	..	..
Australia and New Zealand	..	..	..	..	..	..	..	..	..	..
Asia (non-OECD)	..	..	..	..	..	..	..	..	..	..
Latin America	..	..	..	..	..	..	..	..	..	..

Note: All foreign-owned firms (over 10% of capital share).
Toutes les firmes sous contrôle étranger (plus de 10% du capital détenu par l'étranger).

Table 5. HUNGARY / HONGRIE

VALUE ADDED / VALEUR AJOUTÉE

By industry (ISIC Rev. 3)	FOREIGN AFFILIATES (Billions of Ft)					AS A % OF NATIONAL TOTAL				
	1993	1994	1995	1996	1997	1993	1994	1995	1996	1997
10/14 Mining & quarrying	..	..	..	9	16	..	..	..	..	51.6
15/37 TOTAL MANUFACTURING	**242**	..	..	**790**	**1 140**	**40.6**	..	..	..	**68.3**
15/16 Food, beverages, tobacco	..	..	..	122	154	..	..	..	..	58.8
17/19 Textiles, clothing, leather, footwear	..	..	..	42	58	..	..	..	..	50.4
20/22 Wood and paper products	..	..	..	46	67	..	..	..	..	52.8
20 Wood products	..	..	..	..	..	..	..	..	..	..
21/22 Paper, printing and publishing	..	..	..	..	..	..	..	..	..	..
23/25 Chemicals, Total	..	..	..	287	351	..	..	..	..	87.3
23 Refined petroleum, nuclear fuel	..	..	..	..	..	..	..	..	..	..
24/25 Chemicals, rubber & plastics prod.	..	..	..	..	..	..	..	..	..	..
24 Chemical products	..	..	..	..	..	..	..	..	..	..
2423 Pharmaceuticals	..	..	..	..	..	..	..	..	..	..
25 Rubber and plastics products	..	..	..	..	..	..	..	..	..	..
26 Non-metallic mineral products	..	..	..	38	51	..	..	..	..	69.9
27/28 Basic & fabricated metals	..	..	..	35	54	..	..	..	..	39.1
27 Basic metals	..	..	..	..	..	..	..	..	..	..
28 Fabricated metal products	..	..	..	..	..	..	..	..	..	..
29/32 Machinery, Total	..	..	..	..	..	..	..	..	..	..
29/30 Non-electrical machinery	..	..	..	..	..	..	..	..	..	..
29 Non-electrical machinery nec	..	..	..	..	..	..	..	..	..	..
30 Office and computing machinery	..	..	..	..	..	..	..	..	..	..
31/32 Electrical & electronic equipment	..	..	..	..	..	..	..	..	..	..
31 Electrical machinery nec	..	..	..	..	..	..	..	..	..	..
32 Radio, TV & communications eq.	..	..	..	..	..	..	..	..	..	..
33 Scientific instruments	..	..	..	..	..	..	..	..	..	..
34/35 Transportation equipment	..	..	..	..	..	..	..	..	..	..
34 Motor vehicles	..	..	..	..	..	..	..	..	..	..
35 Other transport equipment	..	..	..	..	..	..	..	..	..	..
351 Shipbuilding & repairing	..	..	..	..	..	..	..	..	..	..
353 Aircraft and spacecraft	..	..	..	..	..	..	..	..	..	..
36/37 Other manufacturing	..	..	..	7	10	..	..	..	..	38.5
40/45 Construction, electricity, gas & water	..	..	..	121	207	..	..	..	..	42.7
50/55 Trade, repair, hotels & restaurants	..	..	..	190	270	..	..	..	..	40.7
65/74 Finance, insurance, business services	..	..	..	65	108	..	..	..	..	26.5
OTHER ACTIVITIES	..	..	..	180	269	..	..	..	..	32.3
01/99 GRAND TOTAL	**448**	**732**	**999**	**1 354**	**2 009**	**30.4**	**33.2**	**38.6**	**42.7**	**49.1**

Grand total by investing country						As a % of grand total by foreign affiliates				
All countries	448	732	999	1 354	2 009	100.0	100.0	100.0	100.0	100.0
United States	..	..	..	..	..	..	..	..	..	..
Canada	..	..	..	..	..	..	..	..	..	..
Mexico	..	..	..	..	..	..	..	..	..	..
Japan	..	..	..	..	..	..	..	..	..	..
Europe	..	..	..	..	..	..	..	..	..	..
European Union (15)	..	..	..	..	..	..	..	..	..	..
Belgium	..	..	..	..	..	..	..	..	..	..
France	..	..	..	..	..	..	..	..	..	..
Germany	..	..	..	..	..	..	..	..	..	..
Italy	..	..	..	..	..	..	..	..	..	..
Netherlands	..	..	..	..	..	..	..	..	..	..
Spain	..	..	..	..	..	..	..	..	..	..
Sweden	..	..	..	..	..	..	..	..	..	..
United Kingdom	..	..	..	..	..	..	..	..	..	..
Switzerland	..	..	..	..	..	..	..	..	..	..
Australia and New Zealand	..	..	..	..	..	..	..	..	..	..
Asia (non-OECD)	..	..	..	..	..	..	..	..	..	..
Latin America	..	..	..	..	..	..	..	..	..	..

Note: All foreign-owned firms (over 10% of capital share).
Toutes les firmes sous contrôle étranger (plus de 10% du capital détenu par l'étranger).

Table 6. HUNGARY / HONGRIE

WAGES AND SALARIES / SALAIRES ET TRAITEMENTS

By industry (ISIC Rev. 3)		FOREIGN AFFILIATES (Billions of Ft)					AS A % OF NATIONAL TOTAL				
		1993	1994	1995	1996	1997	1993	1994	1995	1996	1997
10/14	Mining & quarrying	1 239	1 424	1 618	6 037	5 968	7.6	12.1	12.4	38.0	41.6
15/37	**TOTAL MANUFACTURING**	**104 183**	**146 780**	**184 191**	**235 536**	**324 973**	**36.7**	**42.8**	**46.8**	**50.8**	**56.5**
15/16	Food, beverages, tobacco	24 254	31 189	37 826	43 243	50 142	44.4	45.5	50.4	49.3	51.7
17/19	Textiles, clothing, leather, footwear	10 849	12 795	16 145	20 677	28 544	33.0	33.9	38.8	41.1	46.6
20/22	Wood and paper products	10 579	12 226	15 055	17 757	22 529	36.5	35.2	40.1	42.7	46.5
20	Wood products	..	..	..	..	..	..	..	..	..	..
21/22	Paper, printing and publishing	..	..	..	..	..	..	..	..	..	..
23/25	Chemicals, Total	15 252	36 007	44 143	55 252	77 828	33.1	63.2	66.2	75.6	78.5
23	Refined petroleum, nuclear fuel	..	..	..	..	..	..	..	..	..	..
24/25	Chemicals, rubber & plastics prod.	..	..	..	..	..	..	..	..	..	..
24	Chemical products	..	..	..	..	..	..	..	..	..	..
2423	Pharmaceuticals	..	..	..	..	..	..	..	..	..	..
25	Rubber and plastics products	..	..	..	..	..	..	..	..	..	..
26	Non-metallic mineral products	5 362	6 721	9 940	11 993	15 609	42.4	45.0	54.4	54.9	59.8
27/28	Basic & fabricated metals	7 000	9 207	12 171	15 451	21 792	23.6	24.8	25.9	30.0	34.2
27	Basic metals	..	..	..	..	..	..	..	..	..	..
28	Fabricated metal products	..	..	..	..	..	..	..	..	..	..
29/32	Machinery, Total	..	..	..	..	..	..	..	..	..	..
29/30	Non-electrical machinery	..	..	..	..	..	..	..	..	..	..
29	Non-electrical machinery nec	..	..	..	..	..	..	..	..	..	..
30	Office and computing machinery	..	..	..	..	..	..	..	..	..	..
31/32	Electrical & electronic equipment	..	..	..	..	..	..	..	..	..	..
31	Electrical machinery nec	..	..	..	..	..	..	..	..	..	..
32	Radio, TV & communications eq.	..	..	..	..	..	..	..	..	..	..
33	Scientific instruments	..	..	..	..	..	..	..	..	..	..
34/35	Transportation equipment	..	..	..	..	..	..	..	..	..	..
34	Motor vehicles	..	..	..	..	..	..	..	..	..	..
35	Other transport equipment	..	..	..	..	..	..	..	..	..	..
351	Shipbuilding & repairing	..	..	..	..	..	..	..	..	..	..
353	Aircraft and spacecraft	..	..	..	..	..	..	..	..	..	..
36/37	Other manufacturing	1 859	2 397	2 841	3 475	4 140	23.6	26.3	30.1	30.8	32.6
40/45	Construction, electricity, gas & water	15 667	18 359	42 981	51 771	59 731	12.9	13.8	31.0	33.1	34.3
50/55	Trade, repair, hotels & restaurants	38 320	52 289	58 070	74 237	95 282	26.5	30.2	32.8	34.7	38.3
65/74	Finance, insurance, business services	13 797	16 446	18 576	24 491	36 217	20.6	17.4	21.5	22.5	27.1
	OTHER ACTIVITIES	25 388	31 515	38 839	50 741	66 432	14.6	14.2	15.7	17.6	19.3
01/99	**GRAND TOTAL**	**198 594**	**266 813**	**344 273**	**442 813**	**588 603**	**25.3**	**27.3**	**32.6**	**35.5**	**39.5**

Grand total by investing country						As a % of grand total by foreign affiliates				
All countries	198 594	266 813	344 273	442 813	588 603	100.0	100.0	100.0	100.0	100.0
United States	..	..	..	..	..	..	..	..	..	..
Canada	..	..	..	..	..	..	..	..	..	..
Mexico	..	..	..	..	..	..	..	..	..	..
Japan	..	..	..	..	..	..	..	..	..	..
Europe	..	..	..	..	..	..	..	..	..	..
European Union (15)	..	..	..	..	..	..	..	..	..	..
Belgium	..	..	..	..	..	..	..	..	..	..
France	..	..	..	..	..	..	..	..	..	..
Germany	..	..	..	..	..	..	..	..	..	..
Italy	..	..	..	..	..	..	..	..	..	..
Netherlands	..	..	..	..	..	..	..	..	..	..
Spain	..	..	..	..	..	..	..	..	..	..
Sweden	..	..	..	..	..	..	..	..	..	..
United Kingdom	..	..	..	..	..	..	..	..	..	..
Switzerland	..	..	..	..	..	..	..	..	..	..
Australia and New Zealand	..	..	..	..	..	..	..	..	..	..
Asia (non-OECD)	..	..	..	..	..	..	..	..	..	..
Latin America	..	..	..	..	..	..	..	..	..	..

Note: All foreign-owned firms (over 10% of capital share). *Financial intermediation* (ISIC 65 to 67) is excluded.
Toutes les firmes sous contrôle étranger (plus de 10% du capital détenu par l'étranger). Les *Activités financières* (CITI 65 à 67) sont exclues.

Table 7. HUNGARY / HONGRIE

R&D EXPENDITURE / DÉPENSES DE R-D

By industry (ISIC Rev. 3)	FOREIGN AFFILIATES (Billions of Ft)					AS A % OF NATIONAL TOTAL				
	1993	1994	1995	1996	1997	1993	1994	1995	1996	1997
10/14 Mining & quarrying	..	..	..	..	0.0	..	..	..	..	0.0
15/37 TOTAL MANUFACTURING	..	..	..	..	**15.4**	..	..	..	..	**77.1**
15/16 Food, beverages, tobacco	..	..	..	..	0.2	..	..	..	..	26.3
17/19 Textiles, clothing, leather, footwear	..	..	..	..	0.0	..	..	..	..	49.0
20/22 Wood and paper products	..	..	..	..	0.0	..	..	..	..	11.3
20 Wood products	..	..	..	..	..	..	..	..	..	..
21/22 Paper, printing and publishing	..	..	..	..	..	..	..	..	..	..
23/25 Chemicals, Total	..	..	..	..	11.9	..	..	..	..	85.5
23 Refined petroleum, nuclear fuel	..	..	..	..	..	..	..	..	..	..
24/25 Chemicals, rubber & plastics prod.	..	..	..	..	..	..	..	..	..	..
24 Chemical products	..	..	..	..	..	..	..	..	..	..
2423 Pharmaceuticals	..	..	..	..	..	..	..	..	..	..
25 Rubber and plastics products	..	..	..	..	..	..	..	..	..	..
26 Non-metallic mineral products	..	..	..	..	0.0	..	..	..	..	20.6
27/28 Basic & fabricated metals	..	..	..	..	0.1	..	..	..	..	30.1
27 Basic metals	..	..	..	..	..	..	..	..	..	..
28 Fabricated metal products	..	..	..	..	..	..	..	..	..	..
29/32 Machinery, Total	..	..	..	..	..	..	..	..	..	..
29/30 Non-electrical machinery	..	..	..	..	..	..	..	..	..	..
29 Non-electrical machinery nec	..	..	..	..	..	..	..	..	..	..
30 Office and computing machinery	..	..	..	..	..	..	..	..	..	..
31/32 Electrical & electronic equipment	..	..	..	..	..	..	..	..	..	..
31 Electrical machinery nec	..	..	..	..	..	..	..	..	..	..
32 Radio, TV & communications eq.	..	..	..	..	..	..	..	..	..	..
33 Scientific instruments	..	..	..	..	..	..	..	..	..	..
34/35 Transportation equipment	..	..	..	..	..	..	..	..	..	..
34 Motor vehicles	..	..	..	..	..	..	..	..	..	..
35 Other transport equipment	..	..	..	..	..	..	..	..	..	..
351 Shipbuilding & repairing	..	..	..	..	..	..	..	..	..	..
353 Aircraft and spacecraft	..	..	..	..	..	..	..	..	..	..
36/37 Other manufacturing	..	..	..	..	0.0	..	..	..	..	0.0
40/45 Construction, electricity, gas & water	..	..	..	..	0.1	..	..	..	..	6.5
50/55 Trade, repair, hotels & restaurants	..	..	..	..	0.1	..	..	..	..	71.4
65/74 Finance, insurance, business services	..	..	..	..	0.4	..	..	..	..	32.2
OTHER ACTIVITIES	..	..	..	..	0.8	..	..	..	..	22.0
01/99 GRAND TOTAL	**1.4**	**3.1**	**3.9**	**8.6**	**16.7**	..	**22.6**	**21.8**	**44.4**	**65.3**

Grand total by investing country						As a % of grand total by foreign affiliates				
All countries	1.4	3.1	3.9	8.6	16.7	100.0	100.0	100.0	100.0	100.0
United States	..	..	..	..	..	..	..	..	..	..
Canada	..	..	..	..	..	..	..	..	..	..
Mexico	..	..	..	..	..	..	..	..	..	..
Japan	..	..	..	..	..	..	..	..	..	..
Europe	..	..	..	..	..	..	..	..	..	..
European Union (15)	..	..	..	..	..	..	..	..	..	..
Belgium	..	..	..	..	..	..	..	..	..	..
France	..	..	..	..	..	..	..	..	..	..
Germany	..	..	..	..	..	..	..	..	..	..
Italy	..	..	..	..	..	..	..	..	..	..
Netherlands	..	..	..	..	..	..	..	..	..	..
Spain	..	..	..	..	..	..	..	..	..	..
Sweden	..	..	..	..	..	..	..	..	..	..
United Kingdom	..	..	..	..	..	..	..	..	..	..
Switzerland	..	..	..	..	..	..	..	..	..	..
Australia and New Zealand	..	..	..	..	..	..	..	..	..	..
Asia (non-OECD)	..	..	..	..	..	..	..	..	..	..
Latin America	..	..	..	..	..	..	..	..	..	..

Note: All foreign-owned firms (over 10% of capital share).
Toutes les firmes sous contrôle étranger (plus de 10% du capital détenu par l'étranger).

Table 9. HUNGARY / HONGRIE

GROSS FIXED CAPITAL FORMATION / FORMATION BRUTE DE CAPITAL FIXE

By industry (ISIC Rev. 3)		FOREIGN AFFILIATES (Billions of Ft)					AS A % OF NATIONAL TOTAL				
		1993	1994	1995	1996	1997	1993	1994	1995	1996	1997
10/14	Mining & quarrying	1	1	2	2	3	..	..	..	..	..
15/37	**TOTAL MANUFACTURING**	73	123	173	215	316	..	..	..	..	..
15/16	Food, beverages, tobacco	23	33	42	30	45	..	..	..	..	..
17/19	Textiles, clothing, leather, footwear	4	4	4	4	15	..	..	..	..	..
20/22	Wood and paper products	5	6	6	8	13	..	..	..	..	..
20	Wood products	..	..	..	..	..	..	..	..	..	..
21/22	Paper, printing and publishing	..	..	..	..	..	..	..	..	..	..
23/25	Chemicals, Total	14	47	61	67	99	..	..	..	..	..
23	Refined petroleum, nuclear fuel	..	..	..	..	..	..	..	..	..	..
24/25	Chemicals, rubber & plastics prod.	..	..	..	..	..	..	..	..	..	..
24	Chemical products	..	..	..	..	..	..	..	..	..	..
2423	Pharmaceuticals	..	..	..	..	..	..	..	..	..	..
25	Rubber and plastics products	..	..	..	..	..	..	..	..	..	..
26	Non-metallic mineral products	4	5	9	10	17	..	..	..	..	..
27/28	Basic & fabricated metals	4	6	8	18	20	..	..	..	..	..
27	Basic metals	..	..	..	..	..	..	..	..	..	..
28	Fabricated metal products	..	..	..	..	..	..	..	..	..	..
29/32	Machinery, Total	..	..	..	..	..	..	..	..	..	..
29/30	Non-electrical machinery	..	..	..	..	..	..	..	..	..	..
29	Non-electrical machinery nec	..	..	..	..	..	..	..	..	..	..
30	Office and computing machinery	..	..	..	..	..	..	..	..	..	..
31/32	Electrical & electronic equipment	..	..	..	..	..	..	..	..	..	..
31	Electrical machinery nec	..	..	..	..	..	..	..	..	..	..
32	Radio, TV & communications eq.	..	..	..	..	..	..	..	..	..	..
33	Scientific instruments	..	..	..	..	..	..	..	..	..	..
34/35	Transportation equipment	..	..	..	..	..	..	..	..	..	..
34	Motor vehicles	..	..	..	..	..	..	..	..	..	..
35	Other transport equipment	..	..	..	..	..	..	..	..	..	..
351	Shipbuilding & repairing	..	..	..	..	..	..	..	..	..	..
353	Aircraft and spacecraft	..	..	..	..	..	..	..	..	..	..
36/37	Other manufacturing	2	1	1	1	5	..	..	..	..	..
40/45	Construction, electricity, gas & water	5	7	60	61	73	..	..	..	..	..
50/55	Trade, repair, hotels & restaurants	14	22	25	57	46	..	..	..	..	..
65/74	Finance, insurance, business services	12	14	14	12	12	..	..	..	..	..
	OTHER ACTIVITIES	64	83	100	109	195	..	..	..	..	..
01/99	**GRAND TOTAL**	169	250	374	456	645	34.0	38.0	55.0	54.0	60.0

Grand total by investing country						As a % of grand total by foreign affiliates				
All countries	169	250	402	456	645	100.0	100.0	100.0	100.0	100.0
United States	..	..	..	..	..	..	..	..	..	..
Canada	..	..	..	..	..	..	..	..	..	..
Mexico	..	..	..	..	..	..	..	..	..	..
Japan	..	..	..	..	..	..	..	..	..	..
Europe	..	..	..	..	..	..	..	..	..	..
European Union (15)	..	..	..	..	..	..	..	..	..	..
Belgium	..	..	..	..	..	..	..	..	..	..
France	..	..	..	..	..	..	..	..	..	..
Germany	..	..	..	..	..	..	..	..	..	..
Italy	..	..	..	..	..	..	..	..	..	..
Netherlands	..	..	..	..	..	..	..	..	..	..
Spain	..	..	..	..	..	..	..	..	..	..
Sweden	..	..	..	..	..	..	..	..	..	..
United Kingdom	..	..	..	..	..	..	..	..	..	..
Switzerland	..	..	..	..	..	..	..	..	..	..
Australia and New Zealand	..	..	..	..	..	..	..	..	..	..
Asia (non-OECD)	..	..	..	..	..	..	..	..	..	..
Latin America	..	..	..	..	..	..	..	..	..	..

Note: All foreign-owned firms (over 10% of capital share).
Toutes les firmes sous contrôle étranger (plus de 10% du capital détenu par l'étranger).

Table 10. HUNGARY / HONGRIE

TOTAL EXPORTS / EXPORTATIONS TOTALES

By industry (ISIC Rev. 3)	FOREIGN AFFILIATES (Billions of Ft)					AS A % OF NATIONAL TOTAL				
	1993	1994	1995	1996	1997	1993	1994	1995	1996	1997
10/14 Mining & quarrying	..	..	..	..	..	..	..	..	..	..
15/37 TOTAL MANUFACTURING	**265**	..	..	..	..	..	..	..	..	..
15/16 Food, beverages, tobacco	..	..	..	..	..	..	..	..	..	..
17/19 Textiles, clothing, leather, footwear	..	..	..	..	..	..	..	..	..	..
20/22 Wood and paper products	..	..	..	..	..	..	..	..	..	..
20 Wood products	..	..	..	..	..	..	..	..	..	..
21/22 Paper, printing and publishing	..	..	..	..	..	..	..	..	..	..
23/25 Chemicals, Total	..	..	..	..	..	..	..	..	..	..
23 Refined petroleum, nuclear fuel	..	..	..	..	..	..	..	..	..	..
24/25 Chemicals, rubber & plastics prod.	..	..	..	..	..	..	..	..	..	..
24 Chemical products	..	..	..	..	..	..	..	..	..	..
2423 Pharmaceuticals	..	..	..	..	..	..	..	..	..	..
25 Rubber and plastics products	..	..	..	..	..	..	..	..	..	..
26 Non-metallic mineral products	..	..	..	..	..	..	..	..	..	..
27/28 Basic & fabricated metals	..	..	..	..	..	..	..	..	..	..
27 Basic metals	..	..	..	..	..	..	..	..	..	..
28 Fabricated metal products	..	..	..	..	..	..	..	..	..	..
29/32 Machinery, Total	..	..	..	..	..	..	..	..	..	..
29/30 Non-electrical machinery	..	..	..	..	..	..	..	..	..	..
29 Non-electrical machinery nec	..	..	..	..	..	..	..	..	..	..
30 Office and computing machinery	..	..	..	..	..	..	..	..	..	..
31/32 Electrical & electronic equipment	..	..	..	..	..	..	..	..	..	..
31 Electrical machinery nec	..	..	..	..	..	..	..	..	..	..
32 Radio, TV & communications eq.	..	..	..	..	..	..	..	..	..	..
33 Scientific instruments	..	..	..	..	..	..	..	..	..	..
34/35 Transportation equipment	..	..	..	..	..	..	..	..	..	..
34 Motor vehicles	..	..	..	..	..	..	..	..	..	..
35 Other transport equipment	..	..	..	..	..	..	..	..	..	..
351 Shipbuilding & repairing	..	..	..	..	..	..	..	..	..	..
353 Aircraft and spacecraft	..	..	..	..	..	..	..	..	..	..
36/37 Other manufacturing	..	..	..	..	..	..	..	..	..	..
40/45 Construction, electricity, gas & water	..	..	..	..	..	..	..	..	..	..
50/55 Trade, repair, hotels & restaurants	..	..	..	..	..	..	..	..	..	..
65/74 Finance, insurance, business services	..	..	..	..	..	..	..	..	..	..
OTHER ACTIVITIES	..	..	..	..	..	..	..	..	..	..
01/99 GRAND TOTAL	**357**	**614**	**937**	**1 639**	**2 691**	**43.6**	**54.4**	**57.8**	**68.5**	**75.4**

Grand total by investing country						As a % of grand total by foreign affiliates				
All countries	357	614	937	1 639	2 691	100.0	100.0	100.0	100.0	100.0
United States	15	21	29	46	89	4.2	3.4	3.1	2.8	3.3
Canada	..	..	..	..	6	..	..	..	..	0.2
Mexico	..	..	..	..	1	..	..	..	..	0.0
Japan	..	..	..	..	10	..	..	..	..	0.4
Europe	..	..	..	..	..	..	..	..	..	..
European Union (15)	..	..	603	1 183	1 979	..	..	64.4	72.2	73.5
Belgium	..	..	..	..	58	..	..	..	..	2.1
France	12	21	40	65	103	3.4	3.4	4.2	4.0	3.8
Germany	95	169	272	566	1 085	26.6	27.5	29.0	34.5	40.3
Italy	27	50	78	111	143	7.6	8.1	8.4	6.7	5.3
Netherlands	7	14	28	48	77	2.0	2.3	3.0	2.9	2.9
Spain	..	..	..	..	46	..	..	..	..	1.7
Sweden	..	..	..	..	19	..	..	..	..	0.7
United Kingdom	..	..	..	..	100	..	..	..	..	3.7
Switzerland	7	10	14	21	32	2.0	1.6	1.5	1.3	1.2
Australia and New Zealand	..	..	..	..	3	..	..	..	..	0.1
Asia (non-OECD)	..	..	..	..	..	..	..	..	..	..
Latin America	..	..	..	..	..	..	..	..	..	..

Note: All foreign-owned firms (over 10% of capital share).
Toutes les firmes sous contrôle étranger (plus de 10% du capital détenu par l'étranger).

Table 11. HUNGARY / HONGRIE

TOTAL IMPORTS / IMPORTATIONS TOTALES

By industry (ISIC Rev. 3)	FOREIGN AFFILIATES (Billions of Ft)					AS A % OF NATIONAL TOTAL				
	1993	1994	1995	1996	1997	1993	1994	1995	1996	1997
10/14 Mining & quarrying	..	..	..	..	..	..	..	..	..	..
15/37 TOTAL MANUFACTURING	..	..	..	..	..	..	..	..	..	..
15/16 Food, beverages, tobacco	..	..	..	..	..	..	..	..	..	..
17/19 Textiles, clothing, leather, footwear	..	..	..	..	..	..	..	..	..	..
20/22 Wood and paper products	..	..	..	..	..	..	..	..	..	..
20 Wood products	..	..	..	..	..	..	..	..	..	..
21/22 Paper, printing and publishing	..	..	..	..	..	..	..	..	..	..
23/25 Chemicals, Total	..	..	..	..	..	..	..	..	..	..
23 Refined petroleum, nuclear fuel	..	..	..	..	..	..	..	..	..	..
24/25 Chemicals, rubber & plastics prod.	..	..	..	..	..	..	..	..	..	..
24 Chemical products	..	..	..	..	..	..	..	..	..	..
2423 Pharmaceuticals	..	..	..	..	..	..	..	..	..	..
25 Rubber and plastics products	..	..	..	..	..	..	..	..	..	..
26 Non-metallic mineral products	..	..	..	..	..	..	..	..	..	..
27/28 Basic & fabricated metals	..	..	..	..	..	..	..	..	..	..
27 Basic metals	..	..	..	..	..	..	..	..	..	..
28 Fabricated metal products	..	..	..	..	..	..	..	..	..	..
29/32 Machinery, Total	..	..	..	..	..	..	..	..	..	..
29/30 Non-electrical machinery	..	..	..	..	..	..	..	..	..	..
29 Non-electrical machinery nec	..	..	..	..	..	..	..	..	..	..
30 Office and computing machinery	..	..	..	..	..	..	..	..	..	..
31/32 Electrical & electronic equipment	..	..	..	..	..	..	..	..	..	..
31 Electrical machinery nec	..	..	..	..	..	..	..	..	..	..
32 Radio, TV & communications eq.	..	..	..	..	..	..	..	..	..	..
33 Scientific instruments	..	..	..	..	..	..	..	..	..	..
34/35 Transportation equipment	..	..	..	..	..	..	..	..	..	..
34 Motor vehicles	..	..	..	..	..	..	..	..	..	..
35 Other transport equipment	..	..	..	..	..	..	..	..	..	..
351 Shipbuilding & repairing	..	..	..	..	..	..	..	..	..	..
353 Aircraft and spacecraft	..	..	..	..	..	..	..	..	..	..
36/37 Other manufacturing	..	..	..	..	..	..	..	..	..	..
40/45 Construction, electricity, gas & water	..	..	..	..	..	..	..	..	..	..
50/55 Trade, repair, hotels & restaurants	..	..	..	..	..	..	..	..	..	..
65/74 Finance, insurance, business services	..	..	..	..	..	..	..	..	..	..
OTHER ACTIVITIES	..	..	..	..	..	..	..	..	..	..
01/99 GRAND TOTAL	**515**	**880**	**1 217**	**1 941**	**2 941**	**44.3**	**57.3**	**62.9**	**70.2**	**74.3**

Grand total by investing country						As a % of grand total by foreign affiliates				
All countries	**515**	**880**	**1 217**	**1 941**	**2 941**	**100.0**	**100.0**	**100.0**	**100.0**	**100.0**
United States	30	28	38	60	112	5.8	3.2	3.1	3.1	3.8
Canada	..	..	..	..	13	..	..	..	..	0.4
Mexico	..	..	..	..	12	..	..	..	..	0.4
Japan	..	..	..	..	106	..	..	..	..	3.6
Europe	..	..	..	..	..	..	..	..	..	..
European Union (15)	..	..	759	1 206	1 869	..	..	62.3	62.2	63.5
Belgium	..	..	..	..	51	..	..	..	..	1.7
France	23	34	55	82	136	4.5	3.9	4.5	4.2	4.6
Germany	138	220	292	519	834	26.8	25.0	24.0	26.7	28.4
Italy	37	62	95	129	187	7.2	7.0	7.8	6.6	6.4
Netherlands	17	27	37	46	72	3.3	3.1	3.0	2.4	2.4
Spain	..	..	..	..	39	..	..	..	..	1.3
Sweden	..	..	..	..	39	..	..	..	..	1.3
United Kingdom	..	..	..	..	102	..	..	..	..	3.5
Switzerland	15	22	29	36	49	2.9	2.5	2.4	1.9	1.7
Australia and New Zealand	..	..	..	..	3	..	..	..	..	0.1
Asia (non-OECD)	..	..	..	..	..	..	..	..	..	..
Latin America	..	..	..	..	..	..	..	..	..	..

Note: All foreign-owned firms (over 10% of capital share).
Toutes les firmes sous contrôle étranger (plus de 10% du capital détenu par l'étranger).

Table 17. HUNGARY / HONGRIE

STOCK OF FOREIGN DIRECT INVESTMENT / STOCK D'INVESTISSEMENT DIRECT ÉTRANGER

						FOREIGN AFFILIATES *(Billions of Ft)*					
By industry (ISIC Rev. 3)		**1988**	**1989**	**1990**	**1991**	**1992**	**1993**	**1994**	**1995**	**1996**	**1997**
10/14	Mining & quarrying	..	..	..	..	7	9	9	11	20	23
15/37	**TOTAL MANUFACTURING**	..	..	..	..	**218**	**331**	**405**	**555**	**640**	**805**
15/16	Food, beverages, tobacco	..	..	..	..	78	112	132	157	147	212
17/19	Textiles, clothing, leather, footwear	..	..	..	..	10	14	17	26	32	37
20/22	Wood and paper products	..	..	..	..	15	22	26	38	43	51
20	Wood products	..	..	..	..	..	..	..	..	..	..
21/22	Paper, printing and publishing	..	..	..	..	..	..	..	..	..	..
23/25	Chemicals, Total	..	..	..	..	29	37	54	109	140	170
23	Refined petroleum, nuclear fuel	..	..	..	..	..	..	..	..	31	..
24/25	Chemicals, rubber & plastics prod.	..	..	..	..	..	..	..	..	109	..
24	Chemical products	..	..	..	..	..	..	..	..	80	..
2423	Pharmaceuticals	..	..	..	..	..	..	..	..	34	..
25	Rubber and plastics products	..	..	..	..	..	..	..	..	28	..
26	Non-metallic mineral products	..	..	..	..	19	28	33	41	45	51
27/28	Basic & fabricated metals	..	..	..	..	15	23	26	34	40	60
27	Basic metals	..	..	..	..	..	..	..	..	23	..
28	Fabricated metal products	..	..	..	..	..	..	..	..	18	..
29/32	Machinery, Total	..	..	..	..	..	..	..	..	121	..
29/30	Non-electrical machinery	..	..	..	..	..	..	..	..	34	..
29	Non-electrical machinery nec	..	..	..	..	..	..	..	..	32	..
30	Office and computing machinery	..	..	..	..	..	..	..	..	2	..
31/32	Electrical & electronic equipment	..	..	..	..	..	..	..	..	87	..
31	Electrical machinery nec	..	..	..	..	..	..	..	..	71	..
32	Radio, TV & communications eq.	..	..	..	..	..	..	..	..	16	..
33	Scientific instruments	..	..	..	..	..	..	..	..	8	..
34/35	Transportation equipment	..	..	..	..	..	..	..	..	56	..
34	Motor vehicles	..	..	..	..	..	..	..	..	54	..
35	Other transport equipment	..	..	..	..	..	..	..	..	2	..
351	Shipbuilding & repairing	..	..	..	..	..	..	..	..	0	..
353	Aircraft and spacecraft	..	..	..	..	..	..	..	..	1	..
36/37	Other manufacturing	..	..	..	..	3	5	6	6	7	9
40/45	Construction, electricity, gas & water	..	..	..	..	19	31	43	218	289	332
50/55	Trade, repair, hotels & restaurants	..	..	..	..	70	116	157	189	231	315
65/74	Finance, insurance, business services	..	..	..	..	74	104	146	189	263	387
	OTHER ACTIVITIES	..	..	..	..	14	72	74	143	159	192
01/99	**GRAND TOTAL**	..	..	**93**	**215**	**402**	**663**	**834**	**1 305**	**1 603**	**2 054**

Grand Total by investing country										
All countries	..	..	**93**	**215**	**402**	**663**	**834**	**1 305**	**1 603**	**2 054**
United States	..	..	..	..	46	135	118	209	265	317
Canada	..	..	..	..	2	4	7	8	6	22
Mexico	..	..	..	..	..	..	..	..	..	..
Japan	..	..	..	..	10	17	16	17	25	31
Europe	..	..	..	..	281	452	641	995	1 145	1 577
European Union (15)	..	..	..	..	166	332	435	735	862	1 266
Belgium	..	..	..	..	11	28	32	55	58	88
France	..	..	..	..	19	31	43	106	121	118
Germany	..	..	..	..	69	183	184	322	368	508
Italy	..	..	..	..	12	25	39	49	59	68
Netherlands	..	..	..	..	33	36	92	137	148	297
Spain	..	..	..	..	0	1	1	2	2	2
Sweden	..	..	..	..	4	5	9	9	10	18
United Kingdom	..	..	..	..	18	25	37	50	90	156
Switzerland	..	..	..	..	16	13	32	38	35	55
Australia and New Zealand	..	..	..	..	7	9	1	0	2	0
Asia (non-OECD)	..	..	..	..	4	3	3	26	38	26
Latin America	..	..	..	..	0	..	..	6	5	3

Note: All foreign-owned firms (over 10% of capital share).
Toutes les firmes sous contrôle étranger (plus de 10% du capital détenu par l'étranger).

HUNGARY

Source

The data are prepared by the Financial Statistical Department of the Hungarian Central Statistical Office (HCSO). The annual corporation-tax declarations, the annual investment survey and the external trade data collection of FDI are the most important data sources. In Hungary, all enterprises with legal entity and unincorporated enterprises with more than $500 000 turnover have to submit a detailed corporation-tax declaration. This includes the value of the stock of foreign direct investment and its distribution by industrial sector, but does not provide any information on the country of origin. Therefore, the HCSO organises an annual survey on FDI enterprises. In 1997, the sample included 5 000 enterprises selected on the corporation-tax declarations, covering 88% of the total stocks of FDI. The results are published in *Foreign Direct Investment in Hungary*.

National totals:

- *Number of enterprises*, *Number of employees*, *Turnover*, *Value added*, *Wages and salaries* and *Gross fixed capital formation:* provided by the HCSO and compatible with foreign affiliates' data.

- *Total exports* and *imports:* data come from the *Statistical Handbook of Hungary*.

- *R&D expenditure:* data are extracted from the OECD R&D database.

Industrial classification

For all variables, the data are classified according to the principal industrial activity of the affiliate.

The industrial classification used is the national classification (TEÁOR 92) converted to ISIC Revision 3.

For *Number of employees* and *Wages and salaries*, *Financial intermediation* (ISIC 65/67) is excluded from *Finance, insurance and business services* (65/74).

Variables

- *Number of enterprises* refers to incorporated or unincorporated enterprises with more than 10% foreign capital share which submitted a corporation-tax declaration.

- *Number of employees:* the number of persons in a legal work relationship exceeding five working days with the employer.

- *Gross fixed capital formation* consists of the value of outlays which change or extend the stock of fixed assets. Non-deductible VAT is included.

Geographical breakdown

The breakdown by country of origin is only available for the variables *Total exports* and *imports* and *Stock of foreign direct investment*. The breakdown is for the *Grand total* (all activities) and not for *Total manufacturing* as is the case for other countries. The investor's country is the country of the immediate controller.

HONGRIE

Source

Les données émanent du Département des statistiques financières de l'office central des statistiques hongrois (HCSO). Les déclarations fiscales annuelles des entreprises, l'enquête annuelle sur les investissements et la collecte des données du commerce extérieur sont les principales sources de données. En Hongrie, toutes les entreprises ayant un statut légal ainsi que les entreprises individuelles présentant un chiffre d'affaires annuel supérieur à 500 000 dollars des États-Unis sont tenues d'établir des déclarations fiscales détaillées. Celles-ci comprennent la valeur du capital et sa répartition par secteur industriel, mais ne fournissent aucune information relative au pays d'origine. En conséquence, le HCSO mène une enquête annuelle auprès des entreprises concernées par l'investissement direct. En 1997, l'échantillon comprenait 5 000 entreprises sélectionnées sur la base des déclarations fiscales, couvrant plus de 88 % du total de l'encours de l'IDE. Les résultats sont publiés dans *Foreign Direct Investment in Hungary*.

Totaux nationaux :

- *Nombre d'entreprises, Nombre de salariés, Chiffre d'affaires, Valeur ajoutée, Salaires* et *Formation brute de capital fixe* : fournis par le HCSO et compatibles avec les données relatives aux filiales étrangères.

- *Exportations* et *Importations totales* : les données proviennent de la publication *Statistical Handbook of Hungary*.

- *Dépenses de R-D* : les données sont extraites de la base de données R-D de l'OCDE.

Classification industrielle

Pour toutes les variables, les données sont classées selon l'activité industrielle principale de l'entreprise affiliée.

La classification industrielle utilisée est la classification nationale (TEÁOR 92) adaptée pour correspondre à la CITI révision 3.

Pour les variables *Nombre de salariés* et *Salaires*, les *Activités financières* (CITI 65/67) ne sont pas comprises dans *Finance, assurance et services aux entreprises* (65/74).

Variables

- Le *Nombre d'entreprises* fait référence aux sociétés et entreprises individuelles dont plus de 10 % du capital est détenu par l'étranger et ayant rempli une déclaration fiscale.

- Le *Nombre de salariés* est le nombre de personnes ayant un contrat de travail légal de plus de cinq jours avec l'employeur. Il est exprimé en équivalent plein-temps.

- La *Formation brute de capital fixe* consiste dans la valeur des dépenses effectuées pour modifier ou acquérir le stock d'actifs fixes. La TVA non déductible est incluse.

Ventilation géographique

La ventilation par pays d'origine est seulement disponible pour les variables *Exportations* et *Importations totales* et *Stock d'investissement direct étranger*. La ventilation concerne le *Total général* (toutes activités) et non le *Total manufacturier* comme pour les autres pays. Le pays investisseur est celui où se situe le contrôle immédiat.

IRELAND

IRLANDE

Table 1. IRELAND / IRLANDE

NUMBER OF ESTABLISHMENTS / NOMBRE D'ÉTABLISSEMENTS

By industry (ISIC Rev. 3)	FOREIGN AFFILIATES (Units)					AS A % OF NATIONAL TOTAL				
	1992	1993	1994	1995	1996	1992	1993	1994	1995	1996
10/14 Mining & quarrying	..	..	..	..	..	..	..	..	..	..
15/37 TOTAL MANUFACTURING	**720**	**690**	**726**	**725**	**728**	**15.9**	**15.2**	**15.8**	**15.7**	**15.8**
15/16 Food, beverages, tobacco	72	69	89	86	85	9.0	8.8	11.1	10.3	10.2
17/19 Textiles, clothing, leather, footwear	82	74	71	64	62	17.6	16.2	15.9	15.2	15.5
20/22 Wood and paper products	40	37	45	54	52	5.5	4.9	5.9	7.2	6.9
20 Wood products	6	5	7	7	7	2.6	2.3	3.3	3.4	3.3
21/22 Paper, printing and publishing	34	32	38	47	45	6.8	6.0	7.0	8.6	8.3
23/25 Chemicals, Total	155	152	161	159	160	33.0	31.9	33.3	33.5	33.5
23 Refined petroleum, nuclear fuel	..	..	..	..	..	..	..	..	..	..
24/25 Chemicals, rubber & plastics prod.	155	152	161	159	160	33.0	31.9	33.3	33.5	33.5
24 Chemical products	101	100	107	110	112	43.5	41.8	43.7	45.3	47.3
2423 Pharmaceuticals	37	40	43	43	41	69.8	65.6	67.2	68.3	65.1
25 Rubber and plastics products	54	52	54	49	48	22.7	21.8	22.7	21.2	19.9
26 Non-metallic mineral products	19	18	14	16	16	6.9	6.4	4.8	5.7	5.7
27/28 Basic & fabricated metals	52	50	53	49	46	9.6	9.2	9.5	9.1	8.6
27 Basic metals	..	..	..	..	..	..	..	..	..	..
28 Fabricated metal products	..	..	..	..	..	..	..	..	..	..
29/32 Machinery, Total	181	175	179	182	187	30.4	29.4	29.5	29.5	29.2
29/30 Non-electrical machinery	98	91	100	98	103	25.1	23.2	24.6	24.0	24.4
29 Non-electrical machinery nec	63	59	64	64	68	19.4	18.2	19.1	19.0	19.3
30 Office and computing machinery	35	32	36	34	35	53.0	46.4	50.7	47.9	50.0
31/32 Electrical & electronic equipment	83	84	79	84	84	40.7	41.4	39.3	40.4	38.4
31 Electrical machinery nec	57	57	52	58	58	38.0	38.0	35.1	37.4	34.9
32 Radio, TV & communications eq.	26	27	27	26	26	48.1	50.9	50.9	49.1	49.1
33 Scientific instruments	71	68	68	69	70	51.8	52.7	51.9	51.1	50.4
34/35 Transportation equipment	19	20	19	18	21	12.8	14.1	13.7	12.2	14.7
34 Motor vehicles	9	9	9	9	11	8.7	9.6	9.8	9.1	11.6
35 Other transport equipment	10	11	10	9	10	21.7	22.9	21.3	18.8	20.8
351 Shipbuilding & repairing	..	..	..	..	..	..	..	..	..	..
353 Aircraft and spacecraft	..	..	..	..	..	..	..	..	..	..
36/37 Other manufacturing	29	27	27	28	29	7.8	7.1	7.0	7.0	7.3
40/45 Construction, electricity, gas & water	..	..	..	..	..	..	..	..	..	..
50/55 Trade, repair, hotels & restaurants	..	..	..	..	..	..	..	..	..	..
65/74 Finance, insurance, business services	..	..	..	..	..	..	..	..	..	..
OTHER ACTIVITIES	..	..	..	..	..	..	..	..	..	..
01/99 GRAND TOTAL	..	..	..	..	..	..	..	..	..	..

Total manufacturing by investing country						*As a % of total manufacturing by foreign affiliates*				
All countries	**720**	**690**	**726**	**725**	**728**	**100.0**	**100.0**	**100.0**	**100.0**	**100.0**
United States	266	267	285	289	286	36.9	38.7	39.3	39.9	39.3
Canada	13	12	13	13	17	1.8	1.7	1.8	1.8	2.3
Mexico	..	..	..	..	..	..	..	..	..	..
Japan	18	19	19	21	23	2.5	2.8	2.6	2.9	3.2
Europe	..	..	..	..	..	..	..	..	..	..
European Union (15)	340	318	328	346	344	47.2	46.1	45.2	47.7	47.3
Belgium	12	11	10	11	11	1.7	1.6	1.4	1.5	1.5
France	37	31	35	36	33	5.1	4.5	4.8	5.0	4.5
Germany	108	100	97	99	98	15.0	14.5	13.4	13.7	13.5
Italy	..	..	..	..	..	..	..	..	..	..
Netherlands	39	41	41	41	42	5.4	5.9	5.6	5.7	5.8
Spain	..	..	..	..	..	..	..	..	..	..
Sweden	16	12	13	13	14	2.2	1.7	1.8	1.8	1.9
United Kingdom	121	112	124	117	117	16.8	16.2	17.1	16.1	16.1
Switzerland	29	30	29	29	31	4.0	4.3	4.0	4.0	4.3
Australia and New Zealand	..	..	..	..	..	..	..	..	..	..
Asia (non-OECD)	..	..	..	..	..	..	..	..	..	..
Latin America	..	..	..	..	..	..	..	..	..	..

Note: Majority foreign-owned establishments. ISIC 23/25 excludes *Refined petroleum products* (232) which is included in ISIC 36/37.
Etablissements sous contrôle étranger majoritaire. La CITI 23/25 exclut les *Produits pétroliers raffinés* (232), qui sont compris dans la CITI 36/37.

Table 2. IRELAND / IRLANDE

NUMBER OF EMPLOYEES / NOMBRE DE SALARIÉS

By industry (ISIC Rev. 3)		FOREIGN AFFILIATES (Units)					AS A % OF NATIONAL TOTAL				
		1992	1993	1994	1995	1996	1992	1993	1994	1995	1996
10/14	Mining & quarrying	..	..	..	..	..	..	..	..	..	..
15/37	**TOTAL MANUFACTURING**	**87 572**	**88 836**	**95 715**	**103 864**	**106 410**	**44.0**	**44.4**	**46.6**	**47.1**	**47.0**
15/16	Food, beverages, tobacco	11 963	11 969	12 806	12 535	12 673	26.7	26.8	28.9	27.5	27.3
17/19	Textiles, clothing, leather, footwear	9 547	9 314	9 753	9 257	8 472	43.8	44.9	46.6	45.2	44.7
20/22	Wood and paper products	3 927	3 587	4 878	6 136	6 754	18.2	16.1	21.1	24.9	26.7
20	Wood products	480	446	574	615	617	11.3	10.8	14.0	13.7	13.4
21/22	Paper, printing and publishing	3 447	3 141	4 304	5 521	6 137	19.9	17.3	22.6	27.5	29.6
23/25	Chemicals, Total	16 488	16 949	18 485	19 269	20 635	69.4	68.4	70.3	69.6	69.2
23	Refined petroleum, nuclear fuel	..	..	..	..	..	..	..	..	..	..
24/25	Chemicals, rubber & plastics prod.	16 488	16 949	18 485	19 269	20 635	69.4	68.4	70.3	69.6	69.2
24	Chemical products	12 022	12 413	13 793	14 391	15 560	78.5	76.2	79.0	79.3	80.0
2423	Pharmaceuticals	3 368	3 721	4 534	4 801	5 345	81.0	76.3	82.8	82.3	82.4
25	Rubber and plastics products	4 466	4 536	4 692	4 878	5 075	53.0	53.3	53.0	51.1	49.0
26	Non-metallic mineral products	1 754	1 543	979	1 406	1 457	18.3	16.8	10.6	14.9	15.2
27/28	Basic & fabricated metals	3 385	3 318	3 322	3 252	3 356	27.0	27.1	26.6	25.4	24.3
27	Basic metals	..	..	..	..	..	..	..	..	..	..
28	Fabricated metal products	..	..	..	..	..	..	..	..	..	..
29/32	Machinery, Total	25 491	26 643	29 231	34 897	35 414	70.0	70.6	71.1	72.3	71.0
29/30	Non-electrical machinery	13 642	14 039	15 838	19 709	20 381	66.3	65.6	66.5	68.8	68.9
29	Non-electrical machinery nec	6 969	6 552	7 238	7 331	7 104	55.2	52.4	53.3	51.6	49.6
30	Office and computing machinery	6 673	7 487	8 600	12 378	13 277	84.0	84.2	84.0	85.8	87.1
31/32	Electrical & electronic equipment	11 849	12 604	13 393	15 188	15 033	74.9	77.2	77.5	77.4	74.1
31	Electrical machinery nec	7 792	7 349	7 055	9 031	8 306	73.3	71.8	69.8	72.9	69.1
32	Radio, TV & communications eq.	4 057	5 255	6 338	6 157	6 727	78.0	86.2	88.2	85.2	81.4
33	Scientific instruments	8 842	9 272	9 439	10 544	11 133	91.5	91.0	88.9	89.2	86.3
34/35	Transportation equipment	2 453	2 529	2 811	2 291	2 453	25.4	28.9	36.6	23.9	25.8
34	Motor vehicles	1 265	1 308	1 568	1 582	1 615	32.5	39.7	42.7	35.7	37.0
35	Other transport equipment	1 188	1 221	1 243	709	838	20.7	22.3	31.0	13.7	16.3
351	Shipbuilding & repairing	..	..	..	..	..	..	..	..	..	..
353	Aircraft and spacecraft	..	..	..	..	..	..	..	..	..	..
36/37	Other manufacturing	3 722	3 712	4 011	4 277	4 063	40.1	39.5	41.9	42.0	38.6
40/45	Construction, electricity, gas & water	..	..	..	..	..	..	..	..	..	..
50/55	Trade, repair, hotels & restaurants	..	..	..	..	..	..	..	..	..	..
65/74	Finance, insurance, business services	..	..	..	..	..	..	..	..	..	..
	OTHER ACTIVITIES	..	..	..	..	..	..	..	..	..	..
01/99	**GRAND TOTAL**	..	..	..	..	..	..	..	..	..	..

Total manufacturing by investing country	1992	1993	1994	1995	1996	As a % of total manufacturing by foreign affiliates				
						1992	1993	1994	1995	1996
All countries	**87 572**	**88 836**	**95 715**	**103 864**	**106 410**	**100.0**	**100.0**	**100.0**	**100.0**	**100.0**
United States	39 811	42 806	47 040	54 624	54 167	45.5	48.2	49.1	52.6	50.9
Canada	2 390	2 349	2 051	2 067	2 392	2.7	2.6	2.1	2.0	2.2
Mexico	..	..	..	..	..	..	..	..	..	..
Japan	2 656	2 591	3 227	3 691	3 893	3.0	2.9	3.4	3.6	3.7
Europe	..	..	..	..	..	..	..	..	..	..
European Union (15)	33 881	33 345	34 399	36 043	37 114	38.7	37.5	35.9	34.7	34.9
Belgium	1 275	1 098	966	1 252	1 229	1.5	1.2	1.0	1.2	1.2
France	4 329	3 661	4 313	4 515	4 525	4.9	4.1	4.5	4.3	4.3
Germany	11 530	10 866	10 987	11 483	10 684	13.2	12.2	11.5	11.1	10.0
Italy	..	..	..	..	..	..	..	..	..	..
Netherlands	2 623	2 987	3 528	3 008	4 327	3.0	3.4	3.7	2.9	4.1
Spain	..	..	..	..	..	..	..	..	..	..
Sweden	1 463	1 017	1 410	1 252	1 288	1.7	1.1	1.5	1.2	1.2
United Kingdom	12 351	12 763	12 779	11 765	12 283	14.1	14.4	13.4	11.3	11.5
Switzerland	3 513	3 706	3 745	4 121	4 412	4.0	4.2	3.9	4.0	4.1
Australia and New Zealand	..	..	..	..	..	..	..	..	..	..
Asia (non-OECD)	..	..	..	..	..	..	..	..	..	..
Latin America	..	..	..	..	..	..	..	..	..	..

Note: Majority foreign-owned establishments. ISIC 23/25 excludes *Refined petroleum products* (232) which is included in ISIC 36/37.
Etablissements sous contrôle étranger majoritaire. La CITI 23/25 exclut les *Produits pétroliers raffinés* (232), qui sont compris dans la CITI 36/37.

133

Table 3. IRELAND / IRLANDE

PRODUCTION

By industry (ISIC Rev. 3)	FOREIGN AFFILIATES *(Millions of Ir£)*					AS A % OF NATIONAL TOTAL				
	1992	1993	1994	1995	1996	1992	1993	1994	1995	1996
10/14 Mining & quarrying	..	..	..	..	..	..	..	..	..	..
15/37 TOTAL MANUFACTURING	**12 410**	**14 525**	**17 123**	**21 896**	**24 108**	**55.5**	**58.3**	**61.6**	**65.2**	**66.4**
15/16 Food, beverages, tobacco	2 618	2 898	3 201	3 538	3 786	32.0	33.3	35.8	36.1	38.1
17/19 Textiles, clothing, leather, footwear	381	416	445	452	447	48.8	52.7	52.2	52.5	54.0
20/22 Wood and paper products	1 050	1 142	1 680	2 097	2 635	50.5	49.6	58.2	62.4	66.8
20 Wood products	57	56	77	93	92	24.1	23.2	27.3	28.8	26.8
21/22 Paper, printing and publishing	993	1 086	1 603	2 005	2 543	54.0	52.7	61.6	65.9	70.6
23/25 Chemicals, Total	3 102	3 681	4 505	5 345	6 097	82.2	84.3	85.9	86.5	85.9
23 Refined petroleum, nuclear fuel	..	..	..	..	..	..	..	..	..	..
24/25 Chemicals, rubber & plastics prod.	3 102	3 681	4 505	5 345	6 097	82.2	84.3	85.9	86.5	85.9
24 Chemical products	2 788	3 361	4 141	4 925	5 696	86.3	88.2	89.7	90.4	90.0
2423 Pharmaceuticals	458	598	1 026	1 242	1 257	90.7	91.9	94.5	95.1	94.5
25 Rubber and plastics products	314	320	364	421	401	57.5	57.2	58.0	57.3	51.8
26 Non-metallic mineral products	109	105	72	112	116	19.6	18.0	11.0	15.7	15.3
27/28 Basic & fabricated metals	339	370	383	397	413	42.1	44.2	42.4	39.9	37.8
27 Basic metals	..	..	..	..	..	..	..	..	..	..
28 Fabricated metal products	..	..	..	..	..	..	..	..	..	..
29/32 Machinery, Total	3 780	4 709	5 496	8 495	8 955	87.9	89.6	89.5	92.1	90.7
29/30 Non-electrical machinery	2 883	3 534	4 031	6 556	6 935	89.4	90.5	89.9	92.8	91.8
29 Non-electrical machinery nec	499	496	589	708	663	66.0	64.5	63.8	66.0	59.9
30 Office and computing machinery	2 384	3 038	3 443	5 848	6 272	96.5	96.9	96.7	97.6	97.2
31/32 Electrical & electronic equipment	897	1 175	1 465	1 939	2 019	83.4	87.2	88.4	89.7	87.3
31 Electrical machinery nec	463	481	524	831	910	78.9	78.7	77.1	82.3	82.5
32 Radio, TV & communications eq.	434	695	941	1 108	1 109	88.8	94.3	96.2	96.3	91.7
33 Scientific instruments	656	779	835	930	1 085	93.8	93.1	92.4	92.6	91.5
34/35 Transportation equipment	114	139	186	200	211	27.7	33.5	41.1	38.1	36.5
34 Motor vehicles	78	93	132	153	161	43.8	49.7	56.9	54.7	55.9
35 Other transport equipment	35	47	55	47	49	15.0	20.5	24.9	19.2	16.9
351 Shipbuilding & repairing	..	..	..	..	..	..	..	..	..	..
353 Aircraft and spacecraft	..	..	..	..	..	..	..	..	..	..
36/37 Other manufacturing	260	286	319	330	363	33.3	35.4	39.0	36.4	36.2
40/45 Construction, electricity, gas & water	..	..	..	..	..	..	..	..	..	..
50/55 Trade, repair, hotels & restaurants	..	..	..	..	..	..	..	..	..	..
65/74 Finance, insurance, business services	..	..	..	..	..	..	..	..	..	..
OTHER ACTIVITIES	..	..	..	..	..	..	..	..	..	..
01/99 GRAND TOTAL	..	..	..	..	..	..	..	..	..	..

Total manufacturing by investing country						*As a % of total manufacturing by foreign affiliates*				
All countries	12 410	14 525	17 123	21 896	24 108	100.0	100.0	100.0	100.0	100.0
United States	7 438	8 814	10 599	14 620	15 814	59.9	60.7	61.9	66.8	65.6
Canada	282	331	417	463	658	2.3	2.3	2.4	2.1	2.7
Mexico	..	..	..	..	..	..	..	..	..	..
Japan	365	545	708	980	720	2.9	3.8	4.1	4.5	3.0
Europe	..	..	..	..	..	..	..	..	..	..
European Union (15)	3 257	3 373	3 964	4 242	4 765	26.2	23.2	23.2	19.4	19.8
Belgium	106	97	102	137	143	0.9	0.7	0.6	0.6	0.6
France	497	416	587	613	645	4.0	2.9	3.4	2.8	2.7
Germany	638	636	757	890	855	5.1	4.4	4.4	4.1	3.5
Italy	..	..	..	..	..	..	..	..	..	..
Netherlands	373	453	631	461	751	3.0	3.1	3.7	2.1	3.1
Spain	..	..	..	..	..	..	..	..	..	..
Sweden	100	90	106	110	119	0.8	0.6	0.6	0.5	0.5
United Kingdom	1 476	1 575	1 680	1 726	1 960	11.9	10.8	9.8	7.9	8.1
Switzerland	672	1 098	934	1 091	1 394	5.4	7.6	5.5	5.0	5.8
Australia and New Zealand	..	..	..	..	..	..	..	..	..	..
Asia (non-OECD)	..	..	..	..	..	..	..	..	..	..
Latin America	..	..	..	..	..	..	..	..	..	..

Note: Majority foreign-owned establishments. ISIC 23/25 excludes *Refined petroleum products* (232) which is included in ISIC 36/37.
Etablissements sous contrôle étranger majoritaire. La CITI 23/25 exclut les *Produits pétroliers raffinés* (232), qui sont compris dans la CITI 36/37.

Table 5. IRELAND / IRLANDE

VALUE ADDED / VALEUR AJOUTÉE

By industry (ISIC Rev. 3)	FOREIGN AFFILIATES (Millions of Ir£)					AS A % OF NATIONAL TOTAL				
	1992	1993	1994	1995	1996	1992	1993	1994	1995	1996
10/14 Mining & quarrying	..	..	..	..	..	..	..	..	..	..
15/37 TOTAL MANUFACTURING	**7 288**	**8 303**	**9 818**	**12 490**	**13 975**	**69.5**	**70.8**	**73.7**	**76.9**	**77.1**
15/16 Food, beverages, tobacco	1 792	1 987	2 269	2 484	2 654	60.6	61.0	65.0	65.6	65.5
17/19 Textiles, clothing, leather, footwear	153	188	199	189	187	45.4	51.2	52.4	50.4	51.1
20/22 Wood and paper products	741	856	1 260	1 649	2 137	57.1	58.5	66.4	71.8	75.6
20 Wood products	23	25	33	36	33	24.0	26.3	30.6	31.0	26.2
21/22 Paper, printing and publishing	718	831	1 227	1 613	2 104	59.8	60.7	68.5	73.9	78.0
23/25 Chemicals, Total	2 218	2 672	3 268	3 881	4 459	89.9	91.1	91.4	92.3	91.5
23 Refined petroleum, nuclear fuel	..	..	..	..	..					
24/25 Chemicals, rubber & plastics prod.	2 218	2 672	3 268	3 881	4 459	89.9	91.1	91.4	92.3	91.5
24 Chemical products	2 048	2 499	3 068	3 666	4 258	93.5	94.2	94.3	95.0	94.5
2423 Pharmaceuticals	298	400	685	849	871	92.5	93.9	95.4	95.9	95.1
25 Rubber and plastics products	170	173	199	215	201	61.4	61.6	61.6	61.8	55.1
26 Non-metallic mineral products	56	55	42	56	57	17.7	15.7	11.1	13.8	13.5
27/28 Basic & fabricated metals	107	142	134	146	145	33.9	39.9	38.6	37.6	34.1
27 Basic metals	..	..	..	..	..	..	..	..	..	..
28 Fabricated metal products	..	..	..	..	..	..	..	..	..	..
29/32 Machinery, Total	1 581	1 642	1 827	3 231	3 387	87.1	86.7	86.0	91.1	89.5
29/30 Non-electrical machinery	1 159	1 145	1 243	2 465	2 410	87.8	86.5	85.3	91.9	89.8
29 Non-electrical machinery nec	265	265	295	354	331	68.5	66.1	64.6	68.3	61.6
30 Office and computing machinery	894	880	948	2 111	2 079	95.8	95.3	94.7	97.6	96.9
31/32 Electrical & electronic equipment	422	497	583	766	977	85.3	87.2	87.4	88.6	88.7
31 Electrical machinery nec	251	250	290	448	532	82.6	82.5	81.7	85.6	86.5
32 Radio, TV & communications eq.	171	247	293	318	446	89.5	92.5	93.9	93.2	91.4
33 Scientific instruments	435	523	532	578	655	94.4	93.6	93.0	93.5	90.8
34/35 Transportation equipment	54	63	88	93	82	25.4	30.1	41.7	37.4	31.7
34 Motor vehicles	36	40	59	62	51	43.4	47.6	61.5	53.1	48.6
35 Other transport equipment	19	24	29	32	31	14.6	19.2	25.2	23.8	20.0
351 Shipbuilding & repairing	..	..	..	..	..	..	..	..	..	..
353 Aircraft and spacecraft	..	..	..	..	..	..	..	..	..	..
36/37 Other manufacturing	151	175	199	184	212	49.3	52.6	57.8	50.4	52.2
40/45 Construction, electricity, gas & water	..	..	..	..	..	..	..	..	..	..
50/55 Trade, repair, hotels & restaurants	..	..	..	..	..	..	..	..	..	..
65/74 Finance, insurance, business services	..	..	..	..	..	..	..	..	..	..
OTHER ACTIVITIES	..	..	..	..	..	..	..	..	..	..
01/99 GRAND TOTAL	..	..	..	..	..	..	..	..	..	..

Total manufacturing by investing country						As a % of total manufacturing by foreign affiliates				
All countries	**7 288**	**8 303**	**9 818**	**12 490**	**13 975**	**100.0**	**100.0**	**100.0**	**100.0**	**100.0**
United States	4 542	5 401	6 294	8 615	9 636	62.3	65.0	64.1	69.0	69.0
Canada	78	130	186	245	359	1.1	1.6	1.9	2.0	2.6
Mexico	..	..	..	..	..	..	..	..	..	..
Japan	181	197	243	306	230	2.5	2.4	2.5	2.4	1.6
Europe	..	..	..	..	..	..	..	..	..	..
European Union (15)	1 848	1 845	2 176	2 264	2 422	25.4	22.2	22.2	18.1	17.3
Belgium	52	48	46	63	54	0.7	0.6	0.5	0.5	0.4
France	236	218	310	301	336	3.2	2.6	3.2	2.4	2.4
Germany	334	333	392	453	383	4.6	4.0	4.0	3.6	2.7
Italy	..	..	..	..	..	..	..	..	..	..
Netherlands	195	232	310	247	368	2.7	2.8	3.2	2.0	2.6
Spain	..	..	..	..	..	..	..	..	..	..
Sweden	50	45	56	52	57	0.7	0.5	0.6	0.4	0.4
United Kingdom	941	908	1 003	992	1 074	12.9	10.9	10.2	7.9	7.7
Switzerland	428	557	692	834	1 149	5.9	6.7	7.0	6.7	8.2
Australia and New Zealand	..	..	..	..	..	..	..	..	..	..
Asia (non-OECD)	..	..	..	..	..	..	..	..	..	..
Latin America	..	..	..	..	..	..	..	..	..	..

Note: Majority foreign-owned establishments. ISIC 23/25 excludes Refined petroleum products (232) which is included in ISIC 36/37.
Etablissements sous contrôle étranger majoritaire. La CITI 23/25 exclut les Produits pétroliers raffinés (232), qui sont compris dans la CITI 36/37.

Table 6. IRELAND / IRLANDE

WAGES AND SALARIES / SALAIRES ET TRAITEMENTS

By industry (ISIC Rev. 3)	FOREIGN AFFILIATES (Millions of Ir£)					AS A % OF NATIONAL TOTAL				
	1992	1993	1994	1995	1996	1992	1993	1994	1995	1996
10/14 Mining & quarrying	..	..	..	..	..	..	..	..	..	..
15/37 **TOTAL MANUFACTURING**	1 370	1 437	1 590	1 757	1 868	49.6	49.8	52.1	52.6	52.0
15/16 Food, beverages, tobacco	234	243	265	275	279	36.4	36.6	39.0	38.2	37.2
17/19 Textiles, clothing, leather, footwear	98	104	110	110	101	48.5	51.7	52.1	51.3	49.5
20/22 Wood and paper products	68	63	87	110	124	20.5	17.5	22.9	26.7	28.1
20 Wood products	8	6	10	11	11	18.6	14.0	22.7	21.5	20.4
21/22 Paper, printing and publishing	60	57	77	99	113	20.8	17.9	22.9	27.4	29.1
23/25 Chemicals, Total	297	313	351	386	413	75.8	73.5	75.5	75.9	74.7
23 Refined petroleum, nuclear fuel	..	..	..	..	..	..	..	..	..	..
24/25 Chemicals, rubber & plastics prod.	297	313	351	386	413	75.8	73.5	75.5	75.9	74.7
24 Chemical products	229	243	276	304	328	82.1	78.9	81.4	82.4	82.0
2423 Pharmaceuticals	58	69	86	97	106	84.1	80.2	86.9	87.4	86.9
25 Rubber and plastics products	68	70	75	82	84	60.2	59.8	59.5	58.7	54.9
26 Non-metallic mineral products	29	27	17	25	27	20.9	18.5	11.3	16.5	16.6
27/28 Basic & fabricated metals	55	56	57	59	62	34.8	34.8	33.7	33.2	31.3
27 Basic metals	..	..	..	..	..	..	..	..	..	..
28 Fabricated metal products	..	..	..	..	..	..	..	..	..	..
29/32 Machinery, Total	385	412	464	545	594	75.8	76.9	76.3	77.1	76.2
29/30 Non-electrical machinery	220	233	267	308	343	73.6	73.3	73.2	73.8	73.8
29 Non-electrical machinery nec	102	100	115	123	121	62.2	60.6	60.5	59.7	55.8
30 Office and computing machinery	118	133	152	185	221	86.8	86.9	86.9	87.6	89.1
31/32 Electrical & electronic equipment	165	179	197	237	251	78.9	82.1	81.1	81.8	79.7
31 Electrical machinery nec	108	104	103	137	137	78.8	77.6	74.1	76.9	77.0
32 Radio, TV & communications eq.	57	75	94	100	114	79.2	89.3	90.4	89.7	83.2
33 Scientific instruments	122	132	141	155	169	92.4	92.3	91.0	90.2	88.0
34/35 Transportation equipment	30	34	41	34	40	20.7	26.2	34.7	22.3	23.3
34 Motor vehicles	14	14	20	21	26	29.8	35.9	42.6	35.7	40.0
35 Other transport equipment	16	19	21	12	14	16.2	20.9	29.6	13.6	13.0
351 Shipbuilding & repairing	..	..	..	..	..	..	..	..	..	..
353 Aircraft and spacecraft	..	..	..	..	..	..	..	..	..	..
36/37 Other manufacturing	51	53	57	59	59	45.5	44.9	48.3	47.1	43.1
40/45 Construction, electricity, gas & water	..	..	..	..	..	..	..	..	..	..
50/55 Trade, repair, hotels & restaurants	..	..	..	..	..	..	..	..	..	..
65/74 Finance, insurance, business services	..	..	..	..	..	..	..	..	..	..
OTHER ACTIVITIES	..	..	..	..	..	..	..	..	..	..
01/99 **GRAND TOTAL**	..	..	..	..	..	..	..	..	..	..

Total manufacturing by investing country						*As a % of total manufacturing by foreign affiliates*				
All countries	1 370	1 437	1 590	1 757	1 868	100.0	100.0	100.0	100.0	100.0
United States	635	700	791	906	946	46.4	48.7	49.7	51.6	50.6
Canada	41	42	37	40	46	3.0	2.9	2.3	2.3	2.5
Mexico	..	..	..	..	..	..	..	..	..	..
Japan	37	39	46	63	65	2.7	2.7	2.9	3.6	3.5
Europe	..	..	..	..	..	..	..	..	..	..
European Union (15)	524	534	566	610	658	38.2	37.2	35.6	34.8	35.2
Belgium	20	17	16	21	21	1.5	1.2	1.0	1.2	1.1
France	63	58	69	73	79	4.6	4.0	4.3	4.2	4.2
Germany	150	146	158	167	168	10.9	10.2	9.9	9.5	9.0
Italy	..	..	..	..	..	..	..	..	..	..
Netherlands	41	46	56	53	80	3.0	3.2	3.5	3.0	4.3
Spain	..	..	..	..	..	..	..	..	..	..
Sweden	18	14	20	20	21	1.3	1.0	1.3	1.1	1.1
United Kingdom	223	234	233	230	242	16.3	16.3	14.7	13.1	13.0
Switzerland	58	62	68	82	92	4.2	4.3	4.3	4.7	4.9
Australia and New Zealand	..	..	..	..	..	..	..	..	..	..
Asia (non-OECD)	..	..	..	..	..	..	..	..	..	..
Latin America	..	..	..	..	..	..	..	..	..	..

Note: Majority foreign-owned establishments. ISIC 23/25 excludes *Refined petroleum products* (232) which is included in ISIC 36/37.
Etablissements sous contrôle étranger majoritaire. La CITI 23/25 exclut les *Produits pétroliers raffinés* (232), qui sont compris dans la CITI 36/37.

Table 7. IRELAND / IRLANDE

R&D EXPENDITURE / DÉPENSES DE R-D

By industry (ISIC Rev. 3)		FOREIGN AFFILIATES (Millions of Ir£)					AS A % OF NATIONAL TOTAL				
		1992	1993	1994	1995	1996	1992	1993	1994	1995	1996
10/14	Mining & quarrying	..	0.9	..	..	..	..	92.9	..	..	..
15/37	**TOTAL MANUFACTURING**	..	**138.1**	..	..	..	..	**68.0**	..	..	..
15/16	Food, beverages, tobacco	..	8.8	..	..	..	..	25.1	..	..	..
17/19	Textiles, clothing, leather, footwear	..	5.4	..	..	..	..	73.0	..	..	..
20/22	Wood and paper products	..	0.8	..	..	..	..	28.3	..	..	..
20	Wood products	..	0.2	..	..	..	..	65.4	..	..	..
21/22	Paper, printing and publishing	..	0.7	..	..	..	..	24.7	..	..	..
23/25	Chemicals, Total	..	55.4	..	..	..	..	89.2	..	..	..
23	Refined petroleum, nuclear fuel	..	0.0	..	..	..	..	..	..	..	..
24/25	Chemicals, rubber & plastics prod.	..	55.4	..	..	..	..	89.2	..	..	..
24	Chemical products	..	54.2	..	..	..	..	92.9	..	..	..
2423	Pharmaceuticals	..	45.9	..	..	..	..	94.9	..	..	..
25	Rubber and plastics products	..	1.2	..	..	..	..	31.5	..	..	..
26	Non-metallic mineral products	..	1.1	..	..	..	..	26.7	..	..	..
27/28	Basic & fabricated metals	..	1.7	..	..	..	..	32.6	..	..	..
27	Basic metals	..	0.5	..	..	..	..	49.5	..	..	..
28	Fabricated metal products	..	1.2	..	..	..	..	28.1	..	..	..
29/32	Machinery, Total	..	48.1	..	..	..	..	75.0	..	..	..
29/30	Non-electrical machinery	..	6.7	..	..	..	..	45.4	..	..	..
29	Non-electrical machinery nec	..	2.6	..	..	..	..	32.7	..	..	..
30	Office and computing machinery	..	4.1	..	..	..	..	60.6	..	..	..
31/32	Electrical & electronic equipment	..	41.5	..	..	..	..	83.8	..	..	..
31	Electrical machinery nec	..	4.6	..	..	..	..	62.5	..	..	..
32	Radio, TV & communications eq.	..	36.9	..	..	..	..	87.4	..	..	..
33	Scientific instruments	..	13.3	..	..	..	..	88.5	..	..	..
34/35	Transportation equipment	..	3.0	..	..	..	..	66.6	..	..	..
34	Motor vehicles	..	2.5	..	..	..	..	63.3	..	..	..
35	Other transport equipment	..	0.5	..	..	..	..	89.5	..	..	..
351	Shipbuilding & repairing	..	0.5	..	..	..	..	96.2	..	..	..
353	Aircraft and spacecraft	..	0.0	..	..	..	..	0.0	..	..	..
36/37	Other manufacturing	..	0.4	..	..	..	..	16.1	..	..	..
40/45	Construction, electricity, gas & water	..	0.0	..	..	..	..	0.0	..	..	..
50/55	Trade, repair, hotels & restaurants	..	0.0	..	..	..	..	0.0	..	..	..
65/74	Finance, insurance, business services	..	45.4	..	..	..	..	72.4	..	..	..
	OTHER ACTIVITIES	..	0.0	..	..	..	..	0.0	..	..	..
01/99	**GRAND TOTAL**	..	**184.5**	..	..	..	..	**68.0**	..	..	..

Total manufacturing by investing country						As a % of total manufacturing by foreign affiliates				
All countries	..	**138.1**	..	..	..	..	**100.0**	..	..	..
United States	..	99.8	..	..	..	..	72.2	..	..	..
Canada	..	..	..	..	..	..	..	..	..	..
Mexico	..	..	..	..	..	..	..	..	..	..
Japan	..	1.6	..	..	..	..	1.2	..	..	..
Europe	..	26.0	..	..	..	..	18.8	..	..	..
European Union (15)	..	..	..	..	..	..	..	..	..	..
Belgium	..	..	..	..	..	..	..	..	..	..
France	..	1.3	..	..	..	..	1.0	..	..	..
Germany	..	4.0	..	..	..	..	2.9	..	..	..
Italy	..	0.4	..	..	..	..	0.3	..	..	..
Netherlands	..	1.6	..	..	..	..	1.1	..	..	..
Spain	..	..	..	..	..	..	..	..	..	..
Sweden	..	..	..	..	..	..	..	..	..	..
United Kingdom	..	11.0	..	..	..	..	8.0	..	..	..
Switzerland	..	..	..	..	..	..	..	..	..	..
Australia and New Zealand	..	..	..	..	..	..	..	..	..	..
Asia (non-OECD)	..	..	..	..	..	..	..	..	..	..
Latin America	..	..	..	..	..	..	..	..	..	..

Note: Majority foreign-owned firms.
Firmes sous contrôle étranger majoritaire.

Table 10. IRELAND / IRLANDE

TOTAL EXPORTS / EXPORTATIONS TOTALES

By industry (ISIC Rev. 3)	FOREIGN AFFILIATES (Millions of Ir£)					AS A % OF NATIONAL TOTAL				
	1992	1993	1994	1995	1996	1992	1993	1994	1995	1996
10/14 Mining & quarrying	..	..	..	..	..	..	..	..	..	..
15/37 TOTAL MANUFACTURING	**10 806**	**12 441**	**14 969**	**19 478**	**21 531**	**76.7**	**77.3**	**80.0**	**82.3**	**83.9**
15/16 Food, beverages, tobacco	1 717	1 860	2 062	2 442	2 565	46.3	44.9	47.8	48.9	53.8
17/19 Textiles, clothing, leather, footwear	339	380	401	401	381	69.3	74.1	72.9	71.2	71.1
20/22 Wood and paper products	926	1 065	1 545	1 892	2 415	86.3	85.0	87.8	90.9	92.3
20 Wood products	36	34	50	64	63	59.0	54.0	62.5	64.6	58.9
21/22 Paper, printing and publishing	890	1 031	1 495	1 828	2 352	87.9	86.6	89.0	92.2	93.7
23/25 Chemicals, Total	2 925	3 508	4 284	5 118	5 865	94.3	94.8	95.3	95.3	94.7
23 Refined petroleum, nuclear fuel	..	..	..	..	..	..	..	..	..	..
24/25 Chemicals, rubber & plastics prod.	2 925	3 508	4 284	5 118	5 865	94.3	94.8	95.3	95.3	94.7
24 Chemical products	2 659	3 235	3 993	4 781	5 545	96.0	96.5	96.9	96.9	96.5
2423 Pharmaceuticals	..	..	..	..	..	..	..	..	..	..
25 Rubber and plastics products	266	274	291	337	320	79.9	79.0	78.0	77.1	71.9
26 Non-metallic mineral products	69	70	56	82	82	45.1	42.2	33.5	45.3	39.4
27/28 Basic & fabricated metals	299	327	336	347	368	65.0	67.4	66.0	62.4	62.2
27 Basic metals	..	..	..	..	..	..	..	..	..	..
28 Fabricated metal products	..	..	..	..	..	..	..	..	..	..
29/32 Machinery, Total	..	4 915	5 797	8 667	9 303	..	94.5	94.4	95.8	95.1
29/30 Non-electrical machinery	..	..	..	..	..	..	..	..	..	..
29 Non-electrical machinery nec	..	464	556	678	619	..	80.8	79.9	82.5	75.0
30 Office and computing machinery	..	..	..	..	..	..	..	..	..	..
31/32 Electrical & electronic equipment	..	..	..	..	..	..	..	..	..	..
31 Electrical machinery nec	..	..	..	..	..	..	..	..	..	..
32 Radio, TV & communications eq.	..	..	..	..	..	..	..	..	..	..
33 Scientific instruments	..	..	..	..	..	..	..	..	..	..
34/35 Transportation equipment	..	133	178	197	202	..	57.1	64.7	58.6	51.7
34 Motor vehicles	..	..	..	..	..	..	..	..	..	..
35 Other transport equipment	..	..	..	..	..	..	..	..	..	..
351 Shipbuilding & repairing	..	..	..	..	..	..	..	..	..	..
353 Aircraft and spacecraft	..	..	..	..	..	..	..	..	..	..
36/37 Other manufacturing	244	183	310	332	350	55.1	44.6	61.0	60.6	60.8
40/45 Construction, electricity, gas & water	..	..	..	..	..	..	..	..	..	..
50/55 Trade, repair, hotels & restaurants	..	..	..	..	..	..	..	..	..	..
65/74 Finance, insurance, business services	..	..	..	..	..	..	..	..	..	..
OTHER ACTIVITIES	..	..	..	..	..	..	..	..	..	..
01/99 GRAND TOTAL	..	..	..	..	..	..	..	..	..	..

Total manufacturing by investing country						As a % of total manufacturing by foreign affiliates				
All countries	10 806	12 441	14 969	19 478	21 531	100.0	100.0	100.0	100.0	100.0
United States	7 145	8 461	10 075	13 873	15 067	66.1	68.0	67.3	71.2	70.0
Canada	..	307	..	..	..	..	2.5	..	..	..
Mexico	..	..	..	..	..	..	..	..	..	..
Japan	..	415	..	..	..	..	3.3	..	..	..
Europe	..	..	..	..	..	..	..	..	..	..
European Union (15)	2 121	2 087	2 610	2 929	3 359	19.6	16.8	17.4	15.0	15.6
Belgium	..	36	..	..	..	..	0.3	..	..	..
France	374	304	430	448	479	3.5	2.4	2.9	2.3	2.2
Germany	600	587	711	842	798	5.6	4.7	4.7	4.3	3.7
Italy	..	..	..	..	..	..	..	..	..	..
Netherlands	..	374	537	..	..	..	3.0	3.6	..	..
Spain	..	..	..	..	..	..	..	..	..	..
Sweden	..	83	90	81	89	..	0.7	0.6	0.4	0.4
United Kingdom	688	614	726	879	1 048	6.4	4.9	4.9	4.5	4.9
Switzerland	643	853	892	1 005	1 290	6.0	6.9	6.0	5.2	6.0
Australia and New Zealand	..	..	..	..	..	..	..	..	..	..
Asia (non-OECD)	..	..	..	..	..	..	..	..	..	..
Latin America	..	..	..	..	..	..	..	..	..	..

Note: Majority foreign-owned establishments. ISIC 29/32 includes *Scientific instruments* (33). ISIC 36/37 includes *Leather and footwear* (19) and *Refined petroleum products* (232).
Etablissements sous contrôle étranger majoritaire. La CITI 29/32 comprend *Instruments* (33). La CITI 36/37 comprend *Cuir et chaussures* (19) et *Produits pétroliers raffinés* (232).

Table 11. IRELAND / IRLANDE

TOTAL IMPORTS / IMPORTATIONS TOTALES

By industry (ISIC Rev. 3)	FOREIGN AFFILIATES (Millions of Ir£)					AS A % OF NATIONAL TOTAL				
	1992	1993	1994	1995	1996	1992	1993	1994	1995	1996
10/14 Mining & quarrying	..	..	..	..	..	..	..	..	..	..
15/37 TOTAL MANUFACTURING	**3 157**	**3 632**	**4 299**	**5 683**	**5 622**	**69.2**	**72.8**	**74.1**	**77.8**	**75.4**
15/16 Food, beverages, tobacco	290	351	343	343	342	48.3	50.8	47.2	47.4	47.3
17/19 Textiles, clothing, leather, footwear	120	133	154	166	162	51.5	56.1	55.6	55.7	54.5
20/22 Wood and paper products	111	90	136	128	172	31.9	30.2	38.4	35.5	42.2
20 Wood products	13	13	20	20	27	27.7	34.2	38.5	39.2	40.9
21/22 Paper, printing and publishing	98	77	116	108	145	32.6	29.6	38.3	34.8	42.4
23/25 Chemicals, Total	647	672	841	1 062	1 140	72.7	74.5	77.4	80.0	78.2
23 Refined petroleum, nuclear fuel	..	..	..	..	..	..	..	..	..	..
24/25 Chemicals, rubber & plastics prod.	647	672	841	1 062	1 140	72.7	74.5	77.4	80.0	78.2
24 Chemical products	539	566	723	908	1 002	77.0	79.3	81.1	84.2	83.3
2423 Pharmaceuticals	..	..	..	..	..	..	..	..	..	..
25 Rubber and plastics products	107	106	118	154	138	56.3	56.1	60.8	61.4	54.5
26 Non-metallic mineral products	25	26	16	36	40	35.7	35.1	22.2	37.1	36.7
27/28 Basic & fabricated metals	123	112	136	138	126	51.5	52.1	53.8	48.3	43.0
27 Basic metals	..	..	..	..	..	..	..	..	..	..
28 Fabricated metal products	..	..	..	..	..	..	..	..	..	..
29/32 Machinery, Total	..	2 115	2 511	3 611	3 428	..	93.0	92.7	94.1	92.0
29/30 Non-electrical machinery	..	..	..	..	..	..	..	..	..	..
29 Non-electrical machinery nec	..	142	202	253	235	..	71.4	74.0	76.7	69.1
30 Office and computing machinery	..	..	..	..	..	..	..	..	..	..
31/32 Electrical & electronic equipment	..	..	..	..	..	..	..	..	..	..
31 Electrical machinery nec	..	..	..	..	..	..	..	..	..	..
32 Radio, TV & communications eq.	..	..	..	..	..	..	..	..	..	..
33 Scientific instruments	..	..	..	..	..	..	..	..	..	..
34/35 Transportation equipment	..	68	83	92	110	..	50.0	51.2	52.0	51.6
34 Motor vehicles	..	..	..	..	..	..	..	..	..	..
35 Other transport equipment	..	..	..	..	..	..	..	..	..	..
351 Shipbuilding & repairing	..	..	..	..	..	..	..	..	..	..
353 Aircraft and spacecraft	..	..	..	..	..	..	..	..	..	..
36/37 Other manufacturing	69	65	79	107	102	43.7	39.9	49.4	52.5	44.7
40/45 Construction, electricity, gas & water	..	..	..	..	..	..	..	..	..	..
50/55 Trade, repair, hotels & restaurants	..	..	..	..	..	..	..	..	..	..
65/74 Finance, insurance, business services	..	..	..	..	..	..	..	..	..	..
OTHER ACTIVITIES	..	..	..	..	..	..	..	..	..	..
01/99 GRAND TOTAL	..	..	..	..	..	..	..	..	..	..

Total manufacturing by investing country						As a % of total manufacturing by foreign affiliates				
All countries	3 157	3 632	4 299	5 683	5 622	100.0	100.0	100.0	100.0	100.0
United States	1 897	2 145	2 354	3 407	3 090	60.1	59.1	54.8	60.0	55.0
Canada	..	76	..	..	..	..	2.1	..	..	..
Mexico	..	..	..	..	..	..	..	..	..	..
Japan	..	317	..	..	..	..	8.7	..	..	..
Europe	..	..	..	..	..	..	..	..	..	..
European Union (15)	735	792	1 054	1 154	1 377	23.3	21.8	24.5	20.3	24.5
Belgium	..	29	..	..	..	..	0.8	..	..	..
France	107	100	148	186	173	3.4	2.8	3.4	3.3	3.1
Germany	234	224	285	346	347	7.4	6.2	6.6	6.1	6.2
Italy	..	..	..	..	..	..	..	..	..	..
Netherlands	..	115	245	..	..	..	3.2	5.7	..	..
Spain	..	..	..	..	..	..	..	..	..	..
Sweden	..	33	40	43	45	..	0.9	0.9	0.8	0.8
United Kingdom	207	258	267	297	413	6.6	7.1	6.2	5.2	7.3
Switzerland	163	159	162	159	156	5.2	4.4	3.8	2.8	2.8
Australia and New Zealand	..	..	..	..	..	..	..	..	..	..
Asia (non-OECD)	..	..	..	..	..	..	..	..	..	..
Latin America	..	..	..	..	..	..	..	..	..	..

Note: Majority foreign-owned establishments. ISIC 29/32 includes *Scientific instruments* (33). ISIC 36/37 includes *Leather and footwear* (19) and *Refined petroleum products* (232).
Etablissements sous contrôle étranger majoritaire. La CITI 29/32 comprend *Instruments* (33). La CITI 36/37 comprend *Cuir et chaussures* (19) et *Produits pétroliers raffinés* (232).

IRELAND

Source

The data are prepared by the Irish Central Statistics Office (CSO) for all variables except *R&D expenditure*. The CSO conducts an annual survey on industrial production which covers separately companies which employ at least three persons and where 50% or more of the share capital is held by non-Irish residents. The *local unit* is the basic unit used in this survey.

R&D data are provided by the Irish Science and Technology Agency (EOLAS), on the basis of an annual survey which covers separately R&D-performing companies where 50% or more of the equity is held by non-Irish residents. The *enterprise* is the basic unit used in this survey.

National totals: provided by CSO and EOLAS and fully compatible with foreign affiliates' data.

Industrial classification

The data are classified according to the principal industrial activity of the affiliate.

The industrial classification is NACE Revision 1.

For all variables except *R&D expenditure,* data are available only for manufacturing industries. *Chemicals, Total* (23/25) excludes *Refined petroleum products* (232), which is included in *Other manufacturing* (36/37).

For *Total exports* and *imports*, *Other manufacturing* (36/37) includes *Leather and footwear* (19) and *Machinery and equipment, total* (29/32) includes *Scientific instruments* (33).

Variables

- *Number of establishments* refers to the number of local units. A local unit is defined as an enterprise or part thereof situated in a geographically identified place. The number includes all the separate industrial local units of multi-location enterprises.

- *Number of employees* consists of the total number of persons who are paid a fixed wage or salary (including part-time workers). Outside piece-workers are excluded.

- *Production* (gross output) represents the net selling value of all goods manufactured in the year, whether sold or not, including work done. From 1991, the value of capital work done on own account is included. Operating subsidies related to the production or sales of output are included in the value of gross output; excise duty and VAT are excluded.

- *Value added* is defined as net output, *i.e.* as the difference between gross output and industrial input. Industrial input consists of the industrial materials, industrial services, fuel and power used in the production of the output. Valuation is exclusive of deductible VAT.

- *Wages and salaries* are defined as the gross amount paid to employees before deduction of income tax, employees' contributions to social security, etc. Payments to outside piece-workers are included.

- *Total exports* represents the value of output which was exported.

- *Total imports* is defined as the value of purchased materials which were imported.

Geographical breakdown

The investor's country is that of the "ultimate beneficial owner". Prior to 1995, the European Union totals include only the former 12 member states.

IRLANDE

Source

Les données sont fournies par le *Central Statistics Office* (Office central des statistiques d'Irlande) pour toutes les variables, sauf les *Dépenses de R-D*. Le CSO mène une enquête annuelle sur la production industrielle qui distingue les sociétés employant au moins trois personnes et où 50 % ou plus du capital est détenu par des résidents non irlandais. L'unité de base utilisée dans cette enquête est l'*unité locale*.

Les données de R-D émanent de l'Agence irlandaise pour la science et la technologie (EOLAS) et s'appuient sur une enquête annuelle qui concerne les sociétés exécutant la R-D, où 50 % ou plus du capital est détenu par des résidents non irlandais. Dans cette enquête, l'*entreprise* est l'unité de base.

Totaux nationaux : fournis par le CSO et l'EOLAS et entièrement compatibles avec les données relatives aux filiales étrangères.

Classification industrielle

Les données sont classées selon l'activité industrielle principale de l'entreprise affiliée.

La classification industrielle est la NACE révision 1.

Pour toutes les variables à l'exception des *Dépenses de R-D*, seules les données de l'industrie manufacturière sont disponibles. *Produits chimiques, total* (23/25) exclut *Produits pétroliers raffinés* (232), qui est compris dans *Autres industries manufacturières* (36/37).

Pour les *Exportations* et *Importations totales*, *Autres industries manufacturières* (36/37) comprend *Cuir et chaussures* (19) et *Machines et matériel, total* (29/32) comprend *Instruments* (33).

Variables

- Le *Nombre d'établissements* correspond au nombre d'unités locales. L'unité locale est définie comme une entreprise ou une partie d'entreprise située à un endroit géographiquement déterminé. Les établissements dénombrés comprennent toutes les unités locales distinctes des entreprises implantées sur plusieurs sites de production.

- Le *Nombre de salariés* correspond à l'ensemble des personnes qui reçoivent un salaire ou un traitement fixe (y compris les employés à temps partiel). Les travailleurs extérieurs rémunérés à la pièce ne sont pas pris en compte.

- La *Production* (production brute) représente la valeur marchande nette de tous les biens fabriqués au cours de l'année, qu'ils soient ou non vendus, et la valeur du travail exécuté. Depuis 1991, la valeur des travaux d'équipement effectués pour compte propre est incluse. Les subventions d'exploitation relatives à la production ou à la vente de la production sont comprises dans la valeur de la production brute ; les droits d'accise et la TVA en sont exclus.

- La *Valeur ajoutée* se définit en tant que production nette, c'est-à-dire comme différence entre la production brute et la consommation intermédiaire de l'industrie. Celle-ci comprend les matériaux industriels, les services industriels ainsi que le combustible et l'énergie utilisés dans la production. L'évaluation ne tient pas compte de la TVA déductible.

- Les *Salaires* sont définis comme le montant brut payé aux employés avant déduction des impôts sur le revenu, des cotisation de sécurité sociale dues par les salariés, etc. La rémunération des travailleurs à domicile est comprise.

- Les *Exportations totales* représentent la valeur de la production qui est exportée.

- Les *Importations totales* sont définies comme la valeur des matériaux qui sont importés.

Ventilation géographique

Le pays de l'investisseur est le pays du "bénéficiaire ultime de l'investissement". Avant 1995, les données de l'Union européenne ne comprennent que les 12 anciens États membres.

ITALY

ITALIE

Table 1. ITALY / ITALIE

NUMBER OF ENTERPRISES / NOMBRE D'ENTREPRISES

By industry (ISIC Rev. 3)	FOREIGN AFFILIATES (Units)					AS A % OF NATIONAL TOTAL				
	1993	1994	1995	1996	1997	1993	1994	1995	1996	1997
10/14 Mining & quarrying	9	..	8	..	10	..	..	..	..	..
15/37 **TOTAL MANUFACTURING**	1 363	..	1 403	..	1 522	..	..	0.3	..	..
15/16 Food, beverages, tobacco	110	..	113	..	102	..	..	0.2	..	..
17/19 Textiles, clothing, leather, footwear	58	..	58	..	59	..	..	0.1	..	..
20/22 Wood and paper products	69	..	73	..	90	..	..	0.1	..	..
20 Wood products	..	..	..	..	..	..	..	..	..	..
21/22 Paper, printing and publishing	..	..	..	..	..	..	..	..	..	..
23/25 Chemicals, Total	416	..	413	..	440	..	..	2.2	..	..
23 Refined petroleum, nuclear fuel	14	..	14	..	15	..	..	3.5	..	..
24/25 Chemicals, rubber & plastics prod.	402	..	399	..	425	..	..	2.2	..	..
24 Chemical products	303	..	295	..	306	..	..	5.2	..	..
2423 Pharmaceuticals	103	..	96	..	86	..	..	34.9	..	..
25 Rubber and plastics products	99	..	104	..	119	..	..	0.8	..	..
26 Non-metallic mineral products	61	..	66	..	78	..	..	0.3	..	..
27/28 Basic & fabricated metals	121	..	136	..	151	..	..	0.1	..	..
27 Basic metals	31	..	37	..	45	..	..	1.1	..	..
28 Fabricated metal products	90	..	99	..	106	..	..	0.1	..	..
29/32 Machinery, Total	371	..	380	..	416	..	..	0.6	..	..
29/30 Non-electrical machinery	233	..	240	..	265	..	..	0.6	..	..
29 Non-electrical machinery nec	227	..	232	..	256	..	..	0.6	..	..
30 Office and computing machinery	6	..	8	..	9	..	..	0.7	..	..
31/32 Electrical & electronic equipment	138	..	140	..	151	..	..	0.6	..	..
31 Electrical machinery nec	105	..	108	..	111	..	..	0.7	..	..
32 Radio, TV & communications eq.	33	..	32	..	40	..	..	0.4	..	..
33 Scientific instruments	72	..	71	..	73	..	..	0.3	..	..
34/35 Transportation equipment	60	..	63	..	81	..	..	1.1	..	..
34 Motor vehicles	48	..	52	..	67	..	..	2.6	..	..
35 Other transport equipment	12	..	11	..	14	..	..	0.3	..	..
351 Shipbuilding & repairing	3	..	2	..	2	..	..	0.1	..	..
353 Aircraft and spacecraft	0	..	0	..	0	..	..	0.0	..	..
36/37 Other manufacturing	25	..	30	..	32	..	..	0.1	..	..
40/45 Construction, electricity, gas & water	..	..	..	..	..	..	..	..	..	..
50/55 Trade, repair, hotels & restaurants	..	..	..	..	..	..	..	..	..	..
65/74 Finance, insurance, business services	..	..	..	..	..	..	..	..	..	..
OTHER ACTIVITIES	..	..	..	..	..	..	..	..	..	..
01/99 **GRAND TOTAL**	..	..	..	..	..	..	..	..	..	..

Total manufacturing by investing country						*As a % of total manufacturing by foreign affiliates*				
All countries	1 363	..	1 403	..	1 522	100.0	..	100.0	..	100.0
United States	323	..	346	..	384	23.7	..	24.7	..	25.2
Canada	..	..	..	..	..	..	..	..	..	..
Mexico	..	..	0	..	0	..	..	0.0	..	0.0
Japan	39	..	38	..	46	2.9	..	2.7	..	3.0
Europe	..	..	..	..	..	..	..	..	..	..
European Union (15)	825	..	847	..	915	60.5	..	60.4	..	60.1
Belgium	..	..	..	..	..	..	..	..	..	..
France	228	..	225	..	230	16.7	..	16.0	..	15.1
Germany	211	..	229	..	247	15.5	..	16.3	..	16.2
Italy	..	..	..	..	..	..	..	..	..	..
Netherlands	67	..	73	..	79	4.9	..	5.2	..	5.2
Spain	..	..	..	..	..	..	..	..	..	..
Sweden	..	..	..	..	..	..	..	..	..	..
United Kingdom	152	..	153	..	176	11.2	..	10.9	..	11.6
Switzerland	132	..	126	..	126	9.7	..	9.0	..	8.3
Australia and New Zealand	..	..	..	..	..	..	..	..	..	..
Asia (non-OECD)	9	..	9	..	10	0.7	..	0.6	..	0.7
Latin America	3	..	3	..	4	0.2	..	0.2	..	0.3

Note: Majority foreign-owned firms.
Firmes sous contrôle étranger majoritaire.

Table 2. ITALY / ITALIE

NUMBER OF EMPLOYEES / NOMBRE DE SALARIÉS

By industry (ISIC Rev. 3)	FOREIGN AFFILIATES (Full-time Eq.)					AS A % OF NATIONAL TOTAL				
	1993	1994	1995	1996	1997	1993	1994	1995	1996	1997
10/14 Mining & quarrying	925	..	905	..	862	..	..	..	..	..
15/37 TOTAL MANUFACTURING	**411 518**	..	**423 590**	..	**457 829**	..	..	**8.9**	..	..
15/16 Food, beverages, tobacco	40 200	..	38 379	..	37 362	..	..	11.9	..	..
17/19 Textiles, clothing, leather, footwear	12 024	..	11 603	..	11 840	..	..	1.5	..	..
20/22 Wood and paper products	13 595	..	14 963	..	16 206	..	..	4.7	..	..
20 Wood products	..	..	..	..	..	..	..	..	..	..
21/22 Paper, printing and publishing	..	..	..	..	..	..	..	..	..	..
23/25 Chemicals, Total	120 365	..	116 504	..	123 064	..	..	29.6	..	..
23 Refined petroleum, nuclear fuel	4 621	..	4 701	..	4 550	..	..	18.9	..	..
24/25 Chemicals, rubber & plastics prod.	115 744	..	111 803	..	118 514	..	..	30.3	..	..
24 Chemical products	91 677	..	87 347	..	90 593	..	..	43.4	..	..
2423 Pharmaceuticals	42 034	..	35 766	..	36 388	..	..	54.8	..	..
25 Rubber and plastics products	24 067	..	24 456	..	27 921	..	..	14.6	..	..
26 Non-metallic mineral products	18 405	..	19 089	..	21 506	..	..	9.2	..	..
27/28 Basic & fabricated metals	17 943	..	25 015	..	34 148	..	..	4.2	..	..
27 Basic metals	6 056	..	11 575	..	18 323	..	..	9.0	..	..
28 Fabricated metal products	11 887	..	13 440	..	15 825	..	..	2.9	..	..
29/32 Machinery, Total	159 959	..	162 081	..	171 817	..	..	19.1	..	..
29/30 Non-electrical machinery	81 714	..	89 290	..	97 945	..	..	15.3	..	..
29 Non-electrical machinery nec	64 978	..	74 893	..	82 370	..	..	13.6	..	..
30 Office and computing machinery	16 736	..	14 397	..	15 575	..	..	45.7	..	..
31/32 Electrical & electronic equipment	78 245	..	72 791	..	73 872	..	..	27.1	..	..
31 Electrical machinery nec	43 056	..	43 142	..	45 236	..	..	24.9	..	..
32 Radio, TV & communications eq.	35 189	..	29 649	..	28 636	..	..	31.1	..	..
33 Scientific instruments	10 824	..	11 436	..	11 203	..	..	13.0	..	..
34/35 Transportation equipment	15 176	..	18 521	..	24 425	..	..	6.5	..	..
34 Motor vehicles	12 952	..	15 633	..	20 710	..	..	8.4	..	..
35 Other transport equipment	2 224	..	2 888	..	3 715	..	..	3.0	..	..
351 Shipbuilding & repairing	287	..	183	..	142	..	..	0.7	..	..
353 Aircraft and spacecraft	0	..	0	..	0	..	..	0.0	..	..
36/37 Other manufacturing	3 027	..	5 999	..	6 258	..	..	2.6	..	..
40/45 Construction, electricity, gas & water	..	..	..	..	..	..	..	..	..	..
50/55 Trade, repair, hotels & restaurants	..	..	..	..	..	..	..	..	..	..
65/74 Finance, insurance, business services	..	..	..	..	..	..	..	..	..	..
OTHER ACTIVITIES	..	..	..	..	..	..	..	..	..	..
01/99 GRAND TOTAL	..	..	..	..	..	..	..	..	..	..

Total manufacturing by investing country						As a % of total manufacturing by foreign affiliates				
All countries	**411 518**	..	**423 590**	..	**457 829**	**100.0**	..	**100.0**	..	**100.0**
United States	116 032	..	124 606	..	142 252	28.2	..	29.4	..	31.1
Canada	..	..	3 545	..	3 150	..	..	0.8	..	0.7
Mexico	..	..	0	..	0	..	..	0.0	..	0.0
Japan	6 807	..	7 583	..	10 621	1.7	..	1.8	..	2.3
Europe	..	..	281 172	..	291 437	..	..	66.4	..	63.7
European Union (15)	244 362	..	247 951	..	254 421	59.4	..	58.5	..	55.6
Belgium	..	..	4 365	..	3 892	..	..	1.0	..	0.9
France	74 023	..	70 368	..	67 698	18.0	..	16.6	..	14.8
Germany	54 084	..	57 113	..	60 529	13.1	..	13.5	..	13.2
Italy	..	..	..	..	..	..	..	..	..	..
Netherlands	18 654	..	20 729	..	22 273	4.5	..	4.9	..	4.9
Spain	..	..	1 519	..	1 514	..	..	0.4	..	0.3
Sweden	..	..	48 937	..	47 036	..	..	11.6	..	10.3
United Kingdom	35 532	..	35 603	..	40 358	8.6	..	8.4	..	8.8
Switzerland	34 683	..	31 718	..	34 642	8.4	..	7.5	..	7.6
Australia and New Zealand	..	..	78	..	508	..	..	0.0	..	0.1
Asia (non-OECD)	3 259	..	2 970	..	2 159	0.8	..	0.7	..	0.5
Latin America	644	..	2 570	..	6 822	0.2	..	0.6	..	1.5

Note: Majority foreign-owned firms.
Firmes sous contrôle étranger majoritaire.

Table 4. ITALY / ITALIE

TURNOVER / CHIFFRE D'AFFAIRES

By industry (ISIC Rev. 3)	FOREIGN AFFILIATES (Billions of L)					AS A % OF NATIONAL TOTAL				
	1993	1994	1995	1996	1997	1993	1994	1995	1996	1997
10/14 Mining & quarrying	1 004	..	862	..	1 039	..	..	..	..	..
15/37 TOTAL MANUFACTURING	**142 620**	..	**186 438**	..	**216 126**	..	..	**11.9**	..	..
15/16 Food, beverages, tobacco	18 487	..	20 315	..	21 718	..	..	12.0	..	..
17/19 Textiles, clothing, leather, footwear	2 865	..	3 551	..	3 593	..	..	2.1	..	..
20/22 Wood and paper products	4 853	..	7 374	..	8 150	..	..	7.6	..	..
20 Wood products	..	..	..	..	..	..	..	..	..	..
21/22 Paper, printing and publishing	..	..	..	..	..	..	..	..	..	..
23/25 Chemicals, Total	54 985	..	70 483	..	81 118	..	..	29.8	..	..
23 Refined petroleum, nuclear fuel	6 025	..	11 947	..	14 140	..	..	16.0	..	..
24/25 Chemicals, rubber & plastics prod.	48 961	..	58 537	..	66 978	..	..	36.2	..	..
24 Chemical products	43 069	..	51 233	..	57 965	..	..	45.8	..	..
2423 Pharmaceuticals	16 330	..	16 249	..	18 615	..	..	55.0	..	..
25 Rubber and plastics products	5 891	..	7 303	..	9 013	..	..	14.6	..	..
26 Non-metallic mineral products	4 135	..	5 329	..	7 176	..	..	10.1	..	..
27/28 Basic & fabricated metals	5 212	..	11 023	..	13 978	..	..	6.6	..	..
27 Basic metals	2 148	..	6 695	..	8 691	..	..	10.1	..	..
28 Fabricated metal products	3 064	..	4 328	..	5 286	..	..	4.3	..	..
29/32 Machinery, Total	43 704	..	56 905	..	65 626	..	..	21.8	..	..
29/30 Non-electrical machinery	25 778	..	34 860	..	40 024	..	..	18.4	..	..
29 Non-electrical machinery nec	14 924	..	22 801	..	28 600	..	..	13.4	..	..
30 Office and computing machinery	10 854	..	12 059	..	11 424	..	..	65.6	..	..
31/32 Electrical & electronic equipment	17 926	..	22 045	..	25 603	..	..	30.7	..	..
31 Electrical machinery nec	10 274	..	13 070	..	14 539	..	..	27.7	..	..
32 Radio, TV & communications eq.	7 652	..	8 975	..	11 064	..	..	36.4	..	..
33 Scientific instruments	3 512	..	3 643	..	3 824	..	..	17.9	..	..
34/35 Transportation equipment	3 687	..	5 145	..	8 528	..	..	5.8	..	..
34 Motor vehicles	2 546	..	3 844	..	6 243	..	..	5.8	..	..
35 Other transport equipment	1 141	..	1 301	..	2 285	..	..	5.6	..	..
351 Shipbuilding & repairing	107	..	40	..	22	..	..	0.6	..	..
353 Aircraft and spacecraft	0	..	0	..	0	..	..	0.0	..	..
36/37 Other manufacturing	1 179	..	2 669	..	2 414	..	..	4.5	..	..
40/45 Construction, electricity, gas & water	..	..	..	..	..	..	..	..	..	..
50/55 Trade, repair, hotels & restaurants	..	..	..	..	..	..	..	..	..	..
65/74 Finance, insurance, business services	..	..	..	..	..	..	..	..	..	..
OTHER ACTIVITIES	..	..	..	..	..	..	..	..	..	..
01/99 GRAND TOTAL	..	..	..	..	..	..	..	..	..	..

Total manufacturing by investing country						As a % of total manufacturing by foreign affiliates				
All countries	**142 620**	..	**186 438**	..	**216 126**	**100.0**	..	**100.0**	..	**100.0**
United States	48 579	..	66 474	..	78 375	34.1	..	35.7	..	36.3
Canada	..	..	1 484	..	1 450	..	..	0.8	..	0.7
Mexico	..	..	0	..	0	..	..	0.0	..	0.0
Japan	2 868	..	3 685	..	5 467	2.0	..	2.0	..	2.5
Europe	..	..	112 556	..	127 427	..	..	60.4	..	59.0
European Union (15)	76 194	..	98 583	..	110 463	53.4	..	52.9	..	51.1
Belgium	..	..	2 593	..	2 080	..	..	1.4	..	1.0
France	21 101	..	25 581	..	27 142	14.8	..	13.7	..	12.6
Germany	16 927	..	24 311	..	27 245	11.9	..	13.0	..	12.6
Italy	..	..	..	..	..	..	..	..	..	..
Netherlands	9 771	..	13 827	..	17 033	6.9	..	7.4	..	7.9
Spain	..	..	1 094	..	1 075	..	..	0.6	..	0.5
Sweden	..	..	15 515	..	17 776	..	..	8.3	..	8.2
United Kingdom	10 871	..	12 759	..	14 711	7.6	..	6.8	..	6.8
Switzerland	11 755	..	13 466	..	15 583	8.2	..	7.2	..	7.2
Australia and New Zealand	..	..	12	..	188	..	..	0.0	..	0.1
Asia (non-OECD)	993	..	1 011	..	726	0.7	..	0.5	..	0.3
Latin America	178	..	683	..	2 004	0.1	..	0.4	..	0.9

Note: Majority foreign-owned firms.
Firmes sous contrôle étranger majoritaire.

Table 7. ITALY / ITALIE

R&D EXPENDITURE / DÉPENSES DE R-D

By industry (ISIC Rev. 3)	FOREIGN AFFILIATES (Billions of L)					AS A % OF NATIONAL TOTAL				
	1992	1993	1994	1995	1996	1992	1993	1994	1995	1996
10/14 Mining & quarrying	..	..	..	..	..	..	..	..	..	..
15/37 TOTAL MANUFACTURING	1 791	..	..	..	..	23.1	..	..	..	..
15/16 Food, beverages, tobacco	3	..	..	..	..	2.6	..	..	..	..
17/19 Textiles, clothing, leather, footwear	6	..	..	..	..	4.9	..	..	..	..
20/22 Wood and paper products	4	..	..	..	..	6.8	..	..	..	..
20 Wood products	3	..	..	..	..	15.3	..	..	..	..
21/22 Paper, printing and publishing	0	..	..	..	..	0.6	..	..	..	..
23/25 Chemicals, Total	478	..	..	..	..	34.0	..	..	..	..
23 Refined petroleum, nuclear fuel	7	..	..	..	..	18.5	..	..	..	..
24/25 Chemicals, rubber & plastics prod.	470	..	..	..	..	34.4	..	..	..	..
24 Chemical products	461	..	..	..	..	35.7	..	..	..	..
2423 Pharmaceuticals	374	..	..	..	..	46.3	..	..	..	..
25 Rubber and plastics products	9	..	..	..	..	12.4	..	..	..	..
26 Non-metallic mineral products	9	..	..	..	..	11.5	..	..	..	..
27/28 Basic & fabricated metals	11	..	..	..	..	5.6	..	..	..	..
27 Basic metals	..	..	..	..	..	..	..	..	..	..
28 Fabricated metal products	..	..	..	..	..	..	..	..	..	..
29/32 Machinery, Total	1 212	..	..	..	..	42.8	..	..	..	..
29/30 Non-electrical machinery	329	..	..	..	..	24.7	..	..	..	..
29 Non-electrical machinery nec	87	..	..	..	..	13.5	..	..	..	..
30 Office and computing machinery	242	..	..	..	..	35.5	..	..	..	..
31/32 Electrical & electronic equipment	883	..	..	..	..	58.7	..	..	..	..
31 Electrical machinery nec	31	..	..	..	..	12.2	..	..	..	..
32 Radio, TV & communications eq.	851	..	..	..	..	68.2	..	..	..	..
33 Scientific instruments	26	..	..	..	..	14.1	..	..	..	..
34/35 Transportation equipment	40	..	..	..	..	1.9	..	..	..	..
34 Motor vehicles	28	..	..	..	..	1.6	..	..	..	..
35 Other transport equipment	13	..	..	..	..	2.9	..	..	..	..
351 Shipbuilding & repairing	..	..	..	..	..	..	..	..	..	..
353 Aircraft and spacecraft	..	..	..	..	..	..	..	..	..	..
36/37 Other manufacturing	2	..	..	..	..	0.3	..	..	..	..
40/45 Construction, electricity, gas & water	..	..	..	..	..	..	..	..	..	..
50/55 Trade, repair, hotels & restaurants	..	..	..	..	..	..	..	..	..	..
65/74 Finance, insurance, business services	..	..	..	..	..	..	..	..	..	..
OTHER ACTIVITIES	..	..	..	..	..	..	..	..	..	..
01/99 GRAND TOTAL	..	..	..	..	..	..	..	..	..	..

Total manufacturing by investing country						As a % of total manufacturing by foreign affiliates				
All countries	1 791	..	..	..	..	100.0	..	..	..	..
United States	..	..	..	..	..	..	..	..	..	..
Canada	..	..	..	..	..	..	..	..	..	..
Mexico	..	..	..	..	..	..	..	..	..	..
Japan	..	..	..	..	..	..	..	..	..	..
Europe	..	..	..	..	..	..	..	..	..	..
European Union (15)	..	..	..	..	..	..	..	..	..	..
Belgium	..	..	..	..	..	..	..	..	..	..
France	..	..	..	..	..	..	..	..	..	..
Germany	..	..	..	..	..	..	..	..	..	..
Italy	..	..	..	..	..	..	..	..	..	..
Netherlands	..	..	..	..	..	..	..	..	..	..
Spain	..	..	..	..	..	..	..	..	..	..
Sweden	..	..	..	..	..	..	..	..	..	..
United Kingdom	..	..	..	..	..	..	..	..	..	..
Switzerland	..	..	..	..	..	..	..	..	..	..
Australia and New Zealand	..	..	..	..	..	..	..	..	..	..
Asia (non-OECD)	..	..	..	..	..	..	..	..	..	..
Latin America	..	..	..	..	..	..	..	..	..	..

Note: Preliminary data.
Données préliminaires.

ITALY

Source

The data are extracted from the Reprint database, developed at the Department of Economics and Production of the *Politecnico de Milano* with the support of CNEL (the Italian National Council for Economy and Labour). They are based on a survey (*Italia Multinazionale*) which covers all Italian enterprises in mining and manufacturing industries in which a foreign person owned or controlled a direct or indirect interest of 50% or more at the end of the fiscal year. The surveys are conducted every two years.

R&D data have been compiled by matching the Reprint database with the ISTAT database on technological innovation. A sample of 731 foreign industrial affiliates with a total of 272 000 employees was used to produce the results.

National totals: for all variables except *R&D expenditure*, data come from the OECD SME database and are only available for the year 1995.

Industrial classification

For all variables, the data are classified according to the principal industrial activity of the affiliate.

The data are converted from the national industry classification to ISIC Revision 3.

Variables

- *Number of enterprises*: all enterprises in the mining and manufacturing industries in which a foreign person owned or controlled a direct or indirect interest of 50% or more at the end of the fiscal year.

- *Number of employees* is the number of full-time equivalent employees on the payroll at the end of the year.

Geographical breakdown

The country of origin is the country of the "ultimate beneficial owner".

ITALIE

Source

Les données sont extraites de la base de données Reprint établie par le Département d'économie et de production du *Politecnico di Milano* avec le soutien du CNEL (Conseil national italien de l'économie et de la main d'oeuvre). Elles s'appuient sur une enquête (*Italia Multinazionale*) qui couvre toutes les entreprises italiennes de l'industrie minière et manufacturière dans lesquelles des intérêts étrangers possèdent ou contrôlent directement ou indirectement 50 % ou plus du capital à la fin de l'exercice budgétaire. Les enquêtes sont effectuées tous les deux ans.

Les données sur la R-D ont été assemblées en comparant la base de données Reprint avec la base de données sur l'innovation technologique de l'ISTAT. Les résultats ont été obtenus à partir d'un échantillon de 731 filiales étrangères industrielles, qui totalisent 272 000 salariés.

Totaux nationaux : pour toutes les variables sauf les *Dépenses de R-D*, les données proviennent de la base de données PME de l'OCDE, et sont seulement disponibles pour l'année 1995.

Classification industrielle

Pour toutes les variables, les données sont classées selon l'activité industrielle principale de l'entreprise affiliée.

Les données de la classification industrielle nationale sont adaptées à la CITI révision 3.

Variables

- *Nombre d'entreprises* : toutes les entreprises des industries minières et manufacturières dans lesquelles des intérêts étrangers possèdent ou contrôlent directement ou indirectement 50 % ou plus du capital à la fin de l'exercice budgétaire.

- *Nombre de salariés* : nombre de personnes employées en équivalent plein-temps à la fin de l'année.

Ventilation géographique

Le pays d'origine est le pays du "bénéficiaire ultime de l'investissement".

JAPAN

Sources and Methods

JAPON

Sources et méthodes

Table 1. JAPAN / JAPON

NUMBER OF ENTERPRISES / NOMBRE D'ENTREPRISES

By industry (ISIC Rev. 3)		FOREIGN AFFILIATES (Units)					AS A % OF NATIONAL TOTAL				
		1992	1993	1994	1995	1996	1992	1993	1994	1995	1996
10/14	Mining & quarrying	0	1	0	0	1	0.0	0.0	0.0	0.0	0.0
15/37	**TOTAL MANUFACTURING**	**430**	**355**	**341**	**275**	**285**	**0.1**	**0.1**	**0.1**	**0.1**	**0.1**
15/16	Food, beverages, tobacco	14	13	15	8	6	0.0	0.0	0.0	0.0	0.0
17/19	Textiles, clothing, leather, footwear	6	5	9	10	9	0.0	0.0	0.0	0.0	0.0
20/22	Wood and paper products	15	10	11	14	20	0.0	0.0	0.0	0.0	0.0
20	Wood products	..	..	..	..	..	..	..	..	..	..
21/22	Paper, printing and publishing	..	..	..	..	..	..	..	..	..	..
23/25	Chemicals, Total	111	98	97	82	81	0.9	0.7	0.7	0.6	0.6
23	Refined petroleum, nuclear fuel	3	4	10	4	4	0.3	0.5	1.1	0.4	0.4
24/25	Chemicals, rubber & plastics prod.	108	94	87	78	77	0.9	0.8	0.7	0.6	0.7
24	Chemical products	99	87	78	69	64	..	..	..	..	..
2423	Pharmaceuticals	39	36	33	21	19	..	..	..	..	..
25	Rubber and plastics products	9	7	9	9	13	..	..	..	..	..
26	Non-metallic mineral products	9	5	5	3	2	0.1	0.0	0.0	0.0	0.0
27/28	Basic & fabricated metals	17	12	16	14	14	0.0	0.0	0.0	0.0	0.0
27	Basic metals	10	9	10	8	10	0.1	0.1	0.1	0.1	0.1
28	Fabricated metal products	7	3	6	6	4	0.0	0.0	0.0	0.0	0.0
29/32	Machinery, Total	153	131	119	79	87	0.2	0.2	0.1	0.1	0.1
29/30	Non-electrical machinery	72	65	54	42	48	0.2	0.1	0.1	0.1	0.1
29	Non-electrical machinery nec	70	62	54	33	36	..	..	..	..	..
30	Office and computing machinery	2	3	0	9	12	..	..	..	..	..
31/32	Electrical & electronic equipment	81	66	65	37	39	0.2	0.2	0.2	0.1	0.1
31	Electrical machinery nec	26	19	20	12	12	..	..	..	..	..
32	Radio, TV & communications eq.	55	47	45	25	27	..	..	..	..	..
33	Scientific instruments	65	48	36	31	31	0.6	0.4	0.3	0.3	0.3
34/35	Transportation equipment	22	15	16	15	14	0.1	0.1	0.1	0.1	0.1
34	Motor vehicles	16	12	11	11	10	..	..	..	..	..
35	Other transport equipment	6	3	5	4	4	..	..	..	..	..
351	Shipbuilding & repairing	..	..	..	..	..	..	..	..	..	..
353	Aircraft and spacecraft	1	1	2	1	1	..	..	..	..	..
36/37	Other manufacturing	18	18	17	19	21	0.0	0.0	0.0	0.0	0.0
40/45	Construction, electricity, gas & water	2	3	2	4	4	0.0	0.0	0.0	0.0	0.0
50/55	Trade, repair, hotels & restaurants	484	388	479	587	602	0.1	0.0	0.1	0.1	0.1
65/74	Finance, insurance, business services	97	73	88	88	109	0.0	0.1	0.0	0.1	0.1
	OTHER ACTIVITIES	58	40	46	67	79	0.0	0.0	0.0	0.0	0.0
01/99	**GRAND TOTAL**	**1 071**	**860**	**956**	**1 021**	**1 080**	**0.0**	**0.0**	**0.0**	**0.0**	**0.0**

Total manufacturing by investing country	1992	1993	1994	1995	1996	As a % of total manufacturing by foreign affiliates				
						1992	1993	1994	1995	1996
All countries	430	355	341	275	285	100.0	100.0	100.0	100.0	100.0
United States	216	163	160	127	132	50.2	45.9	46.9	46.2	46.3
Canada	..	..	..	..	..	..	..	..	..	..
Mexico	..	..	..	..	..	..	..	..	..	..
Japan	..	..	..	..	..	..	..	..	..	..
Europe	..	..	..	..	..	..	..	..	..	..
European Union (15)	151	133	120	89	91	35.1	37.5	35.2	32.4	31.9
Belgium	..	..	..	..	..	..	..	..	..	..
France	15	13	17	8	6	3.5	3.7	5.0	2.9	2.1
Germany	59	45	36	27	30	13.7	12.7	10.6	9.8	10.5
Italy	..	..	..	..	..	..	..	..	..	..
Netherlands	20	22	20	18	18	4.7	6.2	5.9	6.5	6.3
Spain	..	..	..	..	..	..	..	..	..	..
Sweden	..	..	..	..	..	..	..	..	..	..
United Kingdom	18	18	17	13	17	4.2	5.1	5.0	4.7	6.0
Switzerland	23	22	23	21	23	5.3	6.2	6.7	7.6	8.1
Australia and New Zealand	..	..	..	..	..	..	..	..	..	..
Asia (non-OECD)	20	24	23	23	21	4.7	6.8	6.7	8.4	7.4
Latin America	4	1	2	2	1	0.9	0.3	0.6	0.7	0.4

Note: Majority foreign-owned firms.
Firmes sous contrôle étranger majoritaire.

Table 2. JAPAN / JAPON

NUMBER OF EMPLOYEES / NOMBRE DE SALARIÉS

By industry (ISIC Rev. 3)	FOREIGN AFFILIATES (Full-time Eq.)					AS A % OF NATIONAL TOTAL				
	1992	1993	1994	1995	1996	1992	1993	1994	1995	1996
10/14 Mining & quarrying	0	14	0	0	..	0.0	0.0	0.0	0.0	..
15/37 TOTAL MANUFACTURING	109 489	98 094	96 220	86 703	86 469	0.9	0.8	0.8	0.7	0.8
15/16 Food, beverages, tobacco	1 418	2 071	1 436	1 497	1 422	0.1	0.1	0.1	0.1	0.1
17/19 Textiles, clothing, leather, footwear	1 530	1 504	1 796	1 782	1 763	0.1	0.1	0.2	0.2	0.2
20/22 Wood and paper products	617	468	921	578	757	0.0	0.0	0.1	0.0	0.1
20 Wood products	..	..	..	..	..	..	..	..	..	..
21/22 Paper, printing and publishing	..	..	..	..	..	..	..	..	..	..
23/25 Chemicals, Total	34 831	31 273	37 284	31 165	32 536	4.3	3.8	4.7	4.2	4.3
23 Refined petroleum, nuclear fuel	8	76	1 554	186	219	0.0	0.1	2.9	0.4	0.4
24/25 Chemicals, rubber & plastics prod.	34 823	31 197	35 730	30 979	32 317	4.6	4.1	4.8	4.4	4.6
24 Chemical products	34 160	29 180	33 605	30 066	29 782	..	..	..	..	..
2423 Pharmaceuticals	20 989	17 371	20 503	14 509	16 490	..	..	..	..	..
25 Rubber and plastics products	663	2 017	2 125	913	2 535	..	..	..	..	..
26 Non-metallic mineral products	1 197	701	1 044	129	64	0.3	0.2	0.2	0.0	0.0
27/28 Basic & fabricated metals	5 946	5 379	1 404	5 806	5 256	0.4	0.4	0.1	0.4	0.4
27 Basic metals	5 341	5 185	1 113	5 337	4 772	0.9	0.9	0.2	1.0	0.9
28 Fabricated metal products	605	194	291	469	484	0.1	0.0	0.0	0.0	0.1
29/32 Machinery, Total	53 208	49 792	45 621	38 973	38 872	1.6	1.5	1.4	1.2	1.4
29/30 Non-electrical machinery	6 920	7 275	6 610	30 660	29 868	0.7	0.7	0.6	3.1	3.2
29 Non-electrical machinery nec	6 843	7 214	6 610	5 785	5 081	..	..	..	..	..
30 Office and computing machinery	77	61	0	24 875	24 787	..	..	..	..	..
31/32 Electrical & electronic equipment	46 288	42 517	39 011	8 313	9 004	2.1	1.8	1.8	0.4	0.5
31 Electrical machinery nec	1 782	3 610	1 316	780	1 018	..	..	..	..	..
32 Radio, TV & communications eq.	44 506	38 907	37 695	7 533	7 986	..	..	..	..	..
33 Scientific instruments	7 024	4 301	3 201	2 606	3 349	2.0	1.3	0.9	0.8	1.1
34/35 Transportation equipment	2 377	1 364	1 630	1 517	666	0.2	0.1	0.1	0.1	0.1
34 Motor vehicles	2 252	1 304	1 394	1 316	462	..	..	..	..	..
35 Other transport equipment	125	60	236	201	204	..	..	..	..	..
351 Shipbuilding & repairing	..	..	..	..	..	..	..	..	..	..
353 Aircraft and spacecraft	2	30	37	28	28	..	..	..	..	..
36/37 Other manufacturing	1 341	1 241	1 883	2 650	1 784	0.1	0.1	0.1	0.2	0.2
40/45 Construction, electricity, gas & water	34	164	19	108	25	0.0	0.0	0.0	0.0	0.0
50/55 Trade, repair, hotels & restaurants	24 866	19 698	27 909	37 972	35 088	0.2	0.2	0.3	0.4	0.3
65/74 Finance, insurance, business services	3 798	2 023	6 205	3 908	3 843	0.1	0.1	0.2	0.1	0.1
OTHER ACTIVITIES	2 726	1 975	3 266	4 060	4 746	0.0	0.0	0.0	0.1	0.1
01/99 GRAND TOTAL	140 913	121 968	133 619	132 751	130 171	0.4	0.3	0.3	0.4	0.4

Total manufacturing by investing country						As a % of total manufacturing by foreign affiliates				
All countries	109 489	98 094	96 220	86 703	86 469	100.0	100.0	100.0	100.0	100.0
United States	79 827	70 943	69 849	56 556	56 057	72.9	72.3	72.6	65.2	64.8
Canada	..	..	..	..	4 794	..	..	..	..	5.5
Mexico	..	..	..	..	..	..	..	..	..	..
Japan	..	..	..	..	..	..	..	..	..	..
Europe	..	..	..	..	23 835	..	..	..	..	27.6
European Union (15)	15 634	11 938	17 183	16 544	16 193	14.3	12.2	17.9	19.1	18.7
Belgium	..	..	..	..	132	..	..	..	..	0.2
France	676	763	1 083	636	85	0.6	0.8	1.1	0.7	0.1
Germany	7 085	5 161	8 278	5 278	6 093	6.5	5.3	8.6	6.1	7.0
Italy	..	..	..	..	22	..	..	..	..	0.0
Netherlands	2 771	1 635	1 599	5 041	5 498	2.5	1.7	1.7	5.8	6.4
Spain	..	..	..	..	..	..	..	..	..	..
Sweden	..	..	..	..	701	..	..	..	..	0.8
United Kingdom	2 359	2 494	3 978	1 738	3 415	2.2	2.5	4.1	2.0	3.9
Switzerland	5 409	7 005	4 680	4 663	5 770	4.9	7.1	4.9	5.4	6.7
Australia and New Zealand	..	..	..	..	383	..	..	..	..	0.4
Asia (non-OECD)	484	1 391	397	420	394	0.4	1.4	0.4	0.5	0.5
Latin America	1 204	3	949	885	907	1.1	0.0	1.0	1.0	1.0

Note: Majority foreign-owned firms.
Firmes sous contrôle étranger majoritaire.

Table 4. JAPAN / JAPON

TURNOVER / CHIFFRE D'AFFAIRES

By industry (ISIC Rev. 3)		FOREIGN AFFILIATES (Billions of yen)					AS A % OF NATIONAL TOTAL				
		1992	1993	1994	1995	1996	1992	1993	1994	1995	1996
10/14	Mining & quarrying	0	0	0	0	0	0.0	0.0	0.0	0.0	0.0
15/37	**TOTAL MANUFACTURING**	**5 040**	**4 707**	**5 489**	**5 183**	**4 990**	**1.2**	**1.2**	**1.4**	**1.3**	**1.2**
15/16	Food, beverages, tobacco	32	97	320	337	370	0.1	0.2	0.7	0.7	0.9
17/19	Textiles, clothing, leather, footwear	26	26	67	36	40	0.1	0.1	0.3	0.2	0.2
20/22	Wood and paper products	50	17	17	23	30	0.1	0.0	0.0	0.1	0.1
20	Wood products	..	..	..	..	..	..	..	..	..	..
21/22	Paper, printing and publishing	..	..	..	..	..	..	..	..	..	..
23/25	Chemicals, Total	1 633	1 491	2 346	1 741	1 429	3.5	3.3	5.1	3.9	2.9
23	Refined petroleum, nuclear fuel	1	51	577	210	18	0.0	0.4	4.8	1.8	0.1
24/25	Chemicals, rubber & plastics prod.	1 633	1 440	1 769	1 531	1 411	4.7	4.3	5.2	4.6	3.9
24	Chemical products	1 593	1 372	1 684	1 495	1 290	..	..	..	..	..
2423	Pharmaceuticals	930	773	944	723	720	..	..	..	..	..
25	Rubber and plastics products	40	68	85	36	122	..	..	..	..	..
26	Non-metallic mineral products	49	25	33	8	4	0.4	0.2	0.2	0.1	0.0
27/28	Basic & fabricated metals	325	285	68	312	349	0.7	0.6	0.2	0.6	0.7
27	Basic metals	307	280	53	306	334	1.2	1.2	0.2	1.2	1.4
28	Fabricated metal products	18	4	16	6	15	0.1	0.0	0.1	0.0	0.1
29/32	Machinery, Total	2 269	2 323	2 270	2 385	2 454	2.3	2.5	2.3	2.3	2.3
29/30	Non-electrical machinery	276	290	244	1 956	1 954	0.9	1.1	0.9	7.1	6.9
29	Non-electrical machinery nec	274	288	244	372	179	..	..	..	..	..
30	Office and computing machinery	2	2	0	1 584	1 775	..	..	..	..	..
31/32	Electrical & electronic equipment	1 994	2 034	2 026	428	500	2.9	3.0	2.9	0.6	0.6
31	Electrical machinery nec	44	152	68	60	96	..	..	..	..	..
32	Radio, TV & communications eq.	1 949	1 882	1 958	368	403	..	..	..	..	..
33	Scientific instruments	343	198	149	84	124	4.1	2.6	1.7	0.9	1.3
34/35	Transportation equipment	156	117	83	63	51	0.3	0.2	0.2	0.1	0.1
34	Motor vehicles	150	115	78	58	45	..	..	..	..	..
35	Other transport equipment	5	3	5	5	6	..	..	..	..	..
351	Shipbuilding & repairing	..	..	..	..	..	..	..	..	..	..
353	Aircraft and spacecraft	0	1	1	1	1	..	..	..	..	..
36/37	Other manufacturing	157	128	135	196	139	0.5	0.4	0.4	0.6	0.4
40/45	Construction, electricity, gas & water	1	1	1	5	1	0.0	0.0	0.0	0.0	0.0
50/55	Trade, repair, hotels & restaurants	4 557	3 613	4 568	4 903	4 974	0.7	0.6	0.7	0.8	0.8
65/74	Finance, insurance, business services	223	92	294	184	208	0.3	0.1	0.3	0.3	0.3
	OTHER ACTIVITIES	106	62	81	375	302	0.1	0.0	0.1	0.2	0.2
01/99	**GRAND TOTAL**	**9 927**	**8 476**	**10 434**	**10 650**	**10 474**	**0.7**	**0.6**	**0.7**	**0.7**	**0.7**

Total manufacturing by investing country	1992	1993	1994	1995	1996	As a % of total manufacturing by foreign affiliates				
						1992	1993	1994	1995	1996
All countries	5 040	4 707	5 489	5 183	4 990	100.0	100.0	100.0	100.0	100.0
United States	3 311	3 139	3 902	3 463	3 438	65.7	66.7	71.1	66.8	68.9
Canada	..	..	..	..	338	..	..	..	..	6.8
Mexico	..	..	..	..	..	..	..	..	..	..
Japan	..	..	..	..	..	..	..	..	..	..
Europe	..	..	..	..	1 101	..	..	..	..	22.1
European Union (15)	962	793	1 205	823	815	19.1	16.8	22.0	15.9	16.3
Belgium	..	..	..	..	5	..	..	..	..	0.1
France	80	41	90	50	41	1.6	0.9	1.6	1.0	0.8
Germany	408	332	452	244	266	8.1	7.1	8.2	4.7	5.3
Italy	..	..	..	..	1	..	..	..	..	0.0
Netherlands	141	106	194	232	246	2.8	2.3	3.5	4.5	4.9
Spain	..	..	..	..	..	..	..	..	..	..
Sweden	..	..	..	..	80	..	..	..	..	1.6
United Kingdom	172	210	299	106	172	3.4	4.5	5.5	2.0	3.4
Switzerland	270	304	201	271	251	5.4	6.5	3.7	5.2	5.0
Australia and New Zealand	..	..	..	..	11	..	..	..	..	0.2
Asia (non-OECD)	76	167	65	46	70	1.5	3.6	1.2	0.9	1.4
Latin America	63	1	37	225	29	1.3	0.0	0.7	4.3	0.6

Note: Majority foreign-owned firms.
Firmes sous contrôle étranger majoritaire.

Table 5. JAPAN / JAPON

VALUE ADDED / VALEUR AJOUTÉE

By industry (ISIC Rev. 3)	FOREIGN AFFILIATES (Billions of yen)					AS A % OF NATIONAL TOTAL				
	1992	1993	1994	1995	1996	1992	1993	1994	1995	1996
10/14 Mining & quarrying	..	..	0	0	0	..	..	0.0	0.0	0.0
15/37 TOTAL MANUFACTURING	..	..	**911**	**1 111**	**1 053**	..	..	**1.0**	**1.2**	**1.2**
15/16 Food, beverages, tobacco	..	..	85	84	79	..	..	0.9	0.9	1.0
17/19 Textiles, clothing, leather, footwear	..	..	10	9	9	..	..	0.2	0.2	0.2
20/22 Wood and paper products	..	..	4	5	7	..	..	0.0	0.1	0.1
20 Wood products	..	..	..	..	..	..	..	..	..	..
21/22 Paper, printing and publishing	..	..	..	..	..	..	..	..	..	..
23/25 Chemicals, Total	..	..	431	388	331	..	..	4.6	4.1	3.4
23 Refined petroleum, nuclear fuel	..	..	45	3	3	..	..	3.2	0.2	0.3
24/25 Chemicals, rubber & plastics prod.	..	..	387	385	328	..	..	4.8	4.7	3.8
24 Chemical products	..	..	373	374	300	..	..	..	..	..
2423 Pharmaceuticals	..	..	240	215	190	..	..	..	..	..
25 Rubber and plastics products	..	..	14	11	28	..	..	..	..	..
26 Non-metallic mineral products	..	..	5	2	1	..	..	0.2	0.1	0.0
27/28 Basic & fabricated metals	..	..	12	48	51	..	..	0.1	0.4	0.4
27 Basic metals	..	..	10	47	47	..	..	0.2	0.9	0.9
28 Fabricated metal products	..	..	2	1	4	..	..	0.0	0.0	0.1
29/32 Machinery, Total	..	..	300	501	516	..	..	1.3	2.1	2.2
29/30 Non-electrical machinery	..	..	41	394	419	..	..	0.5	5.4	5.1
29 Non-electrical machinery nec	..	..	41	39	41	..	..	..	..	..
30 Office and computing machinery	..	..	0	354	378	..	..	..	..	..
31/32 Electrical & electronic equipment	..	..	258	108	97	..	..	1.7	0.6	0.6
31 Electrical machinery nec	..	..	10	16	12	..	..	..	..	..
32 Radio, TV & communications eq.	..	..	248	92	86	..	..	..	..	..
33 Scientific instruments	..	..	30	25	34	..	..	1.2	1.0	1.4
34/35 Transportation equipment	..	..	14	8	6	..	..	0.1	0.1	0.1
34 Motor vehicles	..	..	14	7	4	..	..	..	..	..
35 Other transport equipment	..	..	1	1	2	..	..	..	..	..
351 Shipbuilding & repairing	..	..	..	..	..	..	..	..	..	..
353 Aircraft and spacecraft	..	..	0	0	0	..	..	..	..	..
36/37 Other manufacturing	..	..	20	41	19	..	..	0.2	0.5	0.2
40/45 Construction, electricity, gas & water	..	..	0	1	0	..	..	0.0	0.0	0.0
50/55 Trade, repair, hotels & restaurants	..	..	455	532	539	..	..	0.7	0.8	0.8
65/74 Finance, insurance, business services	..	..	49	44	39	..	..	0.2	0.3	0.3
OTHER ACTIVITIES	..	..	29	38	51	..	..	0.1	0.1	0.1
01/99 GRAND TOTAL	..	..	**1 445**	**1 726**	**1 682**	..	..	**0.5**	**0.6**	**0.6**

Total manufacturing by investing country						*As a % of total manufacturing by foreign affiliates*				
All countries	..	..	**911**	**1 111**	**1 053**	..	..	**100.0**	**100.0**	**100.0**
United States	..	..	623	794	764	..	..	68.3	71.4	72.5
Canada	..	..	..	..	..	..	..	..	..	..
Mexico	..	..	..	..	..	..	..	..	..	..
Japan	..	..	..	..	..	..	..	..	..	..
Europe	..	..	..	..	..	..	..	..	..	..
European Union (15)	..	..	218	183	159	..	..	23.9	16.5	15.1
Belgium	..	..	..	..	..	..	..	..	..	..
France	..	..	11	3	1	..	..	1.2	0.3	0.1
Germany	..	..	97	60	66	..	..	10.7	5.4	6.3
Italy	..	..	..	..	..	..	..	..	..	..
Netherlands	..	..	34	42	49	..	..	3.7	3.8	4.6
Spain	..	..	..	..	..	..	..	..	..	..
Sweden	..	..	..	..	..	..	..	..	..	..
United Kingdom	..	..	48	14	32	..	..	5.3	1.3	3.0
Switzerland	..	..	41	61	56	..	..	4.5	5.5	5.3
Australia and New Zealand	..	..	..	..	..	..	..	..	..	..
Asia (non-OECD)	..	..	5	3	4	..	..	0.5	0.3	0.3
Latin America	..	..	6	7	6	..	..	0.6	0.7	0.5

Note: Majority foreign-owned firms.
Firmes sous contrôle étranger majoritaire.

Table 6. JAPAN / JAPON

WAGES AND SALARIES / SALAIRES ET TRAITEMENTS

By industry (ISIC Rev. 3)		FOREIGN AFFILIATES (Billions of yen)					AS A % OF NATIONAL TOTAL				
		1992	1993	1994	1995	1996	1992	1993	1994	1995	1996
10/14	Mining & quarrying	..	..	0	0	0	..	..	0.0	0.0	0.0
15/37	**TOTAL MANUFACTURING**	..	..	**447**	**629**	**591**	..	..	**0.7**	**1.1**	**1.0**
15/16	Food, beverages, tobacco	..	..	10	12	10	..	..	0.2	0.2	0.2
17/19	Textiles, clothing, leather, footwear	..	..	7	7	8	..	..	0.2	0.2	0.3
20/22	Wood and paper products	..	..	2	4	4	..	..	0.0	0.1	0.1
20	Wood products	..	..	..	..	..	..	..	..	..	..
21/22	Paper, printing and publishing	..	..	..	..	..	..	..	..	..	..
23/25	Chemicals, Total	..	..	246	236	196	..	..	5.1	5.0	4.0
23	Refined petroleum, nuclear fuel	..	..	15	2	2	..	..	3.8	0.4	0.4
24/25	Chemicals, rubber & plastics prod.	..	..	230	234	194	..	..	5.2	5.4	4.3
24	Chemical products	..	..	218	229	177	..	..	..	..	..
2423	Pharmaceuticals	..	..	140	127	110	..	..	..	..	..
25	Rubber and plastics products	..	..	13	5	17	..	..	..	..	..
26	Non-metallic mineral products	..	..	3	1	1	..	..	0.2	0.1	0.0
27/28	Basic & fabricated metals	..	..	9	34	37	..	..	0.1	0.4	0.5
27	Basic metals	..	..	7	33	34	..	..	0.2	1.0	1.2
28	Fabricated metal products	..	..	2	1	3	..	..	0.0	0.0	0.1
29/32	Machinery, Total	..	..	136	295	299	..	..	0.9	1.9	2.0
29/30	Non-electrical machinery	..	..	23	235	239	..	..	0.4	4.7	4.7
29	Non-electrical machinery nec	..	..	23	23	26	..	..	..	..	..
30	Office and computing machinery	..	..	0	212	213	..	..	..	..	..
31/32	Electrical & electronic equipment	..	..	113	60	60	..	..	1.1	0.6	0.6
31	Electrical machinery nec	..	..	6	3	6	..	..	..	..	..
32	Radio, TV & communications eq.	..	..	107	56	54	..	..	..	..	..
33	Scientific instruments	..	..	17	15	20	..	..	1.0	0.9	1.3
34/35	Transportation equipment	..	..	9	7	3	..	..	0.1	0.1	0.1
34	Motor vehicles	..	..	8	6	2	..	..	..	..	..
35	Other transport equipment	..	..	1	1	1	..	..	..	..	..
351	Shipbuilding & repairing	..	..	..	..	..	..	..	..	..	..
353	Aircraft and spacecraft	..	..	0	0	0	..	..	..	..	..
36/37	Other manufacturing	..	..	8	19	13	..	..	0.1	0.4	0.2
40/45	Construction, electricity, gas & water	..	..	0	1	0	..	..	0.0	0.0	0.0
50/55	Trade, repair, hotels & restaurants	..	..	198	268	252	..	..	0.4	0.6	0.6
65/74	Finance, insurance, business services	..	..	39	24	29	..	..	0.3	0.2	0.3
	OTHER ACTIVITIES	..	..	19	29	35	..	..	0.1	0.1	0.1
01/99	**GRAND TOTAL**	..	..	**702**	**951**	**906**	..	..	**0.4**	**0.5**	**0.5**

Total manufacturing by investing country						As a % of total manufacturing by foreign affiliates				
All countries	..	..	**447**	**629**	**591**	..	..	**100.0**	**100.0**	**100.0**
United States	..	..	274	438	395	..	..	61.3	69.6	66.8
Canada	..	..	..	..	..	..	..	..	..	..
Mexico	..	..	..	..	..	..	..	..	..	..
Japan	..	..	..	..	..	..	..	..	..	..
Europe	..	..	..	..	..	..	..	..	..	..
European Union (15)	..	..	121	105	104	..	..	27.0	16.8	17.5
Belgium	..	..	..	..	..	..	..	..	..	..
France	..	..	5	3	1	..	..	1.2	0.5	0.1
Germany	..	..	63	40	45	..	..	14.1	6.4	7.6
Italy	..	..	..	..	..	..	..	..	..	..
Netherlands	..	..	10	17	32	..	..	2.3	2.7	5.3
Spain	..	..	..	..	..	..	..	..	..	..
Sweden	..	..	..	..	..	..	..	..	..	..
United Kingdom	..	..	26	12	21	..	..	5.9	1.9	3.5
Switzerland	..	..	28	32	38	..	..	6.3	5.1	6.4
Australia and New Zealand	..	..	..	..	..	..	..	..	..	..
Asia (non-OECD)	..	..	4	2	3	..	..	0.8	0.4	0.5
Latin America	..	..	6	6	7	..	..	1.4	1.0	1.2

Note: Majority foreign-owned firms.
Firmes sous contrôle étranger majoritaire.

Table 7. JAPAN / JAPON

R&D EXPENDITURE / DÉPENSES DE R-D

By industry (ISIC Rev. 3)	FOREIGN AFFILIATES (Billions of yen)					AS A % OF NATIONAL TOTAL				
	1992	1993	1994	1995	1996	1992	1993	1994	1995	1996
10/14 Mining & quarrying	0.0	0.0	0.0	0.0	0.0	..	..	..	..	..
15/37 **TOTAL MANUFACTURING**	401.7	72.4	126.6	118.5	88.0	4.4	0.8	1.5	1.3	0.9
15/16 Food, beverages, tobacco	0.0	1.3	0.5	0.4	0.4	0.0	0.5	0.2	0.2	0.2
17/19 Textiles, clothing, leather, footwear	0.0	0.0	0.0	0.0	0.1	0.0	0.0	0.0	0.0	0.2
20/22 Wood and paper products	0.1	0.0	0.0	0.1	0.1	0.1	0.0	0.0	0.1	0.1
20 Wood products	..	..	..	..	..	..	..	..	..	..
21/22 Paper, printing and publishing	..	..	..	..	..	..	..	..	..	..
23/25 Chemicals, Total	307.3	54.0	66.9	61.3	61.6	15.8	2.9	3.6	3.3	3.2
23 Refined petroleum, nuclear fuel	0.0	0.0	2.6	0.9	1.2	0.0	0.0	3.3	1.3	1.9
24/25 Chemicals, rubber & plastics prod.	307.3	54.0	64.3	60.4	60.4	16.6	3.0	3.6	3.4	3.3
24 Chemical products	307.3	53.6	63.3	59.9	58.8	19.1	3.4	4.1	3.9	3.7
2423 Pharmaceuticals	44.0	43.3	42.4	37.4	45.4	6.8	6.9	6.7	5.8	6.8
25 Rubber and plastics products	0.0	0.4	1.0	0.5	1.6	0.0	0.2	0.4	0.2	0.6
26 Non-metallic mineral products	0.5	0.0	0.3	0.1	0.0	0.2	0.0	0.2	0.1	0.0
27/28 Basic & fabricated metals	2.9	1.6	1.0	2.8	2.9	0.5	0.3	0.2	0.6	0.6
27 Basic metals	2.2	1.6	0.9	2.8	2.7	0.5	0.4	0.2	0.8	0.8
28 Fabricated metal products	0.7	0.0	0.1	0.0	0.1	0.6	0.0	0.1	0.0	0.1
29/32 Machinery, Total	88.3	13.3	55.1	51.0	20.7	2.1	0.3	1.3	1.2	0.5
29/30 Non-electrical machinery	2.5	2.2	2.1	39.5	6.6	0.2	0.1	0.1	2.3	0.4
29 Non-electrical machinery nec	2.5	2.2	2.1	1.9	1.9	0.3	0.3	0.3	0.2	0.2
30 Office and computing machinery	0.0	0.0	0.0	37.6	4.7	0.0	0.0	0.0	4.4	0.5
31/32 Electrical & electronic equipment	85.8	11.1	52.9	11.5	14.1	3.3	0.5	2.1	0.4	0.5
31 Electrical machinery nec	1.2	0.0	0.2	0.6	1.0	0.1	0.0	0.0	0.1	0.1
32 Radio, TV & communications eq.	84.6	11.0	52.8	10.9	13.1	5.3	0.8	3.6	0.7	0.8
33 Scientific instruments	1.9	1.0	1.8	1.2	1.7	0.6	0.3	0.5	0.3	0.5
34/35 Transportation equipment	0.7	1.0	0.8	0.5	0.4	0.0	0.1	0.1	0.0	0.0
34 Motor vehicles	0.7	1.0	0.8	0.5	0.4	0.1	0.1	0.1	0.0	0.0
35 Other transport equipment	0.0	0.0	0.0	0.0	0.0	0.0	0.0	0.0	0.0	0.0
351 Shipbuilding & repairing	..	..	..	..	..	..	..	..	..	..
353 Aircraft and spacecraft	0.0	0.0	..	0.0	..	0.0	0.0	..	0.0	..
36/37 Other manufacturing	0.1	0.3	0.1	1.1	0.2	0.1	0.4	0.1	1.4	0.2
40/45 Construction, electricity, gas & water	0.0	0.0	0.0	0.1	0.0	..	..	..	..	..
50/55 Trade, repair, hotels & restaurants	9.1	4.0	6.5	8.4	4.4	..	..	..	..	..
65/74 Finance, insurance, business services	4.3	1.1	1.2	0.4	0.4	..	..	..	..	..
OTHER ACTIVITIES	0.4	0.6	0.5	1.0	0.9	..	..	..	..	..
01/99 **GRAND TOTAL**	415.6	78.1	134.8	128.4	93.8	4.3	0.9	1.5	1.4	0.9

Total manufacturing by investing country						As a % of total manufacturing by foreign affiliates				
All countries	401.7	72.4	126.6	118.5	88.0	100.0	100.0	100.0	100.0	100.0
United States	116.1	46.9	94.5	77.1	46.1	28.9	64.8	74.6	65.1	52.4
Canada	..	..	..	..	..	..	..	..	..	..
Mexico	..	..	..	..	..	..	..	..	..	..
Japan	..	..	..	..	..	..	..	..	..	..
Europe	..	..	..	..	..	..	..	..	..	..
European Union (15)	268.5	11.5	21.8	25.2	19.8	66.8	15.9	17.2	21.2	22.5
Belgium	..	..	..	..	..	..	..	..	..	..
France	2.3	0.4	2.9	0.4	0.4	0.6	0.6	2.3	0.4	0.4
Germany	261.3	4.1	14.2	11.0	9.7	65.0	5.6	11.2	9.3	11.0
Italy	..	..	..	..	..	..	..	..	..	..
Netherlands	2.7	2.5	0.8	4.2	6.6	0.7	3.4	0.6	3.6	7.5
Spain	..	..	..	..	..	..	..	..	..	..
Sweden	..	..	..	..	..	..	..	..	..	..
United Kingdom	1.8	4.3	3.2	1.3	3.0	0.5	5.9	2.6	1.1	3.4
Switzerland	9.8	11.9	7.6	9.2	14.8	2.4	16.5	6.0	7.7	16.8
Australia and New Zealand	..	..	..	..	..	..	..	..	..	..
Asia (non-OECD)	0.0	0.4	0.1	0.5	0.6	0.0	0.6	0.1	0.4	0.6
Latin America	5.1	0.0	1.8	2.7	3.0	1.3	0.0	1.4	2.3	3.4

Note: Majority foreign-owned firms.
Firmes sous contrôle étranger majoritaire.

Table 8. JAPAN / JAPON

NUMBER OF RESEARCHERS / NOMBRE DE CHERCHEURS

		FOREIGN AFFILIATES *(Units)*					AS A % OF NATIONAL TOTAL				
By industry (ISIC Rev. 3)		1992	1993	1994	1995	1996	1992	1993	1994	1995	1996
10/14	Mining & quarrying	0	0	0	..	..	..	..	..	..	..
15/37	**TOTAL MANUFACTURING**	**5 960**	**4 838**	**3 903**	..	..	**1.7**	**1.4**	**1.1**	..	..
15/16	Food, beverages, tobacco	0	44	28	..	..	0.0	0.4	0.2	..	..
17/19	Textiles, clothing, leather, footwear	0	0	0	..	..	0.0	0.0	0.0	..	..
20/22	Wood and paper products	11	10	6	..	..	0.2	0.2	0.1	..	..
20	Wood products	..	..	..	..	..	..	..	..	..	..
21/22	Paper, printing and publishing	..	..	..	..	..	..	..	..	..	..
23/25	Chemicals, Total	2 042	1 512	1 838	..	..	2.9	2.1	2.4	..	..
23	Refined petroleum, nuclear fuel	0	0	120	..	..	0.0	0.0	5.7	..	..
24/25	Chemicals, rubber & plastics prod.	2 042	1 512	1 718	..	..	3.0	2.1	2.3	..	..
24	Chemical products	2 042	1 507	1 701	..	..	3.5	2.5	2.8	..	..
2423	Pharmaceuticals	1 092	773	1 184	..	..	6.0	4.2	5.9	..	..
25	Rubber and plastics products	0	5	17	..	..	0.0	0.0	0.1	..	..
26	Non-metallic mineral products	15	0	10	..	..	0.2	0.0	0.1	..	..
27/28	Basic & fabricated metals	188	103	76	..	..	1.1	0.5	0.4	..	..
27	Basic metals	178	103	76	..	..	1.6	0.9	0.7	..	..
28	Fabricated metal products	10	0	0	..	..	0.2	0.0	0.0	..	..
29/32	Machinery, Total	3 533	2 913	1 884	..	..	2.0	1.6	1.0	..	..
29/30	Non-electrical machinery	164	154	104	..	..	0.2	0.2	0.1	..	..
29	Non-electrical machinery nec	164	154	104	..	..	0.5	0.5	0.3	..	..
30	Office and computing machinery	0	0	0	..	..	0.0	0.0	0.0	..	..
31/32	Electrical & electronic equipment	3 369	2 759	1 780	..	..	3.2	2.6	1.6	..	..
31	Electrical machinery nec	88	8	29	..	..	0.2	0.0	0.1	..	..
32	Radio, TV & communications eq.	3 281	2 751	1 751	..	..	4.8	4.1	2.5	..	..
33	Scientific instruments	151	202	21	..	..	0.9	1.1	0.1	..	..
34/35	Transportation equipment	20	49	29	..	..	0.1	0.1	0.1	..	..
34	Motor vehicles	20	49	26	..	..	0.1	0.2	0.1	..	..
35	Other transport equipment	0	0	3	..	..	0.0	0.0	0.1	..	..
351	Shipbuilding & repairing	..	..	..	..	..	..	..	..	..	..
353	Aircraft and spacecraft	0	0	3	..	..	0.0	0.0	0.2	..	..
36/37	Other manufacturing	0	5	11	..	..	0.0	0.1	0.2	..	..
40/45	Construction, electricity, gas & water	0	0	0	..	..	..	..	..	..	..
50/55	Trade, repair, hotels & restaurants	314	254	306	..	..	..	..	..	..	..
65/74	Finance, insurance, business services	113	84	186	..	..	..	..	..	..	..
	OTHER ACTIVITIES	5	5	5	..	..	..	..	..	..	..
01/99	**GRAND TOTAL**	**6 392**	**5 181**	**4 400**	..	..	**1.8**	**1.4**	**1.2**	..	..

Total manufacturing by investing country						As a % of total manufacturing by foreign affiliates				
All countries	5960	4838	3903	..	..	100.0	100.0	100.0	..	..
United States	4671	4237	3084	..	..	78.4	87.6	79.0	..	..
Canada	..	..	..	..	..	..	..	..	..	..
Mexico	..	..	..	..	..	..	..	..	..	..
Japan	..	..	..	..	..	..	..	..	..	..
Europe	..	..	..	..	..	..	..	..	..	..
European Union (15)	512	299	524	..	..	8.6	6.2	13.4	..	..
Belgium	..	..	..	..	..	..	..	..	..	..
France	41	17	62	..	..	0.7	0.4	1.6	..	..
Germany	332	190	294	..	..	5.6	3.9	7.5	..	..
Italy	..	..	..	..	..	..	..	..	..	..
Netherlands	76	60	43	..	..	1.3	1.2	1.1	..	..
Spain	..	..	..	..	..	..	..	..	..	..
Sweden	..	..	..	..	..	..	..	..	..	..
United Kingdom	59	28	119	..	..	1.0	0.6	3.0	..	..
Switzerland	478	165	181	..	..	8.0	3.4	4.6	..	..
Australia and New Zealand	..	..	..	..	..	..	..	..	..	..
Asia (non-OECD)	8	20	11	..	..	0.1	0.4	0.3	..	..
Latin America	102	0	21	..	..	1.7	0.0	0.5	..	..

Note: Majority foreign-owned firms.
Firmes sous contrôle étranger majoritaire.

Table 9. JAPAN / JAPON

GROSS FIXED CAPITAL FORMATION / FORMATION BRUTE DE CAPITAL FIXE

By industry (ISIC Rev. 3)		FOREIGN AFFILIATES (Billions of yen)					AS A % OF NATIONAL TOTAL				
		1992	1993	1994	1995	1996	1992	1993	1994	1995	1996
10/14	Mining & quarrying	0	0	0	0	0	..	..	..	..	..
15/37	**TOTAL MANUFACTURING**	307	208	203	231	304	1.6	1.4	1.6	1.7	2.1
15/16	Food, beverages, tobacco	1	2	2	1	8	0.0	0.1	0.1	0.0	0.7
17/19	Textiles, clothing, leather, footwear	0	1	3	2	0	..	..	..	..	..
20/22	Wood and paper products	0	0	0	0	0	0.0	..	..	..	..
20	Wood products	..	..	..	..	..	..	..	..	..	..
21/22	Paper, printing and publishing	..	..	..	..	..	..	..	..	..	..
23/25	Chemicals, Total	60	54	51	39	53	2.2	2.6	2.6	2.3	2.9
23	Refined petroleum, nuclear fuel	0	0	13	2	0	0.0	0.0	3.2	0.5	0.1
24/25	Chemicals, rubber & plastics prod.	60	54	38	37	52	2.9	3.5	2.5	3.0	3.5
24	Chemical products	60	51	36	36	49	..	..	..	..	..
2423	Pharmaceuticals	33	18	14	15	27	..	..	..	..	..
25	Rubber and plastics products	0	3	2	1	3	..	..	..	..	..
26	Non-metallic mineral products	2	0	11	0	0	..	..	..	..	..
27/28	Basic & fabricated metals	38	8	2	14	19	1.7	..	..	..	..
27	Basic metals	38	8	1	13	19	2.6	0.7	0.1	1.7	2.6
28	Fabricated metal products	0	0	1	0	0	0.0	..	..	..	..
29/32	Machinery, Total	179	130	130	171	219	4.8	4.5	4.3	4.3	5.8
29/30	Non-electrical machinery	12	3	3	101	131	1.2	0.4	0.4	14.3	19.7
29	Non-electrical machinery nec	12	3	3	3	4	..	..	..	..	..
30	Office and computing machinery	0	0	0	98	127	..	..	..	..	..
31/32	Electrical & electronic equipment	167	127	127	70	88	6.2	6.0	5.2	2.1	2.9
31	Electrical machinery nec	2	0	0	1	1	..	..	..	..	..
32	Radio, TV & communications eq.	165	127	127	69	87	..	..	..	..	..
33	Scientific instruments	7	3	1	2	2	..	..	..	..	..
34/35	Transportation equipment	17	2	3	1	1	0.7	0.1	0.2	0.1	0.0
34	Motor vehicles	16	2	1	1	0	..	..	..	..	..
35	Other transport equipment	1	0	2	0	0	..	..	..	..	..
351	Shipbuilding & repairing	..	..	..	..	..	..	..	..	..	..
353	Aircraft and spacecraft	..	0	2	0	..	..	..	..	..	..
36/37	Other manufacturing	2	8	1	1	1	..	..	..	..	..
40/45	Construction, electricity, gas & water	0	1	0	0	0	0.0	0.0	0.0	0.0	0.0
50/55	Trade, repair, hotels & restaurants	57	32	54	78	55	0.9	0.6	1.1	1.6	1.1
65/74	Finance, insurance, business services	24	6	3	15	1	..	..	..	..	..
	OTHER ACTIVITIES	4	1	0	2	5	0.0	..	..	..	..
01/99	**GRAND TOTAL**	392	248	261	326	365	0.7	0.5	0.6	0.7	0.8

Total manufacturing by investing country	1992	1993	1994	1995	1996	*As a % of total manufacturing by foreign affiliates*				
All countries	307	208	203	231	304	100.0	100.0	100.0	100.0	100.0
United States	215	178	175	171	238	70.0	85.6	85.8	73.7	78.3
Canada	..	..	..	..	..	..	..	..	..	..
Mexico	..	..	..	..	..	..	..	..	..	..
Japan	..	..	..	..	..	..	..	..	..	..
Europe	..	..	..	..	..	..	..	..	..	..
European Union (15)	41	7	22	40	31	13.4	3.3	10.9	17.2	10.2
Belgium	..	..	..	..	..	..	..	..	..	..
France	1	0	0	0	0	0.3	0.2	0.1	0.0	0.0
Germany	29	3	12	7	6	9.5	1.4	5.9	2.9	2.1
Italy	..	..	..	..	..	..	..	..	..	..
Netherlands	3	1	1	28	22	0.8	0.3	0.4	12.1	7.1
Spain	..	..	..	..	..	..	..	..	..	..
Sweden	..	..	..	..	..	..	..	..	..	..
United Kingdom	6	2	8	0	2	2.0	1.1	3.8	0.2	0.5
Switzerland	11	14	2	6	18	3.7	6.8	1.2	2.4	6.0
Australia and New Zealand	..	..	..	..	..	..	..	..	..	..
Asia (non-OECD)	0	0	0	0	0	0.1	0.2	0.2	0.2	0.1
Latin America	2	0	0	1	0	0.5	0.0	0.0	0.3	0.1

Note: Majority foreign-owned firms.
Firmes sous contrôle étranger majoritaire.

Table 10. JAPAN / JAPON

TOTAL EXPORTS / EXPORTATIONS TOTALES

By industry (ISIC Rev. 3)		FOREIGN AFFILIATES (Billions of yen)					AS A % OF NATIONAL TOTAL				
		1992	1993	1994	1995	1996	1992	1993	1994	1995	1996
10/14	Mining & quarrying	0	0	0	0	0	..	..	..	..	..
15/37	**TOTAL MANUFACTURING**	**727**	**684**	**657**	**591**	**652**	**1.7**	**1.7**	**1.7**	**1.5**	**1.5**
15/16	Food, beverages, tobacco	3	1	2	2	3	1.3	0.3	0.8	1.1	1.3
17/19	Textiles, clothing, leather, footwear	0	1	0	0	0	0.0	0.1	0.0	0.1	0.0
20/22	Wood and paper products	0	2	0	3	3	0.0	0.5	0.0	0.9	0.8
20	Wood products	..	..	..	..	..	..	..	..	..	..
21/22	Paper, printing and publishing	..	..	..	..	..	..	..	..	..	..
23/25	Chemicals, Total	88	136	130	92	96	2.1	3.5	3.2	2.0	1.9
23	Refined petroleum, nuclear fuel	0	49	39	1	3	0.0	20.7	15.2	0.4	1.3
24/25	Chemicals, rubber & plastics prod.	88	86	90	91	93	2.2	2.4	2.4	2.1	1.9
24	Chemical products	80	74	75	89	67	2.4	2.4	2.3	2.4	1.6
2423	Pharmaceuticals	32	36	34	42	22	19.1	22.7	22.5	24.9	10.8
25	Rubber and plastics products	8	12	16	3	25	1.2	2.1	2.7	0.4	3.5
26	Non-metallic mineral products	2	1	3	2	1	0.4	0.3	0.5	0.3	0.1
27/28	Basic & fabricated metals	17	21	7	23	27	0.6	0.7	0.2	0.7	0.9
27	Basic metals	16	21	6	23	27	0.8	1.1	0.3	1.1	1.3
28	Fabricated metal products	0	0	1	0	0	0.0	0.0	0.1	0.0	0.0
29/32	Machinery, Total	565	499	497	436	481	3.1	2.9	2.8	2.3	2.4
29/30	Non-electrical machinery	44	33	29	325	319	0.5	0.4	0.3	3.7	3.3
29	Non-electrical machinery nec	44	33	29	23	22	0.8	0.6	0.5	0.4	0.3
30	Office and computing machinery	0	0	0	302	297	0.0	0.0	0.0	10.4	9.3
31/32	Electrical & electronic equipment	520	466	468	112	162	5.6	5.2	5.0	1.1	1.6
31	Electrical machinery nec	9	22	17	13	12	0.3	0.8	0.6	0.4	0.4
32	Radio, TV & communications eq.	512	444	451	99	150	8.0	7.4	7.1	1.5	2.2
33	Scientific instruments	36	17	13	3	7	1.5	0.7	0.6	0.1	0.2
34/35	Transportation equipment	15	5	5	28	33	0.1	0.0	0.1	0.3	0.3
34	Motor vehicles	13	5	5	26	31	0.1	0.1	0.1	0.3	0.4
35	Other transport equipment	1	0	1	2	2	0.1	0.0	0.0	0.1	0.1
351	Shipbuilding & repairing	..	..	..	..	..	..	..	..	..	..
353	Aircraft and spacecraft	0	0	..	0	..	0.0	0.0	..	0.0	..
36/37	Other manufacturing	2	2	1	1	2	0.3	0.4	0.2	0.3	0.4
40/45	Construction, electricity, gas & water	0	0	0	0	0	..	..	..	..	..
50/55	Trade, repair, hotels & restaurants	808	524	537	444	411	..	..	..	..	..
65/74	Finance, insurance, business services	18	19	14	12	13	..	..	..	..	..
	OTHER ACTIVITIES	33	28	37	88	96	..	..	..	..	..
01/99	**GRAND TOTAL**	**1 586**	**1 255**	**1 245**	**1 135**	**1 173**	..	..	..	..	..

Total manufacturing by investing country						*As a % of total manufacturing by foreign affiliates*				
All countries	**727**	**684**	**657**	**591**	**652**	**100.0**	**100.0**	**100.0**	**100.0**	**100.0**
United States	592	524	504	425	483	81.4	76.6	76.8	71.9	74.2
Canada	..	..	..	..	33	..	..	..	..	5.1
Mexico	..	..	..	..	..	..	..	..	..	..
Japan	..	..	..	..	..	..	..	..	..	..
Europe	..	..	..	..	99	..	..	..	..	15.2
European Union (15)	53	52	73	68	66	7.3	7.6	11.1	11.5	10.1
Belgium	..	..	..	..	0	..	..	..	..	0.0
France	1	1	1	1	0	0.2	0.2	0.2	0.2	0.1
Germany	17	14	14	7	10	2.3	2.0	2.1	1.2	1.6
Italy	..	..	..	..	..	..	..	..	..	..
Netherlands	5	15	12	38	43	0.6	2.2	1.8	6.5	6.5
Spain	..	..	..	..	..	..	..	..	..	..
Sweden	..	..	..	..	1	..	..	..	..	0.2
United Kingdom	17	16	14	8	8	2.3	2.4	2.1	1.4	1.2
Switzerland	28	34	32	37	32	3.8	5.0	4.9	6.3	4.9
Australia and New Zealand	..	..	..	..	2	..	..	..	..	0.3
Asia (non-OECD)	22	53	41	26	33	3.1	7.8	6.2	4.3	5.1
Latin America	15	1	0	0	..	2.0	0.1	0.0	0.0	..

Note: Majority foreign-owned firms.
Firmes sous contrôle étranger majoritaire.

163

Table 11. JAPAN / JAPON

TOTAL IMPORTS / IMPORTATIONS TOTALES

By industry (ISIC Rev. 3)		FOREIGN AFFILIATES (Billions of yen)					AS A % OF NATIONAL TOTAL				
		1992	1993	1994	1995	1996	1992	1993	1994	1995	1996
10/14	Mining & quarrying	0	0	0	0	0	..	..	..	..	..
15/37	**TOTAL MANUFACTURING**	1 518	1 109	1 113	944	1 125	7.7	6.1	5.6	4.0	4.0
15/16	Food, beverages, tobacco	5	6	17	6	8	0.1	0.2	0.5	0.2	0.2
17/19	Textiles, clothing, leather, footwear	8	7	15	16	13	0.3	0.3	0.6	0.5	0.4
20/22	Wood and paper products	32	5	3	4	6	2.2	0.3	0.2	0.2	0.3
20	Wood products	..	..	..	..	..	..	..	..	..	..
21/22	Paper, printing and publishing	..	..	..	..	..	..	..	..	..	..
23/25	Chemicals, Total	794	471	547	384	398	20.4	14.1	16.4	10.3	8.9
23	Refined petroleum, nuclear fuel	0	42	68	7	9	0.0	4.4	8.0	0.7	0.7
24/25	Chemicals, rubber & plastics prod.	794	429	478	377	389	30.5	17.9	19.3	13.5	12.4
24	Chemical products	781	420	468	371	367	35.1	20.6	22.2	15.8	14.1
2423	Pharmaceuticals	558	231	307	211	224	..	58.4	79.0	49.7	49.4
25	Rubber and plastics products	13	10	11	5	22	3.5	2.7	2.9	1.2	4.1
26	Non-metallic mineral products	12	6	10	2	1	5.0	3.2	4.6	0.9	0.4
27/28	Basic & fabricated metals	11	23	14	62	66	0.6	1.5	0.8	3.0	3.1
27	Basic metals	10	23	11	61	64	0.7	1.8	0.8	3.7	4.1
28	Fabricated metal products	1	0	3	1	2	0.2	0.0	0.8	0.2	0.3
29/32	Machinery, Total	425	412	396	436	565	12.7	12.4	10.0	7.8	7.7
29/30	Non-electrical machinery	42	48	42	324	431	2.5	3.1	2.4	13.2	13.0
29	Non-electrical machinery nec	42	48	42	20	30	4.6	6.2	5.2	2.1	2.4
30	Office and computing machinery	0	0	0	304	401	0.0	0.1	0.0	20.5	19.4
31/32	Electrical & electronic equipment	383	364	354	112	134	22.9	20.4	15.9	3.6	3.3
31	Electrical machinery nec	10	6	24	1	2	1.6	1.1	3.4	0.2	0.2
32	Radio, TV & communications eq.	373	357	330	111	132	35.1	29.9	21.6	5.0	4.6
33	Scientific instruments	148	86	68	27	49	18.8	11.2	7.9	2.7	3.7
34/35	Transportation equipment	56	59	27	6	6	3.9	4.7	1.9	0.4	0.3
34	Motor vehicles	54	58	27	5	4	6.5	7.8	3.0	0.4	0.3
35	Other transport equipment	2	1	1	1	2	0.3	0.2	0.1	0.3	0.4
351	Shipbuilding & repairing	..	..	..	..	..	..	..	..	..	..
353	Aircraft and spacecraft	0	0	0	0	1	0.0	0.1	0.1	0.1	0.2
36/37	Other manufacturing	27	34	16	2	12	3.5	4.7	2.1	0.3	1.3
40/45	Construction, electricity, gas & water	0	15	0	0	0	..	..	..	..	..
50/55	Trade, repair, hotels & restaurants	1 202	1 009	1 478	1 627	1 803	..	..	..	..	..
65/74	Finance, insurance, business services	29	23	29	16	4	..	..	..	..	..
	OTHER ACTIVITIES	13	10	4	52	89	..	..	..	..	..
01/99	**GRAND TOTAL**	2 763	2 167	2 625	2 639	3 021	..	..	..	..	..

Total manufacturing by investing country	As a % of total manufacturing by foreign affiliates									
All countries	1518	1109	1113	944	1125	100.0	100.0	100.0	100.0	100.0
United States	715	630	649	636	773	47.1	56.8	58.3	67.3	68.7
Canada	..	..	..	..	57	..	..	..	..	5.1
Mexico	..	..	..	..	..	..	..	..	..	..
Japan	..	..	..	..	..	..	..	..	..	..
Europe	..	..	..	..	261	..	..	..	..	23.2
European Union (15)	595	299	351	143	159	39.2	27.0	31.5	15.1	14.2
Belgium	..	..	..	..	1	..	..	..	..	0.1
France	28	20	23	2	2	1.8	1.8	2.1	0.2	0.1
Germany	417	143	153	72	78	27.4	12.9	13.7	7.6	6.9
Italy	..	..	..	..	0	..	..	..	..	0.0
Netherlands	27	43	35	14	29	1.8	3.9	3.1	1.5	2.6
Spain	..	..	..	..	..	..	..	..	..	..
Sweden	..	..	..	..	5	..	..	..	..	0.4
United Kingdom	61	61	112	29	42	4.0	5.5	10.1	3.1	3.8
Switzerland	97	96	59	82	93	6.4	8.7	5.3	8.7	8.2
Australia and New Zealand	..	..	..	..	0	..	..	..	..	0.0
Asia (non-OECD)	45	59	30	14	24	3.0	5.4	2.7	1.5	2.2
Latin America	31	0	13	6	9	2.0	0.0	1.2	0.7	0.8

Note: Majority foreign-owned firms.
Firmes sous contrôle étranger majoritaire.

Table 12. JAPAN / JAPON

INTRA-FIRM EXPORTS / EXPORTATIONS INTRA-FIRME

		FOREIGN AFFILIATES *(Billions of yen)*								
By industry (ISIC Rev. 3)		1987	1988	1989	1990	1991	1992	1993	1994	1995	1996
10/14	Mining & quarrying	..	..	..	..	0.0	0.0	0.0	0.0	0.0	0.0
15/37	**TOTAL MANUFACTURING**	..	..	..	..	**320.7**	**341.4**	**362.5**	**337.7**	**331.0**	**177.7**
15/16	Food, beverages, tobacco	..	..	..	..	0.9	0.2	0.0	0.9	0.3	2.3
17/19	Textiles, clothing, leather, footwear	..	..	..	..	0.0	0.0	0.0	0.0	0.3	0.0
20/22	Wood and paper products	..	..	..	..	0.2	0.0	0.0	0.0	0.5	0.8
20	Wood products	..	..	..	..	..	..	..	..	..	..
21/22	Paper, printing and publishing	..	..	..	..	..	..	..	..	..	..
23/25	Chemicals, Total	..	..	..	..	32.4	35.1	70.8	80.3	45.2	55.0
23	Refined petroleum, nuclear fuel	..	..	..	..	0.0	0.0	39.1	33.7	0.2	2.7
24/25	Chemicals, rubber & plastics prod.	..	..	..	..	32.4	35.1	31.7	46.7	45.0	52.2
24	Chemical products	..	..	..	..	31.3	32.2	31.4	38.6	44.7	33.5
2423	Pharmaceuticals	..	..	..	..	15.1	19.3	16.5	19.1	26.2	18.0
25	Rubber and plastics products	..	..	..	..	1.1	2.9	0.3	8.1	0.3	18.7
26	Non-metallic mineral products	..	..	..	..	0.3	0.5	0.2	0.4	0.9	0.3
27/28	Basic & fabricated metals	..	..	..	..	0.9	0.1	0.2	1.4	7.7	1.9
27	Basic metals	..	..	..	..	0.7	0.0	0.1	1.3	7.6	1.8
28	Fabricated metal products	..	..	..	..	0.3	0.1	0.0	0.1	0.1	0.2
29/32	Machinery, Total	..	..	..	..	257.6	273.3	288.4	248.1	254.2	89.8
29/30	Non-electrical machinery	..	..	..	..	8.6	11.4	8.1	1.8	208.4	32.6
29	Non-electrical machinery nec	..	..	..	..	8.6	11.4	8.1	1.8	2.9	11.4
30	Office and computing machinery	..	..	..	..	0.0	0.0	0.0	0.0	205.5	21.3
31/32	Electrical & electronic equipment	..	..	..	..	249.1	261.9	280.3	246.3	45.8	57.1
31	Electrical machinery nec	..	..	..	..	1.1	2.2	20.2	7.4	2.1	2.0
32	Radio, TV & communications eq.	..	..	..	..	248.0	259.8	260.2	238.9	43.7	55.1
33	Scientific instruments	..	..	..	..	27.8	31.1	1.4	2.1	2.6	2.8
34/35	Transportation equipment	..	..	..	..	0.0	0.6	1.1	4.3	19.3	24.7
34	Motor vehicles	..	..	..	..	0.0	0.6	1.1	4.1	19.1	24.6
35	Other transport equipment	..	..	..	..	0.0	0.0	0.0	0.1	0.2	0.2
351	Shipbuilding & repairing	..	..	..	..	..	..	..	..	..	..
353	Aircraft and spacecraft	..	..	..	..	0.0	0.0	..	..	..	..
36/37	Other manufacturing	..	..	..	..	0.5	0.4	0.4	0.1	0.0	0.0
40/45	Construction, electricity, gas & water	..	..	..	..	0.0	0.0	0.0	0.0	0.0	0.0
50/55	Trade, repair, hotels & restaurants	..	..	..	..	483.2	347.6	206.1	153.0	228.8	135.5
65/74	Finance, insurance, business services	..	..	..	..	7.9	13.6	11.5	3.8	9.4	6.7
	OTHER ACTIVITIES	..	..	..	..	5.0	9.6	6.8	3.5	67.8	52.8
01/99	**GRAND TOTAL**	..	..	..	..	**816.9**	**712.3**	**586.9**	**498.1**	**637.0**	**372.8**

Total manufacturing by investing country

	1987	1988	1989	1990	1991	1992	1993	1994	1995	1996
All countries	..	..	..	..	320.7	341.4	362.5	337.7	331.0	177.7
United States	..	..	..	..	280.5	50.2	45.9	46.9	46.2	46.3
Canada	..	..	..	..	0.1	..	..	..	..	..
Mexico	..	..	..	..	..	..	..	..	..	..
Japan	..	..	..	..	..	..	..	..	..	..
Europe	..	..	..	..	31.8	..	..	..	..	..
European Union (15)	..	..	..	..	20.4	35.1	37.5	35.2	32.4	31.9
Belgium	..	..	..	..	1.0	..	..	..	..	..
France	..	..	..	..	0.0	3.5	3.7	5.0	2.9	2.1
Germany	..	..	..	..	3.8	13.7	12.7	10.6	9.8	10.5
Italy	..	..	..	..	0.1	..	..	..	..	..
Netherlands	..	..	..	..	6.6	4.7	6.2	5.9	6.5	6.3
Spain	..	..	..	..	..	..	..	..	..	..
Sweden	..	..	..	..	0.6	..	..	..	..	..
United Kingdom	..	..	..	..	8.1	4.2	5.1	5.0	4.7	6.0
Switzerland	..	..	..	..	11.4	5.3	6.2	6.7	7.6	8.1
Australia and New Zealand	..	..	..	..	..	..	..	..	..	..
Asia (non-OECD)	..	..	..	..	5.1	4.7	6.8	6.7	8.4	7.4
Latin America	..	..	..	..	3.2	0.9	0.3	0.6	0.7	0.4

Note: Majority foreign-owned firms.
Firmes sous contrôle étranger majoritaire.

Table 13. JAPAN / JAPON

INTRA-FIRM IMPORTS / IMPORTATIONS INTRA-FIRME

By industry (ISIC Rev. 3)		FOREIGN AFFILIATES *(Billions of yen)*								
		1987	1988	1989	1990	1991	1992	1993	1994	1995	1996
10/14	Mining & quarrying	..	..	..	..	0.0	0.0	0.0	0.0	0.0	0.0
15/37	**TOTAL MANUFACTURING**	..	..	..	..	929.4	1 114.9	725.2	746.7	629.4	670.9
15/16	Food, beverages, tobacco	..	..	..	..	5.4	1.8	0.4	14.7	3.7	0.8
17/19	Textiles, clothing, leather, footwear	..	..	..	..	11.1	7.4	6.2	12.0	13.9	11.2
20/22	Wood and paper products	..	..	..	..	6.4	30.2	4.3	1.7	2.6	4.0
20	Wood products	..	..	..	..	..	..	..	..	..	..
21/22	Paper, printing and publishing	..	..	..	..	..	..	..	..	..	..
23/25	Chemicals, Total	..	..	..	..	483.7	599.8	281.8	351.6	258.2	304.2
23	Refined petroleum, nuclear fuel	..	..	..	..	62.4	0.1	2.6	20.5	4.8	6.5
24/25	Chemicals, rubber & plastics prod.	..	..	..	..	421.3	599.7	279.2	331.1	253.3	297.7
24	Chemical products	..	..	..	..	414.3	588.8	277.7	322.6	249.3	276.6
2423	Pharmaceuticals	..	..	..	..	260.0	462.8	146.2	215.8	152.0	186.3
25	Rubber and plastics products	..	..	..	..	7.0	10.9	1.5	8.5	4.0	21.1
26	Non-metallic mineral products	..	..	..	..	11.0	9.3	4.6	7.7	1.5	1.1
27/28	Basic & fabricated metals	..	..	..	..	9.7	6.4	21.1	6.9	24.6	12.1
27	Basic metals	..	..	..	..	8.6	5.8	21.1	6.5	23.7	11.6
28	Fabricated metal products	..	..	..	..	1.1	0.6	0.0	0.4	1.0	0.6
29/32	Machinery, Total	..	..	..	..	298.8	283.2	297.9	270.1	307.0	305.7
29/30	Non-electrical machinery	..	..	..	..	28.9	26.6	26.5	29.9	274.6	257.6
29	Non-electrical machinery nec	..	..	..	..	28.7	26.4	26.4	29.9	15.1	28.3
30	Office and computing machinery	..	..	..	..	0.2	0.2	0.0	0.0	259.6	229.4
31/32	Electrical & electronic equipment	..	..	..	..	269.9	256.6	271.4	240.2	32.4	48.1
31	Electrical machinery nec	..	..	..	..	7.4	7.3	5.5	22.7	0.9	0.5
32	Radio, TV & communications eq.	..	..	..	..	262.5	249.3	265.9	217.6	31.5	47.6
33	Scientific instruments	..	..	..	..	89.0	101.1	44.2	43.5	12.7	19.4
34/35	Transportation equipment	..	..	..	..	12.3	54.1	51.7	23.6	4.2	3.9
34	Motor vehicles	..	..	..	..	10.6	52.9	50.7	23.2	4.1	3.2
35	Other transport equipment	..	..	..	..	1.6	1.2	1.0	0.4	0.2	0.6
351	Shipbuilding & repairing	..	..	..	..	..	..	..	..	..	..
353	Aircraft and spacecraft	..	..	..	..	0.0	0.1	0.3	0.4	0.2	0.6
36/37	Other manufacturing	..	..	..	..	2.1	21.6	12.9	15.1	1.0	8.3
40/45	Construction, electricity, gas & water	..	..	..	..	0.0	0.0	14.8	0.0	0.1	0.0
50/55	Trade, repair, hotels & restaurants	..	..	..	..	1 306.0	737.4	739.1	1 040.7	1 226.6	1 356.7
65/74	Finance, insurance, business services	..	..	..	..	19.2	23.8	21.2	22.9	14.6	2.2
	OTHER ACTIVITIES	..	..	..	..	1.3	3.9	4.2	2.9	29.9	71.6
01/99	**GRAND TOTAL**	..	..	..	..	**2 255.9**	**1 880.0**	**1 504.4**	**1 813.2**	**1 900.7**	**2 101.4**

Total manufacturing by investing country

	1987	1988	1989	1990	1991	1992	1993	1994	1995	1996
All countries	..	..	..	..	929.4	1 114.9	725.2	746.7	629.4	670.9
United States	..	..	..	..	546.9	50.2	45.9	46.9	46.2	46.3
Canada	..	..	..	..	0.6	..	..	..	..	..
Mexico	..	..	..	..	..	..	..	..	..	..
Japan	..	..	..	..	..	..	..	..	..	..
Europe	..	..	..	..	345.8	..	..	..	..	..
European Union (15)	..	..	..	..	243.5	35.1	37.5	35.2	32.4	31.9
Belgium	..	..	..	..	4.2	..	..	..	..	..
France	..	..	..	..	3.3	3.5	3.7	5.0	2.9	2.1
Germany	..	..	..	..	159.0	13.7	12.7	10.6	9.8	10.5
Italy	..	..	..	..	0.6	..	..	..	..	..
Netherlands	..	..	..	..	6.3	4.7	6.2	5.9	6.5	6.3
Spain	..	..	..	..	..	..	..	..	..	..
Sweden	..	..	..	..	20.4	..	..	..	..	..
United Kingdom	..	..	..	..	39.0	4.2	5.1	5.0	4.7	6.0
Switzerland	..	..	..	..	98.2	5.3	6.2	6.7	7.6	8.1
Australia and New Zealand	..	..	..	..	..	..	..	..	..	..
Asia (non-OECD)	..	..	..	..	33.5	4.7	6.8	6.7	8.4	7.4
Latin America	..	..	..	..	2.8	0.9	0.3	0.6	0.7	0.4

Note: Majority foreign-owned firms.
Firmes sous contrôle étranger majoritaire.

Table 14. JAPAN / JAPON

GROSS OPERATING SURPLUS / EXCÉDENT BRUT D'EXPLOITATION

By industry (ISIC Rev. 3)	FOREIGN AFFILIATES (Billions of yen)					AS A % OF NATIONAL TOTAL				
	1992	1993	1994	1995	1996	1992	1993	1994	1995	1996
10/14 Mining & quarrying	0	0	0	0	0	..	..	..	..	..
15/37 TOTAL MANUFACTURING	**397**	**397**	**411**	**570**	**583**	..	..	..	..	..
15/16 Food, beverages, tobacco	6	6	63	69	70	..	..	..	..	..
17/19 Textiles, clothing, leather, footwear	1	1	6	1	1	..	..	..	..	..
20/22 Wood and paper products	1	1	2	2	3	..	..	..	..	..
20 Wood products	..	..	..	..	..	..	..	..	..	..
21/22 Paper, printing and publishing	..	..	..	..	..	..	..	..	..	..
23/25 Chemicals, Total	89	89	156	146	137	..	..	..	..	..
23 Refined petroleum, nuclear fuel	0	0	33	2	1	..	..	..	..	..
24/25 Chemicals, rubber & plastics prod.	89	89	123	144	135	..	..	..	..	..
24 Chemical products	91	91	121	138	123	..	..	..	..	..
2423 Pharmaceuticals	61	61	87	85	84	..	..	..	..	..
25 Rubber and plastics products	-2	-2	1	5	13	..	..	..	..	..
26 Non-metallic mineral products	2	2	2	1	0	..	..	..	..	..
27/28 Basic & fabricated metals	18	18	3	18	22	..	..	..	..	..
27 Basic metals	17	17	2	18	20	..	..	..	..	..
28 Fabricated metal products	0	0	1	0	1	..	..	..	..	..
29/32 Machinery, Total	260	260	161	302	328	..	..	..	..	..
29/30 Non-electrical machinery	16	16	15	241	263	..	..	..	..	..
29 Non-electrical machinery nec	16	16	15	18	14	..	..	..	..	..
30 Office and computing machinery	0	0	0	223	249	..	..	..	..	..
31/32 Electrical & electronic equipment	245	245	146	61	65	..	..	..	..	..
31 Electrical machinery nec	11	11	2	2	4	..	..	..	..	..
32 Radio, TV & communications eq.	234	234	144	59	61	..	..	..	..	..
33 Scientific instruments	19	19	11	8	15	..	..	..	..	..
34/35 Transportation equipment	-2	-2	5	5	2	..	..	..	..	..
34 Motor vehicles	-2	-2	5	4	2	..	..	..	..	..
35 Other transport equipment	0	0	0	2	0	..	..	..	..	..
351 Shipbuilding & repairing	..	..	..	..	..	..	..	..	..	..
353 Aircraft and spacecraft	0	0	0	0	0	..	..	..	..	..
36/37 Other manufacturing	3	3	3	18	5	..	..	..	..	..
40/45 Construction, electricity, gas & water	-2	-2	0	0	0	..	..	..	..	..
50/55 Trade, repair, hotels & restaurants	118	118	191	221	239	..	..	..	..	..
65/74 Finance, insurance, business services	5	5	8	8	2	..	..	..	..	..
OTHER ACTIVITIES	2	2	5	15	15	..	..	..	..	..
01/99 GRAND TOTAL	**520**	**520**	**615**	**814**	**839**	..	..	..	..	..

Total manufacturing by investing country						As a % of total manufacturing by foreign affiliates				
All countries	397	397	411	570	583	100.0	100.0	100.0	100.0	100.0
United States	332	332	330	452	475	83.6	83.6	80.2	79.3	81.5
Canada	..	..	..	..	..	..	..	..	..	..
Mexico	..	..	..	..	..	..	..	..	..	..
Japan	..	..	..	..	..	..	..	..	..	..
Europe	..	..	..	..	..	..	..	..	..	..
European Union (15)	24	24	70	63	61	6.0	6.0	16.9	11.1	10.5
Belgium	..	..	..	..	..	..	..	..	..	..
France	1	1	4	0	0	0.2	0.2	1.0	0.0	0.0
Germany	5	5	35	19	25	1.3	1.3	8.6	3.4	4.3
Italy	..	..	..	..	..	..	..	..	..	..
Netherlands	3	3	2	19	22	0.7	0.7	0.6	3.3	3.7
Spain	..	..	..	..	..	..	..	..	..	..
Sweden	..	..	..	..	..	..	..	..	..	..
United Kingdom	8	8	17	3	11	1.9	1.9	4.1	0.5	1.8
Switzerland	19	19	12	29	22	4.7	4.7	2.8	5.0	3.8
Australia and New Zealand	..	..	..	..	..	..	..	..	..	..
Asia (non-OECD)	5	5	-3	1	0	1.2	1.2	-0.7	0.2	0.0
Latin America	0	0	-2	0	-2	0.0	0.0	-0.4	0.0	-0.4

Note: Majority foreign-owned firms.
Firmes sous contrôle étranger majoritaire.

Table 15. JAPAN / JAPON

TECHNOLOGICAL PAYMENTS / PAIEMENTS TECHNOLOGIQUES

By industry (ISIC Rev. 3)		FOREIGN AFFILIATES (Billions of yen)					AS A % OF NATIONAL TOTAL				
		1992	1993	1994	1995	1996	1992	1993	1994	1995	1996
10/14	Mining & quarrying	0.0	0.0	0.0	0.0	0.0	0.0	0.0	0.0	0.0	0.0
15/37	**TOTAL MANUFACTURING**	**160.7**	**124.9**	**138.8**	**173.7**	**193.3**	**39.1**	**34.7**	**37.7**	**44.7**	**44.0**
15/16	Food, beverages, tobacco	0.3	0.5	0.5	0.5	0.7	3.6	5.8	6.1	5.7	8.2
17/19	Textiles, clothing, leather, footwear	0.4	0.4	1.5	0.6	0.7	6.6	7.1	19.0	7.1	6.4
20/22	Wood and paper products	0.4	0.2	0.7	0.7	0.9	37.0	17.3	93.6	46.6	71.7
20	Wood products	..	..	..	..	..	..	..	..	..	..
21/22	Paper, printing and publishing	..	..	..	..	..	..	..	..	..	..
23/25	Chemicals, Total	15.5	16.9	20.1	23.7	25.2	19.0	24.0	29.4	31.8	32.6
23	Refined petroleum, nuclear fuel	0.0	0.0	0.5	0.4	0.4	0.0	0.0	13.0	15.0	16.4
24/25	Chemicals, rubber & plastics prod.	15.5	16.9	19.6	23.3	24.8	19.8	25.1	30.4	32.4	33.1
24	Chemical products	15.3	15.4	18.5	22.8	22.8	21.6	25.1	31.3	34.4	32.6
2423	Pharmaceuticals	7.8	8.7	9.4	11.6	9.6	22.7	25.3	28.8	31.5	26.0
25	Rubber and plastics products	0.3	1.5	1.1	0.5	2.0	3.6	25.2	20.2	9.2	40.3
26	Non-metallic mineral products	0.7	0.5	0.6	0.1	0.1	9.0	13.5	25.8	3.8	1.8
27/28	Basic & fabricated metals	0.5	0.0	0.0	0.1	0.3	4.5	0.6	0.1	0.8	3.4
27	Basic metals	0.1	0.0	0.0	0.0	0.3	1.3	0.3	0.2	0.2	3.7
28	Fabricated metal products	0.4	0.0	0.0	0.1	0.0	22.3	1.8	0.0	3.1	2.2
29/32	Machinery, Total	135.3	95.5	101.9	131.6	149.2	65.4	51.7	50.8	59.6	60.8
29/30	Non-electrical machinery	3.2	1.5	1.8	130.7	138.7	..	..	..	..	..
29	Non-electrical machinery nec	3.1	1.5	1.8	4.2	4.1	..	..	..	..	..
30	Office and computing machinery	0.0	0.0	0.0	126.5	134.6	..	..	..	..	..
31/32	Electrical & electronic equipment	132.1	94.0	100.1	1.0	10.6	..	..	..	..	..
31	Electrical machinery nec	0.2	0.2	0.3	0.0	2.9	..	..	..	..	..
32	Radio, TV & communications eq.	131.9	93.8	99.8	1.0	7.7	..	..	..	..	..
33	Scientific instruments	2.3	0.4	0.7	2.0	3.7	10.2	1.7	6.5	16.4	28.4
34/35	Transportation equipment	1.8	0.7	1.0	0.9	0.4	3.3	1.7	2.7	2.8	0.9
34	Motor vehicles	1.8	0.7	1.0	0.9	0.4	10.3	7.9	11.2	12.0	4.5
35	Other transport equipment	0.0	0.0	0.0	0.0	0.0	0.0	0.0	0.0	0.0	0.0
351	Shipbuilding & repairing	..	..	..	..	..	..	..	..	..	..
353	Aircraft and spacecraft	0.0	0.0	0.0	0.0	0.0	..	..	..	..	..
36/37	Other manufacturing	3.4	9.7	11.9	13.6	12.2	29.3	72.0	44.7	71.9	44.4
40/45	Construction, electricity, gas & water	0.0	0.0	0.0	0.0	0.0	..	..	..	..	..
50/55	Trade, repair, hotels & restaurants	5.1	3.8	9.1	15.7	13.1	..	..	..	..	..
65/74	Finance, insurance, business services	7.6	6.3	7.5	12.3	6.8	..	..	..	..	..
	OTHER ACTIVITIES	9.5	0.4	2.1	2.1	17.4	..	..	..	..	..
01/99	**GRAND TOTAL**	**182.8**	**135.4**	**157.5**	**203.8**	**230.6**	**44.2**	**37.3**	**42.5**	**52.0**	**51.1**

Total manufacturing by investing country						*As a % of total manufacturing by foreign affiliates*				
All countries	160.7	124.9	138.8	173.7	193.3	100.0	100.0	100.0	100.0	100.0
United States	150.3	107.6	124.0	150.0	172.8	93.6	86.2	89.4	86.3	89.4
Canada	..	..	..	..	..	..	..	..	..	..
Mexico	..	..	..	..	..	..	..	..	..	..
Japan	..	..	..	..	..	..	..	..	..	..
Europe	..	..	..	..	..	..	..	..	..	..
European Union (15)	8.1	5.3	13.0	18.5	14.2	5.1	4.2	9.4	10.6	7.3
Belgium	..	..	..	..	..	..	..	..	..	..
France	0.1	0.7	0.2	0.4	..	0.0	0.6	0.1	0.2	..
Germany	4.2	1.0	5.5	6.5	2.5	2.6	0.8	4.0	3.7	1.3
Italy	..	..	..	..	..	..	..	..	..	..
Netherlands	0.8	0.8	5.5	9.0	11.1	0.5	0.6	4.0	5.2	5.7
Spain	..	..	..	..	..	..	..	..	..	..
Sweden	..	..	..	..	..	..	..	..	..	..
United Kingdom	2.1	2.4	1.4	0.0	0.6	1.3	1.9	1.0	0.0	0.3
Switzerland	1.3	2.4	0.8	3.9	5.0	0.8	1.9	0.5	2.2	2.6
Australia and New Zealand	..	..	..	..	..	..	..	..	..	..
Asia (non-OECD)	0.1	9.1	0.1	0.1	..	0.1	7.3	0.1	0.0	..
Latin America	0.0	0.0	0.0	0.0	..	0.0	0.0	0.0	0.0	..

Note: Majority foreign-owned firms.
Firmes sous contrôle étranger majoritaire.

Table 17. JAPAN / JAPON

STOCK OF FOREIGN DIRECT INVESTMENT / STOCK D'INVESTISSEMENT DIRECT ÉTRANGER

By industry (ISIC Rev. 3)		1987	1988	1989	1990	1991	1992	1993	1994	1995	1996
		FOREIGN AFFILIATES *(Billions of yen)*									
10/14	Mining & quarrying	..	..	..	..	..	0.0	0.7	0.0	0.0	0.0
15/37	**TOTAL MANUFACTURING**	..	..	..	..	..	**581.1**	**576.3**	**524.2**	**510.4**	**522.8**
15/16	Food, beverages, tobacco	..	..	..	..	..	8.3	6.0	9.9	9.7	9.5
17/19	Textiles, clothing, leather, footwear	..	..	..	..	..	3.3	2.6	7.1	2.8	3.0
20/22	Wood and paper products	..	..	..	..	..	3.0	1.8	5.9	5.5	4.7
20	Wood products	..	..	..	..	..					
21/22	Paper, printing and publishing	..	..	..	..	..	..	..	..	..	..
23/25	Chemicals, Total	..	..	..	..	..	233.5	238.7	242.3	221.9	243.0
23	Refined petroleum, nuclear fuel	..	..	..	..	..	0.1	0.1	11.8	1.4	1.0
24/25	Chemicals, rubber & plastics prod.	..	..	..	..	..	233.4	238.6	230.5	220.5	242.1
24	Chemical products	..	..	..	..	..	230.4	211.5	196.1	216.9	196.3
2423	Pharmaceuticals	..	..	..	..	..	127.6	102.3	113.1	122.1	118.3
25	Rubber and plastics products	..	..	..	..	..	3.0	27.1	34.4	3.7	45.8
26	Non-metallic mineral products	..	..	..	..	..	6.9	5.7	7.4	3.5	1.8
27/28	Basic & fabricated metals	..	..	..	..	..	24.4	23.2	11.0	24.1	24.9
27	Basic metals	..	..	..	..	..	23.1	22.4	4.1	23.4	24.0
28	Fabricated metal products	..	..	..	..	..	1.3	0.8	6.9	0.7	0.9
29/32	Machinery, Total	..	..	..	..	..	241.0	243.3	217.0	223.7	214.9
29/30	Non-electrical machinery	..	..	..	..	..	21.6	20.9	16.2	165.3	154.5
29	Non-electrical machinery nec	..	..	..	..	..	21.5	19.5	16.2	17.9	12.1
30	Office and computing machinery	..	..	..	..	..	0.1	1.4	0.0	147.4	142.4
31/32	Electrical & electronic equipment	..	..	..	..	..	219.4	222.4	200.7	58.4	60.4
31	Electrical machinery nec	..	..	..	..	..	4.0	17.1	4.2	1.5	2.8
32	Radio, TV & communications eq.	..	..	..	..	..	215.4	205.3	196.5	56.9	57.5
33	Scientific instruments	..	..	..	..	..	27.8	19.8	14.0	6.8	8.5
34/35	Transportation equipment	..	..	..	..	..	23.0	26.8	6.5	3.5	3.0
34	Motor vehicles	..	..	..	..	..	21.2	26.3	5.4	3.2	2.5
35	Other transport equipment	..	..	..	..	..	1.8	0.4	1.0	0.3	0.5
351	Shipbuilding & repairing	..	..	..	..	..	..	..	..	..	..
353	Aircraft and spacecraft	..	..	..	..	..	0.0	0.0	0.5	0.0	0.0
36/37	Other manufacturing	..	..	..	..	..	9.9	8.3	3.2	8.9	9.5
40/45	Construction, electricity, gas & water	..	..	..	..	..	0.2	0.5	0.1	0.2	0.4
50/55	Trade, repair, hotels & restaurants	..	..	..	..	..	239.9	154.0	232.4	242.4	259.2
65/74	Finance, insurance, business services	..	..	..	..	..	49.5	20.4	26.6	9.3	15.3
	OTHER ACTIVITIES	..	..	..	..	..	7.6	18.4	119.8	32.5	39.5
01/99	**GRAND TOTAL**	..	..	..	..	..	**878.3**	**770.4**	**903.1**	**794.9**	**837.2**

Total manufacturing by investing country

	1987	1988	1989	1990	1991	1992	1993	1994	1995	1996
All countries	..	..	..	..	..	**581.1**	**576.3**	**524.2**	**510.4**	**522.8**
United States	..	..	..	..	..	50.2	45.9	46.9	46.2	46.3
Canada	..	..	..	..	..	..	..	..	..	..
Mexico	..	..	..	..	..	..	..	..	..	..
Japan	..	..	..	..	..	..	..	..	..	..
Europe	..	..	..	..	..	..	..	..	..	..
European Union (15)	..	..	..	..	..	35.1	37.5	35.2	32.4	31.9
Belgium	..	..	..	..	..	..	..	..	..	..
France	..	..	..	..	..	3.5	3.7	5.0	2.9	2.1
Germany	..	..	..	..	..	13.7	12.7	10.6	9.8	10.5
Italy	..	..	..	..	..	..	..	..	..	..
Netherlands	..	..	..	..	..	4.7	6.2	5.9	6.5	6.3
Spain	..	..	..	..	..	..	..	..	..	..
Sweden	..	..	..	..	..	..	..	..	..	..
United Kingdom	..	..	..	..	..	4.2	5.1	5.0	4.7	6.0
Switzerland	..	..	..	..	..	5.3	6.2	6.7	7.6	8.1
Australia and New Zealand	..	..	..	..	..	..	..	..	..	..
Asia (non-OECD)	..	..	..	..	..	4.7	6.8	6.7	8.4	7.4
Latin America	..	..	..	..	..	0.9	0.3	0.6	0.7	0.4

Note: Majority foreign-owned firms.
Firmes sous contrôle étranger majoritaire.

Table 18. JAPAN / JAPON

CAPITAL UNDER FOREIGN INFLUENCE / CAPITAL SOUS INFLUENCE ÉTRANGÈRE

By industry (ISIC Rev. 3)		FOREIGN AFFILIATES (Billions of yen)									
		1987	1988	1989	1990	1991	1992	1993	1994	1995	1996
10/14	Mining & quarrying	..	..	..	..	0.0	0.0	0.8	0.0	0.0	0.0
15/37	**TOTAL MANUFACTURING**	..	..	..	..	**701.3**	**590.7**	**600.7**	**540.7**	**530.8**	**552.2**
15/16	Food, beverages, tobacco	..	..	..	..	11.3	8.3	6.0	9.9	9.7	9.5
17/19	Textiles, clothing, leather, footwear	..	..	..	..	7.9	3.3	2.7	7.4	2.8	3.0
20/22	Wood and paper products	..	..	..	..	2.7	3.0	1.8	5.9	5.5	4.7
20	Wood products	..	..	..	..						
21/22	Paper, printing and publishing	..	..	..	..	..	..	..	..	..	..
23/25	Chemicals, Total	..	..	..	..	390.3	236.1	254.8	255.0	233.3	262.9
23	Refined petroleum, nuclear fuel	..	..	..	..	4.6	0.1	0.1	12.5	1.4	1.0
24/25	Chemicals, rubber & plastics prod.	..	..	..	..	385.7	236.1	254.7	242.5	231.9	262.0
24	Chemical products	..	..	..	..	383.3	233.1	227.6	208.1	228.2	216.2
2423	Pharmaceuticals	..	..	..	..	225.7	127.6	113.0	123.8	131.3	135.8
25	Rubber and plastics products	..	..	..	..	2.4	3.0	27.1	34.4	3.7	45.8
26	Non-metallic mineral products	..	..	..	..	4.3	6.9	5.7	7.4	3.5	1.8
27/28	Basic & fabricated metals	..	..	..	..	26.3	28.2	29.6	11.3	33.5	33.7
27	Basic metals	..	..	..	..	25.1	26.9	28.8	4.4	32.8	32.7
28	Fabricated metal products	..	..	..	..	1.2	1.4	0.8	6.9	0.7	0.9
29/32	Machinery, Total	..	..	..	..	206.1	242.5	244.7	220.2	223.0	215.3
29/30	Non-electrical machinery	..	..	..	..	23.7	22.5	22.2	16.3	164.3	154.6
29	Non-electrical machinery nec	..	..	..	..	23.4	22.4	20.9	16.3	18.0	12.1
30	Office and computing machinery	..	..	..	..	0.3	0.1	1.4	0.0	146.3	142.4
31/32	Electrical & electronic equipment	..	..	..	..	182.4	220.0	222.4	203.9	58.8	60.7
31	Electrical machinery nec	..	..	..	..	2.7	4.0	17.2	4.3	1.5	2.9
32	Radio, TV & communications eq.	..	..	..	..	179.8	216.0	205.3	199.6	57.2	57.8
33	Scientific instruments	..	..	..	..	26.9	29.0	20.3	14.0	6.8	8.5
34/35	Transportation equipment	..	..	..	..	18.4	23.0	26.8	6.5	3.5	3.0
34	Motor vehicles	..	..	..	..	18.1	21.2	26.3	5.5	3.2	2.5
35	Other transport equipment	..	..	..	..	0.3	1.8	0.5	1.1	0.3	0.5
351	Shipbuilding & repairing	..	..	..	..	..	..	..	..	..	..
353	Aircraft and spacecraft	..	..	..	..	0.0	0.0	0.0	0.5	0.0	0.0
36/37	Other manufacturing	..	..	..	..	7.0	10.3	8.3	3.2	9.2	9.8
40/45	Construction, electricity, gas & water	..	..	..	..	0.0	0.2	0.5	0.1	0.2	0.4
50/55	Trade, repair, hotels & restaurants	..	..	..	..	193.9	254.3	164.6	239.7	253.3	270.2
65/74	Finance, insurance, business services	..	..	..	..	21.8	49.8	20.9	26.8	9.6	15.4
	OTHER ACTIVITIES	..	..	..	..	14.6	7.8	18.5	190.3	32.7	40.3
01/99	**GRAND TOTAL**	..	..	..	..	**931.7**	**902.7**	**806.0**	**997.5**	**826.6**	**878.4**

Total manufacturing by investing country

		1987	1988	1989	1990	1991	1992	1993	1994	1995	1996
	All countries	..	..	..	..	**701.3**	**590.7**	**600.7**	**540.7**	**530.8**	**552.2**
	United States	..	..	..	..	413.5	50.2	45.9	46.9	46.2	46.3
	Canada	..	..	..	..						
	Mexico	..	..	..	..						
	Japan	..	..	..	..						
	Europe	..	..	..	..						
	European Union (15)	..	..	..	..	217.2	35.1	37.5	35.2	32.4	31.9
	Belgium	..	..	..	..						
	France	..	..	..	..	3.7	3.5	3.7	5.0	2.9	2.1
	Germany	..	..	..	..	162.7	13.7	12.7	10.6	9.8	10.5
	Italy	..	..	..	..						
	Netherlands	..	..	..	..	5.3	4.7	6.2	5.9	6.5	6.3
	Spain	..	..	..	..						
	Sweden	..	..	..	..						
	United Kingdom	..	..	..	..	25.7	4.2	5.1	5.0	4.7	6.0
	Switzerland	..	..	..	..	32.0	5.3	6.2	6.7	7.6	8.1
	Australia and New Zealand	..	..	..	..						
	Asia (non-OECD)	..	..	..	..	3.2	4.7	6.8	6.7	8.4	7.4
	Latin America	..	..	..	..	6.1	0.9	0.3	0.6	0.7	0.4

Note: Majority foreign-owned firms.
Firmes sous contrôle étranger majoritaire.

JAPAN

Source

The data are prepared by the Enterprise Statistics Division, Research and Statistics Department and the International Business Affairs Division, Industrial Policy Bureau, MITI, based on the annual survey on Trends in Business Activities of Foreign Affiliates in Japan. The data presented in this publication refer to majority foreign-owned firms. The period covered is the fiscal year ending on the 31 March. The results are published in *Trends of Foreign Affiliates in Japan.*

National totals:

- *Number of enterprises*, *Number of employees*, *Turnover*, *Value added*, *Wages and salaries* and *Gross fixed capital formation:* the results come from a survey conducted by the Ministry of Finance (Financial statements of incorporated businesses).

- *Total exports* and *imports:* data come from the OECD STAN database and are converted from ISIC Revision 2 to ISIC Revision 3. Thus there may be some sectoral inconsistencies between foreign affiliates' and national data.

- *R&D expenditure:* data are extracted from the OECD ANBERD database.

- *Number of researchers:* data come from the OECD ANRSE database and are converted from ISIC Revision 2 to ISIC Revision 3.

- *Technological payments*: data come from the R&D survey conducted by the Management and Coordination Agency (MCA).

Industrial classification

For all variables, the data are classified according to the principal industrial activity of the affiliate.

The industrial classification used for these tables is ISIC Revision 3, based on the classification used for the survey. Firms in the finance, insurance and real estate sector are excluded from the survey as from 1995. Up to and including 1994, part of *Office and computing machinery* (30) is included in *Radio, TV and communications equipment* (32). The following notes apply to all years and variables:

- *Food, beverages, tobacco* (15/16) includes parts of *Growing of cereals* (0111) and *Growing of vegetables* (0112).

- *Textiles, clothing, leather, footwear* (17/19) includes part of *Manufacture of other general purpose machinery* (2919) (*e.g.* gasket).

- *Refined petroleum and coal products* (23) includes parts of *Mining and agglomeration of hard coal* (1010) and *Mining of lignite* (1020).

- *Rubber and plastic products* (25) includes parts of *Tanning and dressing of leather* (1911) and *Manufacture of footwear* (1920).

- *Non-metallic mineral products* (26) includes parts of *Manufacture of other fabricated metal products nec* (2899) and *Other manufacturing nec* (3699).

- *Basic metals* (27) includes parts of *Processing of nuclear fuel* (2330), *Forging, pressing and roll-forming of metal* (2891), *Manufacture of insulated wire and cable* (3130) and *Recycling of metal waste and scrap* (3710).

- *Fabricated metal products* (28) includes parts of *Manufacture of ovens, furnaces and furnace burners* (2914), *Manufacture of other general purpose machinery* (2919) and *Manufacture of domestic appliances nec* (2930).

- *Non-electrical machinery* (29) includes parts of *Manufacture of cutlery, handtools and general hardware* (2893), *Manufacture of other fabricated metal products nec* (2899) and *Manufacture of parts and accessories for motor vehicles* (3430).

- *Office and computing machinery* (30) includes parts of *Manufacture of other general purpose machinery* (2919), *Manufacture of machinery for textile, apparel and leather production* (2926) and *Manufacture of other special purpose machinery* (2929).

- *Electrical machinery nec* (31) includes parts of *Manufacture of ovens, furnaces and furnace burners* (2914), *Manufacture of machine-tools* (2922), *Manufacture of medical and surgical equipment* (3311), *Manufacture of instruments* (3312), *Manufacture of industrial process control equipment* (3313), *Manufacture of television and radio receivers, sound and video recording* (3230).

- *Radio, TV and communications equipment* (32) includes parts of *Manufacture of other electrical equipment nec* (3190), *Manufacture of medical and surgical equipment* (3311) (*e.g.* x-ray equipment) and *Manufacture of instruments* (3312).

- *Scientific instruments* (33) includes parts of *Manufacture of luggage, handbags and the like* (1912), *Manufacture of pharmaceuticals* (2423) and *Manufacture of other general purpose machinery* (2919).

- *Motor vehicles* (34) includes part of *Manufacture of motorcycles* (3591).

- *Other transport equipment* (35) includes parts of *Manufacture of engines and turbines* (2911) and *Manufacture of lifting and handling equipment* (2915).

- *Other manufacturing* (36/37) includes parts of *Manufacture of made-up textiles* (1721), *Manufacture of builder's carpentry and joinery* (2022), *Manufacture of articles of cork, straw and plaiting materials* (2029), *Manufacture of other chemical products nec* (2429), *Manufacture of articles of concrete, cement and plaster* (2695) and *Manufacture of watches and clocks* (3330).

- *Construction, electricity gas & water* (40/45) includes parts of *Agricultural and animal husbandry service activities* (0140) and *Sewage and refuse disposal, sanitation and similar activities* (9000).

- *Trade, repair, hotels and restaurants* (50/55) includes part of *Dramatic arts, music and other activities* (9214).

- *Finance, insurance, real estate and business services* (65/74) includes part of *News agency activities* (9220).

- *Other activities* (01/05; 60/64; 75/99) includes parts of *Repair of personal and household goods* (5260) and *Photographic activities* (7494).

Variables

Figures for *Number of researchers* from 1995, *Value added* and *Wages and salaries* until 1993, and *Technological receipts* are not available.

- *Number of employees* is calculated on a full-time equivalent basis.

- *Gross operating surplus* includes the value of fixed capital consumption.

- *Technological payments* refer to payments for royalties and licence fees.

Geographical breakdown

The investor's country is the country of the immediate controller.

JAPON

Source

Les données émanent de la Division des statistiques d'entreprise, Département de la recherche et des statistiques et de la Division des affaires commerciales internationales, Bureau de la politique industrielle, MITI. Elles s'appuient sur l'enquête annuelle concernant les activités industrielles des filiales étrangères au Japon. Les données présentées dans cette publication font référence aux entreprises sous contrôle étranger majoritaire. La période couverte est l'exercice budgétaire se terminant le 31 mars. Les résultats sont publiés dans *Trends of Foreign Affiliates in Japan*.

Totaux nationaux :

- *Nombre d'entreprises*, *Nombre de salariés*, *Chiffre d'affaires*, *Valeur ajoutée*, *Salaires* et *Formation brute de capital fixe* : les résultats proviennent d'une enquête réalisée par le Ministère des Finances (*Financial statements of incorporated businesses*).

- *Exportations* et *Importations totales* : les données proviennent de la base de données STAN de l'OCDE, et sont converties de la CITI révision 2 vers la CITI révision 3. Il peut donc y avoir certaines incohérences sectorielles entre les données des firmes nationales et celles des filiales.

- *Dépenses de R-D* : les données sont extraites de la base de données ANBERD de l'OCDE.

- *Nombre de chercheurs* : les données proviennent de la base de données ANRSE de l'OCDE et sont converties de la CITI révision 2 vers la CITI révision 3.

- *Paiements technologiques* : les données proviennent de l'enquête sur la R-D menée par l'Agence de gestion et de coordination (MCA).

Classification industrielle

Pour toutes les variables, les données sont classées selon l'activité industrielle principale de l'entreprise affiliée.

La classification industrielle utilisée pour ces tableaux est la CITI révision 3, sur la base de la classification utilisée pour l'enquête. Les entreprises des domaines suivants : finance, assurance et immobilier sont exclues de l'enquête à partir de 1995. A compter de 1994, une partie de *Machines de bureau et ordinateurs* (30) est comprise dans *Appareils de radio, télévision et télécommunication* (32). Les notes suivantes concernent toutes les variables et toutes les années :

- *Alimentation, boissons, tabac* (15/16) comprend une partie de *Culture de céréales* (0111) et *Culture de légumes* (0112).

- *Textiles, habillement, cuir, chaussures* (17/19) comprend une partie de *Fabrication d'autres machines d'usage général* (2919) (exemple : joints d'étanchéité).

- *Fabrication de produits pétroliers raffinés et de produits du charbon* (23) comprend une partie de *Extraction et agglomération de la houille* (1010) et *Extraction de lignite* (1020).

- *Caoutchouc et plastiques* (25) comprend une partie de *Apprêt et tannage des cuirs* (1911) et *Fabrication de chaussures* (1920).

- *Produits minéraux non métalliques* (26) comprend une partie de *Fabrication d'autres ouvrages en métaux* (2899) et *Autres industries diverses nca* (3699).

- *Métallurgie de base* (27) comprend une partie de *Traitement de matières nucléaires* (2330), *Forge, emboutissage, estampage ; métallurgie des poudres* (2891), *Fabrication de fils et câbles isolés* (3130) et *Récupération de matières métalliques recyclables* (3710).

- *Ouvrages en métaux* (28) comprend une partie de *Fabrication de fours et brûleurs* (2914), *Fabrication d'autres machines d'usage général* (2919) et *Fabrication d'appareils domestiques* (2930).

- *Machines et matériel non électriques* (29) comprend une partie de *Fabrication de coutellerie, d'outillage et de quincaillerie* (2893), *Fabrication d'autres ouvrages en métaux* (2899) et *Fabrication d'équipements automobiles* (3430).

- *Machines de bureau et ordinateurs* (30) comprend une partie de *Fabrication d'autres machines d'usage général* (2919), *Fabrication de machines pour les industries textiles* (2926) et *Fabrication d'autres machines d'usage spécifique* (2929).

- *Machines et appareils électriques* (31) comprend une partie de *Fabrication de fours et brûleurs* (2914), *Fabrication de machines-outils* (2922), *Fabrication de matériel médico-chirurgical et d'orthopédie* (3311), *Fabrication d'instruments de mesure et de contrôle* (3312), *Fabrication d'équipements de contrôle des processus industriels* (3313), *Fabrication d'appareils de réception, enregistrement ou reproduction du son et de l'image* (3230).

- *Appareils de radio, télévision et télécommunication* (32) comprend une partie de *Fabrication d'autres matériels électriques* (3190), *Fabrication de matériel médico-chirurgical et d'orthopédie* (3311) (exemple : équipements radiologiques) et *Fabrication d'instruments de mesure et de contrôle* (3312).

- *Instruments scientifiques* (33) comprend une partie de *Fabrication d'articles de voyage et de maroquinerie* (1912), *Fabrication de produits pharmaceutiques* (2423) et *Fabrication d'autres machines d'usage général* (2919).

- *Véhicules automobiles* (34) comprend une partie de *Fabrication de motocycles* (3591).

- *Autres matériels de transport* (35) comprend une partie de *Fabrication de moteurs et turbines* (2911) et *Fabrication de matériel de levage et de manutention* (2915).

- *Autres industries manufacturières* (36/37) comprend une partie de *Fabrication d'articles textiles* (1721), *Fabrication de charpentes et de menuiserie* (2022), *Fabrication d'objets en bois, liège et vannerie* (2029), *Fabrication d'autres produits chimiques* (2429), *Fabrication d'ouvrages en béton, ciment ou plâtre* (2695) et *Horlogerie* (3330).

- *Construction, electricité gaz et eau* (40/45) comprend une partie de *Services annexes à l'agriculture* (0140) et *Assainissement, voirie et gestion des déchets* (9000).

- *Commerce, réparation, hôtels et restaurants* (50/55) comprend une partie de *Art dramatique, musique et autres activités* (9214).

- *Finance, assurance, immobilier et services aux entreprises* (65/74) comprend une partie de *Agences de presse* (9220).

- *Autres activités* (01/05 ; 60/64 ; 75/99) comprend une partie de *Réparation d'articles personnels et domestiques* (5260) et *Activités photographiques* (7494).

Variables

Les données pour *Nombre de chercheurs* à partir de 1995, *Valeur ajoutée* et *Salaires* jusqu'en 1993, et *Recettes technologiques* ne sont pas disponibles.

- Le *Nombre de salariés* est calculé sur la base d'un équivalent plein-temps.

- L'*Excédent brut d'exploitation* comprend la valeur de la consommation de capital fixe.

- Les *Paiements technologiques* concernent les paiements au titre des redevances et droits de licence.

Ventilation géographique

Le pays investisseur est celui où se situe le contrôle immédiat.

MEXICO

MEXIQUE

Sources et méthodes

Table 1. MEXICO / MEXIQUE

NUMBER OF ENTERPRISES / NOMBRE D'ENTREPRISES

By industry (ISIC Rev. 3)		FOREIGN AFFILIATES (Units)									
		1987	1988	1989	1990	1991	1992	1993	1994	1995	1996
10/14	Mining & quarrying	..	..	..	..	..	..	31	..	..	..
15/37	**TOTAL MANUFACTURING**	**1 178**	..	**1 408**	**1 435**	**1 558**	**1 687**	**1 927**	..	..	..
15/16	Food, beverages, tobacco	..	..	..	..	..	..	171	..	..	..
17/19	Textiles, clothing, leather, footwear	..	..	..	..	..	..	137	..	..	..
20/22	Wood and paper products	..	..	..	..	..	..	140	..	..	..
20	Wood products	..	..	..	..	..	..	..	..	..	..
21/22	Paper, printing and publishing	..	..	..	..	..	..	..	..	..	..
23/25	Chemicals, Total	..	..	..	..	..	..	419	..	..	..
23	Refined petroleum, nuclear fuel	..	..	..	..	..	..	15	..	..	..
24/25	Chemicals, rubber & plastics prod.	..	..	..	..	..	..	404	..	..	..
24	Chemical products	..	..	..	..	..	..	313	..	..	..
2423	Pharmaceuticals	..	..	..	..	..	..	107	..	..	..
25	Rubber and plastics products	..	..	..	..	..	..	91	..	..	..
26	Non-metallic mineral products	..	..	..	..	..	..	64	..	..	..
27/28	Basic & fabricated metals	..	..	..	..	..	..	144	..	..	..
27	Basic metals	..	..	..	..	..	..	45	..	..	..
28	Fabricated metal products	..	..	..	..	..	..	99	..	..	..
29/32	Machinery, Total	..	..	..	..	..	..	558	..	..	..
29/30	Non-electrical machinery	..	..	..	..	..	..	212	..	..	..
29	Non-electrical machinery nec	..	..	..	..	..	..	175	..	..	..
30	Office and computing machinery	..	..	..	..	..	..	37	..	..	..
31/32	Electrical & electronic equipment	..	..	..	..	..	..	346	..	..	..
31	Electrical machinery nec	..	..	..	..	..	..	202	..	..	..
32	Radio, TV & communications eq.	..	..	..	..	..	..	144	..	..	..
33	Scientific instruments	..	..	..	..	..	..	57	..	..	..
34/35	Transportation equipment	..	..	..	..	..	..	137	..	..	..
34	Motor vehicles	..	..	..	..	..	..	123	..	..	..
35	Other transport equipment	..	..	..	..	..	..	14	..	..	..
351	Shipbuilding & repairing	..	..	..	..	..	..	3	..	..	..
353	Aircraft and spacecraft	..	..	..	..	..	..	0	..	..	..
36/37	Other manufacturing	..	..	..	..	..	..	100	..	..	..
40/45	Construction, electricity, gas & water	..	..	..	..	..	..	72	..	..	..
50/55	Trade, repair, hotels & restaurants	..	..	..	..	..	..	887	..	..	..
65/74	Finance, insurance, business services	..	..	..	..	..	..	348	..	..	..
	OTHER ACTIVITIES	..	..	..	..	..	..	722	..	..	..
01/99	**GRAND TOTAL**	..	..	..	..	..	..	**4 019**	..	..	..

Total manufacturing by investing country	1987	1988	1989	1990	1991	1992	1993	1994	1995	1996
All countries	1 178	..	1 408	1 435	1 558	1 687	1 927	..	..	..
United States	851	..	1 003	993	1 043	1 113	1 292	..	..	..
Canada	20	..	22	24	26	30	41	..	..	..
Mexico	0	..	0	0	0	0	0	..	..	..
Japan	18	..	24	27	31	32	39	..	..	..
Europe	0	..	2	2	4	5	3	..	..	..
European Union (15)	189	..	242	263	303	346	366	..	..	..
Belgium	0	..	2	3	3	3	4	..	..	..
France	31	..	39	42	50	57	62	..	..	..
Germany	56	..	68	74	84	99	101	..	..	..
Italy	6	..	4	5	10	9	7	..	..	..
Netherlands	14	..	24	31	38	43	60	..	..	..
Spain	13	..	17	23	28	39	37	..	..	..
Sweden	23	..	26	23	22	23	23	..	..	..
United Kingdom	29	..	41	40	44	47	47	..	..	..
Switzerland	27	..	33	41	51	49	48	..	..	..
Australia and New Zealand	1	..	0	0	0	0	0	..	..	..
Asia (non-OECD)	2	..	3	3	3	6	12	..	..	..
Latin America	35	..	44	46	59	66	76	..	..	..

Note: Majority foreign-owned firms.
Firmes sous contrôle étranger majoritaire.

Table 2. MEXICO / MEXIQUE

NUMBER OF EMPLOYEES / NOMBRE DE SALARIÉS

By industry (ISIC Rev. 3)		FOREIGN AFFILIATES (Units)									
		1987	1988	1989	1990	1991	1992	1993	1994	1995	1996
10/14	Mining & quarrying	..	..	..	..	..	..	601	..	..	..
15/37	**TOTAL MANUFACTURING**	**533 591**	..	**647 768**	**709 026**	**801 944**	**875 222**	**906 614**	..	..	..
15/16	Food, beverages, tobacco	..	..	..	..	..	..	105 189	..	..	..
17/19	Textiles, clothing, leather, footwear	..	..	..	..	..	..	59 779	..	..	..
20/22	Wood and paper products	..	..	..	..	..	..	36 320	..	..	..
20	Wood products	..	..	..	..	..	..		..	..	..
21/22	Paper, printing and publishing	..	..	..	..	..	..		..	..	..
23/25	Chemicals, Total	..	..	..	..	..	..	130 139	..	..	..
23	Refined petroleum, nuclear fuel	..	..	..	..	..	..	1 607	..	..	..
24/25	Chemicals, rubber & plastics prod.	..	..	..	..	..	..	128 532	..	..	..
24	Chemical products	..	..	..	..	..	..	93 990	..	..	..
2423	Pharmaceuticals	..	..	..	..	..	..	41 174	..	..	..
25	Rubber and plastics products	..	..	..	..	..	..	34 542	..	..	..
26	Non-metallic mineral products	..	..	..	..	..	..	18 396	..	..	..
27/28	Basic & fabricated metals	..	..	..	..	..	..	46 680	..	..	..
27	Basic metals	..	..	..	..	..	..	18 463	..	..	..
28	Fabricated metal products	..	..	..	..	..	..	28 217	..	..	..
29/32	Machinery, Total	..	..	..	..	..	..	338 039	..	..	..
29/30	Non-electrical machinery	..	..	..	..	..	..	65 566	..	..	..
29	Non-electrical machinery nec	..	..	..	..	..	..	51 564	..	..	..
30	Office and computing machinery	..	..	..	..	..	..	14 002	..	..	..
31/32	Electrical & electronic equipment	..	..	..	..	..	..	272 473	..	..	..
31	Electrical machinery nec	..	..	..	..	..	..	148 632	..	..	..
32	Radio, TV & communications eq.	..	..	..	..	..	..	123 841	..	..	..
33	Scientific instruments	..	..	..	..	..	..	19 783	..	..	..
34/35	Transportation equipment	..	..	..	..	..	..	116 770	..	..	..
34	Motor vehicles	..	..	..	..	..	..	112 844	..	..	..
35	Other transport equipment	..	..	..	..	..	..	3 926	..	..	..
351	Shipbuilding & repairing	..	..	..	..	..	..	449	..	..	..
353	Aircraft and spacecraft	..	..	..	..	..	..	0	..	..	..
36/37	Other manufacturing	..	..	..	..	..	..	35 519	..	..	..
40/45	Construction, electricity, gas & water	..	..	..	..	..	..	10 902	..	..	..
50/55	Trade, repair, hotels & restaurants	..	..	..	..	..	..	92 748	..	..	..
65/74	Finance, insurance, business services	..	..	..	..	..	..	18 664	..	..	..
	OTHER ACTIVITIES	..	..	..	..	..	..	64 385	..	..	..
01/99	**GRAND TOTAL**	..	..	..	..	..	..	**1 097 870**	..	..	..

Total manufacturing by investing country

	1987	1988	1989	1990	1991	1992	1993	1994	1995	1996
All countries	**533 591**	..	**647 768**	**709 026**	**801 944**	**875 222**	**906 614**	..	..	..
United States	372 754	..	484 820	524 700	593 513	653 443	675 086	..	..	..
Canada	9 107	..	10 450	13 135	13 785	15 417	16 528	..	..	..
Mexico	0	..	0	0	0	0	0	..	..	..
Japan	12 163	..	14 947	17 850	19 882	20 884	23 176	..	..	..
Europe	0	..	198	110	125	8 082	131	..	..	..
European Union (15)	88 667	..	99 163	111 190	117 411	125 780	123 484	..	..	..
Belgium	0	..	30	596	977	926	1 522	..	..	..
France	15 290	..	7 932	10 102	12 204	14 730	16 336	..	..	..
Germany	26 366	..	38 642	47 900	48 543	48 936	43 263	..	..	..
Italy	1 045	..	1 040	535	922	889	780	..	..	..
Netherlands	7 815	..	12 722	15 162	17 510	19 899	20 893	..	..	..
Spain	541	..	771	2 356	2 511	3 742	3 445	..	..	..
Sweden	5 734	..	8 078	6 898	7 043	7 030	6 119	..	..	..
United Kingdom	12 350	..	17 660	18 563	21 953	23 901	26 230	..	..	..
Switzerland	33 536	..	12 514	12 961	16 534	15 714	15 635	..	..	..
Australia and New Zealand	447	..	0	0	0	0	0	..	..	..
Asia (non-OECD)	1 303	..	1 806	1 936	2 148	3 385	4 565	..	..	..
Latin America	8 121	..	11 014	11 566	17 215	16 777	20 992	..	..	..

Note: Majority foreign-owned firms.
Firmes sous contrôle étranger majoritaire.

Table 3. MEXICO / MEXIQUE

PRODUCTION

By industry (ISIC Rev. 3)		1987	1988	1989	1990	1991	1992	1993	1994	1995	1996
		FOREIGN AFFILIATES *(Millions of dollars)*									
10/14	Mining & quarrying	2	..	..	..	..	..	7	..	..	..
15/37	**TOTAL MANUFACTURING**	**11 851**	..	**36 426**	**24 061**	**29 785**	**34 879**	**42 320**	..	..	..
15/16	Food, beverages, tobacco	647	..	..	..	..	..	4 319	..	..	..
17/19	Textiles, clothing, leather, footwear	771	..	..	..	..	..	1 306	..	..	..
20/22	Wood and paper products	754	..	..	..	..	..	929	..	..	..
20	Wood products	..	..	..	..	..	..	..	..	..	..
21/22	Paper, printing and publishing	..	..	..	..	..	..	..	..	..	..
23/25	Chemicals, Total	2 151	..	..	..	..	..	6 448	..	..	..
23	Refined petroleum, nuclear fuel	18	..	..	..	..	..	154	..	..	..
24/25	Chemicals, rubber & plastics prod.	2 133	..	..	..	..	..	6 294	..	..	..
24	Chemical products	1 946	..	..	..	..	..	5 361	..	..	..
2423	Pharmaceuticals	835	..	..	..	..	..	1 834	..	..	..
25	Rubber and plastics products	187	..	..	..	..	..	933	..	..	..
26	Non-metallic mineral products	53	..	..	..	..	..	706	..	..	..
27/28	Basic & fabricated metals	1 028	..	..	..	..	..	1 100	..	..	..
27	Basic metals	25	..	..	..	..	..	622	..	..	..
28	Fabricated metal products	1 002	..	..	..	..	..	477	..	..	..
29/32	Machinery, Total	2 528	..	..	..	..	..	8 046	..	..	..
29/30	Non-electrical machinery	1 216	..	..	..	..	..	2 309	..	..	..
29	Non-electrical machinery nec	931	..	..	..	..	..	1 556	..	..	..
30	Office and computing machinery	284	..	..	..	..	..	753	..	..	..
31/32	Electrical & electronic equipment	1 312	..	..	..	..	..	5 737	..	..	..
31	Electrical machinery nec	617	..	..	..	..	..	2 964	..	..	..
32	Radio, TV & communications eq.	696	..	..	..	..	..	2 773	..	..	..
33	Scientific instruments	133	..	..	..	..	..	469	..	..	..
34/35	Transportation equipment	3 030	..	..	..	..	..	18 196	..	..	..
34	Motor vehicles	3 020	..	..	..	..	..	17 872	..	..	..
35	Other transport equipment	10	..	..	..	..	..	323	..	..	..
351	Shipbuilding & repairing	5	..	..	..	..	..	12	..	..	..
353	Aircraft and spacecraft	0	..	..	..	..	..	0	..	..	..
36/37	Other manufacturing	756	..	..	..	..	..	801	..	..	..
40/45	Construction, electricity, gas & water	4	..	..	..	..	..	200	..	..	..
50/55	Trade, repair, hotels & restaurants	64	..	..	..	..	..	2 437	..	..	..
65/74	Finance, insurance, business services	48	..	..	..	..	..	94	..	..	..
	OTHER ACTIVITIES	99	..	..	..	..	..	277	..	..	..
01/99	**GRAND TOTAL**	**12 072**	..	..	..	..	..	**45 482**	..	..	..

Total Manufacturing by investing country	1987	1988	1989	1990	1991	1992	1993	1994	1995	1996
All countries	11 851	..	36 426	24 061	29 785	34 879	42 320	..	..	..
United States	9 086	..	20 151	17 203	20 213	23 828	29 882	..	..	..
Canada	164	..	255	428	544	656	765	..	..	..
Mexico	0	..	0	0	0	0	0	..	..	..
Japan	630	..	1 116	1 343	1 732	2 272	2 752	..	..	..
Europe	0	..	5	4	4	12	0	..	..	..
European Union (15)	1 102	..	13 957	4 027	5 619	6 153	6 367	..	..	..
Belgium	0	..	0	11	30	28	61	..	..	..
France	147	..	230	295	555	620	620	..	..	..
Germany	659	..	12 816	2 254	3 179	3 444	3 432	..	..	..
Italy	12	..	6	11	17	16	5	..	..	..
Netherlands	37	..	309	505	591	700	1 012	..	..	..
Spain	9	..	14	161	212	244	237	..	..	..
Sweden	98	..	227	286	334	364	173	..	..	..
United Kingdom	105	..	208	277	372	391	464	..	..	..
Switzerland	467	..	616	708	1 060	1 098	1 216	..	..	..
Australia and New Zealand	1	..	0	0	0	0	0	..	..	..
Asia (non-OECD)	0	..	1	0	0	198	335	..	..	..
Latin America	66	..	238	248	431	474	634	..	..	..

Note: Majority foreign-owned firms.
Firmes sous contrôle étranger majoritaire.

181

Table 4. MEXICO / MEXIQUE

TURNOVER / CHIFFRE D'AFFAIRES

By industry (ISIC Rev. 3)		FOREIGN AFFILIATES (Millions of dollars)									
		1987	1988	1989	1990	1991	1992	1993	1994	1995	1996
10/14	Mining & quarrying	..	..	..	..	..	..	12	..	..	..
15/37	**TOTAL MANUFACTURING**	**15 497**	..	**25 858**	**30 915**	**38 414**	**46 071**	**51 971**	..	..	..
15/16	Food, beverages, tobacco	..	..	..	..	..	..	7 724	..	..	..
17/19	Textiles, clothing, leather, footwear	..	..	..	..	..	..	694	..	..	..
20/22	Wood and paper products	..	..	..	..	..	..	954	..	..	..
20	Wood products	..	..	..	..	..	..	..	..	..	..
21/22	Paper, printing and publishing	..	..	..	..	..	..	..	..	..	..
23/25	Chemicals, Total	..	..	..	..	..	..	13 055	..	..	..
23	Refined petroleum, nuclear fuel	..	..	..	..	..	..	252	..	..	..
24/25	Chemicals, rubber & plastics prod.	..	..	..	..	..	..	12 803	..	..	..
24	Chemical products	..	..	..	..	..	..	11 608	..	..	..
2423	Pharmaceuticals	..	..	..	..	..	..	3 717	..	..	..
25	Rubber and plastics products	..	..	..	..	..	..	1 195	..	..	..
26	Non-metallic mineral products	..	..	..	..	..	..	989	..	..	..
27/28	Basic & fabricated metals	..	..	..	..	..	..	1 293	..	..	..
27	Basic metals	..	..	..	..	..	..	741	..	..	..
28	Fabricated metal products	..	..	..	..	..	..	553	..	..	..
29/32	Machinery, Total	..	..	..	..	..	..	8 977	..	..	..
29/30	Non-electrical machinery	..	..	..	..	..	..	3 886	..	..	..
29	Non-electrical machinery nec	..	..	..	..	..	..	1 973	..	..	..
30	Office and computing machinery	..	..	..	..	..	..	1 913	..	..	..
31/32	Electrical & electronic equipment	..	..	..	..	..	..	5 091	..	..	..
31	Electrical machinery nec	..	..	..	..	..	..	1 808	..	..	..
32	Radio, TV & communications eq.	..	..	..	..	..	..	3 283	..	..	..
33	Scientific instruments	..	..	..	..	..	..	450	..	..	..
34/35	Transportation equipment	..	..	..	..	..	..	16 904	..	..	..
34	Motor vehicles	..	..	..	..	..	..	16 724	..	..	..
35	Other transport equipment	..	..	..	..	..	..	180	..	..	..
351	Shipbuilding & repairing	..	..	..	..	..	..	15	..	..	..
353	Aircraft and spacecraft	..	..	..	..	..	..	0	..	..	..
36/37	Other manufacturing	..	..	..	..	..	..	932	..	..	..
40/45	Construction, electricity, gas & water	..	..	..	..	..	..	475	..	..	..
50/55	Trade, repair, hotels & restaurants	..	..	..	..	..	..	10 182	..	..	..
65/74	Finance, insurance, business services	..	..	..	..	..	..	24 094	..	..	..
	OTHER ACTIVITIES	..	..	..	..	..	..	4 464	..	..	..
01/99	**GRAND TOTAL**	..	..	..	..	..	..	**91 299**	..	..	..

Total manufacturing by investing country

	1987	1988	1989	1990	1991	1992	1993	1994	1995	1996
All countries	**15 497**	..	**25 858**	**30 915**	**38 414**	**46 071**	**51 971**	..	..	..
United States	10 789	..	16 771	19 633	24 631	29 958	34 084	..	..	..
Canada	414	..	502	642	780	970	1 135	..	..	..
Mexico	0	..	0	0	0	0	0	..	..	..
Japan	754	..	1 611	2 134	1 744	2 162	2 346	..	..	..
Europe	0	..	20	4	8	14	4	..	..	..
European Union (15)	2 501	..	5 237	6 411	8 247	9 631	10 203	..	..	..
Belgium	0	..	7	23	34	42	86	..	..	..
France	290	..	620	807	1 002	1 420	1 449	..	..	..
Germany	1 156	..	2 667	3 066	3 947	4 488	4 793	..	..	..
Italy	56	..	68	26	33	39	40	..	..	..
Netherlands	143	..	452	694	877	1 011	1 199	..	..	..
Spain	14	..	33	208	276	325	371	..	..	..
Sweden	283	..	489	533	671	633	488	..	..	..
United Kingdom	318	..	503	581	764	945	1 086	..	..	..
Switzerland	684	..	1 209	1 408	1 834	1 945	1 969	..	..	..
Australia and New Zealand	0	..	0	0	0	0	0	..	..	..
Asia (non-OECD)	3	..	5	5	5	192	335	..	..	..
Latin America	227	..	321	441	772	736	1 208	..	..	..

Note: Majority foreign-owned firms.
Firmes sous contrôle étranger majoritaire.

Table 5. MEXICO / MEXIQUE

VALUE ADDED / VALEUR AJOUTÉE

By industry (ISIC Rev. 3)		FOREIGN AFFILIATES (Millions of dollars)									
		1987	1988	1989	1990	1991	1992	1993	1994	1995	1996
10/14	Mining & quarrying	..	..	..	..	..	..	- 2	..	..	..
15/37	**TOTAL MANUFACTURING**	**403**	..	**9 273**	**9 228**	**13 345**	**15 501**	**18 398**	..	..	..
15/16	Food, beverages, tobacco	..	..	..	..	..	..	2 897	..	..	..
17/19	Textiles, clothing, leather, footwear	..	..	..	..	..	..	335	..	..	..
20/22	Wood and paper products	..	..	..	..	..	..	403	..	..	..
20	Wood products	..	..	..	..	..	..	..	..	..	..
21/22	Paper, printing and publishing	..	..	..	..	..	..	..	..	..	..
23/25	Chemicals, Total	..	..	..	..	..	..	5 298	..	..	..
23	Refined petroleum, nuclear fuel	..	..	..	..	..	..	66	..	..	..
24/25	Chemicals, rubber & plastics prod.	..	..	..	..	..	..	5 232	..	..	..
24	Chemical products	..	..	..	..	..	..	4 710	..	..	..
2423	Pharmaceuticals	..	..	..	..	..	..	1 494	..	..	..
25	Rubber and plastics products	..	..	..	..	..	..	522	..	..	..
26	Non-metallic mineral products	..	..	..	..	..	..	2 095	..	..	..
27/28	Basic & fabricated metals	..	..	..	..	..	..	493	..	..	..
27	Basic metals	..	..	..	..	..	..	241	..	..	..
28	Fabricated metal products	..	..	..	..	..	..	253	..	..	..
29/32	Machinery, Total	..	..	..	..	..	..	3 666	..	..	..
29/30	Non-electrical machinery	..	..	..	..	..	..	1 244	..	..	..
29	Non-electrical machinery nec	..	..	..	..	..	..	858	..	..	..
30	Office and computing machinery	..	..	..	..	..	..	387	..	..	..
31/32	Electrical & electronic equipment	..	..	..	..	..	..	2 421	..	..	..
31	Electrical machinery nec	..	..	..	..	..	..	1 014	..	..	..
32	Radio, TV & communications eq.	..	..	..	..	..	..	1 408	..	..	..
33	Scientific instruments	..	..	..	..	..	..	166	..	..	..
34/35	Transportation equipment	..	..	..	..	..	..	2 727	..	..	..
34	Motor vehicles	..	..	..	..	..	..	2 648	..	..	..
35	Other transport equipment	..	..	..	..	..	..	79	..	..	..
351	Shipbuilding & repairing	..	..	..	..	..	..	8	..	..	..
353	Aircraft and spacecraft	..	..	..	..	..	..	0	..	..	..
36/37	Other manufacturing	..	..	..	..	..	..	318	..	..	..
40/45	Construction, electricity, gas & water	..	..	..	..	..	..	170	..	..	..
50/55	Trade, repair, hotels & restaurants	..	..	..	..	..	..	2 265	..	..	..
65/74	Finance, insurance, business services	..	..	..	..	..	..	781	..	..	..
	OTHER ACTIVITIES	..	..	..	..	..	..	2 717	..	..	..
01/99	**GRAND TOTAL**	..	..	..	..	..	..	**24 364**	..	..	..

Total manufacturing by investing country

	1987	1988	1989	1990	1991	1992	1993	1994	1995	1996
All countries	**403**	..	**9 273**	**9 228**	**13 345**	**15 501**	**18 398**	..	..	..
United States	173	..	6 565	5 804	8 439	9 569	12 113	..	..	..
Canada	124	..	173	195	284	317	454	..	..	..
Mexico	0	..	0	0	0	0	0	..	..	..
Japan	- 334	..	116	73	194	292	304	..	..	..
Europe	0	..	7	1	3	- 4	1	..	..	..
European Union (15)	230	..	1 961	1 722	2 382	3 025	2 639	..	..	..
Belgium	0	..	3	5	14	11	21	..	..	..
France	- 310	..	86	146	131	400	324	..	..	..
Germany	274	..	1 137	835	1 051	1 412	963	..	..	..
Italy	7	..	16	35	15	27	24	..	..	..
Netherlands	38	..	155	230	275	289	346	..	..	..
Spain	4	..	6	41	62	92	74	..	..	..
Sweden	127	..	269	69	298	161	151	..	..	..
United Kingdom	56	..	142	197	318	370	476	..	..	..
Switzerland	164	..	417	534	558	483	429	..	..	..
Australia and New Zealand	- 1	..	0	0	0	0	0	..	..	..
Asia (non-OECD)	0	..	1	1	0	- 1	38	..	..	..
Latin America	52	..	- 6	136	315	287	472	..	..	..

Note: Majority foreign-owned firms.
Firmes sous contrôle étranger majoritaire.

Table 6. MEXICO / MEXIQUE

WAGES AND SALARIES / SALAIRES ET TRAITEMENTS

By industry (ISIC Rev. 3)	FOREIGN AFFILIATES (Millions of dollars)									
	1987	1988	1989	1990	1991	1992	1993	1994	1995	1996
10/14 Mining & quarrying	..	..	..	..	..	..	5	..	..	..
15/37 **TOTAL MANUFACTURING**	1 883	..	3 411	3 921	5 337	6 388	8 088	..	..	..
15/16 Food, beverages, tobacco	..	..	..	..	..	..	1 143	..	..	..
17/19 Textiles, clothing, leather, footwear	..	..	..	..	..	..	221	..	..	..
20/22 Wood and paper products	..	..	..	..	..	..	251	..	..	..
20 Wood products	..	..	..	..	..	..	..	..	..	..
21/22 Paper, printing and publishing	..	..	..	..	..	..	..	..	..	..
23/25 Chemicals, Total	..	..	..	..	..	..	2 112	..	..	..
23 Refined petroleum, nuclear fuel	..	..	..	..	..	..	25	..	..	..
24/25 Chemicals, rubber & plastics prod.	..	..	..	..	..	..	2 087	..	..	..
24 Chemical products	..	..	..	..	..	..	1 772	..	..	..
2423 Pharmaceuticals	..	..	..	..	..	..	762	..	..	..
25 Rubber and plastics products	..	..	..	..	..	..	315	..	..	..
26 Non-metallic mineral products	..	..	..	..	..	..	159	..	..	..
27/28 Basic & fabricated metals	..	..	..	..	..	..	254	..	..	..
27 Basic metals	..	..	..	..	..	..	97	..	..	..
28 Fabricated metal products	..	..	..	..	..	..	157	..	..	..
29/32 Machinery, Total	..	..	..	..	..	..	2 111	..	..	..
29/30 Non-electrical machinery	..	..	..	..	..	..	663	..	..	..
29 Non-electrical machinery nec	..	..	..	..	..	..	432	..	..	..
30 Office and computing machinery	..	..	..	..	..	..	231	..	..	..
31/32 Electrical & electronic equipment	..	..	..	..	..	..	1 448	..	..	..
31 Electrical machinery nec	..	..	..	..	..	..	727	..	..	..
32 Radio, TV & communications eq.	..	..	..	..	..	..	721	..	..	..
33 Scientific instruments	..	..	..	..	..	..	108	..	..	..
34/35 Transportation equipment	..	..	..	..	..	..	1 492	..	..	..
34 Motor vehicles	..	..	..	..	..	..	1 439	..	..	..
35 Other transport equipment	..	..	..	..	..	..	52	..	..	..
351 Shipbuilding & repairing	..	..	..	..	..	..	5	..	..	..
353 Aircraft and spacecraft	..	..	..	..	..	..	0	..	..	..
36/37 Other manufacturing	..	..	..	..	..	..	236	..	..	..
40/45 Construction, electricity, gas & water	..	..	..	..	..	..	103	..	..	..
50/55 Trade, repair, hotels & restaurants	..	..	..	..	..	..	847	..	..	..
65/74 Finance, insurance, business services	..	..	..	..	..	..	153	..	..	..
OTHER ACTIVITIES	..	..	..	..	..	..	577	..	..	..
01/99 **GRAND TOTAL**	..	..	..	..	..	..	9 785	..	..	..

Total manufacturing by investing country										
All countries	1 883	..	3 411	3 921	5 337	6 388	8 088	..	..	..
United States	1 359	..	2 452	2 622	3 407	4 078	5 330	..	..	..
Canada	39	..	59	76	111	141	177	..	..	..
Mexico	0	..	0	0	0	0	0	..	..	..
Japan	54	..	99	123	220	247	320	..	..	..
Europe	0	..	1	1	1	2	1	..	..	..
European Union (15)	314	..	608	855	1 188	1 425	1 499	..	..	..
Belgium	0	..	0	5	8	9	20	..	..	..
France	33	..	59	65	96	130	135	..	..	..
Germany	173	..	331	474	646	757	725	..	..	..
Italy	5	..	6	25	7	7	7	..	..	..
Netherlands	16	..	50	109	143	179	207	..	..	..
Spain	2	..	3	13	20	31	38	..	..	..
Sweden	35	..	51	44	94	87	105	..	..	..
United Kingdom	37	..	75	70	101	142	177	..	..	..
Switzerland	69	..	120	144	215	236	328	..	..	..
Australia and New Zealand	1	..	0	0	0	0	0	..	..	..
Asia (non-OECD)	0	..	0	0	0	17	21	..	..	..
Latin America	28	..	48	76	137	160	249	..	..	..

Note: Majority foreign-owned firms.
Firmes sous contrôle étranger majoritaire.

Table 9. MEXICO / MEXIQUE

GROSS FIXED CAPITAL FORMATION / FORMATION BRUTE DE CAPITAL FIXE

By industry (ISIC Rev. 3)		FOREIGN AFFILIATES (Millions of dollars)									
		1987	1988	1989	1990	1991	1992	1993	1994	1995	1996
10/14	Mining & quarrying	..	..	..	..	..	..	7	..	..	..
15/37	**TOTAL MANUFACTURING**	**3 856**	..	**1 364**	**2 437**	**2 912**	**5 009**	**7 735**	..	..	..
15/16	Food, beverages, tobacco	..	..	..	..	..	..	1 684	..	..	..
17/19	Textiles, clothing, leather, footwear	..	..	..	..	..	..	82	..	..	..
20/22	Wood and paper products	..	..	..	..	..	..	99	..	..	..
20	Wood products	..	..	..	..	..	..		..	..	..
21/22	Paper, printing and publishing	..	..	..	..	..	..	..	..	..	..
23/25	Chemicals, Total	..	..	..	..	..	..	1 040	..	..	..
23	Refined petroleum, nuclear fuel	..	..	..	..	..	..	8	..	..	..
24/25	Chemicals, rubber & plastics prod.	..	..	..	..	..	..	1 032	..	..	..
24	Chemical products	..	..	..	..	..	..	669	..	..	..
2423	Pharmaceuticals	..	..	..	..	..	..	212	..	..	..
25	Rubber and plastics products	..	..	..	..	..	..	362	..	..	..
26	Non-metallic mineral products	..	..	..	..	..	..	18	..	..	..
27/28	Basic & fabricated metals	..	..	..	..	..	..	835	..	..	..
27	Basic metals	..	..	..	..	..	..	817	..	..	..
28	Fabricated metal products	..	..	..	..	..	..	19	..	..	..
29/32	Machinery, Total	..	..	..	..	..	..	378	..	..	..
29/30	Non-electrical machinery	..	..	..	..	..	..	195	..	..	..
29	Non-electrical machinery nec	..	..	..	..	..	..	254	..	..	..
30	Office and computing machinery	..	..	..	..	..	..	- 59	..	..	..
31/32	Electrical & electronic equipment	..	..	..	..	..	..	183	..	..	..
31	Electrical machinery nec	..	..	..	..	..	..	106	..	..	..
32	Radio, TV & communications eq.	..	..	..	..	..	..	77	..	..	..
33	Scientific instruments	..	..	..	..	..	..	5	..	..	..
34/35	Transportation equipment	..	..	..	..	..	..	3 557	..	..	..
34	Motor vehicles	..	..	..	..	..	..	3 552	..	..	..
35	Other transport equipment	..	..	..	..	..	..	5	..	..	..
351	Shipbuilding & repairing	..	..	..	..	..	..	2	..	..	..
353	Aircraft and spacecraft	..	..	..	..	..	..	0	..	..	..
36/37	Other manufacturing	..	..	..	..	..	..	36	..	..	..
40/45	Construction, electricity, gas & water	..	..	..	..	..	..	29	..	..	..
50/55	Trade, repair, hotels & restaurants	..	..	..	..	..	..	862	..	..	..
65/74	Finance, insurance, business services	..	..	..	..	..	..	3 331	..	..	..
	OTHER ACTIVITIES	..	..	..	..	..	..	261	..	..	..
01/99	**GRAND TOTAL**	..	..	..	..	..	..	**12 273**	..	..	..

Total manufacturing by investing country

	1987	1988	1989	1990	1991	1992	1993	1994	1995	1996
All countries	**3 856**	..	**1 364**	**2 437**	**2 912**	**5 009**	**7 735**	..	..	..
United States	2 251	..	701	962	1 456	2 389	2 980	..	..	..
Canada	130	..	98	98	128	215	179	..	..	..
Mexico	0	..	0	0	0	0	0	..	..	..
Japan	533	..	132	170	322	623	304	..	..	..
Europe	0	..	1	0	1	6	- 1	..	..	..
European Union (15)	746	..	255	754	355	715	2 845	..	..	..
Belgium	0	..	0	1	1	0	- 1	..	..	..
France	215	..	28	47	39	72	0	..	..	..
Germany	260	..	75	249	71	398	2 502	..	..	..
Italy	3	..	2	27	3	3	4	..	..	..
Netherlands	7	..	63	294	138	109	209	..	..	..
Spain	2	..	0	44	28	35	33	..	..	..
Sweden	143	..	43	12	15	23	- 3	..	..	..
United Kingdom	65	..	23	34	42	47	39	..	..	..
Switzerland	125	..	72	348	504	532	457	..	..	..
Australia and New Zealand	0	..	0	0	0	0	0	..	..	..
Asia (non-OECD)	0	..	0	0	0	404	734	..	..	..
Latin America	32	..	59	36	70	54	195	..	..	..

Note: Majority foreign-owned firms.
Firmes sous contrôle étranger majoritaire.

185

Table 10. MEXICO / MEXIQUE

TOTAL EXPORTS / EXPORTATIONS TOTALES

By industry (ISIC Rev. 3)		FOREIGN AFFILIATES *(Millions of dollars)*								
		1987	1988	1989	1990	1991	1992	1993	1994	1995	1996
10/14	Mining & quarrying	..	..	..	1	..	..	1	..	..	..
15/37	**TOTAL MANUFACTURING**	..	..	..	**6 006**	**7 466**	**8 293**	**10 949**	..	..	..
15/16	Food, beverages, tobacco	..	..	..	113	..	..	265	..	..	..
17/19	Textiles, clothing, leather, footwear	..	..	..	35	..	..	60	..	..	..
20/22	Wood and paper products	..	..	..	18	..	..	33	..	..	..
20	Wood products	..	..	..	..	..	..	..	..	..	..
21/22	Paper, printing and publishing	..	..	..	..	..	..	..	..	..	..
23/25	Chemicals, Total	..	..	..	360	..	..	581	..	..	..
23	Refined petroleum, nuclear fuel	..	..	..	0	..	..	5	..	..	..
24/25	Chemicals, rubber & plastics prod.	..	..	..	360	..	..	576	..	..	..
24	Chemical products	..	..	..	325	..	..	521	..	..	..
2423	Pharmaceuticals	..	..	..	115	..	..	212	..	..	..
25	Rubber and plastics products	..	..	..	36	..	..	54	..	..	..
26	Non-metallic mineral products	..	..	..	44	..	..	105	..	..	..
27/28	Basic & fabricated metals	..	..	..	124	..	..	684	..	..	..
27	Basic metals	..	..	..	97	..	..	414	..	..	..
28	Fabricated metal products	..	..	..	27	..	..	270	..	..	..
29/32	Machinery, Total	..	..	..	1 022	..	..	2 095	..	..	..
29/30	Non-electrical machinery	..	..	..	714	..	..	1 281	..	..	..
29	Non-electrical machinery nec	..	..	..	250	..	..	475	..	..	..
30	Office and computing machinery	..	..	..	465	..	..	807	..	..	..
31/32	Electrical & electronic equipment	..	..	..	308	..	..	814	..	..	..
31	Electrical machinery nec	..	..	..	76	..	..	385	..	..	..
32	Radio, TV & communications eq.	..	..	..	232	..	..	429	..	..	..
33	Scientific instruments	..	..	..	30	..	..	98	..	..	..
34/35	Transportation equipment	..	..	..	4 196	..	..	6 870	..	..	..
34	Motor vehicles	..	..	..	4 196	..	..	6 850	..	..	..
35	Other transport equipment	..	..	..	1	..	..	20	..	..	..
351	Shipbuilding & repairing	..	..	..	0	..	..	0	..	..	..
353	Aircraft and spacecraft	..	..	..	0	..	..	0	..	..	..
36/37	Other manufacturing	..	..	..	64	..	..	158	..	..	..
40/45	Construction, electricity, gas & water	..	..	..	0	..	..	3	..	..	..
50/55	Trade, repair, hotels & restaurants	..	..	..	49	..	..	161	..	..	..
65/74	Finance, insurance, business services	..	..	..	9	..	..	18	..	..	..
	OTHER ACTIVITIES	..	..	..	25	..	..	29	..	..	..
01/99	**GRAND TOTAL**	..	..	..	**6 093**	..	..	**11 174**	..	..	..

Total manufacturing by investing country

	1987	1988	1989	1990	1991	1992	1993	1994	1995	1996
All countries	..	..	..	**6 006**	**7 466**	**8 293**	**10 949**	..	..	..
United States	..	..	..	4 237	5 442	6 030	7 628	..	..	..
Canada	..	..	..	63	57	87	110	..	..	..
Mexico	..	..	..	0	0	0	0	..	..	..
Japan	..	..	..	486	387	528	780	..	..	..
Europe	..	..	..	0	1	4	0	..	..	..
European Union (15)	..	..	..	1 142	1 446	1 535	1 991	..	..	..
Belgium	..	..	..	..	..	..	..	..	..	..
France	..	..	..	140	281	377	261	..	..	..
Germany	..	..	..	707	821	755	1 202	..	..	..
Italy	..	..	..	1	1	1	2	..	..	..
Netherlands	..	..	..	52	37	55	126	..	..	..
Spain	..	..	..	..	..	..	..	..	..	..
Sweden	..	..	..	45	29	41	61	..	..	..
United Kingdom	..	..	..	26	47	47	52	..	..	..
Switzerland	..	..	..	42	64	71	93	..	..	..
Australia and New Zealand	..	..	..	0	0	0	0	..	..	..
Asia (non-OECD)	..	..	..	0	0	0	257	..	..	..
Latin America	..	..	..	72	100	87	77	..	..	..

Note: Majority foreign-owned firms.
Firmes sous contrôle étranger majoritaire.

Table 11. MEXICO / MEXIQUE

TOTAL IMPORTS / IMPORTATIONS TOTALES

By industry (ISIC Rev. 3)	FOREIGN AFFILIATES (Millions of dollars)									
	1987	1988	1989	1990	1991	1992	1993	1994	1995	1996
10/14 Mining & quarrying	..	..	..	0	..	..	2	..	..	..
15/37 TOTAL MANUFACTURING	..	..	..	8 545	10 907	13 616	16 461	..	..	..
15/16 Food, beverages, tobacco	..	..	..	345	..	..	693	..	..	..
17/19 Textiles, clothing, leather, footwear	..	..	..	65	..	..	149	..	..	..
20/22 Wood and paper products	..	..	..	43	..	..	158	..	..	..
20 Wood products	..	..	..	..	..	..	..	..	..	..
21/22 Paper, printing and publishing	..	..	..	..	..	..	..	..	..	..
23/25 Chemicals, Total	..	..	..	1 321	..	..	2 447	..	..	..
23 Refined petroleum, nuclear fuel	..	..	..	24	..	..	53	..	..	..
24/25 Chemicals, rubber & plastics prod.	..	..	..	1 298	..	..	2 393	..	..	..
24 Chemical products	..	..	..	1 095	..	..	2 148	..	..	..
2423 Pharmaceuticals	..	..	..	566	..	..	1 035	..	..	..
25 Rubber and plastics products	..	..	..	203	..	..	246	..	..	..
26 Non-metallic mineral products	..	..	..	47	..	..	124	..	..	..
27/28 Basic & fabricated metals	..	..	..	219	..	..	416	..	..	..
27 Basic metals	..	..	..	141	..	..	127	..	..	..
28 Fabricated metal products	..	..	..	78	..	..	289	..	..	..
29/32 Machinery, Total	..	..	..	1 737	..	..	3 299	..	..	..
29/30 Non-electrical machinery	..	..	..	903	..	..	1 706	..	..	..
29 Non-electrical machinery nec	..	..	..	266	..	..	440	..	..	..
30 Office and computing machinery	..	..	..	637	..	..	1 265	..	..	..
31/32 Electrical & electronic equipment	..	..	..	834	..	..	1 593	..	..	..
31 Electrical machinery nec	..	..	..	203	..	..	703	..	..	..
32 Radio, TV & communications eq.	..	..	..	631	..	..	890	..	..	..
33 Scientific instruments	..	..	..	66	..	..	131	..	..	..
34/35 Transportation equipment	..	..	..	4 578	..	..	8 772	..	..	..
34 Motor vehicles	..	..	..	4 576	..	..	8 731	..	..	..
35 Other transport equipment	..	..	..	2	..	..	41	..	..	..
351 Shipbuilding & repairing	..	..	..	0	..	..	2	..	..	..
353 Aircraft and spacecraft	..	..	..	0	..	..	0	..	..	..
36/37 Other manufacturing	..	..	..	125	..	..	272	..	..	..
40/45 Construction, electricity, gas & water	..	..	..	10	..	..	41	..	..	..
50/55 Trade, repair, hotels & restaurants	..	..	..	419	..	..	1 300	..	..	..
65/74 Finance, insurance, business services	..	..	..	38	..	..	129	..	..	..
OTHER ACTIVITIES	..	..	..	27	..	..	105	..	..	..
01/99 GRAND TOTAL	..	..	..	9 059	..	..	18 081	..	..	..

Total manufacturing by investing country										
All countries	..	..	..	8 545	10 907	13 616	16 461	..	..	..
United States	..	..	..	5 567	6 943	9 021	11 095	..	..	..
Canada	..	..	..	199	219	281	315	..	..	..
Mexico	..	..	..	0	0	0	0	..	..	..
Japan	..	..	..	415	700	1 156	1 309	..	..	..
Europe	..	..	..	2	2	19	1	..	..	..
European Union (15)	..	..	..	2 224	2 841	2 914	3 397	..	..	..
Belgium	..	..	..	..	..	..	..	..	..	..
France	..	..	..	235	268	329	320	..	..	..
Germany	..	..	..	1 057	1 450	1 420	1 841	..	..	..
Italy	..	..	..	3	4	9	8	..	..	..
Netherlands	..	..	..	81	143	112	257	..	..	..
Spain	..	..	..	..	..	..	..	..	..	..
Sweden	..	..	..	322	296	257	224	..	..	..
United Kingdom	..	..	..	93	130	171	167	..	..	..
Switzerland	..	..	..	248	323	387	389	..	..	..
Australia and New Zealand	..	..	..	0	0	0	0	..	..	..
Asia (non-OECD)	..	..	..	0	0	2	5	..	..	..
Latin America	..	..	..	105	122	133	162	..	..	..

Note: Majority foreign-owned firms.
Firmes sous contrôle étranger majoritaire.

Table 14. MEXICO / MEXIQUE

GROSS OPERATING SURPLUS / EXCÉDENT BRUT D'EXPLOITATION

By industry (ISIC Rev. 3)	FOREIGN AFFILIATES *(Millions of dollars)*									
	1987	1988	1989	1990	1991	1992	1993	1994	1995	1996
10/14 Mining & quarrying	..	..	..	..	..	..	9	..	..	..
15/37 **TOTAL MANUFACTURING**	1 985	..	3 530	4 295	5 204	6 008	7 549	..	..	..
15/16 Food, beverages, tobacco	..	..	..	..	..	..	828	..	..	..
17/19 Textiles, clothing, leather, footwear	..	..	..	..	..	..	83	..	..	..
20/22 Wood and paper products	..	..	..	..	..	..	121	..	..	..
20 Wood products	..	..	..	..	..	..	..	..	..	..
21/22 Paper, printing and publishing	..	..	..	..	..	..	..	..	..	..
23/25 Chemicals, Total	..	..	..	..	..	..	1 444	..	..	..
23 Refined petroleum, nuclear fuel	..	..	..	..	..	..	23	..	..	..
24/25 Chemicals, rubber & plastics prod.	..	..	..	..	..	..	1 421	..	..	..
24 Chemical products	..	..	..	..	..	..	1 213	..	..	..
2423 Pharmaceuticals	..	..	..	..	..	..	358	..	..	..
25 Rubber and plastics products	..	..	..	..	..	..	208	..	..	..
26 Non-metallic mineral products	..	..	..	..	..	..	67	..	..	..
27/28 Basic & fabricated metals	..	..	..	..	..	..	125	..	..	..
27 Basic metals	..	..	..	..	..	..	72	..	..	..
28 Fabricated metal products	..	..	..	..	..	..	53	..	..	..
29/32 Machinery, Total	..	..	..	..	..	..	2 879	..	..	..
29/30 Non-electrical machinery	..	..	..	..	..	..	2 530	..	..	..
29 Non-electrical machinery nec	..	..	..	..	..	..	257	..	..	..
30 Office and computing machinery	..	..	..	..	..	..	2 273	..	..	..
31/32 Electrical & electronic equipment	..	..	..	..	..	..	349	..	..	..
31 Electrical machinery nec	..	..	..	..	..	..	210	..	..	..
32 Radio, TV & communications eq.	..	..	..	..	..	..	139	..	..	..
33 Scientific instruments	..	..	..	..	..	..	50	..	..	..
34/35 Transportation equipment	..	..	..	..	..	..	1 842	..	..	..
34 Motor vehicles	..	..	..	..	..	..	1 811	..	..	..
35 Other transport equipment	..	..	..	..	..	..	31	..	..	..
351 Shipbuilding & repairing	..	..	..	..	..	..	1	..	..	..
353 Aircraft and spacecraft	..	..	..	..	..	..	0	..	..	..
36/37 Other manufacturing	..	..	..	..	..	..	110	..	..	..
40/45 Construction, electricity, gas & water	..	..	..	..	..	..	44	..	..	..
50/55 Trade, repair, hotels & restaurants	..	..	..	..	..	..	743	..	..	..
65/74 Finance, insurance, business services	..	..	..	..	..	..	493	..	..	..
OTHER ACTIVITIES	..	..	..	..	..	..	1 230	..	..	..
01/99 **GRAND TOTAL**	..	..	..	..	..	..	10 098	..	..	..

Total manufacturing by investing country

	1987	1988	1989	1990	1991	1992	1993	1994	1995	1996
All countries	1 985	..	3 530	4 295	5 204	6 008	7 549	..	..	..
United States	1 291	..	2 678	3 239	3 991	4 265	5 568	..	..	..
Canada	39	..	71	82	60	66	101	..	..	..
Mexico	0	..	0	0	0	0	0	..	..	..
Japan	25	..	122	62	49	81	253	..	..	..
Europe	0	..	2	0	0	2	2	..	..	..
European Union (15)	524	..	522	794	870	1 217	1 110	..	..	..
Belgium	0	..	0	2	1	1	5	..	..	..
France	305	..	117	266	349	440	528	..	..	..
Germany	88	..	154	168	195	299	181	..	..	..
Italy	4	..	7	56	4	7	5	..	..	..
Netherlands	11	..	56	62	65	90	91	..	..	..
Spain	2	..	3	27	26	27	33	..	..	..
Sweden	34	..	50	49	19	99	34	..	..	..
United Kingdom	52	..	81	92	108	132	121	..	..	..
Switzerland	63	..	92	55	123	167	170	..	..	..
Australia and New Zealand	0	..	0	0	0	0	0	..	..	..
Asia (non-OECD)	0	..	1	0	0	26	21	..	..	..
Latin America	21	..	31	37	64	57	190	..	..	..

Note: Majority foreign-owned firms.
Firmes sous contrôle étranger majoritaire.

Table 15. MEXICO / MEXIQUE

TECHNOLOGICAL PAYMENTS / PAIEMENTS TECHNOLOGIQUES

By industry (ISIC Rev. 3)		FOREIGN AFFILIATES *(Millions of dollars)*									
		1987	1988	1989	1990	1991	1992	1993	1994	1995	1996
10/14	Mining & quarrying	..	..	..	..	..	..	0	..	..	..
15/37	**TOTAL MANUFACTURING**	**177**	..	**260**	**320**	**472**	**634**	**757**	..	..	..
15/16	Food, beverages, tobacco	..	..	..	..	..	..	111	..	..	..
17/19	Textiles, clothing, leather, footwear	..	..	..	..	..	..	8	..	..	..
20/22	Wood and paper products	..	..	..	..	..	..	8	..	..	..
20	Wood products	..	..	..	..	..	..	..	..	..	..
21/22	Paper, printing and publishing	..	..	..	..	..	..	..	..	..	..
23/25	Chemicals, Total	..	..	..	..	..	..	269	..	..	..
23	Refined petroleum, nuclear fuel	..	..	..	..	..	..	2	..	..	..
24/25	Chemicals, rubber & plastics prod.	..	..	..	..	..	..	267	..	..	..
24	Chemical products	..	..	..	..	..	..	231	..	..	..
2423	Pharmaceuticals	..	..	..	..	..	..	79	..	..	..
25	Rubber and plastics products	..	..	..	..	..	..	36	..	..	..
26	Non-metallic mineral products	..	..	..	..	..	..	10	..	..	..
27/28	Basic & fabricated metals	..	..	..	..	..	..	10	..	..	..
27	Basic metals	..	..	..	..	..	..	2	..	..	..
28	Fabricated metal products	..	..	..	..	..	..	7	..	..	..
29/32	Machinery, Total	..	..	..	..	..	..	179	..	..	..
29/30	Non-electrical machinery	..	..	..	..	..	..	114	..	..	..
29	Non-electrical machinery nec	..	..	..	..	..	..	22	..	..	..
30	Office and computing machinery	..	..	..	..	..	..	92	..	..	..
31/32	Electrical & electronic equipment	..	..	..	..	..	..	65	..	..	..
31	Electrical machinery nec	..	..	..	..	..	..	50	..	..	..
32	Radio, TV & communications eq.	..	..	..	..	..	..	15	..	..	..
33	Scientific instruments	..	..	..	..	..	..	1	..	..	..
34/35	Transportation equipment	..	..	..	..	..	..	151	..	..	..
34	Motor vehicles	..	..	..	..	..	..	147	..	..	..
35	Other transport equipment	..	..	..	..	..	..	4	..	..	..
351	Shipbuilding & repairing	..	..	..	..	..	..	0	..	..	..
353	Aircraft and spacecraft	..	..	..	..	..	..	0	..	..	..
36/37	Other manufacturing	..	..	..	..	..	..	10	..	..	..
40/45	Construction, electricity, gas & water	..	..	..	..	..	..	11	..	..	..
50/55	Trade, repair, hotels & restaurants	..	..	..	..	..	..	58	..	..	..
65/74	Finance, insurance, business services	..	..	..	..	..	..	18	..	..	..
	OTHER ACTIVITIES	..	..	..	..	..	..	73	..	..	..
01/99	**GRAND TOTAL**	..	..	..	..	..	..	**916**	..	..	..

Total manufacturing by investing country

	1987	1988	1989	1990	1991	1992	1993	1994	1995	1996
All countries	**177**	..	**260**	**320**	**472**	**634**	**757**	..	..	..
United States	139	..	181	221	334	459	546	..	..	..
Canada	7	..	12	15	22	30	29	..	..	..
Mexico	0	..	0	0	0	0	0	..	..	..
Japan	1	..	3	3	4	4	16	..	..	..
Europe	0	..	0	0	1	1	1	..	..	..
European Union (15)	14	..	36	47	63	85	109	..	..	..
Belgium	0	..	0	0	0	0	0	..	..	..
France	3	..	6	7	14	19	26	..	..	..
Germany	5	..	18	22	27	38	46	..	..	..
Italy	0	..	0	0	0	0	0	..	..	..
Netherlands	1	..	5	9	11	13	18	..	..	..
Spain	0	..	0	1	1	3	3	..	..	..
Sweden	2	..	3	2	2	3	5	..	..	..
United Kingdom	2	..	3	3	5	5	8	..	..	..
Switzerland	13	..	24	29	38	44	44	..	..	..
Australia and New Zealand	0	..	0	0	0	0	0	..	..	..
Asia (non-OECD)	0	..	0	0	0	0	0	..	..	..
Latin America	1	..	2	4	6	7	8	..	..	..

Note: Majority foreign-owned firms.
Firmes sous contrôle étranger majoritaire.

Table 16. MEXICO / MEXIQUE

TECHNOLOGICAL RECEIPTS / RECETTES TECHNOLOGIQUES

By industry (ISIC Rev. 3)	FOREIGN AFFILIATES (Millions of dollars)									
	1987	1988	1989	1990	1991	1992	1993	1994	1995	1996
10/14 Mining & quarrying	..	..	..	..	..	..	0	..	..	..
15/37 TOTAL MANUFACTURING	**15**	..	**20**	**22**	**26**	**34**	**37**	..	..	..
15/16 Food, beverages, tobacco	..	..	..	..	..	..	1	..	..	..
17/19 Textiles, clothing, leather, footwear	..	..	..	..	..	..	1	..	..	..
20/22 Wood and paper products	..	..	..	..	..	..	0	..	..	..
20 Wood products	..	..	..	..	..	..	..	..	..	..
21/22 Paper, printing and publishing	..	..	..	..	..	..	..	..	..	..
23/25 Chemicals, Total	..	..	..	..	..	..	13	..	..	..
23 Refined petroleum, nuclear fuel	..	..	..	..	..	..	0	..	..	..
24/25 Chemicals, rubber & plastics prod.	..	..	..	..	..	..	13	..	..	..
24 Chemical products	..	..	..	..	..	..	12	..	..	..
2423 Pharmaceuticals	..	..	..	..	..	..	4	..	..	..
25 Rubber and plastics products	..	..	..	..	..	..	1	..	..	..
26 Non-metallic mineral products	..	..	..	..	..	..	1	..	..	..
27/28 Basic & fabricated metals	..	..	..	..	..	..	2	..	..	..
27 Basic metals	..	..	..	..	..	..	1	..	..	..
28 Fabricated metal products	..	..	..	..	..	..	0	..	..	..
29/32 Machinery, Total	..	..	..	..	..	..	19	..	..	..
29/30 Non-electrical machinery	..	..	..	..	..	..	4	..	..	..
29 Non-electrical machinery nec	..	..	..	..	..	..	1	..	..	..
30 Office and computing machinery	..	..	..	..	..	..	3	..	..	..
31/32 Electrical & electronic equipment	..	..	..	..	..	..	15	..	..	..
31 Electrical machinery nec	..	..	..	..	..	..	4	..	..	..
32 Radio, TV & communications eq.	..	..	..	..	..	..	11	..	..	..
33 Scientific instruments	..	..	..	..	..	..	0	..	..	..
34/35 Transportation equipment	..	..	..	..	..	..	1	..	..	..
34 Motor vehicles	..	..	..	..	..	..	1	..	..	..
35 Other transport equipment	..	..	..	..	..	..	0	..	..	..
351 Shipbuilding & repairing	..	..	..	..	..	..	0	..	..	..
353 Aircraft and spacecraft	..	..	..	..	..	..	0	..	..	..
36/37 Other manufacturing	..	..	..	..	..	..	0	..	..	..
40/45 Construction, electricity, gas & water	..	..	..	..	..	..	1	..	..	..
50/55 Trade, repair, hotels & restaurants	..	..	..	..	..	..	51	..	..	..
65/74 Finance, insurance, business services	..	..	..	..	..	..	3	..	..	..
OTHER ACTIVITIES	..	..	..	..	..	..	40	..	..	..
01/99 GRAND TOTAL	..	..	..	..	..	..	**133**	..	..	..

Total manufacturing by investing country

	1987	1988	1989	1990	1991	1992	1993	1994	1995	1996
All countries	**15**	..	**20**	**22**	**26**	**34**	**37**	..	..	..
United States	8	..	8	8	9	11	17	..	..	..
Canada	0	..	0	0	0	0	0	..	..	..
Mexico	0	..	0	0	0	0	0	..	..	..
Japan	0	..	1	1	1	1	1	..	..	..
Europe	0	..	0	0	0	0	0	..	..	..
European Union (15)	7	..	10	12	14	20	17	..	..	..
Belgium	0	..	0	0	0	0	0	..	..	..
France	1	..	1	2	2	2	2	..	..	..
Germany	0	..	0	0	0	1	1	..	..	..
Italy	2	..	2	0	0	0	0	..	..	..
Netherlands	0	..	0	0	0	2	1	..	..	..
Spain	0	..	0	0	0	0	0	..	..	..
Sweden	3	..	6	7	8	11	13	..	..	..
United Kingdom	0	..	0	0	0	0	0	..	..	..
Switzerland	0	..	0	0	1	1	1	..	..	..
Australia and New Zealand	0	..	0	0	0	0	0	..	..	..
Asia (non-OECD)	0	..	0	0	0	0	0	..	..	..
Latin America	0	..	1	1	1	1	2	..	..	..

Note: Majority foreign-owned firms.
    Firmes sous contrôle étranger majoritaire.

Table 17. MEXICO / MEXIQUE

STOCK OF FOREIGN DIRECT INVESTMENT / STOCK D'INVESTISSEMENT DIRECT ÉTRANGER

By industry (ISIC Rev. 3)		FOREIGN AFFILIATES (Millions of dollars)									
		1987	1988	1989	1990	1991	1992	1993	1994	1995	1996
10/14	Mining & quarrying	..	..	..	..	..	..	23	..	..	..
15/37	**TOTAL MANUFACTURING**	**4 052**	..	**8 158**	**14 727**	**18 935**	**21 767**	**27 864**	..	..	..
15/16	Food, beverages, tobacco	..	..	..	..	..	..	5 462	..	..	..
17/19	Textiles, clothing, leather, footwear	..	..	..	..	..	..	543	..	..	..
20/22	Wood and paper products	..	..	..	..	..	..	578	..	..	..
20	Wood products	..	..	..	..	..	..		..	..	..
21/22	Paper, printing and publishing	..	..	..	..	..	..	..	..	..	..
23/25	Chemicals, Total	..	..	..	..	..	..	5 844	..	..	..
23	Refined petroleum, nuclear fuel	..	..	..	..	..	..	60	..	..	..
24/25	Chemicals, rubber & plastics prod.	..	..	..	..	..	..	5 784	..	..	..
24	Chemical products	..	..	..	..	..	..	5 147	..	..	..
2423	Pharmaceuticals	..	..	..	..	..	..	2 027	..	..	..
25	Rubber and plastics products	..	..	..	..	..	..	637	..	..	..
26	Non-metallic mineral products	..	..	..	..	..	..	815	..	..	..
27/28	Basic & fabricated metals	..	..	..	..	..	..	1 952	..	..	..
27	Basic metals	..	..	..	..	..	..	1 660	..	..	..
28	Fabricated metal products	..	..	..	..	..	..	291	..	..	..
29/32	Machinery, Total	..	..	..	..	..	..	5 275	..	..	..
29/30	Non-electrical machinery	..	..	..	..	..	..	3 703	..	..	..
29	Non-electrical machinery nec	..	..	..	..	..	..	1 471	..	..	..
30	Office and computing machinery	..	..	..	..	..	..	2 231	..	..	..
31/32	Electrical & electronic equipment	..	..	..	..	..	..	1 572	..	..	..
31	Electrical machinery nec	..	..	..	..	..	..	892	..	..	..
32	Radio, TV & communications eq.	..	..	..	..	..	..	680	..	..	..
33	Scientific instruments	..	..	..	..	..	..	222	..	..	..
34/35	Transportation equipment	..	..	..	..	..	..	6 846	..	..	..
34	Motor vehicles	..	..	..	..	..	..	6 750	..	..	..
35	Other transport equipment	..	..	..	..	..	..	95	..	..	..
351	Shipbuilding & repairing	..	..	..	..	..	..	4	..	..	..
353	Aircraft and spacecraft	..	..	..	..	..	..	0	..	..	..
36/37	Other manufacturing	..	..	..	..	..	..	329	..	..	..
40/45	Construction, electricity, gas & water	..	..	..	..	..	..	188	..	..	..
50/55	Trade, repair, hotels & restaurants	..	..	..	..	..	..	4 910	..	..	..
65/74	Finance, insurance, business services	..	..	..	..	..	..	3 753	..	..	..
	OTHER ACTIVITIES	..	..	..	..	..	..	5 256	..	..	..
01/99	**GRAND TOTAL**	..	..	..	..	..	..	**42 226**	..	..	..

Total manufacturing by investing country	1987	1988	1989	1990	1991	1992	1993	1994	1995	1996
All countries	4 052	..	8 158	14 727	18 935	21 767	27 864	..	..	..
United States	2 221	..	4 736	8 948	11 704	13 395	17 221	..	..	..
Canada	242	..	351	469	497	658	800	..	..	..
Mexico	0	..	0	0	0	0	0	..	..	..
Japan	257	..	502	805	900	946	739	..	..	..
Europe	0	..	5	14	7	17	4	..	..	..
European Union (15)	1 074	..	1 933	3 523	4 213	4 640	5 410	..	..	..
Belgium	0	..	- 3	7	11	20	42	..	..	..
France	- 19	..	72	218	306	371	439	..	..	..
Germany	495	..	720	1 373	1 409	1 518	1 772	..	..	..
Italy	15	..	35	- 19	15	95	135	..	..	..
Netherlands	31	..	313	609	673	718	960	..	..	..
Spain	6	..	8	118	142	190	212	..	..	..
Sweden	256	..	257	253	406	357	393	..	..	..
United Kingdom	87	..	240	422	563	620	624	..	..	..
Switzerland	175	..	440	659	800	760	977	..	..	..
Australia and New Zealand	0	..	0	0	0	0	0	..	..	..
Asia (non-OECD)	1	..	1	1	2	465	1 215	..	..	..
Latin America	42	..	110	198	296	274	718	..	..	..

Note: Majority foreign-owned firms.
Firmes sous contrôle étranger majoritaire.

Table 18. MEXICO / MEXIQUE

CAPITAL UNDER FOREIGN INFLUENCE / CAPITAL SOUS INFLUENCE ÉTRANGÈRE

By industry (ISIC Rev. 3)		**FOREIGN AFFILIATES** *(Millions of dollars)*									
		1987	1988	1989	1990	1991	1992	1993	1994	1995	1996
10/14	Mining & quarrying	..	..	..	..	..	..	27	..	..	..
15/37	**TOTAL MANUFACTURING**	**15 702**	..	**23 517**	**26 095**	**33 561**	**41 834**	**52 446**	..	..	..
15/16	Food, beverages, tobacco	..	..	..	..	..	..	8 379	..	..	..
17/19	Textiles, clothing, leather, footwear	..	..	..	..	..	..	761	..	..	..
20/22	Wood and paper products	..	..	..	..	..	..	1 214	..	..	..
20	Wood products	..	..	..	..	..	..	..	..	..	..
21/22	Paper, printing and publishing	..	..	..	..	..	..	..	..	..	..
23/25	Chemicals, Total	..	..	..	..	..	..	9 679	..	..	..
23	Refined petroleum, nuclear fuel	..	..	..	..	..	..	142	..	..	..
24/25	Chemicals, rubber & plastics prod.	..	..	..	..	..	..	9 537	..	..	..
24	Chemical products	..	..	..	..	..	..	8 356	..	..	..
2423	Pharmaceuticals	..	..	..	..	..	..	3 122	..	..	..
25	Rubber and plastics products	..	..	..	..	..	..	1 181	..	..	..
26	Non-metallic mineral products	..	..	..	..	..	..	1 099	..	..	..
27/28	Basic & fabricated metals	..	..	..	..	..	..	3 398	..	..	..
27	Basic metals	..	..	..	..	..	..	2 975	..	..	..
28	Fabricated metal products	..	..	..	..	..	..	422	..	..	..
29/32	Machinery, Total	..	..	..	..	..	..	10 551	..	..	..
29/30	Non-electrical machinery	..	..	..	..	..	..	7 182	..	..	..
29	Non-electrical machinery nec	..	..	..	..	..	..	2 381	..	..	..
30	Office and computing machinery	..	..	..	..	..	..	4 800	..	..	..
31/32	Electrical & electronic equipment	..	..	..	..	..	..	3 370	..	..	..
31	Electrical machinery nec	..	..	..	..	..	..	1 475	..	..	..
32	Radio, TV & communications eq.	..	..	..	..	..	..	1 895	..	..	..
33	Scientific instruments	..	..	..	..	..	..	322	..	..	..
34/35	Transportation equipment	..	..	..	..	..	..	16 415	..	..	..
34	Motor vehicles	..	..	..	..	..	..	16 116	..	..	..
35	Other transport equipment	..	..	..	..	..	..	300	..	..	..
351	Shipbuilding & repairing	..	..	..	..	..	..	10	..	..	..
353	Aircraft and spacecraft	..	..	..	..	..	..	0	..	..	..
36/37	Other manufacturing	..	..	..	..	..	..	628	..	..	..
40/45	Construction, electricity, gas & water	..	..	..	..	..	..	426	..	..	..
50/55	Trade, repair, hotels & restaurants	..	..	..	..	..	..	9 109	..	..	..
65/74	Finance, insurance, business services	..	..	..	..	..	..	6 611	..	..	..
	OTHER ACTIVITIES	..	..	..	..	..	..	9 418	..	..	..
01/99	**GRAND TOTAL**	..	..	..	..	..	..	**78 303**	..	..	..

Total manufacturing by investing country

	1987	1988	1989	1990	1991	1992	1993	1994	1995	1996
All countries	**15 702**	..	**23 517**	**26 095**	**33 561**	**41 834**	**52 446**	..	..	..
United States	9 227	..	12 994	15 055	19 497	24 134	30 277	..	..	..
Canada	599	..	767	843	931	1 204	1 378	..	..	..
Mexico	0	..	0	0	0	0	0	..	..	..
Japan	1 130	..	1 376	1 427	1 832	2 574	3 288	..	..	..
Europe	0	..	18	20	16	91	16	..	..	..
European Union (15)	3 910	..	6 446	6 892	8 385	9 800	11 052	..	..	..
Belgium	0	..	4	15	32	39	92	..	..	..
France	516	..	830	1 054	1 301	1 497	1 678	..	..	..
Germany	2 055	..	2 933	2 395	3 017	3 996	4 421	..	..	..
Italy	38	..	52	166	28	39	45	..	..	..
Netherlands	102	..	625	746	872	968	1 310	..	..	..
Spain	17	..	33	412	520	588	630	..	..	..
Sweden	499	..	699	655	753	690	682	..	..	..
United Kingdom	332	..	686	684	859	884	1 022	..	..	..
Switzerland	521	..	1 121	1 141	1 525	1 466	1 792	..	..	..
Australia and New Zealand	1	..	0	0	0	0	0	..	..	..
Asia (non-OECD)	2	..	3	2	2	1 037	1 949	..	..	..
Latin America	130	..	501	352	557	553	1 404	..	..	..

Note: Majority foreign-owned firms.
Firmes sous contrôle étranger majoritaire.

MEXICO

Source

The data are prepared by the *Secretaria de Comercio y Fomento Industrial* and the *Banco de Mexico* from an annual survey covering all domestic firms with foreign participation. The final results cover 85% of all firms.

National totals: no data compatible with foreign affiliates' data are available.

Industrial classification

For all variables, the data are classified according to the principal industrial activity of the affiliate.

The industrial classification used for Mexican tables is the national classification (*Clasificación Mexicana de Actividades y Productos*) converted to ISIC Revision 3.

Variables

- *Wages and salaries* include employers' contributions to health and pension funds.

Geographical breakdown

The investor's country is the country of the immediate controller.

MEXIQUE

Source

Les données sont fournies par le *Secretaria de Comercio y Fomento Industrial* et le *Banco de Mexico* à partir d'une enquête annuelle couvrant toutes les entreprises mexicaines à participation étrangère. Le résultat final est une couverture à 85 % des entreprises.

Totaux nationaux : aucune donnée comparable à celles des filiales étrangères n'est disponible.

Classification industrielle

Pour toutes les variables, les données sont classées selon l'activité principale industrielle de l'entreprise affiliée.

La classification industrielle utilisée pour les tableaux mexicains est la classification nationale (*Clasificación Mexicana de Actividades y Productos*) adaptée pour correspondre à la CITI révision 3.

Variables

- Les *Salaires* comprennent les cotisations patronales à l'assurance maladie et aux fonds de pension.

Ventilation géographique

Le pays de l'investisseur est le pays où s'exerce le contrôle immédiat.

NETHERLANDS

PAYS-BAS

Table 1. NETHERLANDS / PAYS-BAS

NUMBER OF ENTERPRISES / NOMBRE D'ENTREPRISES

By industry (ISIC Rev. 3)	FOREIGN AFFILIATES (Units)					AS A % OF NATIONAL TOTAL				
	1993	1994	1995	1996	1997	1993	1994	1995	1996	1997
10/14 Mining & quarrying	..	..	96	64	..	..	..	38.2	22.1	..
15/37 TOTAL MANUFACTURING	..	..	**827**	**844**	..	..	..	**2.4**	**2.6**	..
15/16 Food, beverages, tobacco	..	..	125	112	..	..	..	2.2	2.0	..
17/19 Textiles, clothing, leather, footwear	..	..	36	34	..	..	..	1.5	1.5	..
20/22 Wood and paper products	..	..	93	108	..	..	..	1.3	1.6	..
20 Wood products	..	..	..	..	..	..	..	..	..	..
21/22 Paper, printing and publishing	..	..	..	..	..	..	..	..	..	..
23/25 Chemicals, Total	..	..	192	218	..	..	..	10.2	12.2	..
23 Refined petroleum, nuclear fuel	..	..	9	10	..	..	..	40.9	35.2	..
24/25 Chemicals, rubber & plastics prod.	..	..	183	208	..	..	..	9.9	11.9	..
24 Chemical products	..	..	123	131	..	..	..	16.0	18.2	..
2423 Pharmaceuticals	..	..	15	14	..	..	..	13.4	13.1	..
25 Rubber and plastics products	..	..	60	77	..	..	..	5.5	7.5	..
26 Non-metallic mineral products	..	..	89	89	..	..	..	7.5	8.0	..
27/28 Basic & fabricated metals	..	..	92	83	..	..	..	1.7	1.7	..
27 Basic metals	..	..	24	22	..	..	..	10.8	10.6	..
28 Fabricated metal products	..	..	68	61	..	..	..	1.3	1.3	..
29/32 Machinery, Total	..	..	131	128	..	..	..	3.0	3.1	..
29/30 Non-electrical machinery	..	..	110	108	..	..	..	3.3	3.4	..
29 Non-electrical machinery nec	..	..	105	103	..	..	..	3.3	3.4	..
30 Office and computing machinery	..	..	5	5	..	..	..	2.6	3.4	..
31/32 Electrical & electronic equipment	..	..	21	20	..	..	..	2.1	2.1	..
31 Electrical machinery nec	..	..	17	17	..	..	..	2.2	2.3	..
32 Radio, TV & communications eq.	..	..	4	3	..	..	..	2.0	1.6	..
33 Scientific instruments	..	..	27	28	..	..	..	2.1	2.3	..
34/35 Transportation equipment	..	..	26	28	..	..	..	1.6	1.8	..
34 Motor vehicles	..	..	16	21	..	..	..	2.5	3.5	..
35 Other transport equipment	..	..	10	7	..	..	..	1.0	0.8	..
351 Shipbuilding & repairing	..	..	1	1	..	..	..	0.1	0.1	..
353 Aircraft and spacecraft	..	..	7	3	..	..	..	43.8	7.4	..
36/37 Other manufacturing	..	..	16	16	..	..	..	0.5	0.6	..
40/45 Construction, electricity, gas & water	..	..	70	79	..	..	..	0.2	0.3	..
50/55 Trade, repair, hotels & restaurants	..	..	1 140	1 102	..	..	..	0.5	0.4	..
65/74 Finance, insurance, business services	..	..	629	566	..	..	..	0.6	0.5	..
OTHER ACTIVITIES	..	..	243	266	..	..	..	0.5	0.4	..
01/99 GRAND TOTAL	..	..	**3 005**	**2 921**	..	..	..	**0.7**	**0.6**	..

Total manufacturing by investing country						*As a % of total manufacturing by foreign affiliates*				
All countries	..	..	827	844	..	..	..	100.0	100.0	..
United States	..	..	175	180	..	..	..	21.2	21.3	..
Canada	..	..	..	..	..	..	..	..	..	..
Mexico	..	..	..	..	..	..	..	..	..	..
Japan	..	..	15	21	..	..	..	1.8	2.5	..
Europe	..	..	..	..	..	..	..	..	..	..
European Union (15)	..	..	483	492	..	..	..	58.4	58.3	..
Belgium	..	..	..	..	..	..	..	..	..	..
France	..	..	42	37	..	..	..	5.1	4.4	..
Germany	..	..	108	99	..	..	..	13.1	11.7	..
Italy	..	..	..	..	..	..	..	..	..	..
Netherlands	..	..	..	..	..	..	..	..	..	..
Spain	..	..	0	0	..	..	..	0.0	0.0	..
Sweden	..	..	..	..	..	..	..	..	..	..
United Kingdom	..	..	157	163	..	..	..	19.0	19.3	..
Switzerland	..	..	54	52	..	..	..	6.5	6.2	..
Australia and New Zealand	..	..	..	..	..	..	..	..	..	..
Asia (non-OECD)	..	..	3	7	..	..	..	0.4	0.8	..
Latin America	..	..	66	77	..	..	..	8.0	9.1	..

Note: Majority foreign-owned firms.
Firmes sous contrôle étranger majoritaire.

Table 2. NETHERLANDS / PAYS-BAS

NUMBER OF EMPLOYEES / NOMBRE DE SALARIÉS

By industry (ISIC Rev. 3)		FOREIGN AFFILIATES (Units)					AS A % OF NATIONAL TOTAL				
		1993	1994	1995	1996	1997	1993	1994	1995	1996	1997
10/14	Mining & quarrying	..	..	61	381	..	..	..	5.7	17.3	..
15/37	**TOTAL MANUFACTURING**	..	..	**168 401**	**160 487**	..	..	..	**20.1**	**19.0**	..
15/16	Food, beverages, tobacco	..	..	29 008	29 486	..	..	..	19.9	19.8	..
17/19	Textiles, clothing, leather, footwear	..	..	4 595	3 945	..	..	..	14.1	12.2	..
20/22	Wood and paper products	..	..	15 673	15 754	..	..	..	12.6	12.4	..
20	Wood products	..	..	..	..	..	..	..	..	..	..
21/22	Paper, printing and publishing	..	..	..	..	..	..	..	..	..	..
23/25	Chemicals, Total	..	..	39 782	39 674	..	..	..	34.6	34.9	..
23	Refined petroleum, nuclear fuel	..	..	4 226	4 087	..	..	..	60.3	59.4	..
24/25	Chemicals, rubber & plastics prod.	..	..	35 556	35 587	..	..	..	32.9	33.3	..
24	Chemical products	..	..	29 652	28 583	..	..	..	39.2	38.3	..
2423	Pharmaceuticals	..	..	3 990	3 039	..	..	..	28.9	22.7	..
25	Rubber and plastics products	..	..	5 904	7 004	..	..	..	18.3	21.8	..
26	Non-metallic mineral products	..	..	13 031	14 277	..	..	..	39.8	43.8	..
27/28	Basic & fabricated metals	..	..	16 975	16 454	..	..	..	14.3	13.8	..
27	Basic metals	..	..	7 804	7 315	..	..	..	28.9	28.5	..
28	Fabricated metal products	..	..	9 171	9 139	..	..	..	10.0	9.7	..
29/32	Machinery, Total	..	..	25 573	25 246	..	..	..	16.1	15.6	..
29/30	Non-electrical machinery	..	..	17 340	17 526	..	..	..	19.1	18.9	..
29	Non-electrical machinery nec	..	..	15 326	15 659	..	..	..	18.5	18.4	..
30	Office and computing machinery	..	..	2 014	1 867	..	..	..	25.4	24.2	..
31/32	Electrical & electronic equipment	..	..	8 233	7 720	..	..	..	12.2	11.2	..
31	Electrical machinery nec	..	..	4 742	4 186	..	..	..	23.0	19.9	..
32	Radio, TV & communications eq.	..	..	3 491	3 534	..	..	..	7.4	7.4	..
33	Scientific instruments	..	..	7 167	7 594	..	..	..	32.2	32.1	..
34/35	Transportation equipment	..	..	14 768	6 011	..	..	..	27.9	12.3	..
34	Motor vehicles	..	..	4 770	5 171	..	..	..	19.4	20.1	..
35	Other transport equipment	..	..	9 998	840	..	..	..	35.2	3.6	..
351	Shipbuilding & repairing	..	..	10	72	..	..	..	0.1	0.5	..
353	Aircraft and spacecraft	..	..	9 413	157	..	..	..	95.8	3.5	..
36/37	Other manufacturing	..	..	1 829	2 047	..	..	..	5.3	5.7	..
40/45	Construction, electricity, gas & water	..	..	8 403	9 645	..	..	..	2.1	2.4	..
50/55	Trade, repair, hotels & restaurants	..	..	101 179	101 052	..	..	..	8.2	7.9	..
65/74	Finance, insurance, business services	..	..	31 268	36 568	..	..	..	6.0	6.0	..
	OTHER ACTIVITIES	..	..	15 145	18 805	..	..	..	4.6	4.4	..
01/99	**GRAND TOTAL**	..	..	**324 458**	**326 939**	..	..	..	**9.8**	**9.1**	..

Total manufacturing by investing country						As a % of total manufacturing by foreign affiliates				
All countries	..	..	**168 401**	**160 487**	..	..	..	**100.0**	**100.0**	..
United States	..	..	49 781	49 189	..	..	..	29.6	30.6	..
Canada	..	..	424	328	..	..	..	0.3	0.2	..
Mexico	..	..	..	..	..	..	..	..	..	..
Japan	..	..	3 021	3 555	..	..	..	1.8	2.2	..
Europe	..	..	103 958	95 316	..	..	..	61.7	59.4	..
European Union (15)	..	..	90 627	81 566	..	..	..	53.8	50.8	..
Belgium	..	..	11 843	13 192	..	..	..	7.0	8.2	..
France	..	..	9 411	9 305	..	..	..	5.6	5.8	..
Germany	..	..	28 249	18 495	..	..	..	16.8	11.5	..
Italy	..	..	29	4	..	..	..	0.0	0.0	..
Netherlands	..	..	..	..	..	..	..	..	..	..
Spain	..	..	0	0	..	..	..	0.0	0.0	..
Sweden	..	..	7 574	7 985	..	..	..	4.5	5.0	..
United Kingdom	..	..	20 134	20 035	..	..	..	12.0	12.5	..
Switzerland	..	..	11 941	12 318	..	..	..	7.1	7.7	..
Australia and New Zealand	..	..	3 185	3 045	..	..	..	1.9	1.9	..
Asia (non-OECD)	..	..	329	1 080	..	..	..	0.2	0.7	..
Latin America	..	..	7 703	7 973	..	..	..	4.6	5.0	..

Note: Majority foreign-owned firms.
Firmes sous contrôle étranger majoritaire.

Table 3. NETHERLANDS / PAYS-BAS

PRODUCTION

By industry (ISIC Rev. 3)	FOREIGN AFFILIATES (Millions of Gld)					AS A % OF NATIONAL TOTAL				
	1993	1994	1995	1996	1997	1993	1994	1995	1996	1997
10/14 Mining & quarrying	..	..	..	20 083	..	..	..	..	46.3	..
15/37 TOTAL MANUFACTURING	..	..	..	**113 020**	..	..	..	..	**29.7**	..
15/16 Food, beverages, tobacco	..	..	..	29 322	..	..	..	..	29.3	..
17/19 Textiles, clothing, leather, footwear	..	..	..	1 757	..	..	..	..	20.5	..
20/22 Wood and paper products	..	..	..	7 874	..	..	..	..	20.3	..
20 Wood products	..	..	..	..	..	..	..	..	..	..
21/22 Paper, printing and publishing	..	..	..	..	..	..	..	..	..	..
23/25 Chemicals, Total	..	..	..	45 322	..	..	..	..	48.7	..
23 Refined petroleum, nuclear fuel	..	..	..	13 546	..	..	..	..	59.5	..
24/25 Chemicals, rubber & plastics prod.	..	..	..	31 777	..	..	..	..	45.2	..
24 Chemical products	..	..	..	28 970	..	..	..	..	48.5	..
2423 Pharmaceuticals	..	..	..	4 790	..	..	..	..	49.6	..
25 Rubber and plastics products	..	..	..	2 807	..	..	..	..	26.4	..
26 Non-metallic mineral products	..	..	..	5 131	..	..	..	..	45.4	..
27/28 Basic & fabricated metals	..	..	..	7 302	..	..	..	..	20.9	..
27 Basic metals	..	..	..	3 371	..	..	..	..	32.9	..
28 Fabricated metal products	..	..	..	3 931	..	..	..	..	15.9	..
29/32 Machinery, Total	..	..	..	10 394	..	..	..	..	17.8	..
29/30 Non-electrical machinery	..	..	..	7 053	..	..	..	..	23.7	..
29 Non-electrical machinery nec	..	..	..	5 512	..	..	..	..	21.3	..
30 Office and computing machinery	..	..	..	1 541	..	..	..	..	39.6	..
31/32 Electrical & electronic equipment	..	..	..	3 341	..	..	..	..	11.7	..
31 Electrical machinery nec	..	..	..	1 876	..	..	..	..	26.6	..
32 Radio, TV & communications eq.	..	..	..	1 466	..	..	..	..	6.8	..
33 Scientific instruments	..	..	..	3 166	..	..	..	..	45.9	..
34/35 Transportation equipment	..	..	..	1 870	..	..	..	..	9.4	..
34 Motor vehicles	..	..	..	1 487	..	..	..	..	12.4	..
35 Other transport equipment	..	..	..	384	..	..	..	..	4.9	..
351 Shipbuilding & repairing	..	..	..	29	..	..	..	..	0.5	..
353 Aircraft and spacecraft	..	..	..	67	..	..	..	..	4.5	..
36/37 Other manufacturing	..	..	..	881	..	..	..	..	10.1	..
40/45 Construction, electricity, gas & water	..	..	..	4 765	..	..	..	..	3.3	..
50/55 Trade, repair, hotels & restaurants	..	..	..	109 114	..	..	..	..	17.8	..
65/74 Finance, insurance, business services	..	..	..	10 996	..	..	..	..	10.4	..
OTHER ACTIVITIES	..	..	..	6 439	..	..	..	..	5.8	..
01/99 GRAND TOTAL	..	..	..	**264 416**	..	..	..	..	**18.9**	..

Total manufacturing by investing country						As a % of total manufacturing by foreign affiliates				
All countries	..	..	..	**113 020**	..	..	..	..	**100.0**	..
United States	..	..	..	51 795	..	..	..	..	45.8	..
Canada	..	..	..	91	..	..	..	..	0.1	..
Mexico	..	..	..	..	..	..	..	..	..	..
Japan	..	..	..	2 184	..	..	..	..	1.9	..
Europe	..	..	..	51 434	..	..	..	..	45.5	..
European Union (15)	..	..	..	38 534	..	..	..	..	34.1	..
Belgium	..	..	..	7 805	..	..	..	..	6.9	..
France	..	..	..	4 292	..	..	..	..	3.8	..
Germany	..	..	..	7 576	..	..	..	..	6.7	..
Italy	..	..	..	1	..	..	..	..	0.0	..
Netherlands	..	..	..	..	..	..	..	..	..	..
Spain	..	..	..	0	..	..	..	..	0.0	..
Sweden	..	..	..	3 364	..	..	..	..	3.0	..
United Kingdom	..	..	..	9 668	..	..	..	..	8.6	..
Switzerland	..	..	..	11 513	..	..	..	..	10.2	..
Australia and New Zealand	..	..	..	2 015	..	..	..	..	1.8	..
Asia (non-OECD)	..	..	..	848	..	..	..	..	0.8	..
Latin America	..	..	..	4 652	..	..	..	..	4.1	..

Note: Majority foreign-owned firms.
Firmes sous contrôle étranger majoritaire.

Table 4. NETHERLANDS / PAYS-BAS

TURNOVER / CHIFFRE D'AFFAIRES

By industry (ISIC Rev. 3)		FOREIGN AFFILIATES *(Millions of Gld)*					AS A % OF NATIONAL TOTAL				
		1993	1994	1995	1996	1997	1993	1994	1995	1996	1997
10/14	Mining & quarrying	..	..	1 561	20 065	..	..	..	4.1	46.3	..
15/37	**TOTAL MANUFACTURING**	..	..	**110 225**	**111 438**	..	..	..	**30.3**	**29.7**	..
15/16	Food, beverages, tobacco	..	..	27 407	28 822	..	..	..	28.8	29.4	..
17/19	Textiles, clothing, leather, footwear	..	..	1 932	1 755	..	..	..	21.6	20.6	..
20/22	Wood and paper products	..	..	7 637	7 761	..	..	..	19.8	20.1	..
20	Wood products	..	..	..	..	..	..	..	..	..	..
21/22	Paper, printing and publishing	..	..	..	..	..	..	..	..	..	..
23/25	Chemicals, Total	..	..	40 620	44 597	..	..	..	47.3	49.1	..
23	Refined petroleum, nuclear fuel	..	..	10 807	13 397	..	..	..	60.9	59.9	..
24/25	Chemicals, rubber & plastics prod.	..	..	29 813	31 201	..	..	..	43.8	45.6	..
24	Chemical products	..	..	27 360	28 430	..	..	..	47.7	49.1	..
2423	Pharmaceuticals	..	..	3 546	4 524	..	..	..	46.1	49.8	..
25	Rubber and plastics products	..	..	2 453	2 771	..	..	..	23.0	26.4	..
26	Non-metallic mineral products	..	..	4 515	5 087	..	..	..	41.2	45.4	..
27/28	Basic & fabricated metals	..	..	7 207	7 388	..	..	..	21.4	21.2	..
27	Basic metals	..	..	3 633	3 392	..	..	..	33.7	33.3	..
28	Fabricated metal products	..	..	3 574	3 997	..	..	..	15.6	16.2	..
29/32	Machinery, Total	..	..	11 200	10 267	..	..	..	20.4	17.9	..
29/30	Non-electrical machinery	..	..	6 300	6 970	..	..	..	22.9	24.0	..
29	Non-electrical machinery nec	..	..	4 644	5 457	..	..	..	19.8	21.6	..
30	Office and computing machinery	..	..	1 656	1 513	..	..	..	40.6	39.7	..
31/32	Electrical & electronic equipment	..	..	4 900	3 297	..	..	..	17.8	11.7	..
31	Electrical machinery nec	..	..	3 191	1 823	..	..	..	40.7	26.4	..
32	Radio, TV & communications eq.	..	..	1 709	1 474	..	..	..	8.7	6.9	..
33	Scientific instruments	..	..	2 841	3 060	..	..	..	45.9	45.9	..
34/35	Transportation equipment	..	..	6 210	1 833	..	..	..	29.8	9.1	..
34	Motor vehicles	..	..	2 999	1 458	..	..	..	25.2	12.6	..
35	Other transport equipment	..	..	3 212	375	..	..	..	36.0	4.4	..
351	Shipbuilding & repairing	..	..	3	29	..	..	..	0.1	0.6	..
353	Aircraft and spacecraft	..	..	2 955	68	..	..	..	95.2	2.6	..
36/37	Other manufacturing	..	..	656	868	..	..	..	7.6	10.0	..
40/45	Construction, electricity, gas & water	..	..	2 992	4 736	..	..	..	2.2	3.4	..
50/55	Trade, repair, hotels & restaurants	..	..	94 106	108 160	..	..	..	16.6	17.8	..
65/74	Finance, insurance, business services	..	..	8 906	10 537	..	..	..	9.7	10.3	..
	OTHER ACTIVITIES	..	..	4 898	6 321	..	..	..	6.4	6.1	..
01/99	**GRAND TOTAL**	..	..	**222 688**	**261 257**	..	..	..	**17.5**	**19.0**	..

Total manufacturing by investing country						As a % of total manufacturing by foreign affiliates					
All countries		..	..	**110 225**	**111 438**	..	..	..	**100.0**	**100.0**	..
United States		..	..	47 706	51 123	..	..	..	43.3	45.9	..
Canada		..	..	111	90	..	..	..	0.1	0.1	..
Mexico		..	..	..	..	..	..	..	..	..	..
Japan		..	..	1 640	2 174	..	..	..	1.5	2.0	..
Europe		..	..	54 205	50 534	..	..	..	49.2	45.3	..
European Union (15)		..	..	42 423	38 097	..	..	..	38.5	34.2	..
Belgium		..	..	6 642	7 747	..	..	..	6.0	7.0	..
France		..	..	3 868	4 199	..	..	..	3.5	3.8	..
Germany		..	..	10 483	7 513	..	..	..	9.5	6.7	..
Italy		..	..	14	1	..	..	..	0.0	0.0	..
Netherlands		..	..	..	..	..	..	..	..	..	..
Spain		..	..	0	0	..	..	..	0.0	0.0	..
Sweden		..	..	4 962	3 326	..	..	..	4.5	3.0	..
United Kingdom		..	..	8 693	9 521	..	..	..	7.9	8.5	..
Switzerland		..	..	10 512	11 153	..	..	..	9.5	10.0	..
Australia and New Zealand		..	..	1 796	1 942	..	..	..	1.6	1.7	..
Asia (non-OECD)		..	..	346	833	..	..	..	0.3	0.7	..
Latin America		..	..	4 421	4 741	..	..	..	4.0	4.3	..

Note: Majority foreign-owned firms.
Firmes sous contrôle étranger majoritaire.

Table 5. NETHERLANDS / PAYS-BAS

VALUE ADDED / VALEUR AJOUTÉE

By industry (ISIC Rev. 3)	FOREIGN AFFILIATES (Millions of Gld)					AS A % OF NATIONAL TOTAL				
	1993	1994	1995	1996	1997	1993	1994	1995	1996	1997
10/14 Mining & quarrying	..	..	1 541	19 887	..	..	..	4.1	47.1	..
15/37 TOTAL MANUFACTURING	..	..	**28 103**	**28 624**	..	..	..	**27.3**	**28.5**	..
15/16 Food, beverages, tobacco	..	..	5 939	6 532	..	..	..	31.5	34.3	..
17/19 Textiles, clothing, leather, footwear	..	..	551	518	..	..	..	22.3	21.0	..
20/22 Wood and paper products	..	..	2 525	2 612	..	..	..	17.3	17.9	..
20 Wood products	..	..	..	..	..	..	..	..	..	..
21/22 Paper, printing and publishing	..	..	..	..	..	..	..	..	..	..
23/25 Chemicals, Total	..	..	10 048	9 852	..	..	..	44.0	46.3	..
23 Refined petroleum, nuclear fuel	..	..	1 191	1 414	..	..	..	62.7	58.3	..
24/25 Chemicals, rubber & plastics prod.	..	..	8 857	8 438	..	..	..	42.4	44.8	..
24 Chemical products	..	..	8 167	7 496	..	..	..	46.8	49.1	..
2423 Pharmaceuticals	..	..	893	708	..	..	..	35.3	30.9	..
25 Rubber and plastics products	..	..	690	942	..	..	..	19.9	26.4	..
26 Non-metallic mineral products	..	..	1 947	2 162	..	..	..	44.2	52.6	..
27/28 Basic & fabricated metals	..	..	2 030	1 955	..	..	..	16.1	15.6	..
27 Basic metals	..	..	1 012	886	..	..	..	24.8	24.6	..
28 Fabricated metal products	..	..	1 018	1 070	..	..	..	12.0	12.0	..
29/32 Machinery, Total	..	..	3 137	3 024	..	..	..	18.3	18.1	..
29/30 Non-electrical machinery	..	..	1 945	1 949	..	..	..	21.0	21.2	..
29 Non-electrical machinery nec	..	..	1 601	1 644	..	..	..	19.1	19.7	..
30 Office and computing machinery	..	..	343	304	..	..	..	38.6	36.0	..
31/32 Electrical & electronic equipment	..	..	1 192	1 075	..	..	..	15.1	14.3	..
31 Electrical machinery nec	..	..	606	645	..	..	..	27.2	27.4	..
32 Radio, TV & communications eq.	..	..	585	430	..	..	..	10.4	8.3	..
33 Scientific instruments	..	..	952	1 044	..	..	..	40.6	43.0	..
34/35 Transportation equipment	..	..	744	649	..	..	..	16.3	14.3	..
34 Motor vehicles	..	..	510	525	..	..	..	19.2	19.6	..
35 Other transport equipment	..	..	235	124	..	..	..	12.2	6.7	..
351 Shipbuilding & repairing	..	..	1	6	..	..	..	0.0	0.4	..
353 Aircraft and spacecraft	..	..	164	27	..	..	..	75.1	8.7	..
36/37 Other manufacturing	..	..	229	276	..	..	..	7.3	10.5	..
40/45 Construction, electricity, gas & water	..	..	821	967	..	..	..	2.0	2.2	..
50/55 Trade, repair, hotels & restaurants	..	..	12 019	11 897	..	..	..	14.2	13.9	..
65/74 Finance, insurance, business services	..	..	3 757	4 185	..	..	..	7.8	8.2	..
OTHER ACTIVITIES	..	..	1 774	2 084	..	..	..	5.2	4.5	..
01/99 GRAND TOTAL	..	..	**48 016**	**67 645**	..	..	..	**13.7**	**18.3**	..

Total manufacturing by investing country						As a % of total manufacturing by foreign affiliates				
All countries	..	..	**28 103**	**28 624**	..	..	..	**100.0**	**100.0**	..
United States	..	..	11 141	10 908	..	..	..	39.6	38.1	..
Canada	..	..	..	..	..	..	..	..	..	..
Mexico	..	..	..	..	..	..	..	..	..	..
Japan	..	..	564	614	..	..	..	2.0	2.1	..
Europe	..	..	..	..	..	..	..	..	..	..
European Union (15)	..	..	11 583	11 565	..	..	..	41.2	40.4	..
Belgium	..	..	..	..	..	..	..	..	..	..
France	..	..	1 419	1 367	..	..	..	5.0	4.8	..
Germany	..	..	2 554	2 377	..	..	..	9.1	8.3	..
Italy	..	..	..	..	..	..	..	..	..	..
Netherlands	..	..	..	..	..	..	..	..	..	..
Spain	..	..	0	0	..	..	..	0.0	0.0	..
Sweden	..	..	..	..	..	..	..	..	..	..
United Kingdom	..	..	2 770	2 958	..	..	..	9.9	10.3	..
Switzerland	..	..	2 942	3 282	..	..	..	10.5	11.5	..
Australia and New Zealand	..	..	..	..	..	..	..	..	..	..
Asia (non-OECD)	..	..	65	319	..	..	..	0.2	1.1	..
Latin America	..	..	891	979	..	..	..	3.2	3.4	..

Note: Majority foreign-owned firms.
Firmes sous contrôle étranger majoritaire.

Table 6. NETHERLANDS / PAYS-BAS

WAGES AND SALARIES / SALAIRES ET TRAITEMENTS

By industry (ISIC Rev. 3)		FOREIGN AFFILIATES (Millions of Gld)					AS A % OF NATIONAL TOTAL				
		1993	1994	1995	1996	1997	1993	1994	1995	1996	1997
10/14	Mining & quarrying	..	..	4	31	..	..	..	4.2	11.7	..
15/37	**TOTAL MANUFACTURING**	..	..	**15 763**	**15 634**	..	..	..	**23.8**	**23.4**	..
15/16	Food, beverages, tobacco	..	..	2 778	2 964	..	..	..	25.2	26.5	..
17/19	Textiles, clothing, leather, footwear	..	..	364	318	..	..	..	18.8	17.5	..
20/22	Wood and paper products	..	..	1 403	1 475	..	..	..	14.8	15.1	..
20	Wood products	..	..	..	..	..	..	..	..	..	..
21/22	Paper, printing and publishing	..	..	..	..	..	..	..	..	..	..
23/25	Chemicals, Total	..	..	4 377	4 535	..	..	..	39.0	39.7	..
23	Refined petroleum, nuclear fuel	..	..	576	562	..	..	..	57.7	53.3	..
24/25	Chemicals, rubber & plastics prod.	..	..	3 801	3 974	..	..	..	37.2	38.3	..
24	Chemical products	..	..	3 293	3 377	..	..	..	42.2	42.5	..
2423	Pharmaceuticals	..	..	419	332	..	..	..	31.5	25.4	..
25	Rubber and plastics products	..	..	507	596	..	..	..	21.0	24.5	..
26	Non-metallic mineral products	..	..	1 175	1 285	..	..	..	45.2	49.9	..
27/28	Basic & fabricated metals	..	..	1 468	1 443	..	..	..	16.4	16.1	..
27	Basic metals	..	..	656	637	..	..	..	27.0	26.9	..
28	Fabricated metal products	..	..	812	806	..	..	..	12.4	12.3	..
29/32	Machinery, Total	..	..	2 239	2 275	..	..	..	17.3	17.3	..
29/30	Non-electrical machinery	..	..	1 493	1 532	..	..	..	21.2	21.0	..
29	Non-electrical machinery nec	..	..	1 288	1 343	..	..	..	20.2	20.2	..
30	Office and computing machinery	..	..	205	189	..	..	..	31.0	28.6	..
31/32	Electrical & electronic equipment	..	..	746	743	..	..	..	12.6	12.6	..
31	Electrical machinery nec	..	..	448	414	..	..	..	27.9	25.1	..
32	Radio, TV & communications eq.	..	..	298	329	..	..	..	6.9	7.8	..
33	Scientific instruments	..	..	628	679	..	..	..	37.8	38.1	..
34/35	Transportation equipment	..	..	1 178	483	..	..	..	27.8	11.9	..
34	Motor vehicles	..	..	372	417	..	..	..	19.2	19.3	..
35	Other transport equipment	..	..	806	66	..	..	..	35.1	3.5	..
351	Shipbuilding & repairing	..	..	0	3	..	..	..	0.0	0.3	..
353	Aircraft and spacecraft	..	..	765	17	..	..	..	94.7	4.2	..
36/37	Other manufacturing	..	..	153	176	..	..	..	7.2	8.4	..
40/45	Construction, electricity, gas & water	..	..	691	789	..	..	..	2.5	2.7	..
50/55	Trade, repair, hotels & restaurants	..	..	7 538	7 470	..	..	..	14.8	14.2	..
65/74	Finance, insurance, business services	..	..	2 990	3 362	..	..	..	8.5	8.6	..
	OTHER ACTIVITIES	..	..	1 176	1 515	..	..	..	5.2	5.2	..
01/99	**GRAND TOTAL**	..	..	**28 162**	**28 800**	..	..	..	**13.9**	**13.3**	..

Total manufacturing by investing country	1993	1994	1995	1996	1997	As a % of total manufacturing by foreign affiliates				
						1993	1994	1995	1996	1997
All countries	..	..	**15 763**	**15 634**	..	..	..	**100.0**	**100.0**	..
United States	..	..	5 075	5 262	..	..	..	32.2	33.7	..
Canada	..	..	..	..	..	..	..	..	..	..
Mexico	..	..	..	..	..	..	..	..	..	..
Japan	..	..	287	340	..	..	..	1.8	2.2	..
Europe	..	..	..	..	..	..	..	..	..	..
European Union (15)	..	..	8 047	7 495	..	..	..	51.1	47.9	..
Belgium	..	..	..	..	..	..	..	..	..	..
France	..	..	900	927	..	..	..	5.7	5.9	..
Germany	..	..	2 400	1 591	..	..	..	15.2	10.2	..
Italy	..	..	..	..	..	..	..	..	..	..
Netherlands	..	..	..	..	..	..	..	..	..	..
Spain	..	..	0	0	..	..	..	0.0	0.0	..
Sweden	..	..	..	..	..	..	..	..	..	..
United Kingdom	..	..	1 647	1 766	..	..	..	10.4	11.3	..
Switzerland	..	..	1 173	1 257	..	..	..	7.4	8.0	..
Australia and New Zealand	..	..	..	..	..	..	..	..	..	..
Asia (non-OECD)	..	..	35	108	..	..	..	0.2	0.7	..
Latin America	..	..	695	697	..	..	..	4.4	4.5	..

Note: Majority foreign-owned firms.
Firmes sous contrôle étranger majoritaire.

Table 7. NETHERLANDS / PAYS-BAS

R&D EXPENDITURE / DÉPENSES DE R-D

By industry (ISIC Rev. 3)	FOREIGN AFFILIATES (Millions of Gld)					AS A % OF NATIONAL TOTAL				
	1993	1994	1995	1996	1997	1993	1994	1995	1996	1997
10/14 Mining & quarrying	..	..	..	5	..	..	..	..	2.4	..
15/37 TOTAL MANUFACTURING	..	..	..	**2 368**	..	..	..	..	**24.1**	..
15/16 Food, beverages, tobacco	..	..	..	314	..	..	..	..	23.6	..
17/19 Textiles, clothing, leather, footwear	..	..	..	23	..	..	..	..	25.3	..
20/22 Wood and paper products	..	..	..	363	..	..	..	..	36.1	..
20 Wood products	..	..	..	..	..	..	..	..	..	..
21/22 Paper, printing and publishing	..	..	..	..	..	..	..	..	..	..
23/25 Chemicals, Total	..	..	..	669	..	..	..	..	17.4	..
23 Refined petroleum, nuclear fuel	..	..	..	77	..	..	..	..	57.9	..
24/25 Chemicals, rubber & plastics prod.	..	..	..	592	..	..	..	..	16.0	..
24 Chemical products	..	..	..	505	..	..	..	..	14.9	..
2423 Pharmaceuticals	..	..	..	120	..	..	..	..	19.1	..
25 Rubber and plastics products	..	..	..	87	..	..	..	..	28.1	..
26 Non-metallic mineral products	..	..	..	155	..	..	..	..	45.5	..
27/28 Basic & fabricated metals	..	..	..	125	..	..	..	..	22.8	..
27 Basic metals	..	..	..	49	..	..	..	..	27.4	..
28 Fabricated metal products	..	..	..	76	..	..	..	..	20.6	..
29/32 Machinery, Total	..	..	..	337	..	..	..	..	22.8	..
29/30 Non-electrical machinery	..	..	..	203	..	..	..	..	19.0	..
29 Non-electrical machinery nec	..	..	..	169	..	..	..	..	22.6	..
30 Office and computing machinery	..	..	..	34	..	..	..	..	10.6	..
31/32 Electrical & electronic equipment	..	..	..	134	..	..	..	..	33.0	..
31 Electrical machinery nec	..	..	..	88	..	..	..	..	47.2	..
32 Radio, TV & communications eq.	..	..	..	46	..	..	..	..	20.9	..
33 Scientific instruments	..	..	..	272	..	..	..	..	56.0	..
34/35 Transportation equipment	..	..	..	72	..	..	..	..	12.5	..
34 Motor vehicles	..	..	..	70	..	..	..	..	17.9	..
35 Other transport equipment	..	..	..	2	..	..	..	..	1.0	..
351 Shipbuilding & repairing	..	..	..	0	..	..	..	..	0.0	..
353 Aircraft and spacecraft	..	..	..	0	..	..	..	..	20.4	..
36/37 Other manufacturing	..	..	..	39	..	..	..	..	23.6	..
40/45 Construction, electricity, gas & water	..	..	..	25	..	..	..	..	3.6	..
50/55 Trade, repair, hotels & restaurants	..	..	..	787	..	..	..	..	36.1	..
65/74 Finance, insurance, business services	..	..	..	486	..	..	..	..	6.9	..
OTHER ACTIVITIES	..	..	..	217	..	..	..	..	9.7	..
01/99 GRAND TOTAL	..	..	..	**3 889**	..	..	..	..	**17.5**	..

Total manufacturing by investing country						As a % of total manufacturing by foreign affiliates				
All countries	..	..	..	**2 368**	..	..	..	..	**100.0**	..
United States	..	..	..	704	..	..	..	..	29.7	..
Canada	..	..	..	..	..	..	..	..	..	..
Mexico	..	..	..	..	..	..	..	..	..	..
Japan	..	..	..	36	..	..	..	..	1.5	..
Europe	..	..	..	..	..	..	..	..	..	..
European Union (15)	..	..	..	1 316	..	..	..	..	55.6	..
Belgium	..	..	..	..	..	..	..	..	..	..
France	..	..	..	145	..	..	..	..	6.1	..
Germany	..	..	..	267	..	..	..	..	11.3	..
Italy	..	..	..	..	..	..	..	..	..	..
Netherlands	..	..	..	..	..	..	..	..	..	..
Spain	..	..	..	0	..	..	..	..	0.0	..
Sweden	..	..	..	..	..	..	..	..	..	..
United Kingdom	..	..	..	190	..	..	..	..	8.0	..
Switzerland	..	..	..	133	..	..	..	..	5.6	..
Australia and New Zealand	..	..	..	..	..	..	..	..	..	..
Asia (non-OECD)	..	..	..	6	..	..	..	..	0.2	..
Latin America	..	..	..	104	..	..	..	..	4.4	..

Note: Majority foreign-owned firms.
Firmes sous contrôle étranger majoritaire.

Table 9. NETHERLANDS / PAYS-BAS

GROSS FIXED CAPITAL FORMATION / FORMATION BRUTE DE CAPITAL FIXE

By industry (ISIC Rev. 3)		FOREIGN AFFILIATES (Millions of Gld)					AS A % OF NATIONAL TOTAL				
		1993	1994	1995	1996	1997	1993	1994	1995	1996	1997
10/14	Mining & quarrying	..	..	616	463	..	..	..	35.8	28.8	..
15/37	**TOTAL MANUFACTURING**	..	..	**3 379**	**4 200**	..	..	..	**24.4**	**27.9**	..
15/16	Food, beverages, tobacco	..	..	695	812	..	..	..	27.2	29.0	..
17/19	Textiles, clothing, leather, footwear	..	..	60	62	..	..	..	26.7	27.5	..
20/22	Wood and paper products	..	..	337	350	..	..	..	17.7	17.0	..
20	Wood products	..	..	..	..	..	..	..	..	..	..
21/22	Paper, printing and publishing	..	..	..	..	..	..	..	..	..	..
23/25	Chemicals, Total	..	..	1 239	1 767	..	..	..	35.1	42.7	..
23	Refined petroleum, nuclear fuel	..	..	160	254	..	..	..	35.7	52.1	..
24/25	Chemicals, rubber & plastics prod.	..	..	1 079	1 513	..	..	..	35.0	41.4	..
24	Chemical products	..	..	984	1 277	..	..	..	38.9	43.6	..
2423	Pharmaceuticals	..	..	132	71	..	..	..	30.8	21.3	..
25	Rubber and plastics products	..	..	95	236	..	..	..	17.2	32.6	..
26	Non-metallic mineral products	..	..	373	362	..	..	..	48.5	50.9	..
27/28	Basic & fabricated metals	..	..	218	254	..	..	..	18.4	19.0	..
27	Basic metals	..	..	94	149	..	..	..	26.2	30.5	..
28	Fabricated metal products	..	..	123	106	..	..	..	14.9	12.4	..
29/32	Machinery, Total	..	..	292	360	..	..	..	16.9	13.5	..
29/30	Non-electrical machinery	..	..	164	272	..	..	..	20.7	26.7	..
29	Non-electrical machinery nec	..	..	151	243	..	..	..	21.8	27.1	..
30	Office and computing machinery	..	..	13	29	..	..	..	12.8	24.1	..
31/32	Electrical & electronic equipment	..	..	128	88	..	..	..	13.8	5.3	..
31	Electrical machinery nec	..	..	101	72	..	..	..	43.8	32.2	..
32	Radio, TV & communications eq.	..	..	26	16	..	..	..	3.8	1.1	..
33	Scientific instruments	..	..	67	89	..	..	..	40.1	37.7	..
34/35	Transportation equipment	..	..	75	84	..	..	..	4.7	14.7	..
34	Motor vehicles	..	..	54	76	..	..	..	3.7	17.6	..
35	Other transport equipment	..	..	21	8	..	..	..	16.0	5.6	..
351	Shipbuilding & repairing	..	..	0	0	..	..	..	0.0	0.0	..
353	Aircraft and spacecraft	..	..	16	1	..	..	..	99.4	4.8	..
36/37	Other manufacturing	..	..	24	60	..	..	..	10.5	20.1	..
40/45	Construction, electricity, gas & water	..	..	72	122	..	..	..	1.1	1.2	..
50/55	Trade, repair, hotels & restaurants	..	..	1 948	2 511	..	..	..	14.3	45.0	..
65/74	Finance, insurance, business services	..	..	974	10	..	..	..	10.4	11.7	..
	OTHER ACTIVITIES	..	..	330	167	..	..	..	3.5	0.6	..
01/99	**GRAND TOTAL**	..	..	**7 319**	**7 473**	..	..	..	**13.5**	**12.6**	..

Total manufacturing by investing country						As a % of total manufacturing by foreign affiliates				
All countries	..	..	**3 379**	**4 200**	..	..	..	**100.0**	**100.0**	..
United States	..	..	1 121	1 360	..	..	..	33.2	32.4	..
Canada	..	..	..	..	..	..	..	..	..	..
Mexico	..	..	..	..	..	..	..	..	..	..
Japan	..	..	136	110	..	..	..	4.0	2.6	..
Europe	..	..	..	..	..	..	..	..	..	..
European Union (15)	..	..	1 657	1 995	..	..	..	49.0	47.5	..
Belgium	..	..	..	..	..	..	..	..	..	..
France	..	..	151	206	..	..	..	4.5	4.9	..
Germany	..	..	299	308	..	..	..	8.8	7.3	..
Italy	..	..	..	..	..	..	..	..	..	..
Netherlands	..	..	..	..	..	..	..	..	..	..
Spain	..	..	0	0	..	..	..	0.0	0.0	..
Sweden	..	..	..	..	..	..	..	..	..	..
United Kingdom	..	..	404	568	..	..	..	11.9	13.5	..
Switzerland	..	..	295	382	..	..	..	8.7	9.1	..
Australia and New Zealand	..	..	..	..	..	..	..	..	..	..
Asia (non-OECD)	..	..	13	70	..	..	..	0.4	1.7	..
Latin America	..	..	81	94	..	..	..	2.4	2.2	..

Note: Majority foreign-owned firms.
Firmes sous contrôle étranger majoritaire.

Table 10. NETHERLANDS / PAYS-BAS

TOTAL EXPORTS / EXPORTATIONS TOTALES

By industry (ISIC Rev. 3)	FOREIGN AFFILIATES (Millions of Gld)					AS A % OF NATIONAL TOTAL				
	1993	1994	1995	1996	1997	1993	1994	1995	1996	1997
10/14 Mining & quarrying	..	..	..	739	..	..	..	..	4.4	..
15/37 TOTAL MANUFACTURING	..	..	..	**72 421**	..	..	..	..	**42.4**	..
15/16 Food, beverages, tobacco	..	..	..	12 684	..	..	..	..	37.4	..
17/19 Textiles, clothing, leather, footwear	..	..	..	1 321	..	..	..	..	33.5	..
20/22 Wood and paper products	..	..	..	3 025	..	..	..	..	26.2	..
20 Wood products	..	..	..	..	..	..	..	..	..	..
21/22 Paper, printing and publishing	..	..	..	..	..	..	..	..	..	..
23/25 Chemicals, Total	..	..	..	35 710	..	..	..	..	61.6	..
23 Refined petroleum, nuclear fuel	..	..	..	10 139	..	..	..	..	75.1	..
24/25 Chemicals, rubber & plastics prod.	..	..	..	25 571	..	..	..	..	57.5	..
24 Chemical products	..	..	..	23 757	..	..	..	..	59.6	..
2423 Pharmaceuticals	..	..	..	3 130	..	..	..	..	52.9	..
25 Rubber and plastics products	..	..	..	1 814	..	..	..	..	39.1	..
26 Non-metallic mineral products	..	..	..	1 078	..	..	..	..	45.2	..
27/28 Basic & fabricated metals	..	..	..	3 951	..	..	..	..	26.0	..
27 Basic metals	..	..	..	1 873	..	..	..	..	35.0	..
28 Fabricated metal products	..	..	..	2 077	..	..	..	..	21.0	..
29/32 Machinery, Total	..	..	..	9 521	..	..	..	..	29.3	..
29/30 Non-electrical machinery	..	..	..	5 161	..	..	..	..	36.7	..
29 Non-electrical machinery nec	..	..	..	2 649	..	..	..	..	25.4	..
30 Office and computing machinery	..	..	..	2 512	..	..	..	..	69.5	..
31/32 Electrical & electronic equipment	..	..	..	4 360	..	..	..	..	23.6	..
31 Electrical machinery nec	..	..	..	3 475	..	..	..	..	71.4	..
32 Radio, TV & communications eq.	..	..	..	886	..	..	..	..	6.5	..
33 Scientific instruments	..	..	..	2 348	..	..	..	..	61.5	..
34/35 Transportation equipment	..	..	..	2 654	..	..	..	..	36.3	..
34 Motor vehicles	..	..	..	2 380	..	..	..	..	43.0	..
35 Other transport equipment	..	..	..	273	..	..	..	..	15.5	..
351 Shipbuilding & repairing	..	..	..	0	..	..	..	..	0.0	..
353 Aircraft and spacecraft	..	..	..	149	..	..	..	..	33.9	..
36/37 Other manufacturing	..	..	..	129	..	..	..	..	5.5	..
40/45 Construction, electricity, gas & water	..	..	..	186	..	..	..	..	0.7	..
50/55 Trade, repair, hotels & restaurants	..	..	..	64 502	..	..	..	..	45.7	..
65/74 Finance, insurance, business services	..	..	..	6 832	..	..	..	..	13.4	..
OTHER ACTIVITIES	..	..	..	11 033	..	..	..	..	21.1	..
01/99 GRAND TOTAL	..	..	..	**155 712**	..	..	..	..	**34.0**	..

Total manufacturing by investing country						As a % of total manufacturing by foreign affiliates				
All countries	..	..	..	**72 421**	..	..	..	..	**100.0**	..
United States	..	..	..	37 837	..	..	..	..	52.2	..
Canada	..	..	..	9	..	..	..	..	0.0	..
Mexico	..	..	..	..	..	..	..	..	..	..
Japan	..	..	..	2 228	..	..	..	..	3.1	..
Europe	..	..	..	29 440	..	..	..	..	40.7	..
European Union (15)	..	..	..	22 648	..	..	..	..	31.3	..
Belgium	..	..	..	4 707	..	..	..	..	6.5	..
France	..	..	..	2 777	..	..	..	..	3.8	..
Germany	..	..	..	3 401	..	..	..	..	4.7	..
Italy	..	..	..	0	..	..	..	..	0.0	..
Netherlands	..	..	..	..	..	..	..	..	..	..
Spain	..	..	..	0	..	..	..	..	0.0	..
Sweden	..	..	..	3 011	..	..	..	..	4.2	..
United Kingdom	..	..	..	4 548	..	..	..	..	6.3	..
Switzerland	..	..	..	6 217	..	..	..	..	8.6	..
Australia and New Zealand	..	..	..	264	..	..	..	..	0.4	..
Asia (non-OECD)	..	..	..	562	..	..	..	..	0.8	..
Latin America	..	..	..	2 080	..	..	..	..	2.9	..

Note: Majority foreign-owned firms.
Firmes sous contrôle étranger majoritaire.

Table 11. NETHERLANDS / PAYS-BAS

TOTAL IMPORTS / IMPORTATIONS TOTALES

By industry (ISIC Rev. 3)		FOREIGN AFFILIATES (Millions of Gld)					AS A % OF NATIONAL TOTAL				
		1993	1994	1995	1996	1997	1993	1994	1995	1996	1997
10/14	Mining & quarrying	..	..	..	1 049	..	..	..	..	10.5	..
15/37	**TOTAL MANUFACTURING**	..	..	..	**57 163**	..	..	..	..	**43.2**	..
15/16	Food, beverages, tobacco	..	..	..	10 052	..	..	..	..	45.5	..
17/19	Textiles, clothing, leather, footwear	..	..	..	775	..	..	..	..	24.5	..
20/22	Wood and paper products	..	..	..	2 251	..	..	..	..	21.6	..
20	Wood products	..	..	..	..	..	..	..	..	..	..
21/22	Paper, printing and publishing	..	..	..	..	..	..	..	..	..	..
23/25	Chemicals, Total	..	..	..	28 350	..	..	..	..	65.4	..
23	Refined petroleum, nuclear fuel	..	..	..	10 235	..	..	..	..	76.8	..
24/25	Chemicals, rubber & plastics prod.	..	..	..	18 115	..	..	..	..	60.3	..
24	Chemical products	..	..	..	16 899	..	..	..	..	63.4	..
2423	Pharmaceuticals	..	..	..	2 660	..	..	..	..	65.5	..
25	Rubber and plastics products	..	..	..	1 216	..	..	..	..	35.7	..
26	Non-metallic mineral products	..	..	..	874	..	..	..	..	40.8	..
27/28	Basic & fabricated metals	..	..	..	3 087	..	..	..	..	25.0	..
27	Basic metals	..	..	..	1 105	..	..	..	..	32.7	..
28	Fabricated metal products	..	..	..	1 982	..	..	..	..	22.1	..
29/32	Machinery, Total	..	..	..	7 145	..	..	..	..	29.0	..
29/30	Non-electrical machinery	..	..	..	4 193	..	..	..	..	38.5	..
29	Non-electrical machinery nec	..	..	..	1 864	..	..	..	..	22.9	..
30	Office and computing machinery	..	..	..	2 329	..	..	..	..	84.8	..
31/32	Electrical & electronic equipment	..	..	..	2 952	..	..	..	..	21.5	..
31	Electrical machinery nec	..	..	..	2 336	..	..	..	..	59.3	..
32	Radio, TV & communications eq.	..	..	..	616	..	..	..	..	6.3	..
33	Scientific instruments	..	..	..	1 854	..	..	..	..	59.8	..
34/35	Transportation equipment	..	..	..	2 463	..	..	..	..	28.4	..
34	Motor vehicles	..	..	..	2 230	..	..	..	..	31.6	..
35	Other transport equipment	..	..	..	232	..	..	..	..	14.4	..
351	Shipbuilding & repairing	..	..	..	0	..	..	..	..	0.0	..
353	Aircraft and spacecraft	..	..	..	152	..	..	..	..	34.8	..
36/37	Other manufacturing	..	..	..	312	..	..	..	..	13.3	..
40/45	Construction, electricity, gas & water	..	..	..	734	..	..	..	..	2.9	..
50/55	Trade, repair, hotels & restaurants	..	..	..	75 866	..	..	..	..	47.5	..
65/74	Finance, insurance, business services	..	..	..	6 686	..	..	..	..	14.0	..
	OTHER ACTIVITIES	..	..	..	9 644	..	..	..	..	21.6	..
01/99	**GRAND TOTAL**	..	..	..	**151 142**	..	..	..	..	**36.0**	..

Total manufacturing by investing country							As a % of total manufacturing by foreign affiliates				
All countries		..	..	..	**57 163**	..	..	..	..	**100.0**	..
United States		..	..	..	30 510	..	..	..	..	53.4	..
Canada		..	..	..	15	..	..	..	..	0.0	..
Mexico		..	..	..	..	..	..	..	..	..	..
Japan		..	..	..	1 555	..	..	..	..	2.7	..
Europe		..	..	..	22 049	..	..	..	..	38.6	..
European Union (15)		..	..	..	17 652	..	..	..	..	30.9	..
Belgium		..	..	..	3 936	..	..	..	..	6.9	..
France		..	..	..	2 064	..	..	..	..	3.6	..
Germany		..	..	..	2 641	..	..	..	..	4.6	..
Italy		..	..	..	0	..	..	..	..	0.0	..
Netherlands		..	..	..	..	..	..	..	..	..	..
Spain		..	..	..	0	..	..	..	..	0.0	..
Sweden		..	..	..	2 935	..	..	..	..	5.1	..
United Kingdom		..	..	..	3 464	..	..	..	..	6.1	..
Switzerland		..	..	..	4 091	..	..	..	..	7.2	..
Australia and New Zealand		..	..	..	604	..	..	..	..	1.1	..
Asia (non-OECD)		..	..	..	313	..	..	..	..	0.5	..
Latin America		..	..	..	2 118	..	..	..	..	3.7	..

Note: Majority foreign-owned firms.
Firmes sous contrôle étranger majoritaire.

Table 14. NETHERLANDS / PAYS-BAS

GROSS OPERATING SURPLUS / EXCÉDENT BRUT D'EXPLOITATION

By industry (ISIC Rev. 3)	FOREIGN AFFILIATES (Millions of Gld)					AS A % OF NATIONAL TOTAL				
	1993	1994	1995	1996	1997	1993	1994	1995	1996	1997
10/14 Mining & quarrying	..	..	1 537	19 813	..	..	..	4.1	47.3	..
15/37 TOTAL MANUFACTURING	..	..	**13 950**	**14 734**	..	..	..	**33.1**	**37.3**	..
15/16 Food, beverages, tobacco	..	..	3 424	3 898	..	..	..	38.8	43.3	..
17/19 Textiles, clothing, leather, footwear	..	..	217	226	..	..	..	34.3	30.2	..
20/22 Wood and paper products	..	..	1 246	1 302	..	..	..	22.1	23.9	..
20 Wood products	..	..	..	..	..	..	..	..	..	..
21/22 Paper, printing and publishing	..	..	..	..	..	..	..	..	..	..
23/25 Chemicals, Total	..	..	6 067	5 792	..	..	..	48.3	53.1	..
23 Refined petroleum, nuclear fuel	..	..	648	881	..	..	..	62.9	57.5	..
24/25 Chemicals, rubber & plastics prod.	..	..	5 419	4 911	..	..	..	47.0	52.3	..
24 Chemical products	..	..	5 185	4 502	..	..	..	50.5	56.2	..
2423 Pharmaceuticals	..	..	515	418	..	..	..	39.9	38.3	..
25 Rubber and plastics products	..	..	234	409	..	..	..	18.3	29.7	..
26 Non-metallic mineral products	..	..	893	1 008	..	..	..	44.2	57.1	..
27/28 Basic & fabricated metals	..	..	778	699	..	..	..	18.0	16.3	..
27 Basic metals	..	..	438	314	..	..	..	24.3	22.9	..
28 Fabricated metal products	..	..	340	385	..	..	..	13.5	13.2	..
29/32 Machinery, Total	..	..	1 148	1 008	..	..	..	21.7	21.2	..
29/30 Non-electrical machinery	..	..	603	583	..	..	..	21.2	22.4	..
29 Non-electrical machinery nec	..	..	442	446	..	..	..	17.4	19.0	..
30 Office and computing machinery	..	..	162	137	..	..	..	54.5	52.3	..
31/32 Electrical & electronic equipment	..	..	545	425	..	..	..	22.3	19.8	..
31 Electrical machinery nec	..	..	230	287	..	..	..	29.4	33.7	..
32 Radio, TV & communications eq.	..	..	315	138	..	..	..	19.0	10.6	..
33 Scientific instruments	..	..	383	436	..	..	..	48.7	55.7	..
34/35 Transportation equipment	..	..	- 294	241	..	..	..	-32.6	21.6	..
34 Motor vehicles	..	..	195	177	..	..	..	20.0	20.0	..
35 Other transport equipment	..	..	- 489	64	..	..	..	627.9	27.8	..
351 Shipbuilding & repairing	..	..	0	2	..	..	..	0.1	1.2	..
353 Aircraft and spacecraft	..	..	- 520	15	..	..	..	102.6	-27.9	..
36/37 Other manufacturing	..	..	89	123	..	..	..	7.8	17.7	..
40/45 Construction, electricity, gas & water	..	..	143	187	..	..	..	1.5	1.7	..
50/55 Trade, repair, hotels & restaurants	..	..	5 193	5 169	..	..	..	14.0	14.4	..
65/74 Finance, insurance, business services	..	..	1 161	1 301	..	..	..	7.8	8.8	..
OTHER ACTIVITIES	..	..	731	797	..	..	..	5.4	3.9	..
01/99 GRAND TOTAL	..	..	**22 714**	**42 002**	..	..	..	**14.6**	**25.7**	..

Total manufacturing by investing country						As a % of total manufacturing by foreign affiliates				
All countries	..	..	**13 950**	**14 734**	..	..	..	**100.0**	**100.0**	..
United States	..	..	6 524	6 167	..	..	..	46.8	41.9	..
Canada	..	..	..	..	..	..	..	..	..	..
Mexico	..	..	..	..	..	..	..	..	..	..
Japan	..	..	306	320	..	..	..	2.2	2.2	..
Europe	..	..	..	..	..	..	..	..	..	..
European Union (15)	..	..	4 396	4 934	..	..	..	31.5	33.5	..
Belgium	..	..	..	..	..	..	..	..	..	..
France	..	..	610	543	..	..	..	4.4	3.7	..
Germany	..	..	403	938	..	..	..	2.9	6.4	..
Italy	..	..	..	..	..	..	..	..	..	..
Netherlands	..	..	..	..	..	..	..	..	..	..
Spain	..	..	0	0	..	..	..	0.0	0.0	..
Sweden	..	..	..	..	..	..	..	..	..	..
United Kingdom	..	..	1 292	1 411	..	..	..	9.3	9.6	..
Switzerland	..	..	1 871	2 177	..	..	..	13.4	14.8	..
Australia and New Zealand	..	..	..	..	..	..	..	..	..	..
Asia (non-OECD)	..	..	34	223	..	..	..	0.2	1.5	..
Latin America	..	..	316	382	..	..	..	2.3	2.6	..

Note: Majority foreign-owned firms.
Firmes sous contrôle étranger majoritaire.

NETHERLANDS

Source

The data are prepared by the Department for Statistics on Capital Stocks and Balance Sheets, Central Bureau of Statistics. The data are based on an annual questionnaire on the finances of non-financial enterprises (SFGO). This questionnaire covers all domestic non-financial enterprise groups with a balance sheet total of more than 25 million Dutch guilders. Statistics cover 2 500 enterprise groups, totalising 12 000 non-financial enterprises. Majority foreign-owned enterprises are available separately since 1983. The results are published under the title *Establishment Trade*.

National totals: provided by the Central Bureau of Statistics and compatible with foreign affiliates' data. Smaller enterprises (not belonging to a group or within a group with a balance sheet of less than 25 million guilders) are included.

Industrial classification

For all variables, the data are classified according to the principal industrial activity of the affiliate.

The industrial classification used for the tables is the national classification converted to ISIC Revision 3.

Variables

- *Number of enterprises* is defined as the number of domestic non-financial enterprise groups with a balance sheet total of more than 25 million Dutch guilders, and a foreign shareholding of more than 50%.

- *Number of employees* is the number of employees at the end of September.

- *Turnover* is defined as net turnover.

- *Wages and salaries* is in fact compensation of employees, which consists of wages, salaries, social security and pension contributions.

- *R&D expenditure* refer to expenditure by the affiliate itself.

- *Gross operating surplus* is in fact net income.

Geographical breakdown

The investor's country is the country of the immediate controller.

Data for Latin America refer to Netherlands Antilles/Aruba.

PAYS-BAS

Source

Les données émanent du Département de statistiques sur le stock de capital et les bilans, Bureau central des statistiques. Elles s'appuient sur un questionnaire annuel concernant les finances des entreprises non financières (SFGO). Ce questionnaire couvre tous les groupes néerlandais non financiers dont le total du bilan dépasse 25 millions de florins. Les statistiques couvrent 2 500 groupes, ce qui représente environ 12 000 entreprises non financières. Les entreprises à participation étrangère majoritaire sont disponibles séparément depuis 1983. Les résultats sont publiés sous le titre *Establishment Trade*.

Totaux nationaux : fournis par le Bureau central des statistiques, et compatibles avec les données relatives aux filiales étrangères. Les petites entreprises (n'appartenant pas à un groupe ou au sein d'un groupe dont le bilan est inférieur à 25 millions de florins) sont incluses.

Classification industrielle

Pour toutes les variables, les données sont classées selon la principale activité industrielle de l'entreprise affiliée.

La classification industrielle utilisée pour les tableaux est la classification nationale adaptée de façon à correspondre à la CITI révision 3.

Variables

- Le *Nombre d'entreprises* est défini comme le nombre de groupes néerlandais non financiers dont le total du bilan dépasse 25 millions de florins et dont la participation étrangère dans le capital est de plus de 50 %.

- Le *Nombre de salariés* correspond aux effectifs à fin septembre.

- Le *Chiffre d'affaires* est défini comme le chiffre d'affaires net.

- Les *Salaires* correspondent en fait à la rémunération des salariés, qui se compose des traitements, salaires, cotisations à la sécurité sociale et au système de retraite.

- L'*Excédent brut d'exploitation* est en fait le revenu net.

Ventilation géographique

Le pays d'origine est celui où s'exerce le contrôle immédiat.

Les données pour l'Amérique latine correspondent en fait à celles des Antilles néerlandaises/Aruba.

NORWAY

NORVÈGE

Table 1. NORWAY / NORVÈGE

NUMBER OF ESTABLISHMENTS / NOMBRE D'ÉTABLISSEMENTS

By industry (ISIC Rev. 3)		FOREIGN AFFILIATES (Units)					AS A % OF NATIONAL TOTAL				
		1992	1993	1994	1995	1996	1992	1993	1994	1995	1996
10/14	Mining & quarrying	6	8	9	11	19	8.1	9.5	10.8	11.8	5.3
15/37	TOTAL MANUFACTURING	193	206	232	348	516	5.0	5.3	5.7	8.4	4.7
15/16	Food, beverages, tobacco	19	19	23	39	44	2.1	2.1	2.5	4.3	2.5
17/19	Textiles, clothing, leather, footwear	5	5	5	6	10	2.5	2.6	2.6	3.2	1.9
20/22	Wood and paper products	26	27	30	51	75	3.1	3.3	3.5	5.7	2.5
20	Wood products	..	..	4	4	..	..	..	1.3	1.2	..
21/22	Paper, printing and publishing	..	..	26	47	..	..	..	4.6	8.4	..
23/25	Chemicals, Total	31	39	49	57	66	13.7	13.7	15.8	18.9	12.2
23	Refined petroleum, nuclear fuel	5	11	12	11	3	45.5	18.6	18.5	18.3	37.5
24/25	Chemicals, rubber & plastics prod.	26	28	37	46	63	12.0	12.4	15.0	19.0	11.8
24	Chemical products	12	13	18	26	36	12.0	13.1	17.6	25.0	20.3
2423	Pharmaceuticals	0	0	3	..	6	0.0	0.0	21.4	..	26.1
25	Rubber and plastics products	14	15	19	20	27	12.1	11.9	13.2	14.5	7.6
26	Non-metallic mineral products	18	18	22	35	61	12.6	10.2	12.7	18.7	10.2
27/28	Basic & fabricated metals	20	20	24	30	48	4.2	4.4	5.3	6.3	3.7
27	Basic metals	9	8	9	11	16	13.8	11.9	10.8	14.7	13.2
28	Fabricated metal products	11	12	15	19	32	2.7	3.1	4.1	4.7	2.7
29/32	Machinery, Total	42	45	47	..	144	8.8	9.7	9.7	..	9.1
29/30	Non-electrical machinery	24	25	26	..	87	7.8	8.3	8.0	..	7.3
29	Non-electrical machinery nec	24	25	26	34	85	8.0	8.5	8.2	10.0	7.3
30	Office and computing machinery	0	0	0	..	2	0.0	0.0	0.0	..	8.0
31/32	Electrical & electronic equipment	18	20	21	..	57	10.7	12.3	13.0	..	14.6
31	Electrical machinery nec	13	13	15	..	46	10.2	10.9	12.8	..	14.6
32	Radio, TV & communications eq.	5	7	6	..	11	11.9	15.9	13.6	..	14.7
33	Scientific instruments	5	7	6	..	19	9.1	12.7	10.9	..	5.7
34/35	Transportation equipment	21	22	20	34	34	6.2	6.3	5.8	9.3	4.8
34	Motor vehicles	2	2	2	..	4	3.5	3.8	3.7	..	4.1
35	Other transport equipment	19	20	18	..	30	6.7	6.7	6.2	..	4.9
351	Shipbuilding & repairing	16	17	15	..	26	6.3	6.3	5.7	..	4.6
353	Aircraft and spacecraft	0	0	0	..	0	0.0	0.0	0.0	..	0.0
36/37	Other manufacturing	6	4	6	11	15	2.6	1.8	2.5	4.3	2.0
40/45	Construction, electricity, gas & water	..	..	..	..	..	..	..	..	..	..
50/55	Trade, repair, hotels & restaurants	..	..	..	..	..	..	..	..	..	..
65/74	Finance, insurance, business services	..	..	..	..	..	..	..	..	..	..
	OTHER ACTIVITIES	..	..	..	..	..	..	..	..	..	..
01/99	GRAND TOTAL	..	..	..	..	..	..	..	..	..	..

Total manufacturing by investing country						As a % of total manufacturing by foreign affiliates				
All countries	193	206	232	..	375	100.0	100.0	100.0	..	100.0
United States	15	15	23	..	34	7.8	7.3	9.9	..	9.1
Canada	3	4	3	..	..	1.6	1.9	1.3	..	..
Mexico	0	0	0	..	..	0.0	0.0	0.0	..	..
Japan	1	0	0	..	0	0.5	0.0	0.0	..	0.0
Europe	174	187	206	..	..	90.2	90.8	88.8	..	..
European Union (15)	155	167	187	..	314	80.3	81.1	80.6	..	83.7
Belgium	5	5	5	..	..	2.6	2.4	2.2	..	..
France	2	3	5	..	5	1.0	1.5	2.2	..	1.3
Germany	8	11	10	..	20	4.1	5.3	4.3	..	5.3
Italy	0	1	1	..	..	0.0	0.5	0.4	..	..
Netherlands	14	12	14	..	18	7.3	5.8	6.0	..	4.8
Spain	1	1	1	..	..	0.5	0.5	0.4	..	..
Sweden	61	64	73	..	..	31.6	31.1	31.5	..	..
United Kingdom	12	16	17	..	22	6.2	7.8	7.3	..	5.9
Switzerland	19	19	19	..	19	9.8	9.2	8.2	..	5.1
Australia and New Zealand	0	0	0	..	..	0.0	0.0	0.0	..	..
Asia (non-OECD)	0	0	0	..	0	0.0	0.0	0.0	..	0.0
Latin America	0	0	0	..	3	0.0	0.0	0.0	..	0.8

Note: Majority foreign-owned establishments. *Crude petroleum and natural gas extraction* (ISIC 11) is excluded from *Mining and quarrying* (10/14). From 1995 onwards sectoral data include indirectly from abroad owned establishments.
Etablissements sous contrôle étranger majoritaire. L'*Extraction de pétrole et de gaz naturel* (CITI 11) est exclue des *Industries extractives* (10/14). Les données sectorielles à partir de 1995 comprennent les établissements contrôlés indirectement par l'étranger.

Table 2. NORWAY / NORVÈGE

NUMBER OF EMPLOYEES / NOMBRE DE SALARIÉS

By industry (ISIC Rev. 3)	FOREIGN AFFILIATES (Units)					AS A % OF NATIONAL TOTAL				
	1992	1993	1994	1995	1996	1992	1993	1994	1995	1996
10/14 Mining & quarrying	390	464	457	807	889	10.3	13.1	13.3	23.8	20.6
15/37 TOTAL MANUFACTURING	**18 035**	**19 352**	**21 664**	**37 237**	**40 348**	**7.7**	**8.2**	**9.0**	**15.0**	**14.3**
15/16 Food, beverages, tobacco	1 310	1 501	1 908	6 787	6 697	3.0	3.4	4.1	14.5	12.8
17/19 Textiles, clothing, leather, footwear	619	548	462	276	431	8.5	7.9	6.5	4.1	5.2
20/22 Wood and paper products	1 799	1 781	1 904	3 654	3 059	3.6	3.6	3.7	6.9	5.0
20 Wood products	..	..	181	190	..	..	..	1.6	1.6	..
21/22 Paper, printing and publishing	..	..	1 723	3 464	..	..	..	4.3	8.4	..
23/25 Chemicals, Total	2 895	2 887	3 832	4 883	5 031	14.9	14.6	18.8	23.8	23.2
23 Refined petroleum, nuclear fuel	456	478	485	478	392	34.7	30.4	29.6	32.0	32.5
24/25 Chemicals, rubber & plastics prod.	2 439	2 409	3 347	4 405	4 639	13.4	13.2	17.9	23.2	22.7
24 Chemical products	1 333	1 313	2 303	3 052	3 198	10.0	9.9	17.4	22.4	23.1
2423 Pharmaceuticals	0	0	386	..	737	0.0	0.0	16.1	..	28.2
25 Rubber and plastics products	1 106	1 096	1 044	1 353	1 441	22.7	21.8	19.1	25.0	21.8
26 Non-metallic mineral products	1 207	1 305	1 569	2 561	3 326	17.9	20.0	23.5	36.2	35.2
27/28 Basic & fabricated metals	3 686	3 822	4 076	4 799	5 098	13.7	14.7	15.0	16.7	15.5
27 Basic metals	2 874	2 704	2 953	3 135	3 293	20.7	20.4	20.2	21.0	21.8
28 Fabricated metal products	812	1 118	1 123	1 664	1 805	6.2	8.8	9.0	12.1	10.1
29/32 Machinery, Total	3 900	4 251	4 654	..	10 063	12.4	13.7	14.9	..	26.7
29/30 Non-electrical machinery	1 994	1 848	1 943	..	3 411	10.4	9.8	10.2	..	14.4
29 Non-electrical machinery nec	1 994	1 848	1 943	2 742	3 377	10.9	10.2	10.6	14.5	14.8
30 Office and computing machinery	0	0	0	..	34	0.0	0.0	0.0	..	4.6
31/32 Electrical & electronic equipment	1 906	2 403	2 711	..	6 652	15.6	19.8	22.4	..	47.3
31 Electrical machinery nec	910	1 256	1 491	..	4 724	10.6	15.2	18.6	..	49.3
32 Radio, TV & communications eq.	996	1 147	1 220	..	1 928	27.6	29.7	29.8	..	43.1
33 Scientific instruments	240	594	559	..	1 107	7.4	17.4	15.7	..	20.5
34/35 Transportation equipment	1 878	2 334	2 381	5 298	4 998	5.1	6.2	6.4	13.5	12.5
34 Motor vehicles	93	100	109	..	413	3.0	3.1	3.4	..	8.5
35 Other transport equipment	1 785	2 234	2 272	..	4 585	5.3	6.5	6.7	..	13.1
351 Shipbuilding & repairing	1 385	1 826	1 854	..	3 913	4.9	6.2	6.4	..	12.9
353 Aircraft and spacecraft	0	0	0	..	0	0.0	0.0	0.0	..	0.0
36/37 Other manufacturing	501	329	319	468	538	5.4	3.6	3.3	4.5	4.2
40/45 Construction, electricity, gas & water	..	..	..	..	..	..	..	..	..	..
50/55 Trade, repair, hotels & restaurants	..	..	..	..	..	..	..	..	..	..
65/74 Finance, insurance, business services	..	..	..	..	..	..	..	..	..	..
OTHER ACTIVITIES	..	..	..	..	..	..	..	..	..	..
01/99 GRAND TOTAL	..	..	..	..	..	..	..	..	..	..

Total manufacturing by investing country						As a % of total manufacturing by foreign affiliates				
All countries	18 035	19 352	21 664	..	28 824	100.0	100.0	100.0	..	100.0
United States	1 679	1 752	2 518	..	2 962	9.3	9.1	11.6	..	10.3
Canada	745	778	694	..	622	4.1	4.0	3.2	..	2.2
Mexico	0	0	0	..	..	0.0	0.0	0.0	..	..
Japan	17	0	0	..	0	0.1	0.0	0.0	..	0.0
Europe	15 594	16 822	18 452	..	25 117	86.5	86.9	85.2	..	87.1
European Union (15)	13 277	14 001	15 692	..	23 130	73.6	72.3	72.4	..	80.2
Belgium	247	323	416	..	464	1.4	1.7	1.9	..	1.6
France	128	163	270	..	184	0.7	0.8	1.2	..	0.6
Germany	442	560	481	..	2 509	2.5	2.9	2.2	..	8.7
Italy	0	38	39	..	53	0.0	0.2	0.2	..	0.2
Netherlands	1 557	1 113	1 491	..	1 604	8.6	5.8	6.9	..	5.6
Spain	24	29	29	..	41	0.1	0.1	0.1	..	0.1
Sweden	5 610	6 283	6 887	..	12 793	31.1	32.5	31.8	..	44.4
United Kingdom	1 589	1 998	1 884	..	1 293	8.8	10.3	8.7	..	4.5
Switzerland	1 805	2 319	2 760	..	1 976	10.0	12.0	12.7	..	6.9
Australia and New Zealand	0	0	0	..	64	0.0	0.0	0.0	..	0.2
Asia (non-OECD)	0	0	0	..	0	0.0	0.0	0.0	..	0.0
Latin America	0	0	0	..	59	0.0	0.0	0.0	..	0.2

Note: Majority foreign-owned establishments. *Crude petroleum and natural gas extraction* (ISIC 11) is excluded from *Mining and quarrying* (10/14). From 1995 onwards sectoral data include indirectly from abroad owned establishments.
Etablissements sous contrôle étranger majoritaire. L'*Extraction de pétrole et de gaz naturel* (CITI 11) est exclue des *Industries extractives* (10/14). Les données sectorielles à partir de 1995 comprennent les établissements contrôlés indirectement par l'étranger.

Table 3. NORWAY / NORVÈGE

PRODUCTION

By industry (ISIC Rev. 3)	FOREIGN AFFILIATES (Millions of Kr)					AS A % OF NATIONAL TOTAL				
	1992	1993	1994	1995	1996	1992	1993	1994	1995	1996
10/14 Mining & quarrying	329	379	445	964	1 232	9.8	12.0	12.7	26.3	23.9
15/37 TOTAL MANUFACTURING	**29 933**	**32 687**	**41 395**	**66 988**	**74 264**	**10.5**	**11.2**	**13.0**	**19.5**	**19.0**
15/16 Food, beverages, tobacco	2 285	2 545	3 242	11 526	11 206	2.9	3.2	3.8	13.2	11.6
17/19 Textiles, clothing, leather, footwear	478	438	378	233	327	10.1	9.2	7.4	4.9	5.6
20/22 Wood and paper products	2 051	1 970	2 273	5 153	4 717	4.7	4.5	4.6	9.2	7.5
20 Wood products	..	..	207	224	..	..	..	1.7	1.8	..
21/22 Paper, printing and publishing	..	..	2 066	4 929	..	..	..	5.5	11.4	..
23/25 Chemicals, Total	9 130	9 545	13 304	14 866	17 248	21.8	21.1	27.8	31.0	30.8
23 Refined petroleum, nuclear fuel	6 662	7 009	6 837	6 490	9 229	45.1	42.4	43.6	49.1	49.0
24/25 Chemicals, rubber & plastics prod.	2 468	2 536	6 467	8 376	8 019	9.1	8.8	20.1	24.1	21.6
24 Chemical products	1 504	1 542	5 368	6 932	6 296	6.6	6.3	19.9	23.8	20.9
2423 Pharmaceuticals	0	0	..	..	972	0.0	0.0	..	..	17.3
25 Rubber and plastics products	964	994	1 099	1 444	1 723	22.2	22.4	21.4	25.8	24.4
26 Non-metallic mineral products	1 333	1 571	2 018	2 996	5 247	20.1	23.5	26.6	35.0	42.0
27/28 Basic & fabricated metals	7 973	7 790	10 266	11 928	12 342	22.9	22.3	24.6	24.7	24.6
27 Basic metals	7 428	6 776	9 130	10 222	10 225	29.5	26.7	28.8	27.9	28.8
28 Fabricated metal products	545	1 014	1 136	1 706	2 117	5.7	10.7	11.4	14.7	14.4
29/32 Machinery, Total	4 266	4 677	6 206	..	..	14.2	15.7	18.3	..	..
29/30 Non-electrical machinery	2 023	1 752	2 146	..	..	11.5	10.1	10.7	..	..
29 Non-electrical machinery nec	2 023	1 752	2 146	3 889	4 472	12.2	10.6	11.6	18.1	17.0
30 Office and computing machinery	0	0	0	..	..	0.0	0.0	0.0	..	..
31/32 Electrical & electronic equipment	2 243	2 925	4 060	..	9 273	17.9	23.4	29.2	..	52.5
31 Electrical machinery nec	859	1 485	2 224	..	6 392	9.7	17.1	23.8	..	56.7
32 Radio, TV & communications eq.	1 384	1 440	1 836	..	2 881	37.4	38.2	40.3	..	44.9
33 Scientific instruments	352	752	656	..	..	10.0	19.6	15.5	..	..
34/35 Transportation equipment	1 609	3 169	2 735	7 272	6 513	4.7	8.8	7.5	18.5	14.7
34 Motor vehicles	..	..	..	..	422	..	..	..	..	8.6
35 Other transport equipment	..	..	..	..	6 091	..	..	..	..	15.4
351 Shipbuilding & repairing	1 214	2 803	2 313	..	5 439	4.3	9.5	8.0	..	15.7
353 Aircraft and spacecraft	0	0	0	..	0	0.0	0.0	0.0	..	0.0
36/37 Other manufacturing	456	230	318	470	580	6.9	3.5	4.3	5.5	5.5
40/45 Construction, electricity, gas & water	..	..	..	..	..	..	..	..	..	..
50/55 Trade, repair, hotels & restaurants	..	..	..	..	..	..	..	..	..	..
65/74 Finance, insurance, business services	..	..	..	..	..	..	..	..	..	..
OTHER ACTIVITIES	..	..	..	..	..	..	..	..	..	..
01/99 GRAND TOTAL	..	..	..	..	..	..	..	..	..	..

Total manufacturing by investing country						As a % of total manufacturing by foreign affiliates				
All countries	**29 933**	**32 687**	**41 395**	..	**55 351**	**100.0**	**100.0**	**100.0**	..	**100.0**
United States	5 434	6 149	7 859	..	10 112	18.2	18.8	19.0	..	18.3
Canada	..	3 769	5 121	..	..	..	11.5	12.4	..	..
Mexico	0	0	0	..	..	0.0	0.0	0.0	..	..
Japan	..	0	0	..	0	..	0.0	0.0	..	0.0
Europe	20 433	22 769	28 414	..	..	68.3	69.7	68.6	..	..
European Union (15)	17 890	19 632	24 870	..	36 487	59.8	60.1	60.1	..	65.9
Belgium	291	376	394	..	..	1.0	1.2	1.0	..	..
France	..	213	327	..	258	..	0.7	0.8	..	0.5
Germany	467	587	567	..	2 224	1.6	1.8	1.4	..	4.0
Italy	0	..	..	..	..	0.0	..	..	..	..
Netherlands	2 521	1 959	2 472	..	1 938	8.4	6.0	6.0	..	3.5
Spain	..	..	..	..	..	..	..	..	..	..
Sweden	6 141	7 115	8 313	..	19 172	20.5	21.8	20.1	..	34.6
United Kingdom	4 685	6 089	5 797	..	5 409	15.7	18.6	14.0	..	9.8
Switzerland	1 813	2 365	3 544	..	3 605	6.1	7.2	8.6	..	6.5
Australia and New Zealand	0	0	0	..	..	0.0	0.0	0.0	..	..
Asia (non-OECD)	0	0	0	..	0	0.0	0.0	0.0	..	0.0
Latin America	0	0	0	..	22	0.0	0.0	0.0	..	0.0

Note: Majority foreign-owned establishments. *Crude petroleum and natural gas extraction* (ISIC 11) is excluded from *Mining and quarrying* (10/14). From 1995 onwards sectoral data include indirectly from abroad owned establishments.

Etablissements sous contrôle étranger majoritaire. L'*Extraction de pétrole et de gaz naturel* (CITI 11) est exclue des *Industries extractives* (10/14). Les données sectorielles à partir de 1995 comprennent les établissements contrôlés indirectement par l'étranger.

Table 4. NORWAY / NORVÈGE

TURNOVER / CHIFFRE D'AFFAIRES

By industry (ISIC Rev. 3)		FOREIGN AFFILIATES (Millions of Kr)					AS A % OF NATIONAL TOTAL				
		1992	1993	1994	1995	1996	1992	1993	1994	1995	1996
10/14	Mining & quarrying	..	..	..	..	1 186	..	..	..	..	22.9
15/37	**TOTAL MANUFACTURING**	..	..	..	..	**74 690**	..	..	..	..	**18.9**
15/16	Food, beverages, tobacco	..	..	..	..	11 290	..	..	..	..	11.5
17/19	Textiles, clothing, leather, footwear	..	..	..	..	346	..	..	..	..	5.7
20/22	Wood and paper products	..	..	..	..	4 791	..	..	..	..	7.5
20	Wood products	..	..	..	..	..	..	..	..	..	..
21/22	Paper, printing and publishing	..	..	..	..	..	..	..	..	..	..
23/25	Chemicals, Total	..	..	..	..	17 142	..	..	..	..	30.8
23	Refined petroleum, nuclear fuel	..	..	..	..	9 026	..	..	..	..	48.3
24/25	Chemicals, rubber & plastics prod.	..	..	..	..	8 116	..	..	..	..	21.9
24	Chemical products	..	..	..	..	6 396	..	..	..	..	21.5
2423	Pharmaceuticals	..	..	..	..	970	..	..	..	..	19.5
25	Rubber and plastics products	..	..	..	..	1 721	..	..	..	..	23.7
26	Non-metallic mineral products	..	..	..	..	5 285	..	..	..	..	41.4
27/28	Basic & fabricated metals	..	..	..	..	12 542	..	..	..	..	24.8
27	Basic metals	..	..	..	..	10 436	..	..	..	..	29.1
28	Fabricated metal products	..	..	..	..	2 106	..	..	..	..	14.3
29/32	Machinery, Total	..	..	..	..	13 823	..	..	..	..	30.3
29/30	Non-electrical machinery	..	..	..	..	..	..	..	..	..	..
29	Non-electrical machinery nec	..	..	..	..	4 396	..	..	..	..	16.6
30	Office and computing machinery	..	..	..	..	..	..	..	..	..	..
31/32	Electrical & electronic equipment	..	..	..	..	..	..	..	..	..	..
31	Electrical machinery nec	..	..	..	..	6 560	..	..	..	..	56.5
32	Radio, TV & communications eq.	..	..	..	..	..	..	..	..	..	..
33	Scientific instruments	..	..	..	..	2 248	..	..	..	..	34.5
34/35	Transportation equipment	..	..	..	..	6 620	..	..	..	..	14.5
34	Motor vehicles	..	..	..	..	390	..	..	..	..	8.0
35	Other transport equipment	..	..	..	..	6 230	..	..	..	..	15.3
351	Shipbuilding & repairing	..	..	..	..	5 519	..	..	..	..	15.5
353	Aircraft and spacecraft	..	..	..	..	0	..	..	..	..	0.0
36/37	Other manufacturing	..	..	..	..	603	..	..	..	..	5.6
40/45	Construction, electricity, gas & water	..	..	..	..	..	..	..	..	..	..
50/55	Trade, repair, hotels & restaurants	..	..	..	..	..	..	..	..	..	..
65/74	Finance, insurance, business services	..	..	..	..	..	..	..	..	..	..
	OTHER ACTIVITIES	..	..	..	..	..	..	..	..	..	..
01/99	**GRAND TOTAL**	..	..	..	..	..	..	..	..	..	..

Total manufacturing by investing country	1992	1993	1994	1995	1996	As a % of total manufacturing by foreign affiliates				
All countries	..	..	..	..	**55 724**	..	..	..	..	**100.0**
United States	..	..	..	..	9 808	..	..	..	..	17.6
Canada	..	..	..	..	..	..	..	..	..	..
Mexico	..	..	..	..	..	..	..	..	..	..
Japan	..	..	..	..	0	..	..	..	..	0.0
Europe	..	..	..	..	..	..	..	..	..	..
European Union (15)	..	..	..	..	37 209	..	..	..	..	66.8
Belgium	..	..	..	..	..	..	..	..	..	..
France	..	..	..	..	258	..	..	..	..	0.5
Germany	..	..	..	..	2 536	..	..	..	..	4.6
Italy	..	..	..	..	..	..	..	..	..	..
Netherlands	..	..	..	..	1 918	..	..	..	..	3.4
Spain	..	..	..	..	..	..	..	..	..	..
Sweden	..	..	..	..	..	..	..	..	..	..
United Kingdom	..	..	..	..	5 350	..	..	..	..	9.6
Switzerland	..	..	..	..	3 566	..	..	..	..	6.4
Australia and New Zealand	..	..	..	..	..	..	..	..	..	..
Asia (non-OECD)	..	..	..	..	0	..	..	..	..	0.0
Latin America	..	..	..	..	21	..	..	..	..	0.0

Note: Majority foreign-owned establishments. *Crude petroleum and natural gas extraction* (ISIC 11) is excluded from *Mining and quarrying* (10/14). The sectoral data include indirectly from abroad owned establishments.
Etablissements sous contrôle étranger majoritaire. L'*Extraction de pétrole et de gaz naturel* (CITI 11) est exclue des *Industries extractives* (10/14). Les données sectorielles comprennent les établissements contrôlés indirectement par l'étranger.

Table 5. NORWAY / NORVÈGE

VALUE ADDED / VALEUR AJOUTÉE

By industry (ISIC Rev. 3)	FOREIGN AFFILIATES (Millions of Kr)					AS A % OF NATIONAL TOTAL				
	1992	1993	1994	1995	1996	1992	1993	1994	1995	1996
10/14 Mining & quarrying	142	159	224	435	449	10.3	13.1	15.0	28.9	23.9
15/37 TOTAL MANUFACTURING	**6 715**	**8 156**	**9 867**	**20 775**	**21 497**	**8.1**	**9.2**	**10.4**	**19.5**	**18.6**
15/16 Food, beverages, tobacco	669	777	923	5 940	5 507	3.5	3.9	4.5	27.0	23.3
17/19 Textiles, clothing, leather, footwear	210	180	100	77	91	11.4	9.8	5.4	4.5	4.2
20/22 Wood and paper products	731	649	704	1 775	1 429	4.9	4.1	4.0	8.6	6.5
20 Wood products	..	..	72	55	..	..	..	2.0	1.5	..
21/22 Paper, printing and publishing	..	..	632	1 720	..	..	..	4.5	10.1	..
23/25 Chemicals, Total	1 164	1 639	2 492	3 412	3 516	12.0	14.5	20.5	25.4	24.3
23 Refined petroleum, nuclear fuel	220	693	702	394	839	23.4	38.4	45.0	47.4	51.6
24/25 Chemicals, rubber & plastics prod.	944	946	1 790	3 018	2 677	10.8	9.9	16.9	24.0	20.9
24 Chemical products	571	571	1 424	2 511	2 157	8.1	7.3	16.3	23.7	20.8
2423 Pharmaceuticals	0	0	..	..	381	0.0	0.0	..	..	13.7
25 Rubber and plastics products	373	375	365	507	521	22.2	22.0	19.5	25.5	21.1
26 Non-metallic mineral products	523	644	820	1 216	1 819	21.7	23.4	27.2	35.8	43.6
27/28 Basic & fabricated metals	1 221	1 692	1 886	2 281	2 275	13.0	17.1	16.3	15.9	15.6
27 Basic metals	994	1 225	1 355	1 665	1 500	17.9	20.4	18.0	17.0	17.9
28 Fabricated metal products	227	467	531	616	775	6.0	12.0	13.1	13.6	12.5
29/32 Machinery, Total	1 336	1 436	1 732	..	4 381	12.4	13.1	14.8	..	29.6
29/30 Non-electrical machinery	673	587	672	..	..	10.6	9.5	10.0	..	..
29 Non-electrical machinery nec	673	587	672	1 100	1 351	11.2	9.9	10.6	15.6	16.0
30 Office and computing machinery	0	0	0	..	..	0.0	0.0	0.0	..	..
31/32 Electrical & electronic equipment	663	849	1 060	..	..	14.8	17.9	21.3	..	..
31 Electrical machinery nec	256	392	542	..	2 128	8.2	12.0	16.3	..	55.9
32 Radio, TV & communications eq.	407	457	518	..	..	30.4	30.9	31.2	..	..
33 Scientific instruments	131	237	266	..	528	9.7	16.8	16.7	..	24.2
34/35 Transportation equipment	612	818	826	1 866	1 733	5.5	6.5	6.8	14.2	12.5
34 Motor vehicles	..	..	..	..	122	..	..	..	..	7.8
35 Other transport equipment	..	..	..	..	1 611	..	..	..	..	13.1
351 Shipbuilding & repairing	470	698	672	..	1 462	5.4	7.0	7.1	..	14.2
353 Aircraft and spacecraft	0	0	0	..	0	0.0	0.0	0.0	..	0.0
36/37 Other manufacturing	118	84	117	170	218	4.8	3.4	4.1	5.3	5.9
40/45 Construction, electricity, gas & water	..	..	..	..	..	..	..	..	..	..
50/55 Trade, repair, hotels & restaurants	..	..	..	..	..	..	..	..	..	..
65/74 Finance, insurance, business services	..	..	..	..	..	..	..	..	..	..
OTHER ACTIVITIES	..	..	..	..	..	..	..	..	..	..
01/99 GRAND TOTAL	..	..	..	..	..	..	..	..	..	..

Total manufacturing by investing country						As a % of total manufacturing by foreign affiliates				
All countries	6 715	8 156	9 867	..	16 142	100.0	100.0	100.0	..	100.0
United States	690	1 011	1 499	..	1 975	10.3	12.4	15.2	..	12.2
Canada	..	..	322	..	..	..	..	3.3	..	..
Mexico	0	0	0	..	..	0.0	0.0	0.0	..	..
Japan	..	0	0	..	0	..	0.0	0.0	..	0.0
Europe	..	..	8 046	..	..	..	..	81.5	..	..
European Union (15)	4 945	5 748	6 812	..	12 759	73.6	70.5	69.0	..	79.0
Belgium	..	78	145	..	..	..	1.0	1.5	..	..
France	..	..	104	..	69	..	..	1.1	..	0.4
Germany	174	213	208	..	817	2.6	2.6	2.1	..	5.1
Italy	..	..	..	..	..	..	..	..	..	..
Netherlands	743	676	820	..	703	11.1	8.3	8.3	..	4.4
Spain	..	..	..	..	..	..	..	..	..	..
Sweden	..	..	2 713	..	..	..	..	27.5	..	..
United Kingdom	635	1 166	1 078	..	902	9.5	14.3	10.9	..	5.6
Switzerland	680	912	1 234	..	1 033	10.1	11.2	12.5	..	6.4
Australia and New Zealand	0	0	0	..	..	0.0	0.0	0.0	..	..
Asia (non-OECD)	0	0	0	..	0	0.0	0.0	0.0	..	0.0
Latin America	0	0	0	..	6	0.0	0.0	0.0	..	0.0

Note: Majority foreign-owned establishments. *Crude petroleum and natural gas extraction* (ISIC 11) is excluded from *Mining and quarrying* (10/14). From 1995 onwards sectoral data include indirectly from abroad owned establishments.

Etablissements sous contrôle étranger majoritaire. L'*Extraction de pétrole et de gaz naturel* (CITI 11) est exclue des *Industries extractives* (10/14). Les données sectorielles à partir de 1995 comprennent les établissements contrôlés indirectement par l'étranger.

Table 6. NORWAY / NORVÈGE

WAGES AND SALARIES / SALAIRES ET TRAITEMENTS

By industry (ISIC Rev. 3)		FOREIGN AFFILIATES *(Millions of Kr)*					AS A % OF NATIONAL TOTAL				
		1992	1993	1994	1995	1996	1992	1993	1994	1995	1996
10/14	Mining & quarrying	94	113	115	237	276	9.7	11.8	11.3	24.4	22.9
15/37	**TOTAL MANUFACTURING**	**4 873**	**5 392**	**6 335**	**11 488**	**13 101**	**8.4**	**9.1**	**10.0**	**17.0**	**16.8**
15/16	Food, beverages, tobacco	308	361	445	1 894	1 976	3.2	3.6	4.1	17.0	15.5
17/19	Textiles, clothing, leather, footwear	133	119	119	61	95	10.2	9.3	8.8	4.6	5.8
20/22	Wood and paper products	480	441	496	1 186	984	4.3	3.9	4.1	9.1	6.3
20	Wood products	..	..	43	45	..	..	..	1.8	1.7	..
21/22	Paper, printing and publishing	..	..	453	1 141	..	..	..	4.7	11.1	..
23/25	Chemicals, Total	852	887	1 304	1 665	1 759	14.9	14.9	20.7	24.6	24.5
23	Refined petroleum, nuclear fuel	197	196	186	193	179	39.7	33.6	29.8	32.3	36.1
24/25	Chemicals, rubber & plastics prod.	655	691	1 118	1 472	1 580	12.5	12.9	19.7	23.8	23.6
24	Chemical products	390	414	838	1 105	1 169	9.5	9.9	19.3	23.1	23.7
2423	Pharmaceuticals	0	0	..	..	267	0.0	0.0	..	..	28.7
25	Rubber and plastics products	265	277	280	367	411	23.8	23.6	21.1	26.3	23.5
26	Non-metallic mineral products	306	330	423	715	1 018	17.5	19.8	23.9	36.9	38.9
27/28	Basic & fabricated metals	952	1 026	1 148	1 345	1 509	13.3	14.6	15.0	16.2	15.6
27	Basic metals	764	760	839	920	990	18.8	18.9	18.5	19.4	19.9
28	Fabricated metal products	188	266	309	425	519	6.1	8.8	9.9	12.0	11.0
29/32	Machinery, Total	1 113	1 241	1 432	..	3 580	12.9	14.2	15.5	..	30.4
29/30	Non-electrical machinery	545	489	566	..	..	10.5	9.4	10.2	..	..
29	Non-electrical machinery nec	545	489	566	872	1 123	11.1	9.9	10.7	15.5	16.4
30	Office and computing machinery	0	0	0	..	..	0.0	0.0	0.0	..	..
31/32	Electrical & electronic equipment	568	752	866	..	..	16.4	21.4	23.5	..	..
31	Electrical machinery nec	249	386	457	..	1 711	10.3	16.1	18.9	..	56.2
32	Radio, TV & communications eq.	319	366	409	..	..	30.5	32.7	32.2	..	..
33	Scientific instruments	76	178	176	..	446	7.1	15.6	14.2	..	24.2
34/35	Transportation equipment	536	735	716	1 613	1 603	5.5	7.0	6.8	14.1	13.5
34	Motor vehicles	..	..	..	..	110	..	..	..	..	8.4
35	Other transport equipment	..	..	..	..	1 493	..	..	..	..	14.1
351	Shipbuilding & repairing	429	621	591	..	1 299	5.6	7.6	7.2	..	14.3
353	Aircraft and spacecraft	0	0	0	..	0	0.0	0.0	0.0	..	0.0
36/37	Other manufacturing	117	74	76	110	131	6.1	3.9	3.6	4.7	4.5
40/45	Construction, electricity, gas & water	..	..	..	..	..	..	..	..	..	..
50/55	Trade, repair, hotels & restaurants	..	..	..	..	..	..	..	..	..	..
65/74	Finance, insurance, business services	..	..	..	..	..	..	..	..	..	..
	OTHER ACTIVITIES	..	..	..	..	..	..	..	..	..	..
01/99	**GRAND TOTAL**	..	..	..	..	..	..	..	..	..	..

Total manufacturing by investing country	1992	1993	1994	1995	1996	*As a % of total manufacturing by foreign affiliates*				
All countries	**4 873**	**5 392**	**6 335**	**..**	**9 137**	**100.0**	**100.0**	**100.0**	**..**	**100.0**
United States	530	575	774	..	1 047	10.9	10.7	12.2	..	11.5
Canada	..	..	216	..	..	..	..	3.4	..	..
Mexico	0	0	0	..	..	0.0	0.0	0.0	..	..
Japan	..	0	0	..	0	..	0.0	0.0	..	0.0
Europe	..	..	5 344	..	..	..	..	84.4	..	..
European Union (15)	3 553	3 831	4 555	..	7 254	72.9	71.0	71.9	..	79.4
Belgium	..	..	125	..	..	..	..	2.0	..	..
France	..	45	66	..	55	..	0.8	1.0	..	0.6
Germany	119	150	137	..	794	2.4	2.8	2.2	..	8.7
Italy	..	..	..	..	..	..	..	..	..	..
Netherlands	454	273	391	..	429	9.3	5.1	6.2	..	4.7
Spain	..	..	..	..	..	..	..	..	..	..
Sweden	..	..	1 969	..	..	..	..	31.1	..	..
United Kingdom	511	660	643	..	498	10.5	12.2	10.1	..	5.5
Switzerland	466	629	789	..	593	9.6	11.7	12.5	..	6.5
Australia and New Zealand	0	0	0	..	..	0.0	0.0	0.0	..	..
Asia (non-OECD)	0	0	0	..	0	0.0	0.0	0.0	..	0.0
Latin America	0	0	0	..	12	0.0	0.0	0.0	..	0.1

Note: Majority foreign-owned establishments. *Crude petroleum and natural gas extraction* (ISIC 11) is excluded from *Mining and quarrying* (10/14). From 1995 onwards sectoral data include indirectly from abroad owned establishments.

Etablissements sous contrôle étranger majoritaire. L'*Extraction de pétrole et de gaz naturel* (CITI 11) est exclue des *Industries extractives* (10/14). Les données sectorielles à partir de 1995 comprennent les établissements contrôlés indirectement par l'étranger.

Table 9. NORWAY / NORVÈGE

GROSS FIXED CAPITAL FORMATION / FORMATION BRUTE DE CAPITAL FIXE

By industry (ISIC Rev. 3)		FOREIGN AFFILIATES (Millions of Kr)					AS A % OF NATIONAL TOTAL				
		1992	1993	1994	1995	1996	1992	1993	1994	1995	1996
10/14	Mining & quarrying	12	9	16	82	63	4.6	3.9	6.6	24.2	17.3
15/37	**TOTAL MANUFACTURING**	**1 123**	**1 262**	**1 513**	**2 773**	**2 942**	**9.8**	**13.5**	**14.8**	**22.2**	**16.7**
15/16	Food, beverages, tobacco	69	107	123	522	543	3.0	4.3	4.8	20.2	15.6
17/19	Textiles, clothing, leather, footwear	14	82	30	3	4	13.7	45.8	16.3	1.4	1.9
20/22	Wood and paper products	49	56	65	145	200	1.2	3.0	3.1	4.9	5.4
20	Wood products	..	..	6	3	..	..	..	1.1	0.5	..
21/22	Paper, printing and publishing	..	..	59	142	..	..	..	3.9	6.2	..
23/25	Chemicals, Total	189	443	430	531	580	12.4	28.1	25.3	32.3	14.4
23	Refined petroleum, nuclear fuel	86	296	138	154	72	41.7	85.8	52.9	87.5	14.9
24/25	Chemicals, rubber & plastics prod.	103	147	292	377	508	7.8	12.0	20.3	25.6	14.4
24	Chemical products	72	78	238	276	428	6.2	7.6	20.3	24.7	13.5
2423	Pharmaceuticals	0	0	..	..	101	0.0	0.0	..	..	41.1
25	Rubber and plastics products	31	69	53	101	80	20.0	33.8	19.7	28.7	21.9
26	Non-metallic mineral products	252	131	256	506	648	..	45.6	54.3	65.6	66.7
27/28	Basic & fabricated metals	361	216	318	514	723	27.1	28.2	28.2	32.9	26.8
27	Basic metals	351	144	255	411	581	39.1	27.7	28.4	36.2	27.9
28	Fabricated metal products	10	72	63	103	142	2.3	29.3	27.2	24.0	23.2
29/32	Machinery, Total	124	119	176	..	97	13.9	15.0	22.3	..	14.3
29/30	Non-electrical machinery	52	38	62	..	..	10.6	8.8	14.8	..	..
29	Non-electrical machinery nec	52	38	62	116	87	10.8	9.0	15.8	17.9	18.8
30	Office and computing machinery	0	0	0	..	..	0.0	0.0	0.0	..	..
31/32	Electrical & electronic equipment	72	81	114	..	..	17.8	22.4	30.8	..	..
31	Electrical machinery nec	16	27	42	..	- 41	5.4	11.8	21.0	..	-33.9
32	Radio, TV & communications eq.	56	54	72	..	..	50.9	40.3	42.4	..	..
33	Scientific instruments	9	21	87	..	28	7.6	17.9	50.1	..	9.7
34/35	Transportation equipment	59	79	22	158	57	6.4	7.4	2.4	15.3	5.5
34	Motor vehicles	..	..	..	..	7	..	..	..	..	2.6
35	Other transport equipment	..	..	..	..	50	..	..	..	..	6.5
351	Shipbuilding & repairing	54	62	17	..	102	7.3	8.5	2.6	..	14.2
353	Aircraft and spacecraft	0	0	0	..	0	0.0	0.0	0.0	..	0.0
36/37	Other manufacturing	- 3	8	6	10	62	-1.7	3.8	2.3	2.9	12.3
40/45	Construction, electricity, gas & water	..	..	..	..	..	..	..	..	..	..
50/55	Trade, repair, hotels & restaurants	..	..	..	..	..	..	..	..	..	..
65/74	Finance, insurance, business services	..	..	..	..	..	..	..	..	..	..
	OTHER ACTIVITIES	..	..	..	..	..	..	..	..	..	..
01/99	**GRAND TOTAL**	..	..	..	..	..	..	..	..	..	..

Total manufacturing by investing country	1992	1993	1994	1995	1996	As a % of total manufacturing by foreign affiliates				
						1992	1993	1994	1995	1996
All countries	1 123	1 262	1 513	..	2 389	100.0	100.0	100.0	..	100.0
United States	85	345	143	..	226	7.6	27.3	9.5	..	9.5
Canada	..	..	101	..	..	..	..	6.7	..	..
Mexico	0	0	0	..	..	0.0	0.0	0.0	..	..
Japan	..	0	0	..	0	..	0.0	0.0	..	0.0
Europe	..	..	1 269	..	..	..	..	83.9	..	..
European Union (15)	516	672	977	..	1 272	45.9	53.2	64.6	..	53.2
Belgium	..	..	6	..	..	..	..	0.4	..	..
France	..	2	2	..	19	..	0.2	0.1	..	0.8
Germany	26	24	53	..	38	2.3	1.9	3.5	..	1.6
Italy	..	..	..	..	..	..	..	..	..	..
Netherlands	52	96	108	..	119	4.6	7.6	7.1	..	5.0
Spain	..	..	..	..	..	..	..	..	..	..
Sweden	..	..	398	..	..	..	..	26.3	..	..
United Kingdom	122	114	155	..	143	10.9	9.0	10.2	..	6.0
Switzerland	239	153	292	..	706	21.3	12.1	19.3	..	29.6
Australia and New Zealand	0	0	0	..	..	0.0	0.0	0.0	..	..
Asia (non-OECD)	0	0	0	..	0	0.0	0.0	0.0	..	0.0
Latin America	0	0	0	..	1	0.0	0.0	0.0	..	0.0

Note: Majority foreign-owned establishments. *Crude petroleum and natural gas extraction* (ISIC 11) is excluded from *Mining and quarrying* (10/14). From 1995 onwards sectoral data include indirectly from abroad owned establishments.
Etablissements sous contrôle étranger majoritaire. L'*Extraction de pétrole et de gaz naturel* (CITI 11) est exclue des *Industries extractives* (10/14). Les données sectorielles à partir de 1995 comprennent les établissements contrôlés indirectement par l'étranger.

Table 14. NORWAY / NORVÈGE

GROSS OPERATING SURPLUS / EXCÉDENT BRUT D'EXPLOITATION

By industry (ISIC Rev. 3)	FOREIGN AFFILIATES (Millions of Kr)					AS A % OF NATIONAL TOTAL				
	1992	1993	1994	1995	1996	1992	1993	1994	1995	1996
10/14 Mining & quarrying	48	48	109	198	174	7.8	12.1	..	27.0	20.8
15/37 TOTAL MANUFACTURING	**1 848**	**2 680**	**3 460**	**6 692**	**5 440**	**8.7**	**10.5**	**..**	**19.1**	**16.8**
15/16 Food, beverages, tobacco	363	319	361	1 412	551	6.7	5.8	..	22.6	10.7
17/19 Textiles, clothing, leather, footwear	78	62	- 18	16	- 4	14.5	10.9	..	4.0	-0.7
20/22 Wood and paper products	252	208	208	589	446	6.5	4.5	..	7.4	6.8
20 Wood products	..	..	28	10	..	..	..	..	1.1	..
21/22 Paper, printing and publishing	..	..	179	579	..	..	..	..	8.3	..
23/25 Chemicals, Total	313	753	1 217	1 756	1 762	7.9	13.9	..	26.3	24.1
23 Refined petroleum, nuclear fuel	22	495	524	201	660	5.0	40.5	..	83.4	58.4
24/25 Chemicals, rubber & plastics prod.	291	258	693	1 555	1 102	8.3	6.1	..	24.1	17.8
24 Chemical products	182	158	606	1 413	990	6.2	4.3	..	24.2	18.2
2423 Pharmaceuticals	0	0	..	..	115	0.0	0.0	..	..	6.2
25 Rubber and plastics products	109	100	87	142	112	19.1	18.6	..	23.6	15.3
26 Non-metallic mineral products	218	314	408	502	801	32.8	28.8	..	34.4	51.2
27/28 Basic & fabricated metals	270	670	739	937	767	11.9	23.0	..	15.5	15.6
27 Basic metals	231	468	517	745	510	15.4	23.2	..	14.8	15.0
28 Fabricated metal products	39	202	222	192	257	5.1	22.6	..	18.8	16.9
29/32 Machinery, Total	224	196	302	..	806	10.2	8.7	..	..	26.0
29/30 Non-electrical machinery	129	98	107	..	..	11.3	9.8	..	..	..
29 Non-electrical machinery nec	129	98	107	228	229	12.0	10.1	..	15.8	14.3
30 Office and computing machinery	0	0	0	..	..	0.0	0.0	..	..	..
31/32 Electrical & electronic equipment	95	98	195	..	..	8.9	7.9	..	..	..
31 Electrical machinery nec	7	6	86	..	421	0.9	0.7	..	..	54.4
32 Radio, TV & communications eq.	88	92	109	..	..	29.9	25.6	..	..	..
33 Scientific instruments	55	63	90	..	83	18.9	22.2	..	..	23.6
34/35 Transportation equipment	73	84	111	277	141	4.7	3.8	..	14.8	6.4
34 Motor vehicles	..	..	..	..	12	..	..	..	..	4.5
35 Other transport equipment	..	..	..	..	129	..	..	..	..	6.6
351 Shipbuilding & repairing	41	80	81	..	172	3.2	4.3	..	..	12.4
353 Aircraft and spacecraft	0	0	0	..	0	0.0	0.0	..	..	0.0
36/37 Other manufacturing	2	11	41	60	87	0.4	1.9	..	7.2	11.1
40/45 Construction, electricity, gas & water	..	..	..	..	..	..	..	..	..	..
50/55 Trade, repair, hotels & restaurants	..	..	..	..	..	..	..	..	..	..
65/74 Finance, insurance, business services	..	..	..	..	..	..	..	..	..	..
OTHER ACTIVITIES	..	..	..	..	..	..	..	..	..	..
01/99 GRAND TOTAL	**..**	**..**	**..**	**..**	**..**	**..**	**..**	**..**	**..**	**..**

Total manufacturing by investing country						As a % of total manufacturing by foreign affiliates				
All countries	**1 848**	**2 680**	**3 460**	**..**	**4 265**	**100.0**	**100.0**	**100.0**	**..**	**100.0**
United States	162	437	733	..	929	8.8	16.3	21.2	..	21.8
Canada	..	..	114	..	..	..	..	3.3	..	..
Mexico	0	0	0	..	..	0.0	0.0	0.0	..	..
Japan	..	0	0	..	0	..	0.0	0.0	..	0.0
Europe	..	..	2 612	..	..	..	..	75.5	..	..
European Union (15)	1 397	1 828	2 167	..	2 760	75.6	68.2	62.6	..	64.7
Belgium	..	..	20	..	..	..	..	0.6	..	..
France	..	33	38	..	14	..	1.2	1.1	..	0.3
Germany	55	62	71	..	26	3.0	2.3	2.1	..	0.6
Italy	..	..	..	..	..	..	..	..	..	..
Netherlands	289	405	429	..	274	15.6	15.1	12.4	..	6.4
Spain	..	..	..	..	..	..	..	..	..	..
Sweden	..	..	637	..	..	..	..	18.4	..	..
United Kingdom	124	509	438	..	405	6.7	19.0	12.7	..	9.5
Switzerland	215	285	446	..	443	11.6	10.6	12.9	..	10.4
Australia and New Zealand	0	0	0	..	..	0.0	0.0	0.0	..	..
Asia (non-OECD)	0	0	0	..	0	0.0	0.0	0.0	..	0.0
Latin America	0	0	0	..	- 5	0.0	0.0	0.0	..	-0.1

Note: Majority foreign-owned establishments. *Crude petroleum and natural gas extraction* (ISIC 11) is excluded from *Mining and quarrying* (10/14). From 1995 onwards sectoral data include indirectly from abroad owned establishments.
Etablissements sous contrôle étranger majoritaire. L'*Extraction de pétrole et de gaz naturel* (CITI 11) est exclue des *Industries extractives* (10/14). Les données sectorielles à partir de 1995 comprennent les établissements contrôlés indirectement par l'étranger.

NORWAY

Source

The data are prepared by Statistics Norway (*Statistik sentralbyrå*). They are based on a yearly survey of mining and manufacturing industries, which covers all manufacturing establishments from 1996. Previous surveys covered all establishments employing five or more persons up to 1991, and employing more than ten persons for the period 1992-95. The SIFON register, which includes Norwegian joint-stock companies where the entire share capital or parts of it are in foreign hands, is also used. Indirectly foreign-owned establishments are included from 1995 in the data broken down by industrial sector. The results are published every year in *Industristatistikk*.

National totals: provided by Statistics Norway and fully compatible with foreign affiliates' data.

Industrial classification

For all variables, the data are classified according to the principal industrial activity of the establishment.

Data are provided in ISIC Revision 3, from the equivalent NACE Revision 1.

Crude petroleum and natural gas extraction (ISIC 11) is excluded.

Variables

- *Number of establishments*: all majority foreign-controlled establishments in the mining and manufacturing industries, except *Crude petroleum and natural gas extraction*.

- *Number of employees* is the number of persons employed (owners and employees) not expressed on a full-time equivalent basis. Figures are annual averages.

- *Value added* is valued in market prices and equals gross value of production less costs of goods and services consumed, excluding VAT.

- *Wages and salaries* is in fact compensation of employees. It comprises salaries and wages in cash and kind, employers' contributions to private pension and family allowance schemes and social expenses levied by law.

- *Gross fixed capital formation* is defined as the acquisition of new and used fixed durable assets, with an expected productive life of more than one year, less receipts from sales of such assets.

- *Gross operating surplus* is defined as gross value added at factor cost less wages and salaries.

Geographical breakdown

The investor's country is the country of the immediate controller.

NORVÈGE

Source

Les données émanent de l'office norvégien de statistiques (*Statistik sentralbyrå*). Elles proviennent de l'enquête annuelle sur les industries extractives et manufacturières, qui couvre à partir de 1996 tous les établissements manufacturiers. Les enquêtes précédentes couvraient tous les établissements de plus de cinq salariés jusqu'en 1991, et plus de dix personnes pour la période 1992-95. Le registre SIFON, qui recense les entreprises norvégiennes dans lesquelles tout le capital ou une partie de celui-ci est en mains étrangères, est également utilisé. Les établissements détenus ou contrôlés indirectement par l'étranger sont inclus à partir de 1995 dans les données ventilées par secteur d'activité. Les résultats sont publiés chaque année dans *Industristatistikk*.

Totaux nationaux : fournis par l'office norvégien de statistiques et entièrement compatibles avec les données relatives aux filiales étrangères.

Classification industrielle

Pour toutes les variables, les données sont classées selon l'activité industrielle principale de l'établissement.

Les données sont fournies en CITI révision 3, à partir de la classification équivalente NACE révision 1.

Extraction de pétrole brut et de gaz naturel (CITI 11) ne figure pas dans les résultats.

Variables

- *Nombre d'établissements* : tous les établissements sous contrôle étranger majoritaire dans les industries extractives et manufacturières, à l'exception de l'*Extraction de pétrole brut et de gaz naturel*.

- *Nombre de salariés* : nombre de personnes employées (patrons et salariés) non exprimé en équivalent plein-temps. Les chiffres sont une moyenne annuelle.

- La *Valeur ajoutée* est évaluée au prix du marché, et correspond à la valeur brute de la production moins le coût des biens et services consommés hors TVA.

- Les *Salaires et traitements* sont en fait la rémunération des salariés. Celle-ci comprend les traitements et salaires en espèces et en nature, les cotisations patronales aux régimes de retraite et d'allocations familiales et les dépenses sociales légales.

- La *Formation brute de capital fixe* est définie comme la valeur des acquisitions d'actifs fixes neufs et usagés dont la durée de vie productive est supérieure à un an, déduction faite de la valeur des ventes de ces mêmes actifs.

- L'*Excédent brut d'exploitation* est défini comme la valeur ajoutée brute au coût des facteurs, moins les salaires et traitements.

Ventilation géographique

Le pays de l'investisseur est celui où se situe le contrôle immédiat.

SWEDEN

Sources and Methods

SUÈDE

NUMBER OF ENTERPRISES / NOMBRE D'ENTREPRISES

By industry (ISIC Rev. 3)		FOREIGN AFFILIATES (Units)					AS A % OF NATIONAL TOTAL				
		1992	1993	1994	1995	1996	1992	1993	1994	1995	1996
10/14	Mining & quarrying	5	7	9	12	13	0.7	1.2	1.6	2.0	2.2
15/37	**TOTAL MANUFACTURING**	**683**	**646**	**684**	**780**	**789**	**1.6**	**1.6**	**1.6**	**1.8**	**1.7**
15/16	Food, beverages, tobacco	47	49	52	53	48	1.7	1.9	2.0	2.0	1.8
17/19	Textiles, clothing, leather, footwear	25	28	26	25	22	0.9	1.2	1.0	0.9	0.7
20/22	Wood and paper products	75	91	112	114	126	0.7	0.8	0.9	0.9	1.0
20	Wood products	..	13	15	15	17	..	0.3	0.3	0.3	0.3
21/22	Paper, printing and publishing	..	78	97	99	109	..	1.2	1.4	1.3	1.4
23/25	Chemicals, Total	120	97	112	129	126	5.6	4.8	5.3	6.0	5.7
23	Refined petroleum, nuclear fuel	5	3	4	5	6	9.8	9.4	10.8	14.7	16.7
24/25	Chemicals, rubber & plastics prod.	115	94	108	124	120	5.5	4.7	5.2	5.9	5.6
24	Chemical products	72	54	71	82	79	9.2	9.3	11.1	12.0	10.7
2423	Pharmaceuticals	10	8	10	12	9	11.4	10.4	11.6	12.8	8.5
25	Rubber and plastics products	33	40	37	42	41	2.5	2.8	2.6	2.9	2.9
26	Non-metallic mineral products	30	28	28	34	31	2.5	2.4	2.4	2.8	2.4
27/28	Basic & fabricated metals	113	79	79	97	96	1.2	1.0	0.9	1.1	1.0
27	Basic metals	24	21	26	38	31	6.0	6.6	7.6	10.3	8.2
28	Fabricated metal products	89	58	53	59	65	1.0	0.7	0.7	0.7	0.7
29/32	Machinery, Total	192	185	188	219	212	2.4	3.0	2.9	3.4	3.2
29/30	Non-electrical machinery	134	137	140	161	156	2.3	2.9	2.9	3.3	3.1
29	Non-electrical machinery nec	125	126	132	153	148	2.4	3.0	3.0	3.4	3.2
30	Office and computing machinery	9	11	8	8	8	2.2	2.5	1.8	1.9	1.9
31/32	Electrical & electronic equipment	58	48	48	58	56	2.7	3.3	3.1	3.6	3.4
31	Electrical machinery nec	50	38	39	44	45	3.8	3.7	3.6	3.9	3.9
32	Radio, TV & communications eq.	8	10	9	14	11	0.9	2.3	2.0	2.9	2.2
33	Scientific instruments	17	18	21	25	53	2.2	1.2	1.3	1.4	2.8
34/35	Transportation equipment	41	39	35	43	38	2.7	2.5	2.2	2.6	2.1
34	Motor vehicles	23	23	24	32	26	4.9	4.6	4.6	5.6	4.3
35	Other transport equipment	18	16	11	11	12	1.7	1.5	1.0	1.0	1.0
351	Shipbuilding & repairing	..	4	3	3	..	..	0.4	0.3	0.3	..
353	Aircraft and spacecraft	..	3	..	..	..	..	4.1	..	..	..
36/37	Other manufacturing	23	32	31	41	37	0.8	1.1	0.9	1.1	0.9
40/45	Construction, electricity, gas & water	..	66	93	78	122	..	0.1	0.2	0.2	0.2
50/55	Trade, repair, hotels & restaurants	1 088	1 185	1 304	1 369	1 461	0.9	1.0	1.0	1.1	1.1
65/74	Finance, insurance, business services	430	535	660	756	830	0.5	0.5	0.6	0.6	0.6
	OTHER ACTIVITIES	231	279	324	349	398	0.1	0.2	0.2	0.2	0.2
01/99	**GRAND TOTAL**	**2 437**	**2 718**	**3 074**	**3 344**	**3 613**	**0.5**	**0.6**	**0.6**	**0.6**	**0.6**

Total manufacturing by investing country						As a % of total manufacturing by foreign affiliates				
All countries	683	646	684	780	789	100.0	100.0	100.0	100.0	100.0
United States	63	70	69	85	98	9.2	10.8	10.1	10.9	12.4
Canada	..	..	..	..	..	..	..	..	..	..
Mexico	..	..	..	..	..	..	..	..	..	..
Japan	..	6	7	12	11	..	0.9	1.0	1.5	1.4
Europe	611	562	589	663	662	89.5	87.0	86.1	85.0	83.9
European Union (15)	429	412	446	484	491	62.8	63.8	65.2	62.1	62.2
Belgium	..	..	..	..	..	..	..	..	..	..
France	25	25	25	24	29	3.7	3.9	3.7	3.1	3.7
Germany	45	42	51	52	60	6.6	6.5	7.5	6.7	7.6
Italy	..	..	..	..	..	..	..	..	..	..
Netherlands	87	91	117	122	110	12.7	14.1	17.1	15.6	13.9
Spain	..	..	..	..	..	..	..	..	..	..
Sweden	..	..	..	..	..	..	..	..	..	..
United Kingdom	61	58	72	96	92	8.9	9.0	10.5	12.3	11.7
Switzerland	102	85	73	90	77	14.9	13.2	10.7	11.5	9.8
Australia and New Zealand	..	..	..	..	..	..	..	..	..	..
Asia (non-OECD)	..	..	..	..	6	..	..	..	..	0.8
Latin America	..	..	..	..	..	..	..	..	..	..

Note: **All** majority foreign-owned firms. Source: NUTEK's Statistics on Foreign-owned Enterprises. In 1992, ISIC 20/22 includes part of *Furniture* (361), small part of ISIC 353 and 35 is included in ISIC 29/32 and ISIC 40/45 is included in *Other activities*. See country notes.
Toutes les firmes sous contrôle étranger majoritaire. Source : Statistiques de NUTEK sur les entreprises à capitaux étrangers. En 1992, la CITI 20/22 comprend une partie de *Meubles* (361), une petite partie de la CITI 353 et 35 est comprise dans la CITI 29/32 et la CITI 40/45 est comprise dans *Autres activités*. Voir les notes par pays.

Table 1b. SWEDEN / SUÈDE

NUMBER OF ENTERPRISES / NOMBRE D'ENTREPRISES

By industry (ISIC Rev. 3)		FOREIGN AFFILIATES (Units)					AS A % OF NATIONAL TOTAL				
		1992	1993	1994	1995	1996	1992	1993	1994	1995	1996
10/14	Mining & quarrying	3	5	5	7	12	0.7	1.2	1.2	1.6	2.4
15/37	**TOTAL MANUFACTURING**	**658**	**662**	**714**	**821**	**757**	**2.3**	**2.4**	**2.6**	**2.9**	**2.3**
15/16	Food, beverages, tobacco	42	42	45	46	48	2.3	2.2	2.4	2.4	2.3
17/19	Textiles, clothing, leather, footwear	23	14	31	18	21	1.5	1.0	2.3	1.4	1.4
20/22	Wood and paper products	58	120	113	157	114	0.8	1.6	1.5	2.0	1.2
20	Wood products	..	8	8	8	16	..	0.3	0.3	0.3	0.5
21/22	Paper, printing and publishing	..	112	105	149	98	..	2.3	2.1	3.0	1.6
23/25	Chemicals, Total	95	98	96	111	122	5.5	6.0	5.7	7.0	6.5
23	Refined petroleum, nuclear fuel	4	..	3	5	7	10.8	..	10.7	17.2	21.9
24/25	Chemicals, rubber & plastics prod.	91	98	93	106	115	5.4	6.1	5.6	6.8	6.2
24	Chemical products	68	47	66	77	76	10.8	10.1	13.2	14.9	11.8
2423	Pharmaceuticals	9	8	4	8	6	14.3	13.8	6.5	11.9	6.3
25	Rubber and plastics products	23	51	27	29	39	2.2	4.5	2.3	2.8	3.3
26	Non-metallic mineral products	27	33	34	36	29	3.3	4.1	4.4	4.7	3.3
27/28	Basic & fabricated metals	82	67	62	83	93	1.2	1.2	1.1	1.4	1.4
27	Basic metals	27	29	24	33	30	8.6	11.3	8.6	10.9	9.1
28	Fabricated metal products	55	38	38	50	63	0.9	0.7	0.7	0.9	1.0
29/32	Machinery, Total	266	196	192	195	207	5.0	4.4	4.2	4.2	3.9
29/30	Non-electrical machinery	216	136	134	143	148	5.6	4.1	3.9	4.1	3.8
29	Non-electrical machinery nec	209	130	127	137	142	5.9	4.4	4.1	4.4	4.0
30	Office and computing machinery	7	6	7	6	6	2.4	1.8	2.2	1.9	1.6
31/32	Electrical & electronic equipment	50	60	58	52	59	3.3	5.4	5.1	4.4	4.2
31	Electrical machinery nec	43	51	50	38	49	4.6	6.4	6.0	4.5	5.0
32	Radio, TV & communications eq.	7	9	8	14	10	1.3	2.9	2.6	4.2	2.4
33	Scientific instruments	13	13	13	24	51	2.4	1.1	1.1	1.9	3.4
34/35	Transportation equipment	34	30	36	37	37	3.2	2.8	3.4	3.4	2.8
34	Motor vehicles	19	19	17	27	25	5.0	4.6	4.1	6.1	4.7
35	Other transport equipment	15	11	19	10	12	2.2	1.7	3.0	1.5	1.5
351	Shipbuilding & repairing	..	..	..	..	..	..	..	..	..	..
353	Aircraft and spacecraft	..	..	..	..	..	..	..	..	..	..
36/37	Other manufacturing	17	47	90	113	35	1.2	3.0	5.6	6.9	1.6
40/45	Construction, electricity, gas & water	..	39	98	43	113	..	0.1	0.4	0.2	0.4
50/55	Trade, repair, hotels & restaurants	726	622	984	1 510	1 283	1.1	0.8	1.3	2.0	1.4
65/74	Finance, insurance, business services	203	256	437	457	498	0.6	0.6	0.9	0.9	0.8
	OTHER ACTIVITIES	248	100	118	130	242	0.4	0.4	0.4	0.4	0.5
01/99	**GRAND TOTAL**	**1 839**	**1 684**	**2 357**	**2 967**	**2 905**	**0.9**	**0.8**	**1.1**	**1.4**	**1.1**

Total manufacturing by investing country	1992	1993	1994	1995	1996	As a % of total manufacturing by foreign affiliates				
						1992	1993	1994	1995	1996
All countries	658	662	714	821	757	100.0	100.0	100.0	100.0	100.0
United States	67	58	55	74	92	10.2	8.8	7.7	9.0	12.2
Canada	..	..	..	..	..	..	..	..	..	..
Mexico	..	..	..	..	..	..	..	..	..	..
Japan	..	..	..	35	11	..	..	..	4.3	1.5
Europe	479	567	614	700	638	72.8	85.6	86.0	85.3	84.3
European Union (15)	335	441	446	508	466	50.9	66.6	62.5	61.9	61.6
Belgium	..	..	..	..	..	..	..	..	..	..
France	23	20	20	21	29	3.5	3.0	2.8	2.6	3.8
Germany	34	44	51	77	59	5.2	6.6	7.1	9.4	7.8
Italy	..	..	..	..	..	..	..	..	..	..
Netherlands	59	51	77	97	99	9.0	7.7	10.8	11.8	13.1
Spain	..	..	..	..	..	..	..	..	..	..
Sweden	..	..	..	..	..	..	..	..	..	..
United Kingdom	62	63	67	73	89	9.4	9.5	9.4	8.9	11.8
Switzerland	87	74	67	75	79	13.2	11.2	9.4	9.1	10.4
Australia and New Zealand	..	..	..	..	..	..	..	..	..	..
Asia (non-OECD)	..	..	..	..	6	..	..	..	..	0.8
Latin America	..	..	..	..	..	..	..	..	..	..

Note: Majority foreign-owned **non-financial** firms. Source: Statistics Sweden's Structural Business Statistics. In 1992, ISIC 20/22 includes part of *Furniture* (361), small part of ISIC 353 and 35 is included in ISIC 29/32 and ISIC 40/45 is included in *Other activities*. See country notes.
Firmes **non financières** sous contrôle étranger majoritaire. Source : Statistiques structurelles d'entreprises de l'office suédois de statistiques. En 1992, la CITI 20/22 comprend une partie de *Meubles* (361), une petite partie de la CITI 353 et 35 est comprise dans la CITI 29/32 et la CITI 40/45 est comprise dans *Autres activités*. Voir les notes par pays.

NUMBER OF EMPLOYEES / NOMBRE DE SALARIÉS

		FOREIGN AFFILIATES *(Units)*					AS A % OF NATIONAL TOTAL				
By industry (ISIC Rev. 3)		1992	1993	1994	1995	1996	1992	1993	1994	1995	1996
10/14	Mining & quarrying	340	507	389	712	819	3.1	5.0	4.1	7.5	8.6
15/37	**TOTAL MANUFACTURING**	**127 046**	**107 631**	**108 648**	**132 239**	**137 097**	**16.9**	**15.6**	**16.2**	**19.2**	**19.3**
15/16	Food, beverages, tobacco	15 029	13 392	13 127	14 098	18 040	21.8	20.0	20.0	21.2	26.9
17/19	Textiles, clothing, leather, footwear	2 053	1 975	2 272	2 425	2 418	11.1	13.2	13.6	14.4	15.2
20/22	Wood and paper products	9 898	8 093	8 379	9 705	10 776	6.6	5.9	6.1	7.1	7.8
20	Wood products	..	811	894	969	2 630	..	2.5	2.6	2.7	7.2
21/22	Paper, printing and publishing	..	7 282	7 485	8 736	8 146	..	7.0	7.4	8.6	8.0
23/25	Chemicals, Total	15 780	14 129	18 214	25 319	25 272	26.5	26.4	34.5	46.8	45.8
23	Refined petroleum, nuclear fuel	720	1 472	1 844	2 073	1 517	29.9	49.7	69.7	78.1	91.8
24/25	Chemicals, rubber & plastics prod.	15 060	12 657	16 370	23 246	23 755	26.3	25.1	32.7	45.2	44.4
24	Chemical products	11 393	8 008	12 529	18 847	18 928	30.2	28.9	44.8	66.0	64.9
2423	Pharmaceuticals	282	256	542	6 023	6 655	3.0	3.0	6.4	63.0	63.7
25	Rubber and plastics products	3 385	4 649	3 841	4 399	4 827	17.3	20.4	17.4	19.3	19.8
26	Non-metallic mineral products	6 715	6 181	5 637	6 318	6 272	30.6	29.0	31.4	34.9	35.4
27/28	Basic & fabricated metals	12 548	8 304	8 497	14 434	13 404	9.2	7.4	8.0	12.8	11.2
27	Basic metals	5 533	4 814	5 152	10 584	9 453	15.7	14.2	16.0	32.0	28.0
28	Fabricated metal products	7 015	3 490	3 345	3 850	3 951	7.0	4.5	4.5	4.9	4.6
29/32	Machinery, Total	49 306	40 116	38 278	42 009	41 378	29.1	25.6	25.8	27.5	26.0
29/30	Non-electrical machinery	33 425	27 534	28 166	31 584	31 114	31.4	26.2	28.6	31.7	30.1
29	Non-electrical machinery nec	27 405	25 973	26 243	30 571	30 145	28.8	26.4	28.7	32.3	30.4
30	Office and computing machinery	6 020	1 561	1 923	1 013	969	53.5	22.4	26.5	20.5	22.7
31/32	Electrical & electronic equipment	15 881	12 582	10 112	10 425	10 264	25.2	24.5	20.3	19.7	18.4
31	Electrical machinery nec	14 236	10 375	8 230	8 348	8 335	46.6	47.0	44.6	42.7	35.9
32	Radio, TV & communications eq.	1 645	2 207	1 882	2 077	1 929	5.1	7.5	6.0	6.2	5.9
33	Scientific instruments	6 365	5 597	6 499	6 385	7 043	44.2	29.5	32.4	29.5	32.5
34/35	Transportation equipment	8 375	7 568	5 126	7 451	8 253	9.6	9.4	6.1	8.8	9.1
34	Motor vehicles	5 099	4 736	3 177	5 375	6 070	6.7	7.0	5.1	8.3	8.7
35	Other transport equipment	3 276	2 832	1 949	2 076	2 183	28.5	22.8	9.1	10.5	10.5
351	Shipbuilding & repairing	..	195	158	157	..	..	7.1	3.6	3.5	..
353	Aircraft and spacecraft	..	612	..	..	..	..	11.9	..	..	..
36/37	Other manufacturing	977	2 276	2 619	4 095	4 241	3.6	8.8	11.7	16.4	16.7
40/45	Construction, electricity, gas & water	..	7 533	8 136	8 547	9 833	..	3.5	4.3	4.5	5.1
50/55	Trade, repair, hotels & restaurants	46 086	48 864	49 671	54 284	61 047	9.5	10.2	10.6	11.3	12.5
65/74	Finance, insurance, business services	13 516	25 001	27 113	29 237	40 403	4.4	7.5	8.0	8.3	10.9
	OTHER ACTIVITIES	32 164	20 702	20 057	20 999	28 816	4.7	5.3	5.4	5.5	7.5
01/99	**GRAND TOTAL**	**219 152**	**210 238**	**214 014**	**246 018**	**278 016**	**9.8**	**9.9**	**10.5**	**11.7**	**12.9**

Total manufacturing by investing country	1992	1993	1994	1995	1996	*As a % of total manufacturing by foreign affiliates*				
All countries	127 046	107 631	108 648	132 239	137 097	100.0	100.0	100.0	100.0	100.0
United States	13 492	9 995	10 852	20 062	24 067	10.6	9.3	10.0	15.2	17.6
Canada	..	..	..	..	..	..	..	..	..	..
Mexico	..	..	..	..	..	..	..	..	..	..
Japan	..	383	411	528	618	..	0.4	0.4	0.4	0.5
Europe	112 889	96 791	95 597	110 081	110 929	88.9	89.9	88.0	83.2	80.9
European Union (15)	71 119	62 256	65 689	73 391	71 963	56.0	57.8	60.5	55.5	52.5
Belgium	..	..	..	..	..	..	..	..	..	..
France	5 463	4 575	4 606	4 907	5 000	4.3	4.3	4.2	3.7	3.6
Germany	6 347	5 624	6 171	5 955	7 538	5.0	5.2	5.7	4.5	5.5
Italy	..	..	..	..	..	..	..	..	..	..
Netherlands	21 090	18 665	23 600	20 980	16 910	16.6	17.3	21.7	15.9	12.3
Spain	..	..	..	..	..	..	..	..	..	..
Sweden	..	..	..	..	..	..	..	..	..	..
United Kingdom	6 693	6 261	7 059	13 439	13 560	5.3	5.8	6.5	10.2	9.9
Switzerland	29 096	26 108	23 892	25 766	23 707	22.9	24.3	22.0	19.5	17.3
Australia and New Zealand	..	..	..	..	..	..	..	..	..	..
Asia (non-OECD)	..	..	..	..	949	..	..	..	..	0.7
Latin America	..	..	..	..	..	..	..	..	..	..

Note: **All** majority foreign-owned firms. Source: NUTEK's Statistics on Foreign-owned Enterprises. In 1992, ISIC 20/22 includes part of *Furniture* (361), small part of ISIC 353 and 35 is included in ISIC 29/32 and ISIC 40/45 is included in *Other activities* . See country notes.

Toutes les firmes sous contrôle étranger majoritaire. Source : Statistiques de NUTEK sur les entreprises à capitaux étrangers. En 1992, la CITI 20/22 comprend une partie de *Meubles* (361), une petite partie de la CITI 353 et 35 est comprise dans la CITI 29/32 et la CITI 40/45 est comprise dans *Autres activités* . Voir les notes par pays.

NUMBER OF EMPLOYEES / NOMBRE DE SALARIÉS

By industry (ISIC Rev. 3)	FOREIGN AFFILIATES (Full-time Eq.)					AS A % OF NATIONAL TOTAL				
	1992	1993	1994	1995	1996	1992	1993	1994	1995	1996
10/14 Mining & quarrying	307	455	350	772	743	3.0	4.7	3.6	7.7	8.0
15/37 TOTAL MANUFACTURING	**114 156**	**99 582**	**101 999**	**132 054**	**134 372**	**16.9**	**15.9**	**16.1**	**19.9**	**19.9**
15/16 Food, beverages, tobacco	12 391	12 665	12 711	13 441	17 734	19.0	19.7	20.1	20.6	27.9
17/19 Textiles, clothing, leather, footwear	1 934	1 826	2 449	2 256	2 254	12.3	13.6	18.2	17.1	17.1
20/22 Wood and paper products	9 762	10 153	7 210	8 995	9 879	6.8	7.9	5.6	7.1	7.7
20 Wood products	..	742	837	898	2 326	..	2.4	2.5	2.7	7.3
21/22 Paper, printing and publishing	..	9 411	6 373	8 097	7 553	..	9.7	6.7	8.7	7.9
23/25 Chemicals, Total	14 326	13 260	17 305	24 491	25 133	24.2	24.7	31.7	43.4	42.9
23 Refined petroleum, nuclear fuel	499	..	1 523	1 851	2 323	22.7	..	63.8	78.2	94.5
24/25 Chemicals, rubber & plastics prod.	13 827	11 973	15 782	22 640	22 810	24.2	23.4	30.2	41.9	40.6
24 Chemical products	10 576	7 398	12 037	18 376	18 588	27.9	25.1	39.5	58.3	56.1
2423 Pharmaceuticals	281	271	509	5 634	5 893	2.6	2.6	4.4	45.9	44.3
25 Rubber and plastics products	3 251	4 575	3 745	4 264	4 222	17.0	21.1	17.2	18.9	18.3
26 Non-metallic mineral products	6 097	5 454	5 288	6 127	5 961	30.8	27.5	30.3	34.7	34.0
27/28 Basic & fabricated metals	11 204	7 723	7 971	14 110	12 766	10.5	9.1	9.0	14.9	13.1
27 Basic metals	4 905	4 766	4 928	10 062	8 902	16.6	17.1	17.5	35.7	31.4
28 Fabricated metal products	6 299	2 957	3 043	4 048	3 864	8.2	5.2	5.1	6.1	5.6
29/32 Machinery, Total	44 855	35 005	35 917	44 835	41 764	29.3	24.0	23.6	28.0	25.1
29/30 Non-electrical machinery	31 105	21 588	24 493	33 157	30 299	32.2	23.2	24.4	31.8	28.6
29 Non-electrical machinery nec	26 071	20 666	22 929	32 320	29 414	30.3	24.1	24.5	32.5	28.9
30 Office and computing machinery	5 034	922	1 564	837	885	47.7	12.6	23.1	18.2	20.9
31/32 Electrical & electronic equipment	13 750	13 417	11 424	11 678	11 465	24.4	25.5	22.2	20.9	19.0
31 Electrical machinery nec	12 437	11 624	9 601	9 534	9 475	46.6	53.1	47.1	44.9	38.4
32 Radio, TV & communications eq.	1 313	1 793	1 823	2 144	1 990	4.4	5.8	5.8	6.2	5.6
33 Scientific instruments	5 233	4 716	5 623	6 213	6 719	42.3	27.1	29.0	28.8	31.2
34/35 Transportation equipment	7 297	6 685	4 861	7 622	8 120	8.3	8.5	6.2	8.9	9.2
34 Motor vehicles	4 226	3 981	2 767	5 545	5 979	6.2	6.2	4.6	8.4	8.8
35 Other transport equipment	3 071	2 704	2 094	2 077	2 141	16.0	18.5	11.1	10.8	10.7
351 Shipbuilding & repairing	..	..	..	..	..	..	..	..	..	..
353 Aircraft and spacecraft	..	..	..	..	..	..	..	..	..	..
36/37 Other manufacturing	1 057	2 095	2 664	3 964	4 042	7.8	11.0	13.5	18.8	18.7
40/45 Construction, electricity, gas & water	..	6 421	7 004	7 946	9 871	..	3.2	3.7	4.1	5.1
50/55 Trade, repair, hotels & restaurants	39 522	39 625	43 393	48 432	54 707	8.9	9.2	9.7	10.7	12.2
65/74 Finance, insurance, business services	9 741	19 013	21 680	24 033	33 335	5.9	10.1	10.9	11.3	14.8
OTHER ACTIVITIES	24 582	10 617	12 820	13 255	22 516	4.7	4.4	4.3	4.2	6.5
01/99 GRAND TOTAL	**188 308**	**175 713**	**187 246**	**226 492**	**255 544**	**10.4**	**10.4**	**10.5**	**12.3**	**13.5**

Total manufacturing by investing country						*As a % of total manufacturing by foreign affiliates*				
All countries	**114 156**	**99 582**	**101 999**	**132 054**	**134 372**	**100.0**	**100.0**	**100.0**	**100.0**	**100.0**
United States	12 403	9 332	10 539	19 542	23 004	10.9	9.4	10.3	14.8	17.1
Canada	..	..	..	422	305	..	..	..	0.3	0.2
Mexico	..	..	..	..	..	..	..	..	..	..
Japan	..	549	..	679	633	..	0.6	..	0.5	0.5
Europe	100 662	89 298	89 302	110 191	109 433	88.2	89.7	87.6	83.4	81.4
European Union (15)	63 760	57 915	60 159	74 185	70 417	55.9	58.2	59.0	56.2	52.4
Belgium	..	..	..	633	642	..	..	..	0.5	0.5
France	4 856	4 278	4 455	4 791	5 016	4.3	4.3	4.4	3.6	3.7
Germany	5 507	5 643	6 226	6 333	7 168	4.8	5.7	6.1	4.8	5.3
Italy	..	..	..	319	529	..	..	..	0.2	0.4
Netherlands	19 874	16 503	19 020	22 264	17 843	17.4	16.6	18.6	16.9	13.3
Spain	..	..	..	..	86	..	..	..	..	0.1
Sweden	..	..	..	..	..	..	..	..	..	..
United Kingdom	6 160	5 520	6 752	12 779	12 869	5.4	5.5	6.6	9.7	9.6
Switzerland	25 968	24 031	23 309	25 278	24 504	22.7	24.1	22.9	19.1	18.2
Australia and New Zealand	..	..	..	..	..	..	..	..	..	..
Asia (non-OECD)	..	..	..	..	832	..	..	..	..	0.6
Latin America	..	..	..	..	..	..	..	..	..	..

Note: Majority foreign-owned **non-financial** firms. Source: Statistics Sweden's Structural Business Statistics. In 1992, ISIC 20/22 includes part of *Furniture* (361), small part of ISIC 353 and 35 is included in *Other activities*. See country notes.

Firmes **non financières** sous contrôle étranger majoritaire. Source : Statistiques structurelles d'entreprises de l'office suédois de statistiques. En 1992, la CITI 20/22 comprend une partie de *Meubles* (361), une petite partie de la CITI 353 et 35 est comprise dans la CITI 29/32 et la CITI 40/45 est comprise dans *Autres activités* . Voir les notes par pays.

Table 4. SWEDEN / SUÈDE

TURNOVER / CHIFFRE D'AFFAIRES

By industry (ISIC Rev. 3)		FOREIGN AFFILIATES (Millions of SKr)					AS A % OF NATIONAL TOTAL				
		1992	1993	1994	1995	1996	1992	1993	1994	1995	1996
10/14	Mining & quarrying	426	532	633	1 115	1 017	3.6	4.4	4.6	7.0	6.7
15/37	**TOTAL MANUFACTURING**	**138 090**	**139 415**	**164 535**	**235 987**	**229 976**	**18.0**	**17.4**	**17.4**	**21.6**	**20.8**
15/16	Food, beverages, tobacco	16 320	18 376	20 128	23 517	32 277	14.8	16.6	17.4	19.9	26.9
17/19	Textiles, clothing, leather, footwear	1 880	1 902	2 600	2 544	2 768	15.8	15.7	20.5	17.6	20.9
20/22	Wood and paper products	13 867	17 226	11 671	16 034	16 658	8.1	10.1	6.1	7.5	8.2
20	Wood products	..	1 111	1 493	1 640	3 907	..	2.8	3.1	3.1	8.0
21/22	Paper, printing and publishing	..	16 115	10 178	14 394	12 751	..	12.3	7.1	8.9	8.3
23/25	Chemicals, Total	23 958	26 343	36 808	54 971	54 731	28.7	29.9	36.8	49.5	49.1
23	Refined petroleum, nuclear fuel	690	..	1 949	2 719	4 561	15.3	..	42.1	57.3	88.9
24/25	Chemicals, rubber & plastics prod.	23 268	24 785	34 859	52 252	50 170	29.4	29.9	36.6	49.1	47.2
24	Chemical products	19 634	18 124	29 221	46 094	44 514	32.4	30.3	42.0	59.5	58.0
2423	Pharmaceuticals	477	618	1 072	10 799	11 256	2.6	2.6	3.9	36.3	36.6
25	Rubber and plastics products	3 633	6 660	5 639	6 158	5 657	19.7	29.0	21.8	21.3	19.1
26	Non-metallic mineral products	5 778	5 632	6 546	7 825	7 314	30.3	28.6	33.6	37.1	34.4
27/28	Basic & fabricated metals	12 607	11 890	15 346	33 774	28 392	13.6	13.5	14.1	25.8	22.3
27	Basic metals	6 812	8 517	11 034	27 501	22 286	20.5	20.8	21.5	44.2	40.4
28	Fabricated metal products	5 795	3 373	4 312	6 273	6 106	9.7	7.2	7.5	9.2	8.5
29/32	Machinery, Total	50 373	42 972	53 517	71 411	61 378	33.0	26.2	25.4	28.9	22.1
29/30	Non-electrical machinery	35 401	25 883	36 962	54 292	44 096	37.7	26.3	28.6	37.7	29.3
29	Non-electrical machinery nec	25 468	24 975	34 901	52 961	42 621	32.1	27.6	29.2	38.3	29.4
30	Office and computing machinery	9 933	908	2 061	1 331	1 475	67.6	11.6	20.9	23.5	25.8
31/32	Electrical & electronic equipment	14 972	17 089	16 555	17 119	17 282	25.6	26.1	20.3	16.6	13.6
31	Electrical machinery nec	13 958	15 544	14 230	14 532	14 956	54.0	62.8	56.5	53.4	45.7
32	Radio, TV & communications eq.	1 014	1 545	2 325	2 587	2 326	3.1	3.8	4.1	3.4	2.5
33	Scientific instruments	5 096	5 155	7 616	9 480	10 738	46.1	29.6	34.4	34.1	39.4
34/35	Transportation equipment	7 250	7 449	7 054	11 340	10 656	7.1	6.7	4.8	6.2	5.9
34	Motor vehicles	3 510	4 129	3 509	7 437	7 359	4.1	4.2	2.7	4.7	4.7
35	Other transport equipment	3 740	3 320	3 545	3 903	3 297	21.9	24.4	19.6	17.3	13.5
351	Shipbuilding & repairing	..	..	..	..	..	..	..	..	..	..
353	Aircraft and spacecraft	..	..	..	..	..	..	..	..	..	..
36/37	Other manufacturing	961	2 470	3 249	5 091	5 066	7.7	14.1	16.4	21.1	20.3
40/45	Construction, electricity, gas & water	..	6 631	8 770	8 485	20 493	..	2.4	3.1	2.9	6.3
50/55	Trade, repair, hotels & restaurants	105 546	130 732	174 316	206 163	247 602	11.5	13.4	16.3	17.6	20.6
65/74	Finance, insurance, business services	13 809	18 706	31 846	38 068	43 334	9.2	11.0	15.8	17.3	18.2
	OTHER ACTIVITIES	23 131	24 045	27 659	34 341	40 837	3.9	9.0	8.3	9.5	9.5
01/99	**GRAND TOTAL**	**281 002**	**320 062**	**407 760**	**524 159**	**583 258**	**11.5**	**12.8**	**14.3**	**16.6**	**17.6**

Total manufacturing by investing country						As a % of total manufacturing by foreign affiliates				
All countries	138 090	139 415	164 535	235 987	229 976	100.0	100.0	100.0	100.0	100.0
United States	19 374	13 500	17 514	35 445	39 720	14.0	9.7	10.6	15.0	17.3
Canada	..	..	..	564	515	..	..	..	0.2	0.2
Mexico	..	..	..	..	..	..	..	..	..	..
Japan	..	..	..	1 460	1 124	..	..	..	0.6	0.5
Europe	117 037	124 511	143 837	196 977	187 236	84.8	89.3	87.4	83.5	81.4
European Union (15)	73 111	80 194	97 607	133 861	120 211	52.9	57.5	59.3	56.7	52.3
Belgium	..	..	..	736	683	..	..	..	0.3	0.3
France	5 019	5 072	6 274	7 570	7 357	3.6	3.6	3.8	3.2	3.2
Germany	7 019	7 802	10 497	12 102	12 222	5.1	5.6	6.4	5.1	5.3
Italy	..	..	..	729	1 064	..	..	..	0.3	0.5
Netherlands	24 234	25 522	33 320	40 527	30 263	17.5	18.3	20.3	17.2	13.2
Spain	..	..	..	..	161	..	..	..	..	0.1
Sweden	..	..	..	..	..	..	..	..	..	..
United Kingdom	6 134	6 300	8 605	25 689	25 907	4.4	4.5	5.2	10.9	11.3
Switzerland	30 658	33 660	36 196	42 933	40 785	22.2	24.1	22.0	18.2	17.7
Australia and New Zealand	..	..	..	..	..	..	..	..	..	..
Asia (non-OECD)	..	..	..	..	1 111	..	..	..	..	0.5
Latin America	..	..	..	..	..	..	..	..	..	..

Note: Majority foreign-owned **non-financial** firms. Source: Statistics Sweden's Structural Business Statistics. In 1992, ISIC 20/22 includes part of *Furniture* (361), small part of ISIC 353 and 35 is included in ISIC 29/32 and ISIC 40/45 is included in *Other activities*. See country notes.

Firmes **non financières** sous contrôle étranger majoritaire. Source : Statistiques structurelles d'entreprises de l'office suédois de statistiques. En 1992, la CITI 20/22 comprend une partie de *Meubles* (361), une petite partie de la CITI 353 et 35 est comprise dans la CITI 29/32 et la CITI 40/45 est comprise dans *Autres activités*. Voir les notes par pays.

Table 5. SWEDEN / SUÈDE

VALUE ADDED / VALEUR AJOUTÉE

By industry (ISIC Rev. 3)	FOREIGN AFFILIATES (Millions of SKr)					AS A % OF NATIONAL TOTAL				
	1992	1993	1994	1995	1996	1992	1993	1994	1995	1996
10/14 Mining & quarrying	156	215	282	516	417	3.4	5.1	5.7	8.7	7.9
15/37 TOTAL MANUFACTURING	41 920	41 344	48 824	69 534	68 281	18.3	17.0	15.6	21.2	21.8
15/16 Food, beverages, tobacco	5 001	5 866	6 008	5 763	9 192	20.7	23.9	24.0	23.3	33.9
17/19 Textiles, clothing, leather, footwear	716	736	1 119	969	1 124	17.5	18.7	25.6	19.6	24.5
20/22 Wood and paper products	3 885	4 462	3 497	4 655	4 960	7.6	8.5	5.0	6.1	8.2
20 Wood products	..	294	422	425	1 166	..	2.8	2.9	2.9	10.6
21/22 Paper, printing and publishing	..	4 168	3 075	4 230	3 794	..	9.9	5.6	6.9	7.6
23/25 Chemicals, Total	5 948	7 130	10 836	18 000	16 474	20.4	23.4	30.1	48.1	45.6
23 Refined petroleum, nuclear fuel	284	..	1 054	1 369	1 750	17.5	..	62.0	81.9	92.5
24/25 Chemicals, rubber & plastics prod.	5 664	6 359	9 782	16 631	14 724	20.5	22.3	28.5	46.5	43.0
24 Chemical products	4 635	4 459	8 317	14 770	12 901	21.6	20.6	32.8	56.5	52.4
2423 Pharmaceuticals	106	146	368	5 115	4 298	1.1	1.3	2.7	39.0	35.4
25 Rubber and plastics products	1 029	1 900	1 465	1 861	1 823	16.8	27.9	16.4	19.4	18.9
26 Non-metallic mineral products	1 909	1 905	2 103	2 589	2 600	28.9	27.5	31.9	36.1	34.7
27/28 Basic & fabricated metals	3 290	2 977	3 705	8 638	5 932	10.5	9.9	9.7	18.5	13.9
27 Basic metals	1 479	1 933	2 513	6 984	4 289	16.9	16.8	16.5	36.9	29.4
28 Fabricated metal products	1 811	1 044	1 192	1 654	1 643	8.0	5.6	5.2	6.0	5.8
29/32 Machinery, Total	16 605	13 449	16 237	21 385	19 821	31.7	24.7	24.1	28.7	25.3
29/30 Non-electrical machinery	11 592	7 971	11 191	16 203	14 613	35.1	23.3	24.7	33.3	29.8
29 Non-electrical machinery nec	7 995	7 651	10 515	15 757	14 191	29.2	24.3	25.0	33.5	30.2
30 Office and computing machinery	3 597	320	676	446	422	64.0	11.7	21.0	28.5	20.9
31/32 Electrical & electronic equipment	5 013	5 478	5 046	5 182	5 208	25.9	27.2	22.9	20.1	17.7
31 Electrical machinery nec	4 578	4 932	4 436	4 407	4 613	50.2	57.6	53.0	49.2	42.1
32 Radio, TV & communications eq.	435	546	610	775	595	4.3	4.7	4.4	4.6	3.2
33 Scientific instruments	2 032	2 083	2 705	3 341	3 679	47.2	28.8	31.1	32.1	33.7
34/35 Transportation equipment	2 218	2 164	2 085	3 005	2 924	9.8	8.1	4.0	7.8	7.8
34 Motor vehicles	1 190	1 238	1 088	2 170	2 004	7.1	5.7	3.9	6.9	6.6
35 Other transport equipment	1 028	926	997	835	920	17.5	18.6	4.1	12.3	12.4
351 Shipbuilding & repairing	..	..	70	..	..	..	..	5.4	..	..
353 Aircraft and spacecraft	..	..	43	..	..	..	..	0.2	..	..
36/37 Other manufacturing	315	574	528	1 189	1 574	8.0	9.8	8.4	15.8	19.8
40/45 Construction, electricity, gas & water	..	2 004	2 822	3 217	6 281	..	2.3	3.2	3.5	6.4
50/55 Trade, repair, hotels & restaurants	16 523	20 146	26 011	28 387	32 060	12.8	14.4	16.8	17.2	18.6
65/74 Finance, insurance, business services	4 701	7 355	10 507	12 586	14 524	7.4	10.2	13.0	13.3	14.9
OTHER ACTIVITIES	7 561	4 211	5 579	4 686	8 213	4.1	4.9	5.0	3.9	6.1
01/99 GRAND TOTAL	70 861	75 275	94 025	118 926	129 776	11.6	11.9	12.5	14.8	15.8

Total manufacturing by investing country						As a % of total manufacturing by foreign affiliates				
All countries	41 920	41 344	48 824	69 534	68 281	100.0	100.0	100.0	100.0	100.0
United States	6 144	3 811	4 899	11 247	13 053	14.7	9.2	10.0	16.2	19.1
Canada	..	..	..	..	..	..	..	..	..	..
Mexico	..	..	..	..	..	..	..	..	..	..
Japan	..	..	..	471	322	..	..	..	0.7	0.5
Europe	35 222	37 128	42 616	56 795	54 029	84.0	89.8	87.3	81.7	79.1
European Union (15)	21 664	23 831	29 067	38 941	34 760	51.7	57.6	59.5	56.0	50.9
Belgium	..	..	..	..	..	..	..	..	..	..
France	1 791	1 790	2 136	2 321	2 405	4.3	4.3	4.4	3.3	3.5
Germany	2 166	2 522	3 283	3 763	3 746	5.2	6.1	6.7	5.4	5.5
Italy	..	..	..	..	..	..	..	..	..	..
Netherlands	6 801	7 578	9 938	11 810	9 465	16.2	18.3	20.4	17.0	13.9
Spain	..	..	..	..	..	..	..	..	..	..
Sweden	..	..	..	..	..	..	..	..	..	..
United Kingdom	2 048	1 888	2 822	7 979	6 463	4.9	4.6	5.8	11.5	9.5
Switzerland	9 432	10 205	10 782	11 855	12 371	22.5	24.7	22.1	17.0	18.1
Australia and New Zealand	..	..	..	..	..	..	..	..	..	..
Asia (non-OECD)	..	..	..	..	683	..	..	..	..	1.0
Latin America	..	..	..	..	..	..	..	..	..	..

Note: Majority foreign-owned **non-financial** firms. Source: Statistics Sweden's Structural Business Statistics. In 1992, ISIC 20/22 includes part of *Furniture* (361), small part of ISIC 353 and 35 is included in ISIC 29/32 and ISIC 40/45 is included in *Other activities*. See country notes.
Firmes **non financières** sous contrôle étranger majoritaire. Source : Statistiques structurelles d'entreprises de l'office suédois de statistiques. En 1992, la CITI 20/22 comprend une partie de *Meubles* (361), une petite partie de la CITI 353 et 35 est comprise dans la CITI 29/32 et la CITI 40/45 est comprise dans *Autres activités*. Voir les notes par pays.

Table 6. SWEDEN / SUÈDE

WAGES AND SALARIES / SALAIRES ET TRAITEMENTS

By industry (ISIC Rev. 3)		FOREIGN AFFILIATES (Millions of SKr)					AS A % OF NATIONAL TOTAL				
		1992	1993	1994	1995	1996	1992	1993	1994	1995	1996
10/14	Mining & quarrying	87	125	103	235	271	2.8	4.4	3.4	7.2	8.4
15/37	**TOTAL MANUFACTURING**	**33 685**	**29 366**	**31 466**	**44 003**	**47 441**	**18.3**	**17.0**	**17.2**	**21.6**	**21.4**
15/16	Food, beverages, tobacco	3 260	3 514	3 567	4 021	5 643	20.3	21.9	22.0	23.1	30.7
17/19	Textiles, clothing, leather, footwear	511	521	712	680	739	15.1	17.6	23.5	20.5	21.8
20/22	Wood and paper products	2 709	3 080	2 130	3 094	3 454	6.8	8.5	5.7	7.8	8.2
20	Wood products	..	191	225	263	771	..	2.5	2.7	3.0	8.8
21/22	Paper, printing and publishing	..	2 889	1 905	2 831	2 683	..	10.1	6.5	9.2	8.1
23/25	Chemicals, Total	4 302	4 143	5 656	8 894	9 888	24.3	25.8	32.4	46.9	46.9
23	Refined petroleum, nuclear fuel	171	..	563	745	974	24.4	..	66.0	80.6	95.6
24/25	Chemicals, rubber & plastics prod.	4 131	3 658	5 093	8 149	8 914	24.3	24.1	30.6	45.2	44.4
24	Chemical products	3 257	2 430	3 992	6 942	7 627	26.7	25.0	37.5	59.3	58.1
2423	Pharmaceuticals	103	103	172	2 431	2 808	2.6	2.7	3.8	47.6	47.6
25	Rubber and plastics products	873	1 228	1 101	1 207	1 287	18.3	22.5	18.4	19.1	18.5
26	Non-metallic mineral products	1 613	1 477	1 468	1 816	1 886	31.6	28.9	31.0	35.3	34.7
27/28	Basic & fabricated metals	2 938	2 065	2 366	4 402	4 343	11.0	9.4	9.9	15.9	14.5
27	Basic metals	1 346	1 295	1 477	3 221	3 124	16.3	16.4	17.7	35.6	32.4
28	Fabricated metal products	1 592	770	889	1 181	1 219	8.6	5.5	5.7	6.3	6.0
29/32	Machinery, Total	14 466	10 768	11 630	15 691	15 371	32.8	25.8	25.3	30.4	26.6
29/30	Non-electrical machinery	10 263	6 544	8 024	11 653	11 159	36.7	24.4	26.3	35.0	30.8
29	Non-electrical machinery nec	7 787	6 175	7 426	11 322	10 860	32.8	25.3	26.4	35.8	31.3
30	Office and computing machinery	2 476	369	598	331	299	59.0	15.3	25.2	20.7	19.4
31/32	Electrical & electronic equipment	4 203	4 224	3 606	4 038	4 212	26.1	28.2	23.3	22.1	19.5
31	Electrical machinery nec	3 824	3 762	3 107	3 396	3 623	50.1	58.5	52.3	51.0	43.9
32	Radio, TV & communications eq.	379	462	499	642	589	4.5	5.4	5.2	5.5	4.4
33	Scientific instruments	1 671	1 468	1 822	2 149	2 451	46.1	28.3	31.0	30.1	32.5
34/35	Transportation equipment	1 949	1 837	1 454	2 258	2 524	7.9	8.1	6.1	8.1	8.3
34	Motor vehicles	1 064	1 052	788	1 561	1 723	5.5	5.6	4.4	7.2	7.3
35	Other transport equipment	885	785	666	697	801	17.2	20.4	11.6	11.3	11.7
351	Shipbuilding & repairing	..	..	..	..	..	..	..	..	..	..
353	Aircraft and spacecraft	..	..	..	..	..	..	..	..	..	..
36/37	Other manufacturing	267	493	661	998	1 143	8.5	11.1	13.9	18.8	19.7
40/45	Construction, electricity, gas & water	..	1 987	2 347	2 627	3 571	..	3.8	4.5	4.9	6.1
50/55	Trade, repair, hotels & restaurants	13 130	14 344	16 265	18 674	21 029	12.7	13.8	14.7	15.7	17.0
65/74	Finance, insurance, business services	3 567	5 688	7 303	8 495	11 996	7.1	10.4	12.1	12.3	15.6
	OTHER ACTIVITIES	6 559	2 895	3 828	4 012	6 841	4.9	4.6	4.7	4.5	6.7
01/99	**GRAND TOTAL**	**57 029**	**54 406**	**61 311**	**78 046**	**91 148**	**12.0**	**12.1**	**12.5**	**14.5**	**15.5**

Total manufacturing by investing country						As a % of total manufacturing by foreign affiliates				
All countries	33 685	29 366	31 466	44 003	47 441	100.0	100.0	100.0	100.0	100.0
United States	4 330	2 726	3 201	6 948	8 812	12.9	9.3	10.2	15.8	18.6
Canada	..	..	..	..	..	..	..	..	..	..
Mexico	..	..	..	..	..	..	..	..	..	..
Japan	..	..	..	278	219	..	..	..	0.6	0.5
Europe	28 872	26 309	27 554	36 249	37 942	85.7	89.6	87.6	82.4	80.0
European Union (15)	17 862	16 477	18 030	23 993	23 955	53.0	56.1	57.3	54.5	50.5
Belgium	..	..	..	..	..	..	..	..	..	..
France	1 341	1 164	1 268	1 443	1 596	4.0	4.0	4.0	3.3	3.4
Germany	1 617	1 649	1 945	2 330	2 459	4.8	5.6	6.2	5.3	5.2
Italy	..	..	..	..	..	..	..	..	..	..
Netherlands	5 748	4 918	5 961	7 558	6 516	17.1	16.7	18.9	17.2	13.7
Spain	..	..	..	..	..	..	..	..	..	..
Sweden	..	..	..	..	..	..	..	..	..	..
United Kingdom	1 777	1 521	1 966	4 053	4 476	5.3	5.2	6.2	9.2	9.4
Switzerland	7 999	7 731	7 713	8 890	9 371	23.7	26.3	24.5	20.2	19.8
Australia and New Zealand	..	..	..	..	..	..	..	..	..	..
Asia (non-OECD)	..	..	..	..	314	..	..	..	..	0.7
Latin America	..	..	..	..	..	..	..	..	..	..

Note: Majority foreign-owned **non-financial** firms. Source: Statistics Sweden's Structural Business Statistics. In 1992, ISIC 20/22 includes part of *Furniture* (361), small part of ISIC 353 and 35 is included in ISIC 29/32 and ISIC 40/45 is included in *Other activities* . See country notes.

Firmes **non financières** sous contrôle étranger majoritaire. Source : Statistiques structurelles d'entreprises de l'office suédois de statistiques. En 1992, la CITI 20/22 comprend une partie de *Meubles* (361), une petite partie de la CITI 353 et 35 est comprise dans la CITI 29/32 et la CITI 40/45 est comprise dans *Autres activités* . Voir les notes par pays.

Table 7. SWEDEN / SUÈDE

R&D EXPENDITURE / DÉPENSES DE R-D

By industry (ISIC Rev. 3)		FOREIGN AFFILIATES (Millions of SKr)					AS A % OF NATIONAL TOTAL				
		1992	1993	1994	1995	1996	1992	1993	1994	1995	1996
10/14	Mining & quarrying	3	3	..	..	3	3.5	3.7	..	..	3.5
15/37	**TOTAL MANUFACTURING**	4 187	3 856	3 933	7 725	7 517	17.3	13.7	9.1	19.0	18.7
15/16	Food, beverages, tobacco	55	89	66	76	91	21.3	31.8	25.0	28.3	29.3
17/19	Textiles, clothing, leather, footwear	22	15	33	50	48	51.7	37.7	60.9	71.7	55.2
20/22	Wood and paper products	675	807	18	25	35	47.2	53.9	2.4	3.2	3.5
20	Wood products	..	..	1	1	..	..	..	1.6	1.8	..
21/22	Paper, printing and publishing	..	807	17	24	..	..	55.3	2.5	3.3	..
23/25	Chemicals, Total	264	360	648	2 606	2 730	6.0	7.5	11.4	34.0	31.5
23	Refined petroleum, nuclear fuel	3	..	78	89	18	13.0	..	100.0	87.4	85.7
24/25	Chemicals, rubber & plastics prod.	261	271	570	2 517	2 712	6.0	5.8	10.1	33.3	31.4
24	Chemical products	226	181	410	2 440	2 617	5.3	4.2	7.9	34.1	31.8
2423	Pharmaceuticals	3	3	50	1 953	2 060	0.1	0.1	1.1	30.3	27.8
25	Rubber and plastics products	35	90	160	77	96	30.4	26.6	36.9	18.6	23.0
26	Non-metallic mineral products	70	55	51	60	57	43.2	35.0	36.0	33.8	31.1
27/28	Basic & fabricated metals	90	65	80	116	146	9.4	7.6	8.6	22.4	13.0
27	Basic metals	52	49	58	95	109	25.6	17.3	17.9	29.4	28.6
28	Fabricated metal products	38	16	22	21	37	5.0	2.9	3.7	10.7	5.0
29/32	Machinery, Total	2 409	1 864	2 000	3 517	2 867	24.7	15.5	7.7	19.8	14.0
29/30	Non-electrical machinery	1 563	937	1 296	2 642	1 942	49.9	23.4	8.0	49.9	36.5
29	Non-electrical machinery nec	1 153	860	1 121	2 493	1 797	46.0	28.3	29.8	50.0	35.6
30	Office and computing machinery	410	76	174	149	145	65.5	8.0	1.4	48.4	54.3
31/32	Electrical & electronic equipment	846	927	704	875	925	12.8	11.6	7.3	7.0	6.1
31	Electrical machinery nec	752	828	603	733	865	86.3	93.6	89.9	90.6	52.7
32	Radio, TV & communications eq.	94	99	101	142	60	1.6	1.4	1.1	1.2	0.4
33	Scientific instruments	478	476	885	1 040	1 165	63.2	27.1	36.6	38.2	40.9
34/35	Transportation equipment	118	118	132	175	234	1.8	1.8	1.8	1.7	4.4
34	Motor vehicles		37	36	74	91	..	0.6	0.7	0.9	2.5
35	Other transport equipment	78	80	96	101	143	17.9	17.7	5.1	5.1	8.2
351	Shipbuilding & repairing	..	..	..	..	..	..	..	..	..	..
353	Aircraft and spacecraft	..	..	..	..	..	..	..	..	..	..
36/37	Other manufacturing	7	7	20	60	146	15.9	11.5	20.9	51.7	74.1
40/45	Construction, electricity, gas & water	..	..	84	..	297	..	..	13.8	..	35.8
50/55	Trade, repair, hotels & restaurants	101	131	128	267	285	30.0	40.8	40.1	58.7	59.9
65/74	Finance, insurance, business services	601	474	762	511	1 001	30.4	22.3	26.8	13.5	18.5
	OTHER ACTIVITIES	7	64	84	9	3	8.1	47.8	9.2	0.7	0.2
01/99	**GRAND TOTAL**	4 899	4 528	4 990	8 512	9 106	18.3	14.7	10.4	18.4	18.7

Total manufacturing by investing country	1992	1993	1994	1995	1996	As a % of total manufacturing by foreign affiliates				
						1992	1993	1994	1995	1996
All countries	4 187	3 856	3 933	7 725	7 517	100.0	100.0	100.0	100.0	100.0
United States	175	107	267	2 362	2 758	4.2	2.8	6.8	30.6	36.7
Canada	..	0	1	1	..	..	0.0	0.0	0.0	..
Mexico	..	..	..	..	..	..	..	..	..	..
Japan	13	14	14	7	4	0.3	0.4	0.4	0.1	0.1
Europe	3 998	3 735	3 608	5 349	4 676	95.5	96.9	91.7	69.2	62.2
European Union (15)	2 601	2 079	1 719	2 917	2 103	62.1	53.9	43.7	37.8	28.0
Belgium	1	1	4	4	..	0.0	0.0	0.1	0.0	..
France	69	62	63	84	109	1.7	1.6	1.6	1.1	1.5
Germany	304	374	405	336	441	7.3	9.7	10.3	4.3	5.9
Italy	..	..	11	6	..	..	..	0.3	0.1	..
Netherlands	1 529	1 141	773	1 805	923	36.5	29.6	19.6	23.4	12.3
Spain	..	..	..	..	..	..	..	..	..	..
Sweden	..	..	..	..	..	..	..	..	..	..
United Kingdom	277	106	76	279	295	6.6	2.7	1.9	3.6	3.9
Switzerland	1 399	1 596	1 825	2 249	2 482	33.4	41.4	46.4	29.1	33.0
Australia and New Zealand	..	..	..	..	..	..	..	..	..	..
Asia (non-OECD)	..	..	..	..	0	..	..	..	..	0.0
Latin America	..	..	..	..	..	..	..	..	..	..

Note: Majority foreign-owned **non-financial** firms with 50 or more employees. Source: Statistics Sweden's Structural Business Statistics. In 1992, ISIC 20/22 includes part of *Furniture* (361) and small part of ISIC 353 and 35 is included in ISIC 29/32. Unless given separately, ISIC 40/45 is included in *Other activities*. See country notes.
Firmes **non financières** sous contrôle étranger majoritaire de plus de 50 salariés. Source : Statistiques structurelles d'entreprises de l'office suédois de statistiques. En 1992, la CITI 20/22 comprend une partie de *Meubles* (361) et une petite partie de la CITI 353 et 35 est comprise dans la CITI 29/32. Sauf notification séparée, la CITI 40/45 est comprise dans *Autres activités*. Voir

Table 9. SWEDEN / SUÈDE

GROSS FIXED CAPITAL FORMATION / FORMATION BRUTE DE CAPITAL FIXE

By industry (ISIC Rev. 3)		FOREIGN AFFILIATES (Millions of SKr)					AS A % OF NATIONAL TOTAL				
		1992	1993	1994	1995	1996	1992	1993	1994	1995	1996
10/14	Mining & quarrying	2	8	56	101	90	0.2	0.5	3.3	5.2	5.3
15/37	TOTAL MANUFACTURING	4 227	4 380	5 560	10 973	12 536	14.6	14.1	14.4	20.4	20.1
15/16	Food, beverages, tobacco	782	1 169	1 020	1 171	1 045	23.5	32.3	29.4	28.5	30.5
17/19	Textiles, clothing, leather, footwear	89	95	118	71	89	25.2	27.1	27.8	13.4	13.3
20/22	Wood and paper products	650	555	476	583	795	9.0	6.8	4.6	3.6	4.4
20	Wood products	..	41	51	107	..	..	2.4	2.0	3.6	..
21/22	Paper, printing and publishing	..	514	425	476	..	..	8.0	5.5	3.6	..
23/25	Chemicals, Total	1 343	910	1 666	4 675	5 942	26.0	19.3	28.5	55.2	55.5
23	Refined petroleum, nuclear fuel	161	..	449	764	1 430	35.6	..	73.7	85.4	98.7
24/25	Chemicals, rubber & plastics prod.	1 182	721	1 217	3 911	4 512	25.0	16.9	23.2	51.6	48.7
24	Chemical products	1 071	580	1 024	3 652	4 270	28.8	17.1	26.0	58.8	57.2
2423	Pharmaceuticals	8	4	49	1 125	1 674	0.5	0.2	2.0	36.5	41.0
25	Rubber and plastics products	110	141	193	258	242	11.0	16.1	14.8	18.9	13.5
26	Non-metallic mineral products	135	80	184	383	344	29.5	24.0	37.2	48.7	38.7
27/28	Basic & fabricated metals	266	257	284	1 298	1 045	6.6	9.9	7.4	19.9	14.8
27	Basic metals	165	150	236	1 119	894	13.1	13.2	16.5	39.5	31.0
28	Fabricated metal products	101	107	48	179	151	3.6	7.3	2.0	4.8	3.6
29/32	Machinery, Total	569	924	1 379	2 014	2 244	16.8	19.9	18.8	24.3	26.4
29/30	Non-electrical machinery	208	396	906	1 416	1 667	12.3	16.3	22.4	31.9	32.2
29	Non-electrical machinery nec	178	371	760	1 400	1 641	11.0	16.6	20.9	32.7	33.0
30	Office and computing machinery	30	25	146	16	26	42.3	13.0	36.8	10.3	12.1
31/32	Electrical & electronic equipment	361	528	473	598	577	21.3	23.8	14.4	15.5	17.4
31	Electrical machinery nec	385	449	383	406	424	52.9	71.8	55.8	48.0	35.0
32	Radio, TV & communications eq.	- 24	79	90	192	153	-2.5	4.9	3.5	6.4	7.2
33	Scientific instruments	209	200	153	320	414	39.7	32.1	25.7	34.2	40.4
34/35	Transportation equipment	143	151	214	363	501	3.6	2.9	3.7	5.2	4.6
34	Motor vehicles	116	106	101	225	435	3.4	2.1	2.0	3.5	4.2
35	Other transport equipment	27	45	113	138	66	4.8	14.2	19.8	23.5	10.4
351	Shipbuilding & repairing	..	..	..	..	..	..	..	..	..	..
353	Aircraft and spacecraft	..	..	..	..	..	..	..	..	..	..
36/37	Other manufacturing	41	39	65	96	118	8.0	5.9	8.8	10.6	13.6
40/45	Construction, electricity, gas & water	..	345	87	93	147	..	2.9	0.7	0.6	0.9
50/55	Trade, repair, hotels & restaurants	2 023	2 250	1 930	2 617	3 330	17.0	20.0	15.6	17.2	18.8
65/74	Finance, insurance, business services	394	518	1 761	1 826	612	7.7	53.7	24.6	22.0	6.6
	OTHER ACTIVITIES	896	301	1 657	1 201	1 615	2.9	2.8	8.7	4.9	5.0
01/99	GRAND TOTAL	7 542	7 802	11 050	16 811	18 337	9.7	11.5	12.2	14.2	13.1

Total manufacturing by investing country						As a % of total manufacturing by foreign affiliates				
All countries	4 227	4 380	5 560	10 973	12 536	100.0	100.0	100.0	100.0	100.0
United States	..	624	903	1 962	2 853	..	14.2	16.2	17.9	22.8
Canada	..	..	..	..	..	..	..	..	..	..
Mexico	..	..	..	..	..	..	..	..	..	..
Japan	..	..	..	55	129	..	..	..	0.5	1.0
Europe	3 928	3 740	4 183	8 252	8 090	92.9	85.4	75.2	75.2	64.5
European Union (15)	2 391	2 242	2 681	6 064	6 009	56.6	51.2	48.2	55.3	47.9
Belgium	..	..	..	..	..	..	..	..	..	..
France	..	174	256	198	389	..	4.0	4.6	1.8	3.1
Germany	..	213	191	254	492	..	4.9	3.4	2.3	3.9
Italy	..	..	..	..	..	..	..	..	..	..
Netherlands	..	880	1 065	1 926	2 137	..	20.1	19.2	17.6	17.0
Spain	..	..	..	..	..	..	..	..	..	..
Sweden	..	..	..	..	..	..	..	..	..	..
United Kingdom	..	116	259	1 519	1 006	..	2.6	4.7	13.8	8.0
Switzerland	..	962	1 135	1 340	1 233	..	22.0	20.4	12.2	9.8
Australia and New Zealand	..	..	..	..	..	..	..	..	..	..
Asia (non-OECD)	..	..	..	..	1 111	..	..	..	..	8.9
Latin America	..	..	..	..	..	..	..	..	..	..

Note: Majority foreign-owned **non-financial** firms. Source: Statistics Sweden's Structural Business Statistics. In 1992, ISIC 20/22 includes part of *Furniture* (361), small part of ISIC 353 and 35 is included in ISIC 29/32 and ISIC 40/45 is included in *Other activities*. See country notes.
Firmes **non financières** sous contrôle étranger majoritaire. Source : Statistiques structurelles d'entreprises de l'office suédois de statistiques. En 1992, la CITI 20/22 comprend une partie de *Meubles* (361), une petite partie de la CITI 353 et 35 est comprise dans la CITI 29/32 et la CITI 40/45 est comprise dans *Autres activités*. Voir les notes par pays.

Table 10. SWEDEN / SUÈDE

TOTAL EXPORTS / EXPORTATIONS TOTALES

By industry (ISIC Rev. 3)	FOREIGN AFFILIATES (Millions of SKr)					AS A % OF NATIONAL TOTAL				
	1992	1993	1994	1995	1996	1992	1993	1994	1995	1996
10/14 Mining & quarrying	284	226	272	629	715	5.0	4.5	4.4	9.9	10.1
15/37 **TOTAL MANUFACTURING**	**61 479**	**65 333**	**78 415**	**121 803**	**108 892**	**21.1**	**18.8**	**17.8**	**23.4**	**20.7**
15/16 Food, beverages, tobacco	1 951	2 499	2 929	3 541	3 963	42.8	35.8	35.4	34.8	36.8
17/19 Textiles, clothing, leather, footwear	1 211	1 234	1 442	1 576	1 528	30.4	33.3	33.0	34.4	31.7
20/22 Wood and paper products	6 911	8 768	3 694	4 678	6 105	11.2	12.1	4.6	5.1	7.6
20 Wood products	..	..	..	..	..	..	..	..	..	..
21/22 Paper, printing and publishing	..	..	..	..	..	..	..	..	..	..
23/25 Chemicals, Total	10 769	11 938	18 288	31 770	29 218	29.2	27.9	35.1	55.5	53.4
23 Refined petroleum, nuclear fuel	14		680	828	1 568	0.7		48.3	57.3	96.5
24/25 Chemicals, rubber & plastics prod.	10 755	11 517	17 608	30 942	27 650	30.8	28.2	34.8	55.4	52.0
24 Chemical products	9 246	9 025	15 042	28 429	25 289	30.7	27.6	36.8	63.1	60.1
2423 Pharmaceuticals	101	71	709	8 601	8 734	0.8	0.4	3.2	39.5	39.8
25 Rubber and plastics products	1 510	2 492	2 566	2 512	2 360	31.2	30.4	26.1	23.4	21.4
26 Non-metallic mineral products	1 269	1 482	1 852	2 734	2 624	51.3	47.1	51.0	60.9	58.4
27/28 Basic & fabricated metals	6 199	6 898	8 966	20 479	17 565	17.8	17.9	18.3	35.8	31.8
27 Basic metals	4 336	5 656	7 603	18 294	15 197	23.9	23.5	25.0	50.8	46.2
28 Fabricated metal products	1 863	1 242	1 363	2 185	2 368	11.2	8.6	7.3	10.3	10.6
29/32 Machinery, Total	27 300	25 654	32 281	44 680	35 596	36.7	28.1	25.6	29.9	21.1
29/30 Non-electrical machinery	20 951	18 030	25 806	37 307	27 229	46.6	33.2	34.2	44.2	32.3
29 Non-electrical machinery nec	16 495	17 581	25 039	36 177	25 979	43.0	34.3	34.7	44.4	32.0
30 Office and computing machinery	4 456	449	767	1 130	1 250	67.9	14.8	23.7	37.9	40.0
31/32 Electrical & electronic equipment	6 349	7 624	6 475	7 373	8 367	21.6	20.6	12.8	11.3	9.9
31 Electrical machinery nec	5 898	6 729	4 889	5 727	6 686	62.4	74.2	62.5	62.5	54.5
32 Radio, TV & communications eq.	451	895	1 586	1 646	1 681	2.3	3.2	3.7	2.9	2.3
33 Scientific instruments	3 473	3 843	5 576	6 534	6 558	50.9	38.5	41.8	47.8	44.8
34/35 Transportation equipment	2 196	2 686	2 754	4 789	4 658	3.5	3.6	2.7	3.8	3.7
34 Motor vehicles	1 014	1 478	1 335	2 886	2 669	1.8	2.1	1.4	2.5	2.3
35 Other transport equipment	1 182	1 208	1 419	1 903	1 989	19.8	28.9	23.2	21.1	20.1
351 Shipbuilding & repairing	..	..	..	..	..	..	..	..	..	..
353 Aircraft and spacecraft	..	..	..	..	..	..	..	..	..	..
36/37 Other manufacturing	201	331	634	1 023	1 077	7.6	8.3	12.6	18.1	16.9
40/45 Construction, electricity, gas & water	..	503	485	626	313	..	21.2	17.9	22.0	9.3
50/55 Trade, repair, hotels & restaurants	12 155	16 406	25 967	28 039	36 119	26.1	30.5	41.8	54.8	53.3
65/74 Finance, insurance, business services	2 412	1 649	2 751	2 882	3 117	45.1	30.9	35.6	45.3	37.1
OTHER ACTIVITIES	1 501	1 212	2 081	1 372	2 039	22.6	20.6	34.7	15.9	24.2
01/99 **GRAND TOTAL**	**77 831**	**85 330**	**109 972**	**155 351**	**151 199**	**21.9**	**20.3**	**20.9**	**26.1**	**24.4**

Total manufacturing by investing country						As a % of total manufacturing by foreign affiliates				
All countries	**61 479**	**65 333**	**78 415**	**121 803**	**108 892**	**100.0**	**100.0**	**100.0**	**100.0**	**100.0**
United States	8 645	4 832	6 433	19 267	21 270	14.1	7.4	8.2	15.8	19.5
Canada	..	..	..	..	296	..	..	..	..	0.3
Mexico	..	..	..	..	..	..	..	..	..	..
Japan	..	..	..	421	623	..	..	..	0.3	0.6
Europe	52 252	59 971	68 555	101 404	86 601	85.0	91.8	87.4	83.3	79.5
European Union (15)	35 353	40 288	48 595	69 549	56 885	57.5	61.7	62.0	57.1	52.2
Belgium	..	..	..	254	268	..	..	..	0.2	0.2
France	1 884	1 942	2 513	3 332	2 927	3.1	3.0	3.2	2.7	2.7
Germany	3 939	4 313	5 078	5 772	6 844	6.4	6.6	6.5	4.7	6.3
Italy	..	..	..	541	597	..	..	..	0.4	0.5
Netherlands	13 018	14 838	17 241	21 520	12 210	21.2	22.7	22.0	17.7	11.2
Spain	..	..	..	..	91	..	..	..	..	0.1
Sweden	..	..	..	..	..	..	..	..	..	..
United Kingdom	3 030	3 403	5 078	16 398	16 874	4.9	5.2	6.5	13.5	15.5
Switzerland	12 530	15 601	16 279	20 780	20 498	20.4	23.9	20.8	17.1	18.8
Australia and New Zealand	..	..	..	..	..	..	..	..	..	..
Asia (non-OECD)	..	..	..	..	185	..	..	..	..	0.2
Latin America	..	..	..	..	..	..	..	..	..	..

Note: Majority foreign-owned **non-financial** firms. Source: Statistics Sweden's Structural Business Statistics and Trade Statistics. In 1992, ISIC 20/22 includes part of *Furniture* (361), small part of ISIC 353 and 35 is included in ISIC 29/32 and ISIC 40/45 is included in *Other activities*. See country notes.
Firmes **non financières** sous contrôle étranger majoritaire. Source : office suédois de statistiques, Statistiques structurelles d'entreprises et Statistiques du commerce. En 1992, la CITI 20/22 comprend une partie de *Meubles* (361), une petite partie de la CITI 353 et 35 est comprise dans la CITI 29/32 et la CITI 40/45 est comprise dans *Autres activités*. Voir les notes par pays.

Table 11. SWEDEN / SUÈDE

TOTAL IMPORTS / IMPORTATIONS TOTALES

By industry (ISIC Rev. 3)		FOREIGN AFFILIATES (Millions of SKr)					AS A % OF NATIONAL TOTAL				
		1992	1993	1994	1995	1996	1992	1993	1994	1995	1996
10/14	Mining & quarrying	..	..	..	59	80	..	..	..	3.3	4.8
15/37	TOTAL MANUFACTURING	25 029	28 788	34 503	50 423	50 334	32.4	28.6	28.2	29.4	30.3
15/16	Food, beverages, tobacco	..	..	..	5 246	5 877	..	..	..	44.3	49.7
17/19	Textiles, clothing, leather, footwear	..	..	..	704	859	..	..	..	15.5	23.2
20/22	Wood and paper products	..	..	..	2 121	2 299	..	..	..	19.7	24.4
20	Wood products	..	..	..			..	..	..		
21/22	Paper, printing and publishing	..	..	..	..	..	..	..	..	..	..
23/25	Chemicals, Total	..	..	..	14 513	15 706	..	..	..	54.5	58.2
23	Refined petroleum, nuclear fuel	..	..	..	1 762	2 457	..	..	..	87.2	96.8
24/25	Chemicals, rubber & plastics prod.	..	..	..	12 751	13 249	..	..	..	51.8	54.2
24	Chemical products	..	..	..	11 301	11 736	..	..	..	58.7	61.4
2423	Pharmaceuticals	..	..	..	1 333	1 444	..	..	..	20.6	21.0
25	Rubber and plastics products	..	..	..	1 449	1 513	..	..	..	27.1	28.3
26	Non-metallic mineral products	..	..	..	1 524	1 368	..	..	..	51.9	54.9
27/28	Basic & fabricated metals	..	..	..	10 237	8 749	..	..	..	45.8	44.1
27	Basic metals	..	..	..	8 520	7 382	..	..	..	57.5	56.0
28	Fabricated metal products	..	..	..	1 717	1 367	..	..	..	22.8	20.6
29/32	Machinery, Total	..	..	..	10 566	9 686	..	..	..	27.4	25.2
29/30	Non-electrical machinery	..	..	..	6 652	6 146	..	..	..	33.5	33.7
29	Non-electrical machinery nec	..	..	..	6 432	5 918	..	..	..	33.5	34.0
30	Office and computing machinery	..	..	..	220	228	..	..	..	33.8	28.4
31/32	Electrical & electronic equipment	..	..	..	3 914	3 540	..	..	..	21.0	17.5
31	Electrical machinery nec	..	..	..	2 711	2 431	..	..	..	55.8	44.4
32	Radio, TV & communications eq.	..	..	..	1 203	1 109	..	..	..	8.7	7.5
33	Scientific instruments	..	..	..	2 318	2 513	..	..	..	45.5	51.0
34/35	Transportation equipment	..	..	..	2 192	2 288	..	..	..	4.7	5.0
34	Motor vehicles	..	..	..	1 816	1 855	..	..	..	4.9	5.1
35	Other transport equipment	..	..	..	376	433	..	..	..	4.2	4.7
351	Shipbuilding & repairing	..	..	..	..	..	..	..	..	..	..
353	Aircraft and spacecraft	..	..	..	..	..	..	..	..	..	..
36/37	Other manufacturing	..	..	..	1 001	989	..	..	..	35.2	36.4
40/45	Construction, electricity, gas & water	..	..	..	369	351	..	..	..	10.9	6.5
50/55	Trade, repair, hotels & restaurants	..	..	..	92 001	103 800	..	..	..	47.5	50.6
65/74	Finance, insurance, business services	..	..	..	3 431	2 382	..	..	..	71.9	42.7
	OTHER ACTIVITIES	..	..	..	363	438	..	..	..	3.4	3.8
01/99	GRAND TOTAL	..	..	..	146 645	157 385	..	..	..	38.0	39.8

Total manufacturing by investing country	1992	1993	1994	1995	1996	As a % of total manufacturing by foreign affiliates				
All countries	25 029	28 788	34 503	50 423	50 334	100.0	100.0	100.0	100.0	100.0
United States	..	..	..	..	..	..	..	..	..	..
Canada	..	..	..	..	..	..	..	..	..	..
Mexico	..	..	..	..	..	..	..	..	..	..
Japan	..	..	..	..	..	..	..	..	..	..
Europe	..	..	..	..	..	..	..	..	..	..
European Union (15)	..	..	..	..	..	..	..	..	..	..
Belgium	..	..	..	..	..	..	..	..	..	..
France	..	..	..	..	..	..	..	..	..	..
Germany	..	..	..	..	..	..	..	..	..	..
Italy	..	..	..	..	..	..	..	..	..	..
Netherlands	..	..	..	..	..	..	..	..	..	..
Spain	..	..	..	..	..	..	..	..	..	..
Sweden	..	..	..	..	..	..	..	..	..	..
United Kingdom	..	..	..	..	..	..	..	..	..	..
Switzerland	..	..	..	..	..	..	..	..	..	..
Australia and New Zealand	..	..	..	..	..	..	..	..	..	..
Asia (non-OECD)	..	..	..	..	..	..	..	..	..	..
Latin America	..	..	..	..	..	..	..	..	..	..

Note: Majority foreign-owned **non-financial** firms. Imports of goods. Source: Statistics Sweden's Trade Statistics.
Firmes **non financières** sous contrôle étranger majoritaire. Importations de biens. Source : Statistiques du commerce de l'office suédois de statistiques.

Table 12. SWEDEN / SUÈDE

INTRA-FIRM EXPORTS / EXPORTATIONS INTRA-FIRME

By industry (ISIC Rev. 3)		FOREIGN AFFILIATES (Millions of SKr)									
		1987	1988	1989	1990	1991	1992	1993	1994	1995	1996
10/14	Mining & quarrying	..	..	..	152	164	174	161	20	373	418
15/37	**TOTAL MANUFACTURING**	..	..	..	23 911	24 357	26 700	27 114	33 021	57 021	58 275
15/16	Food, beverages, tobacco	..	..	..	409	549	667	809	1 670	2 325	2 484
17/19	Textiles, clothing, leather, footwear	..	..	..	22	287	308	243	251	432	328
20/22	Wood and paper products	..	..	..	350	327	241	465	620	568	1 820
20	Wood products	..	..	..	..	..	..	60	79	94	..
21/22	Paper, printing and publishing	..	..	..	..	..	..	405	541	474	..
23/25	Chemicals, Total	..	..	..	2 504	3 026	5 259	5 470	8 786	16 511	15 792
23	Refined petroleum, nuclear fuel	..	..	..	4	3	2	..	32	203	355
24/25	Chemicals, rubber & plastics prod.	..	..	..	2 500	3 023	5 257	5 443	8 754	16 308	15 437
24	Chemical products	..	..	..	2 369	2 646	4 576	4 311	7 961	15 052	14 071
2423	Pharmaceuticals	..	..	..	28	19	20	17	429	5 657	5 868
25	Rubber and plastics products	..	..	..	131	377	681	1 149	1 221	1 256	1 366
26	Non-metallic mineral products	..	..	..	558	338	408	400	500	863	859
27/28	Basic & fabricated metals	..	..	..	1 638	2 425	2 041	2 118	3 029	9 874	9 967
27	Basic metals	..	..	..	1 069	1 434	1 368	1 856	2 780	9 212	9 090
28	Fabricated metal products	..	..	..	569	991	673	262	249	662	877
29/32	Machinery, Total	..	..	..	17 271	16 495	14 367	13 932	13 609	19 997	20 579
29/30	Non-electrical machinery	..	..	..	11 874	11 065	10 577	10 107	9 636	15 720	15 361
29	Non-electrical machinery nec	..	..	..	6 394	6 408	6 276	9 743	8 940	14 899	14 523
30	Office and computing machinery	..	..	..	5 480	4 657	4 301	364	696	821	838
31/32	Electrical & electronic equipment	..	..	..	5 397	5 430	3 790	3 825	3 973	4 277	5 218
31	Electrical machinery nec	..	..	..	2 723	3 670	3 692	3 385	2 798	3 264	4 093
32	Radio, TV & communications eq.	..	..	..	2 674	1 760	98	440	1 175	1 013	1 125
33	Scientific instruments	..	..	..	500	405	2 811	2 848	3 606	4 295	4 627
34/35	Transportation equipment	..	..	..	585	461	524	702	712	1 675	1 319
34	Motor vehicles	..	..	..	164	141	151	370	236	966	642
35	Other transport equipment	..	..	..	421	320	373	332	476	709	677
351	Shipbuilding & repairing	..	..	..	..	..	..	16	43	..	..
353	Aircraft and spacecraft	..	..	..	..	..	..	..	..	..	..
36/37	Other manufacturing	..	..	..	73	46	75	129	239	481	502
40/45	Construction, electricity, gas & water	..	..	..	..	..	..	..	..	..	1
50/55	Trade, repair, hotels & restaurants	..	..	..	1 831	1 922	3 027	5 117	4 775	6 142	7 278
65/74	Finance, insurance, business services	..	..	..	313	696	482	555	1 298	992	1 581
	OTHER ACTIVITIES	..	..	..	414	172	274	659	1 048	1 116	1 218
01/99	**GRAND TOTAL**	..	..	..	26 620	27 311	30 656	33 606	40 161	65 644	68 771

Total manufacturing by investing country

	1987	1988	1989	1990	1991	1992	1993	1994	1995	1996
All countries	..	..	..	23 911	24 357	26 700	27 114	33 021	57 021	58 275
United States	..	..	..	6 476	5 722	5 582	1 932	3 152	11 245	12 690
Canada	..	..	..	30	26	23	24	..	24	23
Mexico	..	..	..	..	..	..	..	..	..	..
Japan	..	..	..	..	4	9	31	47	49	134
Europe	..	..	..	17 405	18 605	21 086	25 128	29 552	45 598	45 415
European Union (15)	..	..	..	10 444	10 982	13 869	16 998	19 918	29 027	29 201
Belgium	..	..	..	66	54	22	14	..	49	35
France	..	..	..	116	281	719	963	1 412	1 713	1 699
Germany	..	..	..	1 868	2 248	2 513	2 678	3 142	3 426	4 437
Italy	..	..	..	51	51	55	76	..	63	95
Netherlands	..	..	..	3 060	3 663	4 164	5 223	4 955	5 994	5 678
Spain	..	..	..	..	..	..	..	..	..	..
Sweden	..	..	..	..	..	..	..	..	..	..
United Kingdom	..	..	..	658	820	1 150	1 176	1 707	9 481	9 873
Switzerland	..	..	..	6 061	6 262	6 032	7 216	8 747	11 724	11 621
Australia and New Zealand	..	..	..	..	..	..	..	..	..	..
Asia (non-OECD)	..	..	..	..	..	..	..	..	..	..
Latin America	..	..	..	..	..	..	..	..	..	0

Note: Majority foreign-owned **non-financial** firms. Source: Statistics Sweden's Structural Business Statistics.
Firmes **non financières** sous contrôle étranger majoritaire. Source : Statistiques structurelles d'entreprises de l'office suédois de statistiques.

Table 14. SWEDEN / SUÈDE

GROSS OPERATING SURPLUS / EXCÉDENT BRUT D'EXPLOITATION

By industry (ISIC Rev. 3)		FOREIGN AFFILIATES (Millions of SKr)					AS A % OF NATIONAL TOTAL				
		1992	1993	1994	1995	1996	1992	1993	1994	1995	1996
10/14	Mining & quarrying	68	90	179	275	146	4.4	6.7	9.3	10.1	7.2
15/37	**TOTAL MANUFACTURING**	**8 236**	**11 978**	**17 358**	**25 915**	**20 840**	**18.3**	**17.0**	**13.3**	**20.7**	**22.7**
15/16	Food, beverages, tobacco	1 741	2 352	2 441	2 496	3 549	21.6	27.7	27.5	28.6	40.6
17/19	Textiles, clothing, leather, footwear	205	214	406	306	386	29.5	21.7	30.2	18.7	32.4
20/22	Wood and paper products	1 176	1 382	1 367	1 634	1 506	10.8	8.4	4.3	4.3	8.0
20	Wood products	..	103	197	161	..	..	3.3	3.1	2.8	..
21/22	Paper, printing and publishing	..	1 279	1 170	1 473	..	..	9.6	4.6	4.6	..
23/25	Chemicals, Total	1 647	2 986	5 180	8 334	6 586	14.3	20.7	28.0	44.8	43.7
23	Refined petroleum, nuclear fuel	113	..	491	611	776	12.3	..	57.9	82.9	88.8
24/25	Chemicals, rubber & plastics prod.	1 534	2 701	4 689	7 723	5 810	14.5	20.3	26.5	43.3	41.0
24	Chemical products	1 378	2 029	4 325	7 061	5 273	14.9	16.9	29.3	51.5	45.9
2423	Pharmaceuticals	3	43	197	1 810	1 491	0.1	0.6	2.2	25.3	23.9
25	Rubber and plastics products	155	672	364	662	536	11.4	50.3	12.4	16.0	19.9
26	Non-metallic mineral products	296	427	635	788	714	19.8	23.7	34.2	37.5	34.7
27/28	Basic & fabricated metals	352	911	1 339	4 438	1 589	7.5	11.0	9.5	23.1	12.4
27	Basic metals	133	637	1 036	3 953	1 165	25.9	17.5	15.0	39.0	23.6
28	Fabricated metal products	219	274	303	485	424	5.2	5.9	4.2	5.4	5.4
29/32	Machinery, Total	2 139	2 682	4 608	5 669	4 449	25.8	21.2	21.5	26.3	21.6
29/30	Non-electrical machinery	1 328	1 428	3 167	4 382	3 454	26.2	19.0	21.4	33.2	26.9
29	Non-electrical machinery nec	207	1 476	3 089	4 246	3 331	5.7	20.5	22.1	32.2	27.0
30	Office and computing machinery	1 121	- 48	78	136	123	79.1	-14.9	9.3	1700.0	26.0
31/32	Electrical & electronic equipment	811	1 254	1 441	1 287	995	25.1	24.5	21.9	15.4	12.8
31	Electrical machinery nec	755	1 170	1 329	1 146	989	50.9	55.0	54.8	37.8	36.7
32	Radio, TV & communications eq.	56	84	112	141	6	3.2	2.8	2.7	2.6	0.1
33	Scientific instruments	361	615	884	1 267	1 228	53.0	30.0	31.3	33.5	36.4
34/35	Transportation equipment	269	328	631	766	401	-13.0	8.3	2.2	8.0	5.6
34	Motor vehicles	126	187	300	620	281	-4.5	6.6	3.0	7.1	4.3
35	Other transport equipment	143	141	331	146	120	19.7	12.6	1.8	17.6	20.6
351	Shipbuilding & repairing	..	..	..	..	..	..	..	..	..	..
353	Aircraft and spacecraft	..	..	..	..	..	..	..	..	..	..
36/37	Other manufacturing	49	81	- 132	217	431	6.2	5.8	-8.5	9.6	19.9
40/45	Construction, electricity, gas & water	..	17	475	608	2 710	..	0.0	1.3	1.4	6.7
50/55	Trade, repair, hotels & restaurants	3 392	5 802	9 746	9 247	11 031	13.6	16.2	21.9	19.4	22.7
65/74	Finance, insurance, business services	1 133	1 667	3 205	3 645	2 529	8.6	9.6	15.7	14.2	12.2
	OTHER ACTIVITIES	1 003	1 316	1 751	633	1 372	1.9	5.7	5.8	2.0	4.2
01/99	**GRAND TOTAL**	**13 832**	**20 869**	**32 714**	**40 323**	**38 628**	**10.0**	**11.4**	**12.4**	**14.6**	**16.4**

Total manufacturing by investing country	1992	1993	1994	1995	1996	As a % of total manufacturing by foreign affiliates				
						1992	1993	1994	1995	1996
All countries	**8 236**	**11 978**	**17 358**	**25 915**	**20 840**	**100.0**	**100.0**	**100.0**	**100.0**	**100.0**
United States	..	1 085	1 699	4 247	4 241	..	9.1	9.8	16.4	20.4
Canada	..	..	..	..	..	..	..	..	..	..
Mexico	..	..	..	..	..	..	..	..	..	..
Japan	..	..	..	195	103	..	..	..	0.8	0.5
Europe	6 350	10 819	15 063	20 998	15 121	77.1	90.3	86.8	81.0	72.6
European Union (15)	3 802	7 354	11 036	15 180	10 805	46.2	61.4	63.6	58.6	51.8
Belgium	..	..	..	..	..	..	..	..	..	..
France	..	626	868	989	809	..	5.2	5.0	3.8	3.9
Germany	..	873	1 339	1 533	1 286	..	7.3	7.7	5.9	6.2
Italy	..	..	..	..	..	..	..	..	..	..
Netherlands	..	2 660	3 977	4 074	2 948	..	22.2	22.9	15.7	14.1
Spain	..	..	..	..	..	..	..	..	..	..
Sweden	..	..	..	..	..	..	..	..	..	..
United Kingdom	..	367	855	3 917	1 987	..	3.1	4.9	15.1	9.5
Switzerland	..	2 473	3 069	3 126	3 000	..	20.6	17.7	12.1	14.4
Australia and New Zealand	..	..	..	..	..	..	..	..	..	..
Asia (non-OECD)	..	..	..	..	370	..	..	..	..	1.8
Latin America	..	..	..	..	..	..	..	..	..	..

Note: Majority foreign-owned **non-financial** firms. Source: Statistics Sweden's Structural Business Statistics. In 1992, ISIC 20/22 includes part of *Furniture* (361), small part of ISIC 353 and 35 is included in ISIC 29/32 and ISIC 40/45 is included in *Other activities*. See country notes.
Firmes **non financières** sous contrôle étranger majoritaire. Source : Statistiques structurelles d'entreprises de l'office suédois de statistiques. En 1992, la CITI 20/22 comprend une partie de *Meubles* (361), une petite partie de la CITI 353 et 35 est comprise dans la CITI 29/32 et la CITI 40/45 est comprise dans *Autres activités*. Voir les notes par pays.

Table 18. SWEDEN / SUÈDE

CAPITAL UNDER FOREIGN INFLUENCE / CAPITAL SOUS INFLUENCE ÉTRANGÈRE

By industry (ISIC Rev. 3)		1987	1988	1989	1990	1991	1992	1993	1994	1995	1996
					FOREIGN AFFILIATES *(Millions of SKr)*						
10/14	Mining & quarrying	..	..	..	418	344	326	615	737	1 094	1 061
15/37	**TOTAL MANUFACTURING**	..	..	..	**117375**	**149412**	**140 980**	**137 635**	**166 307**	**238 636**	**229 865**
15/16	Food, beverages, tobacco	..	..	..	8069	9699	14 708	18 832	19 133	21 420	26 134
17/19	Textiles, clothing, leather, footwear	..	..	..	1736	2057	2 013	2 016	2 473	2 353	2 763
20/22	Wood and paper products	..	..	..	9373	9081	10 290	10 732	7 704	11 244	11 422
20	Wood products	..	..	..	..	..	..	616	794	888	3 000
21/22	Paper, printing and publishing	..	..	..	..	..	..	10 116	6 910	10 356	8 422
23/25	Chemicals, Total	..	..	..	18723	25766	21 864	23 383	51 531	67 502	68 831
23	Refined petroleum, nuclear fuel	..	..	..	504	569	650	..	3 331	4 732	6 911
24/25	Chemicals, rubber & plastics prod.	..	..	..	18219	25197	21 214	23 380	48 200	62 770	61 920
24	Chemical products	..	..	..	16020	22408	19 057	18 152	44 873	59 540	58 696
2423	Pharmaceuticals	..	..	..	762	426	469	451	864	21 926	22 284
25	Rubber and plastics products	..	..	..	2200	2789	2 157	3 498	3 327	3 230	3 224
26	Non-metallic mineral products	..	..	..	5681	5203	5 133	5 270	5 230	5 886	5 711
27/28	Basic & fabricated metals	..	..	..	7533	8330	9 024	7 256	8 391	23 154	22 852
27	Basic metals	..	..	..	2373	3752	4 982	4 787	5 765	19 703	19 322
28	Fabricated metal products	..	..	..	5160	4578	4 042	2 469	2 626	3 451	3 530
29/32	Machinery, Total	..	..	..	60587	82405	67 067	58 653	59 230	89 765	72 989
29/30	Non-electrical machinery	..	..	..	30318	51861	36 492	27 580	32 200	44 661	34 272
29	Non-electrical machinery nec	..	..	..	21988	41664	29 344	26 536	30 357	43 496	33 237
30	Office and computing machinery	..	..	..	8330	10197	7 148	1 044	1 843	1 165	1 035
31/32	Electrical & electronic equipment	..	..	..	30269	30544	30 575	31 073	27 030	45 104	38 717
31	Electrical machinery nec	..	..	..	25305	26855	29 626	29 454	25 409	43 186	36 731
32	Radio, TV & communications eq.	..	..	..	4964	3689	949	1 619	1 621	1 918	1 986
33	Scientific instruments	..	..	..	1093	968	4 365	4 418	5 833	7 360	8 879
34/35	Transportation equipment	..	..	..	3890	5383	5 812	5 840	5 205	7 529	7 407
34	Motor vehicles	..	..	..	1434	1660	1 988	2 238	1 649	3 923	3 743
35	Other transport equipment	..	..	..	2456	3723	3 824	3 602	3 556	3 606	3 664
351	Shipbuilding & repairing	..	..	..	..	..	..	..	..	..	..
353	Aircraft and spacecraft	..	..	..	..	..	..	..	..	..	..
36/37	Other manufacturing	..	..	..	690	520	704	1 235	1 577	2 423	2 877
40/45	Construction, electricity, gas & water	..	..	..	..	..	..	5 284	13 492	6 141	36 598
50/55	Trade, repair, hotels & restaurants	..	..	..	65233	63688	62 245	71 096	91 411	103 215	121 400
65/74	Finance, insurance, business services	..	..	..	20285	21793	20 735	57 034	78 843	86 807	99 121
	OTHER ACTIVITIES	..	..	..	11669	11904	21 657	13 048	15 979	14 050	20 578
01/99	**GRAND TOTAL**	..	..	..	**214981**	**247141**	**245 942**	**284 712**	**366 770**	**449 943**	**508 623**

Total manufacturing by investing country

	1987	1988	1989	1990	1991	1992	1993	1994	1995	1996
All countries	..	..	..	117375	149412	140 980	137 635	166 307	238 636	229 865
United States	..	..	..	..	..	..	..	12 394	39 382	44 325
Canada	..	..	..	..	..	..	..	..	..	..
Mexico	..	..	..	..	..	..	..	..	..	..
Japan	..	..	..	..	..	..	..	965	1 397	1 098
Europe	..	..	..	104052	134435	125 498	126 612	149 757	193 883	173 079
European Union (15)	..	..	..	51310	80426	69 207	75 240	100 972	117 192	105 405
Belgium	..	..	..	..	..	..	..	..	..	..
France	..	..	..	..	..	..	..	4 774	5 257	5 531
Germany	..	..	..	..	..	..	..	7 267	9 025	9 051
Italy	..	..	..	..	..	..	..	..	..	..
Netherlands	..	..	..	..	..	..	..	51 442	47 419	34 155
Spain	..	..	..	..	..	..	..	..	..	..
Sweden	..	..	..	..	..	..	..	..	..	..
United Kingdom	..	..	..	..	..	..	..	6 542	22 109	24 232
Switzerland	..	..	..	..	..	..	..	42 093	62 987	55 922
Australia and New Zealand	..	..	..	..	..	..	..	..	..	..
Asia (non-OECD)	..	..	..	..	..	..	..	2 133	..	4 106
Latin America	..	..	..	..	..	..	..	..	0	0

Note: Majority foreign-owned **non-financial** firms. Source: Statistics Sweden's Structural Business Statistics. Up to 1992, ISIC 20/22 includes part of *Furniture* (361), small part of ISIC 353 and 35 is included in ISIC 29/32 and ISIC 40/45 is included in *Other activities*. See country notes.
Firmes **non financières** sous contrôle étranger majoritaire. Source : Statistiques structurelles d'entreprises de l'office suédois de statistiques. Jusqu'en 1992, la CITI 20/22 comprend une partie de *Meubles* (361), une petite partie de la CITI 353 et 35 est comprise dans la CITI 29/32 et la CITI 40/45 est comprise dans *Autres activités*. Voir les notes par pays.

SWEDEN

Source

As of 1 July 1994, statistics on international business, *i.e.* Swedish groups with subsidiaries abroad and foreign-owned enterprises in Sweden, have an official status and are regularly produced and published. The Swedish National Board for Industrial and Technical Development, NUTEK, is the governmental agency responsible for the production of these official statistics. The surveys are carried out in co-operation with Statistics Sweden.

From reference year 1996, data on foreign-owned affiliates are based on annual questionnaires to all parent companies as well as to all branches located in Sweden. Coverage has been extended over time: questionnaires were sent to 1 in 4 parent companies in the 1980's and the beginning of the 1990's; and to about 1 in 2 in 1995. Greater efforts have also been made to cover new foreign-owned affiliates. The increase in the number of enterprises and the number of employees in 1995 and 1996 partly results from the improved coverage.

The data refer to majority foreign-owned enterprises, *i.e.* enterprises in which a foreign investor owns more than 50% of the voting power. The reporting unit is, in most cases, the enterprise. In 1996, 11% of the units were branches.

NUTEK's Statistics on Foreign-owned Enterprises is based on data from three sources (in addition to the survey on ownership):

1) Statistic Sweden's Central Register of Enterprises and Establishments. The register on Foreign-owned Enterprises includes all foreign-owned enterprises and branches, except for the period 1990-92, when branches were not included. The register is used for the variables *Number of enterprises* (Table 1*a*) and *Number of employees* (Table 2*a*). These tables provide a better coverage on these variables, but should not be mixed with other tables.

2) Statistics Sweden's Structural Business Statistics. All non-financial enterprises with on annual average 20 or more employees (manufacturing industry) and 50 employees or more (service sector) are surveyed annually. These statistics are based on data from annual reports and questionnaires on exports, revenues and costs, R&D expenditure etc. Since the 1996 reference year, enterprises with less than 20 (manufacturing) / 50 employees (services) are surveyed using tax returns. Collection of these data is mandatory for all Swedish enterprises. Data are not included for real estate management (ISIC 70) or for financial enterprises. The Structural Business Statistics have been used for all variables including *Number of enterprises* (Table 1*b*) and *Number of employees* (Table 2*b*).

3) Statistics Sweden's Trade Statistics. Exports of goods for small enterprises and all data regarding imports are taken from this register.

Statistics on International Business are published by NUTEK/Statistics Sweden. Related articles are published in English in NUTEK's annual report *Swedish Industry and Industrial Policy*. All publications from NUTEK are available at NUTEK's homepage, www.nutek.se.

National totals: data are provided by NUTEK/Statistics Sweden and are fully compatible with foreign affiliates' data.

Industrial classification

For all variables, the data are classified according to the principal industrial activity of the affilite in Sweden. The whole business sector is surveyed.

The industrial classification used for Swedish tables is ISIC Revision 3, equivalent to NACE Revision 1.

Conversion to ISIC Revision 3 implies notes to all variables for the year 1992:

- Part of *Furniture* (361) is included in *Wood and paper products* (20/22).

- Part of *Machinery and equipment n.e.c. except electrical* (3829 of ISIC Revision 2) is excluded from *Other transport equipment* (35) and from *Aircraft and spacecraft* (353) and included in *Machinery, Total* (29/32).

- *Construction, electricity, gas and water supply* (40/45) is not available separately and is included in *Other activities*.

Variables

- *Number of enterprises* in Table 1*a* is defined as all foreign-owned enterprises which are controlled by a foreign investor to the extent of more than 50% of the voting power. *Number of enterprises* in Table 1*b* has the same definition but does not include financial enterprises and real estate management. Further, enterprises with no employees and turnover of less than SEK 50 000 according to the VAT register are excluded. The enterprise is the smallest legal unit in the corporate sector for which data on balance sheet and on profit and loss can be obtained.

- *Number of employees* in Table 2*a* is defined as salaried employment in number of persons, *i.e.* no distinction is made between full-time and part-time employees. *Number of employees* in Table 2*b* is calculated on a full-time equivalent basis.

- *Turnover* is defined as sales including part of other operating income.

- *Value added* is calculated as the adjusted gross profit before depreciation, plus labour costs.

- *Wages and salaries* includes employer's social insurance contributions on behalf of the employees.

- *Gross fixed capital formation* corresponds to investment in tangible fixed assets, less sales of such assets.

- *Total exports* includes exports of goods and services from foreign affiliates to parent company and other intra-group firms in Sweden. It excludes services for firms with less than 50 employees.

- *Total imports* includes only imports of goods. The transactions are based on "statistical value" and not on the invoiced price. The lack of data for some years relates to uncertainty regarding the quality of the data.

- *Intra-firm exports* includes exports of goods and services from the parent and other intra-group firms in Sweden to the enterprise group abroad.

- *Gross operating surplus* consists of profit or loss before depreciation.

- *Capital under foreign influence* is the foreign-owned affiliates' share of total capital and adjusted equity according to the balance sheets in the whole corporate sector in Sweden.

Geographical breakdown

The country of origin is that of the "ultimate beneficial owner".

SUÈDE

Source

Depuis le 1er juillet 1994, les statistiques sur les entreprises internationales, c'est-à-dire sur les les groupes suédois ayant des filiales à l'étranger et sur les entreprises étrangères implantées en Suède, ont un statut officiel et sont produites et diffusées régulièrement. Le Conseil national suédois pour le développement industriel et technique (NUTEK) est l'agence responsable de l'élaboration de ces statistiques officielles. Les enquêtes sont menées en collaboration avec l'office suédois de statistiques.

A partir de l'année de référence 1996, les données sur les filiales étrangères sont fondées sur des questionnaires annuels envoyés à toutes les maisons mères ainsi qu'à toutes les succursales situées sur le territoire suédois. La couverture a été élargie au fil du temps : les questionnaires étaient envoyés à une entreprise sur quatre dans les années 80 et au début des années 90, puis à environ la moitié des maisons mères en 1995. Des efforts ont également été faits pour recenser de nouvelles filiales étrangères. L'augmentation du nombre d'entreprises et du nombre de salariés en 1995 et 1996 provient donc en partie de l'amélioration de la couverture.

Les données concernent les entreprises sous contrôle étranger majoritaire, c'est-à-dire dans lesquelles l'investisseur étranger possède plus de 50 % des droits de vote dans l'entreprise. L'unité (reporting) est dans la plupart des cas l'entreprise. En 1996, 11 % de ces unités étaient des succursales.

Les statistiques de NUTEK sur les entreprises à capitaux étrangers sont fondées sur des données provenant de trois sources (sans compter l'enquête sur l'origine de l'investissement) :

1) Le Registre central des entreprises et des établissements de l'office suédois de statistiques. Le registre sur les entreprises à capitaux étrangers prend en compte toutes les entreprises et les succursales à participation étrangère, sauf pour la période 1990-92 où les succursales ne sont pas incluses. Ces registres ont été utilisés pour le *Nombre d'entreprises* (tableau 1*a*) et pour le *Nombre de salariés* (tableau 2*a*). Ces tableaux fournissent une meilleure couverture pour ces variables, mais ils ne doivent pas être mélangés aux autres.

2) Les statistiques structurelles d'entreprises de l'office suédois de statistiques. Toutes les entreprises non financières employant au moins 20 salariés pour l'industrie manufacturière et au moins 50 salariés pour le secteur des services (en moyenne annuelle) sont enquêtées chaque année. Ces statistiques sont fondées sur des données provenant de rapports annuels et d'enquêtes sur les exportations, les revenus et les coûts, les dépenses de R-D, etc. Depuis l'année de référence 1996, les entreprises de moins de 20 salariés (50 dans le cas des services) sont enquêtées à travers les déclarations fiscales. La collecte de ces données est une obligation légale pour toutes les entreprises suédoises. Les données sur les services immobiliers (CITI 70) et les entreprises financières sont exclues. Les statistiques structurelles d'entreprises ont été utilisées pour toutes les variables, y compris *Nombre d'entreprises* (tableau 1*b*) et *Nombre de salariés* (tableau 2*b*).

3) Les statistiques du commerce de l'office suédois de statistiques. Les exportations de biens concernant les petites entreprises et l'ensemble des données sur les importations proviennent de ce registre.

Les statistiques sur les entreprises internationales sont publiées annuellement par NUTEK/office suédois de statistiques. Des articles relatifs à ce domaine sont également publiés en anglais dans le rapport annuel de NUTEK *Swedish Industry and Industrial Policy*. Toutes les publications de NUTEK sont disponibles sur le site Internet, www.nutek.se.

Totaux nationaux : les données sont fournies par NUTEK/office suédois de statistiques et sont entièrement compatibles avec les données relatives aux filiales étrangères.

Classification industrielle

Pour toutes les variables, les données sont classées selon l'activité industrielle principale de l'entreprise affiliée établie en Suède. La totalité du secteur des entreprises est enquêté.

La classification industrielle utilisée pour les tableaux suédois est la CITI révision 3, équivalant à la NACE révision 1.

La conversion vers la CITI révision 3 implique des notes qui s'appliquent à toutes les variables pour l'année 1992 :

- Une partie de *Meubles* (361) est comprise dans *Production et fabrication, bois et papier (20/22)*.

- Une partie de *Machines et matériel n.c.a., à l'exclusion des machines électriques* (3829 dans la CITI révision 2) est exclue de *Autres matériels de transport* (35) et de *Aéronautique et aérospatiale* (353), et comprise dans *Machines, total* (29/32).

- *Construction, production et distribution d'électricité, de gaz et d'eau* (40/45) n'est pas disponible séparément et est inclus dans *Autres activités*.

Variables

- Le *Nombre d'entreprises* du tableau 1*a* est défini comme l'ensemble des entreprises à participation étrangère qui sont contrôlées par un investisseur étranger à hauteur de plus de 50 % des droits de vote. Le *Nombre d'entreprises* du tableau 1*b* est défini de manière identique, mais les entreprises financières et les services immobiliers ne sont pas incluses. De plus, les entreprises sans salariés et dont le chiffre d'affaires est inférieur à 50 000 SEK selon le registre de la TVA sont exclues. L'entreprise est la plus petite unité légale du secteur des entreprises pour laquelle les données du bilan comptable et sur les pertes et profits sont disponibles.

- Le *Nombre de salariés* du tableau 2*a* est défini comme l'emploi salarié en nombre de personnes, c'est-à-dire qu'aucune distinction n'est faite entre les salariés à temps plein et à temps partiel. Le *Nombre de salariés* du tableau 2*b* est exprimé en équivalent plein-temps.

- Le *Chiffre d'affaires* représente les ventes y compris une partie du revenu d'exploitation.

- La *Valeur ajoutée* est calculée comme le profit net ajusté avant amortissement, auquel s'ajoutent les coûts salariaux.

- Les *Salaires* comprennent les cotisations patronales d'assurance sociale pour le compte des salariés.

- La *Formation brute de capital fixe* correspond à l'investissement en actifs tangibles fixes diminué des cessions de ces mêmes actifs.

- Les *Exportations totales* comprennent les exportations de biens et services en provenance des filiales étrangères vers la maison mère et les autres firmes du même groupe en Suède. Elles excluent les services pour les entreprises de moins de 50 salariés.

- Les *Importations totales* correspondent aux importations de biens uniquement. Les transactions sont basées sur une "valeur statistique" et non sur le prix facturé. Le manque de données pour certaines années provient de l'incertitude quant à leur qualité.

- Les *Exportations intra-firme* comprennent les exportations de biens et services en provenance de la maison mère et des autres firmes du même groupe en Suède vers l'entreprise ou le groupe à l'étranger.

- L'*Excédent brut d'exploitation* consiste dans les pertes et profits avant amortissement.

- Le *Capital sous influence étranger* est la part des fonds propres et des actions des entreprises sous contrôle étranger ajustée selon les bilans comptables de l'ensemble du secteur des entreprises suédois.

Ventilation géographique

Le pays de l'investisseur est le pays du "bénéficiaire ultime de l'investissement".

TURKEY

TURQUIE

Table 1. TURKEY / TURQUIE

NUMBER OF ESTABLISHMENTS / NOMBRE D'ÉTABLISSEMENTS

By industry (ISIC Rev. 3)	FOREIGN AFFILIATES (Units)					AS A % OF NATIONAL TOTAL				
	1992	1993	1994	1995	1996	1992	1993	1994	1995	1996
10/14 Mining & quarrying	..	..	..	..	..	..	..	..	..	..
15/37 TOTAL MANUFACTURING	120	153	156	169	170	2.0	1.5	1.5	1.7	1.6
15/16 Food, beverages, tobacco	24	31	31	34	33	2.4	1.6	1.7	1.9	1.8
17/19 Textiles, clothing, leather, footwear	18	21	21	22	21	1.0	0.7	0.7	0.7	0.6
20/22 Wood and paper products	4	4	4	4	5	1.1	0.6	0.7	0.7	0.8
20 Wood products	1	2	0	0	0	0.8	0.8	0.0	0.0	0.0
21/22 Paper, printing and publishing	3	2	4	4	5	1.3	0.5	1.1	1.1	1.3
23/25 Chemicals, Total	29	32	32	35	39	5.4	3.7	3.8	4.1	4.4
23 Refined petroleum, nuclear fuel	3	3	4	4	5	17.6	13.6	17.4	21.1	20.8
24/25 Chemicals, rubber & plastics prod.	26	29	28	31	34	5.0	3.4	3.4	3.7	4.0
24 Chemical products	19	22	22	24	26	7.1	5.7	5.9	6.0	6.5
2423 Pharmaceuticals	9	10	9	9	9	13.6	13.0	12.3	11.4	11.7
25 Rubber and plastics products	7	7	6	7	8	2.8	1.5	1.3	1.6	1.8
26 Non-metallic mineral products	6	11	11	11	5	1.1	1.3	1.3	1.3	0.6
27/28 Basic & fabricated metals	6	12	12	12	14	0.9	1.0	1.1	1.1	1.3
27 Basic metals	1	2	2	2	3	0.4	0.5	0.6	0.5	0.8
28 Fabricated metal products	5	10	10	10	11	1.3	1.3	1.4	1.5	1.5
29/32 Machinery, Total	19	27	30	32	34	2.8	2.1	2.5	2.7	2.7
29/30 Non-electrical machinery	9	13	13	14	15	1.9	1.4	1.5	1.6	1.7
29 Non-electrical machinery nec	9	13	13	14	15	1.9	1.4	1.5	1.6	1.7
30 Office and computing machinery	0	0	0	0	0	0.0	0.0	0.0	0.0	0.0
31/32 Electrical & electronic equipment	10	14	17	18	19	4.8	4.0	5.3	5.3	5.1
31 Electrical machinery nec	7	8	11	11	13	4.5	2.9	4.3	4.1	4.2
32 Radio, TV & communications eq.	3	6	6	7	6	5.9	8.0	9.1	10.3	9.2
33 Scientific instruments	2	2	1	2	2	6.7	2.8	1.4	2.7	2.7
34/35 Transportation equipment	10	10	10	14	14	6.2	4.0	4.0	5.5	5.0
34 Motor vehicles	10	10	10	13	13	7.4	5.2	5.2	6.5	5.9
35 Other transport equipment	0	0	0	1	1	0.0	0.0	0.0	1.9	1.7
351 Shipbuilding & repairing	0	0	0	1	0	0.0	0.0	0.0	3.3	0.0
353 Aircraft and spacecraft	0	0	0	0	0	0.0	0.0	0.0	0.0	0.0
36/37 Other manufacturing	2	3	4	3	3	1.3	0.8	1.2	0.9	0.9
40/45 Construction, electricity, gas & water	..	..	..	..	..	..	..	..	..	..
50/55 Trade, repair, hotels & restaurants	..	..	..	..	..	..	..	..	..	..
65/74 Finance, insurance, business services	..	..	..	..	..	..	..	..	..	..
OTHER ACTIVITIES	..	..	..	..	..	..	..	..	..	..
01/99 GRAND TOTAL	..	..	..	..	..	..	..	..	..	..

Total manufacturing by investing country						As a % of total manufacturing by foreign affiliates				
All countries	120	153	156	169	170	100.0	100.0	100.0	100.0	100.0
United States	14	20	20	20	18	11.7	13.1	12.8	11.8	10.6
Canada	0	1	1	1	0	0.0	0.7	0.6	0.6	0.0
Mexico	0	0	0	0	0	0.0	0.0	0.0	0.0	0.0
Japan	0	0	0	0	1	0.0	0.0	0.0	0.0	0.6
Europe	94	125	131	141	142	78.3	81.7	84.0	83.4	83.5
European Union (15)	85	114	120	129	131	70.8	74.5	76.9	76.3	77.1
Belgium	5	5	5	7	9	4.2	3.3	3.2	4.1	5.3
France	18	21	19	19	21	15.0	13.7	12.2	11.2	12.4
Germany	26	37	41	46	42	21.7	24.2	26.3	27.2	24.7
Italy	8	12	15	14	15	6.7	7.8	9.6	8.3	8.8
Netherlands	12	11	15	17	20	10.0	7.2	9.6	10.1	11.8
Spain	1	3	2	1	1	0.8	2.0	1.3	0.6	0.6
Sweden	0	5	4	4	2	0.0	3.3	2.6	2.4	1.2
United Kingdom	11	13	12	15	15	9.2	8.5	7.7	8.9	8.8
Switzerland	9	12	11	12	12	7.5	7.8	7.1	7.1	7.1
Australia and New Zealand	1	2	1	1	1	0.8	1.3	0.6	0.6	0.6
Asia (non-OECD)	1	1	1	1	2	0.8	0.7	0.6	0.6	1.2
Latin America	0	0	0	0	0	0.0	0.0	0.0	0.0	0.0

Note: Majority foreign-owned firms. From 1993, change in the coverage of the survey. See country notes.
Firmes sous contrôle étranger majoritaire. A partir de 1993, changement dans la couverture de l'enquête. Voir les notes par pays.

Table 2. TURKEY / TURQUIE

NUMBER OF EMPLOYEES / NOMBRE DE SALARIÉS

By industry (ISIC Rev. 3)	FOREIGN AFFILIATES (Units)					AS A % OF NATIONAL TOTAL				
	1992	1993	1994	1995	1996	1992	1993	1994	1995	1996
10/14 Mining & quarrying	..	..	..	..	..	..	..	..	..	..
15/37 **TOTAL MANUFACTURING**	**43 797**	**47 503**	**49 055**	**54 377**	**58 422**	**4.9**	**4.9**	**5.3**	**5.6**	**5.6**
15/16 Food, beverages, tobacco	6 656	6 963	8 602	9 928	10 808	4.0	4.0	5.1	5.9	6.3
17/19 Textiles, clothing, leather, footwear	3 141	3 075	3 124	3 995	4 433	1.2	1.0	1.1	1.2	1.2
20/22 Wood and paper products	334	349	455	352	566	0.7	0.7	1.0	0.8	1.1
20 Wood products	59	147	0	0	0	0.4	1.0	0.0	0.0	0.0
21/22 Paper, printing and publishing	275	202	455	352	566	0.8	0.6	1.3	1.0	1.5
23/25 Chemicals, Total	9 316	9 701	9 721	10 563	10 745	10.9	10.8	11.4	11.9	11.6
23 Refined petroleum, nuclear fuel	532	482	697	825	903	7.5	6.7	9.5	12.0	13.0
24/25 Chemicals, rubber & plastics prod.	8 784	9 219	9 024	9 738	9 842	11.2	11.2	11.6	11.9	11.5
24 Chemical products	5 774	6 189	6 059	6 778	7 567	10.6	11.3	11.7	12.6	14.0
2423 Pharmaceuticals	3 282	3 665	3 247	3 423	4 061	25.4	27.0	25.8	24.1	28.5
25 Rubber and plastics products	3 010	3 030	2 965	2 960	2 275	12.7	10.9	11.2	10.6	7.2
26 Non-metallic mineral products	1 807	1 557	1 597	1 446	814	2.8	2.4	2.5	2.2	1.2
27/28 Basic & fabricated metals	1 278	3 000	1 607	1 588	1 786	1.3	2.6	1.6	1.5	1.7
27 Basic metals	556	556	538	525	558	0.8	0.8	0.9	0.8	1.0
28 Fabricated metal products	722	2 444	1 069	1 063	1 228	2.1	5.5	2.7	2.7	2.7
29/32 Machinery, Total	8 883	11 287	11 993	13 978	15 039	9.0	10.6	12.1	14.1	14.4
29/30 Non-electrical machinery	1 086	2 024	1 836	4 687	5 233	1.8	3.0	2.9	7.5	8.1
29 Non-electrical machinery nec	1 086	2 024	1 836	4 687	5 233	1.8	3.0	2.9	7.5	8.1
30 Office and computing machinery	0	0	0	0	0	0.0	0.0	0.0	0.0	0.0
31/32 Electrical & electronic equipment	7 797	9 263	10 157	9 291	9 806	20.7	23.4	28.6	25.4	24.8
31 Electrical machinery nec	2 635	2 707	2 985	3 135	3 300	13.8	12.5	14.5	13.7	12.8
32 Radio, TV & communications eq.	5 162	6 556	7 172	6 156	6 506	27.8	36.8	48.2	44.9	46.9
33 Scientific instruments	110	117	71	86	90	3.4	2.9	2.0	2.0	2.0
34/35 Transportation equipment	12 056	11 227	11 713	12 318	13 963	21.3	19.0	21.2	22.3	23.2
34 Motor vehicles	12 056	11 227	11 713	12 240	13 905	30.1	25.9	29.0	30.2	30.9
35 Other transport equipment	0	0	0	78	58	0.0	0.0	0.0	0.5	0.4
351 Shipbuilding & repairing	0	0	0	78	0	0.0	0.0	0.0	2.0	0.0
353 Aircraft and spacecraft	0	0	0	0	0	0.0	0.0	0.0	0.0	0.0
36/37 Other manufacturing	216	227	172	123	178	1.9	1.5	1.1	0.7	0.9
40/45 Construction, electricity, gas & water	..	..	..	..	..	..	..	..	..	..
50/55 Trade, repair, hotels & restaurants	..	..	..	..	..	..	..	..	..	..
65/74 Finance, insurance, business services	..	..	..	..	..	..	..	..	..	..
OTHER ACTIVITIES	..	..	..	..	..	..	..	..	..	..
01/99 **GRAND TOTAL**	..	..	..	..	..	..	..	..	..	..

Total manufacturing by investing country						As a % of total manufacturing by foreign affiliates				
All countries	43 797	47 503	49 055	54 377	58 422	100.0	100.0	100.0	100.0	100.0
United States	6 986	7 951	7 350	8 138	7 815	16.0	16.7	15.0	15.0	13.4
Canada	0	1 953	1 722	1 507	0	0.0	4.1	3.5	2.8	0.0
Mexico	0	0	0	0	0	0.0	0.0	0.0	0.0	0.0
Japan	0	0	0	0	58	0.0	0.0	0.0	0.0	0.1
Europe	35 600	36 769	39 621	44 114	49 319	81.3	77.4	80.8	81.1	84.4
European Union (15)	29 737	30 740	37 135	40 189	45 177	67.9	64.7	75.7	73.9	77.3
Belgium	478	495	2 579	2 458	2 762	1.1	1.0	5.3	4.5	4.7
France	9 512	8 353	8 341	6 425	6 775	21.7	17.6	17.0	11.8	11.6
Germany	8 845	11 378	14 797	18 230	19 274	20.2	24.0	30.2	33.5	33.0
Italy	1 855	2 676	3 950	3 678	4 170	4.2	5.6	8.1	6.8	7.1
Netherlands	5 503	4 440	4 161	5 175	7 337	12.6	9.3	8.5	9.5	12.6
Spain	40	90	81	36	41	0.1	0.2	0.2	0.1	0.1
Sweden	0	131	118	103	86	0.0	0.3	0.2	0.2	0.1
United Kingdom	2 773	2 370	2 348	3 357	3 892	6.3	5.0	4.8	6.2	6.7
Switzerland	5 869	6 126	2 464	3 902	4 221	13.4	12.9	5.0	7.2	7.2
Australia and New Zealand	76	186	71	70	79	0.2	0.4	0.1	0.1	0.1
Asia (non-OECD)	81	45	31	17	149	0.2	0.1	0.1	0.0	0.3
Latin America	0	0	0	0	0	0.0	0.0	0.0	0.0	0.0

Note: Majority foreign-owned firms. From 1993, change in the coverage of the survey. See country notes.
Firmes sous contrôle étranger majoritaire. A partir de 1993, changement dans la couverture de l'enquête. Voir les notes par pays.

Table 3. TURKEY / TURQUIE

PRODUCTION

By industry (ISIC Rev. 3)	FOREIGN AFFILIATES (Billions of TL)					AS A % OF NATIONAL TOTAL				
	1992	1993	1994	1995	1996	1992	1993	1994	1995	1996
10/14 Mining & quarrying	..	..	..	..	..	..	..	..	..	..
15/37 TOTAL MANUFACTURING	**56 938**	**120 832**	**243 933**	**545 574**	**963 075**	**10**	**11.5**	**11.1**	**12.1**	**12.7**
15/16 Food, beverages, tobacco	7 842	21 875	55 030	117 466	227 004	7	11.0	13.9	14.9	15.9
17/19 Textiles, clothing, leather, footwear	1 422	2 248	6 128	11 288	17 018	2	1.3	1.4	1.3	1.2
20/22 Wood and paper products	388	647	1 925	3 408	8 327	2	1.2	1.9	1.7	2.4
20 Wood products	25	90	0	0	0	0	0.9	0.0	0.0	0.0
21/22 Paper, printing and publishing	363	556	1 925	3 408	8 327	2	1.3	2.3	2.0	2.9
23/25 Chemicals, Total	21 369	40 014	83 752	199 310	304 763	16	18.0	17.0	19.0	17.5
23 Refined petroleum, nuclear fuel	9 943	18 235	32 600	73 026	126 823	15	18.2	15.1	16.6	16.0
24/25 Chemicals, rubber & plastics prod.	11 426	21 779	51 152	126 285	177 941	17	17.9	18.5	20.8	18.8
24 Chemical products	7 342	14 629	36 523	89 691	147 024	14	15.8	17.4	19.8	21.4
2423 Pharmaceuticals	3 915	9 066	20 445	36 767	65 835	33	38.8	42.2	35.6	40.5
25 Rubber and plastics products	4 084	7 149	14 630	36 593	30 917	27	24.6	21.9	23.5	11.9
26 Non-metallic mineral products	1 646	3 214	5 776	9 442	11 081	5	5.6	4.8	4.3	2.9
27/28 Basic & fabricated metals	2 070	3 949	6 855	16 669	29 814	3	3.0	2.3	2.9	3.5
27 Basic metals	471	896	1 831	3 754	5 682	1	0.9	0.8	0.8	0.9
28 Fabricated metal products	1 599	3 053	5 024	12 915	24 132	11	10.1	9.4	10.6	10.1
29/32 Machinery, Total	8 167	19 181	42 694	96 510	176 650	13	16.5	20.2	22.0	24.1
29/30 Non-electrical machinery	1 521	4 284	10 063	32 491	50 168	4	6.4	8.2	12.5	11.9
29 Non-electrical machinery nec	1 521	4 284	10 063	32 491	50 168	4	6.5	8.2	12.6	12.0
30 Office and computing machinery	0	0	0	0	0	0	0.0	0.0	0.0	0.0
31/32 Electrical & electronic equipment	6 646	14 897	32 630	64 019	126 482	24	30.0	36.8	35.7	40.7
31 Electrical machinery nec	2 324	4 603	11 078	26 421	41 333	20	21.7	24.8	25.5	26.1
32 Radio, TV & communications eq.	4 322	10 294	21 552	37 598	85 148	27	36.1	49.0	49.5	55.8
33 Scientific instruments	34	51	91	219	330	3	2.0	2.3	2.2	2.0
34/35 Transportation equipment	13 920	29 408	41 308	90 934	186 763	32	31.6	32.8	30.5	34.0
34 Motor vehicles	13 920	29 408	41 308	90 847	185 430	35	34.0	36.3	33.1	36.8
35 Other transport equipment	0	0	0	87	1 333	0	0.0	0.0	0.4	2.9
351 Shipbuilding & repairing	0	0	0	87	0	0	0.0	0.0	1.2	0.0
353 Aircraft and spacecraft	0	0	0	0	0	0	0.0	0.0	0.0	0.0
36/37 Other manufacturing	79	247	374	328	1 324	2	3.3	2.6	0.9	1.7
40/45 Construction, electricity, gas & water	..	..	..	..	..	..	..	..	..	..
50/55 Trade, repair, hotels & restaurants	..	..	..	..	..	..	..	..	..	..
65/74 Finance, insurance, business services	..	..	..	..	..	..	..	..	..	..
OTHER ACTIVITIES	..	..	..	..	..	..	..	..	..	..
01/99 GRAND TOTAL	..	..	..	..	..	..	..	..	..	..

Total manufacturing by investing country						As a % of total manufacturing by foreign affiliates				
All countries	**56 938**	**120 832**	**243 933**	**545 574**	**963 075**	**100.0**	**100.0**	**100.0**	**100.0**	**100.0**
United States	16 615	35 285	67 751	136 910	210 186	29.2	29.2	27.8	25.1	21.8
Canada	0	4 708	5 329	8 842	0	0.0	3.9	2.2	1.6	0.0
Mexico	0	0	0	0	0	0.0	0.0	0.0	0.0	0.0
Japan	0	0	0	0	1 333	0.0	0.0	0.0	0.0	0.1
Europe	39 439	79 601	169 427	395 683	740 107	69.3	65.9	69.5	72.5	76.8
European Union (15)	33 308	68 441	157 892	369 721	690 966	58.5	56.6	64.7	67.8	71.7
Belgium	290	496	7 197	12 973	30 792	0.5	0.4	3.0	2.4	3.2
France	10 811	20 759	28 466	56 413	90 869	19.0	17.2	11.7	10.3	9.4
Germany	9 858	24 887	65 660	136 596	263 887	17.3	20.6	26.9	25.0	27.4
Italy	2 190	3 701	14 175	32 835	59 868	3.8	3.1	5.8	6.0	6.2
Netherlands	7 482	13 473	31 783	110 393	204 632	13.1	11.2	13.0	20.2	21.2
Spain	15	48	112	68	103	0.0	0.0	0.0	0.0	0.0
Sweden	0	176	313	646	696	0.0	0.1	0.1	0.1	0.1
United Kingdom	1 984	3 586	8 322	15 765	32 438	3.5	3.0	3.4	2.9	3.4
Switzerland	6 013	11 292	11 121	25 294	49 520	10.6	9.3	4.6	4.6	5.1
Australia and New Zealand	30	381	97	199	379	0.1	0.3	0.0	0.0	0.0
Asia (non-OECD)	7	10	5	14	135	0.0	0.0	0.0	0.0	0.0
Latin America	0	0	0	0	0	0.0	0.0	0.0	0.0	0.0

Note: Majority foreign-owned firms. From 1993, change in the coverage of the survey. See country notes.
        Firmes sous contrôle étranger majoritaire. A partir de 1993, changement dans la couverture de l'enquête. Voir les notes par pays.

Table 4. TURKEY / TURQUIE

TURNOVER / CHIFFRE D'AFFAIRES

By industry (ISIC Rev. 3)	FOREIGN AFFILIATES (Billions of TL)					AS A % OF NATIONAL TOTAL				
	1992	1993	1994	1995	1996	1992	1993	1994	1995	1996
10/14 Mining & quarrying	..	..	..	..	..	..	..	..	..	..
15/37 **TOTAL MANUFACTURING**	55 825	117 690	235 323	534 071	935 921	10.3	11.6	11.1	12.4	12.8
15/16 Food, beverages, tobacco	7 228	20 628	53 226	114 826	218 113	7.6	11.2	14.0	15.4	16.4
17/19 Textiles, clothing, leather, footwear	1 386	2 276	6 004	11 029	16 567	1.5	1.4	1.4	1.3	1.2
20/22 Wood and paper products	384	630	1 896	3 354	8 194	1.7	1.2	1.9	1.7	2.4
20 Wood products	22	81	0	0	0	0.5	0.8	0.0	0.0	0.0
21/22 Paper, printing and publishing	362	549	1 896	3 354	8 194	2.0	1.3	2.2	2.0	2.9
23/25 Chemicals, Total	21 120	39 299	80 968	193 957	298 420	15.9	18.0	16.9	18.9	17.5
23 Refined petroleum, nuclear fuel	9 921	18 177	31 725	72 340	126 796	14.8	18.2	15.0	16.6	16.2
24/25 Chemicals, rubber & plastics prod.	11 199	21 122	49 243	121 617	171 624	17.1	17.8	18.4	20.6	18.7
24 Chemical products	7 170	14 182	35 185	87 093	141 624	14.2	15.8	17.3	19.7	21.2
2423 Pharmaceuticals	3 743	8 746	19 606	34 986	62 201	32.8	38.7	41.7	35.2	40.0
25 Rubber and plastics products	4 030	6 940	14 058	34 525	30 000	26.7	24.5	22.0	23.2	12.0
26 Non-metallic mineral products	1 641	3 194	5 673	9 287	10 823	5.5	5.7	4.9	4.3	2.9
27/28 Basic & fabricated metals	2 044	3 789	6 529	16 311	28 915	3.3	3.0	2.3	3.0	3.5
27 Basic metals	455	841	1 801	3 725	5 451	1.0	0.9	0.8	0.9	0.9
28 Fabricated metal products	1 590	2 948	4 728	12 586	23 464	11.1	10.0	9.2	10.6	10.2
29/32 Machinery, Total	8 128	18 468	40 594	94 030	168 587	13.3	16.3	19.8	22.0	23.8
29/30 Non-electrical machinery	1 536	4 152	9 505	32 679	48 899	4.5	6.4	8.0	12.8	12.0
29 Non-electrical machinery nec	1 536	4 152	9 505	32 679	48 899	4.5	6.4	8.0	13.0	12.1
30 Office and computing machinery	0	0	0	0	0	0.0	0.0	0.0	0.0	0.0
31/32 Electrical & electronic equipment	6 593	14 316	31 089	61 351	119 688	24.4	29.5	36.3	35.3	40.1
31 Electrical machinery nec	2 243	4 428	10 395	25 667	40 251	20.2	21.4	24.1	25.4	26.1
32 Radio, TV & communications eq.	4 350	9 888	20 695	35 684	79 437	27.4	35.5	48.5	49.0	54.9
33 Scientific instruments	31	47	98	217	323	2.9	1.9	2.5	2.3	2.0
34/35 Transportation equipment	13 785	29 124	39 953	90 765	184 804	32.9	32.2	33.0	31.5	34.6
34 Motor vehicles	13 785	29 124	39 953	90 677	183 496	35.7	34.6	36.2	34.0	37.3
35 Other transport equipment	0	0	0	88	1 308	0.0	0.0	0.0	0.4	3.2
351 Shipbuilding & repairing	0	0	0	88	0	0.0	0.0	0.0	1.7	0.0
353 Aircraft and spacecraft	0	0	0	0	0	0.0	0.0	0.0	0.0	0.0
36/37 Other manufacturing	77	235	383	294	1 174	2.3	3.3	2.7	0.9	1.6
40/45 Construction, electricity, gas & water	..	..	..	..	..	..	..	..	..	..
50/55 Trade, repair, hotels & restaurants	..	..	..	..	..	..	..	..	..	..
65/74 Finance, insurance, business services	..	..	..	..	..	..	..	..	..	..
OTHER ACTIVITIES	..	..	..	..	..	..	..	..	..	..
01/99 **GRAND TOTAL**	..	..	..	..	..	..	..	..	..	..

Total manufacturing by investing country						As a % of total manufacturing by foreign affiliates				
All countries	55 825	117 690	235 323	534 071	935 921	100.0	100.0	100.0	100.0	100.0
United States	16 274	34 019	64 378	133 538	205 963	29.2	28.9	27.4	25.0	22.0
Canada	0	4 666	5 267	8 685	0	0.0	4.0	2.2	1.6	0.0
Mexico	0	0	0	0	0	0.0	0.0	0.0	0.0	0.0
Japan	0	0	0	0	1 308	0.0	0.0	0.0	0.0	0.1
Europe	38 651	77 800	164 277	387 749	717 482	69.2	66.1	69.8	72.6	76.7
European Union (15)	32 768	67 282	152 866	364 115	671 436	58.7	57.2	65.0	68.2	71.7
Belgium	274	484	6 916	12 539	30 320	0.5	0.4	2.9	2.3	3.2
France	10 636	20 694	27 905	55 798	88 387	19.1	17.6	11.9	10.4	9.4
Germany	9 660	24 536	62 342	133 237	256 348	17.3	20.8	26.5	24.9	27.4
Italy	2 219	3 595	13 936	32 587	58 669	4.0	3.1	5.9	6.1	6.3
Netherlands	7 415	13 033	31 491	110 220	200 199	13.3	11.1	13.4	20.6	21.4
Spain	15	46	107	68	102	0.0	0.0	0.0	0.0	0.0
Sweden	0	174	311	629	690	0.0	0.1	0.1	0.1	0.1
United Kingdom	1 886	3 501	8 149	15 413	30 605	3.4	3.0	3.5	2.9	3.3
Switzerland	5 775	10 619	10 998	22 979	46 353	10.3	9.0	4.7	4.3	5.0
Australia and New Zealand	28	368	86	198	307	0.0	0.3	0.0	0.0	0.0
Asia (non-OECD)	7	10	5	14	98	0.0	0.0	0.0	0.0	0.0
Latin America	0	0	0	0	0	0.0	0.0	0.0	0.0	0.0

Note: Majority foreign-owned firms. From 1993, change in the coverage of the survey. See country notes.
Firmes sous contrôle étranger majoritaire. A partir de 1993, changement dans la couverture de l'enquête. Voir les notes par pays.

Table 5. TURKEY / TURQUIE

VALUE ADDED / VALEUR AJOUTÉE

By industry (ISIC Rev. 3)	FOREIGN AFFILIATES (Billions of TL)					AS A % OF NATIONAL TOTAL				
	1992	1993	1994	1995	1996	1992	1993	1994	1995	1996
10/14 Mining & quarrying	..	..	..	..	..	..	..	..	..	..
15/37 **TOTAL MANUFACTURING**	25 596	60 155	118 573	255 454	444 994	10.7	13.4	12.9	14.7	15.4
15/16 Food, beverages, tobacco	3 021	10 397	25 247	44 804	97 498	7.2	13.6	18.3	16.5	20.5
17/19 Textiles, clothing, leather, footwear	918	1 334	3 742	4 669	7 755	2.5	2.0	2.3	1.6	1.5
20/22 Wood and paper products	165	307	949	1 565	4 168	1.7	1.4	2.3	2.2	3.3
20 Wood products	12	49	0	0	0	0.7	1.3	0.0	0.0	0.0
21/22 Paper, printing and publishing	153	258	949	1 565	4 168	2.0	1.5	2.6	2.7	3.8
23/25 Chemicals, Total	11 995	22 664	42 905	116 937	181 521	17.9	19.9	17.8	22.7	22.8
23 Refined petroleum, nuclear fuel	5 858	10 793	17 576	49 935	91 941	15.9	18.7	15.9	19.9	23.4
24/25 Chemicals, rubber & plastics prod.	6 137	11 871	25 328	67 002	89 580	20.2	21.1	19.3	25.3	22.2
24 Chemical products	3 811	7 685	17 429	46 925	75 450	16.3	17.9	17.1	23.5	25.0
2423 Pharmaceuticals	2 039	5 001	10 987	18 414	28 524	32.4	37.3	40.4	36.9	35.8
25 Rubber and plastics products	2 327	4 185	7 899	20 076	14 130	33.1	31.7	26.6	30.8	14.1
26 Non-metallic mineral products	832	2 087	3 008	5 145	5 936	4.7	6.0	4.3	4.3	3.0
27/28 Basic & fabricated metals	819	2 083	3 951	7 425	10 726	3.8	4.5	3.6	4.5	4.0
27 Basic metals	174	308	732	1 160	2 056	1.2	0.9	0.9	1.0	1.2
28 Fabricated metal products	644	1 775	3 219	6 265	8 670	10.1	13.5	13.9	12.6	9.5
29/32 Machinery, Total	3 597	11 241	25 885	45 209	80 633	13.0	22.3	26.4	24.9	27.3
29/30 Non-electrical machinery	925	2 566	7 385	14 563	22 136	6.1	9.6	13.1	14.2	13.5
29 Non-electrical machinery nec	925	2 566	7 385	14 563	22 136	6.2	9.6	13.2	14.3	13.6
30 Office and computing machinery	0	0	0	0	0	0.0	0.0	0.0	0.0	0.0
31/32 Electrical & electronic equipment	2 672	8 675	18 500	30 646	58 497	21.4	36.8	44.0	38.9	44.3
31 Electrical machinery nec	946	2 256	4 198	9 024	17 204	19.1	24.2	22.9	22.6	27.9
32 Radio, TV & communications eq.	1 725	6 419	14 302	21 622	41 293	22.9	45.0	60.3	55.6	58.7
33 Scientific instruments	9	15	69	80	114	1.6	1.4	3.1	1.9	2.0
34/35 Transportation equipment	4 191	9 842	12 596	29 496	55 937	25.8	27.3	24.4	28.2	28.6
34 Motor vehicles	4 191	9 842	12 596	29 432	55 139	30.7	31.1	28.7	33.0	32.5
35 Other transport equipment	0	0	0	64	798	0.0	0.0	0.0	0.4	3.0
351 Shipbuilding & repairing	0	0	0	64	0	0.0	0.0	0.0	1.3	0.0
353 Aircraft and spacecraft	0	0	0	0	0	0.0	0.0	0.0	0.0	0.0
36/37 Other manufacturing	48	184	222	125	705	2.9	5.8	3.3	0.9	2.2
40/45 Construction, electricity, gas & water	..	..	..	..	..	..	..	..	..	..
50/55 Trade, repair, hotels & restaurants	..	..	..	..	..	..	..	..	..	..
65/74 Finance, insurance, business services	..	..	..	..	..	..	..	..	..	..
OTHER ACTIVITIES	..	..	..	..	..	..	..	..	..	..
01/99 **GRAND TOTAL**	..	..	..	..	..	..	..	..	..	..

Total manufacturing by investing country						As a % of total manufacturing by foreign affiliates				
All countries	25 596	60 155	118 573	255 454	444 994	100.0	100.0	100.0	100.0	100.0
United States	9 454	21 504	42 025	79 811	127 439	36.9	35.7	35.4	31.2	28.6
Canada	0	3 554	3 704	4 291	0	0.0	5.9	3.1	1.7	0.0
Mexico	0	0	0	0	0	0.0	0.0	0.0	0.0	0.0
Japan	0	0	0	0	798	0.0	0.0	0.0	0.0	0.2
Europe	15 850	34 528	72 481	170 200	312 809	61.9	57.4	61.1	66.6	70.3
European Union (15)	13 488	28 686	67 953	161 071	288 247	52.7	47.7	57.3	63.1	64.8
Belgium	104	194	3 639	5 512	15 288	0.4	0.3	3.1	2.2	3.4
France	3 712	8 598	8 900	19 583	33 596	14.5	14.3	7.5	7.7	7.5
Germany	3 630	9 461	32 655	57 815	92 323	14.2	15.7	27.5	22.6	20.7
Italy	1 422	2 069	5 828	16 232	27 561	5.6	3.4	4.9	6.4	6.2
Netherlands	3 319	5 892	11 409	51 851	99 416	13.0	9.8	9.6	20.3	22.3
Spain	6	20	38	31	49	0.0	0.0	0.0	0.0	0.0
Sweden	0	85	166	217	359	0.0	0.1	0.1	0.1	0.1
United Kingdom	1 065	1 776	4 591	8 561	16 986	4.2	3.0	3.9	3.4	3.8
Switzerland	2 369	6 008	4 361	8 901	24 834	9.3	10.0	3.7	3.5	5.6
Australia and New Zealand	21	241	75	133	272	0.1	0.4	0.1	0.1	0.1
Asia (non-OECD)	3	6	1	6	74	0.0	0.0	0.0	0.0	0.0
Latin America	0	0	0	0	0	0.0	0.0	0.0	0.0	0.0

Note: Majority foreign-owned firms. From 1993, change in the coverage of the survey. See country notes.
Firmes sous contrôle étranger majoritaire. A partir de 1993, changement dans la couverture de l'enquête. Voir les notes par pays.

Table 6. TURKEY / TURQUIE

WAGES AND SALARIES / SALAIRES ET TRAITEMENTS

By industry (ISIC Rev. 3)	FOREIGN AFFILIATES (Billions of TL)					AS A % OF NATIONAL TOTAL				
	1992	1993	1994	1995	1996	1992	1993	1994	1995	1996
10/14 Mining & quarrying	..	..	..	..	..	..	..	..	..	..
15/37 TOTAL MANUFACTURING	**4 364**	**8 652**	**14 522**	**33 536**	**58 983**	**8.1**	**9.3**	**9.8**	**12.6**	**11.9**
15/16 Food, beverages, tobacco	500	1 002	2 249	5 029	9 495	5.0	6.0	8.2	11.1	12.3
17/19 Textiles, clothing, leather, footwear	138	228	333	879	1 915	1.5	1.3	1.2	1.6	1.7
20/22 Wood and paper products	24	45	105	222	631	0.8	1.0	1.4	1.7	2.7
20 Wood products	3	9	0	0	0	0.5	0.8	0.0	0.0	0.0
21/22 Paper, printing and publishing	21	36	105	222	631	1.0	1.0	1.8	2.1	3.2
23/25 Chemicals, Total	1 416	2 614	4 608	10 855	16 228	18.1	19.9	20.4	25.7	22.5
23 Refined petroleum, nuclear fuel	94	150	351	825	1 499	9.6	9.1	12.0	17.1	26.4
24/25 Chemicals, rubber & plastics prod.	1 322	2 464	4 257	10 030	14 729	19.4	21.4	21.7	26.8	22.2
24 Chemical products	791	1 584	2 780	5 964	12 742	15.3	18.4	19.3	22.2	26.2
2423 Pharmaceuticals	460	954	1 509	2 937	6 269	35.1	40.9	40.6	36.6	41.3
25 Rubber and plastics products	531	881	1 477	4 066	1 987	31.8	30.5	28.5	38.7	11.2
26 Non-metallic mineral products	198	273	469	685	791	4.7	4.2	4.5	3.4	2.2
27/28 Basic & fabricated metals	141	478	548	829	1 998	1.7	3.3	2.5	2.5	3.1
27 Basic metals	54	104	154	288	551	0.8	0.9	0.9	1.1	1.2
28 Fabricated metal products	87	373	394	541	1 447	5.7	11.1	8.7	6.5	7.7
29/32 Machinery, Total	866	2 192	3 451	7 998	15 585	12.9	18.8	19.8	24.7	26.1
29/30 Non-electrical machinery	105	294	471	2 123	3 718	2.8	4.6	4.6	11.5	11.4
29 Non-electrical machinery nec	105	294	471	2 123	3 718	2.8	4.6	4.6	11.6	11.4
30 Office and computing machinery	0	0	0	0	0	0.0	0.0	0.0	0.0	0.0
31/32 Electrical & electronic equipment	761	1 899	2 980	5 876	11 867	25.9	36.2	41.4	41.9	43.6
31 Electrical machinery nec	294	478	734	1 670	3 498	23.2	21.0	21.3	24.1	26.3
32 Radio, TV & communications eq.	467	1 421	2 246	4 205	8 369	27.9	47.8	59.8	59.5	60.1
33 Scientific instruments	6	8	13	27	48	3.2	2.5	3.2	3.0	2.5
34/35 Transportation equipment	1 067	1 800	2 731	6 999	12 261	24.3	22.3	22.4	29.0	28.5
34 Motor vehicles	1 067	1 800	2 731	6 974	12 175	35.1	32.2	34.4	40.0	38.6
35 Other transport equipment	0	0	0	25	86	0.0	0.0	0.0	0.4	0.7
351 Shipbuilding & repairing	0	0	0	25	0	0.0	0.0	0.0	1.5	0.0
353 Aircraft and spacecraft	0	0	0	0	0	0.0	0.0	0.0	0.0	0.0
36/37 Other manufacturing	7	12	16	14	31	1.9	1.5	1.3	0.6	0.5
40/45 Construction, electricity, gas & water	..	..	..	..	..	..	..	..	..	..
50/55 Trade, repair, hotels & restaurants	..	..	..	..	..	..	..	..	..	..
65/74 Finance, insurance, business services	..	..	..	..	..	..	..	..	..	..
OTHER ACTIVITIES	..	..	..	..	..	..	..	..	..	..
01/99 GRAND TOTAL	..	..	..	..	..	..	..	..	..	..

Total manufacturing by investing country						As a % of total manufacturing by foreign affiliates				
All countries	55825	117690	235323	534071	935921	100.0	100.0	100.0	100.0	100.0
United States	16274	34019	64378	133538	205963	18.9	18.3	18.2	17.0	12.2
Canada	0	4666	5267	8685	0	0.0	6.0	5.2	4.7	0.0
Mexico	0	0	0	0	0	0.0	0.0	0.0	0.0	0.0
Japan	0	0	0	0	1308	0.0	0.0	0.0	0.0	0.1
Europe	38651	77800	164277	387749	717482	79.4	74.2	76.0	77.7	86.8
European Union (15)	32768	67282	152866	364115	671436	62.5	56.9	69.1	70.8	80.3
Belgium	274	484	6916	12539	30320	0.6	0.6	4.3	4.2	4.3
France	10636	20694	27905	55798	88387	19.1	15.5	13.9	9.4	11.8
Germany	9660	24536	62342	133237	256348	20.8	23.1	30.0	31.8	32.8
Italy	2219	3595	13936	32587	58669	4.6	5.2	9.1	10.5	7.2
Netherlands	7415	13033	31491	110220	200199	11.8	7.9	7.7	10.0	18.3
Spain	15	46	107	68	102	0.0	0.0	0.0	0.0	0.0
Sweden	0	174	311	629	690	0.0	0.2	0.2	0.2	0.1
United Kingdom	1886	3501	8149	15413	30605	4.0	3.1	2.7	4.0	4.8
Switzerland	5775	10619	10998	22979	46353	16.8	17.4	6.8	6.8	6.6
Australia and New Zealand	28	368	86	198	307	0.1	0.3	0.1	0.1	0.1
Asia (non-OECD)	7	10	5	14	98	0.0	0.0	0.0	0.0	0.1
Latin America	0	0	0	0	0	0.0	0.0	0.0	0.0	0.0

Note: Majority foreign-owned firms. From 1993, change in the coverage of the survey. See country notes.
Firmes sous contrôle étranger majoritaire. A partir de 1993, changement dans la couverture de l'enquête. Voir les notes par pays.

Table 7. TURKEY / TURQUIE

R&D EXPENDITURE / DÉPENSES DE R-D

By industry (ISIC Rev. 3)		FOREIGN AFFILIATES (Billions of TL)					AS A % OF NATIONAL TOTAL				
		1992	1993	1994	1995	1996	1992	1993	1994	1995	1996
10/14	Mining & quarrying	..	..	..	..	..	..	..	..	..	..
15/37	**TOTAL MANUFACTURING**	35	327	1 016	2 286	3 680	2.8	16.3	29.4	32.8	21.7
15/16	Food, beverages, tobacco	5	6	21	36	77	7.9	7.5	12.7	12.6	13.1
17/19	Textiles, clothing, leather, footwear	..	..	..	..	..	..	..	..	..	..
20/22	Wood and paper products	..	..	..	..	..	..	..	..	..	..
20	Wood products	..	..	..	..	..	..	..	..	..	..
21/22	Paper, printing and publishing	..	..	..	..	..	..	..	..	..	..
23/25	Chemicals, Total	1	11	75	204	165	0.7	5.5	20.6	30.8	11.4
23	Refined petroleum, nuclear fuel	..	..	22	29	..	..	..	97.8	96.7	..
24/25	Chemicals, rubber & plastics prod.	1	11	53	175	165	0.8	5.8	15.5	27.6	11.5
24	Chemical products	1	11	53	175	165	1.0	7.2	20.1	36.6	16.5
2423	Pharmaceuticals	1	2	12	39	..	3.4	5.9	36.4	42.4	..
25	Rubber and plastics products	..	..	..	..	..	..	..	..	..	..
26	Non-metallic mineral products	..	3	..	..	..	..	4.3	..	..	..
27/28	Basic & fabricated metals	..	..	..	..	..	..	..	..	..	..
27	Basic metals	..	..	..	..	..	..	..	..	..	..
28	Fabricated metal products	..	..	..	0	..	..	..	..	0.0	..
29/32	Machinery, Total	19	279	885	1 943	2 754	3.7	29.7	48.0	51.3	37.3
29/30	Non-electrical machinery	..	..	..	234	70	..	..	..	17.7	2.8
29	Non-electrical machinery nec	..	..	..	234	70	..	..	..	17.7	3.2
30	Office and computing machinery	..	..	..	0	..	..	..	..	..	..
31/32	Electrical & electronic equipment	19	279	885	1 709	2 684	7.1	43.7	74.7	69.4	54.5
31	Electrical machinery nec	12	29	77	192	391	36.8	35.8	63.1	58.2	41.8
32	Radio, TV & communications eq.	7	250	808	1 517	2 293	3.0	44.7	76.0	71.1	57.4
33	Scientific instruments	..	..	..	..	..	..	..	..	..	..
34/35	Transportation equipment	10	28	35	103	684	7.4	9.7	13.0	16.6	31.8
34	Motor vehicles	10	28	35	103	684	7.9	10.6	15.2	19.7	35.9
35	Other transport equipment	..	..	..	..	..	..	..	..	..	..
351	Shipbuilding & repairing	..	..	..	..	..	..	..	..	..	..
353	Aircraft and spacecraft	..	..	..	..	..	..	..	..	..	..
36/37	Other manufacturing	..	..	..	..	..	..	..	..	..	..
40/45	Construction, electricity, gas & water	..	..	..	..	..	..	..	..	..	..
50/55	Trade, repair, hotels & restaurants	..	..	..	..	..	..	..	..	..	..
65/74	Finance, insurance, business services	..	..	..	..	..	..	..	..	..	..
	OTHER ACTIVITIES	..	..	..	..	..	..	..	..	..	..
01/99	**GRAND TOTAL**	..	..	..	..	..	..	..	..	..	..

Total manufacturing by investing country						*As a % of total manufacturing by foreign affiliates*				
All countries	35	327	1 016	2 286	3 680	100.0	100.0	100.0	100.0	100.0
United States	..	..	..	..	..	..	..	..	..	..
Canada	..	..	..	..	..	..	..	..	..	..
Mexico	..	..	..	..	..	..	..	..	..	..
Japan	..	..	..	..	..	..	..	..	..	..
Europe	..	..	..	..	..	..	..	..	..	..
European Union (15)	..	..	..	..	..	..	..	..	..	..
Belgium	..	..	..	..	..	..	..	..	..	..
France	..	..	..	..	..	..	..	..	..	..
Germany	..	..	..	..	..	..	..	..	..	..
Italy	..	..	..	..	..	..	..	..	..	..
Netherlands	..	..	..	..	..	..	..	..	..	..
Spain	..	..	..	..	..	..	..	..	..	..
Sweden	..	..	..	..	..	..	..	..	..	..
United Kingdom	..	..	..	..	..	..	..	..	..	..
Switzerland	..	..	..	..	..	..	..	..	..	..
Australia and New Zealand	..	..	..	..	..	..	..	..	..	..
Asia (non-OECD)	..	..	..	..	..	..	..	..	..	..
Latin America	..	..	..	..	..	..	..	..	..	..

Note: Majority foreign-owned firms. *Radio, TV and communications equipment* (ISIC 32) excludes *Electronic components* (321). *Food, beverages and tobacco* (ISIC 15/16) excludes *Tobacco* (16).
Firmes sous contrôle étranger majoritaire. *Radio, TV et télécommunications* (CITI 32) exclut *Composants électroniques* (321). *Alimentation, boissons, tabac* (CITI 15/16) exclut *Tabac* (16).

Table 8. TURKEY / TURQUIE

NUMBER OF RESEARCHERS / NOMBRE DE CHERCHEURS

By industry (ISIC Rev. 3)	FOREIGN AFFILIATES (Full-time Eq.)					AS A % OF NATIONAL TOTAL				
	1992	1993	1994	1995	1996	1992	1993	1994	1995	1996
10/14 Mining & quarrying	..	..	..	..	..	..	..	..	..	..
15/37 TOTAL MANUFACTURING	**69**	**351**	**413**	**498**	**490**	**9.6**	**21.9**	**20.7**	**22.5**	**20.0**
15/16 Food, beverages, tobacco	11	4	18	22	10	11.6	4.4	18.8	20.6	11.2
17/19 Textiles, clothing, leather, footwear	..	..	..	..	..	..	..	..	..	..
20/22 Wood and paper products	..	..	..	..	..	..	..	..	..	..
20 Wood products	..	..	..	..	..	..	..	..	..	..
21/22 Paper, printing and publishing	..	..	..	..	..	..	..	..	..	..
23/25 Chemicals, Total	3	13	18	47	38	2.7	6.6	10.8	24.1	14.9
23 Refined petroleum, nuclear fuel	..	..	..	..	..	..	..	..	..	..
24/25 Chemicals, rubber & plastics prod.	3	13	18	47	38	2.7	6.8	10.9	24.2	15.0
24 Chemical products	3	13	18	47	38	3.2	8.3	13.8	30.5	18.7
2423 Pharmaceuticals	3	4	5	7	..	15.0	10.5	16.7	18.9	..
25 Rubber and plastics products	..	..	..	..	..	..	..	..	..	..
26 Non-metallic mineral products	..	2	..	..	..	..	2.6	..	..	..
27/28 Basic & fabricated metals	..	..	..	..	..	..	..	..	..	..
27 Basic metals	..	..	..	..	..	..	..	..	..	..
28 Fabricated metal products	..	..	..	..	..	..	..	..	..	..
29/32 Machinery, Total	45	314	356	404	401	14.4	42.3	36.1	37.0	35.3
29/30 Non-electrical machinery	..	..	..	19	23	..	..	..	7.1	6.9
29 Non-electrical machinery nec	..	..	..	19	23	..	..	..	7.1	7.6
30 Office and computing machinery	..	..	..	..	..	..	..	..	..	..
31/32 Electrical & electronic equipment	45	314	356	385	378	21.1	50.2	46.2	46.7	47.1
31 Electrical machinery nec	22	10	6	15	74	66.7	33.3	14.6	23.8	48.7
32 Radio, TV & communications eq.	23	304	350	370	304	12.8	51.0	48.0	48.6	46.7
33 Scientific instruments	..	..	..	..	..	..	..	..	..	..
34/35 Transportation equipment	10	20	21	25	41	20.8	17.7	14.8	14.0	21.8
34 Motor vehicles	10	20	21	25	41	71.4	26.3	17.2	17.2	28.1
35 Other transport equipment	..	..	..	..	..	..	..	..	..	..
351 Shipbuilding & repairing	..	..	..	..	..	..	..	..	..	..
353 Aircraft and spacecraft	..	..	..	..	..	..	..	..	..	..
36/37 Other manufacturing	..	..	..	..	..	..	..	..	..	..
40/45 Construction, electricity, gas & water	..	..	..	..	..	..	..	..	..	..
50/55 Trade, repair, hotels & restaurants	..	..	..	..	..	..	..	..	..	..
65/74 Finance, insurance, business services	..	..	..	..	..	..	..	..	..	..
OTHER ACTIVITIES	..	..	..	..	..	..	..	..	..	..
01/99 GRAND TOTAL	..	..	..	..	..	..	..	..	..	..

Total manufacturing by investing country						As a % of total manufacturing by foreign affiliates				
All countries	69	351	413	498	490	100.0	100.0	100.0	100.0	100.0
United States	..	..	..	..	..	..	..	..	..	..
Canada	..	..	..	..	..	..	..	..	..	..
Mexico	..	..	..	..	..	..	..	..	..	..
Japan	..	..	..	..	..	..	..	..	..	..
Europe	..	..	..	..	..	..	..	..	..	..
European Union (15)	..	..	..	..	..	..	..	..	..	..
Belgium	..	..	..	..	..	..	..	..	..	..
France	..	..	..	..	..	..	..	..	..	..
Germany	..	..	..	..	..	..	..	..	..	..
Italy	..	..	..	..	..	..	..	..	..	..
Netherlands	..	..	..	..	..	..	..	..	..	..
Spain	..	..	..	..	..	..	..	..	..	..
Sweden	..	..	..	..	..	..	..	..	..	..
United Kingdom	..	..	..	..	..	..	..	..	..	..
Switzerland	..	..	..	..	..	..	..	..	..	..
Australia and New Zealand	..	..	..	..	..	..	..	..	..	..
Asia (non-OECD)	..	..	..	..	..	..	..	..	..	..
Latin America	..	..	..	..	..	..	..	..	..	..

Note: Majority foreign-owned firms. *Radio, TV and communications equipment* (ISIC 32) excludes *Electronic components* (321). *Food, beverages and tobacco* (ISIC 15/16) excludes *Tobacco* (16).
Firmes sous contrôle étranger majoritaire. *Radio, TV et télécommunications* (CITI 32) exclut *Composants électroniques* (321). *Alimentation, boissons, tabac* (CITI 15/16) exclut *Tabac* (16).

Table 9. TURKEY / TURQUIE

GROSS FIXED CAPITAL FORMATION / FORMATION BRUTE DE CAPITAL FIXE

By industry (ISIC Rev. 3)	FOREIGN AFFILIATES (Billions of TL)					AS A % OF NATIONAL TOTAL				
	1992	1993	1994	1995	1996	1992	1993	1994	1995	1996
10/14 Mining & quarrying	..	..	..	..	..	..	..	..	..	..
15/37 TOTAL MANUFACTURING	**1 581**	**6 253**	**10 280**	**20 823**	**53 211**	**5.5**	**13.2**	**10.0**	**9.8**	**10.3**
15/16 Food, beverages, tobacco	332	1 799	2 081	6 607	15 634	13.7	25.4	20.4	31.2	31.9
17/19 Textiles, clothing, leather, footwear	37	49	150	399	640	0.5	0.6	0.7	0.7	0.5
20/22 Wood and paper products	23	53	226	229	330	2.1	1.6	3.5	1.7	1.5
20 Wood products	1	1	0	0	0	0.3	0.2	0.0	0.0	0.0
21/22 Paper, printing and publishing	23	52	226	229	330	2.8	1.8	4.3	2.2	2.0
23/25 Chemicals, Total	429	1 353	2 045	5 633	11 850	10.4	20.4	12.6	14.0	14.8
23 Refined petroleum, nuclear fuel	144	159	623	1 346	4 377	9.5	20.8	71.4	10.2	15.2
24/25 Chemicals, rubber & plastics prod.	284	1 194	1 422	4 287	7 474	10.9	20.3	9.2	15.8	14.6
24 Chemical products	183	895	953	2 558	3 574	9.3	22.6	13.1	18.9	13.7
2423 Pharmaceuticals	130	714	418	1 245	1 546	30.7	52.0	32.3	34.3	21.4
25 Rubber and plastics products	102	300	468	1 729	3 900	15.6	15.7	5.8	12.7	15.5
26 Non-metallic mineral products	130	239	868	502	2 552	4.6	5.6	7.1	2.6	5.1
27/28 Basic & fabricated metals	62	670	704	359	2 595	1.9	8.7	6.0	1.2	2.7
27 Basic metals	21	7	6	108	455	0.8	0.1	0.1	0.5	0.6
28 Fabricated metal products	42	663	698	251	2 140	7.4	28.0	27.8	3.5	11.8
29/32 Machinery, Total	188	553	1 674	3 291	9 163	3.3	10.5	16.0	20.0	19.5
29/30 Non-electrical machinery	55	32	126	527	877	1.2	1.0	2.2	5.7	3.2
29 Non-electrical machinery nec	55	32	126	527	877	1.2	1.0	2.2	5.7	3.2
30 Office and computing machinery	0	0	0	0	0	0.0	0.0	0.0	0.0	0.0
31/32 Electrical & electronic equipment	134	521	1 547	2 764	8 286	13.0	25.3	32.8	38.8	42.5
31 Electrical machinery nec	135	201	656	822	2 053	22.3	16.4	21.5	19.0	19.3
32 Radio, TV & communications eq.	- 2	320	891	1 942	6 233	-0.4	38.1	53.9	69.4	70.3
33 Scientific instruments	1	0	2	6	9	0.7	0.3	0.5	0.8	0.4
34/35 Transportation equipment	379	1 537	2 506	3 786	10 411	18.4	34.5	19.5	27.0	42.4
34 Motor vehicles	379	1 537	2 506	3 783	10 295	19.7	37.3	20.3	28.8	47.2
35 Other transport equipment	0	0	0	3	116	0.0	0.0	0.0	0.4	4.2
351 Shipbuilding & repairing	0	0	0	3	0	0.0	0.0	0.0	0.7	0.0
353 Aircraft and spacecraft	0	0	0	0	0	0.0	0.0	0.0	0.0	0.0
36/37 Other manufacturing	0	0	25	11	27	0.0	0.0	4.0	0.7	0.7
40/45 Construction, electricity, gas & water	..	..	..	..	..	..	..	..	..	..
50/55 Trade, repair, hotels & restaurants	..	..	..	..	..	..	..	..	..	..
65/74 Finance, insurance, business services	..	..	..	..	..	..	..	..	..	..
OTHER ACTIVITIES	..	..	..	..	..	..	..	..	..	..
01/99 GRAND TOTAL	..	..	..	..	..	..	..	..	..	..

Total manufacturing by investing country						As a % of total manufacturing by foreign affiliates				
All countries	**1 581**	**6 253**	**10 280**	**20 823**	**53 211**	**100.0**	**100.0**	**100.0**	**100.0**	**100.0**
United States	282	1 574	1 372	2 442	10 342	17.8	25.2	13.3	11.7	19.4
Canada	0	105	466	539	0	0.0	1.7	4.5	2.6	0.0
Mexico	0	0	0	0	0	0.0	0.0	0.0	0.0	0.0
Japan	0	0	0	0	116	0.0	0.0	0.0	0.0	0.2
Europe	1 282	4 546	8 435	17 361	42 319	81.1	72.7	82.1	83.4	79.5
European Union (15)	1 123	3 987	8 222	16 376	41 684	71.0	63.8	80.0	78.6	78.3
Belgium	12	3	189	1 942	2 694	0.8	0.0	1.8	9.3	5.1
France	449	2 230	3 611	3 265	10 462	28.4	35.7	35.1	15.7	19.7
Germany	409	1 029	2 384	5 305	13 045	25.9	16.5	23.2	25.5	24.5
Italy	62	109	989	1 795	2 343	3.9	1.7	9.6	8.6	4.4
Netherlands	159	412	551	3 563	8 310	10.0	6.6	5.4	17.1	15.6
Spain	0	4	1	5	22	0.0	0.1	0.0	0.0	0.0
Sweden	0	3	5	9	18	0.0	0.0	0.1	0.0	0.0
United Kingdom	15	176	423	335	4 711	0.9	2.8	4.1	1.6	8.9
Switzerland	155	560	185	987	688	9.8	9.0	1.8	4.7	1.3
Australia and New Zealand	0	7	1	31	52	0.0	0.1	0.0	0.1	0.1
Asia (non-OECD)	0	0	0	0	0	0.0	0.0	0.0	0.0	0.0
Latin America	0	0	0	0	0	0.0	0.0	0.0	0.0	0.0

Note: Majority foreign-owned firms. From 1993, change in the coverage of the survey. See country notes.
Firmes sous contrôle étranger majoritaire. A partir de 1993, changement dans la couverture de l'enquête. Voir les notes par pays.

TURKEY

Source

The data are prepared by the Turkish State Institute of Statistics. For all variables except *R&D expenditure* and *Number of researchers*, they are derived from the annual manufacturing survey. Prior to 1993, all manufacturing establishments in the public sector and establishments employing 25 or more persons in the private sector were covered; from 1993 onwards, establishments employing ten or more persons in the private sector are covered. Data are available separately for majority foreign-owned firms, minority foreign-owned firms and national firms. The data in this publication refer to majority foreign-owned establishments, which have a foreign capital share of more than 50%. Data on *R&D expenditure* and *Number of researchers* come from the R&D survey and the establishment is the basic unit.

National totals: data are provided by the State Institute of Statistics and are fully compatible with foreign affiliates' data.

Industrial classification

For all variables, the data are classified according to the principal industrial activity of the affiliate.

Data are only available for manufacturing industries.

The industrial classification used for the Turkish tables is the national industrial classification converted to ISIC Revision 3.

Variables

Up to 1992, figures for *Number of employees, Production, Turnover, Value added, Wages and salaries* are weighted by the percentage of foreign-held equity in each sector.

- *Number of employees* is the number of persons engaged, defined as the arithmetic average of the number of employees in February, May, August and November, plus the number of owners, partners and unpaid family workers active in November. This number is calculated on a full-time equivalent basis.

- *Production* is the value of output calculated by subtracting the value of the beginning-of-year stock (finished and semi-finished goods) from the total of receipts from sales and services rendered to others, receipts from sales of transfers of electricity plus the end-of-year stock (finished and semi-finished goods) and the production value of fixed assets produced by the establishment's staff for own use.

- *Value added* is obtained by subtracting the value of inputs from output. The value of inputs is calculated by subtracting the value of the end-of-year stock (raw materials, supplementary materials, packaging materials and fuel) from the total value of goods and services purchased or transferred, electricity purchased and the beginning-of-year stock (raw materials, supplementary materials, packaging materials and fuel).

- *Wages and salaries* are defined as annual payments to employees, which include all payments on the payroll and per diems gross of income tax, social security and pension fund premiums. It also includes overtime payments, bonuses, indemnities and payments in kind. It excludes social security and pension contributions paid by the employer.

- *R&D expenditure* is intramural expenditure on R&D performed by foreign affiliates, whatever the source of funds.

- *Gross fixed capital formation* is calculated by subtracting the sales value of fixed assets sold during the year from total expenditures made on new or used fixed assets purchased from the domestic market, fixed assets imported new or used, fixed assets produced by the establishment's own staff, parts of fixed assets installed during the year and bought at an auction, major repairs and expenditures made on fixed assets, studies and plans, drawings, machinery, equipment, motor vehicle and building, other construction, office equipment and furniture (used by the establishment and expected to have a productive life of more than one year and recorded in the capital accounts) and expenditures on land and land improvements.

Geographical breakdown

The breakdown by foreign investor's country is available for all variables. It is not possible to identify whether the investor's country is that of the immediate controller or that of the "ultimate beneficial owner".

TURQUIE

Source

Les données émanent de l'Institut de statistique de l'État turc. Pour toutes les variables à l'exception des *Dépenses de R-D* et du *Nombre de chercheurs*, les données proviennent de l'enquête annuelle auprès de l'industrie manufacturière. Jusqu'en 1992, tous les établissements du secteur manufacturier public étaient couverts, ainsi que ceux du secteur privé employant au moins 25 personnes ; à partir de 1993, tous les établissements du secteur privé employant dix personnes ou plus sont couverts. Des données sont disponibles séparément pour les entreprises à participation étrangère majoritaire, minoritaire, ainsi que pour les entreprises nationales. Les données de cette publication font référence aux établissements sous contrôle étranger où la part du capital en mains étrangères est de plus de 50 %. Pour les *Dépenses de R-D* et le *Nombre de chercheurs*, les données proviennent de l'enquête sur la R-D et l'unité de base est l'établissement.

Totaux nationaux : les données sont fournies par l'Institut de statistique sur la même base que les données relatives aux filiales étrangères.

Classification industrielle

Pour toutes les variables, les données sont classées selon l'activité industrielle principale de l'entreprise affiliée.

On ne dispose de données que pour l'industrie manufacturière.

La classification industrielle utilisée pour les tableaux turcs est la classification nationale adaptée à la CITI révision 3.

Variables

Pour *Nombre de salariés, Production brute, Chiffre d'affaires, Valeur ajoutée, Salaires*, les données jusqu'en 1992 sont pondérées par le pourcentage de capital détenu par l'étranger dans chaque secteur.

- Le *Nombre de salariés* est le nombre de personnes employées, défini comme la moyenne arithmétique du nombre de salariés aux mois de février, mai, août et novembre, plus le nombre de propriétaires exploitants, partenaires et travailleurs familiaux non rémunérés actifs au mois de novembre. Ce nombre est calculé en équivalent plein-temps.

- La *Production* est donnée par la valeur totale des ventes de biens et services et des transferts d'électricité, à laquelle on ajoute la valeur des stocks (de produits finis et semi-finis) en fin d'année et celle des actifs fixes produits par l'unité pour son propre usage et dont on déduit la valeur des stocks en début d'année (de produits finis et semi-finis).

- La *Valeur ajoutée* est donnée par la production déduction faite de la valeur des consommations intermédiaires. Cette dernière correspond à la valeur totale des produits et services achetés ou transférés, de l'électricité achetée et de la valeur des stocks en début d'année après déduction de la valeur des stocks en fin d'année (matières premières, fournitures, matériel d'emballage et combustibles).

- Les *Salaires* sont définis comme les paiements annuels aux salariés et comprennent tous les versements qui figurent sur la feuille de paie, les indemnités journalières avant déduction de l'impôt sur le revenu, ainsi que les cotisations de sécurité sociale et de retraite. Cette variable comprend également le paiement des heures supplémentaires, les primes, indemnités et paiements en nature. Elle ne comprend pas les cotisations de sécurité sociale et de retraite versées par l'employeur.

- Les *Dépenses de R-D* sont les dépenses intramuros de R-D réalisées par les filiales étrangères, quelle que soit la source de financement.

- La *Formation brute de capital fixe* est donnée par le coût total des actifs fixes neufs ou usagés acquis sur le marché intérieur, des actifs fixes neufs ou usagés importés, des actifs fixes produits par le personnel de l'établissement, des actifs fixes installés pendant l'année et achetés aux enchères, des grosses réparations et des dépenses faites sur les actifs fixes, des études, plans et dessins, des machines, équipement, véhicules et construction, du matériel et mobilier de bureau (à condition qu'ils soient utilisés dans l'établissement, qu'ils aient une espérance de vie productive supérieure à un an et qu'ils soient portés au compte de capital) et aux dépenses d'acquisition et d'amélioration des terrains, déduction faite des ventes.

Ventilation géographique

La ventilation par pays d'origine de l'investissement est disponible pour toutes les variables. Il n'est pas possible d'identifier si le pays de l'investisseur est celui où se situe le contrôle immédiat ou bien si c'est celui du "bénéficiaire ultime de l'investissement".

UNITED KINGDOM

ROYAUME-UNI

Table 1. UNITED KINGDOM / ROYAUME-UNI

NUMBER OF ENTERPRISES / NOMBRE D'ENTREPRISES

By industry (ISIC Rev. 3)	FOREIGN AFFILIATES (Units)					AS A % OF NATIONAL TOTAL				
	1993	1994	1995	1996	1997	1993	1994	1995	1996	1997
10/14 Mining & quarrying	..	..	..	26	..	..	..	..	2.4	..
15/37 **TOTAL MANUFACTURING**	**2 394**	**2 633**	**2 397**	**2 686**	**2 462**	**1.5**	**1.7**	**1.4**	**1.6**	..
15/16 Food, beverages, tobacco	..	..	..	151	..	..	..	..	1.8	..
17/19 Textiles, clothing, leather, footwear	..	..	..	78	..	..	..	..	0.5	..
20/22 Wood and paper products	302	361	316	358	..	0.9	1.0	0.8	0.9	..
20 Wood products	23	31	25	..	..	0.3	0.4	0.3	..	..
21/22 Paper, printing and publishing	279	330	291	..	..	1.0	1.2	1.0	..	..
23/25 Chemicals, Total	479	503	458	514	..	5.3	5.2	3.8	4.4	..
23 Refined petroleum, nuclear fuel	21	20	28	25	..	10.6	9.0	6.3	8.5	..
24/25 Chemicals, rubber & plastics prod.	458	483	430	489	..	5.1	5.1	3.7	4.3	..
24 Chemical products	283	308	281	296	..	7.4	8.0	6.2	7.0	..
2423 Pharmaceuticals	..	..	..	53	..	..	..	..	10.4	..
25 Rubber and plastics products	175	175	149	193	..	3.4	3.1	2.2	2.7	..
26 Non-metallic mineral products	70	79	67	90	..	2.4	2.5	1.3	1.8	..
27/28 Basic & fabricated metals	296	314	301	305	..	1.0	1.0	1.0	1.0	..
27 Basic metals	95	101	95	92	..	2.7	4.2	3.4	3.3	..
28 Fabricated metal products	201	213	206	213	..	0.8	0.8	0.7	0.7	..
29/32 Machinery, Total	651	699	651	746	..	3.0	2.9	2.4	3.1	..
29/30 Non-electrical machinery	414	443	396	455	..	3.1	3.1	2.2	3.0	..
29 Non-electrical machinery nec	372	403	355	410	..	3.2	3.1	2.3	3.0	..
30 Office and computing machinery	42	40	41	45	..	2.6	2.4	1.9	3.2	..
31/32 Electrical & electronic equipment	237	256	255	291	..	2.8	2.7	2.9	3.4	..
31 Electrical machinery nec	135	144	144	179	..	2.4	2.4	2.5	3.2	..
32 Radio, TV & communications eq.	102	112	111	112	..	3.3	3.3	3.4	3.8	..
33 Scientific instruments	149	177	158	175	..	4.1	4.1	2.4	3.1	..
34/35 Transportation equipment	165	178	157	171	..	4.5	4.1	2.3	3.3	..
34 Motor vehicles	111	122	107	109	..	7.5	6.9	2.8	4.4	..
35 Other transport equipment	54	56	50	62	..	2.4	2.2	1.6	2.3	..
351 Shipbuilding & repairing	..	..	..	5	..	..	..	..	0.3	..
353 Aircraft and spacecraft	..	..	..	32	..	..	..	..	4.2	..
36/37 Other manufacturing	57	94	82	98	..	0.4	0.5	0.4	0.5	..
40/45 Construction, electricity, gas & water	..	..	..	203	..	..	..	..	0.1	..
50/55 Trade, repair, hotels & restaurants	..	..	..	..	..	..	..	..	..	..
65/74 Finance, insurance, business services	..	..	..	..	..	..	..	..	..	..
OTHER ACTIVITIES	..	..	..	..	..	..	..	..	..	..
01/99 **GRAND TOTAL**	..	..	..	..	..	..	..	..	..	..

Total manufacturing by investing country						As a % of total manufacturing by foreign affiliates				
All countries	2 394	2 633	2 397	2 686	2 462	100.0	100.0	100.0	100.0	100.0
United States	..	..	873	1 067	..	..	..	36.4	39.7	..
Canada	..	..	118	80	..	..	..	4.9	3.0	..
Mexico	..	..	..	..	..	..	..	..	..	..
Japan	..	..	138	139	..	..	..	5.8	5.2	..
Europe	..	..	..	..	..	..	..	..	..	..
European Union (15)	..	..	798	1 044	..	..	..	33.3	38.9	..
Belgium	..	..	..	27	..	..	..	..	1.0	..
France	..	..	151	155	..	..	..	6.3	5.8	..
Germany	..	..	256	265	..	..	..	10.7	9.9	..
Italy	..	..	..	25	..	..	..	..	0.9	..
Netherlands	..	..	161	177	..	..	..	6.7	6.6	..
Spain	..	..	..	..	..	..	..	..	..	..
Sweden	..	..	127	118	..	..	..	5.3	4.4	..
United Kingdom	..	..	..	..	..	..	..	..	..	..
Switzerland	..	..	153	157	..	..	..	6.4	5.8	..
Australia and New Zealand	..	..	56	63	..	..	..	2.3	2.3	..
Asia (non-OECD)	..	..	..	31	..	..	..	..	1.2	..
Latin America	..	..	..	0	..	..	..	..	0.0	..

Note: Majority foreign-owned firms.
Firmes sous contrôle étranger majoritaire.

Table 2. UNITED KINGDOM / ROYAUME-UNI

NUMBER OF EMPLOYEES / NOMBRE DE SALARIÉS

By industry (ISIC Rev. 3)		FOREIGN AFFILIATES (Units)					AS A % OF NATIONAL TOTAL				
		1993	1994	1995	1996	1997	1993	1994	1995	1996	1997
10/14	Mining & quarrying	..	..	..	3 449	..	..	..	..	6.3	..
15/37	TOTAL MANUFACTURING	756 000	789 000	718 400	815 161	745 800	18.1	18.6	17.1	19.2	..
15/16	Food, beverages, tobacco	..	..	..	74 639	..	..	..	..	15.0	..
17/19	Textiles, clothing, leather, footwear	..	..	..	21 787	..	..	..	..	5.5	..
20/22	Wood and paper products	64 600	67 100	55 700	58 879	..	12.8	12.5	10.9	10.6	..
20	Wood products	3 100	3 300	2 500	..	..	4.4	4.2	3.4	..	..
21/22	Paper, printing and publishing	61 500	63 800	53 200	..	..	14.1	14.0	12.1	..	..
23/25	Chemicals, Total	149 300	139 600	133 300	151 217	..	28.2	26.5	24.7	27.7	..
23	Refined petroleum, nuclear fuel	5 400	4 600	5 900	6 189	..	18.2	16.5	22.1	22.2	..
24/25	Chemicals, rubber & plastics prod.	143 900	135 000	127 400	145 028	..	28.8	27.1	24.9	28.0	..
24	Chemical products	98 400	95 100	87 600	97 310	..	36.4	35.9	31.7	36.4	..
2423	Pharmaceuticals	..	..	..	30 419	..	..	..	..	46.9	..
25	Rubber and plastics products	45 500	39 900	39 800	47 718	..	19.8	17.1	16.9	19.1	..
26	Non-metallic mineral products	18 400	19 100	15 400	19 049	..	13.6	13.3	9.7	12.1	..
27/28	Basic & fabricated metals	60 500	58 200	54 800	56 737	..	12.5	11.7	10.4	10.3	..
27	Basic metals	27 600	22 700	22 200	22 129	..	22.5	19.6	16.6	15.9	..
28	Fabricated metal products	32 900	35 500	32 600	34 608	..	9.1	9.3	8.3	8.4	..
29/32	Machinery, Total	209 400	208 900	188 000	225 168	..	27.6	26.5	24.0	28.4	..
29/30	Non-electrical machinery	131 700	124 100	106 100	127 861	..	28.9	26.9	22.9	27.9	..
29	Non-electrical machinery nec	88 900	86 100	81 500	97 982	..	23.0	21.9	20.3	24.5	..
30	Office and computing machinery	42 800	38 000	24 600	29 879	..	61.3	56.0	38.8	50.8	..
31/32	Electrical & electronic equipment	77 700	84 800	81 900	97 307	..	25.7	25.9	25.5	29.3	..
31	Electrical machinery nec	36 200	39 800	33 300	45 007	..	19.6	20.4	18.1	23.1	..
32	Radio, TV & communications eq.	41 500	45 000	48 600	52 301	..	35.4	34.0	35.5	37.9	..
33	Scientific instruments	27 400	24 100	20 900	28 587	..	19.3	18.1	15.5	20.2	..
34/35	Transportation equipment	123 200	158 900	148 600	163 333	..	29.6	39.3	36.6	40.2	..
34	Motor vehicles	92 600	126 300	122 300	134 126	..	42.1	55.6	51.0	54.7	..
35	Other transport equipment	30 600	32 600	26 300	29 207	..	15.6	18.4	15.8	18.1	..
351	Shipbuilding & repairing	..	..	..	1 471	..	..	..	..	3.8	..
353	Aircraft and spacecraft	..	..	..	16 523	..	..	..	..	16.1	..
36/37	Other manufacturing	9 400	12 400	9 370	15 765	..	5.1	5.8	4.8	7.4	..
40/45	Construction, electricity, gas & water	..	..	..	28 497	..	..	..	..	2.5	..
50/55	Trade, repair, hotels & restaurants	..	..	..	..	..	..	..	..	..	..
65/74	Finance, insurance, business services	..	..	..	..	..	..	..	..	..	..
	OTHER ACTIVITIES	..	..	..	..	..	..	..	..	..	..
01/99	GRAND TOTAL	..	..	..	..	..	..	..	..	..	..

Total manufacturing by investing country						As a % of total manufacturing by foreign affiliates				
All countries	756 000	789 000	718 400	815 161	745 800	100.0	100.0	100.0	100.0	100.0
United States	..	..	323 100	379 370	..	..	..	45.0	46.5	..
Canada	..	..	36 400	31 700	..	..	..	5.1	3.9	..
Mexico	..	..	..	..	..	..	..	..	..	..
Japan	..	..	51 700	56 862	..	..	..	7.2	7.0	..
Europe	..	..	..	325 500	..	..	..	..	39.9	..
European Union (15)	..	..	208 200	267 606	..	..	..	29.0	32.8	..
Belgium	..	..	..	5 800	..	..	..	..	0.7	..
France	..	..	51 400	56 689	..	..	..	7.2	7.0	..
Germany	..	..	78 400	85 106	..	..	..	10.9	10.4	..
Italy	..	..	..	9 800	..	..	..	..	1.2	..
Netherlands	..	..	38 800	39 390	..	..	..	5.4	4.8	..
Spain	..	..	..	..	..	..	..	..	..	..
Sweden	..	..	23 600	20 900	..	..	..	3.3	2.6	..
United Kingdom	..	..	..	..	..	..	..	..	..	..
Switzerland	..	..	43 100	43 645	..	..	..	6.0	5.4	..
Australia and New Zealand	..	..	15 800	12 400	..	..	..	2.2	1.5	..
Asia (non-OECD)	..	..	..	4 554	..	..	..	..	0.6	..
Latin America	..	..	..	0	..	..	..	..	0.0	..

Note: Majority foreign-owned firms.
Firmes sous contrôle étranger majoritaire.

Table 3. UNITED KINGDOM / ROYAUME-UNI

PRODUCTION

By industry (ISIC Rev. 3)		FOREIGN AFFILIATES (Millions of £)					AS A % OF NATIONAL TOTAL				
		1993	1994	1995	1996	1997	1993	1994	1995	1996	1997
10/14	Mining & quarrying	..	..	..	398	..	..	..	..	6.7	..
15/37	**TOTAL MANUFACTURING**	**102 423**	**116 853**	**123 113**	**146 979**	**141 733**	**29.2**	**30.7**	**30.5**	**33.2**	..
15/16	Food, beverages, tobacco	..	..	..	17 956	..	..	..	..	23.7	..
17/19	Textiles, clothing, leather, footwear				1 636	..				8.3	..
20/22	Wood and paper products	6 757	7 485	7 133	8 076	..	18.8	18.7	17.4	17.5	..
20	Wood products	417	475	465	..	..	9.4	9.0	9.3	..	..
21/22	Paper, printing and publishing	6 340	7 010	6 668	..	..	20.2	20.2	18.5	..	..
23/25	Chemicals, Total	30 511	29 398	32 416	40 054	..	41.1	37.7	39.3	44.1	..
23	Refined petroleum, nuclear fuel	11 925	10 268	11 578	16 365	..	54.0	47.0	53.7	63.0	..
24/25	Chemicals, rubber & plastics prod.	18 586	19 130	20 838	23 689	..	35.6	34.1	34.2	36.6	..
24	Chemical products	14 913	15 567	16 698	19 009	..	39.8	39.1	38.2	41.7	..
2423	Pharmaceuticals	..	..	..	5 069	..	..	..	..	52.6	..
25	Rubber and plastics products	3 673	3 562	4 140	4 680	..	25.0	21.9	24.0	24.4	..
26	Non-metallic mineral products	1 234	1 514	1 299	1 617	..	15.4	15.9	11.4	14.2	..
27/28	Basic & fabricated metals	6 317	6 971	7 775	7 348	..	19.5	19.3	19.4	16.8	..
27	Basic metals	3 709	3 741	4 450	3 794	..	26.1	23.9	23.6	19.8	..
28	Fabricated metal products	2 607	3 230	3 325	3 554	..	14.4	15.8	15.7	14.5	..
29/32	Machinery, Total	24 249	25 951	28 987	35 643	..	42.0	41.0	40.4	45.3	..
29/30	Non-electrical machinery	16 497	16 274	18 022	22 731	..	44.7	41.8	40.2	46.5	..
29	Non-electrical machinery nec	7 459	8 061	8 990	11 235	..	29.0	28.6	28.0	32.4	..
30	Office and computing machinery	9 039	8 213	9 032	11 497	..	81.1	76.7	71.2	81.2	..
31/32	Electrical & electronic equipment	7 751	9 677	10 964	12 912	..	37.3	39.7	40.7	43.4	..
31	Electrical machinery nec	2 690	3 061	2 621	3 845	..	24.1	25.5	21.8	28.1	..
32	Radio, TV & communications eq.	5 061	6 616	8 343	9 067	..	52.6	53.4	55.9	56.4	..
33	Scientific instruments	2 185	2 040	1 901	3 129	..	26.2	23.8	20.5	28.8	..
34/35	Transportation equipment	18 298	25 483	25 512	30 071	..	45.5	56.3	54.5	58.0	..
34	Motor vehicles	16 184	23 102	23 417	27 213	..	60.6	74.5	69.7	74.0	..
35	Other transport equipment	2 114	2 381	2 095	2 858	..	15.6	16.7	15.8	19.0	..
351	Shipbuilding & repairing	..	..	..	115	..	..	..	..	4.2	..
353	Aircraft and spacecraft	..	..	..	1 716	..	..	..	..	16.0	..
36/37	Other manufacturing	589	1 018	988	1 450	..	6.2	8.5	8.2	10.4	..
40/45	Construction, electricity, gas & water	..	..	..	3 946	..	..	..	..	3.1	..
50/55	Trade, repair, hotels & restaurants	..	..	..	..	..	..	..	..	..	..
65/74	Finance, insurance, business services	..	..	..	..	..	..	..	..	..	..
	OTHER ACTIVITIES	..	..	..	..	..	..	..	..	..	..
01/99	**GRAND TOTAL**	..	..	..	..	..	..	..	..	..	..

Total manufacturing by investing country							*As a % of total manufacturing by foreign affiliates*				
All countries	102 423	116 853	123 113	146 979	141 733		100.0	100.0	100.0	100.0	100.0
United States	..	..	68 481	83 982	..		..	..	55.6	57.1	..
Canada	..	..	5 080	4 805	..		..	..	4.1	3.3	..
Mexico	..	..	..	..	..		..	..	..	..	..
Japan	..	..	7 881	9 333	..		..	..	6.4	6.3	..
Europe	..	..	..	..	..		..	..	..	..	..
European Union (15)	..	..	27 791	38 272	..		..	..	22.6	26.0	..
Belgium	..	..	..	2 138	..		..	..	..	1.5	..
France	..	..	7 589	9 916	..		..	..	6.2	6.7	..
Germany	..	..	10 006	10 736	..		..	..	8.1	7.3	..
Italy	..	..	..	2 353	..		..	..	..	1.6	..
Netherlands	..	..	3 741	4 067	..		..	..	3.0	2.8	..
Spain	..	..	..	..	..		..	..	..	..	..
Sweden	..	..	2 975	2 564	..		..	..	2.4	1.7	..
United Kingdom	..	..	..	..	..		..	..	..	..	..
Switzerland	..	..	5 747	6 215	..		..	..	4.7	4.2	..
Australia and New Zealand	..	..	2 914	1 731	..		..	..	2.4	1.2	..
Asia (non-OECD)	..	..	..	512	..		..	..	..	0.3	..
Latin America	..	..	..	0	..		..	..	..	0.0	..

Note: Majority foreign-owned firms.
Firmes sous contrôle étranger majoritaire.

Table 4. UNITED KINGDOM / ROYAUME-UNI

TURNOVER / CHIFFRE D'AFFAIRES

By industry (ISIC Rev. 3)	FOREIGN AFFILIATES (Millions of £)					AS A % OF NATIONAL TOTAL				
	1993	1994	1995	1996	1997	1993	1994	1995	1996	1997
10/14 Mining & quarrying	..	..	..	393	..	..	..	..	6.5	..
15/37 **TOTAL MANUFACTURING**	102 036	116 363	121 872	146 969	141 883	..	..	30.6	33.2	..
15/16 Food, beverages, tobacco	..	..	..	17 864	..	..	..	..	23.7	..
17/19 Textiles, clothing, leather, footwear	..	..	..	1 626	..	..	..	..	8.3	..
20/22 Wood and paper products	6 750	7 436	7 080	8 107	..	..	..	..	17.5	..
20 Wood products	419	473	460	..	..	..	..	..	..	..
21/22 Paper, printing and publishing	6 330	6 963	6 620	..	..	..	..	..	..	..
23/25 Chemicals, Total	30 475	29 353	32 145	39 884	..	..	..	..	44.1	..
23 Refined petroleum, nuclear fuel	11 965	10 255	11 535	16 366	..	..	..	..	63.1	..
24/25 Chemicals, rubber & plastics prod.	18 510	19 098	20 609	23 518	..	..	..	..	36.5	..
24 Chemical products	14 842	15 546	16 506	18 825	..	..	..	..	41.6	..
2423 Pharmaceuticals	..	..	..	5 062	..	..	..	..	52.8	..
25 Rubber and plastics products	3 668	3 552	4 103	4 693	..	..	..	..	24.5	..
26 Non-metallic mineral products	1 239	1 516	1 298	1 594	..	..	..	..	14.2	..
27/28 Basic & fabricated metals	6 344	6 952	7 681	7 329	..	..	..	..	16.8	..
27 Basic metals	3 725	3 731	4 401	3 790	..	..	..	..	19.8	..
28 Fabricated metal products	2 619	3 221	3 280	3 539	..	..	..	..	14.4	..
29/32 Machinery, Total	24 195	26 081	28 713	35 807	..	..	..	..	45.6	..
29/30 Non-electrical machinery	16 504	16 454	17 862	22 871	..	..	..	..	46.8	..
29 Non-electrical machinery nec	7 465	8 028	8 887	11 248	..	..	..	..	32.5	..
30 Office and computing machinery	9 039	8 426	8 975	11 623	..	..	..	..	81.5	..
31/32 Electrical & electronic equipment	7 691	9 627	10 851	12 936	..	..	..	..	43.6	..
31 Electrical machinery nec	2 716	3 051	2 600	3 850	..	..	..	..	28.2	..
32 Radio, TV & communications eq.	4 975	6 576	8 251	9 086	..	..	..	..	56.6	..
33 Scientific instruments	2 197	2 031	1 899	3 112	..	..	..	..	28.8	..
34/35 Transportation equipment	18 004	25 058	25 019	30 203	..	..	..	..	57.8	..
34 Motor vehicles	15 831	22 729	23 041	27 323	..	..	..	..	74.1	..
35 Other transport equipment	2 172	2 329	1 978	2 880	..	..	..	..	18.7	..
351 Shipbuilding & repairing	..	..	..	132	..	..	..	..	5.1	..
353 Aircraft and spacecraft	..	..	..	1 705	..	..	..	..	15.2	..
36/37 Other manufacturing	593	1 012	982	1 443	..	..	..	..	10.5	..
40/45 Construction, electricity, gas & water	..	..	..	3 918	..	..	..	..	3.1	..
50/55 Trade, repair, hotels & restaurants	..	..	..	..	..	..	..	..	..	..
65/74 Finance, insurance, business services	..	..	..	..	..	..	..	..	..	..
OTHER ACTIVITIES	..	..	..	..	..	..	..	..	..	..
01/99 **GRAND TOTAL**	..	..	..	..	..	..	..	..	..	..

Total manufacturing by investing country						As a % of total manufacturing by foreign affiliates				
All countries	102 036	116 363	121 872	146 969	141 883	100.0	100.0	100.0	100.0	100.0
United States	..	..	67 871	84 102	..	..	..	55.7	57.2	..
Canada	..	..	5 010	4 760	..	..	..	4.1	3.2	..
Mexico	..	..	..	..	..	..	..	..	..	..
Japan	..	..	7 807	9 303	..	..	..	6.4	6.3	..
Europe	..	..	..	45 808	..	..	..	..	31.2	..
European Union (15)	..	..	27 511	37 971	..	..	..	22.6	25.8	..
Belgium	..	..	..	2 142	..	..	..	..	1.5	..
France	..	..	7 622	9 887	..	..	..	6.3	6.7	..
Germany	..	..	9 784	10 732	..	..	..	8.0	7.3	..
Italy	..	..	..	2 365	..	..	..	..	1.6	..
Netherlands	..	..	3 680	3 942	..	..	..	3.0	2.7	..
Spain	..	..	..	..	..	..	..	..	..	..
Sweden	..	..	2 949	2 569	..	..	..	2.4	1.7	..
United Kingdom	..	..	..	..	..	..	..	..	..	..
Switzerland	..	..	5 585	6 298	..	..	..	4.6	4.3	..
Australia and New Zealand	..	..	2 912	2 017	..	..	..	2.4	1.4	..
Asia (non-OECD)	..	..	..	517	..	..	..	..	0.4	..
Latin America	..	..	..	0	..	..	..	..	0.0	..

Note: Majority foreign-owned firms.
Firmes sous contrôle étranger majoritaire.

Table 5. UNITED KINGDOM / ROYAUME-UNI

VALUE ADDED / VALEUR AJOUTÉE

By industry (ISIC Rev. 3)	FOREIGN AFFILIATES (Millions of £)					AS A % OF NATIONAL TOTAL				
	1993	1994	1995	1996	1997	1993	1994	1995	1996	1997
10/14 Mining & quarrying	..	..	..	253	..	..	..	..	..	..
15/37 **TOTAL MANUFACTURING**	**35 534**	**40 908**	**42 093**	**50 420**	..	**24.3**	**25.6**	**32.6**	..	..
15/16 Food, beverages, tobacco	..	..	..	6 828	..	..	..	..	..	..
17/19 Textiles, clothing, leather, footwear	..	..	..	837	..	..	..	..	..	..
20/22 Wood and paper products	3 554	3 930	3 639	4 126	..	18.0	18.0	22.1	..	..
20 Wood products	156	194	201	100	..	8.4	9.1	12.8	..	..
21/22 Paper, printing and publishing	3 398	3 736	3 438	4 026	..	19.0	19.0	23.1	..	..
23/25 Chemicals, Total	9 625	9 577	10 207	11 963	..	35.2	32.8	42.2	..	..
23 Refined petroleum, nuclear fuel	1 197	923	1 083	1 167	..	38.5	29.5	38.1	..	..
24/25 Chemicals, rubber & plastics prod.	8 428	8 655	9 124	10 796	..	34.7	33.2	42.7	..	..
24 Chemical products	6 726	6 970	7 298	8 607	..	39.6	38.5	48.3	..	..
2423 Pharmaceuticals	..	..	..	2 634	..	..	..	..	..	..
25 Rubber and plastics products	1 702	1 685	1 826	2 189	..	23.4	21.1	29.2	..	..
26 Non-metallic mineral products	628	793	699	897	..	14.1	14.7	14.7	..	..
27/28 Basic & fabricated metals	2 335	2 612	2 844	2 662	..	16.1	16.4	19.6	..	..
27 Basic metals	1 151	1 232	1 432	1 202	..	23.6	22.5	26.0	..	..
28 Fabricated metal products	1 185	1 380	1 413	1 460	..	12.3	13.2	15.7	..	..
29/32 Machinery, Total	8 153	8 980	9 708	11 891	..	33.7	33.0	40.8	..	..
29/30 Non-electrical machinery	5 118	5 335	5 610	7 134	..	34.3	33.0	39.3	..	..
29 Non-electrical machinery nec	3 098	3 267	3 434	4 353	..	26.2	25.3	30.1	..	..
30 Office and computing machinery	2 019	2 068	2 176	2 781	..	65.1	63.2	75.8	..	..
31/32 Electrical & electronic equipment	3 035	3 645	4 098	4 757	..	32.8	33.1	42.9	..	..
31 Electrical machinery nec	1 227	1 319	1 182	1 654	..	23.9	22.8	25.7	..	..
32 Radio, TV & communications eq.	1 809	2 326	2 916	3 103	..	43.9	44.6	58.9	..	..
33 Scientific instruments	1 078	1 087	995	1 332	..	24.3	23.1	26.0	..	..
34/35 Transportation equipment	4 909	7 273	7 448	9 221	..	30.8	43.3	55.8	..	..
34 Motor vehicles	4 026	6 208	6 706	8 191	..	44.3	66.2	80.7	..	..
35 Other transport equipment	883	1 065	742	1 030	..	12.9	14.4	14.7	..	..
351 Shipbuilding & repairing	..	..	..	28	..	..	..	..	..	..
353 Aircraft and spacecraft	..	..	..	601	..	..	..	..	..	..
36/37 Other manufacturing	285	433	409	663	..	6.1	7.4	9.9	..	..
40/45 Construction, electricity, gas & water	..	..	..	1 775	..	..	..	..	..	..
50/55 Trade, repair, hotels & restaurants	..	..	..	..	..	..	..	..	..	..
65/74 Finance, insurance, business services	..	..	..	..	..	..	..	..	..	..
OTHER ACTIVITIES	..	..	..	..	..	..	..	..	..	..
01/99 **GRAND TOTAL**	..	..	..	..	..	..	..	..	..	..

Total manufacturing by investing country						As a % of total manufacturing by foreign affiliates				
All countries	**35 534**	**40 908**	**42 093**	**50 420**	..	**100.0**	**100.0**	**100.0**	**100.0**	..
United States	..	..	22 015	27 430	..	..	..	52.3	54.4	..
Canada	..	..	2 142	2 183	..	..	..	5.1	4.3	..
Mexico	..	..	..	..	..	..	..	..	..	..
Japan	..	..	2 581	2 641	..	..	..	6.1	5.2	..
Europe	..	..	..	..	..	..	..	..	..	..
European Union (15)	..	..	9 758	13 341	..	..	..	23.2	26.5	..
Belgium	..	..	..	289	..	..	..	..	0.6	..
France	..	..	2 757	3 399	..	..	..	6.5	6.7	..
Germany	..	..	3 658	3 868	..	..	..	8.7	7.7	..
Italy	..	..	..	761	..	..	..	..	1.5	..
Netherlands	..	..	1 613	1 771	..	..	..	3.8	3.5	..
Spain	..	..	..	..	..	..	..	..	..	..
Sweden	..	..	1 099	942	..	..	..	2.6	1.9	..
United Kingdom	..	..	..	..	..	..	..	..	..	..
Switzerland	..	..	2 544	2 933	..	..	..	6.0	5.8	..
Australia and New Zealand	..	..	1 075	892	..	..	..	2.6	1.8	..
Asia (non-OECD)	..	..	..	152	..	..	..	..	0.3	..
Latin America	..	..	..	0	..	..	..	..	0.0	..

Note: Majority foreign-owned firms.
Firmes sous contrôle étranger majoritaire.

Table 6. UNITED KINGDOM / ROYAUME-UNI

WAGES AND SALARIES / SALAIRES ET TRAITEMENTS

By industry (ISIC Rev. 3)	FOREIGN AFFILIATES (Millions of £)					AS A % OF NATIONAL TOTAL				
	1993	1994	1995	1996	1997	1993	1994	1995	1996	1997
10/14 Mining & quarrying	..	..	..	73	..	..	..	..	7.2	..
15/37 TOTAL MANUFACTURING	**13 461**	**14 463**	**13 791**	**16 356**	**16 048**	**21.9**	**22.5**	**21.5**	**23.4**	**..**
15/16 Food, beverages, tobacco	..	..	..	1 462	..	..	..	..	19.4	..
17/19 Textiles, clothing, leather, footwear	..	..	..	300	..	..	..	..	7.0	..
20/22 Wood and paper products	1 172	1 284	1 122	1 262	..	14.9	14.6	13.5	12.9	..
20 Wood products	48	54	43	..	..	5.7	5.5	4.6	..	..
21/22 Paper, printing and publishing	1 124	1 230	1 079	..	..	16.0	15.8	14.7	..	..
23/25 Chemicals, Total	2 920	2 778	2 801	3 333	..	32.3	29.9	28.8	32.5	..
23 Refined petroleum, nuclear fuel	143	125	160	182	..	21.4	18.6	24.3	25.5	..
24/25 Chemicals, rubber & plastics prod.	2 776	2 653	2 641	3 150	..	33.1	30.8	29.1	33.0	..
24 Chemical products	2 010	1 960	1 920	2 266	..	38.8	37.4	34.1	39.7	..
2423 Pharmaceuticals	..	..	..	761	..	..	..	..	49.4	..
25 Rubber and plastics products	766	693	721	884	..	24.0	20.6	21.0	23.0	..
26 Non-metallic mineral products	276	303	255	319	..	14.7	14.8	11.0	13.4	..
27/28 Basic & fabricated metals	994	995	998	1 082	..	13.6	13.2	12.7	12.2	..
27 Basic metals	473	405	424	435	..	23.3	20.2	17.7	16.8	..
28 Fabricated metal products	521	590	574	647	..	9.9	10.7	10.5	10.3	..
29/32 Machinery, Total	3 776	3 722	3 436	4 293	..	31.6	29.4	27.1	31.6	..
29/30 Non-electrical machinery	2 571	2 345	2 001	2 516	..	33.9	30.3	25.7	30.9	..
29 Non-electrical machinery nec	1 498	1 489	1 488	1 863	..	24.7	23.2	22.5	26.6	..
30 Office and computing machinery	1 073	856	512	653	..	71.2	64.3	44.3	56.5	..
31/32 Electrical & electronic equipment	1 205	1 377	1 435	1 777	..	27.6	28.1	29.2	32.7	..
31 Electrical machinery nec	582	630	537	782	..	22.2	22.9	20.1	26.2	..
32 Radio, TV & communications eq.	624	747	899	995	..	35.6	34.6	40.0	40.6	..
33 Scientific instruments	466	409	366	550	..	21.3	19.4	17.2	23.0	..
34/35 Transportation equipment	2 279	3 078	3 032	3 506	..	31.7	42.8	41.1	44.6	..
34 Motor vehicles	1 747	2 497	2 524	2 914	..	47.3	61.9	58.5	61.8	..
35 Other transport equipment	531	581	508	592	..	15.2	18.4	16.6	18.8	..
351 Shipbuilding & repairing	..	..	..	25	..	..	..	..	3.6	..
353 Aircraft and spacecraft	..	..	..	369	..	..	..	..	17.4	..
36/37 Other manufacturing	123	177	148	249	..	5.6	6.6	6.1	8.7	..
40/45 Construction, electricity, gas & water	..	..	..	552	..	..	..	..	3.1	..
50/55 Trade, repair, hotels & restaurants	..	..	..	..	..	..	..	..	..	..
65/74 Finance, insurance, business services	..	..	..	..	..	..	..	..	..	..
OTHER ACTIVITIES	..	..	..	..	..	..	..	..	..	..
01/99 GRAND TOTAL	**..**	**..**	**..**	**..**	**..**	**..**	**..**	**..**	**..**	**..**

Total manufacturing by investing country						As a % of total manufacturing by foreign affiliates				
All countries	13 461	14 463	13 791	16 356	16 048	100.0	100.0	100.0	100.0	100.0
United States	..	..	6 513	7 967	..	..	..	47.2	48.7	..
Canada	..	..	717	704	..	..	..	5.2	4.3	..
Mexico	..	..	..	..	..	..	..	..	..	..
Japan	..	..	815	952	..	..	..	5.9	5.8	..
Europe	..	..	..	..	..	..	..	..	..	..
European Union (15)	..	..	3 824	5 160	..	..	..	27.7	31.5	..
Belgium	..	..	..	120	..	..	..	..	0.7	..
France	..	..	987	1 182	..	..	..	7.2	7.2	..
Germany	..	..	1 513	1 701	..	..	..	11.0	10.4	..
Italy	..	..	..	219	..	..	..	..	1.3	..
Netherlands	..	..	677	731	..	..	..	4.9	4.5	..
Spain	..	..	..	..	..	..	..	..	..	..
Sweden	..	..	407	372	..	..	..	2.9	2.3	..
United Kingdom	..	..	..	..	..	..	..	..	..	..
Switzerland	..	..	842	885	..	..	..	6.1	5.4	..
Australia and New Zealand	..	..	387	253	..	..	..	2.8	1.5	..
Asia (non-OECD)	..	..	..	66	..	..	..	..	0.4	..
Latin America	..	..	..	0	..	..	..	..	0.0	..

Note: Majority foreign-owned firms.
Firmes sous contrôle étranger majoritaire.

Table 7. UNITED KINGDOM / ROYAUME-UNI

R&D EXPENDITURE / DÉPENSES DE R-D

By industry (ISIC Rev. 3)	FOREIGN AFFILIATES (Millions of £)					AS A % OF NATIONAL TOTAL				
	1993	1994	1995	1996	1997	1993	1994	1995	1996	1997
10/14 Mining & quarrying	..	10	8	11	9	..	13.9	12.3	17.2	20.5
15/37 TOTAL MANUFACTURING	..	**2 530**	**2 567**	**2 907**	..	..	**33.7**	**36.7**	**39.5**	..
15/16 Food, beverages, tobacco	..	142	58	78	76	..	40.1	33.7	39.4	42.2
17/19 Textiles, clothing, leather, footwear	..	18	6	13	15	..	40.0	31.6	48.1	45.5
20/22 Wood and paper products	..	18	22	36	33	..	35.3	48.9	63.2	75.0
20 Wood products	..	1	5	..	..	..	12.5	31.3	..	..
21/22 Paper, printing and publishing	..	17	17	..	..	..	39.5	58.6	..	..
23/25 Chemicals, Total	..	763	861	1 007	1 336	..	27.4	31.2	34.6	41.2
23 Refined petroleum, nuclear fuel	..	14	14	25	77	..	25.9	23.0	6.9	22.1
24/25 Chemicals, rubber & plastics prod.	..	749	847	982	1 259	..	27.4	31.3	38.6	43.5
24 Chemical products	..	715	812	946	1 237	..	27.0	30.7	38.2	43.7
2423 Pharmaceuticals	..	461	557	694	943	..	25.3	31.2	37.5	43.8
25 Rubber and plastics products	..	34	35	36	22	..	42.0	58.3	53.7	36.7
26 Non-metallic mineral products	..	6	8	11	6	..	15.4	17.0	18.3	12.8
27/28 Basic & fabricated metals	..	73	63	39	..	..	44.0	38.0	26.9	..
27 Basic metals	..	31	17	14	..	..	34.8	25.8	25.9	..
28 Fabricated metal products	..	42	46	25	24	..	54.5	46.0	27.5	27.3
29/32 Machinery, Total	..	790	635	742	720	..	38.5	35.4	40.6	41.5
29/30 Non-electrical machinery	..	404	285	356	361	..	48.0	40.2	52.7	55.2
29 Non-electrical machinery nec	..	137	173	232	293	..	26.8	30.9	45.1	53.1
30 Office and computing machinery	..	267	112	124	68	..	81.2	74.7	77.0	66.7
31/32 Electrical & electronic equipment	..	386	350	386	359	..	31.8	32.3	33.5	33.3
31 Electrical machinery nec	..	124	151	118	82	..	21.2	30.6	24.1	19.3
32 Radio, TV & communications eq.	..	262	199	268	277	..	41.7	33.7	40.5	42.3
33 Scientific instruments	..	121	159	151	155	..	47.6	52.5	49.2	46.1
34/35 Transportation equipment	..	596	751	822	883	..	34.2	44.4	45.5	46.5
34 Motor vehicles	..	487	604	731	786	..	75.9	80.0	77.3	81.6
35 Other transport equipment	..	109	147	91	97	..	9.9	16.0	10.6	10.4
351 Shipbuilding & repairing	..	1	3	2	3	..	5.9	15.0	10.0	20.0
353 Aircraft and spacecraft	..	98	132	71	82	..	9.3	15.0	8.7	9.2
36/37 Other manufacturing	..	3	4	8	11	..	21.4	57.1	47.1	44.0
40/45 Construction, electricity, gas & water	..	6	2	3	..	..	2.9	1.2	1.9	..
50/55 Trade, repair, hotels & restaurants	..	1	6	2	2	..	20.0	66.7	50.0	40.0
65/74 Finance, insurance, business services	..	495	751	736	636	..	36.9	46.7	57.5	55.4
OTHER ACTIVITIES	..	35	182	176	..	..	8.8	34.0	35.0	..
01/99 GRAND TOTAL	..	**3 079**	**3 516**	**3 835**	**4 126**	..	**32.3**	**37.5**	**41.0**	**43.2**

Grand total by investing country						As a % of grand total by foreign affiliates				
All countries	..	**3 079**	**3 516**	**3 835**	**4 126**	..	**100.0**	**100.0**	**100.0**	**100.0**
United States	..	1 378	1 385	1 472	1 664	..	44.8	39.4	38.4	40.3
Canada	..	..	..	..	..	..	..	..	..	..
Mexico	..	..	..	..	..	..	..	..	..	..
Japan	..	341	296	323	244	..	11.1	8.4	8.4	5.9
Europe	..	..	..	..	..	..	..	..	..	..
European Union (15)	..	665	736	801	887	..	21.6	20.9	20.9	21.5
Belgium	..	..	..	..	..	..	..	..	..	..
France	..	148	175	151	94	..	4.8	5.0	3.9	2.3
Germany	..	266	288	301	213	..	8.6	8.2	7.8	5.2
Italy	..	..	..	..	..	..	..	..	..	..
Netherlands	..	..	..	..	..	..	..	..	..	..
Spain	..	..	..	..	..	..	..	..	..	..
Sweden	..	..	..	..	..	..	..	..	..	..
United Kingdom	..	..	..	..	..	..	..	..	..	..
Switzerland	..	..	..	..	..	..	..	..	..	..
Australia and New Zealand	..	..	..	..	..	..	..	..	..	..
Asia (non-OECD)	..	..	..	..	..	..	..	..	..	..
Latin America	..	..	..	..	..	..	..	..	..	..

Note: Majority foreign-owned firms.
Firmes sous contrôle étranger majoritaire.

Table 9. UNITED KINGDOM / ROYAUME-UNI

GROSS FIXED CAPITAL FORMATION / FORMATION BRUTE DE CAPITAL FIXE

By industry (ISIC Rev. 3)		FOREIGN AFFILIATES (Millions of £)					AS A % OF NATIONAL TOTAL				
		1993	1994	1995	1996	1997	1993	1994	1995	1996	1997
10/14	Mining & quarrying	..	..	..	34	..	..	..	..	..	..
15/37	**TOTAL MANUFACTURING**	**3 807**	**4 175**	**5 340**	**5 859**	**..**	**29.7**	**30.5**	**31.8**	**..**	**..**
15/16	Food, beverages, tobacco	..	..	..	449	..	..	..	..	..	..
17/19	Textiles, clothing, leather, footwear	..	..	..	73	..	..	..	..	..	..
20/22	Wood and paper products	382	273	274	311	..	22.0	14.8	13.2	..	..
20	Wood products	47	32	26	9	..	36.6	25.9	18.3	..	..
21/22	Paper, printing and publishing	336	240	248	302	..	20.9	14.0	12.8	..	..
23/25	Chemicals, Total	1 180	956	1 166	1 488	..	35.4	30.0	29.7	..	..
23	Refined petroleum, nuclear fuel	212	122	213	199	..	29.4	21.1	28.8	..	..
24/25	Chemicals, rubber & plastics prod.	968	834	953	1 289	..	37.0	32.0	30.0	..	..
24	Chemical products	805	691	805	1 078	..	43.3	37.2	35.4	..	..
2423	Pharmaceuticals	..	..	..	297	..	..	..	..	..	..
25	Rubber and plastics products	163	143	148	211	..	21.6	19.1	16.4	..	..
26	Non-metallic mineral products	39	71	89	87	..	10.3	18.6	15.4	..	..
27/28	Basic & fabricated metals	188	204	291	267	..	20.9	19.6	23.0	..	..
27	Basic metals	99	76	144	136	..	30.7	22.9	28.7	..	..
28	Fabricated metal products	89	129	147	132	..	15.4	18.0	19.3	..	..
29/32	Machinery, Total	865	1 057	1 398	1 419	..	46.2	47.2	45.9	..	..
29/30	Non-electrical machinery	421	511	495	544	..	44.9	44.0	35.6	..	..
29	Non-electrical machinery nec	242	276	271	368	..	34.4	32.6	26.4	..	..
30	Office and computing machinery	179	235	224	177	..	76.1	75.0	61.6	..	..
31/32	Electrical & electronic equipment	445	546	903	875	..	47.6	50.6	54.6	..	..
31	Electrical machinery nec	101	105	98	164	..	25.5	30.8	25.6	..	..
32	Radio, TV & communications eq.	344	441	805	711	..	63.6	59.8	63.4	..	..
33	Scientific instruments	66	87	81	123	..	24.5	24.5	25.2	..	..
34/35	Transportation equipment	593	1 025	1 564	1 598	..	45.8	68.2	67.9	..	..
34	Motor vehicles	535	986	1 448	1 529	..	54.5	78.3	74.8	..	..
35	Other transport equipment	58	39	116	70	..	18.6	16.0	31.7	..	..
351	Shipbuilding & repairing	..	..	..	0	..	..	..	..	..	..
353	Aircraft and spacecraft	..	..	..	52	..	..	..	..	..	..
36/37	Other manufacturing	16	38	26	42	..	6.9	11.9	6.8	..	..
40/45	Construction, electricity, gas & water	..	..	..	263	..	..	..	..	..	..
50/55	Trade, repair, hotels & restaurants	..	..	..	..	..	..	..	..	..	..
65/74	Finance, insurance, business services	..	..	..	..	..	..	..	..	..	..
	OTHER ACTIVITIES	..	..	..	..	..	..	..	..	..	..
01/99	**GRAND TOTAL**	**..**	**..**	**..**	**..**	**..**	**..**	**..**	**..**	**..**	**..**

Total manufacturing by investing country	1993	1994	1995	1996	1997	As a % of total manufacturing by foreign affiliates				
						1993	1994	1995	1996	1997
All countries	3 807	4 175	5 340	5 859	..	100.0	100.0	100.0	100.0	..
United States	..	..	2 586	2 829	..	..	..	48.4	48.3	..
Canada	..	..	163	187	..	..	..	3.1	3.2	..
Mexico	..	..	..	..	..	..	..	..	..	..
Japan	..	..	776	637	..	..	..	14.5	10.9	..
Europe	..	..	..	..	..	..	..	..	..	..
European Union (15)	..	..	1 305	1 697	..	..	..	24.4	29.0	..
Belgium	..	..	..	55	..	..	..	..	0.9	..
France	..	..	268	268	..	..	..	5.0	4.6	..
Germany	..	..	707	780	..	..	..	13.2	13.3	..
Italy	..	..	..	63	..	..	..	..	1.1	..
Netherlands	..	..	150	224	..	..	..	2.8	3.8	..
Spain	..	..	..	..	..	..	..	..	..	..
Sweden	..	..	99	102	..	..	..	1.9	1.7	..
United Kingdom	..	..	..	..	..	..	..	..	..	..
Switzerland	..	..	267	266	..	..	..	5.0	4.5	..
Australia and New Zealand	..	..	63	28	..	..	..	1.2	0.5	..
Asia (non-OECD)	..	..	..	18	..	..	..	..	0.3	..
Latin America	..	..	..	0	..	..	..	..	0.0	..

Note: Majority foreign-owned firms.
Firmes sous contrôle étranger majoritaire.

Table 14. UNITED KINGDOM / ROYAUME-UNI

GROSS OPERATING SURPLUS / EXCÉDENT BRUT D'EXPLOITATION

By industry (ISIC Rev. 3)	FOREIGN AFFILIATES (Millions of £)					AS A % OF NATIONAL TOTAL				
	1993	1994	1995	1996	1997	1993	1994	1995	1996	1997
10/14 Mining & quarrying	..	..	..	91	..	..	..	..	5.8	..
15/37 **TOTAL MANUFACTURING**	**13 362**	**16 490**	**18 544**	**22 387**	**20 127**	..	..	**28.9**	**31.5**	..
15/16 Food, beverages, tobacco	..	..	..	3 493	..	..	..	..	29.6	..
17/19 Textiles, clothing, leather, footwear				353	..				10.4	..
20/22 Wood and paper products	1 332	1 499	1 524	1 697					19.5	
20 Wood products	71	97	121							
21/22 Paper, printing and publishing	1 262	1 403	1 403	..					..	
23/25 Chemicals, Total	4 395	4 335	4 938	5 792					39.0	
23 Refined petroleum, nuclear fuel	887	660	718	716					38.8	
24/25 Chemicals, rubber & plastics prod.	3 508	3 675	4 221	5 076					39.0	
24 Chemical products	2 906	3 048	3 423	4 200					43.1	
2423 Pharmaceuticals	..	..		1 111					42.2	
25 Rubber and plastics products	602	627	798	876					26.7	
26 Non-metallic mineral products	172	294	266	358					13.8	
27/28 Basic & fabricated metals	865	1 111	1 297	1 070					16.5	
27 Basic metals	446	613	739	555					21.8	
28 Fabricated metal products	419	497	558	514					13.1	
29/32 Machinery, Total	2 569	3 302	4 416	5 083					42.3	
29/30 Non-electrical machinery	1 256	1 789	2 580	3 108					42.5	
29 Non-electrical machinery nec	933	1 142	1 333	1 603					29.2	
30 Office and computing machinery	323	648	1 247	1 505					82.1	
31/32 Electrical & electronic equipment	1 313	1 513	1 837	1 975					42.0	
31 Electrical machinery nec	437	421	434	524					25.5	
32 Radio, TV & communications eq.	876	1 092	1 403	1 451					54.9	
33 Scientific instruments	381	498	444	493					25.0	
34/35 Transportation equipment	1 442	2 318	2 572	3 794					54.5	
34 Motor vehicles	1 247	2 050	2 487	3 555					72.8	
35 Other transport equipment	195	269	85	239					11.5	
351 Shipbuilding & repairing	..	..	..	- 2					-0.4	
353 Aircraft and spacecraft	..	..	..	112					8.2	
36/37 Other manufacturing	90	164	186	255					11.1	
40/45 Construction, electricity, gas & water	..	..	..	707	..	..	..	..	2.9	
50/55 Trade, repair, hotels & restaurants	..	..	..	..	..	..	..	..	..	
65/74 Finance, insurance, business services	..	..	..	..	..	..	..	..	..	..
OTHER ACTIVITIES	..	..	..	..	..	..	..	..	..	..
01/99 **GRAND TOTAL**	..	..	..	..	..	..	..	..	..	..

Total manufacturing by investing country						As a % of total manufacturing by foreign affiliates				
All countries	13 362	16 490	18 544	22 387	20 127	100.0	100.0	100.0	100.0	100.0
United States	..	..	10 290	13 603	..	..	..	55.5	60.8	..
Canada	..	..	995	1 006	..	..	..	5.4	4.5	..
Mexico	..	..	..	..	..	..	..	..	..	..
Japan	..	..	1 331	1 082	..	..	..	7.2	4.8	..
Europe	..	..	..	..	..	..	..	..	..	..
European Union (15)	..	..	3 480	4 449	..	..	..	18.8	19.9	..
Belgium	..	..	..	58	..	..	..	..	0.3	..
France	..	..	1 152	1 205	..	..	..	6.2	5.4	..
Germany	..	..	1 117	1 040	..	..	..	6.0	4.6	..
Italy	..	..	..	312	..	..	..	..	1.4	..
Netherlands	..	..	551	639	..	..	..	3.0	2.9	..
Spain	..	..	..	..	..	..	..	..	..	..
Sweden	..	..	434	331	..	..	..	2.3	1.5	..
United Kingdom	..	..	..	..	..	..	..	..	..	..
Switzerland	..	..	1 189	1 402	..	..	..	6.4	6.3	..
Australia and New Zealand	..	..	423	499	..	..	..	2.3	2.2	..
Asia (non-OECD)	..	..	..	51	..	..	..	..	0.2	..
Latin America	..	..	..	0	..	..	..	..	0.0	..

Note: Majority foreign-owned firms.
Firmes sous contrôle étranger majoritaire.

UNITED KINGDOM

Source

The data are prepared by the Office for National Statistics and are based on the Annual Business Inquiry, which replaced the annual Census of Production in 1993. This inquiry covers United Kingdom (except Channel Islands and Isle of Man) "enterprises" engaged in industrial production, *i.e.* mining and quarrying, manufacturing, construction, and electricity, gas and water supply industries (Sections C to F of SIC92). Up to 1995, data for foreign enterprises, *i.e.* controlled or owned by companies incorporated overseas (majority foreign ownership), are available separately for manufacturing industries only.

The reporting unit is the *company*, with the exception of large mixed activity companies which are asked to make separate returns to the inquiry for each of their production activities on an establishment basis. These reporting units are referred to as "enterprises".

Forms are in general despatched to all businesses with 100 or more employees, samples of one-in-four and one-in-two respectively being taken for businesses in the 20-49 and 50-99 employment size bands. Estimates are made for non-responders, unsatisfactory returns and enterprises not selected for the Inquiry. The data are published every year in *Business Monitor – Production and Construction Inquiry, Summary Volume (PA 1002)* and PACSTAT CD Rom.

For *R&D expenditure*, data come from the Survey of Business Enterprise R&D and are published by the Office for National Statistics in *Research and Development in UK Business*.

National totals: for all variables except *R&D expenditure*, data come from the OECD ISIS database until 1995. From 1996, they have been provided by the NSO and are fully compatible with foreign affiliates' data.

Industrial classification

For all variables, data are classified according to the principal industrial activity of the enterprise.

Since 1993, the inquiry has been conducted on the Standard Industrial Classification Revised (SIC92), based on ISIC Revision 3.

Variables

- *Number of employees* consists of the average number of administrative, technical and clerical employees and operatives on the payroll and the number of working proprietors employed during the year of return. Full-time and part-time employees are included but outworkers and casual employees are excluded.

- *Production* is defined as gross output and is calculated by adjusting the value of total sales and work done by the change during the year of work in progress and goods on hand for sale.

269

- *Value added* is defined as net output, which is calculated by deducting from gross output the cost of purchases of materials for use in production and packaging and fuel and purchases of goods for merchanting or factoring, the cost of industrial services received, and is adjusted for net duties and levies, etc., where applicable. Purchases are adjusted for changes during the year of stocks of materials, stores and fuel.

- *Wages and salaries* represent amounts paid during the year to administrative, technical and clerical employees and to operatives. All overtime payments, bonuses, commissions, holiday pay and redundancy payments less any amounts reimbursed for this purpose from government sources are included. No deduction is made for income tax or employees' national insurance contributions, etc. Payments to working proprietors, payments in kind, travelling expenses, lodging allowances, etc., and employers' national insurance contributions, etc., are excluded.

- *Gross fixed capital formation* is defined as net capital expenditure, which is calculated by adding to the value of new building work acquisitions less disposals of land and existing buildings, vehicles and plant and machinery.

- *Gross operating surplus* is defined as gross value added at factor cost less wages and salaries.

Geographical breakdown

The country of origin is the country of the "ultimate beneficial owner".

Prior to 1996, the European Union consists of its 12 former member states and the figures for Australia and New Zealand concern Australia only.

For *R&D expenditure*, the breakdown by country of origin is available for the *Grand total* and not for *Total manufacturing* as for other variables.

ROYAUME-UNI

Source

Les données émanent de l'Office national des statistiques et sont basées sur l'Enquête annuelle sur les entreprises qui a remplacé en 1993 le Recensement annuel de la production. Cette enquête couvre au Royaume-Uni (à l'exception des îles anglo-normandes et de l'île de Man) les "entreprises" engagées dans la production industrielle, c'est-à-dire les industries extractives, le secteur manufacturier, la construction, la production et la distribution d'électricité, de gaz et d'eau (Divisions C à F de la SIC92). Jusqu'en 1995, les données concernant les entreprises étrangères, c'est-à-dire contrôlées par ou appartenant à des sociétés immatriculées à l'étranger (participation étrangère majoritaire), sont disponibles séparément pour l'industrie manufacturière seulement.

L'unité employée pour le recensement est la *société*, à l'exception des grandes sociétés à l'activité mixte qui sont tenues, dans ce cadre, de faire des rapports séparés pour chacune de leurs activités de production sur la base de l'établissement. Il est fait référence à ces unités sous le terme d'"entreprises".

Des formulaires sont en général envoyés à toutes les entreprises de 100 salariés ou plus. Pour les autres, on tire un échantillon : 1 sur 4 dans le groupe des entreprises de 20 à 49 salariés, et 1 sur 2 dans celui des entreprises de 50 à 99 salariés. On fait des estimations pour les non réponses, les déclarations non satisfaisantes et les entreprises non sélectionnées pour l'enquête. Les données sont publiées chaque année dans *Business Monitor – Production and Construction Inquiry, Summary Volume (PA 1002)* et dans le CD-Rom PACSTAT.

Pour les *Dépenses de R-D*, les données proviennent de l'enquête sur la R-D des entreprises et sont publiées par l'ONS dans *Research and Development in UK Business*.

Totaux nationaux : pour toutes les variables à l'exception des *Dépenses de R-D*, les données proviennent de la base de données SISI de l'OCDE jusqu'en 1995. A partir de 1996, elles sont fournies par l'ONS et sont entièrement compatibles avec les données relatives aux filiales étrangères.

Classification industrielle

Pour toutes les variables, les données sont classées selon l'activité industrielle principale de l'entreprise.

Depuis 1993, les données sont classées selon la Classification industrielle standard révisée (SIC92), basée sur la CITI révision 3.

Variables

- Le *Nombre de salariés* est le nombre moyen d'employés de bureau, personnel administratif et technique et d'ouvriers, et le nombre de propriétaires exploitants employés pendant l'exercice considéré. Sont pris en compte les salariés à plein temps et à temps partiel, mais sont exclus les travailleurs à domicile et occasionnels.

- La *Production* est définie en tant que production brute et est calculée en ajustant la valeur des ventes totales et travaux effectués aux variations durant l'année des travaux en cours et biens disponibles à la vente.

- La *Valeur ajoutée* est en fait la production nette qui est calculée en déduisant de la production brute le coût des achats de matériels à utiliser dans la production et l'emballage ainsi que de fuel, et des achats pour courtage sur marchandises ou affacturage, le coût des services industriels reçus, et est ajustée des droits et prélèvements nets, etc., le cas échéant. Les achats sont ajustés des variations survenues pendant l'année des stocks de matériels, approvisionnements et fuel.

- Les *Salaires et traitements* représentent les montants versés pendant l'année aux employés de bureau, au personnel administratif et technique et aux ouvriers. Toutes les heures supplémentaires, primes, commissions, congés payés et indemnités pour perte d'emploi sont inclus, déduction faite de tout montant de source publique remboursé à cette fin. Aucune déduction n'est faite pour l'impôt sur le revenu ou les cotisations salariales au régime national d'assurance. Les versements aux propriétaires exploitants, paiements en nature, frais de voyage, indemnités de logement, etc., et les cotisations patronales au régime d'assurance sociale sont exclus.

- La *Formation brute de capital fixe* est définie comme les dépenses nettes en capital qui sont calculées en ajoutant à la valeur des constructions nouvelles les acquisitions moins les cessions de terrains et bâtiments existants, véhicules, installations et équipements.

- L'*Excédent brut d'exploitation* est défini comme la valeur ajoutée brute au coût des facteurs, moins les salaires et traitements.

Ventilation géographique

Le pays d'origine est le pays du bénéficiaire ultime de l'investissement.

Avant 1996, l'Union européenne ne comprend que les 12 anciens États membres, et les chiffres pour Australie et Nouvelle-Zélande concernent l'Australie seulement.

Pour les *Dépenses de R-D*, la ventilation par pays d'origine est disponible pour le *Total général* et non pour le *Total manufacturier* comme pour les autres variables.

UNITED STATES

ÉTATS-UNIS

Sources et méthodes

Table 1a. UNITED STATES / ÉTATS-UNIS

NUMBER OF ENTERPRISES / NOMBRE D'ENTREPRISES

By industry (ISIC Rev. 3)		FOREIGN AFFILIATES (Units)									
		1987	1988	1989	1990	1991	1992	1993	1994	1995	1996
10/14	Mining & quarrying	108	109	109	114	119	110	110	112	113	108
15/37	**TOTAL MANUFACTURING**	**1 739**	**1 912**	**2 143**	**2 431**	**2 563**	**2 808**	**2 866**	**2 926**	**3 019**	**2 950**
15/16	Food, beverages, tobacco	139	168	197	226	231	258	264	260	258	257
17/19	Textiles, clothing, leather, footwear	81	94	95	104	111	131	133	139	139	130
20/22	Wood and paper products	166	170	175	202	216	239	245	252	259	254
20	Wood products	44	46	47	60	67	78	76	75	76	73
21/22	Paper, printing and publishing	122	124	128	142	149	161	169	177	183	181
23/25	Chemicals, Total	292	315	341	392	412	485	498	524	550	542
23	Refined petroleum, nuclear fuel	..	..	..	..	..	..	..	..	..	..
24/25	Chemicals, rubber & plastics prod.	292	315	341	392	412	485	498	524	550	542
24	Chemical products	190	203	214	253	260	304	314	332	346	338
2423	Pharmaceuticals	46	50	49	52	59	62	70	80	85	84
25	Rubber and plastics products	102	112	127	139	152	181	184	192	204	204
26	Non-metallic mineral products	107	112	122	125	129	130	131	129	138	130
27/28	Basic & fabricated metals	227	254	286	345	368	396	399	401	404	407
27	Basic metals	88	90	108	143	147	159	162	170	168	173
28	Fabricated metal products	139	164	178	202	221	237	237	231	236	234
29/32	Machinery, Total	475	525	600	672	708	715	735	745	773	736
29/30	Non-electrical machinery	294	318	360	399	423	430	447	451	466	447
29	Non-electrical machinery nec	255	270	293	312	337	358	360	365	374	362
30	Office and computing machinery	39	48	67	87	86	72	87	86	92	85
31/32	Electrical & electronic equipment	181	207	240	273	285	285	288	294	307	289
31	Electrical machinery nec	71	80	87	85	93	102	104	107	107	102
32	Radio, TV & communications eq.	110	127	153	188	192	183	184	187	200	187
33	Scientific instruments	98	107	128	143	145	163	170	175	175	175
34/35	Transportation equipment	76	86	118	134	146	170	174	190	209	200
34	Motor vehicles	48	55	83	97	102	114	117	134	150	148
35	Other transport equipment	28	31	35	37	44	56	57	56	59	52
351	Shipbuilding & repairing	..	..	..	..	..	..	..	..	..	..
353	Aircraft and spacecraft	..	..	..	..	..	..	..	..	..	..
36/37	Other manufacturing	78	81	81	88	97	121	117	111	114	119
40/45	Construction, electricity, gas & water	107	108	116	130	135	140	141	146	144	137
50/55	Trade, repair, hotels & restaurants	1 742	1 786	1 883	1 948	2 014	2 545	2 597	2 602	2 618	2 582
65/74	Finance, insurance, business services	2 952	3 152	3 489	3 804	3 954	4 406	4 488	4 564	4 625	4 575
	OTHER ACTIVITIES	1 462	1 567	1 730	1 855	1 962	2 129	2 187	2 256	2 297	2 274
01/99	**GRAND TOTAL**	**8 110**	**8 634**	**9 470**	**10 282**	**10 747**	**12 138**	**12 389**	**12 606**	**12 816**	**12 626**

Total manufacturing by investing country											
All countries		1 739	1 912	2 143	2 431	2 563	2 808	2 866	2 926	3 019	2 950
United States		..	..	..	..	..	..	..	..	..	..
Canada		..	..	..	..	..	..	..	..	..	..
Mexico		..	..	..	..	..	..	..	..	..	..
Japan		..	..	..	..	..	..	..	..	..	..
Europe		..	..	..	..	..	..	..	..	..	..
European Union (15)		..	..	..	..	..	..	..	..	..	..
Belgium		..	..	..	..	..	..	..	..	..	..
France		..	..	..	..	..	..	..	..	..	..
Germany		..	..	..	..	..	..	..	..	..	..
Italy		..	..	..	..	..	..	..	..	..	..
Netherlands		..	..	..	..	..	..	..	..	..	..
Spain		..	..	..	..	..	..	..	..	..	..
Sweden		..	..	..	..	..	..	..	..	..	..
United Kingdom		..	..	..	..	..	..	..	..	..	..
Switzerland		..	..	..	..	..	..	..	..	..	..
Australia and New Zealand		..	..	..	..	..	..	..	..	..	..
Asia (non-OECD)		..	..	..	..	..	..	..	..	..	..
Latin America		..	..	..	..	..	..	..	..	..	..

Note: **Enterprise-level data.** Defined as the number of non-bank affiliates. See country notes.
Données au niveau de l'entreprise. Défini comme le nombre d'entreprises affiliées du secteur non bancaire. Voir les notes par pays.

NUMBER OF EMPLOYEES / NOMBRE DE SALARIÉS

By industry (ISIC Rev. 3)		FOREIGN AFFILIATES (Thousands)									
		1987	1988	1989	1990	1991	1992	1993	1994	1995	1996
10/14	Mining & quarrying	27.6	26.7	44.1	36.0	44.2	48.1	49.3	46.8	42.0	41.6
15/37	**TOTAL MANUFACTURING**	**1 542.6**	**1 828.6**	**2 138.6**	**2 220.7**	**2 233.6**	**2 252.0**	**2 241.2**	**2 309.5**	**2 281.9**	**2 213.6**
15/16	Food, beverages, tobacco	142.6	177.4	251.3	247.3	241.0	242.3	199.9	234.3	234.6	205.4
17/19	Textiles, clothing, leather, footwear	40.4	50.5	58.9	60.3	63.0	76.3	89.3	100.1	89.7	90.0
20/22	Wood and paper products	137.2	157.7	159.3	190.4	194.6	186.9	214.0	220.5	235.2	222.5
20	Wood products	13.9	17.1	13.3	19.9	23.6	23.1	26.1	27.1	23.9	24.7
21/22	Paper, printing and publishing	123.3	140.6	146.0	170.5	171.0	163.8	187.9	193.4	211.3	197.8
23/25	Chemicals, Total	443.4	471.1	525.1	626.0	610.0	622.2	611.7	619.6	537.7	535.0
23	Refined petroleum, nuclear fuel	..	..	..	..	..	..	..	..	..	..
24/25	Chemicals, rubber & plastics prod.	443.4	471.1	525.1	626.0	610.0	622.2	611.7	619.6	537.7	535.0
24	Chemical products	395.8	390.7	437.1	512.5	508.3	515.6	505.8	508.3	416.7	409.8
2423	Pharmaceuticals	70.8	79.3	93.3	115.0	123.4	127.9	159.8	164.8	151.6	149.6
25	Rubber and plastics products	47.6	80.4	88.0	113.5	101.7	106.6	105.9	111.3	121.0	125.2
26	Non-metallic mineral products	103.2	103.5	115.6	122.8	111.9	114.0	108.9	105.2	120.9	121.0
27/28	Basic & fabricated metals	159.3	199.8	280.2	255.5	270.2	266.0	271.7	261.6	241.4	233.3
27	Basic metals	85.5	87.7	118.4	135.2	149.3	139.5	141.8	123.8	111.2	97.5
28	Fabricated metal products	73.8	112.1	161.8	120.3	120.9	126.5	129.9	137.8	130.1	135.9
29/32	Machinery, Total	326.1	464.8	511.8	509.1	509.0	503.0	498.8	516.3	545.5	536.8
29/30	Non-electrical machinery	109.3	194.1	245.3	219.0	218.6	210.5	211.1	225.1	240.7	235.7
29	Non-electrical machinery nec	74.1	155.5	199.6	157.6	158.7	168.5	175.0	197.8	198.3	197.1
30	Office and computing machinery	35.2	38.5	45.7	61.3	59.9	42.0	36.1	27.3	42.4	38.6
31/32	Electrical & electronic equipment	216.8	270.7	266.6	290.1	290.4	292.5	287.7	291.3	304.8	301.1
31	Electrical machinery nec	82.6	125.0	118.1	135.1	154.1	144.8	147.4	164.5	175.5	167.0
32	Radio, TV & communications eq.	134.3	145.7	148.5	155.1	136.2	147.7	140.3	126.8	129.3	134.1
33	Scientific instruments	64.6	65.3	71.9	90.3	107.4	108.8	110.0	97.8	105.6	97.8
34/35	Transportation equipment	55.7	55.4	74.5	87.8	95.2	101.5	104.4	119.2	141.2	140.6
34	Motor vehicles	33.2	35.8	44.6	57.0	56.2	57.7	64.2	84.2	107.2	110.5
35	Other transport equipment	22.5	19.6	29.9	30.8	39.0	43.8	40.2	35.0	34.0	30.1
351	Shipbuilding & repairing	..	..	..	..	..	..	..	..	..	..
353	Aircraft and spacecraft	..	..	..	..	..	..	..	..	..	..
36/37	Other manufacturing	70.0	83.1	89.8	31.2	31.4	31.2	32.5	34.9	30.2	31.3
40/45	Construction, electricity, gas & water	52.4	56.8	72.5	92.0	82.0	59.1	56.2	54.1	66.6	69.1
50/55	Trade, repair, hotels & restaurants	880.6	1 043.2	1 202.6	1 174.6	1 245.8	1 149.1	1 191.8	1 150.8	1 224.5	1 309.6
65/74	Finance, insurance, business services	205.2	237.0	244.6	230.4	252.4	247.7	238.1	226.7	221.0	228.4
	OTHER ACTIVITIES	515.9	651.9	809.0	980.7	1 014.0	959.3	989.0	1 052.6	1 105.7	1 115.2
01/99	**GRAND TOTAL**	**3 224.3**	**3 844.2**	**4 511.5**	**4 734.5**	**4 871.9**	**4 715.4**	**4 765.6**	**4 840.5**	**4 941.8**	**4 977.5**

Total manufacturing by investing country	1987	1988	1989	1990	1991	1992	1993	1994	1995	1996
All countries	**1 542.6**	**1 828.6**	**2 138.6**	**2 220.7**	**2 233.6**	**2 252.0**	**2 241.2**	**2 309.5**	**2 281.9**	**2 213.6**
United States	10.0	11.9	10.9	3.6	3.6	2.7	1.8	4.9	6.0	9.6
Canada	275.1	295.7	298.1	307.8	299.8	294.2	315.8	357.3	294.8	260.2
Mexico	1.3	1.3	..	11.0	12.3	18.3	18.1	22.3	23.8	22.7
Japan	86.9	170.1	224.1	296.3	311.0	318.5	324.6	333.6	372.4	361.1
Europe	1 034.4	1 218.1	1 452.8	1 457.9	1 468.0	1 479.2	1 427.1	1 439.7	1 434.5	1 410.5
European Union (15)	838.0	989.7	1 167.5	1 173.7	1 184.9	1 180.2	1 152.3	1 160.9	1 256.5	1 234.5
Belgium	9.5	10.6	9.5	10.8	11.4	12.7	10.8	12.4	12.8	12.3
France	110.1	142.0	151.0	193.5	199.9	195.0	192.4	195.6	187.9	198.2
Germany	193.9	216.1	250.0	251.5	247.5	260.4	277.3	283.9	290.7	293.8
Italy	8.0	10.6	14.3	15.3	29.8	32.1	32.8	31.1	27.9	23.7
Netherlands	93.5	113.2	126.6	126.7	115.9	115.4	92.8	88.9	87.9	95.7
Spain	0.3	0.6	0.6	0.6	1.6	1.5	2.7	2.9	2.8	2.8
Sweden	60.0	69.0	68.3	72.5	70.7	75.5	73.0	68.2	81.7	68.1
United Kingdom	391.2	463.2	580.6	535.2	540.9	527.6	507.4	507.0	498.1	477.4
Switzerland	116.0	130.9	185.1	179.3	178.8	192.1	169.7	169.0	166.6	164.7
Australia and New Zealand	39.4	37.3	56.3	60.4	57.0	53.1	52.8	38.9	40.8	41.4
Asia (non-OECD)	20.5	17.7	19.2	26.7	29.6	35.0	37.3	46.0	51.6	43.8
Latin America	54.8	58.2	59.6	55.6	52.2	53.2	54.7	60.0	50.7	47.3

Note: **Enterprise-level data.** Employment **by industry of the affiliate**. See country notes.
Données au niveau de l'entreprise. Emploi par **industrie de la filiale**. Voir les notes par pays.

NUMBER OF EMPLOYEES / NOMBRE DE SALARIÉS

By industry (National classification, ISI)	FOREIGN AFFILIATES (Thousands)					AS A % OF NATIONAL TOTAL				
	1992	1993	1994	1995	1996	1992	1993	1994	1995	1996
Agriculture, forestry and fishing	32	31	32	28	29	1.7	1.7	1.7	1.4	1.4
Mining, excluding oil and gas extraction	68	75	67	63	62	24.0	28.0	25.1	23.8	24.2
Construction	68	64	61	76	72	1.4	1.3	1.2	1.4	1.3
TOTAL MANUFACTURING	**2 140**	**2 149**	**2 193**	**2 159**	**2 148**	**11.5**	**11.6**	**11.7**	**11.4**	**11.4**
Food and kindred products	198	184	188	182	158	11.9	10.9	11.2	10.8	9.3
Textile mill products	45	44	50	46	47	6.7	6.5	7.4	7.0	7.5
Apparel and other textile products	32	46	56	39	41	3.2	4.7	5.7	4.1	4.6
Lumber, wood, furniture and fixtures	31	33	33	27	28	2.6	2.7	2.6	2.1	2.1
Paper and allied products	52	52	51	56	58	7.5	7.5	7.3	8.1	8.5
Printing and publishing	101	113	119	120	113	6.6	7.4	7.6	7.6	7.2
Chemicals and allied products	348	354	354	317	317	32.1	33.0	33.5	30.5	30.7
Petroleum and coal products	89	77	69	54	54	17.4	15.4	14.1	11.7	11.7
Rubber and plastics products	130	130	135	139	144	14.8	14.3	14.1	14.2	14.7
Stone, clay and glass product	107	108	104	113	115	20.8	20.7	19.4	20.9	21.0
Primary metal industries	110	113	116	113	100	15.9	16.6	16.6	15.9	14.1
Fabricated metal products	110	114	117	114	125	8.3	8.5	8.4	7.9	8.6
Industrial machinery and equipment	217	218	221	235	233	11.2	11.2	11.1	11.3	11.0
Electronic and other electric equipment	263	259	268	291	298	17.2	16.9	16.9	17.9	18.0
Motor vehicles and equipment	90	98	113	127	137	11.0	11.7	12.6	13.1	14.2
Other transportation equipment	50	38	32	33	29	4.9	4.2	3.8	4.1	3.6
Instruments and related products	111	112	114	112	110	11.9	12.5	13.3	13.4	12.8
Other manufacturing	56	54	54	42	41	10.2	9.7	9.6	7.5	7.6
Transportation	198	250	250	258	221	5.6	6.8	6.5	6.5	5.4
Communication and public utilities	33	39	80	99	135	1.5	1.7	3.6	4.5	6.0
Wholesale trade	346	359	363	373	377	5.6	5.9	5.8	5.8	5.8
Retail trade	798	831	830	888	925	4.0	4.1	3.9	4.1	4.2
Finance, excluding depository institutions	70	60	63	66	70	6.3	5.0	4.9	5.2	5.2
Insurance	143	140	137	134	136	6.5	6.3	6.1	6.0	6.0
Real estate	32	31	27	27	29	2.4	2.2	1.9	1.9	2.0
Services	**702**	**673**	**676**	**707**	**720**	**2.3**	**2.2**	**2.1**	**2.1**	**2.0**
Hotels and other lodging places	161	133	137	130	112	9.7	7.9	8.0	7.4	6.2
Business services	299	265	275	292	316	5.5	4.5	4.3	4.2	4.2
Motion pictures	24	35	37	40	20	5.9	8.4	8.2	7.8	3.6
Other	217	240	228	246	272	1.0	1.0	1.0	1.0	1.1
GRAND TOTAL	**4 715**	**4 766**	**4 841**	**4 942**	**4 978**	**5.1**	**5.0**	**4.9**	**4.9**	**4.8**

Total manufacturing by investing country						As a % of total manufacturing by foreign affiliates				
All countries	2 140	2 149	2 193	2 159	2 148	100.0	100.0	100.0	100.0	100.0
United States	..	..	..	..	..	..	..	..	..	..
Canada	..	..	..	..	..	..	..	..	..	..
Mexico	..	..	..	..	..	..	..	..	..	..
Japan	..	..	..	..	..	..	..	..	..	..
Europe	..	..	..	..	..	..	..	..	..	..
European Union (15)	..	..	..	..	..	..	..	..	..	..
Belgium	..	..	..	..	..	..	..	..	..	..
France	..	..	..	..	..	..	..	..	..	..
Germany	..	..	..	..	..	..	..	..	..	..
Italy	..	..	..	..	..	..	..	..	..	..
Netherlands	..	..	..	..	..	..	..	..	..	..
Spain	..	..	..	..	..	..	..	..	..	..
Sweden	..	..	..	..	..	..	..	..	..	..
United Kingdom	..	..	..	..	..	..	..	..	..	..
Switzerland	..	..	..	..	..	..	..	..	..	..
Australia and New Zealand	..	..	..	..	..	..	..	..	..	..
Asia (non-OECD)	..	..	..	..	..	..	..	..	..	..
Latin America	..	..	..	..	..	..	..	..	..	..

Note: **Enterprise-level data.** Employment **by industry of sales**. See country notes.
Données au niveau de l'entreprise. Emploi **par secteur des ventes**. Voir les notes par pays.

Table 4a. UNITED STATES / ÉTATS-UNIS

TURNOVER / CHIFFRE D'AFFAIRES

By industry (ISIC Rev. 3)		1987	1988	1989	1990	1991	1992	1993	1994	1995	1996
		FOREIGN AFFILIATES *(Billions of US$)*									
10/14	Mining & quarrying	5.8	6.5	8.5	8.2	9.7	11.2	11.3	11.8	12.0	11.8
15/37	**TOTAL MANUFACTURING**	**225.1**	**280.7**	**353.1**	**396.4**	**405.7**	**431.2**	**468.3**	**524.9**	**559.3**	**552.0**
15/16	Food, beverages, tobacco	22.9	31.2	42.6	47.1	47.7	47.0	46.8	48.9	51.1	49.6
17/19	Textiles, clothing, leather, footwear	3.3	4.7	5.6	5.8	6.6	8.3	9.3	11.0	10.8	10.6
20/22	Wood and paper products	16.8	22.2	24.1	29.4	29.8	31.0	38.6	41.4	47.3	43.2
20	Wood products	1.8	1.9	1.7	2.9	3.1	3.7	4.8	6.0	4.6	4.7
21/22	Paper, printing and publishing	15.0	20.2	22.4	26.5	26.7	27.4	33.8	35.5	42.6	38.5
23/25	Chemicals, Total	78.7	89.6	104.9	127.2	129.5	140.0	147.5	165.2	155.8	157.1
23	Refined petroleum, nuclear fuel	..	..	..	..	..	..	..	..	..	..
24/25	Chemicals, rubber & plastics prod.	78.7	89.6	104.9	127.2	129.5	140.0	147.5	165.2	155.8	157.1
24	Chemical products	72.1	78.8	92.7	110.5	115.0	123.5	129.8	145.1	133.4	134.5
2423	Pharmaceuticals	11.3	13.5	17.5	22.1	24.9	27.9	38.9	42.4	45.6	48.7
25	Rubber and plastics products	6.6	10.8	12.2	16.8	14.5	16.5	17.7	20.1	22.4	22.7
26	Non-metallic mineral products	13.4	14.2	16.8	17.9	16.8	17.6	17.9	19.3	22.8	23.7
27/28	Basic & fabricated metals	26.7	36.8	51.7	50.8	51.0	54.0	57.6	64.7	67.3	62.9
27	Basic metals	18.0	20.9	26.5	32.3	32.2	32.8	36.5	39.7	41.3	36.0
28	Fabricated metal products	8.6	15.8	25.2	18.5	18.8	21.2	21.1	25.0	26.0	26.9
29/32	Machinery, Total	40.3	56.3	71.6	80.0	82.5	88.4	99.8	114.6	123.1	124.1
29/30	Non-electrical machinery	13.8	22.9	35.4	36.7	36.7	36.4	40.9	48.1	58.0	54.1
29	Non-electrical machinery nec	9.5	17.9	27.8	24.7	24.3	27.8	32.2	38.0	39.7	39.6
30	Office and computing machinery	4.2	5.0	7.5	12.1	12.4	8.6	8.8	10.1	18.2	14.5
31/32	Electrical & electronic equipment	26.6	33.4	36.2	43.3	45.8	52.1	58.8	66.6	65.2	70.0
31	Electrical machinery nec	9.5	14.2	14.2	19.4	23.2	22.8	25.8	32.9	34.5	34.8
32	Radio, TV & communications eq.	17.1	19.2	22.0	23.9	22.6	29.3	33.0	33.6	30.6	35.2
33	Scientific instruments	6.8	7.4	8.6	10.8	13.4	15.2	16.4	15.7	17.1	16.7
34/35	Transportation equipment	8.4	9.4	16.4	19.9	21.8	22.9	27.6	35.9	55.9	55.7
34	Motor vehicles	5.5	6.8	12.6	15.8	16.9	16.6	21.4	29.7	50.0	50.1
35	Other transport equipment	2.9	2.7	3.7	4.1	4.9	6.3	6.2	6.2	5.9	5.5
351	Shipbuilding & repairing	..	..	..	..	..	..	..	..	..	..
353	Aircraft and spacecraft	..	..	..	..	..	..	..	..	..	..
36/37	Other manufacturing	7.9	9.0	10.7	7.5	6.7	6.8	6.9	8.2	8.1	8.6
40/45	Construction, electricity, gas & water	7.9	9.1	13.1	16.8	16.4	15.8	15.2	15.3	16.4	17.2
50/55	Trade, repair, hotels & restaurants	327.3	380.8	419.4	451.5	445.9	457.5	495.7	518.9	559.0	560.7
65/74	Finance, insurance, business services	77.2	96.7	113.3	111.1	122.7	121.7	124.1	127.9	142.9	161.8
	OTHER ACTIVITIES	101.5	112.5	149.4	191.9	185.5	194.6	214.8	244.7	255.0	292.5
01/99	**GRAND TOTAL**	**744.6**	**886.4**	**1 056.6**	**1 175.9**	**1 185.9**	**1 232.0**	**1 329.4**	**1 443.5**	**1 544.6**	**1 596.0**

Total manufacturing by investing country

	1987	1988	1989	1990	1991	1992	1993	1994	1995	1996
All countries	**225.1**	**280.7**	**353.1**	**396.4**	**405.7**	**431.2**	**468.3**	**524.9**	**559.3**	**552.0**
United States	1.5	2.1	1.9	0.5	0.4	0.4	0.3	1.1	1.5	2.4
Canada	43.7	49.7	53.9	57.9	55.3	57.6	64.8	70.5	50.4	45.1
Mexico	0.1	0.1	..	1.6	1.7	2.7	2.7	3.5	..	3.5
Japan	15.5	27.1	42.5	61.2	64.9	70.2	79.8	90.7	123.4	118.7
Europe	146.9	182.3	229.8	249.7	259.2	275.1	293.0	327.3	344.8	347.3
European Union (15)	118.2	147.5	182.0	199.7	208.6	220.3	233.3	261.7	298.2	300.6
Belgium	1.6	2.2	2.0	2.4	2.8	2.9	2.5	3.1	3.6	3.7
France	16.9	25.3	29.6	36.4	39.2	41.5	43.4	50.0	49.4	51.7
Germany	30.7	37.0	43.6	45.2	46.7	51.8	58.9	67.7	73.4	75.6
Italy	1.7	3.2	3.9	4.0	6.1	7.5	8.3	9.7	8.8	7.2
Netherlands	14.8	16.8	22.0	24.0	23.9	25.1	24.3	25.2	26.4	29.8
Spain	0.1	0.1	0.1	0.1	0.2	0.3	0.5	0.8	0.7	0.7
Sweden	7.6	8.6	10.0	11.2	10.9	12.8	15.6	17.0	18.1	15.9
United Kingdom	48.0	57.8	75.6	81.8	83.5	85.4	88.8	97.7	103.6	102.5
Switzerland	18.4	21.7	32.5	33.2	33.9	36.0	37.4	39.0	42.3	42.7
Australia and New Zealand	5.3	6.5	10.0	10.7	10.0	9.9	10.2	9.4	9.6	9.7
Asia (non-OECD)	3.0	3.2	3.8	5.1	5.9	6.6	7.3	9.7	12.0	10.5
Latin America	5.9	6.8	7.8	8.0	7.1	8.3	8.5	10.0	8.6	8.6

Note: **Enterprise-level data.** Defined as *Sales*. See country notes.
Données au niveau de l'entreprise. Défini en tant que ventes de biens et services. Voir les notes par pays.

Table 5a. UNITED STATES / ÉTATS-UNIS

VALUE ADDED / VALEUR AJOUTÉE

By industry (ISIC Rev. 3)		FOREIGN AFFILIATES (Billions of US$)									
		1987	1988	1989	1990	1991	1992	1993	1994	1995	1996
10/14	Mining & quarrying	2.3	2.5	3.3	3.5	4.8	5.5	5.0	5.9	6.5	5.5
15/37	**TOTAL MANUFACTURING**	**75.5**	**90.9**	**109.2**	**119.8**	**125.9**	**134.1**	**142.5**	**157.1**	**155.7**	**156.4**
15/16	Food, beverages, tobacco	6.4	8.0	9.9	11.2	12.3	12.3	11.5	12.3	12.1	11.8
17/19	Textiles, clothing, leather, footwear	1.1	1.5	1.7	1.9	2.2	2.9	3.4	3.8	3.6	3.7
20/22	Wood and paper products	6.1	7.3	7.7	9.7	9.9	10.5	12.5	14.2	15.3	15.5
20	Wood products	0.5	0.6	0.5	0.9	0.8	0.9	1.2	1.5	1.2	1.1
21/22	Paper, printing and publishing	5.5	6.7	7.2	8.9	9.2	9.6	11.3	12.6	14.1	14.4
23/25	Chemicals, Total	28.2	31.6	36.2	42.4	43.3	47.4	50.3	55.5	47.8	49.8
23	Refined petroleum, nuclear fuel	..	..	..	..	..	..	..	..	..	..
24/25	Chemicals, rubber & plastics prod.	28.2	31.6	36.2	42.4	43.3	47.4	50.3	55.5	47.8	49.8
24	Chemical products	26.2	28.2	32.4	37.2	39.0	41.9	44.3	48.5	40.6	42.1
2423	Pharmaceuticals	4.2	5.2	6.9	8.9	9.9	11.4	14.2	15.1	15.3	15.7
25	Rubber and plastics products	2.0	3.3	3.8	5.1	4.3	5.5	6.0	6.9	7.3	7.7
26	Non-metallic mineral products	5.3	5.3	5.9	5.8	5.7	6.2	6.5	6.8	8.8	9.1
27/28	Basic & fabricated metals	7.2	10.4	15.7	14.6	14.9	15.0	16.5	16.4	16.9	16.1
27	Basic metals	4.3	5.1	7.0	8.4	8.6	8.7	10.0	9.6	9.7	8.4
28	Fabricated metal products	2.9	5.2	8.7	6.2	6.3	6.3	6.5	6.8	7.1	7.7
29/32	Machinery, Total	12.7	18.1	21.8	23.3	24.8	25.9	26.9	31.4	31.9	31.9
29/30	Non-electrical machinery	4.8	7.6	10.9	10.3	10.5	10.2	10.4	12.9	13.4	12.8
29	Non-electrical machinery nec	..	..	..	..	..	8.0	9.2	11.3	11.5	11.7
30	Office and computing machinery	..	..	..	..	..	2.2	1.2	1.6	1.9	1.1
31/32	Electrical & electronic equipment	7.9	10.5	10.9	13.1	14.4	15.7	16.5	18.5	18.5	19.1
31	Electrical machinery nec	..	..	..	..	..	7.2	7.8	9.9	10.4	10.0
32	Radio, TV & communications eq.	..	..	..	..	..	8.5	8.7	8.6	8.2	9.1
33	Scientific instruments	2.6	2.7	3.2	4.2	5.5	6.1	6.6	6.1	6.3	6.3
34/35	Transportation equipment	2.4	2.0	2.7	3.9	4.7	4.8	5.7	7.5	9.2	8.4
34	Motor vehicles	..	..	..	..	..	2.7	3.7	5.7	7.3	6.7
35	Other transport equipment	..	..	..	..	..	2.2	1.9	1.8	1.9	1.7
351	Shipbuilding & repairing	..	..	..	..	..	..	..	..	..	..
353	Aircraft and spacecraft	..	..	..	..	..	..	..	..	..	..
36/37	Other manufacturing	3.5	4.1	4.3	2.8	2.7	3.0	2.6	3.2	3.7	3.8
40/45	Construction, electricity, gas & water	1.8	2.1	3.0	4.0	4.0	3.2	3.0	3.0	3.4	3.2
50/55	Trade, repair, hotels & restaurants	29.9	35.4	39.7	41.6	49.9	50.9	54.2	57.2	62.5	66.5
65/74	Finance, insurance, business services	18.8	19.8	21.3	16.0	17.9	15.3	16.2	17.7	16.1	21.6
	OTHER ACTIVITIES	29.6	39.7	46.9	54.3	55.1	57.3	64.8	72.2	78.3	86.3
01/99	**GRAND TOTAL**	**157.9**	**190.4**	**223.4**	**239.3**	**257.6**	**266.3**	**285.7**	**313.0**	**322.6**	**339.5**

Total manufacturing by investing country										
All countries	75.5	90.9	109.2	119.8	125.9	134.1	142.5	157.1	155.7	156.4
United States	0.4	0.6	0.4	0.1	..	0.1	0.1	0.3	0.6	1.0
Canada	17.3	18.5	20.2	20.9	..	20.4	23.4	25.4	14.9	14.5
Mexico	..	..	..	..	..	0.9	0.8	1.1	1.1	0.9
Japan	4.4	7.7	10.7	15.0	..	16.9	18.9	21.7	25.0	23.2
Europe	48.0	58.1	70.5	75.0	..	88.8	91.4	100.0	105.1	107.8
European Union (15)	..	..	..	..	..	71.2	73.7	80.3	90.7	92.9
Belgium	..	..	..	..	..	0.9	0.8	1.0	1.1	1.2
France	5.2	7.0	7.8	8.8	..	11.6	12.0	13.6	13.8	15.0
Germany	9.6	11.5	13.4	14.2	..	16.4	19.1	20.6	21.8	23.5
Italy	..	..	..	..	..	1.5	1.7	2.2	2.0	1.6
Netherlands	4.1	5.0	5.8	6.0	..	6.8	6.2	6.6	7.0	7.3
Spain	..	..	..	..	..	0.1	0.1	0.2	0.2	0.2
Sweden	..	..	..	..	..	3.6	4.1	4.6	5.1	4.2
United Kingdom	17.8	21.1	25.4	27.2	..	32.1	31.8	34.0	35.6	35.9
Switzerland	5.6	6.5	10.4	10.7	..	12.3	11.9	12.7	13.6	14.1
Australia and New Zealand	..	..	..	..	..	3.1	3.1	2.4	2.7	2.9
Asia (non-OECD)	..	..	..	..	..	1.2	1.5	2.5	2.9	2.3
Latin America	2.2	2.8	3.0	2.6	..	2.9	2.8	3.2	2.6	2.6

Note: **Enterprise-level data.** Defined as *Gross Product*. See country notes.
Données au niveau de l'entreprise. Représente le produit brut. Voir les notes par pays.

WAGES AND SALARIES / SALAIRES ET TRAITEMENTS

By industry (ISIC Rev. 3)	FOREIGN AFFILIATES (Billions of US$)									
	1987	1988	1989	1990	1991	1992	1993	1994	1995	1996
10/14 Mining & quarrying	1.2	1.2	1.8	1.5	2.3	2.5	2.5	2.7	2.6	2.6
15/37 TOTAL MANUFACTURING	**50.8**	**62.4**	**76.4**	**88.7**	**92.8**	**97.6**	**101.8**	**107.0**	**106.2**	**104.0**
15/16 Food, beverages, tobacco	3.9	5.1	6.6	7.3	7.5	7.5	7.1	7.6	7.5	6.6
17/19 Textiles, clothing, leather, footwear	0.8	1.1	1.4	1.4	1.6	2.0	2.3	2.7	2.6	2.6
20/22 Wood and paper products	4.2	4.9	5.5	6.9	7.2	7.7	9.0	9.6	10.5	10.3
20 Wood products	0.3	0.4	0.3	0.6	0.6	0.6	0.7	0.8	0.7	0.7
21/22 Paper, printing and publishing	3.9	4.5	5.2	6.3	6.6	7.0	8.4	8.8	9.8	9.7
23/25 Chemicals, Total	16.6	19.2	22.0	28.2	29.2	31.7	31.9	33.5	30.4	30.1
23 Refined petroleum, nuclear fuel	..	..	..	..	..	..	..	..	..	..
24/25 Chemicals, rubber & plastics prod.	16.6	19.2	22.0	28.2	29.2	31.7	31.9	33.5	30.4	30.1
24 Chemical products	15.1	16.6	18.9	23.8	25.0	26.9	27.1	28.4	25.1	24.6
2423 Pharmaceuticals	2.7	3.3	4.1	5.4	6.1	6.8	8.9	9.5	10.3	10.2
25 Rubber and plastics products	1.5	2.7	3.1	4.4	4.2	4.8	4.9	5.1	5.3	5.4
26 Non-metallic mineral products	3.4	3.5	4.2	4.8	4.6	4.7	4.6	4.8	5.6	5.6
27/28 Basic & fabricated metals	5.8	7.5	11.5	11.2	11.8	11.6	12.6	12.6	11.7	11.0
27 Basic metals	3.3	3.5	4.7	6.3	6.8	6.8	7.4	6.6	6.2	5.2
28 Fabricated metal products	2.5	4.0	6.8	4.9	5.0	4.8	5.2	5.9	5.5	5.8
29/32 Machinery, Total	10.5	15.0	18.3	21.0	21.7	22.4	23.6	24.8	25.2	25.3
29/30 Non-electrical machinery	4.0	6.1	8.9	9.0	9.4	9.0	9.5	10.1	10.9	10.5
29 Non-electrical machinery nec	2.4	4.3	6.7	6.0	6.3	6.9	7.4	8.5	8.6	8.7
30 Office and computing machinery	1.6	1.8	2.2	3.0	3.1	2.2	2.0	1.6	2.3	1.8
31/32 Electrical & electronic equipment	6.6	9.0	9.4	12.0	12.3	13.4	14.1	14.8	14.3	14.8
31 Electrical machinery nec	2.5	3.8	3.7	5.6	6.6	6.4	6.9	8.4	8.3	8.4
32 Radio, TV & communications eq.	4.1	5.2	5.7	6.3	5.7	7.0	7.1	6.3	6.0	6.4
33 Scientific instruments	2.0	2.1	2.4	3.2	4.0	4.5	4.9	4.5	4.7	4.5
34/35 Transportation equipment	1.9	2.0	2.5	3.3	3.9	4.3	4.6	5.5	6.8	6.6
34 Motor vehicles	1.2	1.2	1.6	2.2	2.4	2.4	2.7	3.8	5.0	5.2
35 Other transport equipment	0.7	0.8	0.9	1.2	1.4	1.9	1.8	1.7	1.8	1.4
351 Shipbuilding & repairing	..	..	..	..	..	..	..	..	..	..
353 Aircraft and spacecraft	..	..	..	..	..	..	..	..	..	..
36/37 Other manufacturing	1.6	2.0	2.1	1.4	1.1	1.2	1.2	1.4	1.3	1.4
40/45 Construction, electricity, gas & water	1.8	2.0	2.7	3.7	3.7	3.0	2.8	2.8	3.4	3.3
50/55 Trade, repair, hotels & restaurants	18.1	22.0	26.1	28.3	32.1	32.2	34.1	34.0	37.6	39.4
65/74 Finance, insurance, business services	10.5	12.7	13.5	11.5	13.4	14.3	14.7	14.4	15.7	18.2
OTHER ACTIVITIES	13.6	19.3	23.6	29.9	31.6	32.5	37.0	39.6	40.9	42.9
01/99 GRAND TOTAL	**96.0**	**119.6**	**144.2**	**163.6**	**176.0**	**182.1**	**193.0**	**200.6**	**206.4**	**210.4**
Total manufacturing by investing country										
All countries	**50.8**	**62.4**	**76.4**	**88.7**	**92.8**	**97.6**	**101.8**	**107.0**	**106.2**	**104.0**
United States	0.3	0.4	0.4	0.1	0.1	0.1	0.0	0.2	0.3	0.5
Canada	10.1	11.2	11.8	13.3	13.4	13.7	15.5	15.6	10.7	10.1
Mexico	..	..	..	..	..	..	..	..	..	..
Japan	3.0	5.9	8.1	11.6	12.9	13.6	14.6	15.1	17.0	15.9
Europe	33.1	40.3	50.6	57.8	60.7	64.2	65.3	69.2	71.1	70.6
European Union (15)	..	..	..	..	..	..	..	..	..	..
Belgium	..	..	..	..	..	..	..	..	..	..
France	3.9	5.3	6.0	8.4	9.2	9.1	9.2	10.2	9.7	10.3
Germany	7.1	8.5	9.8	11.0	11.4	12.6	14.2	15.0	16.0	16.2
Italy	..	..	..	..	..	..	..	..	..	..
Netherlands	3.2	3.9	4.7	5.1	5.0	5.2	4.6	4.3	4.5	5.1
Spain	..	..	..	..	..	..	..	..	..	..
Sweden	..	..	..	..	..	..	..	..	..	..
United Kingdom	11.1	13.4	16.9	19.1	19.8	20.6	20.4	21.4	21.9	21.3
Switzerland	3.9	4.6	7.7	8.0	8.3	9.0	8.7	9.1	9.6	9.5
Australia and New Zealand	..	..	..	..	..	..	..	..	..	..
Asia (non-OECD)	1.6	1.6	2.5	3.1	3.2	3.2	3.3	3.2	3.7	3.4
Latin America	2.0	2.3	2.5	2.3	2.1	2.2	2.3	2.6	2.2	2.0

Note: **Enterprise-level data.** Defined as *Compensation of Employees* (including *Employer expenditures for all employee benefit plans*). See country notes.
Données au niveau de l'entreprise. Représente la rémunération des salariés (y compris les dépenses patronales pour tous les régimes de prestations sociales). Voir les notes par pays.

Table 7. UNITED STATES / ÉTATS-UNIS

R&D EXPENDITURE / DÉPENSES DE R-D

By industry (ISIC Rev. 3)		FOREIGN AFFILIATES (Millions of US$)					AS A % OF NATIONAL TOTAL				
		1992	1993	1994	1995	1996	1992	1993	1994	1995	1996
10/14	Mining & quarrying	22	36	46	45	31	..	..	..	..	..
15/37	**TOTAL MANUFACTURING**	**11 413**	**11 842**	**12 970**	**14 756**	**13 807**	**13.0**	**13.3**	**13.7**	**14.4**	**12.0**
15/16	Food, beverages, tobacco	247	266	294	360	353	17.8	19.8	19.9	23.0	22.6
17/19	Textiles, clothing, leather, footwear	62	44	55	51	55	22.5	13.8	15.4	12.9	11.3
20/22	Wood and paper products	118	119	187	179	176	7.9	6.2	9.3	8.9	6.0
20	Wood products	14	17	34	9	10	5.7	6.4	10.8	3.8	1.3
21/22	Paper, printing and publishing	104	102	153	170	166	8.4	6.2	9.0	9.6	7.6
23/25	Chemicals, Total	6 534	6 836	7 254	8 515	7 652	39.1	36.6	38.0	45.1	37.6
23	Refined petroleum, nuclear fuel	..	..	..	..	..	..	..	..	..	..
24/25	Chemicals, rubber & plastics prod.	6 534	6 836	7 254	8 515	7 652	39.1	36.6	38.0	45.1	37.6
24	Chemical products	6 189	6 580	7 003	8 263	7 366	40.2	37.6	40.1	46.9	39.0
2423	Pharmaceuticals	3 391	4 232	4 506	5 201	5 849	42.7	46.3	46.8	50.9	59.8
25	Rubber and plastics products	345	256	251	252	286	26.1	21.7	15.5	20.1	19.2
26	Non-metallic mineral products	123	106	153	162	159	24.1	19.7	25.9	36.2	34.0
27/28	Basic & fabricated metals	337	373	348	322	286	21.9	20.4	19.3	19.9	12.5
27	Basic metals	191	201	170	161	156	36.6	30.0	24.6	27.2	20.9
28	Fabricated metal products	146	172	178	161	131	14.4	14.9	16.0	15.7	8.4
29/32	Machinery, Total	3 091	3 187	3 567	3 991	3 889	10.9	12.2	12.3	12.2	9.4
29/30	Non-electrical machinery	1 092	1 019	954	1 136	935	7.3	8.0	7.0	8.2	4.9
29	Non-electrical machinery nec	333	395	475	541	533	9.4	11.5	11.9	10.7	8.7
30	Office and computing machinery	759	624	479	595	402	6.7	6.7	5.0	6.7	3.1
31/32	Electrical & electronic equipment	1 999	2 168	2 613	2 855	2 954	15.0	16.2	17.0	15.2	13.1
31	Electrical machinery nec	584	753	969	931	965	21.5	29.7	36.4	26.8	28.7
32	Radio, TV & communications eq.	1 415	1 415	1 643	1 923	1 988	13.3	13.1	13.0	12.6	10.4
33	Scientific instruments	608	581	671	691	720	6.4	5.7	5.9	5.8	5.9
34/35	Transportation equipment	227	266	375	424	454	0.8	1.0	1.3	1.3	1.4
34	Motor vehicles	88	117	203	309	370	0.9	1.0	1.5	2.1	2.3
35	Other transport equipment	139	149	173	115	84	0.8	1.0	1.2	0.7	0.5
351	Shipbuilding & repairing	..	..	..	..	..	..	..	..	..	..
353	Aircraft and spacecraft	..	..	..	..	..	..	..	..	..	..
36/37	Other manufacturing	68	63	66	60	64	10.3	9.4	13.0	12.1	13.1
40/45	Construction, electricity, gas & water	3	1	2	7	5	..	..	..	..	..
50/55	Trade, repair, hotels & restaurants	922	870	1 089	1 437	1 738	..	..	..	..	..
65/74	Finance, insurance, business services	16	12	11	17	17	..	..	..	..	..
	OTHER ACTIVITIES	1 320	1 438	1 448	1 280	1 552	..	..	..	..	..
01/99	**GRAND TOTAL**	**13 695**	**14 199**	**15 566**	**17 542**	**17 150**	**11.5**	**12.1**	**13.0**	**13.3**	**11.9**

Total manufacturing by investing country										
All countries	**11 413**	**11 842**	**12 970**	**14 756**	**13 807**	**13.0**	**13.3**	**13.7**	**14.4**	**12.0**
United States	3	3	..	61	55	..	..	..	..	..
Canada	2 080	2 081	2 263	1 205	1 228	..	..	..	..	..
Mexico	..	..	..	..	..	..	..	..	..	..
Japan	1 189	1 084	1 017	1 199	1 001	..	..	..	..	..
Europe	7 597	8 121	8 980	11 824	11 007	..	..	..	..	..
European Union (15)	..	..	..	..	..	..	..	..	..	..
Belgium	..	..	..	..	..	..	..	..	..	..
France	1 211	1 172	1 400	1 551	1 641	..	..	..	..	..
Germany	1 796	2 032	2 187	3 567	2 767	..	..	..	..	..
Italy	..	..	..	..	..	..	..	..	..	..
Netherlands	472	458	510	612	743	..	..	..	..	..
Spain	..	..	..	..	..	..	..	..	..	..
Sweden	..	..	..	..	..	..	..	..	..	..
United Kingdom	1 826	1 929	2 177	2 211	2 273	..	..	..	..	..
Switzerland	1 874	2 041	2 056	2 735	2 985	..	..	..	..	..
Australia and New Zealand	..	..	..	..	..	..	..	..	..	..
Asia (non-OECD)	..	107	..	169	158	..	..	..	..	..
Latin America	339	388	485	148	182	..	..	..	..	..

Note: **Enterprise-level data.** See country notes.
Données au niveau de l'entreprise. Voir les notes par pays.

Table 8. UNITED STATES / ÉTATS-UNIS

NUMBER OF RESEARCHERS / NOMBRE DE CHERCHEURS

By industry (ISIC Rev. 3)	FOREIGN AFFILIATES (Thousands)					AS A % OF NATIONAL TOTAL				
	1992	1993	1994	1995	1996	1992	1993	1994	1995	1996
10/14 Mining & quarrying	0.2	0.4	0.5	0.4	0.3	..	..	..	..	..
15/37 TOTAL MANUFACTURING	**86.7**	**85.9**	**84.7**	**84.6**	**84.4**	**15.6**	**14.7**	**15.1**	**13.6**	**12.9**
15/16 Food, beverages, tobacco	2.1	2.0	1.9	2.0	2.0	21.9	19.4	21.3	20.4	19.2
17/19 Textiles, clothing, leather, footwear	0.5	0.5	0.7	0.6	0.7	16.1	15.2	24.1	15.8	18.9
20/22 Wood and paper products	1.7	1.3	1.7	1.7	1.9	13.9	9.4	13.2	12.2	13.0
20 Wood products	0.2	0.2	0.5	0.1	0.1	12.5	6.1	21.7	3.4	2.9
21/22 Paper, printing and publishing	1.5	1.1	1.2	1.6	1.8	14.2	10.4	11.3	14.5	16.1
23/25 Chemicals, Total	39.8	42.6	41.6	39.6	37.6	40.0	41.7	38.0	37.9	38.0
23 Refined petroleum, nuclear fuel	..	..	..	..	..	..	..	..	..	..
24/25 Chemicals, rubber & plastics prod.	39.8	42.6	41.6	39.6	37.6	40.0	41.7	38.0	37.9	38.0
24 Chemical products	37.7	40.5	39.8	37.8	35.7	43.6	43.5	40.0	40.1	40.1
2423 Pharmaceuticals	18.4	23.5	22.6	23.2	22.7	43.5	48.5	44.9	47.3	52.7
25 Rubber and plastics products	2.1	2.1	1.8	1.8	1.9	16.2	23.3	18.4	17.6	19.2
26 Non-metallic mineral products	1.2	1.2	0.7	0.7	0.6	23.5	30.0	16.3	17.9	16.2
27/28 Basic & fabricated metals	3.0	3.0	3.0	2.7	2.6	24.0	19.6	19.1	20.5	16.8
27 Basic metals	1.7	1.5	1.2	1.2	1.1	37.0	29.4	18.5	29.3	20.0
28 Fabricated metal products	1.3	1.5	1.7	1.5	1.5	16.5	14.7	18.5	16.5	15.0
29/32 Machinery, Total	29.9	26.6	26.2	28.9	30.2	16.0	14.0	13.5	12.2	12.1
29/30 Non-electrical machinery	9.7	8.2	8.2	9.7	9.1	10.0	8.8	9.1	8.7	8.0
29 Non-electrical machinery nec	4.0	4.6	5.2	5.5	5.5	12.7	12.8	14.1	10.3	12.7
30 Office and computing machinery	5.7	3.6	3.0	4.2	3.6	8.7	6.3	5.6	7.2	5.1
31/32 Electrical & electronic equipment	20.2	18.4	18.0	19.2	21.1	22.6	19.1	17.4	15.3	15.5
31 Electrical machinery nec	4.7	6.6	7.9	8.4	8.2	16.3	33.7	39.5	33.2	38.3
32 Radio, TV & communications eq.	15.6	11.8	10.2	10.8	12.9	25.8	15.3	12.2	10.7	11.3
33 Scientific instruments	5.5	5.3	5.6	5.3	5.2	7.3	5.3	6.6	7.5	8.1
34/35 Transportation equipment	2.4	2.9	2.9	2.8	3.0	1.6	2.2	2.4	1.8	1.9
34 Motor vehicles	0.9	1.2	1.7	2.0	2.4	2.0	2.4	3.3	3.5	3.8
35 Other transport equipment	1.5	1.7	1.2	0.9	0.6	1.5	2.2	1.7	0.9	0.6
351 Shipbuilding & repairing	..	..	..	..	..	..	..	..	..	..
353 Aircraft and spacecraft	..	..	..	..	..	..	..	..	..	..
36/37 Other manufacturing	0.4	0.4	0.4	0.4	0.5	6.9	2.6	5.3	4.9	1.5
40/45 Construction, electricity, gas & water	0.0	0.0	0.0	0.1	0.1	..	..	..	..	..
50/55 Trade, repair, hotels & restaurants	7.6	6.5	9.8	8.9	9.6	..	..	..	..	..
65/74 Finance, insurance, business services	0.0	0.0	0.1	0.1	0.0	..	..	..	..	..
OTHER ACTIVITIES	9.8	9.7	10.2	9.6	11.2	..	..	..	..	..
01/99 GRAND TOTAL	**104.5**	**102.5**	**105.1**	**103.7**	**105.8**	**13.7**	**13.3**	**14.1**	**12.5**	**11.9**

Total manufacturing by investing country										
All countries	**86.7**	**85.9**	**84.7**	**84.6**	**84.4**	**15.6**	**14.7**	**15.1**	**13.6**	**12.9**
United States	0.0	0.0	0.1	0.4	0.4	..	..	..	..	..
Canada	11.1	9.9	10.2	5.8	7.5	..	..	..	..	..
Mexico	..	..	..	..	..	..	..	..	..	..
Japan	8.1	7.5	7.4	8.3	8.3	..	..	..	..	..
Europe	63.0	64.3	62.4	66.5	64.2	..	..	..	..	..
European Union (15)	..	..	..	..	..	..	..	..	..	..
Belgium	..	..	..	..	..	..	..	..	..	..
France	9.9	9.1	9.2	8.8	9.1	..	..	..	..	..
Germany	15.1	16.6	15.7	16.9	16.1	..	..	..	..	..
Italy	..	..	..	..	..	..	..	..	..	..
Netherlands	7.0	4.6	4.4	5.1	6.2	..	..	..	..	..
Spain	..	..	..	..	..	..	..	..	..	..
Sweden	..	..	..	..	..	..	..	..	..	..
United Kingdom	15.9	17.5	15.8	14.7	14.4	..	..	..	..	..
Switzerland	10.8	11.6	11.5	13.5	13.1	..	..	..	..	..
Australia and New Zealand	..	..	..	..	..	..	..	..	..	..
Asia (non-OECD)	1.5	1.3	1.1	1.3	1.4	..	..	..	..	..
Latin America	..	2.4	2.9	1.0	1.2	..	..	..	..	..

Note: **Enterprise-level data.** Defined as *R&D Employment.* See country notes.
Données au niveau de l'entreprise. Défini comme le nombre d'employés travaillant dans la R-D. Voir les notes par pays.

Table 9. UNITED STATES / ÉTATS-UNIS

GROSS FIXED CAPITAL FORMATION / FORMATION BRUTE DE CAPITAL FIXE

By industry (ISIC Rev. 3)		FOREIGN AFFILIATES *(Millions of US$)*									
		1987	1988	1989	1990	1991	1992	1993	1994	1995	1996
10/14	Mining & quarrying	922	1 326	1 107	978	1 405	1 176	1 456	1 910	1 642	1 733
15/37	**TOTAL MANUFACTURING**	**14 162**	**19 111**	**23 268**	**27 869**	**26 190**	**24 505**	**22 628**	**24 549**	**28 001**	**29 725**
15/16	Food, beverages, tobacco	787	1 222	1 450	2 100	1 943	1 748	1 582	2 090	2 007	2 068
17/19	Textiles, clothing, leather, footwear	268	398	771	344	377	476	486	573	572	664
20/22	Wood and paper products	857	1 486	1 683	1 906	1 776	1 400	1 560	1 963	2 178	2 320
20	Wood products	98	160	155	193	155	184	87	170	173	152
21/22	Paper, printing and publishing	759	1 326	1 528	1 713	1 621	1 216	1 473	1 793	2 005	2 168
23/25	Chemicals, Total	5 216	7 120	9 049	12 219	11 221	10 716	9 818	9 654	9 624	10 421
23	Refined petroleum, nuclear fuel	..	..	..	..	..	..	..	..	..	..
24/25	Chemicals, rubber & plastics prod.	5 216	7 120	9 049	12 219	11 221	10 716	9 818	9 654	9 624	10 421
24	Chemical products	4 824	6 441	8 102	10 498	10 066	9 439	8 508	8 314	8 303	9 054
2423	Pharmaceuticals	647	906	1 188	1 694	1 976	2 022	2 077	2 339	2 730	3 024
25	Rubber and plastics products	392	679	947	1 721	1 155	1 277	1 310	1 340	1 321	1 367
26	Non-metallic mineral products	983	1 234	1 278	1 295	1 212	1 064	1 031	1 267	1 742	2 040
27/28	Basic & fabricated metals	1 492	2 143	3 138	3 352	3 329	2 897	2 449	2 989	3 465	3 352
27	Basic metals	1 022	1 485	2 144	2 400	2 393	1 934	1 598	1 935	2 340	2 118
28	Fabricated metal products	470	658	995	952	937	963	851	1 054	1 125	1 235
29/32	Machinery, Total	2 158	3 035	3 792	4 470	3 894	3 903	3 537	3 727	5 570	5 787
29/30	Non-electrical machinery	796	1 179	1 767	1 960	1 597	1 565	1 255	1 337	1 810	1 803
29	Non-electrical machinery nec	383	629	1 141	1 281	830	970	982	1 108	1 285	1 431
30	Office and computing machinery	413	550	626	680	766	595	273	229	525	372
31/32	Electrical & electronic equipment	1 362	1 856	2 025	2 509	2 298	2 338	2 283	2 390	3 760	3 984
31	Electrical machinery nec	460	611	695	845	1 098	1 010	1 044	1 204	1 729	1 596
32	Radio, TV & communications eq.	902	1 245	1 330	1 664	1 200	1 329	1 238	1 185	2 031	2 388
33	Scientific instruments	362	459	524	618	646	520	588	582	603	641
34/35	Transportation equipment	1 676	1 593	1 164	1 165	1 498	1 502	1 251	1 370	1 876	2 052
34	Motor vehicles	1 605	1 536	1 036	1 061	1 358	1 312	1 094	1 260	1 718	1 950
35	Other transport equipment	71	58	128	105	139	190	158	110	158	103
351	Shipbuilding & repairing	..	..	..	..	..	..	..	..	..	..
353	Aircraft and spacecraft	..	..	..	..	..	..	..	..	..	..
36/37	Other manufacturing	363	421	418	401	293	279	326	334	364	379
40/45	Construction, electricity, gas & water	344	160	379	494	328	625	334	537	588	906
50/55	Trade, repair, hotels & restaurants	4 374	5 688	8 076	10 858	12 448	12 332	14 510	17 937	18 726	23 254
65/74	Finance, insurance, business services	5 628	6 145	8 758	10 329	10 005	7 762	7 151	6 735	8 181	9 243
	OTHER ACTIVITIES	7 606	11 892	13 575	19 052	19 440	14 965	17 163	16 512	17 371	19 282
01/99	**GRAND TOTAL**	**33 035**	**44 322**	**55 164**	**69 580**	**69 816**	**61 366**	**63 243**	**68 179**	**74 510**	**84 142**

Total manufacturing by investing country	1987	1988	1989	1990	1991	1992	1993	1994	1995	1996
All countries	**14 162**	**19 111**	**23 268**	**27 869**	**26 190**	**24 505**	**22 628**	**24 549**	**28 001**	**29 725**
United States	90	137	82	23	10	7	4	58	151	..
Canada	3 423	4 175	4 473	5 202	4 311	3 880	3 275	3 643	2 194	2 028
Mexico	..	..	..	..	..	..	..	..	..	..
Japan	2 477	4 159	5 273	6 042	5 601	5 201	4 251	4 314	5 899	6 417
Europe	7 214	9 620	11 772	14 157	13 865	13 229	13 181	14 646	17 536	18 643
European Union (15)	..	..	..	..	..	..	..	..	..	..
Belgium	..	..	..	..	..	..	..	..	..	..
France	752	1 127	1 605	2 281	2 088	2 183	1 893	2 138	2 420	2 834
Germany	1 758	2 352	2 783	3 361	3 456	3 183	3 696	3 727	4 333	5 178
Italy	..	..	..	..	..	..	..	..	..	..
Netherlands	657	894	1 049	1 027	829	840	913	1 082	1 433	1 268
Spain	..	..	..	..	..	..	..	..	..	..
Sweden	..	..	..	..	..	..	..	..	..	..
United Kingdom	2 496	2 867	3 418	4 078	3 871	3 760	3 354	3 746	4 995	5 029
Switzerland	724	996	1 283	1 573	1 760	1 763	1 729	2 082	2 036	2 337
Australia and New Zealand	..	..	..	..	..	..	..	..	..	..
Asia (non-OECD)	527	538	1 189	1 724	1 692	1 511	1 311	1 123	1 370	1 511
Latin America	266	345	332	601	469	478	489	512	511	486

Note: **Enterprise-level data.** Defined as *Expenditure for New Plant & Equipment.* See country notes.
Données au niveau de l'entreprise. Représente les dépenses pour nouveaux équipements et installations. Voir les notes par pays.

Table 10. UNITED STATES / ÉTATS-UNIS

TOTAL EXPORTS / EXPORTATIONS TOTALES

By industry (ISIC Rev. 3)	FOREIGN AFFILIATES (Billions of US$)									
	1987	1988	1989	1990	1991	1992	1993	1994	1995	1996
10/14 Mining & quarrying	0.9	1.0	1.2	1.2	1.4	2.1	1.5	1.9	2.5	2.1
15/37 TOTAL MANUFACTURING	**15.5**	**25.2**	**31.9**	**36.1**	**37.7**	**40.3**	**43.4**	**49.8**	**55.4**	**58.8**
15/16 Food, beverages, tobacco	0.5	1.5	1.4	1.6	1.8	2.0	2.3	2.5	2.8	2.8
17/19 Textiles, clothing, leather, footwear	0.1	0.2	0.3	0.3	0.3	0.5	0.5	0.6	0.6	0.6
20/22 Wood and paper products	0.7	1.0	1.2	1.5	1.6	1.8	2.3	2.3	2.6	2.4
20 Wood products	0.2	0.2	0.3	0.2	0.3	0.3	0.4	0.4	0.4	0.3
21/22 Paper, printing and publishing	0.5	0.8	0.9	1.3	1.4	1.5	1.8	1.8	2.1	2.1
23/25 Chemicals, Total	7.1	9.3	10.2	11.9	12.8	13.7	14.3	16.0	15.9	17.6
23 Refined petroleum, nuclear fuel	..	..	..	..	..	..	..	..	..	..
24/25 Chemicals, rubber & plastics prod.	7.1	9.3	10.2	11.9	12.8	13.7	14.3	16.0	15.9	17.6
24 Chemical products	6.8	8.7	9.6	10.7	11.6	12.5	13.0	14.4	14.1	15.7
2423 Pharmaceuticals	0.8	0.8	1.0	1.1	1.1	1.3	3.0	3.2	4.3	6.0
25 Rubber and plastics products	0.3	0.6	0.6	1.1	1.1	1.2	1.3	1.6	1.8	2.0
26 Non-metallic mineral products	0.2	0.4	0.5	0.6	0.6	0.7	0.7	0.7	0.9	0.7
27/28 Basic & fabricated metals	1.5	1.9	3.5	2.8	3.7	3.5	3.6	4.0	4.2	4.1
27 Basic metals	1.1	1.1	1.7	1.8	2.3	2.1	2.2	2.2	2.3	2.1
28 Fabricated metal products	0.4	0.8	1.9	1.1	1.4	1.3	1.4	1.7	1.8	2.0
29/32 Machinery, Total	3.4	8.6	11.4	13.5	12.2	12.3	13.8	16.8	18.7	20.6
29/30 Non-electrical machinery	1.4	2.4	4.8	5.2	5.0	5.1	5.9	6.4	7.5	8.2
29 Non-electrical machinery nec	0.8	1.6	3.5	3.4	3.2	3.6	4.7	5.2	5.6	6.8
30 Office and computing machinery	0.6	0.8	1.4	1.7	1.8	1.5	1.3	1.2	1.9	1.4
31/32 Electrical & electronic equipment	2.0	6.1	6.6	8.3	7.1	7.2	7.9	10.4	11.2	12.4
31 Electrical machinery nec	0.8	1.3	1.4	2.9	3.9	3.2	3.3	5.4	5.8	5.4
32 Radio, TV & communications eq.	1.2	4.9	5.1	5.4	3.3	4.0	4.6	5.0	5.4	7.0
33 Scientific instruments	0.7	0.9	1.2	1.5	1.8	2.0	2.3	2.8	2.8	3.0
34/35 Transportation equipment	0.6	0.7	1.2	1.2	1.7	2.3	2.3	2.7	4.9	5.2
34 Motor vehicles	0.4	0.5	0.5	0.5	1.0	1.2	1.2	1.8	4.3	4.5
35 Other transport equipment	0.3	0.2	0.7	0.7	0.7	1.1	1.0	0.9	0.6	0.6
351 Shipbuilding & repairing	..	..	..	..	..	..	..	..	..	..
353 Aircraft and spacecraft	..	..	..	..	..	..	..	..	..	..
36/37 Other manufacturing	0.6	0.7	0.9	1.1	1.3	1.4	1.4	1.6	2.1	1.7
40/45 Construction, electricity, gas & water	0.1	0.0	0.2	0.1	0.2	0.0	0.0	0.1	..	0.1
50/55 Trade, repair, hotels & restaurants	30.1	41.2	50.5	51.1	53.4	56.9	57.3	56.3	66.9	64.3
65/74 Finance, insurance, business services	0.0	0.0	0.0	0.0	0.1	0.0	0.0	0.0	0.0	0.0
OTHER ACTIVITIES	1.5	2.0	2.5	3.8	4.1	4.6	4.4	12.5	..	11.2
01/99 GRAND TOTAL	**48.1**	**69.5**	**86.3**	**92.3**	**96.9**	**103.9**	**106.6**	**120.7**	**135.2**	**136.6**

Total manufacturing by investing country

	1987	1988	1989	1990	1991	1992	1993	1994	1995	1996
All countries	**15.5**	**25.2**	**31.9**	**36.1**	**37.7**	**40.3**	**43.4**	**49.8**	**55.4**	**58.8**
United States	0.0	..	0.1	0.0	0.0	0.0	..	..	0.3	0.4
Canada	4.0	4.8	4.9	5.4	5.5	5.9	5.9	6.0	3.4	3.6
Mexico	..	..	..	..	..	..	..	..	..	..
Japan	1.1	2.0	4.1	5.3	6.2	7.5	8.1	8.1	11.8	11.9
Europe	8.9	16.7	20.3	23.0	23.8	24.5	27.2	32.7	36.4	39.7
European Union (15)	..	..	..	..	..	..	..	..	..	..
Belgium	..	..	..	..	..	..	..	..	..	..
France	0.9	4.1	4.9	5.3	3.5	3.6	4.2	5.7	5.7	6.7
Germany	2.8	4.5	5.1	5.3	5.9	6.1	6.6	7.8	8.9	10.7
Italy	..	..	..	..	..	..	..	..	..	..
Netherlands	0.7	1.7	1.5	1.4	1.8	1.9	2.2	2.7	2.6	2.5
Spain	..	..	..	..	..	..	..	..	..	..
Sweden	..	..	..	..	..	..	..	..	..	..
United Kingdom	2.6	3.5	4.9	5.7	6.2	6.6	6.7	7.4	8.5	9.4
Switzerland	0.8	1.1	2.0	2.8	3.3	2.6	2.9	3.6	4.8	4.9
Australia and New Zealand	..	..	..	..	..	..	..	..	..	..
Asia (non-OECD)	0.3	0.5	1.3	1.3	1.3	1.2	1.3	1.4	2.2	1.9
Latin America	0.5	..	0.7	0.5	0.4	0.6	0.5	0.7	0.7	0.8

Note: **Enterprise-level data.** Defined as *US merchandise exports shipped by affiliates.* See country notes.
Données au niveau de l'entreprise. Définies comme les exportations américaines de marchandises expédiées par les entreprises affiliées. Voir les notes par pays.

Table 11. UNITED STATES / ÉTATS-UNIS

TOTAL IMPORTS / IMPORTATIONS TOTALES

By industry (ISIC Rev. 3)		FOREIGN AFFILIATES (Billions of US$)									
		1987	1988	1989	1990	1991	1992	1993	1994	1995	1996
10/14	Mining & quarrying	0.3	0.4	0.2	0.3	0.2	0.2	0.3	0.1	0.1	0.3
15/37	**TOTAL MANUFACTURING**	**24.5**	**32.8**	**40.9**	**47.2**	**47.0**	**53.3**	**59.6**	**68.4**	**81.6**	**78.5**
15/16	Food, beverages, tobacco	1.6	2.1	2.5	2.4	2.9	3.0	3.2	3.2	3.2	3.4
17/19	Textiles, clothing, leather, footwear	0.3	0.6	0.7	0.4	0.4	0.7	0.8	0.7	0.8	0.6
20/22	Wood and paper products	0.7	1.1	1.0	1.2	1.4	1.4	1.6	1.5	1.8	1.7
20	Wood products	0.2	0.2	0.2	0.2	0.2	0.4	0.5	0.3	0.3	0.3
21/22	Paper, printing and publishing	0.5	0.9	0.9	1.0	1.2	1.0	1.2	1.3	1.5	1.4
23/25	Chemicals, Total	6.2	7.5	8.8	11.4	11.5	14.2	15.1	17.3	16.8	17.2
23	Refined petroleum, nuclear fuel	..	..	..	..	..	..	..	..	..	..
24/25	Chemicals, rubber & plastics prod.	6.2	7.5	8.8	11.4	11.5	14.2	15.1	17.3	16.8	17.2
24	Chemical products	5.2	6.4	7.6	9.1	9.6	11.9	12.6	14.3	13.4	14.3
2423	Pharmaceuticals	1.2	1.6	1.8	2.1	2.4	2.9	5.4	5.4	6.1	6.3
25	Rubber and plastics products	1.0	1.1	1.2	2.4	1.9	2.3	2.5	3.0	3.4	2.9
26	Non-metallic mineral products	0.6	0.8	0.8	1.1	0.9	0.9	1.1	1.2	1.4	1.2
27/28	Basic & fabricated metals	3.7	3.9	5.0	5.0	5.1	6.0	6.4	7.6	7.9	7.4
27	Basic metals	2.8	2.9	3.4	3.8	3.8	4.3	4.8	5.3	5.3	4.8
28	Fabricated metal products	0.9	1.1	1.6	1.3	1.3	1.7	1.6	2.3	2.6	2.6
29/32	Machinery, Total	7.6	11.6	14.4	17.9	16.8	19.8	22.5	26.0	30.0	28.7
29/30	Non-electrical machinery	2.9	3.6	6.0	8.4	7.7	7.9	9.2	10.7	14.4	11.7
29	Non-electrical machinery nec	2.0	2.6	4.2	3.9	3.6	5.3	6.5	7.3	7.7	7.4
30	Office and computing machinery	0.8	1.0	1.7	4.5	4.0	2.6	2.7	3.3	6.8	4.4
31/32	Electrical & electronic equipment	4.8	8.0	8.4	9.5	9.2	12.0	13.3	15.3	15.6	17.0
31	Electrical machinery nec	1.5	2.4	1.8	2.4	2.9	2.6	2.8	5.9	6.9	5.9
32	Radio, TV & communications eq.	3.3	5.6	6.6	7.2	6.3	9.3	10.5	9.4	8.7	11.1
33	Scientific instruments	0.8	0.6	0.8	1.0	1.0	1.1	1.3	1.4	1.5	1.4
34/35	Transportation equipment	2.3	3.2	6.1	5.9	5.6	5.5	6.7	8.8	17.6	16.1
34	Motor vehicles	1.6	2.4	5.4	5.4	5.0	4.8	5.9	7.8	17.0	15.5
35	Other transport equipment	0.7	0.8	0.6	0.5	0.6	0.6	0.8	1.0	0.6	0.6
351	Shipbuilding & repairing	..	..	..	..	..	..	..	..	..	..
353	Aircraft and spacecraft	..	..	..	..	..	..	..	..	..	..
36/37	Other manufacturing	0.6	1.2	0.9	0.7	1.4	0.8	0.9	0.7	0.5	0.8
40/45	Construction, electricity, gas & water	0.1	0.1	0.4	..	..	..	..	..	0.1	0.1
50/55	Trade, repair, hotels & restaurants	109.4	113.8	115.9	115.8	114.3	112.5	122.7	145.5	149.3	151.4
65/74	Finance, insurance, business services	0.0	0.0	0.0	0.0	0.0	0.0	0.0	0.0	0.0	0.0
	OTHER ACTIVITIES	9.1	8.5	14.5	..	..	..	..	..	19.8	22.7
01/99	**GRAND TOTAL**	**143.5**	**155.5**	**171.8**	**182.9**	**178.7**	**184.5**	**200.6**	**232.4**	**250.8**	**253.0**

Total manufacturing by investing country	1987	1988	1989	1990	1991	1992	1993	1994	1995	1996
All countries	**24.5**	**32.8**	**40.9**	**47.2**	**47.0**	**53.3**	**59.6**	**68.4**	**81.6**	**78.5**
United States	0.0	0.1	0.1	..	0.0	..	0.0	0.1	..	0.3
Canada	4.3	4.6	5.8	5.8	5.8	6.4	7.1	7.4	6.4	6.2
Mexico	..	..	..	..	..	..	..	..	..	..
Japan	4.2	5.9	10.1	14.1	12.8	14.7	15.9	17.8	31.2	28.0
Europe	14.4	20.6	22.5	24.3	25.0	29.3	33.0	39.2	39.7	40.4
European Union (15)	..	..	..	..	..	..	..	..	..	..
Belgium	..	..	..	..	..	..	..	..	..	..
France	1.8	4.0	4.1	4.9	4.2	5.4	6.2	8.2	7.3	8.1
Germany	4.3	5.3	6.0	6.7	6.7	8.1	8.4	10.8	11.0	11.0
Italy	..	..	..	..	..	..	..	..	..	..
Netherlands	1.4	2.3	2.5	2.6	2.6	2.9	3.5	3.4	3.8	3.9
Spain	..	..	..	..	..	..	..	..	..	..
Sweden	..	..	..	..	..	..	..	..	..	..
United Kingdom	3.3	4.5	5.1	5.1	5.5	6.0	6.7	7.3	7.6	7.4
Switzerland	1.6	2.2	2.3	2.4	2.7	2.9	3.2	3.5	3.9	4.0
Australia and New Zealand	..	..	..	..	..	..	..	..	..	..
Asia (non-OECD)	0.7	0.7	1.4	1.4	2.1	1.7	2.0	1.7	2.2	1.8
Latin America	..	0.4	..	..	0.5	0.6	0.8	1.2	..	1.2

Note: **Enterprise-level data.** Defined as *US merchandise imports shipped to affiliates.* See country notes.
Données au niveau de l'entreprise. Définies comme les importations américaines de marchandises expédiées aux entreprises affiliées. Voir les notes par pays.

Table 12. UNITED STATES / ÉTATS-UNIS

INTRA-FIRM EXPORTS / EXPORTATIONS INTRA-FIRME

By industry (ISIC Rev. 3)		FOREIGN AFFILIATES (Billions of US$)									
		1987	1988	1989	1990	1991	1992	1993	1994	1995	1996
10/14	Mining & quarrying	0.6	0.5	0.6	0.4	0.3	0.4	0.3	0.2	0.2	0.3
15/37	TOTAL MANUFACTURING	7.2	10.7	13.4	15.0	17.3	19.5	20.9	24.6	28.9	29.0
15/16	Food, beverages, tobacco	0.2	0.9	0.5	0.6	0.7	0.9	1.1	1.2	1.3	1.4
17/19	Textiles, clothing, leather, footwear	0.0	0.1	0.1	0.1	0.1	0.2	0.2	0.2	0.2	0.2
20/22	Wood and paper products	0.4	0.4	0.6	0.5	0.5	0.8	0.9	0.9	1.0	1.0
20	Wood products	0.1	0.1	0.2	0.1	0.1	0.1	0.2	0.2	0.1	0.1
21/22	Paper, printing and publishing	0.3	0.4	0.4	0.4	0.5	0.7	0.7	0.8	0.9	1.0
23/25	Chemicals, Total	3.3	4.4	5.2	6.2	6.9	7.8	8.2	9.1	8.8	8.7
23	Refined petroleum, nuclear fuel	..	..	..	..	..	..	..	..	..	..
24/25	Chemicals, rubber & plastics prod.	3.3	4.4	5.2	6.2	6.9	7.8	8.2	9.1	8.8	8.7
24	Chemical products	3.2	4.1	4.9	5.5	6.3	7.0	7.4	8.2	7.7	7.3
2423	Pharmaceuticals	0.6	0.7	0.7	1.0	0.9	1.0	2.3	2.5	3.3	2.9
25	Rubber and plastics products	0.1	0.3	0.3	0.6	0.6	0.8	0.8	0.9	1.1	1.3
26	Non-metallic mineral products	0.0	0.1	0.1	0.2	0.2	0.3	0.4	0.3	0.3	0.3
27/28	Basic & fabricated metals	0.4	0.5	1.1	1.0	1.1	1.0	1.0	1.2	1.5	1.5
27	Basic metals	0.4	0.4	0.7	0.7	0.8	0.6	0.7	0.8	0.9	0.9
28	Fabricated metal products	0.1	0.2	0.4	0.2	0.3	0.3	0.3	0.3	0.5	0.6
29/32	Machinery, Total	2.0	3.2	4.4	5.1	5.8	6.1	6.7	8.6	9.8	10.0
29/30	Non-electrical machinery	0.8	1.3	2.3	2.7	2.6	2.5	2.5	2.6	3.4	3.1
29	Non-electrical machinery nec	0.3	0.6	1.1	1.3	1.2	1.4	1.7	1.9	2.1	2.2
30	Office and computing machinery	0.5	0.7	1.2	1.4	1.4	1.1	0.8	0.7	1.3	0.9
31/32	Electrical & electronic equipment	1.2	2.0	2.0	2.4	3.2	3.6	4.2	6.0	6.4	6.9
31	Electrical machinery nec	0.5	0.6	0.6	0.8	1.3	1.2	1.3	3.0	3.0	2.8
32	Radio, TV & communications eq.	0.7	1.3	1.4	1.5	1.9	2.4	2.9	3.0	3.4	4.1
33	Scientific instruments	0.3	0.4	0.5	0.6	0.9	1.1	1.1	1.3	1.4	1.5
34/35	Transportation equipment	0.2	0.4	0.4	0.4	0.5	0.9	0.9	1.2	3.6	3.7
34	Motor vehicles	0.2	0.2	0.3	0.3	0.4	0.7	0.7	1.0	3.4	3.5
35	Other transport equipment	0.1	0.1	0.1	0.1	0.1	0.3	0.2	0.3	0.2	0.2
351	Shipbuilding & repairing	..	..	..	..	..	..	..	..	..	..
353	Aircraft and spacecraft	..	..	..	..	..	..	..	..	..	..
36/37	Other manufacturing	0.2	0.3	0.4	0.4	0.5	0.5	0.4	0.5	1.1	0.7
40/45	Construction, electricity, gas & water	0.0	0.0	0.1	0.1	0.0	0.0	0.0	0.0	..	0.1
50/55	Trade, repair, hotels & restaurants	14.1	20.0	25.7	28.2	30.3	36.4	35.4	33.5	37.6	37.2
65/74	Finance, insurance, business services	0.0	0.0	0.0	0.0	0.1	0.0	0.0	0.0	0.0	0.0
	OTHER ACTIVITIES	0.7	1.1	1.0	1.7	2.4	2.2	1.8	6.5	..	5.2
01/99	GRAND TOTAL	22.6	32.3	40.7	45.3	50.4	58.6	58.3	64.8	72.2	71.8

Total manufacturing by investing country	1987	1988	1989	1990	1991	1992	1993	1994	1995	1996
All countries	4.5	6.5	7.9	9.1	10.4	11.6	12.1	14.1	18.2	20.0
United States	0.0	..	..	..	..	0.0	..	..	0.1	0.1
Canada	0.4	..	..	..	..	1.1	1.1	1.3	1.5	1.9
Mexico	..	..	..	..	..	..	..	..	..	..
Japan	0.6	..	..	..	..	2.7	2.8	3.1	4.5	5.4
Europe	3.2	..	..	..	..	7.3	7.7	9.1	11.5	12.0
European Union (15)	..	..	..	..	..	..	..	..	..	..
Belgium	..	..	..	..	..	..	..	..	..	..
France	0.3	..	..	..	..	1.0	1.0	1.0	1.2	1.6
Germany	1.1	..	..	..	..	1.9	2.0	2.3	2.8	2.9
Italy	..	..	..	..	..	..	..	..	..	..
Netherlands	0.3	..	..	..	..	0.9	0.9	1.0	1.4	1.4
Spain	..	..	..	..	..	..	..	..	..	..
Sweden	..	..	..	..	..	..	..	..	..	..
United Kingdom	0.9	..	..	..	..	1.5	1.4	1.6	2.3	2.1
Switzerland	0.3	..	..	..	..	1.1	1.3	1.6	1.9	2.1
Australia and New Zealand	..	..	..	..	..	..	..	..	..	..
Asia (non-OECD)	0.1	..	..	..	..	0.2	0.2	0.3	0.3	0.3
Latin America	0.3	..	..	..	..	0.2	0.2	0.2	0.2	0.2

Note: **Enterprise-level data.** Defined as *US merchandise exports shipped by affiliates a) to the foreign parent company + b) to foreign affiliates*. For *Total manufacturing by investing country*, a) only. See country notes.

Données au niveau de l'entreprise. Définies comme les exportations à destination a) du groupe-parent étranger + b) des filiales étrangères. a) uniquement pour le total manufacturier par pays investisseur. Voir les notes par pays.

Table 13. UNITED STATES / ÉTATS-UNIS

INTRA-FIRM IMPORTS / IMPORTATIONS INTRA-FIRME

		FOREIGN AFFILIATES (Billions of US$)									
By industry (ISIC Rev. 3)		1987	1988	1989	1990	1991	1992	1993	1994	1995	1996
10/14	Mining & quarrying	0.3	0.4	0.2	0.3	0.2	0.2	0.2	0.1	0.1	0.3
15/37	**TOTAL MANUFACTURING**	**18.7**	**24.1**	**30.6**	**36.7**	**36.0**	**42.0**	**46.2**	**54.9**	**68.7**	**65.3**
15/16	Food, beverages, tobacco	1.0	1.6	1.2	1.5	1.7	1.8	2.0	2.0	1.9	1.7
17/19	Textiles, clothing, leather, footwear	0.1	0.3	0.4	0.2	0.2	0.4	0.4	0.4	0.4	0.3
20/22	Wood and paper products	0.5	0.7	0.7	0.7	0.8	1.0	1.1	1.0	1.2	1.1
20	Wood products	0.2	0.2	0.1	0.1	0.1	0.4	0.4	0.2	0.2	0.2
21/22	Paper, printing and publishing	0.3	0.5	0.6	0.6	0.7	0.6	0.7	0.8	0.9	0.9
23/25	Chemicals, Total	4.5	6.1	6.9	9.1	9.3	11.7	12.6	14.3	15.1	15.5
23	Refined petroleum, nuclear fuel	..	..	..	..	..	..	..	..	..	..
24/25	Chemicals, rubber & plastics prod.	4.5	6.1	6.9	9.1	9.3	11.7	12.6	14.3	15.1	15.5
24	Chemical products	3.6	5.1	5.8	6.8	7.5	9.5	10.2	11.9	12.2	12.7
2423	Pharmaceuticals	1.1	1.5	1.8	2.0	2.3	2.7	5.1	5.1	5.9	5.7
25	Rubber and plastics products	0.9	1.0	1.1	2.2	1.8	2.2	2.4	2.5	2.8	2.7
26	Non-metallic mineral products	0.4	0.5	0.6	0.8	0.6	0.7	0.9	1.0	1.0	0.9
27/28	Basic & fabricated metals	2.6	2.6	3.4	2.8	3.2	4.1	4.2	5.4	6.0	5.4
27	Basic metals	2.1	2.1	2.4	2.2	2.6	2.9	3.1	3.5	3.7	3.3
28	Fabricated metal products	0.4	0.5	1.1	0.6	0.6	1.2	1.1	1.9	2.3	2.1
29/32	Machinery, Total	6.6	8.5	10.5	14.8	14.4	15.9	17.3	20.9	24.6	23.4
29/30	Non-electrical machinery	2.6	3.1	4.7	7.8	6.8	6.3	6.7	7.5	10.9	9.0
29	Non-electrical machinery nec	1.8	2.2	3.3	3.5	3.1	3.9	4.9	5.8	5.9	5.7
30	Office and computing machinery	0.7	0.9	1.3	4.3	3.7	2.3	1.7	1.7	5.0	3.2
31/32	Electrical & electronic equipment	4.0	5.4	5.8	7.0	7.6	9.6	10.6	13.4	13.7	14.5
31	Electrical machinery nec	1.3	2.2	1.5	2.1	2.5	2.3	2.5	5.0	5.7	5.0
32	Radio, TV & communications eq.	2.7	3.2	4.3	4.9	5.0	7.4	8.1	8.4	8.0	9.4
33	Scientific instruments	0.6	0.5	0.7	0.8	0.8	0.9	1.0	1.1	1.2	1.1
34/35	Transportation equipment	2.2	3.1	5.9	5.7	4.6	5.2	6.3	8.3	17.1	15.6
34	Motor vehicles	1.4	2.3	5.3	5.3	4.1	4.6	5.6	7.3	16.5	15.1
35	Other transport equipment	0.7	0.8	0.6	0.4	0.6	0.6	0.8	1.0	0.6	0.5
351	Shipbuilding & repairing	..	..	..	..	..	..	..	..	..	..
353	Aircraft and spacecraft	..	..	..	..	..	..	..	..	..	..
36/37	Other manufacturing	0.3	0.3	0.3	0.3	0.4	0.4	0.4	0.4	0.3	0.3
40/45	Construction, electricity, gas & water	0.0	0.0	0.3	..	..	..	..	..	0.1	0.1
50/55	Trade, repair, hotels & restaurants	86.6	92.4	95.0	92.9	90.7	91.2	101.9	120.6	123.7	126.4
65/74	Finance, insurance, business services	0.0	0.0	0.0	0.0	0.0	0.0	0.0	0.0	0.0	0.0
	OTHER ACTIVITIES	4.3	4.6	8.2	..	..	..	..	..	11.1	13.1
01/99	**GRAND TOTAL**	**109.9**	**121.5**	**134.3**	**141.8**	**137.0**	**143.9**	**158.9**	**186.0**	**203.7**	**205.1**

Total manufacturing by investing country										
All countries	**17.6**	**22.0**	**27.6**	**33.2**	**32.7**	**37.3**	**39.9**	**47.2**	**60.4**	**56.9**
United States	0.0	..	..	..	..	..	0.0	0.1	..	0.2
Canada	2.7	..	..	..	..	3.7	4.1	4.2	5.1	5.2
Mexico	..	..	..	..	..	..	..	..	..	..
Japan	3.9	..	..	..	..	12.3	13.1	15.0	25.4	22.4
Europe	10.0	..	..	..	..	19.6	20.7	26.1	28.2	27.6
European Union (15)	..	..	..	..	..	..	..	..	..	..
Belgium	..	..	..	..	..	..	..	..	..	..
France	1.4	..	..	..	..	2.4	2.3	3.4	3.8	3.7
Germany	3.2	..	..	..	..	6.5	6.2	8.2	8.8	8.2
Italy	..	..	..	..	..	..	..	..	..	..
Netherlands	0.9	..	..	..	..	1.7	1.8	2.0	2.7	2.9
Spain	..	..	..	..	..	..	..	..	..	..
Sweden	..	..	..	..	..	..	..	..	..	..
United Kingdom	1.9	..	..	..	..	3.9	4.2	4.7	4.7	4.4
Switzerland	1.3	..	..	..	..	2.5	2.7	3.0	3.4	3.4
Australia and New Zealand	..	..	..	..	..	..	..	..	..	..
Asia (non-OECD)	0.3	..	..	..	..	1.1	1.3	1.1	0.8	0.8
Latin America	..	..	..	..	..	0.4	0.5	0.5	..	0.4

Note: **Enterprise-level data.** Defined as *US merchandise imports shipped to affiliates a) from the foreign parent company + b) from foreign affiliates*. For *Total manufacturing by investing country, a)* only. See country notes.

Données au niveau de l'entreprise. Définies comme les importations en provenance a) du groupe parent étranger + b) des filiales étrangères. a) uniquement pour le total manufacturier par pays investisseur. Voir les notes par pays.

Table 14. UNITED STATES / ÉTATS-UNIS

GROSS OPERATING SURPLUS / EXCÉDENT BRUT D'EXPLOITATION

By industry (ISIC Rev. 3)		1987	1988	1989	1990	1991	1992	1993	1994	1995	1996
		FOREIGN AFFILIATES *(Millions of US$)*									
10/14	Mining & quarrying	344	561	46	597	655	- 80	- 2	381	1 202	769
15/37	**TOTAL MANUFACTURING**	**4 985**	**7 542**	**5 698**	**- 31**	**-3 265**	**-9 171**	**-6 351**	**6 432**	**9 189**	**7 153**
15/16	Food, beverages, tobacco	353	831	444	89	210	238	-1 621	- 172	512	3 591
17/19	Textiles, clothing, leather, footwear	161	57	- 42	- 188	- 74	4	148	- 41	21	15
20/22	Wood and paper products	- 22	516	- 76	- 199	- 726	-1 222	- 894	717	819	840
20	Wood products	20	111	73	35	- 22	85	490	331	125	578
21/22	Paper, printing and publishing	- 42	405	- 149	- 234	- 704	-1 307	-1 384	386	694	262
23/25	Chemicals, Total	3 289	4 630	4 857	4 263	2 586	-2 075	2 939	5 240	4 158	1 018
23	Refined petroleum, nuclear fuel	..	..	..	..	..	..	..	..	..	..
24/25	Chemicals, rubber & plastics prod.	3 289	4 630	4 857	4 263	2 586	-2 075	2 939	5 240	4 158	1 018
24	Chemical products	3 145	4 368	4 894	4 923	3 886	-1 281	3 338	5 123	3 834	549
2423	Pharmaceuticals	138	706	1 166	1 847	2 190	2 291	2 178	2 195	2 748	1 734
25	Rubber and plastics products	144	262	- 37	- 660	-1 300	- 794	- 399	117	324	469
26	Non-metallic mineral products	725	445	173	- 659	- 918	-1 005	- 563	- 439	801	382
27/28	Basic & fabricated metals	182	1 088	791	363	-1 072	-2 029	-1 854	384	1 311	1 010
27	Basic metals	526	719	557	312	- 770	-2 014	-1 445	1 025	1 210	807
28	Fabricated metal products	- 344	369	234	51	- 301	- 15	- 408	- 641	101	203
29/32	Machinery, Total	- 328	- 181	- 394	-3 659	-3 105	-2 749	-3 970	66	222	- 737
29/30	Non-electrical machinery	- 12	379	297	-1 464	-1 865	-1 638	-2 193	52	- 384	- 495
29	Non-electrical machinery nec	- 6	272	462	- 437	- 582	- 835	- 625	468	614	825
30	Office and computing machinery	- 6	107	- 166	-1 028	-1 283	- 803	-1 568	- 415	- 998	-1 320
31/32	Electrical & electronic equipment	- 315	- 560	- 691	-2 195	-1 240	-1 112	-1 778	13	607	- 242
31	Electrical machinery nec	- 203	- 241	- 327	- 813	- 747	- 672	- 796	- 234	310	- 226
32	Radio, TV & communications eq.	- 112	- 319	- 364	-1 381	- 493	- 439	- 982	247	297	- 16
33	Scientific instruments	10	169	80	5	416	366	68	132	538	604
34/35	Transportation equipment	111	- 547	- 708	- 792	- 585	- 920	- 683	408	410	168
34	Motor vehicles	- 9	- 371	- 730	- 614	- 465	- 487	- 515	434	529	- 25
35	Other transport equipment	120	- 176	22	- 178	- 120	- 433	- 168	- 26	- 119	193
351	Shipbuilding & repairing	..	..	..	..	..	..	..	..	..	..
353	Aircraft and spacecraft	..	..	..	..	..	..	..	..	..	..
36/37	Other manufacturing	504	533	574	746	1	221	79	137	397	261
40/45	Construction, electricity, gas & water	- 157	- 155	- 70	- 243	- 338	- 413	- 393	- 129	- 386	- 516
50/55	Trade, repair, hotels & restaurants	450	1 713	- 643	-2 153	-1 898	-2 421	- 681	2 769	309	3 216
65/74	Finance, insurance, business services	1 902	1 441	3 139	-1 196	-1 607	-1 803	2 905	1 186	2 699	3 652
	OTHER ACTIVITIES	297	947	1 117	-1 508	-4 564	-7 444	168	-2 507	2 481	6 839
01/99	**GRAND TOTAL**	**7 820**	**12 049**	**9 286**	**-4 535**	**-11 018**	**-21 331**	**-4 354**	**8 132**	**15 493**	**21 110**

Total manufacturing by investing country										
All countries	**4 985**	**7 542**	**5 698**	**- 31**	**-3 265**	**-9 171**	**-6 351**	**6 432**	**9 189**	**7 153**
United States	- 26	- 26	- 65	- 44	- 29	- 2	11	48	113	- 11
Canada	2 371	3 175	3 391	3 116	1 545	-3 421	-1 609	3 206	812	3 992
Mexico	..	..	..	..	..	..	..	..	..	..
Japan	45	- 242	- 632	-1 600	-3 526	-4 059	-3 474	558	1 216	- 77
Europe	2 327	4 628	3 348	- 993	- 837	- 902	- 622	2 547	7 155	3 802
European Union (15)	..	..	..	..	..	..	..	..	..	..
Belgium	..	..	..	..	..	..	..	..	..	..
France	384	255	0	-1 958	- 759	- 554	-1 007	- 554	559	1 001
Germany	142	422	411	53	- 653	- 521	617	1 040	238	1 430
Italy	..	..	..	..	..	..	..	..	..	..
Netherlands	6	177	- 89	- 831	- 353	10	- 428	574	817	304
Spain	..	..	..	..	..	..	..	..	..	..
Sweden	..	..	..	..	..	..	..	..	..	..
United Kingdom	1 245	2 499	2 321	1 976	2 084	1 201	1 906	1 948	3 680	- 76
Switzerland	- 90	385	317	- 54	- 226	- 126	- 444	- 546	324	652
Australia and New Zealand	..	..	..	..	..	..	..	..	..	..
Asia (non-OECD)	497	- 70	- 264	- 539	- 477	- 684	- 168	96	- 102	- 82
Latin America	- 342	- 2	- 33	16	9	- 46	- 491	- 132	- 145	- 583

Note: **Enterprise-level data.** Defined as *Net Income.* See country notes.
Données au niveau de l'entreprise. Représente le revenu net. Voir les notes par pays.

Table 15. UNITED STATES / ÉTATS-UNIS

TECHNOLOGICAL PAYMENTS / PAIEMENTS TECHNOLOGIQUES

By industry (ISIC Rev. 3)		FOREIGN AFFILIATES (Millions of US$)									
		1988	1989	1990	1991	1992	1993	1994	1995	1996	1997
10/14	Mining & quarrying	..	..	..	..	..	..	..	..	..	..
15/37	**TOTAL MANUFACTURING**	**812**	**1 098**	**1 317**	**1 771**	**2 066**	**2 063**	**2 389**	**3 350**	**3 271**	**3 645**
15/16	Food, beverages, tobacco	123	177	155	214	222	227	235	226	268	270
17/19	Textiles, clothing, leather, footwear	..	..	..	..	..	..	..	..	..	..
20/22	Wood and paper products	..	..	..	..	..	..	..	..	..	..
20	Wood products	..	..	..	..	..	..	..	..	..	..
21/22	Paper, printing and publishing	..	..	..	..	..	..	..	..	..	..
23/25	Chemicals, Total	..	..	..	..	..	..	..	..	..	..
23	Refined petroleum, nuclear fuel	..	..	..	..	..	..	..	..	..	..
24/25	Chemicals, rubber & plastics prod.	..	..	..	..	..	..	..	..	..	..
24	Chemical products	451	604	683	1 073	1 267	1 224	1 421	1 949	1 996	2 207
2423	Pharmaceuticals	..	..	..	..	..	..	..	..	..	..
25	Rubber and plastics products	..	..	..	..	..	..	..	..	..	..
26	Non-metallic mineral products	..	..	..	..	..	..	..	..	..	..
27/28	Basic & fabricated metals	24	47	64	51	64	72	70	103	137	146
27	Basic metals	..	..	..	..	..	..	..	..	..	..
28	Fabricated metal products	..	..	..	..	..	..	..	..	..	..
29/32	Machinery, Total	60	103	222	173	222	228	298	301	336	416
29/30	Non-electrical machinery	..	..	..	..	..	..	..	..	..	..
29	Non-electrical machinery nec	..	..	..	..	..	..	..	..	..	..
30	Office and computing machinery	..	..	..	..	..	..	..	..	..	..
31/32	Electrical & electronic equipment	..	..	..	..	..	..	..	..	..	..
31	Electrical machinery nec	..	..	..	..	..	..	..	..	..	..
32	Radio, TV & communications eq.	..	..	..	..	..	..	..	..	..	..
33	Scientific instruments	..	..	..	..	..	..	..	..	..	..
34/35	Transportation equipment	..	..	..	..	..	..	..	..	..	..
34	Motor vehicles	..	..	..	..	..	..	..	..	..	..
35	Other transport equipment	..	..	..	..	..	..	..	..	..	..
351	Shipbuilding & repairing	..	..	..	..	..	..	..	..	..	..
353	Aircraft and spacecraft	..	..	..	..	..	..	..	..	..	..
36/37	Other manufacturing	..	..	..	..	..	..	..	..	..	..
40/45	Construction, electricity, gas & water	..	..	..	..	..	..	..	..	..	..
50/55	Trade, repair, hotels & restaurants	328	358	382	675	789	680	..	..	798	..
65/74	Finance, insurance, business services	..	..	..	..	..	49	44	67	..	67
	OTHER ACTIVITIES	..	..	..	..	..	..	..	..	..	..
01/99	**GRAND TOTAL**	**1 243**	**1 579**	**1 860**	**2 652**	**3 049**	**2 998**	**3 312**	**4 411**	**4 472**	**5 785**

Total manufacturing by investing country											
All countries	812	1 098	1 317	1 771	2 066	2 063	2 389	3 350	3 271	3 645
United States	..	..	..	..	..	..	..	..	..	..
Canada	16	13	9	6	24	..	12	33	53	..
Mexico	0	0	0	0	0	0	2	0	0	..
Japan	57	93	138	185	211	231	276	648	556	517
Europe	726	976	1 159	1 570	1 820	1 801	2 094	2 661	2 652	2 964
European Union (15)	530	707	885	1 225	1 434	1 436	1 638	2 220	2 212	2 478
Belgium	..	24	24	33	31	31	44	63	69	75
France	52	74	110	108	102	106	69	98	106	176
Germany	188	210	209	166	225	230	362	403	403	477
Italy	2	4	15	7	8	8	..	17	16	..
Netherlands	36	72	151	113	157	111	114	283	236	..
Spain	0	0	0	0	0	0	..	..	1	1
Sweden	..	11	15	27	24	29	46	41	39	..
United Kingdom	229	322	374	798	908	945	1 010	1 283	1 316	1 388
Switzerland	185	250	240	309	354	318	383	439	438	485
Australia and New Zealand	5	0	4	4	4	3	4	4	4	..
Asia (non-OECD)	0	7	1	1	0	2	1	1	1	..
Latin America	7	8	5	5	8	..	3	3	2	..

Note: **Enterprise-level data.** Defined as *Royalties and license fees payments by US affiliates.* See country notes.
Données au niveau de l'entreprise. Définis comme les paiements de la filiale américaine au groupe-parent au titre des redevances et droits de licence. Voir les notes par pays.

Table 16. UNITED STATES / ÉTATS-UNIS

TECHNOLOGICAL RECEIPTS / RECETTES TECHNOLOGIQUES

By industry (ISIC Rev. 3)	FOREIGN AFFILIATES (Millions of US$)									
	1988	1989	1990	1991	1992	1993	1994	1995	1996	1997
10/14 Mining & quarrying	..	..	..	..	..	..	..	..	..	..
15/37 TOTAL MANUFACTURING	**109**	**155**	**165**	**200**	**283**	**261**	**403**	**709**	**1 210**	**885**
15/16 Food, beverages, tobacco	16	28	31	30	39	57	46	54	46	76
17/19 Textiles, clothing, leather, footwear	..	..	..	..	..	..	..	..	..	..
20/22 Wood and paper products	..	..	..	..	..	..	..	..	..	..
20 Wood products	..	..	..	..	..	..	..	..	..	..
21/22 Paper, printing and publishing	..	..	..	..	..	..	..	..	..	..
23/25 Chemicals, Total	..	..	..	..	..	..	..	..	..	..
23 Refined petroleum, nuclear fuel	..	..	..	..	..	..	..	..	..	..
24/25 Chemicals, rubber & plastics prod.	..	..	..	..	..	..	..	..	..	..
24 Chemical products	19	24	68	81	58	96	81	149	400	351
2423 Pharmaceuticals	..	..	..	..	..	..	..	..	..	..
25 Rubber and plastics products	..	..	..	..	..	..	..	..	..	..
26 Non-metallic mineral products	..	..	..	..	..	..	..	..	..	..
27/28 Basic & fabricated metals	4	34	7	8	3	9	7	23	27	9
27 Basic metals	..	..	..	..	..	..	..	..	..	..
28 Fabricated metal products	..	..	..	..	..	..	..	..	..	..
29/32 Machinery, Total	46	34	20	36	105	43	222	404	561	201
29/30 Non-electrical machinery	..	..	..	..	..	..	..	..	..	..
29 Non-electrical machinery nec	..	..	..	..	..	..	..	..	..	..
30 Office and computing machinery	..	..	..	..	..	..	..	..	..	..
31/32 Electrical & electronic equipment	..	..	..	..	..	..	..	..	..	..
31 Electrical machinery nec	..	..	..	..	..	..	..	..	..	..
32 Radio, TV & communications eq.	..	..	..	..	..	..	..	..	..	..
33 Scientific instruments	..	..	..	..	..	..	..	..	..	..
34/35 Transportation equipment	..	..	..	..	..	..	..	..	..	..
34 Motor vehicles	..	..	..	..	..	..	..	..	..	..
35 Other transport equipment	..	..	..	..	..	..	..	..	..	..
351 Shipbuilding & repairing	..	..	..	..	..	..	..	..	..	..
353 Aircraft and spacecraft	..	..	..	..	..	..	..	..	..	..
36/37 Other manufacturing	..	..	..	..	..	..	..	..	..	..
40/45 Construction, electricity, gas & water	..	..	..	..	..	..	..	..	..	..
50/55 Trade, repair, hotels & restaurants	77	..	..	..	..	..	..	..	..	..
65/74 Finance, insurance, business services	..	..	..	..	24	19	15	..	..	15
OTHER ACTIVITIES	..	..	..	..	..	..	..	..	..	..
01/99 GRAND TOTAL	**242**	**331**	..	**553**	**697**	**714**	**974**	**1 387**	**1 833**	**1 954**

Total manufacturing by investing country

	1988	1989	1990	1991	1992	1993	1994	1995	1996	1997
All countries	**109**	**155**	**165**	**200**	**283**	**261**	**403**	**709**	**1 210**	**885**
United States	..	..	..	..	..	..	..	..	..	..
Canada	12	15	8	10	10	11	24	18	32	..
Mexico	0	1	1	1	7	6	6	10	8	..
Japan	..	19	25	19	58	57	89	147	171	183
Europe	70	81	119	150	186	161	251	499	959	620
European Union (15)	60	71	108	122	146	141	235	486	921	523
Belgium	0	1	10	4	3	..	7	..	59	16
France	35	23	39	19	51	23	67	189	..	43
Germany	6	13	23	40	30	33	44	56	35	46
Italy	0	0	3	2	3	2	8	..	21	..
Netherlands	3	2	2	6	10	10	11	37	10	..
Spain	0	1	0	0	0	5	9	..	0	0
Sweden	0	0	4	5	2	5	2	1	..	..
United Kingdom	15	31	..	49	44	50	89	171	301	301
Switzerland	9	4	6	18	36	14	11	10	38	94
Australia and New Zealand	..	0	1	8	3	7	..	..	2	1
Asia (non-OECD)	..	36	10	13	19	18	..	..	31	28
Latin America	0	3	1	1	7	7	10	11	9	..

Note: **Enterprise-level data.** Defined as *Royalties and license fees receipts by US affiliates*. See country notes.
Données au niveau de l'entreprise. Définies comme les recettes de la filiale américaine provenant du groupe-parent au titre des redevances et droits de licence. Voir les notes par pays.

Table 17. UNITED STATES / ÉTATS-UNIS

STOCK OF FOREIGN DIRECT INVESTMENT / STOCK D'INVESTISSEMENT DIRECT ÉTRANGER

		FOREIGN AFFILIATES (Billions of US$)									
By industry (ISIC Rev. 3)		1988	1989	1990	1991	1992	1993	1994	1995	1996	1997
10/14	Mining & quarrying	7.4	4.7	8.5	7.9	8.5	10.1	10.6	11.3	10.2	13.1
15/37	TOTAL MANUFACTURING	122.6	150.9	152.8	157.1	160.4	168.1	189.5	214.5	242.3	267.1
15/16	Food, beverages, tobacco	16.5	23.6	22.5	23.9	23.8	22.8	21.4	27.0	27.9	27.5
17/19	Textiles, clothing, leather, footwear	2.1	2.9	1.8	2.1	2.5	2.6	3.2	3.9	4.0	4.9
20/22	Wood and paper products	12.1	13.4	15.4	13.5	14.2	15.7	17.5	20.0	29.5	27.0
20	Wood products	0.6	0.6	0.8	0.5	0.8	2.5	2.8	2.9	2.0	1.5
21/22	Paper, printing and publishing	11.5	12.8	14.7	13.0	13.4	13.2	14.8	17.0	27.5	25.4
23/25	Chemicals, Total	34.9	42.7	51.3	54.7	57.5	63.0	72.7	79.9	86.5	96.4
23	Refined petroleum, nuclear fuel	..	..	..	..	..	..	..	..	..	..
24/25	Chemicals, rubber & plastics prod.	34.9	42.7	51.3	54.7	57.5	63.0	72.7	79.9	86.5	96.4
24	Chemical products	30.9	38.4	45.7	48.6	52.4	56.8	66.0	72.1	76.7	88.8
2423	Pharmaceuticals	6.5	9.0	11.5	11.8	12.2	19.2	24.9	28.6	33.1	41.5
25	Rubber and plastics products	4.0	4.3	5.6	6.1	5.1	6.2	6.6	7.7	9.8	7.7
26	Non-metallic mineral products	9.5	9.4	9.5	9.5	8.1	9.5	10.2	12.0	13.1	14.1
27/28	Basic & fabricated metals	10.9	15.1	13.7	12.9	12.2	12.5	14.3	14.2	17.4	20.5
27	Basic metals	6.3	6.6	7.2	7.9	5.9	5.8	7.6	8.1	8.7	9.6
28	Fabricated metal products	4.5	8.6	6.5	5.0	6.3	6.7	6.7	6.1	8.7	10.9
29/32	Machinery, Total	22.5	27.8	27.6	29.5	30.5	30.2	35.2	37.1	39.1	46.0
29/30	Non-electrical machinery	9.3	12.8	11.5	12.0	11.9	10.8	13.5	15.2	15.7	21.1
29	Non-electrical machinery nec	7.1	9.8	8.9	9.3	10.1	9.6	11.7	12.7	12.7	16.5
30	Office and computing machinery	2.2	3.0	2.6	2.7	1.8	1.2	1.8	2.5	3.0	4.6
31/32	Electrical & electronic equipment	13.2	15.1	16.1	17.6	18.6	19.4	21.7	21.9	23.4	24.9
31	Electrical machinery nec	6.3	6.4	6.8	8.0	7.1	7.4	9.3	10.1	10.0	9.8
32	Radio, TV & communications eq.	6.8	8.7	9.3	9.6	11.5	12.0	12.4	11.8	13.4	15.1
33	Scientific instruments	4.2	5.3	8.1	7.5	7.3	7.7	7.3	8.6	9.8	12.7
34/35	Transportation equipment	2.8	4.8	3.6	4.0	5.1	5.0	7.0	11.1	14.0	17.1
34	Motor vehicles	2.0	3.7	3.1	2.9	3.5	3.4	5.3	8.8	12.2	14.3
35	Other transport equipment	0.8	1.1	0.5	1.2	1.6	1.6	1.7	2.3	1.8	2.8
351	Shipbuilding & repairing	..	..	..	..	..	..	..	..	..	..
353	Aircraft and spacecraft	..	..	..	..	..	..	..	..	..	..
36/37	Other manufacturing	7.2	5.8	- 0.8	- 0.5	- 0.9	- 0.8	0.7	0.8	1.0	1.0
40/45	Construction, electricity, gas & water	1.5	2.4	4.1	3.6	1.6	2.0	2.0	2.0	1.5	2.4
50/55	Trade, repair, hotels & restaurants	53.6	54.0	60.2	65.3	70.6	75.2	75.6	79.4	88.8	103.7
65/74	Finance, insurance, business services	53.0	71.6	70.4	78.3	81.6	110.6	95.6	115.6	125.6	145.7
	OTHER ACTIVITIES	59.7	66.8	80.5	81.9	78.2	76.8	80.3	78.9	93.5	112.6
01/99	GRAND TOTAL	297.8	350.5	376.5	394.2	400.9	442.8	453.5	501.7	561.9	644.6

Total manufacturing by investing country	1988	1989	1990	1991	1992	1993	1994	1995	1996	1997
All countries	122.6	150.9	152.8	157.1	160.4	168.1	189.5	214.5	242.3	267.1
United States	..	..	..	..	..	..	..	..	..	..
Canada	9.7	9.8	9.2	15.7	15.8	16.0	17.4	20.3	22.3	27.8
Mexico	0.0	..	0.2	0.2	0.4	0.5	1.1	1.0	0.5	0.5
Japan	11.1	15.6	17.1	18.2	18.8	18.4	20.6	25.5	35.2	33.4
Europe	95.6	118.1	115.8	114.2	116.1	124.7	138.8	156.5	174.3	195.1
European Union (15)	83.4	101.0	98.6	97.5	99.3	105.9	116.7	141.6	157.1	174.5
Belgium	0.8	0.9	1.4	1.4	1.3	1.8	2.3	2.3	2.2	3.7
France	7.9	10.1	13.0	15.1	17.1	17.7	20.0	21.6	27.0	29.2
Germany	14.0	15.6	15.7	15.7	16.5	18.1	22.4	25.0	28.8	33.1
Italy	0.5	0.6	0.8	2.6	0.8	0.9	1.0	0.9	0.7	0.6
Netherlands	17.8	23.1	24.7	19.5	21.5	22.1	19.8	19.1	25.9	29.4
Spain	0.0	0.1	0.1	0.1	0.2	0.1	0.3	0.4	0.4	0.6
Sweden	3.8	3.9	5.0	4.8	5.0	5.4	5.7	7.1	6.5	7.7
United Kingdom	41.7	50.2	42.4	41.9	40.2	43.2	47.3	56.7	58.6	61.2
Switzerland	7.6	11.8	10.7	10.2	10.0	11.8	13.2	13.5	15.6	18.9
Australia and New Zealand	..	1.3	2.2	2.4	2.5	2.9	3.2	3.0	2.9	3.1
Asia (non-OECD)	..	1.3	1.7	1.5	1.1	1.7	1.7	2.1	2.2	3.2
Latin America	3.8	4.3	6.5	4.7	5.8	4.0	6.7	6.0	4.3	3.9

Note: **Enterprise-level data.** Defined as *Direct Investment Position*. See country notes.
Données au niveau de l'entreprise. Défini comme l'encours d'investissement direct étranger. Voir les notes par pays.

NUMBER OF ESTABLISHMENTS / NOMBRE D'ÉTABLISSEMENTS

By industry (ISIC Rev. 3)	FOREIGN AFFILIATES (Units)						AS A % OF NATIONAL TOTAL					
	1987	1988	1989	1990	1991	1992	1987	1988	1989	1990	1991	1992
10/14 Mining & quarrying	1 299	..	..	..	..	1 604	3.9	..	..	..	..	5.2
15/37 **TOTAL MANUFACTURING**	**8 151**	**9 105**	**10 458**	**11 934**	**12 741**	**12 781**	**2.2**	..	..	..	..	**3.3**
15/16 Food, beverages, tobacco	752	849	947	988	986	1 019	3.6	..	..	..	..	4.9
17/19 Textiles, clothing, leather, footwear	226	200	245	328	313	348	0.7	..	..	..	..	1.1
20/22 Wood and paper products	859	1 019	1 133	1 346	1 337	1 277	0.8	..	..	..	..	1.2
20 Wood products	130	124	135	184	194	152	0.4	..	..	..	..	0.4
21/22 Paper, printing and publishing	729	895	998	1 162	1 143	1 125	1.1	..	..	..	..	1.6
23/25 Chemicals, Total	1 778	1 940	2 210	2 497	2 611	2 737	6.2	..	..	..	..	9.1
23 Refined petroleum, nuclear fuel	213	227	314	319	348	360	9.5	..	..	..	..	16.9
24/25 Chemicals, rubber & plastics prod.	1 565	1 713	1 896	2 178	2 263	2 377	5.9	..	..	..	..	8.5
24 Chemical products	1 148	1 221	1 382	1 520	1 603	1 635	9.5	..	..	..	..	13.6
2423 Pharmaceuticals	108	122	135	166	176	202	8.0	..	..	..	..	14.2
25 Rubber and plastics products	417	492	514	658	660	742	2.9	..	..	..	..	4.7
26 Non-metallic mineral products	849	1 091	1 268	1 421	1 566	1 484	5.2	..	..	..	..	9.1
27/28 Basic & fabricated metals	712	772	893	995	1 082	1 099	1.7	..	..	..	..	2.6
27 Basic metals	311	304	367	402	430	413	4.7	..	..	..	..	6.4
28 Fabricated metal products	401	468	526	593	652	686	1.1	..	..	..	..	1.9
29/32 Machinery, Total	1 237	1 317	1 510	1 705	1 831	1 906	1.8	..	..	..	..	2.7
29/30 Non-electrical machinery	675	706	827	945	1 020	1 094	1.3	..	..	..	..	2.0
29 Non-electrical machinery nec	619	631	748	838	909	982	1.2	..	..	..	..	1.9
30 Office and computing machinery	56	75	79	107	111	112	2.7	..	..	..	..	5.0
31/32 Electrical & electronic equipment	562	611	683	760	811	812	3.5	..	..	..	..	4.8
31 Electrical machinery nec	267	294	328	361	404	385	3.5	..	..	..	..	5.2
32 Radio, TV & communications eq.	295	317	355	399	407	427	3.6	..	..	..	..	4.5
33 Scientific instruments	320	363	388	467	469	481	3.1	..	..	..	..	4.2
34/35 Transportation equipment	163	172	192	274	298	331	1.6	..	..	..	..	2.9
34 Motor vehicles	97	107	124	182	196	207	2.2	..	..	..	..	4.3
35 Other transport equipment	66	65	68	92	102	124	1.1	..	..	..	..	1.9
351 Shipbuilding & repairing	10	7	7	23	16	22	0.4	..	..	..	..	0.7
353 Aircraft and spacecraft	41	46	46	52	67	75	2.5	..	..	..	..	4.3
36/37 Other manufacturing	181	185	185	211	223	270	0.6	..	..	..	..	0.9
40/45 Construction, electricity, gas & water	760	..	..	..	..	1 361	0.1	..	..	..	..	0.2
50/55 Trade, repair, hotels & restaurants	38 051	..	..	..	..	59 456	1.7	..	..	..	..	2.6
65/74 Finance, insurance, business services	12 057	..	..	..	..	18 688	1.2	..	..	..	..	1.6
OTHER ACTIVITIES	..	..	..	..	..	..	..	..	..	..	..	..
01/99 **GRAND TOTAL**	**66 878**	..	..	..	..	**102 958**	**1.1**	..	..	..	..	**1.7**

Total manufacturing by investing country							As a % of total manufacturing by foreign affiliates					
All countries	8 151	9 105	10 458	11 934	12 741	12 781	100.0	100.0	100.0	100.0	100.0	100.0
United States	36	22	57	33	32	38	0.4	0.2	0.5	0.3	0.3	0.3
Canada	1 017	1 098	1 220	1 538	1 531	1 488	12.5	12.1	11.7	12.9	12.0	11.6
Mexico	10	3	36	64	81	108	0.1	0.0	0.3	0.5	0.6	0.8
Japan	718	920	1 136	1 356	1 564	1 767	8.8	10.1	10.9	11.4	12.3	13.8
Europe	5 710	6 403	7 239	8 007	8 426	8 368	70.1	70.3	69.2	67.1	66.1	65.5
European Union (15)	4 811	5 439	6 077	6 735	7 152	7 092	59.0	59.7	58.1	56.4	56.1	55.5
Belgium	114	104	71	95	118	126	1.4	1.1	0.7	0.8	0.9	1.0
France	657	880	986	1 217	1 252	1 202	8.1	9.7	9.4	10.2	9.8	9.4
Germany	754	807	926	1 045	1 157	1 272	9.3	8.9	8.9	8.8	9.1	10.0
Italy	66	100	111	141	195	250	0.8	1.1	1.1	1.2	1.5	2.0
Netherlands	470	532	583	618	597	577	5.8	5.8	5.6	5.2	4.7	4.5
Spain	6	17	16	20	29	28	0.1	0.2	0.2	0.2	0.2	0.2
Sweden	277	283	304	347	368	364	3.4	3.1	2.9	2.9	2.9	2.8
United Kingdom	2 499	2 723	3 122	3 291	3 459	3 311	30.7	29.9	29.9	27.6	27.1	25.9
Switzerland	478	505	656	697	653	655	5.9	5.5	6.3	5.8	5.1	5.1
Australia and New Zealand	308	332	459	548	584	554	3.8	3.6	4.4	4.6	4.6	4.3
Asia (non-OECD)	73	80	65	101	122	162	0.9	0.9	0.6	0.8	1.0	1.3
Latin America	151	147	156	174	169	184	1.9	1.6	1.5	1.5	1.3	1.4

Note: **Establishment-level data.** See country notes.
Données au niveau de l'établissement. Voir les notes par pays.

NUMBER OF EMPLOYEES / NOMBRE DE SALARIÉS

By industry (ISIC Rev. 3)		FOREIGN AFFILIATES (Thousands)						AS A % OF NATIONAL TOTAL					
		1987	1988	1989	1990	1991	1992	1987	1988	1989	1990	1991	1992
10/14	Mining & quarrying	98	..	..	..	..	121	14.0	..	..	..	..	19.0
15/37	**TOTAL MANUFACTURING**	**1 311**	**1 543**	**1 815**	**2 004**	**2 005**	**2 005**	**6.9**	**8.1**	**9.5**	**10.6**	**11.1**	**11.0**
15/16	Food, beverages, tobacco	..	..	..	..	..	..	..	..	..	..	..	..
17/19	Textiles, clothing, leather, footwear	..	50	63	77	75	81	..	2.7	3.5	4.4	4.5	4.7
20/22	Wood and paper products	109	136	155	170	167	158	3.9	4.8	5.5	6.0	6.1	5.7
20	Wood products	14	13	14	17	17	13	2.0	1.9	2.1	2.5	2.6	2.1
21/22	Paper, printing and publishing	95	123	141	153	150	145	4.5	5.8	6.6	7.0	7.1	6.8
23/25	Chemicals, Total	254	297	337	389	376	394	14.4	16.5	18.3	21.2	20.9	21.1
23	Refined petroleum, nuclear fuel	18	22	23	26	26	27	15.7	18.8	20.7	22.9	22.5	23.7
24/25	Chemicals, rubber & plastics prod.	236	275	314	363	351	367	14.3	16.3	18.2	21.1	20.8	20.9
24	Chemical products	172	187	214	242	233	241	21.1	22.6	25.3	28.4	27.5	28.4
2423	Pharmaceuticals	33	39	51	65	55	65	19.4	22.2	27.9	35.7	29.7	33.3
25	Rubber and plastics products	64	88	99	121	118	126	7.7	10.2	11.3	13.9	14.1	13.9
26	Non-metallic mineral products	65	81	96	106	96	93	12.3	15.5	18.4	20.7	20.2	19.8
27/28	Basic & fabricated metals	140	160	188	212	222	215	6.5	7.2	8.6	9.9	10.9	10.6
27	Basic metals	78	81	98	119	121	114	11.1	11.2	13.4	16.7	17.8	17.2
28	Fabricated metal products	61	79	91	93	102	102	4.2	5.3	6.2	6.5	7.5	7.5
29/32	Machinery, Total	286	337	423	420	428	415	8.4	9.7	12.2	12.4	13.4	13.1
29/30	Non-electrical machinery	116	144	191	191	193	190	6.3	7.6	10.0	10.2	10.9	10.9
29	Non-electrical machinery nec	93	120	159	161	160	158	6.1	7.7	9.9	10.1	10.6	10.6
30	Office and computing machinery	23	24	32	31	32	32	7.0	7.2	10.4	10.7	12.2	12.7
31/32	Electrical & electronic equipment	170	193	232	228	235	225	10.9	12.2	15.0	15.2	16.5	15.6
31	Electrical machinery nec	69	85	100	98	105	100	9.7	11.8	14.3	14.8	16.8	16.1
32	Radio, TV & communications eq.	101	108	132	130	130	125	11.9	12.5	15.5	15.6	16.2	15.3
33	Scientific instruments	73	97	108	122	113	107	7.4	9.9	11.2	12.8	12.5	11.8
34/35	Transportation equipment	56	65	79	104	107	115	3.1	3.6	4.4	5.9	6.5	7.0
34	Motor vehicles	40	46	58	73	76	82	5.4	6.3	8.0	10.4	11.7	11.7
35	Other transport equipment	15	19	21	31	31	33	1.4	1.8	2.0	2.9	3.1	3.5
351	Shipbuilding & repairing	..	..	1	6	..	4	..	..	0.8	3.4	..	2.4
353	Aircraft and spacecraft	11	15	18	19	21	22	1.9	2.5	2.9	3.1	3.7	4.1
36/37	Other manufacturing	36	..	..	..	..	..	4.1	..	..	..	..	..
40/45	Construction, electricity, gas & water	57	..	..	..	..	97	1.0	..	..	..	..	1.7
50/55	Trade, repair, hotels & restaurants	1 028	..	..	..	..	1 529	4.0	..	..	..	..	5.5
65/74	Finance, insurance, business services	545	..	..	..	..	798	4.2	..	..	..	..	5.5
	OTHER ACTIVITIES	..	..	..	..	..	..	..	..	..	..	..	..
01/99	**GRAND TOTAL**	**3 229**	..	..	..	..	**4 944**	**3.7**	..	..	..	..	**5.8**

Total manufacturing by investing country							As a % of total manufacturing by foreign affiliates					
All countries	1 311	1 543	1 815	2 004	2 005	2 005	100.0	100.0	100.0	100.0	100.0	100.0
United States	9	9	..	..	..	3	0.7	0.6	..	..	..	0.2
Canada	211	241	247	269	266	251	16.1	15.6	13.6	13.4	13.3	12.5
Mexico	..	..	..	..	12	15	..	..	..	..	0.6	0.7
Japan	109	170	216	291	320	343	8.3	11.0	11.9	14.5	16.0	17.1
Europe	870	1 011	1 212	1 297	1 275	1 272	66.4	65.5	66.8	64.7	63.6	63.4
European Union (15)	714	..	..	..	..	1 024	54.5	..	..	..	..	51.1
Belgium	12	11	11	15	13	12	0.9	0.7	0.6	0.7	0.6	0.6
France	93	123	142	178	181	173	7.1	8.0	7.8	8.9	9.0	8.6
Germany	167	190	215	229	229	235	12.7	12.3	11.9	11.4	11.4	11.7
Italy	6	11	16	17	27	32	0.5	0.7	0.9	0.9	1.3	1.6
Netherlands	100	104	119	123	120	113	7.6	6.7	6.5	6.2	6.0	5.6
Spain	..	0	..	0	1	1	..	0.0	..	0.0	0.1	0.1
Sweden	51	59	71	74	73	73	3.9	3.8	3.9	3.7	3.7	3.7
United Kingdom	310	360	440	457	431	424	23.6	23.4	24.2	22.8	21.5	21.1
Switzerland	85	93	135	134	127	143	6.5	6.1	7.5	6.7	6.3	7.1
Australia and New Zealand	33	36	53	54	52	44	2.5	2.3	2.9	2.7	2.6	2.2
Asia (non-OECD)	14	15	11	18	21	24	1.0	1.0	0.6	0.9	1.1	1.2
Latin America	..	..	..	..	38	35	..	..	..	..	1.9	1.7

Note: **Establishment-level data.** See country notes.
Données au niveau de l'établissement. Voir les notes par pays.

Table 4b. UNITED STATES / ÉTATS-UNIS

TURNOVER / CHIFFRE D'AFFAIRES

By industry (ISIC Rev. 3)	FOREIGN AFFILIATES (Billions of US$)						AS A % OF NATIONAL TOTAL					
	1987	1988	1989	1990	1991	1992	1987	1988	1989	1990	1991	1992
10/14 Mining & quarrying	27	..	..	..	..	31	16.8	..	..	..	..	18.7
15/37 TOTAL MANUFACTURING	**237**	**303**	**372**	**418**	**423**	**436**	**9.6**	**11.3**	**13.3**	**14.5**	**15.0**	**14.5**
15/16 Food, beverages, tobacco	..	..	..	..	..	..	..	..	..	..	..	..
17/19 Textiles, clothing, leather, footwear	..	5	7	8	8	9	..	3.4	4.6	5.7	5.9	6.2
20/22 Wood and paper products	17	22	27	30	30	30	5.3	6.4	7.7	8.3	8.5	7.8
20 Wood products	2	2	2	2	2	2	2.6	2.2	2.5	3.1	3.3	2.9
21/22 Paper, printing and publishing	15	20	26	28	28	27	6.0	7.6	9.1	9.7	9.8	9.1
23/25 Chemicals, Total	89	109	129	152	149	151	20.0	22.4	24.8	27.0	27.0	26.6
23 Refined petroleum, nuclear fuel	26	31	36	46	41	40	20.1	23.6	25.2	26.9	26.1	26.3
24/25 Chemicals, rubber & plastics prod.	63	78	93	105	108	112	19.9	21.9	24.7	27.1	27.4	26.7
24 Chemical products	55	65	79	88	90	92	23.8	25.0	28.2	30.4	30.7	30.2
2423 Pharmaceuticals	9	12	16	19	21	22	23.6	26.3	32.1	36.3	34.4	32.8
25 Rubber and plastics products	8	13	14	18	18	20	9.6	13.5	14.7	17.5	17.7	17.2
26 Non-metallic mineral products	9	12	14	16	15	15	15.1	18.5	22.2	25.9	24.6	24.4
27/28 Basic & fabricated metals	25	36	43	46	46	45	9.4	11.6	13.7	14.8	15.7	14.8
27 Basic metals	18	24	30	32	30	29	14.8	15.8	19.6	21.8	22.8	20.7
28 Fabricated metal products	7	12	13	14	15	16	5.0	7.7	8.1	8.6	9.8	9.8
29/32 Machinery, Total	36	47	64	66	70	73	9.2	11.0	14.3	14.5	15.8	15.4
29/30 Non-electrical machinery	14	21	30	31	31	33	6.6	8.5	11.9	12.1	12.7	12.7
29 Non-electrical machinery nec	11	16	23	24	24	25	6.9	8.9	12.3	12.4	13.0	13.0
30 Office and computing machinery	3	5	7	7	7	8	5.7	7.3	10.8	11.1	11.7	11.7
31/32 Electrical & electronic equipment	21	27	34	35	39	41	12.5	14.3	17.4	17.8	19.7	18.7
31 Electrical machinery nec	8	10	13	13	16	16	9.7	11.6	14.4	15.3	18.7	18.0
32 Radio, TV & communications eq.	14	17	21	21	23	24	14.9	16.5	19.9	19.7	20.5	19.2
33 Scientific instruments	8	12	14	16	16	16	7.2	10.1	11.8	12.8	12.8	11.8
34/35 Transportation equipment	15	18	23	29	33	38	4.4	5.2	6.4	7.8	9.1	9.5
34 Motor vehicles	13	16	20	25	29	33	6.3	7.2	9.0	11.6	14.2	14.0
35 Other transport equipment	2	2	3	4	4	5	1.4	1.8	2.1	2.5	2.4	2.8
351 Shipbuilding & repairing	..	..	0	1	..	0	..	..	1.0	3.7	..	2.9
353 Aircraft and spacecraft	1	2	2	2	2	3	1.7	2.3	2.6	2.3	2.3	2.6
36/37 Other manufacturing	4	..	..	..	..	..	5.4	..	..	..	..	..
40/45 Construction, electricity, gas & water	..	..	..	..	..	24	..	..	..	..	..	2.9
50/55 Trade, repair, hotels & restaurants	437	..	..	..	..	613	10.6	..	..	..	..	11.6
65/74 Finance, insurance, business services	..	..	..	..	..	217	..	..	..	..	..	9.4
OTHER ACTIVITIES	..	..	..	..	..	..	..	..	..	..	..	..
01/99 GRAND TOTAL	..	..	..	..	..	**1 355**	..	..	..	..	..	**10.7**

Total manufacturing by investing country							As a % of total manufacturing by foreign affiliates					
	1987	1988	1989	1990	1991	1992	1987	1988	1989	1990	1991	1992
All countries	**237**	**303**	**372**	**418**	**423**	**436**	**100.0**	**100.0**	**100.0**	**100.0**	**100.0**	**100.0**
United States	2	4	..	..	..	0	0.6	1.3	..	..	..	0.1
Canada	39	50	55	59	56	55	16.6	16.5	14.8	14.1	13.4	12.6
Mexico	..	..	..	..	2	2	..	..	..	..	0.5	0.5
Japan	24	36	49	66	73	83	10.0	11.8	13.2	15.7	17.4	19.1
Europe	152	189	232	251	254	259	64.2	62.4	62.3	60.1	60.0	59.5
European Union (15)	127	..	..	..	..	213	53.4	..	..	..	..	48.8
Belgium	3	4	4	5	4	5	1.4	1.3	1.0	1.2	1.0	1.0
France	15	24	30	36	36	35	6.5	8.0	8.1	8.7	8.6	8.0
Germany	26	33	38	41	42	45	11.1	10.8	10.4	9.7	9.9	10.3
Italy	1	4	4	4	5	6	0.5	1.3	1.0	0.9	1.3	1.5
Netherlands	25	27	33	35	32	34	10.5	9.0	8.9	8.3	7.5	7.7
Spain	..	0	..	0	0	0	..	0.0	..	0.0	0.1	0.1
Sweden	6	8	10	11	11	12	2.7	2.8	2.7	2.6	2.5	2.7
United Kingdom	51	60	74	81	83	82	21.3	19.7	19.8	19.3	19.6	18.7
Switzerland	16	19	26	27	28	29	6.9	6.4	6.9	6.6	6.6	6.6
Australia and New Zealand	6	8	13	14	12	11	2.6	2.6	3.5	3.4	3.0	2.5
Asia (non-OECD)	2	3	3	4	5	6	1.0	1.0	0.9	1.0	1.3	1.4
Latin America	..	..	..	..	12	11	..	..	..	..	2.7	2.5

Note: **Establishment-level data**. See country notes.
Données au niveau de l'établissement. Voir les notes par pays.

Table 5b. UNITED STATES / ÉTATS-UNIS

VALUE ADDED / VALEUR AJOUTÉE

By industry (ISIC Rev. 3)	FOREIGN AFFILIATES (Billions of US$)						AS A % OF NATIONAL TOTAL					
	1987	1988	1989	1990	1991	1992	1987	1988	1989	1990	1991	1992
10/14 Mining & quarrying	..	..	..	..	..	..	..	..	..	..	..	..
15/37 TOTAL MANUFACTURING	..	131.8	161.9	177.4	183.6	194.5	..	10.4	12.4	13.4	14.0	13.7
15/16 Food, beverages, tobacco	..	..	..	..	..	..	..	..	..	..	..	..
17/19 Textiles, clothing, leather, footwear	..	2.0	2.7	3.4	3.6	4.3	..	3.1	4.3	5.3	5.6	6.0
20/22 Wood and paper products	..	11.1	14.5	16.0	16.1	15.9	..	6.1	7.7	8.3	8.5	7.7
20 Wood products	..	0.7	0.8	0.8	0.8	0.9	..	2.4	2.6	2.9	3.0	2.8
21/22 Paper, printing and publishing	..	10.4	13.7	15.1	15.3	15.0	..	6.9	8.6	9.3	9.4	8.7
23/25 Chemicals, Total	..	46.1	55.7	61.7	63.1	67.2	..	22.0	25.3	26.8	27.6	27.3
23 Refined petroleum, nuclear fuel	..	5.0	4.9	4.1	4.3	5.7	..	19.8	18.7	15.1	17.9	24.1
24/25 Chemicals, rubber & plastics prod.	..	41.1	50.8	57.6	58.8	61.6	..	22.3	26.2	28.4	28.7	27.6
24 Chemical products	..	34.9	43.9	48.8	49.9	51.5	..	25.3	30.1	31.9	32.2	31.3
2423 Pharmaceuticals	..	8.2	11.3	14.2	15.2	16.3	..	26.3	33.0	37.2	35.1	33.6
25 Rubber and plastics products	..	6.2	6.9	8.8	9.0	10.1	..	13.3	14.4	17.6	17.8	17.2
26 Non-metallic mineral products	..	6.2	7.6	8.5	7.6	8.2	..	18.1	22.0	24.8	23.9	23.7
27/28 Basic & fabricated metals	..	12.6	14.8	16.6	16.9	18.0	..	9.2	10.9	12.5	13.7	13.3
27 Basic metals	..	7.2	8.6	10.3	9.8	10.3	..	12.8	15.4	19.3	21.0	19.7
28 Fabricated metal products	..	5.3	6.3	6.4	7.2	7.8	..	6.7	7.8	7.9	9.3	9.3
29/32 Machinery, Total	..	22.8	30.1	30.3	32.7	34.2	..	9.8	12.5	12.7	14.2	13.5
29/30 Non-electrical machinery	..	10.1	13.5	13.6	14.1	14.8	..	7.8	10.0	10.3	11.3	11.2
29 Non-electrical machinery nec	..	7.6	10.7	10.6	11.2	11.6	..	8.0	10.6	10.6	11.6	11.2
30 Office and computing machinery	..	2.5	2.8	2.9	2.9	3.2	..	7.3	8.3	9.3	10.4	11.0
31/32 Electrical & electronic equipment	..	12.7	16.6	16.7	18.6	19.4	..	12.3	15.6	15.6	17.5	16.0
31 Electrical machinery nec	..	5.0	6.2	6.3	7.7	8.0	..	11.2	13.7	14.2	17.8	17.0
32 Radio, TV & communications eq.	..	7.7	10.4	10.4	10.9	11.4	..	13.1	17.0	16.6	17.3	15.4
33 Scientific instruments	..	7.3	8.6	9.7	9.8	9.6	..	9.6	10.9	11.9	11.9	10.7
34/35 Transportation equipment	..	4.7	5.7	7.2	8.2	10.8	..	3.3	3.7	4.9	5.4	6.8
34 Motor vehicles	..	3.7	4.6	5.4	6.2	8.6	..	5.1	5.9	7.8	8.5	10.6
35 Other transport equipment	..	1.0	1.2	1.7	2.0	2.2	..	1.4	1.5	2.2	2.5	2.9
351 Shipbuilding & repairing	..	..	0.1	0.3	..	0.2	..	..	0.7	3.4	..	2.3
353 Aircraft and spacecraft	..	0.7	0.9	1.0	1.3	1.5	..	1.8	2.0	2.2	2.7	3.2
36/37 Other manufacturing	..	..	..	..	..	..	..	..	..	..	..	..
40/45 Construction, electricity, gas & water	..	..	..	..	..	..	..	..	..	..	..	..
50/55 Trade, repair, hotels & restaurants	..	..	..	..	..	..	..	..	..	..	..	..
65/74 Finance, insurance, business services	..	..	..	..	..	..	..	..	..	..	..	..
OTHER ACTIVITIES	..	..	..	..	..	..	..	..	..	..	..	..
01/99 GRAND TOTAL	..	..	..	..	..	..	..	..	..	..	..	..

Total manufacturing by investing country							As a % of total manufacturing by foreign affiliates					
All countries	..	131.8	161.9	177.4	183.6	194.5	..	100.0	100.0	100.0	100.0	100.0
United States	..	0.9	..	..	..	0.2	..	0.7	..	..	..	0.1
Canada	..	22.8	25.6	26.9	27.2	26.5	..	17.3	15.8	15.1	14.8	13.6
Mexico	..	..	..	..	1.1	1.3	..	..	..	..	0.6	0.7
Japan	..	12.8	17.3	22.8	24.5	29.7	..	9.7	10.7	12.9	13.3	15.3
Europe	..	87.6	107.7	115.5	120.1	124.2	..	66.5	66.5	65.1	65.4	63.9
European Union (15)	..	..	..	..	..	100.5	..	..	..	..	..	51.7
Belgium	..	1.4	1.3	1.6	1.4	1.5	..	1.1	0.8	0.9	0.7	0.8
France	..	10.1	12.1	15.4	16.7	15.8	..	7.7	7.5	8.7	9.1	8.1
Germany	..	15.7	19.0	20.4	21.0	22.4	..	11.9	11.7	11.5	11.4	11.5
Italy	..	1.1	1.2	1.3	2.0	2.7	..	0.8	0.8	0.7	1.1	1.4
Netherlands	..	11.5	13.7	11.6	11.9	13.1	..	8.7	8.5	6.6	6.5	6.8
Spain	..	0.0	..	0.0	0.1	0.1	..	0.0	..	0.0	0.1	0.1
Sweden	..	3.6	4.3	5.0	4.7	5.5	..	2.8	2.7	2.8	2.5	2.8
United Kingdom	..	29.7	37.0	40.3	41.6	42.2	..	22.6	22.9	22.7	22.7	21.7
Switzerland	..	10.3	13.9	14.8	15.6	15.8	..	7.8	8.6	8.4	8.5	8.1
Australia and New Zealand	..	2.5	4.8	5.1	4.6	4.3	..	1.9	2.9	2.9	2.5	2.2
Asia (non-OECD)	..	1.1	1.0	1.4	1.7	2.2	..	0.8	0.6	0.8	0.9	1.1
Latin America	..	..	..	..	3.9	4.4	..	..	..	..	2.1	2.2

Note: **Establishment-level data.** See country notes.
Données au niveau de l'établissement. Voir les notes par pays.

Table 6b. UNITED STATES / ÉTATS-UNIS

WAGES AND SALARIES / SALAIRES ET TRAITEMENTS

By industry (ISIC Rev. 3)	FOREIGN AFFILIATES (Billions of US$)						AS A % OF NATIONAL TOTAL					
	1987	1988	1989	1990	1991	1992	1987	1988	1989	1990	1991	1992
10/14 Mining & quarrying	3.6	..	..	..	..	5.4	16.8	..	..	..	..	22.4
15/37 TOTAL MANUFACTURING	**36.7**	**45.7**	**55.6**	**63.5**	**66.0**	**69.6**	**7.7**	**..**	**..**	**..**	**..**	**12.5**
15/16 Food, beverages, tobacco	..	..	..	..	..	..	..	..	..	..	..	..
17/19 Textiles, clothing, leather, footwear	..	0.9	1.2	1.4	1.5	..	..	..	..	..	..	..
20/22 Wood and paper products	2.8	3.6	4.4	4.8	4.9	..	4.4	..	..	..	..	..
20 Wood products	0.3	0.3	0.3	0.4	0.4	..	2.2	..	..	..	..	..
21/22 Paper, printing and publishing	2.5	3.4	4.1	4.4	4.6	..	5.0	..	..	..	..	..
23/25 Chemicals, Total	8.0	9.6	11.6	13.7	13.6	..	17.1	..	..	..	..	..
23 Refined petroleum, nuclear fuel	0.7	0.8	0.9	1.1	1.1	..	17.0	..	..	..	..	..
24/25 Chemicals, rubber & plastics prod.	7.3	8.8	10.6	12.6	12.5	..	17.1	..	..	..	..	..
24 Chemical products	5.7	6.5	7.9	9.2	9.1	..	22.9	..	..	..	..	..
2423 Pharmaceuticals	1.1	1.4	2.1	2.7	2.3	..	21.6	..	..	..	..	..
25 Rubber and plastics products	1.6	2.3	2.7	3.4	3.4	..	8.8	..	..	..	..	..
26 Non-metallic mineral products	1.7	2.2	2.6	3.1	2.8	..	13.6	..	..	..	..	..
27/28 Basic & fabricated metals	3.9	4.8	5.7	6.9	7.2	..	7.1	..	..	..	..	..
27 Basic metals	2.3	2.6	3.1	4.1	4.2	..	11.6	..	..	..	..	..
28 Fabricated metal products	1.6	2.3	2.6	2.7	3.0	..	4.6	..	..	..	..	..
29/32 Machinery, Total	7.2	9.3	12.1	12.4	13.1	..	8.1	..	..	..	..	..
29/30 Non-electrical machinery	3.2	4.2	5.8	5.9	6.2	..	6.3	..	..	..	..	..
29 Non-electrical machinery nec	2.5	3.4	4.6	4.8	4.9	..	6.3	..	..	..	..	..
30 Office and computing machinery	0.7	0.9	1.2	1.2	1.3	..	6.4	..	..	..	..	..
31/32 Electrical & electronic equipment	4.0	5.1	6.3	6.4	7.0	..	10.4	..	..	..	..	..
31 Electrical machinery nec	1.6	2.0	2.5	2.5	2.9	..	9.4	..	..	..	..	..
32 Radio, TV & communications eq.	2.5	3.0	3.8	3.9	4.0	..	11.2	..	..	..	..	..
33 Scientific instruments	2.0	2.8	3.3	3.9	3.7	..	6.9	..	..	..	..	..
34/35 Transportation equipment	1.6	2.0	2.4	3.2	3.4	..	2.7	..	..	..	..	..
34 Motor vehicles	1.1	1.4	1.8	2.3	2.4	..	4.8	..	..	..	..	..
35 Other transport equipment	0.4	0.5	0.6	0.9	1.0	..	1.2	..	..	..	..	..
351 Shipbuilding & repairing	..	..	0.0	0.1	..	..	..	..	..	..	..	..
353 Aircraft and spacecraft	0.3	0.4	0.5	0.6	0.7	..	1.6	..	..	..	..	..
36/37 Other manufacturing	0.7	..	..	..	..	..	4.4	..	..	..	..	..
40/45 Construction, electricity, gas & water	1.8	..	..	..	..	3.7	1.3	..	..	..	..	2.4
50/55 Trade, repair, hotels & restaurants	18.9	..	..	..	..	36.0	5.6	..	..	..	..	7.5
65/74 Finance, insurance, business services	16.3	..	..	..	..	28.9	5.6	..	..	..	..	7.1
OTHER ACTIVITIES	..	..	..	..	..	..	..	..	..	..	..	..
01/99 GRAND TOTAL	**81.1**	**..**	**..**	**..**	**..**	**155.0**	**4.7**	**..**	**..**	**..**	**..**	**7.5**

Total manufacturing by investing country							As a % of total manufacturing by foreign affiliates					
All countries	**36.7**	**45.7**	**55.6**	**63.5**	**66.0**	**69.6**	**100.0**	**100.0**	**100.0**	**100.0**	**100.0**	**100.0**
United States	0.3	0.3	..	..	..	0.1	0.8	0.7	..	..	..	0.1
Canada	6.4	7.5	8.0	8.9	9.1	9.1	17.4	16.4	14.4	14.0	13.8	13.1
Mexico	..	..	..	..	0.4	0.4	..	..	..	..	0.5	0.6
Japan	3.1	5.3	6.8	9.4	10.6	11.8	8.4	11.5	12.3	14.8	16.1	17.0
Europe	23.9	29.5	36.5	40.6	41.7	44.0	65.2	64.5	65.7	63.9	63.2	63.2
European Union (15)	19.6	..	..	..	..	35.3	53.3	..	..	..	..	50.7
Belgium	0.3	0.3	0.3	0.4	0.4	0.4	0.9	0.7	0.6	0.7	0.7	0.6
France	2.5	3.6	4.3	5.7	6.0	6.1	6.8	7.9	7.8	8.9	9.1	8.8
Germany	4.9	6.1	7.0	7.7	8.0	8.5	13.5	13.4	12.5	12.1	12.1	12.3
Italy	0.2	0.3	0.5	0.5	0.9	1.0	0.5	0.7	0.9	0.9	1.3	1.5
Netherlands	2.9	3.1	3.6	3.9	4.1	4.1	7.9	6.8	6.4	6.2	6.3	5.9
Spain	..	0.0	..	0.0	0.1	0.1	..	0.0	..	0.0	0.1	0.1
Sweden	1.3	1.5	1.8	2.0	2.0	2.2	3.6	3.2	3.2	3.2	3.1	3.2
United Kingdom	8.0	10.0	12.8	13.7	13.6	14.0	21.8	21.8	23.0	21.5	20.5	20.0
Switzerland	2.6	2.9	4.4	4.6	4.5	5.4	7.1	6.3	7.9	7.2	6.9	7.8
Australia and New Zealand	0.9	0.9	1.6	1.7	1.6	1.4	2.3	2.1	2.9	2.6	2.4	2.1
Asia (non-OECD)	0.3	0.4	0.4	0.5	0.7	0.8	0.8	0.8	0.7	0.8	1.0	1.1
Latin America	..	..	..	..	1.3	1.3	..	..	..	..	2.0	1.8

Note: **Establishment-level data**. See country notes.
Données au niveau de l'établissement. Voir les notes par pays.

UNITED STATES

Source

The data are prepared by the Bureau of Economic Analysis, US Department of Commerce. Most of the data are based on annual and benchmark surveys which cover US business enterprises in which a foreign person owned (or controlled) a direct (or indirect) interest of 10% or more at the end of the US business enterprise's fiscal year. The last benchmark surveys were conducted in 1980, 1987 and 1992. They provide benchmarks for deriving current universe estimates of direct investment from sample data collected in nonbenchmark years. The data are electronically released annually and are also available on the Web site of the Bureau of Economic Analysis (www.bea.doc.gov). They are published every benchmark year in *Foreign Direct Investment in the United States.*

The data on technological payments and receipts (royalties and licence fees) and on the stock of foreign direct investment (direct investment position) are from quarterly surveys conducted by the Bureau of Economic Analysis.

National totals:

Except for R&D variables, no data collected from enterprises are available for the United States. Therefore the Bureau of Economic Analysis produces also an establishment-based data series in order to be compatible with establishment-based data collected by the US Bureau of the Census. This time series is only available for the period 1987-92. The variables covered are *Number of establishments* (Table 1*b*), *Number of employees* (Table 2*c*), *Turnover* (Table 4*b*), *Value added* (Table 5*b*) and *Wages and salaries* (Table 6*b*).

- *R&D expenditure:* data are extracted from the OECD's ANBERD database.

- *Number of researchers:* data come from the OECD's ANRSE database and are converted from ISIC Revision 2 to ISIC Revision 3. The ratio for number of researchers is overestimated, because ANRSE provides only data for researchers, whereas data for the foreign affiliates refer to total R&D employment (including support staff).

Industrial classification

For all variables except *Number of employees* (Table 2*b*), the data are classified according to the principal industrial activity of the affiliate.

The industrial classification used for the US tables is ISI (national classification), converted to ISIC Revision 3. The following notes apply to all years and variables for enterprise-level data, except *Number of employees* (Table 2*b*) which is only available in the national classification:

- *Mining and quarrying* (10/14) excludes *Petroleum and natural gas extraction* (11), which is included in *Other activities* (01/05; 60/64; 75/99).

- *Total manufacturing* (15/37) excludes *Refined petroleum and coal products* (23), which is included in *Other activities* (01/05; 60/64; 75/99).

- *Food, beverages, tobacco* (15/16) excludes *Tobacco* (16), which is included in *Other manufacturing* (36/37).

- *Textiles, clothing, leather, footwear* (17/19) excludes *Leather* (191), which is included in *Other manufacturing* (36/37).

- *Wood and paper products* (20/22) and *Wood products* (20) include *Furniture* (361), which should be included in *Other manufacturing* (36/37).

- *Chemicals, total* (23/25) excludes *Refined petroleum and coal products* (23), which is included in *Other activities* (01/05; 60/64; 75/99).

- *Refined petroleum and coal products* (23) is not available separately. It is included in *Other activities* (01/05; 60/64; 75/99).

- *Shipbuilding* (351) and *Aircraft and spacecraft* (353) are not available separately.

- *Other manufacturing* (36/37) excludes *Furniture* (361); includes *Tobacco* (16) and *Leather* (191).

- *Construction, electricity gas & water* (40/45) excludes *Electricity, gas & water* (40/41), which is included in *Other activities* (01/05; 60/64; 75/99).

- *Trade, repair, hotels and restaurants* (50/55) excludes *Hotels* (551), *Petroleum wholesale trade* (5141) and *Gasoline service stations* (505), which are included in *Other activities* (01/05; 60/64; 75/99).

- *Finance, insurance, real estate and business services* (65/74) excludes *Business services* (71/74), which is included in *Other activities* (01/05; 60/64; 75/99).

- *Other activities* (01/05; 60/64; 75/99) includes all Petroleum activities (extraction, manufacturing, trade, storage and transportation), *Electricity, gas and water* (40/41), *Hotels* (551), *Business services* (71/74).

Variables

- *Number of enterprises* is defined as the number of non-bank affiliates, which means the number of business enterprises located in the United States which are directly or indirectly owned or controlled by a foreign person to the extent of 10% or more of its securities for an incorporated business enterprise or an equivalent interest for an unincorporated business enterprise, including a branch. Each report covers a fully consolidated US business enterprise, which may consist of a number of individual companies. The number of companies consolidated is substantially higher than the number of affiliates. For example, in 1987, for non-bank affiliates, the comparable figures were 22 937 and 8 110. The number of establishments, which is not available from the benchmark survey, would be even higher.

298

- *Number of employees* consists of the number of full-time and part-time employees on the payroll at the end of the fiscal year. In Table *2a* and Table *2c*, data are classified according to the principal industrial activity of the affiliate; in Table *2b*, data are classified by industry of sales, a basis that approximates the disaggregation of the data for all US businesses by industry of establishments.

- *Turnover* is defined as sales of goods and services, plus investment income included in "sales or gross operating revenues" in the income statement (mostly finance and insurance affiliates).

- *Value added* is called gross product, which is defined as the sum of employee compensation, profit-type return, net interest paid, indirect business taxes and capital consumption allowance.

- *Wages and salaries* is in fact the compensation of employees, which consists of wages and salaries of employees and employer expenditures for all employee benefit plans.

- *R&D expenditure* is defined as expenditures for R&D performed by US affiliates. It includes R&D performed by US affiliates for themselves or for others.

- *Number of researchers* is called R&D employment, and consists of all employees engaged in research and development, including managers, scientists, engineers, and other professional and technical employees.

- *Gross fixed capital formation* is defined as expenditure for new plant and equipment.

- *Total exports* is defined as the US merchandise exports shipped by affiliates. It excludes exports of services.

- *Total imports* is defined as the US merchandise imports shipped to affiliates. It excludes imports of services.

- *Intra-firm exports* is defined as the exports shipped to the foreign parent group. It excludes exports of services.

- *Intra-firm imports* is defined as the imports shipped by the foreign parent group. It excludes imports of services.

- *Gross operating surplus* is called net income, and consists of the difference between total income and total costs and expenses of affiliate.

- *Technological payments:* it is defined as US affiliates' payments to the parent group for royalties and licence fees.

- *Technological receipts:* it is defined as US affiliates' receipts from the parent group for royalties and licence fees.

- *Stock of foreign direct investment* is defined as the foreign direct investment position in the United States.

Geographical breakdown

For *Technological payments, Technological receipts* and *Stock of foreign direct investment*, the breakdown of *Total manufacturing* is by country of foreign parent. For all other variables, the breakdown is by country of ultimate beneficial owner.

For *Wages and salaries*, *R&D expenditure*, *Number of researchers*, *Gross fixed capital formation*, *Total exports* and *imports*, *Intra-firm exports* and *imports* and *Gross operating surplus*, data for the Asia (non-OECD) area actually correspond to those of Asia-Pacific excluding Japan.

ÉTATS-UNIS

Source

Les données émanent du Bureau d'analyse économique du *US Department of Commerce*. La plupart des données sont basées sur des enquêtes annuelles et de référence qui couvrent les entreprises américaines dans lesquelles une personne étrangère possède une participation directe (ou indirecte) de 10 % ou plus à la fin de l'exercice (ou exerce un contrôle équivalent). Les dernières enquêtes de référence ont été menées en 1980, 1987 et 1992. Elles fournissent des repères permettant de faire des estimations d'investissements directs à partir de données recueillies par sondage lors des années autres que de référence. Les données sont disponibles annuellement sous forme électronique et sur le site Internet du Bureau d'analyse économique (www.bea.doc.gov). Elles sont publiées chaque année de référence dans *Foreign Direct Investment in the United States*.

Les données sur les paiements et recettes technologiques (redevances et droits de licence) et sur le stock d'investissement direct étranger (encours d'investissement direct) sont tirées d'enquêtes trimestrielles menées par le Bureau d'analyse économique.

Totaux nationaux :

A l'exception des variables relatives à la R-D, aucune donnée collectée au niveau de l'entreprise n'est disponible pour les États-Unis. C'est pourquoi le Bureau d'analyse économique produit également une série de données au niveau de l'établissement, de façon à pouvoir les comparer avec les données collectées au niveau de l'établissement par le Bureau of the Census. Cette série de données est seulement disponible pour la période 1987-92. Les variables couvertes sont *Nombre d'établissements* (tableau 1*b*), *Nombre de salariés* (tableau 2*c*), *Chiffre d'affaires* (tableau 4*b*), *Valeur ajoutée* (tableau 5*b*) et *Salaires* (tableau 6*b*).

- *Dépenses de R-D* : les données sont extraites de la base de données ANBERD de l'OCDE.

- *Nombre de chercheurs* : les données sont été extraites de la base de données ANRSE de l'OCDE, et sont converties de la CITI révision 2 vers la CITI révision 3. Les ratios relatifs au nombre de chercheurs est surestimé, puisque ANRSE fournit des données sur les chercheurs, tandis que les données des filiales font référence à l'emploi total de R-D (y compris le personnel de soutien).

Classification industrielle

Pour toutes les variables à l'exception du *Nombre de salariés* (tableau 2*b*), les données sont classées selon l'activité industrielle principale de l'entreprise affiliée.

La classification industrielle utilisée pour les tableaux américains est la classification nationale (ISI) adaptée pour correspondre à la CITI révision 3. Les notes suivantes s'appliquent à toutes les années et toutes les variables pour les données au niveau de l'entreprise, à l'exception du *Nombre de salariés* (tableau 2*b*) disponible uniquement dans la classification nationale :

- *Activités extractives* (10/14) exclut *Extraction de pétrole et de gaz naturel* (11) qui est inclus dans *Autres activités* (01/05 ; 60/64 ; 75/99).

- *Activités de fabrication* (15/37) exclut *Raffineries de pétrole et dérivés du charbon* (23) qui est inclus dans *Autres activités* (01/05 ; 60/64 ; 75/99).

- *Produits alimentaires, boissons, tabac* (15/16) exclut le *Tabac* (16) qui est inclus dans *Autres activités de fabrication* (36/37).

- *Textiles, habillement, cuirs, chaussures* (17/19) exclut les *Cuirs* (191), inclus dans *Autres activités de fabrication* (36/37).

- *Articles en bois et en papier* (20/22) et *Articles en bois* (20) incluent *Meubles* (361) qui devrait être inclus dans *Autres activités de fabrication* (36/37).

- *Produits chimiques* (23/25) exclut *Raffineries de pétrole et dérivés du charbon* (23) qui est inclus dans *Autres activités* (01/05 ; 60/64 ; 75/99).

- *Raffineries de pétrole et dérivés du charbon* (23) n'est pas disponible séparément. Est inclus dans *Autres activités* (01/05 ; 60/64 ; 75/99).

- *Construction navale* (351) et *Construction aéronautique et spatiale* (353) ne sont pas disponibles séparément.

- *Autres activités de fabrication* (36/37) exclut *Meubles* (361) ; inclut *Tabac* (16) et *Cuirs* (191).

- *Construction, électricité, gaz et eau* (40/45) exclut *Electricité, gaz et eau* (40/41) qui est inclus dans *Autres activités* (01/05 ; 60/64 ; 75/99).

- *Commerce, réparation, hôtels et restaurants* (50/55) exclut *Hôtels* (551), *Commerce de gros de combustibles* (5141) et *Stations de distribution de carburants* (505) qui sont inclus dans *Autres activités* (01/05 ; 60/64 ; 75/99).

- *Finance, assurance, immobilier et services aux entreprises* (65/74) exclut *Activités de service aux entreprises* (71/74) qui est inclus dans *Autres activités* (01/05 ; 60/64 ; 75/99).

- *Autres activités* (01/05 ; 60/64 ; 75/99) inclut toutes les activités concernant le pétrole (extraction, fabrication, commerce, stockage et transport), *Electricité, gaz et eau* (40/41), *Hôtels* (551), *Services aux entreprises* (71/74).

Variables

- Le *Nombre d'entreprises* est défini comme le nombre d'entreprises affiliées du secteur non bancaire situées aux États-Unis, qui appartiennent directement ou indirectement ou qui sont sous le contrôle d'une personne étrangère à hauteur de 10 % ou plus de ses titres pour une entreprise constituée en société ou avec une participation équivalente pour une entreprise non constituée en société, y compris une succursale. Chaque rapport couvre un groupe américain complet qui peut comprendre plusieurs sociétés individuelles. Le nombre de sociétés membres du groupe est beaucoup plus élevé que le nombre de sociétés affiliées. Par exemple, en 1987, pour les entreprises affiliées du secteur non bancaire, les chiffres étaient respectivement de 22 937 et 8 110. Le nombre d'établissements, qui n'est pas disponible dans l'enquête de référence, serait encore plus élevé.

– Le *Nombre de salariés* représente le nombre de personnes employées à plein temps et à temps partiel à la fin de l'exercice budgétaire. Dans les tableaux 2*a* et 2*c*, les données sont classées selon l'activité industrielle principale de l'entreprise affiliée ; dans le tableau 2*b*, les données sont classées selon le secteur des ventes, une base qui est une approximation des données pour l'ensemble des entreprises américaines classées selon l'activité industrielle de l'établissement.

– Le *Chiffre d'affaires* est défini en tant que ventes de biens et services, plus les revenus d'investissement inclus dans les "ventes ou recettes brutes d'exploitation" de la déclaration de revenus (filiales du secteur de la finance ou des assurances pour la plupart).

– La *Valeur ajoutée* est appelée produit brut, et est définie comme la somme de la rémunération des salariés, des bénéfices, des intérêts nets payés, des impôts indirects sur les sociétés et des provisions pour amortissement.

– Les *Salaires* sont en fait la rémunération des salariés, qui se compose des traitements et salaires des personnes employées et des dépenses patronales pour tous les régimes de prestations sociales.

– Les *Dépenses de R-D* sont définies comme les dépenses pour la R-D exécutée par les filiales américaines pour elles-mêmes ou pour d'autres.

– Le *Nombre de chercheurs* est appelé emploi de R-D et comprend tous les salariés travaillant dans la recherche et développement, y compris les dirigeants, scientifiques, ingénieurs et autres professionnels et techniciens.

– La *Formation brute de capital fixe* est définie comme les dépenses pour de nouveaux équipements et installations.

– Les *Exportations totales* sont définies comme les exportations américaines de marchandises expédiées par les entreprises affiliées. Sont exclues les exportations de services.

– Les *Importations totales* sont définies comme les importations américaines de marchandises expédiées aux entreprises affiliées. Sont exclues les importations de services.

– Les *Exportations intra-firme* sont définies comme les exportations à destination du groupe parent étranger. Sont exclues les exportations de services.

– Les *Importations intra-firme* sont définies comme les importations en provenance du groupe parent étranger. Sont exclues les importations de services.

- L'*Excédent brut d'exploitation* est appelé aussi revenu net et résulte de la différence entre le revenu total et l'ensemble des coûts et dépenses de l'entreprise affiliée.

- Les *Paiements technologiques* sont définis comme les paiements de la filiale américaine au groupe parent au titre des redevances et droits de licence.

- Les *Recettes technologiques* sont définies comme les recettes de la filiale américaine provenant du groupe parent au titre des redevances et droits de licence.

- Le *Stock d'investissement direct étranger* est défini comme l'encours d'investissement direct étranger aux États-Unis.

Ventilation géographique

Pour les *Paiements technologiques,* les *Recettes technologiques* et le *Stock d'investissement direct étranger*, la ventilation du *Total manufacturier* s'effectue par pays du parent étranger. Pour toutes les autres variables, la ventilation se fait par pays du bénéficiaire ultime de l'investissement.

Pour les *Salaires et traitements*, les *Dépenses de R-D*, le *Nombre de chercheurs*, la *Formation brute de capital fixe*, les *Exportations* et *Importations totales*, les *Exportations* et *Importations intra-firme* et l'*Excédent brut d'exploitation*, les données pour la zone Asie hors OCDE correspondent en fait à celles de l'Asie-Pacifique, à l'exclusion du Japon.

List of industries in ISIC Revision 3

Liste des industries en CITI révision 3

	Industries in ISIC Revision 3	Industries en CITI révision 3
10/14	Mining and quarrying	Activités extractives
15/37	Total manufacturing	Total manufacturier
15/16	Food, beverages and tobacco	Alimentation, boissons, tabac
17/19	Textiles, wearing apparel, leather, footwear	Textile, habillement, cuir, chaussures
20/22	Wood and paper products, publishing, printing	Produits du bois et du papier, imprimerie, édition
20	Wood and wood products, except furniture	Bois et produits du bois, sauf meubles
21/22	Paper and products, printing and publishing	Papier et produits du papier, imprimerie, édition
23/25	All chemical products	Produits chimiques, total
23	Refined petroleum and coal products	Raffineries de pétrole et dérivés du charbon
24/25	Chemicals, rubber and plastics products	Produits chimiques, caoutchouc et plastiques
24	Chemical products	Produits chimiques
2423	Pharmaceuticals	Produits pharmaceutiques
25	Rubber and plastics products	Caoutchouc et plastiques
26	Non-metallic mineral products	Produits minéraux non métalliques
27/28	Basic and fabricated metal products	Métallurgie et ouvrages en métaux
27	Basic metals	Métallurgie de base
28	Fabricated metal products	Ouvrages en métaux
29/32	Total machinery and equipment	Machines et matériels, total
29/30	Non-electrical machinery and equipment	Machines et matériels non électriques
29	Machinery and equipment n.e.c.	Machines et matériels non électriques n.c.a.
30	Office, accounting and computing machinery	Machines de bureau et ordinateurs
31/32	Electrical machinery and electronic equipment	Machines électriques et électroniques
31	Electrical machinery and apparatus n.e.c.	Machines électriques n.c.a.
32	Radio, TV and communication equipment	Appareil de radio, télévision et télécommunication
33	Medical, precision, opt. instruments, watches	Instruments médicaux, de précision, optique, horlogerie
34/35	Transport equipment	Matériel de transport
34	Motor vehicles	Véhicules automobiles
35	Other transport equipment	Autres matériels de transport
351	Shipbuilding and repairing	Construction navale
353	Aircraft and spacecraft	Construction aéronautique et spatiale
36/37	Furniture, recycling and manufacturing n.e.c.	Meubles, récupération et industries manufacturières n.c.a.
40/45	Electricity, gas and water supply, construction	Électricité, gaz et eau, construction
50/55	Trade, repair, hotels and restaurants	Commerce, réparation, hôtels, restaurants
65/74	Finance, insurance, real estate, business act.	Finance, assurances, immobilier, services aux entreprises
Other activities	Other activities	Autres activités
01/99	TOTAL	TOTAL

OECD PUBLICATIONS, 2, rue André-Pascal, 75775 PARIS CEDEX 16
PRINTED IN FRANCE
(92 1999 08 3 P) ISBN 92-64-05877-X – No. 50937 1999